A STRUCTURED APPROACH TO FORTRAN

A STRUCTURED APPROACH TO FORTRAN

Second Edition

J. Winston Crawley
Charles E. Miller

PRENTICE-HALL, INC.
Englewood Cliffs, New Jersey 07632

Library of Congress Cataloging-in-Publication Data

CRAWLEY, J. WINSTON (date)
A structured approach to FORTRAN.

Includes index.
1. FORTRAN (Computer program language) 2. Structured programming. I. Miller, Charles E. II. Title.
QA76.73.F25C725 1987 005.13'3 86-91451
ISBN 0-13-854183-3

Editorial/production supervision and
interior design: *Carol L. Atkins*
Cover design: *Lundgren Graphics, Ltd.*
Manufacturing buyer: *Ed O'Dougherty*

A Division of Simon & Schuster
Englewood Cliffs, New Jersey 07632

This book was formerly a title of Reston Publishing Company, a division of Prentice-Hall, Inc.

Printed in the United States of America

10 9 8 7 6 5 4 3 2 1

ISBN 0-13-854183-3 025

Prentice-Hall International (UK) Limited, *London*
Prentice-Hall of Australia Pty. Limited, *Sydney*
Prentice-Hall Canada Inc., *Toronto*
Prentice-Hall Hispanoamericana, S.A., *Mexico*
Prentice-Hall of India Private Limited, *New Delhi*
Prentice-Hall of Japan, Inc., *Tokyo*
Prentice-Hall of Southeast Asia Pte. Ltd., *Singapore*
Editora Prentice-Hall do Brasil, Ltda., *Rio de Janeiro*

To our parents,

Winston and Margaret Crawley
and
C. Eugene and Florence Miller

Our wives,

Margaret Crawley
and
Esther Miller

And our children,

Allyson and Winston Crawley
and
Diana and Cynthia Miller

CONTENTS

PREFACE

PREFACE TO THE SECOND EDITION

"No matter how good something is there are ways to improve and enhance it." This is a lesson we try to teach our students in our computer science courses. We try to encourage them to look at the programs they have written, and to see where improvements could be made. This is, in large measure, the reason for grading and returning the programs.

The authors of this text would like to think that the first edition was a good textbook. However, we have taken a close look at that first edition and found several ways to make improvements, both major and minor. Thus the second edition represents not just a rehash of the first edition, but, we hope, a significant enhancement of the first edition.

In making the revisions, we have sought to keep what we viewed as strengths of the text. For example:

1. We have retained the emphasis on a consistent style of program design, using variable lists and pseudocode algorithms as important development tools.
2. We have retained and strengthened the emphasis on subprograms as a design tool.
3. We have retained and enhanced the *Pitfalls* and the *Review* sections following each major unit of the chapters.

4. We have retained the philosophy of providing good models for student programs, by documenting sample programs, by including white space, by using meaningful variable names, and by using consistent indentation strategies to emphasize decision and loop structures.
5. We have retained the spiral approach, which we believe to be pedagogically sound.
6. We have retained the idea of having an exercise set with each section, rather than just at the end of each chapter. As one reviewer of the first edition commented, "this text contains too many exercises!"—we do not agree that it is possible to have too many. Writing programs is a skill best learned by doing. (However, the instructor may wish to choose exercise sets to meet his or her own special criteria.)
7. Perhaps most importantly, we have retained the thorough explanation of major ideas, even though that does make the book rather longish. Feedback from students has indicated that they appreciated the careful explanations. This stands in contrast to too many textbooks which present the material as if the student already understood the subject.

What, then, have we changed? The following is a list of what we view as the major changes in the text:

Getting Started. The topics from Chapters 1–5 of the first edition have been redistributed into six chapters, with a first chapter entitled *Getting Started*. This brief chapter (four sections) introduces just enough of the FORTRAN language to present and write complete looping programs. The first edition introduced the topics, but lacked a unified early treatment of the entire development process. Sections 1.3 and 1.4 provide that treatment through a "case study 0" (not labelled as such), followed by a formal case study 1.

Conversational Approach. The general approach of the second edition is conversational rather than batch. However, batch and file concepts are introduced at various stages, particularly Section 2.4 for some terminology, Section 5.1 for a general discussion of the topics, and Chapter 13 for details on file processing.

Free Format. Free format (list directed) input and output are used to get started with programming. This allows immediate writing of complete looping programs without having to worry about this detail. Formats are introduced later, as a means to take more control of the I/O process.

Case Studies. This has been expanded upon significantly. There are now ten case studies placed throughout the text. These case studies are developed in a manner more indicative of the various steps involved, from "*statement of problem*" through "*algorithm development*" and "*testing*" to "*modifications.*" In addition, many of the case studies are revisited for major enhancements or modifications in later sections.

Antibugging and Debugging. Section 3.4 provides a unified treatment of this topic, which is dealt with in less direct ways in other places, such as the *Pitfalls* subsections.

Program Testing. The first edition had some treatment of program testing in Section 1.7. In this edition, there are *Testing* subsections throughout, similar to the *Pitfalls* sections of both editions. These introduce this important concept gradually in the context of specific types of programs. A unified treatment is also given at a later point in the text (section 3.4).

Subprograms. Subprograms are introduced even earlier than in the first edition, in a "friendly" fashion consistent with the overall spiral approach of the text. The first subprogram is a subroutine to print instructions to the user. It has no parameters. After the student has achieved some familiarity with this, functions with input parameters are introduced to perform calculation steps. A little later the notion that a subroutine could also have an input parameter is brought in. This is followed still later by subroutines with output parameters. Chapter 4 on subprograms (the former Chapter 3) then reviews, enhances, and draws together the student's knowledge of how and why to use subprograms.

LOGICAL Functions. These are covered in Chapter 4 in a more thorough manner.

Random Numbers. Section 3.2 contains a subsection introducing the concept of random number generation. A hypothetical RND(N) function is used in various examples in the next several chapters.

Common Applications of Loops. Three important topics (counting, accumulation, and largest/smallest) have been combined in a unified treatment in Section 3.1.

FORTRAN 77. The Non-77 subsections have been removed. The text is now completely FORTRAN 77.

Multiple Exits. Section 5.3 *(Loop Control: Multiple Exit Conditions)* has been completely rewritten. The emphasis in the first edition involved numbering the exits, and using this after the loop to take appropriate action. In the section edition, the emphasis is on "natural" ways, based on the algorithm logic itself, to determine the appropriate action following loops of this type. We have found that this approach is much less confusing, and that it encourages doing the planning during the algorithm development rather than during coding.

Answer Key. The second edition contains an appendix with answers to selected exercises. In the first edition, this was present only in the instructor's guide.

The book is in two parts. The first part covers what we deem to be the core material for a first course in program design using FORTRAN. In the second part, we have included additional material which may be selected based on the desires of the instructor. As far as a timetable is concerned, each instructor will naturally develop his own pace. In fact, the two co-authors do not follow the same schedule. However, we would suggest the following as a possible starting point. Spend about one week on the first chapter, with appropriate additions concerning the specific computer system to be used, and make a programming assignment based on that chapter. Then proceed at the pace of about one section per day through Chapters 2–6. With allowance for tests, this should leave some time at the end of a 14 week semester for further exploration. This exploration could consist of additional topics from Chapters 7–14, or perhaps in-class development of additional case studies based on the core material.

PREFACE TO THE FIRST EDITION (EXCERPTS)

Preface to the Instructor

This textbook evolves from the authors' experience in teaching the introductory level FORTRAN course at Shippensburg State College. We are of the opinion that, in this introductory course, teaching the art of programming is, if anything, even more important than teaching the details of a particular language. One of the most important consequences resulting from this approach is that the text emphasizes a consistent style of program design, using variable lists and pseudocode algorithms as important program development tools. In addition, we feel that subprograms are one of the most important tools for programming design. As a result, we have covered subprograms early, and they are then consistently used throughout the remainder of the text as an aid in modular design.

There are other implications of this emphasis on the total design process. For one thing, commonly used algorithmic techniques such as counting and searching are covered in detail and are used in a variety of settings throughout the text. In addition, we feel that programming texts should practice good documentation as well as preach it. Accordingly, almost every program example includes numerous comment lines, including blank comment lines to improve readability. In addition, meaningful variable names are used, and consistent indentation patterns emphasize the loop and decision structures present in the program.

To a large degree the text would be suitable for self-study. Especially in the first six chapters, there are a large number of examples worked out in detail, from problem statement through algorithm design to completed program. The techniques used in counting, accumulating, finding largest or smallest value, and searching are covered in detail. In addition to the many examples which involve relatively simple problems, there are a number of case studies which present and solve more complex problems. These case studies feature both numerical applications and business applications.

Two special features are included to aid the student in learning the material. First, there are many *Pitfalls* sections to aid in antibugging and debugging. These sections warn of some of the more common misconceptions or errors, both in algorithm design and in the FORTRAN program itself. Special attention is given to those errors which are not easily located even after being flagged by the compiler, or which would perhaps not be detected by the compiler. In addition, almost every section of the text ends with a *Review*, which outlines the material learned and, where appropriate, gives simple examples of the concepts covered.

We have included an unusually large number of exercises for a programming text. A majority of these are repetitive "drill" type exercises. Their purpose is for the student to reinforce the concepts being studied by using them in a large number of relatively simple problems. In addition, we have included more complex exercises suitable for use as programming projects, either as they are given or with minor modifications or enhancements to suit the instructor.

A "spiral" approach to the presentation of material is used where appropriate.

By a "spiral" approach we mean one which presents a concept in a relatively simple form at first, progressing to the more general form after the student has thoroughly mastered the simpler form. This approach is most notably present in three areas: FORMAT statements, CHARACTER data types, and DO loops. While these are the three most obvious areas where this approach is utilized, the philosophy is apparent throughout the text. Indeed, the repeated emphasis on the fundamental counting, accumulating, finding the largest/smallest, and searching techniques may be viewed as an outgrowth of this philosophy.

In this same vein, one note to the instructor may be in order. There are certain topics in which the full generality of the FORTRAN language is never discussed in detail. Our approach in these areas has been to place restrictions which are not a part of the standard but which are, in our estimation, good programming practices.

Numerous acknowledgements are in order. Portions of the text have been used in classes taught by professors Ronald Hoover, Howard Bell, William McArthur, Glenn Stambaugh, and Tom Benjey, as well as the authors. We are indebted to these colleagues for giving the text a trial run, as well as for their comments and suggestions. A student, Sue Ann Hoke, has done a marvelous job of typing and correcting most of the manuscript. In the process she has made helpful suggestions, and has detected and corrected many errors. We are especially indebted to our colleague Carl Kerr, who read the manuscript in rough draft and offered countless valuable suggestions concerning both content and style. James Sieber, chairman of the Department of Mathematics and Computer Science at Shippensburg State College, made it possible for the manuscript to be used by the various professors teaching the introductory programming course. Finally, we wish to thank Pam Schenzel and the rest of the office staff for handling the distribution of the manuscript to the students in that introductory course.

Preface to the Student

The purpose of this text is to help you learn to program a computer. This involves two major components. For one thing, you must learn the details of how to make the computer perform certain actions. In addition, you must learn how to combine these actions in meaningful ways in order to solve problems.

The computer can perform certain fundamental tasks. It can store data; read the data which is to be stored; print the data which has been stored; and manipulate the stored data, including doing numerical calculations. In addition, it can automatically go back and repeat one or more steps, thus allowing the processing of large amounts of data in a short time. Finally, it can make decisions concerning what steps it should perform, based on the present value of the data which has been stored.

One goal of this text is to present the details of the computer language called FORTRAN. Using the features of this language, you will be able to write commands to cause the computer to perform each of the fundamental tasks described above (read, print, calculate, and so on).

A more important goal, however, is to help you learn how to design programs. By this we mean the following: given a problem to be solved using the computer, you must determine what combination of steps can be used to solve it. You will put together the fundamental operations listed earlier, in more and more complex ways to solve increasingly complex problems. The text develops some tools designed to aid you in the construction of solutions to the problems. Once you have determined what combination of steps can be used to solve the problem, you can then write the FORTRAN needed to accomplish that combination of steps.

The text will, then, have two threads running throughout: 1. how to design programs which solve certain types of problems; and 2. how to use FORTRAN to actually write the programs.

Several other comments about the text may help you make full use of it. First, it contains many examples. When reading the text, and especially the examples, you need to pay close attention to what you are reading. Work through the examples line by line, making sure that you understand each step.

There are a large number of exercises. Most of these are designed to help you practice routine skills. By referring back to the examples as needed to help you get started, you should reach the point where you feel relatively confident in working these routine problems. In addition, a few of the exercises are more complex and will require deeper thought. The intention is that most of the exercises are to be worked out on paper. However, your instructor will no doubt assign certain problems to be done on the computer. In addition, you may wish to try others using the computer. If you have any questions as to how a certain feature works, it is always possible to determine the answer by trying it out using the computer.

Three features have been included to aid you in studying. First, there is a *Review* at the end of almost every section to summarize what you should have learned from the section. Second, there are many *Pitfalls* subsections to warn you of possible misconceptions or errors. Paying close attention to these *Pitfalls* subsections will save you time, both by helping you avoid errors in your programs, and by helping you recognize errors if they are made. Third, an answers key contains solutions or partial solutions to a representative sample of the exercises.

J. Winston Crawley

Charles E. Miller

1

GETTING STARTED

1.1 COMPUTERS AND PROGRAMS

This is a textbook on computer programming. We all have some vague idea of what a computer is and what a computer program is like. For many of us, our ideas may be shaped more by science fiction than by fact. While some of you will have had some experience in programming a computer, we will start in this book with the very basics.

A computer program, loosely speaking, is a list of orders for the computer to carry out in accomplishing a given task. The task may be processing a payroll for a large company, or playing some game such as tic-tac-toe, checkers, or even chess.

Computer programs are written in a form which the computer can use in following the instructions given in the program. We say that the program is written in a **programming language**. There are a large number of programming languages. Some of the more widely used languages are PASCAL, FORTRAN, COBOL, and BASIC. In a beginning course on computer programming, you are likely to concentrate on one of these languages, learning in detail how to make the computer do what you want it to by issuing commands in that particular language.

The language we will utilize in this textbook is FORTRAN. This language is one of the most widely used computer languages today. Knowledge of this language will be beneficial whether you are a computer science or data processing major or just a person interested in taking a few computer courses. However, there is an even more important topic in this text than the FORTRAN programming language. That is, the general topic of computer programming. There are certain ways of thinking and skills that are useful to any programmer, whether she is programming in FORTRAN or in COBOL or in some other language. In this text we will attempt to begin your training in these skills. If you learn these skills (as well as how to implement them in the particular language FORTRAN), they will be of great assistance in your future computer courses. Learning a new computer language will still be a fairly major task, but you will not have to relearn the basic skills. You will be able to build on these skills, adding to your knowledge and ability with each new course.

The Computer

Before we start learning how to program a computer in FORTRAN, we should know something about a computer and what it does. A computer is a machine which processes information. That is, it changes, collects, or reports information. The information can be in the form of text (such as a textbook or a news report), or in the form of numbers (such as weather data or people's ages).

Generally a computer is considered to have five major components (Figure 1.1). The first of these is the **central processing unit (CPU)**, which controls all the other components. The CPU contains a **control unit** which obtains commands from a

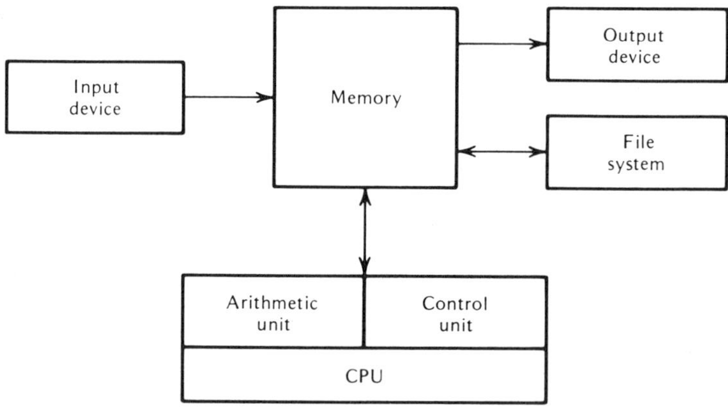

Solid arrows represent flow of data.
CPU controls all other portions.

Figure 1.1

list of commands (the program) and performs the actions required by these commands, one after the other. The CPU also contains an **arithmetic unit**, in which arithmetic operations (such as addition or subtraction) are performed. Thus the two major functions of the CPU are controlling the other components and performing arithmetic operations.

The data used in performing arithmetic operations is stored in another component called the **memory** (or **storage**). The memory consists of a large number of storage locations sometimes called **cells**. In FORTRAN each cell is usually used to store a number. The number may be changed from time to time as the program is running; however, at any given time there is precisely one number stored in a cell. FORTRAN also allows character type data—letters, digits, punctuation marks, and so forth—to be stored in a cell. For now we will consider a cell as a storage place for a number. In modern computers, the program itself is also stored (as a series of numbers) in the memory. This is referred to as a **stored program**. This fact is often used to distinguish between a computer and a programmable calculator. In a programmable calculator, the data memory is usually distinct from the program memory.

Two more major components are the input and output devices. An **input device** provides information to the computer, while an **output device** receives information from the computer. The two are often grouped together and referred to as the **input/output (I/O)** units. Two common input devices are the computer **terminal** and the **card reader**. The computer terminal usually has a keyboard which looks like a typewriter. The terminal can also be used as an output device and can type or display information from the computer. The card reader reads information from a standard IBM card which contains room for 80 characters (letters, digits, punctuation marks). Two common output devices are the **card punch** and the **line printer**. The card punch punches cards for later reading by the card reader. The line printer can print large amounts of information rapidly.

The final major component is the **file system**. Not all computers have file systems, and, in fact, the file system is often considered part of the I/O system. The file system is used for intermediate or long-term storage of data or programs.

Information in the computer is stored in the form of binary numbers, or collections of what are called **bits**. Each bit can be in one of two conditions, which we usually refer to as 0 and 1. Certain combinations of bits are taken to stand for particular numbers, or letters, or machine instructions. (The machine instructions differ from one family of computers to another. The instructions for an IBM 4341 are quite different from the instructions for a Vax 11/780.)

The machine instructions are usually very simple and perform a very simple task. In order to do something useful, we must usually provide a long list of instructions called the **program**. For example, to add the numbers 5 and 6 and place the result in some specific memory location would typically require three instructions. The first would copy the bits representing the first number to a special place in the CPU called an accumulator. The second instruction would cause the arithmetic unit to add the number in the accumulator to the second number from the memory, placing the bit pattern which represents the sum back into the accumulator. The third instruction would then copy this bit pattern representing the sum back into the desired location in the memory.

A program written in the form so that the computer can directly perform each instruction is called a **machine language** program. Writing such a program is very difficult but fortunately is rarely necessary. Machine language programs are not only difficult to write, but are also difficult to understand or modify. In addition, if there is an error (or **bug**) in a machine language program, it can be very difficult to locate or remove.

Fortunately, the FORTRAN language (and others) allows us to write programs in a form more easily understood by people. The FORTRAN command to add 5 and 6 and place the result into a memory location called K is

```
K = 5 + 6
```

In fact, rather complicated computations can be specified simply in FORTRAN. For example,

```
A = (X1 + X2 + X3)/3.0
```

computes the average of the three numbers in the memory locations called X1, X2, and X3, and places the result into the location called A. Notice that we refer to the cells or memory locations by name (K, A, X1, and so on).

A program in FORTRAN is simpler to write than one in machine language. However, the computer can only perform the steps of a machine language program. It cannot work directly with a FORTRAN program. Before the program can be run, it must be translated into machine language. This translation is an involved process which can be and is done by the computer itself under control of a complicated program called a FORTRAN **compiler**. Most computers of any size have a FORTRAN compiler available.

There are two major advantages to writing a program in FORTRAN and having the compiler translate it to machine language. The first, which we have already discussed, is that it is much simpler to write in FORTRAN than in machine language. The second is that, by using FORTRAN compilers for a number of different computers, our program can be translated into machine language and run on any of them.

FORTRAN Programs

The FORTRAN language was one of the first successful "high-level" languages developed. The name FORTRAN stands for FORmula TRANslator. The language was first released by the International Business Machines Corporation (IBM), and was intended for writing scientific or numerical programs. The language has gone through many modifications, and variations in the FORTRAN language are available on different computers. However, there does exist a standard version of FORTRAN, and if one adheres to the standard, it is usually possible to convert the program from one computer to another without too much difficulty. In this text we shall emphasize the standard FORTRAN known as "FORTRAN 77."

Figure 1.2 shows a short but complete FORTRAN program. The numbers to the left of each line are for reference purposes and are not part of the program.

Line 1 is called a comment line. The compiler does not translate such lines into machine language; they are used to explain the program to a human reader. Comment lines start with a "C" in the first position of the line. Blank lines, such as line 2, can be used to separate portions of the program. They also are ignored by the compiler.

Line 3 is a "declaration" statement. It informs the compiler that we will be using three storage locations in this program. In addition, it tells the compiler that we wish to refer to these storage locations using the "variable names" PRICE, TAX, and COST, respectively.When the compiler translates the program into machine language, it will automatically set aside the three requested cells. Finally, the declaration informs the compiler that the numbers to be stored in these cells will be "real" numbers (that is, they will contain decimal points). Line 3 gives information to the compiler. It uses this information in translating the program into machine language, but it does not actually translate the line into machine language.

Lines 4 through 9 contain the actual steps of the program. The program asks the user to enter the price of an item in line 4, then reads that price (line 5), computes a sales tax at 6 percent (line 6), calculates the resulting cost (line 7), prints the resulting cost (line 8), and finally stops (line 9).

Line 10 indicates that there are no more statements in the program.

Figure 1.3 shows the display at the authors' terminal when the program was run. The line Enter Price was the so-called **prompt** written by line 4 of the program. The computer we were using writes the character ">" when it is expecting information from the terminal; we responded with the 4.75. The final line was produced by line 8 in the program.

As we mentioned above, the symbols PRICE, TAX, and COST are called **variables** and are used to name locations in the memory of the computer. The value of a variable, that is, the contents of the memory location, can be changed by the

```
 1 C  THIS PROGRAM ADDS SALES TAX TO PRICE
 2
 3       REAL PRICE, TAX, COST
 4       PRINT *, 'Enter Price'
 5       READ *, PRICE
 6       TAX = 0.06 * PRICE
 7       COST = PRICE + TAX
 8       PRINT *, 'Price is ',PRICE, ' Cost with tax is ', COST
 9       STOP
10       END
```

Figure 1.2

```
Enter price
>4.75
Price is  4.7500000  Cost with tax is  5.0350000
```

Figure 1.3

program. In fact, lines 5, 6, and 7 cause the values of the variables PRICE, TAX, and COST, respectively, to change.

The names of variables may be chosen by the programmer subject to a few restrictions which will be considered later. The compiler attaches no significance to the name of the variable, except that multiple occurrences of the same name refer to the same storage location. The program in Figure 1.4 performs exactly the same operations as that in Figure 1.2. In fact, most compilers would produce exactly the same machine language program as the translation of each of these FORTRAN programs. Notice, however, that it is easy to see what the program in Figure 1.2 is doing. This is not true for Figure 1.4. As a programmer you should choose meaningful names for your variables, not because the compiler attaches significance to the names, but because it makes the program easier for humans to understand.

The symbols REAL, READ, WRITE, STOP, and END are called **key words**. They are used to specify certain FORTRAN statements. The statements can be commands that the computer is to perform, such as the READ, WRITE, and STOP statements. On the other hand, some statements can provide information about the data, the variables, or the program (such as the REAL and END statements).

Needless to say, you are not expected to be able to write a complete FORTRAN program after this brief introduction. The purpose of the example is to give you a feeling of what a FORTRAN program is like. As you begin to learn the details of the FORTRAN language in the next several sections, you should relate those details to this first simple example.

```
C  THIS PROGRAM ADDS SALES TAX TO PRICE

      REAL X, Y, Z
      PRINT *, 'Enter Price'
      READ *, X
      Y = 0.06 * X
      Z = X + Y
      PRINT *, 'Price is ',X, ' Cost with tax is ', Z
      STOP
      END
```

Figure 1.4

Batch and Conversational Jobs

In order to actually run a program on most computer systems, we must submit a "job." There are two common methods for submitting a job to the computer. We will give a brief discussion of each.

For a **batch** job we typically create a deck of cards consisting of our program, the data we wish to use, and some control information. The cards are usually created using a **keypunch**, a mechanical device which punches holes into IBM cards. The cards are then read into the computer utilizing a card reader. Usually one can also create a file with the same information as in the card deck. A job file would usually contain your FORTRAN program, lines containing your data, and so-called **job control language** lines or **JCL**. The JCL lines would usually identify you to the computer system, and control the running of your program. One of the JCL lines would normally be used to tell the system to compile your program and another to run your program. The details vary from system to system and will not be discussed here.

JCL lines are read by a program usually called the **monitor** or **executive** (a part of the **operating system** which controls the overall use of the computer). The compilers and portions of the executive program are usually stored in the file system of the computer and can be loaded into the memory for execution very rapidly.

A **conversational** job has some things in common with a batch job. However, there are some significant differences, of which the most important is that the data for the program is not supplied by the programmer along with the program. Rather, the program will ask for the data as it is needed, at the time the program is running. It is this feature that gives this form of running a job its name of "conversational computing." A person running a job conversationally will typically perform the following steps:

1. "Log on" to the computer terminal. This may involve dialing the computer's number on a phone.
2. Inform the executive that he wishes to use the system's **editor**. The executive will load the editor from the file system. (An editor is a program used for creating files of text, such as programs.)
3. Create the program, one line at a time, in a "conversation" with the editor. If any mistakes are made, it is possible to change them fairly easily.
4. Save a copy of the program on the file system.
5. Inform the executive that he wishes to run the program he has created. The executive will cause the program to be compiled and loaded into the memory. (This step may be postponed until later, if desired. The program saved may be recalled for later use.)
6. The translated program, when it reaches the READ step, will issue a "prompt" to the terminal indicating that data is required. At this time the programmer will type in the data value, and the program will print the answer at the terminal.

7. After the program has finished, the programmer may proceed to other programs, or he may "log off" (leave) the system. At this point the executive will update the amount of computer time used under this user's account number.

Figure 1.5 contains a sample conversational session by a programmer who runs the same program given in Figure 1.2.

In Figure 1.5 we have shaded and numbered the portions typed by the programmer. To simplify the example, we are using a program typed in at an earlier time. Lines labeled 1 and 2 are the programmer's request for service and identification. In line 3 the programmer indicates that he wishes to use a program that already exists, named EX1. Line 4 is a command to display the program at the terminal. Line 5 is the command to run the program after translating it using the FORTRAN (FTN) compiler. Line 6 is the entry of data to the running program and finally lines 7 and 8 are where the programmer indicates that he is finished.

NOTE. If you were to run the same program on your computer, you would probably execute similar actions. However, the details of your commands to the executive and its responses would probably differ from the example.

A major difference between batch and conversational programs is that a conversational program will usually print messages to the output terminal (as we have done) before reading a value from the terminal. A person running a batch job must provide the data in the order expected by the program before the program is run.

NOTE. In the discussion above, we have assumed that the programmer creates both the program and the data. This is generally true up to a point. However, once a programmer is certain that the program works correctly, he usually turns it over to the person who will actually use the program. This user typically makes up the data for the program and runs the program. This is true both for a batch job and for a conversational job.

You have had a brief introduction to what a computer is and how it operates. In addition, you have seen a simple example of what a FORTRAN program looks like. You have been given a very brief introduction to batch and conversational computing.

In the next few sections, we will begin to develop the concepts and skills needed to become a computer programmer. We will also introduce you more formally and in more detail to the FORTRAN concepts hinted at in this section.

REVIEW

Terms and Concepts

programming language
CPU
control unit

```
*TERMINAL INACTIVE*
>$$OPEN DEMAND        ← 1

SESSION PATH OPEN

>ENTER USERID/PASSWORD CLEARANCE LEVEL
>FACMCO2160/XYZ        ← 2


*DESTROY USERID/PASSWORD CLEARANCE LEVEL*
*SPERRY 1100 OPERATING SYSTEM LEV. 39R2A-15  (RSI)*

RUN NUMBER 9

LAST RUN AT: 040885 092845
DATE: 040885   TIME: 093132
IPF 1100 3R1 04/08/85 09:31:34
~C~>OLD EX1        ← 3
~C~>P ALL          ← 4
C  THIS PROGRAM ADDS SALES TAX TO PRICE

      REAL PRICE, TAX, COST
      PRINT *, 'Enter Price'
      READ *, PRICE
      TAX = 0.06 * PRICE
      COST = PRICE + TAX
      PRINT *, 'Price is ',PRICE,' Cost with tax is ', COST
      STOP
      END
'~'C'~'>RUN ,FTN        ← 5
FTN 11R1A   04/08/85-09:33(0,)

END FTN 24 IBANK 33 DBANK
Collector 31R2 (840425 1811:06) 1985 Apr 08 Mon 0933:16
START=005570, PROG SIZE(I/D)=2448/2311
END MAP.  ERRORS: 0  TIME: 25.817  STORAGE: 15906/8/032777/0107377
Enter Price
>4.75      ← 6
Price is 4.7500000  Cost with tax is  5.0350000
'~'C'~'>LOGOFF       ← 7
END IPF
>@FIN      ← 8


 RUNID: FACMCO  ACCT: 5170100000  PROJECT: FACMCO2160
    FACMCO FIN
 TIME:   TOTAL: 00:01:01.838  CBSUPS: 011936016
           CPU:   00:00:00.967  I/O: 00:00:14.304
           CC/ER: 00:00:46.566  WAIT: 00:02:03.233
 SUAS USED:       3.52   SUAS REMAINING:     9974.56
 IMAGES READ:   16       PAGES: 2
 START:  09:31:32 APR 08,1985  FIN: 09:34:07 APR 08,1985
*TERMINAL INACTIVE*
>
```

Figure 1.5

arithmetic unit
memory, storage, cell
stored program
I/O device
card reader
terminal
keypunch
line printer
file system
bit
program
machine language
high-level language
bug
compiler
variable
key words
batch
JCL
monitor, executive, operating system
conversational
editor

1.2 ELEMENTS OF THE FORTRAN LANGUAGE

Speaking in broad terms, we might say that designing a program involves two major steps: (1) constructing an algorithm which solves the given problem and (2) translating this algorithm into an appropriate programming language. In this section we will begin to learn about the details of writing programs in the FORTRAN language. In particular, we will learn about the form of the statements making up a FORTRAN program, and about FORTRAN constants and variables. Throughout this text, a major theme will be this two-step design process. We will learn how to solve increasingly difficult problems and the details of the FORTRAN language needed to write the corresponding programs. The next section will discuss the design process in some detail.

Statement Layout

In the preceding section you saw an example of a FORTRAN program. The lines of such a program fall into three categories—comment lines, blank lines, and statement lines. Comment lines can be identified by the presence of the letter C in the first column of the line. Their purpose is to explain to the reader of the program exactly what the program is doing. They will be printed but otherwise completely ignored by the computer. The information on a comment line may be placed in columns 2–72 of the line.

Blank lines are used to separate parts of the program. Both the comment lines and the blank lines are ignored by the FORTRAN compiler and thus have no effect on the action of a program. They do help the reader and the writer of the program to understand it and therefore should be used as explanatory tools.

The statement line of a FORTRAN program is divided into four separate regions: columns 1–5, column 6, columns 7–72, and columns 73–80. These four regions are sometimes referred to as the "fields" of the line.

The largest field occupies columns 7–72 inclusive. We might call this the "statement field." The actual FORTRAN statement goes in these columns. The statement may be a READ or WRITE statement, an assignment statement such as COST = PRICE + TAX, a declaration such as REAL PRICE, TAX, COST, or any number of other types of FORTRAN statements. (These statement types will be covered in detail in subsequent sections.) Whatever the statement, it must be completely contained in columns 7–72.

NOTE. Most students are concerned about spacing within the FORTRAN statement itself. Must there be blanks on each side of the equals sign? Can there be more than one blank before the plus sign? Fortunately, the answer to these and other similar questions is that it does not matter. Spacing is left to the discretion of the programmer. As far as the compiler is concerned, each of the following statements is identical:

```
      COST = PRICE + TAX
      COST=PRICE+TAX
           COST     =  PRICE+        TAX
        C  O  ST=P   R  ICE+     T A    X
```

Our major concern with spacing is to make the program readable, rather than to satisfy the whims of the compiler. The first two statements above are much more readable than the second two.

Sometimes the FORTRAN statement we would like to write is too long to fit in columns 7–72. In this case we can continue the statement in columns 7–72 of the following line. So that the compiler will know that the second line is a continuation of the first, we place a character (other than zero or space) in column 6 of the second line. This column is called the "continuation column." For example, we could write:

```
      ROOT = (-SECOND+SQRT(SECOND ** 2 - 4.0 * FIRST * THIRD)) /
     $         (2.0 * FIRST)
```

In this text we will consistently use dollar signs (in column 6) to indicate continuation lines. It is possible to continue a statement onto more than one continuation line, and it is not necessary to start the second and subsequent lines in column 7 (as long as they stay within the column 7–72 statement field).

The field occupying columns 1–5 of the line is called the "label field." On most lines, this field will be blank. However, some statements are referred to by other statements in the program. When one statement is referred to by another, a label is placed on the first statement.

The label can be any number which will fit in the five available columns. Thus, it can be any number from 1 to 99999. In addition, it may be placed anywhere in the five columns. For example, each of the following three lines are equivalent:

```
120    Y = X+2.0
 120   Y = X+2.0
   120 Y = X+2.0
```

The third of these lines illustrates a label which is **right justified** in the available columns; it is placed as far to the right as possible in the available space. This is the same way we would usually write down a column of figures for addition:

```
1024
   3
  25
```

In this text we will consistently follow the practice of right justifying all our labels.

There is no rule in FORTRAN concerning the order of the labels in our program. For example, we could have the label 350 on one statement and the label 25 on a statement 15 lines further on in the program. However, this could lead to a program where the statements we need to locate are hard to find. An otherwise understandable program could be made difficult to follow. For this reason, we encourage you to keep your labels in numerical order in your program.

We will not use columns 73–80 in this text. They are available for the programmer to use for any purpose she desires. These columns are most commonly used in batch programs prepared on punched cards. Columns 73–80 are ignored by the compiler. You should make sure that information you are entering into the statement field does not extend past column 72.

Numerical Constants

There are two distinct types of numerical constants we will use in our early FORTRAN programs: INTEGER constants and REAL constants. As you will recall from algebra, an integer is a positive or negative whole number or zero, such as 5, 167, −35, 0, or −4. An integer has no fractional part. An INTEGER constant in FORTRAN is the same—a constant which contains no decimal fraction part. For example, the following are valid INTEGER constants:

```
     5
-47362
     0
100001
```

Notice that in writing numbers in FORTRAN we do not include commas. We write 100001 rather than 100,001.

In contrast, REAL constants are those which contain a fractional part, written as a decimal fraction. For example, these are valid REAL constants:

5.73
−1.502
.273
0.273
6.7
10123.6
−.5
−0.5

Once again, we must write our numbers without commas: 10123.6 rather than 10,123.6. Observe also that we may write either 0.273 or .273, omitting the 0.

What about the constant 5.0? Is it an INTEGER constant or a REAL constant? The answer, since it includes a decimal point, is that it is a REAL constant. The REAL number 5.0 and the INTEGER number 5 will be represented inside the machine using completely different schemes. As we will see later, there are some general guidelines we can follow in trying to decide whether we want to use 5 or 5.0 in a computation. (We comment in passing that the real constant 5.0 may also be written as 5., leaving off the 0.)

NOTES

1. The number of digits allowed in an INTEGER constant is different for different machines. For example, for one type of machine any nine-digit positive or negative number is allowed, while some ten-digit numbers are too large.
2. Likewise, the number of digits of accuracy ("significant digits") in a REAL constant varies from machine to machine. For more digits of accuracy, it is possible to use DOUBLE PRECISION constants, discussed in detail in Chapter 11.
3. The programmer may write REAL constants in exponential, or E notation. This notation is based on scientific notation. The following table indicates the meaning of the exponential notation:

1.5 E 2	is	$1.5 \times 10^{2} = 1.5 \times 100 = 150.0$
1.5 E −2	is	$1.5 \times 10^{-2} = .015$
−3.25 E 3	is	$-3.25 \times 10^{3} = -3250.0$
−0.214 E −01	is	$-0.214 \times 10^{-1} = -0.0214$

The number following the E represents the exponent. To obtain the value of such an expression, we multiply the number before the E by 10 raised to the power indicated by the exponent.

This notation is most useful when dealing with very large numbers (for example 1.6 E 35) or very small numbers (for example, 0.1 E −8).

Variables and Declarations

Just as there are INTEGER and REAL constants, there are both INTEGER and REAL variables. A **variable** is a symbolic quantity which may take on any one of a number of different values. The use of the term "variable" is similar to its use in algebra. For example, in the algebraic expression

$$y = 2x + 1$$

both y and x are variables. Most variables in algebra are written as a single letter, frequently x, y, or z. In FORTRAN, on the other hand, we will generally use a combination of letters or letters and digits for our variable names. For example, the following are valid FORTRAN variable names:

```
PAY
INCOME
STAR3
AVE
HUMID
X
Y
X3Y12A
```

The rules for forming a valid variable name are simple.

1. There must be between 1 and 6 letters or digits.
2. No other characters, such as periods, dashes, or commas, are allowed.
3. The first character must be a letter.
4. No more than 6 characters are allowed.

These are the rules; however, good programming practice requires that we do more than follow the rules. We must choose our variable names so that their names convey the quantities they are intended to represent. Recall how much more understandable the program in Section 1.1 was when we used the variables PRICE, TAX, and COST. The identical program, using X, Y, and Z instead, accomplished the same thing but was much harder to comprehend. Given a choice between XNCM and INCOME as variable names for a variable representing a person's income, it should be obvious which is preferable.

> **COMMENT.** English-speaking people generally have difficulty reading a word with the vowels omitted. Given a choice between CNTYTX and COUNTY as a variable name for "county tax," probably COUNTY is better even though it completely omits any reference to the word "tax."

A variable name represents a location in the computer's memory area. The compiler automatically sets aside space in the memory for each variable we use in our program. As the program runs, numerical values will be placed into these locations. For example, the READ step of the program in Figure 1.2, p. 5, reads a number and places it in the location represented by the variable PRICE. The step TAX = .06* PRICE calculates a value and places it in the TAX memory location. It is possible to change the value in a memory location—hence the term "variable." The value may vary as the program runs, but at any given time there can only be one value stored in a variable.

The values that are stored in a numerical variable may be either integer (6, −3, 0, and so on) or real (5.52, −16.03, 2.0, . . .). If the values contained in a variable will be integers, we should use an INTEGER variable. On the other hand, a REAL variable should be used when working with real quantities. In order to inform the compiler which variables our program will use and what type (INTEGER or REAL) they are, we will include **declarations** at the beginning of the program. In the program of Figure 1.2 there is one declaration statement:

```
REAL PRICE, TAX, COST
```

In this statement we listed every REAL variable we planned to use in the program. If we had used any INTEGER variables, we would have had a similar statement listing all the integer variables. Typically, then, our programs will begin with the following two statements (as for all statements, in columns 7-72):

INTEGER list of integer variables, separated by commas

REAL list of real variables, separated by commas

One of these may be omitted in a program which contains no INTEGER or no REAL variables.

Suppose we are writing a program which reads employee number, hourly rate, and hours worked, and calculates the gross pay. We will decide on the variables needed, and give the appropriate declarations.

Since hourly rate, hours worked, and pay will most likely involve fractions of dollars or hours, we choose REAL variables for these. We will use an integer variable for the employee number. Here is a complete variable list:

Name	Type	Use	Comment
EMPNO	INTEGER	Employee number	
RATE	REAL	Hourly rate	
HOURS	REAL	Hours worked	
PAY	REAL	Gross Pay	

The declarations could be either

```
INTEGER EMPNO
REAL RATE, HOURS, PAY
```

or

```
REAL RATE, HOURS, PAY
INTEGER EMPNO
```

The order of the two statements and the variables within the statements are immaterial.

COMMENT. If we forget to **declare** a variable by including it in one of the declaration statements, the compiler will make a choice itself. If the variable begins with I, J, K, L, M or N the compiler will assume it is INTEGER; otherwise it will assume it is REAL. If this is not what we intended, our program will very likely not work correctly. Many FORTRAN programmers do not declare any of their variables, instead choosing their variable names to take advantage of these assumptions by the compiler. In our experience, this can lead to many hours spent in chasing down errors caused by carelessness in choosing variable names. We advocate, and in this text we will follow, the practice of explicitly declaring all our variables.

CHARACTER Constants and Variables

Frequently you will want to manipulate text information in your programs. For example, you might have to process data containing name and address information. FORTRAN provides a character data type for this purpose. A character constant is written with the character values enclosed in apostrophes (sometimes referred to as single quotes). For example, the following are valid character constants:

```
'ABCD'
'?$#!XAb'
'156'
' '
```

A space in a character constant is significant and occupies a position within the constant. The length of the constant is simply the number of characters between the beginning and ending quotes. The lengths of the constants above are four, seven, three, and one. You should also note that digits are acceptable characters and so the third constant is a valid character constant. Furthermore the constant '156' is handled by the compiler differently from the way an integer 156 is handled. The two are not equal and are not related in any simple direct way.

An apostrophe is represented within a character constant by writing two adjacent apostrophes. For example, the text "John's" would be written as 'John''s' and would have a length of six (since the double apostrophe represents a single character).

Character variables follow the same name rules as numeric variables and are declared using a declaration statement similar to those used to declare INTEGER or REAL variables. In general, it will look like this:

```
CHARACTER*n    list of variables
```

As usual, the variables in the list will be separated by commas if there is more than one variable. Consider the following examples:

```
CHARACTER*1 CODE
CHARACTER*2 CLASS, TITLE
CHARACTER*20 NAME, ADDRESS
CHARACTER*2 STATE
```

The number behind the asterisk, indicated by the "n" in the general description above, indicates how many characters are going to be stored in the variable. Keep in mind that a blank space is considered a character in counting the number of characters in the variable, and two apostrophes are interpreted as one. For example, each of the following character constants consists of exactly ten characters:

```
'0123456789'
'John''s dog'
'J. J. ROHM'
';:*&%=+@!('
```

To store any of these strings, we would need a CHARACTER type variable with the number after the asterisk at least ten.

If the variable is capable of storing 12 characters and we put a string of ten characters into the variable, then the last two characters in the variable will be blanks. This is sometimes referred to as **right padding with blanks**. The rest of the available space will be put in as "padding" at the right end of the string.

In general, we will know exactly how many characters we will be putting into the variable in question, and we will make an appropriate declaration statement using this length after the asterisk. For example, if the variable CODE will be used to contain the sex code from a data line, we will use the declaration statement.

```
CHARACTER*1 CODE
```

In any case, the length of a character variable must be one or more, and less than some maximum value (which depends on your computer system).

Pitfalls

Most of the elements of the FORTRAN language are fairly straightforward once you have had a little practice. However, there are a few problems which can easily arise but are easily fixed if you know where to look. In this section, and in others like it throughout the text, we will try to indicate some potential problems to anticipate. When you have errors in a line or in a program which "looks OK," the problem could be one of those listed. More important, perhaps, by consciously avoiding these pitfalls, you can produce more error-free programs.

1. It is easy to type the letter O in place of the digit 0, or vice versa. This type of error is difficult to locate, since our minds frequently see what they expect to see. In addition, many printers used with computers make very little distinction between the two characters.

   The distinction between the letter l and the 1 can also be difficult to spot. Many experienced typists use a lowercase l for the number 1. On a computer this is not allowed.
2. Columns 73 to 80 are for programmer use. If we inadvertently allow our FORTRAN statement to extend beyond column 72, the line may look correct to us, but those characters beyond column 72 will be ignored by the compiler.

A similar problem can arise if we inadvertently begin our statement in column 6. Since column 6 is the continuation column, the line will be treated as a continuation of the previous line.

Both these errors can lead to strange-seeming compiler diagnostic messages.

3. As we have described earlier, if we forget to declare a variable, we may or may not get the type of variable (INTEGER or REAL) that we intended. We should always double-check our declarations, especially for spelling errors (for example, INDO when we intended IDNO).

   Likewise, misspelling variable names in the program itself is a potential problem which should be avoided.
4. The character string '156' is totally different from the integer 156.
5. In a character constant, two consecutive apostrophes are needed to represent an apostrophe.

REVIEW

Terms and Concepts

right justified
variable
declarations

Statement Layout

Label—columns 1–5
Continuation—column 6
FORTRAN statements—columns 7–72
Programmer use—columns 73–80
Comment statement—C in column 1, comment in columns 2–72

FORTRAN Syntax

Constants
- INTEGER, for example, 34, −4716, 0, 151025
- REAL, for example, −16.26, 143.916, 0.0
- CHARACTER, for example, 'ABC', 'John''s'

Variables
- One to six letters or digits in variable name
- First character must be a letter

Used to store a single numerical quantity. The value of the quantity stored may vary as the program runs. Only one quantity is present at any given time in a given variable.

Declarations
- INTEGER list of integer variables, separated by commas

REAL list of real variables, separated by commas

CHARACTER* length list of character variables, separated by commas

Purpose—inform compiler of the name and type of each variable used in the program

Placement—at beginning of program

Pitfalls

1. O for 0, l for 1, L for l, etc.
2. Statement past column 72, or in column 6.
3. Variables not declared, or misspelled.
4. '156' not same as 156.
5. Two apostrophes to represent one.

EXERCISES

1. Decide whether each of the following is a valid FORTRAN variable name. For those which are not valid, explain why not.

(a) T	**(f)** T123
(b) RHO	**(g)** 18XYZ
(c) TRE.AD	**(h)** TOTAL
(d) AVERAGE	**(i)** COUNTER
(e) XMAS	**(j)** X$

2. Decide whether the following are valid FORTRAN constants. For those which are valid, identify them as real, integer, or character constants.

(a) 123	**(e)** 12318	**(i)** −600	**(m)** 1,340
(b) −.0567	**(f)** 'AB''C'	**(j)** 0.0	**(n)** '?!'x'
(c) −.567	**(g)** 643124	**(k)** −5,342.0	
(d) '−.567'	**(h)** '125'	**(l)** '1,340'	

3. For each of the following, decide on appropriate variable names for the quantities involved, and give the required declarations.

(a) social security number, age, hourly pay, number of hours worked

(b) student name, three test grades, average test grade

(c) section number, number of students, number who passed the course, number who failed, average grade of the class

(d) number of bears in sample, height in centimeters of all the bears, average height in centimeters

(e) state name, population, number of cities over 250,000 population, square miles, population density (population per square mile), percentage of population with high school education or above

1.3 DESIGNING AND WRITING LOOPING PROGRAMS (PART I)

The first two sections of the text have introduced a few fundamentals of the FORTRAN language. They have also discussed some of the components of the computer.

In this section we begin to learn how to design and write a program which will cause the various components of the computer to perform a desired sequence of activities.

Algorithms and Refinement

We may describe a computer program as being a detailed, step-by-step listing of the steps to be performed by the control unit of the computer, written in a computer-oriented language such as FORTRAN. Perhaps the most important words in this description are "detailed" and "computer-oriented." A broad statement of what we plan to do, such as the phrase "calculate the taxes for this person," will be helpful to us as we plan the program. Before we actually have a program, however, we must **refine** this statement to a more detailed set of instructions and convert these instructions into a form the computer can utilize. We might wind up with something like this:

1. Calculate taxable income by subtracting $15 per dependent from the income.
2. Federal tax is 16% of taxable income.
3. State tax is 3% of income.
4. Local tax is 0.5% of income.

This could then be translated into appropriate steps for whatever computer-oriented language we were using. In FORTRAN, for example, this would involve choosing appropriate variable names and writing assignment statements similar to these:

```
TAXINC = INCOME - 15.00 * NUMBER
FEDERAL = .16 * TAXINC
STATE = .03 * INCOME
LOCAL = .005 * INCOME
```

In this form the computer would be able to follow our instructions and perform the desired sequence of steps.

> **NOTE.** As we learned in Section 1.1, the computer itself does not work directly with the FORTRAN program. Instead, the program is translated by a special program called a compiler into machine language, the form the control unit utilizes. However, since this is done for us, we can safely think of the computer as working directly with the FORTRAN program.

In the preceding discussion we have hinted at the concept of an **algorithm**. An algorithm, like a program, is a list of the steps to be performed by the computer. However, it may be written in a combination of English and algebraic notation, rather than in a computer language, in order to be more easily understood by a human being. The purpose of an algorithm is to help us state precisely what must be done to solve the given problem.

This text presents program writing as a two-step process. The first step is planning the program. This involves studying the program description to make sure we understand what is being asked for. We will identify values which are to be calculated and values on which those calculations are based. This will lead to a preliminary list of variables. The algorithm is used to plan the steps needed to obtain the desired results.

For a given problem, our first algorithm may be very rough, giving only a broad outline of what we plan to do. We will then go back and fill in the details. This process, known as "stepwise refinement," may have to be repeated several times before we have an algorithm which is detailed enough to be translated into a computer language. (As the algorithm is refined, it may begin to look more and more like the program will eventually look.) The example on calculating taxes illustrated a refinement of the phrase "calculate the taxes for this person."

Four Programming Techniques

There are four primary processes from which we will build our algorithms, and hence our programs, in this text. They are

1. sequencing
2. looping
3. decision making
4. subprograms

Let us describe each of these concepts briefly.

Sequencing refers to performing one step of the program after another, from first to last. The simplest type of program merely consists of a list of steps, where each step is performed once, in order. The computer would execute the first line of the program, then the second line, then the third line, and so on. The example in Section 1.1 illustrated a program consisting of nothing but sequencing.

Frequently, after reading an input value and calculating and printing an answer, we would like to repeat the whole process for a new input value. It is in fact possible to write a program to do this. The process used is called **looping**. Looping refers to the situation where the computer executes all or part of the program repeatedly. This has helped make the computer practical for such things as payrolls, where there are hundreds or thousands of employees to be processed. The alternative, running the program again for each new employee, would hardly be desirable.

The third technique, **decision making**, is indispensable. As a simple example, for a payroll calculation the formula to be used for pay may depend on whether overtime was earned. If a program is to be used for finding the pay for each employee, it must have some facility for examining the number of hours worked, and performing different calculations for those with overtime and those without.

The fourth technique, **subprograms**, is an extremely useful and convenient tool. It is possible to write small programs which do not use subprograms. However, it is almost imperative that subprograms be used in writing very complex programs. Briefly, the idea will be to divide a large program up into smaller pieces. This helps us concentrate on one smaller problem at a time.

In Chapters 1 and 2, we will learn to write programs which use simple forms of these four techniques. In the remainder of the text, we will build upon these ideas to write increasingly complex programs.

Planning a Looping Program

We will give an example which illustrates sequencing and looping. It also uses a very limited form of decision making. We start with a fairly rough algorithm and refine it. In the process, we introduce a form of algorithm description which we will use throughout this text. This algorithm description language is designed to help bridge the gap between a vague English-language description and the strict rules of a language such as FORTRAN. We will refer to it as **pseudocode**.

Suppose we want to find the areas of a number of rectangles. We begin by analyzing this very brief description of what the program must do. As part of this process, we begin thinking about the variables we will need in order to solve the problem. Some of these variables will represent the answer we are calculating, in this case the area. Others will represent the values upon which that answer is to be based. The problem statement is vague here. However, we recall that the area of a rectangle may be calculated by finding the product of its length and its width. Thus we will need variables representing these quantities. Since these are needed for the calculations, they will be "input" to the program. The person running the program will have to tell the program what the length and width are; the program will calculate the area.

We also begin planning the algorithm. As a first step, we might write something like this, using sequencing to execute the steps in the proper order.

1. Ask the user to enter a length and a width.
2. Read the length and width.
3. Calculate the area.
4. Print the area.

However, something is missing in this description. The program is supposed to find the areas of a number of rectangles. If we write a program based on the four steps above, it will only calculate one area. We need a loop in order to calculate the areas for several rectangles. As will be true for all the loops we write, we will need to include a way to get out of the loop.

It is time to get a little more specific. We write a variable list which looks something like this:

	Name	Type	Use	Comment
Input:	LENGTH	REAL	Length of the rectangle	
	WIDTH	REAL	Width of the rectangle	
Output:	AREA	REAL	Area of the rectangle	

We write a somewhat refined algorithm which uses the variable names and which includes the specific terms **loop** and **endloop** to indicate that a loop is involved.

```
loop
    print a prompt asking for input
    read LENGTH and WIDTH
    leave (exit) the loop if no more rectangles
    calculate AREA
    print AREA
endloop
stop
```

Between the **loop** and **endloop** are placed the "body" of the loop, the steps which are to be repeatedly executed. (To make them stand out better, we indent them.) By the word **exit** we mean "leave the loop," that is, "proceed to the step following the **endloop** step." In this example that is the **stop** statement.

We now have a fairly refined algorithm. The **loop** and **endloop** together state that the steps in between are to be done repeatedly, until there are no more rectangles. After we leave the loop, the program will stop. There are one or two more things to do, however, before we begin writing the program.

First, we need to refine the step which leaves the loop. To do so, we need to ask the question: "How will the program know that there are no more rectangles?" One technique that is frequently used is to ask the user to supply some "dummy" input to indicate that he is through. This is input which could not be confused with actual input. For example, we might ask for a length of zero to terminate the calculations. If so, we can rewrite

```
leave (exit) the loop if no more rectangles
```

as

```
if LENGTH = 0 then
    exit
endif
```

Just as the end of the loop is signalled by an **endloop** line, we use an **endif** line to indicate where the **if** thought ends. Since the only thing we want to do if the length is 0 is to leave the loop (**exit**), we place the **endif** right after the **exit** line.

Unless the user is told that a length of 0 will terminate the process, she will not know. It might, therefore, be a good idea to print some instructions at the very beginning of the program, before we start the looping part of the program. The step to do this, placed before the loop, will be done only once.

Finally, we will write the "calculate AREA" step as an **assignment statement**, as shown here:

```
AREA ← LENGTH × WIDTH
```

This is read as "AREA is assigned the value LENGTH times WIDTH." In our algorithms, we will use the arrow symbol (←) to indicate assigning a value to a variable.

The complete refined algorithm is given below.

```
print instructions
loop
    print a prompt asking for input
    read LENGTH and WIDTH
    if LENGTH = 0 then
        exit
    endif
    AREA ← LENGTH × WIDTH
    print AREA
endloop
stop
```

Writing a Looping Program

Many programs follow the general pattern illustrated by the algorithm we have just developed, as shown in the following example. (For the first portion of the textbook, all the programs will follow this general outline.)

```
print instructions
loop
    print a prompt asking for input
    read input values
    if dummy input value then
        exit
    endif
    perform calculations
    print answers
endloop
stop
```

The pattern involves a loop which repeatedly reads some values and calculates and prints some answers which depend on the input. The user is asked to supply some dummy input value which indicates that she no longer desires to use the program. This dummy input value is used to "control" the loop; that is, to determine when it is time to leave the loop.

To write programs such as this in FORTRAN, we need to learn how to accomplish four major things:

1. print (this includes printing messages such as instructions, and printing values of variables for the answers);
2. read values for variables;
3. perform calculations (assignment statements);
4. control the looping process: cause the repetition to occur, and also leave the loop at the proper time.

The assignment statement (#3 in the list) will be covered in detail in Section 2.1. Reading and printing will be introduced in this section and expanded upon throughout the text. We will cover the looping process in some detail in this section, using the sample algorithm developed in the previous subsection as a guide.

For ease of reference, we have reproduced the variable list and algorithm for the program we are developing in Figure 1.6. In addition, that figure contains the

	Name	Type	Use	Comment
Input:	LENGTH	REAL	Length of the rectangle	
	WIDTH	REAL	Width of the rectangle	
Output:	AREA	REAL	Area of the rectangle	

```
print instructions
loop
  print a prompt asking for input
  read LENGTH and WIDTH
  if LENGTH = 0 then
    exit
  endif
  AREA ← LENGTH × WIDTH
  print AREA
endloop
stop
```

```
      REAL LENGTH,WIDTH,AREA
      PRINT *,'  This program finds areas of rectangles.'
      PRINT *,'  For each rectangle, enter the length and width of'
      PRINT *,'rectangle, separated by a space or a comma.'
      PRINT *,'  When you are ready to quit, enter a length of 0.'
   10 CONTINUE
         PRINT *,' '
         PRINT *,'Enter a length and width.'
         READ *, LENGTH,WIDTH
         IF (LENGTH.EQ.0) THEN
            GO TO 500
         ENDIF
         AREA = LENGTH * WIDTH
         PRINT *,'The area is ',AREA
         GO TO 10
  500 CONTINUE
      STOP
      END
```

Figure 1.6

resulting program. The numbers to the left of the algorithm and program are for reference purposes only. In the following paragraphs, we explain the various steps involved in going from algorithm to program.

The shaded lines in the program (lines 6, 10–12, and 15–16) relate to the loop control referred to earlier. The other lines either declare variables, or are directly related to the individual prints, reads, and assignments of the algorithm. For convenience, we postpone the consideration of the loop control lines until last.

> **NOTE.** Just as in our algorithm, we have indented the body of the loop. Although the compiler does not require this indentation pattern, it does make the program more readable. It is possible to see at a glance which steps are contained in the loop's body. We will follow this practice for the examples in the remainder of this text.

Line 1 of the program declares the variables which are used in the program. The information in the variable list is used to write the declarations. In this program all the variables are REAL, so there are no INTEGER or CHARACTER declarations.

Lines 2 through 5 print the instructions (line 1 of the algorithm). The form of the PRINT statement being used here is

```
PRINT *,message in quotes
```

The asterisk (*) in the statement implies what is called **list directed I/O**, or **free format I/O**. In this form of print, the computer determines the exact form the output will take. When we are simply printing a single message, this means that the message within the quotes will be printed exactly as it appears. Thus the series of four PRINT statements will cause the program, when it is run, to print the following on the terminal:

```
 This program finds areas of rectangles.
 For each rectangle, enter the length and width of
rectangle, separated by a space or a comma.
 When you are ready to quit, enter a length of 0.
```

Lines 7 and 8 print the prompt (line 3 in the algorithm). They are similar to the lines which print the instructions; the computer will print precisely what is contained in the quotes. In particular, line 7 will print a blank line prior to the actual prompt. This technique can help the user mentally form a "break" between the answer for the previous rectangle and the input for the new one. Line 8 is the prompt itself.

Line 13 is the assignment statement. We will be studying assignment statements in more detail in a later section. However, notice that FORTRAN uses an equals sign (=) to perform assignment, and that it uses an asterisk (*) to indicate multiplication. (It uses a plus sign (+) for addition, a minus sign (−) for subtraction, and a slash (/) for division.)

Line 14 prints the answer. It is similar to the PRINT statements we have used before, but it prints two things: the message 'The area is', and the variable AREA.

In general, the form of the PRINT statement may be summarized as:

```
PRINT *,list of things to print
```

The list of things to print may contain messages or variable names, and it may include one or more things. The items in the list are separated by commas. For example, to print the variables X, Y, and Z, we could write

```
PRINT *,X,Y,Z
```

In our program, we are printing the message

```
The area is
```

followed immediately by the value of the variable AREA. A typical output line might look like

```
The area is    17.4
```

Similarly, we could write

```
PRINT *,AREA,' is the area of the rectangle.'
```

to print first the value of the AREA variable, then the message explaining the answer. For this PRINT, a typical output line might look like

```
17.4    is the area of the rectangle.
```

COMMENTS

1. In list-directed I/O, the computer chooses the exact form that the answer takes. This means that if you ran the program, the output line might look a little different. In particular, some computers use the exponential notation to print real variables. On such a computer, the output line might look something like

   ```
   The area is    0.174E+02
   ```

   This form was discussed in the previous section.
2. You might be wondering about the extra space after the word "is" in the message 'The area is '. This makes sure that there is at least one blank space between the word "is" and the answer printed for the area. Similarly, the message ' is the area of the rectangle.' includes a blank before the word "is" to separate it from the number printed for the area.

The remaining lines of the program cause the desired looping (repetition) to take place. Recall that the **loop** in line 2 of the algorithm and the **endloop** in line 10 together state that the lines in between should be repeated. Lines 5–7 of the algorithm "control" the loop, causing the repetition to terminate when the user inputs a length of 0. We now discuss these two issues: how to achieve the repetition, and how to exit from the loop using a dummy entry.

Lines 6 and 15 illustrate how we shall achieve repetition in our programs. At the bottom of the loop, we will use a GO TO statement to cause the computer to branch back up to the top of the loop. At the top of the loop, we will place a CONTINUE statement with a label on it.

The form of the GO TO statement is

```
GO TO label
```

This statement causes the computer to proceed immediately to the step indicated by the label in the GO TO. Thus, line 15 of the program causes the computer to go back up to the line with the label 10 (line 6). From there it proceeds down through lines 7–15 again, thus repeating the loop body.

The CONTINUE statement we place at the top of the loop will have the form

```
label CONTINUE
```

This statement does not actually cause the computer to do anything; it is simply used as a handy place for a label. Although it would be possible to place the label directly on the first line in the loop body (line 7), we will generally use the CONTINUE at the top of the loop as illustrated in this example.

The only thing remaining, then, is to study the technique used to leave the loop. This involves a quick look at the FORTRAN IF/THEN and ENDIF statements. For our purposes, we need only be able to code steps such as

if dummy input value **then**
  exit
endif

This will be coded in the form

```
IF (variable .EQ. dummy value) THEN
   GO TO label
ENDIF
```

Since the word **exit** in the algorithm means "leave the loop," we place a labelled CONTINUE at the bottom of the loop (right after the GO TO, line 16). The **exit** step may then be coded by using a GO TO statement branching to that label.

FORTRAN uses .EQ. to compare two things to see if they are equal. Moreover, the comparison must be placed in parentheses. Thus we have, in line 10,

```
IF (LENGTH.EQ.0) THEN
```

to convey the idea that if the user has input a length of 0 we wish to leave the loop. The ENDIF in line 12 says that that is the end of the list of things to do when the length is 0. If we forget the **endif** in the algorithm, a person might still understand what we mean. If we forget the ENDIF in the program, the compiler will not understand our intention and will generate an error message.

COMMENT. Recall that the particular label numbers used (10 and 500 in this example) are chosen by the programmer. You will want to develop a systematic, orderly method for choosing labels. It will aid in reading a program if you always keep the labels in numerical order.

SUMMARY

We list here a brief summary of the FORTRAN we have looked at in coding this example:

1. Code print statements using PRINT *, list of items.
2. Code read statement using READ *, list of variables.
3. Code assignment statements using FORTRAN assignments. These will use an equals sign (=) to do the assignment.
4. Achieve looping (repetition) by placing

```
10 CONTINUE
```

at the top of the loop, and

```
GO TO 10
```

at the bottom.
5. Achieve loop control (exiting the loop) by placing

```
500 CONTINUE
```

at the bottom of the loop (after the GO TO 10), and using

```
IF (variable .EQ. dummy value) THEN
   GO TO 500
ENDIF
```

to leave the loop when the dummy value is input by the user.

An Aside on Algorithms

In this section we have developed a sample program using a two-step process. The first step was to develop a plan for the program, which we eventually developed to the point of a pseudocode algorithm (together with a list of the variables to be used in the program). The second step was to code this variable list and algorithm as a FORTRAN program.

We will continue to follow this general pattern throughout the text. The algorithms we develop serve at least two important purposes:

1. They are a useful design tool. They allow us to describe what the program is to do in a systematic way. The form used emphasizes looping and decision-making structures, making us conscious of these structures and their presence in our program. In conjunction with a variable list, a carefully designed algorithm encourages us to think about our problem before the coding stage, thus reducing the total time spent in writing and debugging a program.

2. The algorithm and variable list become an important part of the "documentation" of the program. Good documentation can make the job of modifying a program in later years easier. In addition, it can help in finding errors which, in a large program, may only become apparent after months or even years of use.

Both of these benefits become more pronounced as programs become more complicated. One could argue that, for the relatively simple programs we will be writing, the algorithm and variable list are a waste of time. The programs are simple to design, and thus need no documentation. This is perhaps true, especially for the best students. However, we will consistently use the algorithm and variable list tools, even for simple programs. There are two reasons for this:

1. The algorithm form is relatively language-independent. We will translate our algorithms into FORTRAN. However, the same algorithms could be translated into other programming languages, such as ALGOL, COBOL, or PASCAL. If you think in terms of algorithms, it will greatly simplify the program design portion of learning any new language.
2. To learn to use a tool, you must practice in simple settings. If you decide to develop the algorithm tool only when you really need it, it will probably be too late. At the least, it will be a relatively major undertaking. By developing your facility in devising algorithms gradually, you will be able to handle complex problems more easily when they do arise.

REVIEW

Terms and Concepts

refinement
algorithm
pseudocode

Four Important Programming Techniques

1. sequencing
2. looping
3. decision making
4. subprograms

Pseudocode Features

Surrounding body of loop—**loop** and **endloop**

Using dummy input to terminate loop, as

```
if variable = dummy value then
    exit
endif
```

Typical algorithm form

```
print instructions
loop
   prompt for input
   read input variables
   if dummy value entered then
      exit
   endif
   perform calculations
   print answers
endloop
stop
```

FORTRAN Syntax

Reading variables (free format)

```
READ *, list of variables separated by commas
```

Printing strings and variables (free format)

```
PRINT *, list of strings/variables separated by commas
```

String—1 or more characters enclosed in single quotes (that is, apostrophes)

IF statement for loop control

```
If (variable .EQ. dummy value) THEN
  GO TO label
ENDIF
```

GO TO statement for loop control

```
GO TO label (at top of loop or after loop)
```

Labelled statements for loop control

```
label CONTINUE (at top of loop or after loop)
```

Typical program form

```
    declarations
    PRINT statements for instructions
 10 CONTINUE
       PRINT statements for prompt
       READ statement to read input values
       IF (variable .EQ. dummy value) THEN
          GO TO 500
       ENDIF
       assignment statements to calculate answers
       PRINT statement to print answers
       GO TO 10
500 CONTINUE
    STOP
    END
```

EXERCISES

1. By following the example given in this section, and by using the typical algorithm and program form in the Review portion at the end of the section, write programs for the following. You should make a variable list, decide on an appropriate dummy value to terminate the loop, write an algorithm, and finally write the program.
   (a) The area of a square can be found by multiplying the length of a side by itself (side × side). Write a program to find the areas of squares.
   (b) The perimeter of a square is 4 times the length of the side. Write a program to find the perimeters of squares.
   (c) Write a program which repeatedly reads 2 real numbers. For each pair of real numbers it reads, it should calculate and print their sum.
2. What changes would you make to the program in Exercise 1(c) in order to find the difference rather than the sum?
3. What changes would you make to the program in Exercise 1(c) if the numbers were integers rather than real numbers?

1.4 DESIGNING AND WRITING LOOPING PROGRAMS (PART II)

Running the Program

In the previous section, we developed a program for finding the areas of rectangles. For convenience, that program is reproduced below.

```
      REAL LENGTH,WIDTH,AREA
      PRINT *,' This program finds areas of rectangles.'
      PRINT *,' For each rectangle, enter the length and width of'
      PRINT *,'rectangle, separated by a space or a comma.'
      PRINT *,' When you are ready to quit, enter a length of 0.'
   10 CONTINUE
         PRINT *,' '
         PRINT *,'Enter a length and width.'
         READ *,LENGTH,WIDTH
         IF (LENGTH.EQ.0) THEN
            GO TO 500
         ENDIF
         AREA = LENGTH * WIDTH
         PRINT *,'The area is ',AREA
         GO TO 10
  500 CONTINUE
      STOP
      END
```

In Figure 1.7, we show the results of running the program. We are skipping over the details of how you will type in and run the program, since these will be different from computer to computer. Your instructor will supply these details. However, once the program begins to run, what happens is generally pretty much the same no matter what computer you are using. In the following discussion, we will indicate where you may encounter slight differences.

```
   This program finds areas of rectangles.
   For each rectangle, enter the length and width of
rectangle, separated by a space or a comma.
   When you are ready to quit, enter a length of 0.

Enter a length and width.
>10.0,1.3
The area is  13.000000

Enter a length and width.
>.05,.05
The area is  .25000000-002

Enter a length and width.
>50.2,20.0
The area is  1004.0000

Enter a length and width.
>.001 .001
The area is  .10000000-005

Enter a length and width.
>1000.0 1000.0
The area is  1000000.0

Enter a length and width.
>40.0
>30.0
The area is  1200.0000

Enter a length and width.
>145.2,17.5
The area is  2541.0000

Enter a length and width.
>319.92,.045
The area is  14.396400

Enter a length and width.
>-5.0,-4.0
The area is  20.000000

Enter a length and width.
>0.0,0.0
```

Figure 1.7

We begin, then, after the user (the person trying out the program) has requested the computer to run the program. The first action taken by the program is to print the four lines of explanation. The program next enters the loop, where it prints a blank line and then prints the prompts, "Enter a length and width." At this point, the computer pauses and waits for the user to supply the data the program needs for the READ statement.

In the figure, the '>' symbol was printed by the computer as a "prompt character." Some versions of FORTRAN use such a prompt character, while others do not. The prompt character is not necessarily a '>' character; for example, many versions of FORTRAN would use an asterisk (*) as the prompt character. Still others do not issue any prompt character, but simply wait for user input.

In the sample run, we have shaded all user responses. The first line of data input by the user is

```
10.0,1.3
```

Notice that the numbers are REAL, and that they are separated by a comma. The program uses the order of the variables in the READ statement to determine which is the length and which is the width. In this case, the first of the two numbers is read by the computer as the value for the LENGTH variable, the second as the value for the WIDTH variable. The program checks the LENGTH to see if it is 0.0. Since it is not, the AREA is calculated, and the answer is printed in the output line:

```
The area is    13.000000
```

NOTE. The exact form in which the answer is printed may vary from computer to computer. For example, the following are some of the possible ways that the number could appear. All have the same meaning.

```
13.000000
13.0
0.130000E 02
1.3E+01
.13000000+002
```

The exact form used is the choice of the computer when we use free format output. In a later section (Section 2.1) we will learn how to take control of the exact form of the output by using a FORMAT statement.

(The form .13000000+002 is similar to, but not quite the same as, the exponential form discussed in Section 1.2.) The +002 part means "times 10 to the second power, just as E+02 or E 02 would mean.)

After printing the answer, the computer goes back up to the top of the loop (label 10) and repeats the process. This involves printing a blank line, printing the prompt, and waiting for input. This time the user types in the line

```
.05,.05
```

Since the LENGTH value is not 0.0, the AREA is calculated and printed in the message

```
THE AREA IS  .25000000-002
```

which means .25 times 10 to the power −2, or .0025.

This process continues until the user enters a value of 0.0 for the length. In the figure, several such values are entered. We will comment on a few of these.

Of special interest is the sixth entry, in which the user entered only the LENGTH value. Since the READ required two values, another prompt character was issued by the computer and the user had to enter the WIDTH value on the next line.

The fourth and fifth entries illustrate the fact that the two numbers may be separated by a blank space rather than by a comma.

Observe that, since the program was not written to detect erroneous input, the values in the next to last entry (−5.0 for the LENGTH and −4.0 for the WIDTH) were accepted. The answer calculated is, of course, meaningless. Later in the text, we will learn how to write programs which warn the user when he has entered data which does not make sense for the task the program is accomplishing.

Program Testing

Testing a program begins, at least in an informal way, as soon as the planning is begun. In designing an algorithm, we are almost certainly doing some preliminary thinking about how the alogrithm will behave with simple input data. However, prior to announcing that a program is finished, there are at least three phases of testing which may be carried out. The first is a hand test of the algorithm, prior to coding into FORTRAN. The second consists of correcting those errors which the compiler detects for us. The third is a thorough test of the program itself, by entering a variety of input data. In this subsection we discuss each of these topics briefly. There will be PROGRAM TESTING subsections throughout the text, expanding on the ideas involved in testing computer programs.

Hand-tracing an algorithm refers to stepping through the algorithm with a small set of data. For example, we might have stepped through the original algorithm for the sample program under the assumption that the user enters 10.0 and 1.3 as the values for the first read, and then 0.0 and 0.0 for the second read. We will not pursue this issue at length here, but rather we will postpone a thorough discussion to a later section.

Unfortunately, even if the algorithm's logic is perfect, it is easy to make "silly" mistakes when converting the algorithm to FORTRAN. For example, we may encounter one of the pitfalls listed in previous sections, such as typing a zero in place of the letter O, or forgetting to begin the statement at or beyond column 7 of the line. Many of these types of errors will be detected by the compiler and flagged as "syntax errors."

The compiler will generally try to tell us what it thought was wrong with the line; however, we sometimes have to go beyond what it says. For example, consider this program fragment:

```
C   PIECE OF A PROGRAM WITH AN ERROR
          READ *,I,J
QUOT = I/J
```

The programmer has forgotten to indent the assignment statement under the READ statement; it begins in column 1. However, this places the equals sign (=) in column 6. The compiler will think this is a continuation of the previous line. It will therefore interpret the previous line as if it has been

```
READ *,I,JI/J
```

placing the I/J from the second line at the end of the first line. The error messages might say something like "illegal expression in READ statement" (referring to the JI/J), and "label not allowed in columns 1–5 of continuation line" (referring to the QUOT on the second line).

To fix these types of errors, it is necessary to look at what the compiler thinks is wrong, look at what the line and nearby lines look like, and think about what they ought to look like. It may be helpful at this point to review the various "pitfalls" that have been pointed out in the text.

Eventually, we fix all these syntax errors and get a "clean compile." If we are very careful typists, we might even get a clean compile the first time we run the program. At this point, we must avoid the tendency to think that we are done. We still need to test the program for any remaining **bugs** (errors). There are two general types of bugs that we hope to detect by doing this testing. The first involves an error in thinking about the algorithm, and the second involves erroneous coding of the algorithm into FORTRAN. In an attempt to uncover these errors, we run the program with a variety of input data, and we examine the answers carefully to see if they are correct.

The only way to thoroughly test a program would be to run it with every possible combination of input. However, this is impossible in practice. Hence, we must be satisfied with a compromise—a carefully chosen sample of input data.

It is difficult to say what constitutes "adequate" testing, especially for a complex program. As evidence of this, we may point to the fact that bugs in programs are sometimes discovered months or years after the program has been pronounced "correct." However, we can give some general guidelines. This section, and others like it throughout the text, will present some of these guidelines.

In testing the sample program, we used data which illustrates a few of the principles involved. First of all, we included some input for which the answers could easily be verified by doing calculations in our head. If the program contained an error such as adding the length and width rather than multiplying them, these input lines would have allowed us to detect the error quickly. However, not all the data was of this form. Some of the input included some more "realistic" values, such as 145.2 and

17.5. We did, however, use a calculator to make sure that the answers for these input lines were also correct.

A second principle illustrated by the sample test data concerns boundaries. The length and width could be any number from just greater than zero on up. We included data very close to the lower limit, or boundary, for the input. In fact, we included both 0.05 and 0.001 as test data. Although there was no stated upper limit for the length and width, we did also check with some relatively large numbers (1000.0 for each). Experience has shown that errors are more likely to occur for data near boundaries, so these tests may be among the most important that we do.

(However, not all our tests should be boundary tests. We should also include some data which is between the boundaries. In our sample test run, we had a number of values between the very small and the very large.)

A third principle concerns "bad" data. In this example, we entered negative numbers for the length and width. Since the program was not designed to detect negative values, we got a wrong answer. In later programs, where the program is supposed to detect such errors and print warning messages about them, this type of testing will become very important.

There are a number of other important testing principles which we will introduce later in the text, when we write programs for which the principles become pertinent. For now, we can summarize the three ideas we have presented here as:

1. Check all answers. Include some data that is easy to check.
2. Test near boundaries; also test a random sampling away from the boundaries.
3. Include some erroneous input, especially if the program is designed to detect and warn about such errors.

Internal Documentation (Comment Lines)

The program we developed in the previous section was missing one important ingredient—comment lines. These comment lines are used to explain the program, in terms of what it does and also how it does it. Figure 1.8 presents the same program, this time with some comments. This example illustrates a form of documentation we will use consistently throughout this text.

At the top of the program, immediately following the declaration of the variables, we have comments indicating who wrote the program, on what date, and a brief description of what the program does. These comments are sometimes called "header" comments—they explain the program as a whole.

The remaining comments are sometimes called "signpost" comments. They explain pieces of the program, and they convey the structure of the program. Since this program has a structure consisting of a single loop, we include three brief comments, explaining:

1. what is done before the loop begins
2. what is accomplished by the body of the loop
3. what is done after the loop terminates

```
      REAL LENGTH,WIDTH,AREA

C   WRITTEN BY *******, **/**/**

C   THIS PROGRAM FINDS AREAS OF RECTANGLES

C   BEFORE THE LOOP, PRINT INSTRUCTIONS

       PRINT *,'  This program finds areas of rectangles.'
       PRINT *,'  For each rectangle, enter the length and width of'
       PRINT *,'rectangle, separated by a space or a comma.'
       PRINT *,'  When you are ready to quit, enter a length of 0.'

C   IN THE LOOP, READ THE LENGTHS AND WIDTHS OF THE RECTANGLES, ONE
C AT A TIME, AND CALCULATE AND PRINT THE AREA FOR EACH. EXIT WHEN
C A DUMMY LENGTH OF 0 IS INPUT.

    10 CONTINUE
          PRINT *,' '
          PRINT *,'Enter a length and width.'
          READ *, LENGTH,WIDTH
          IF (LENGTH.EQ.0) THEN
             GO TO 500
          ENDIF
          AREA = LENGTH * WIDTH
          PRINT *,'The area is ',AREA
          GO TO 10

C   AFTER THE LOOP, STOP THE PROGRAM

  500 CONTINUE
      STOP
      END
```

Figure 1.8

A person reading our program can use these signpost comments to obtain a quick understanding of the program, prior to digging into the code itself to get a more thorough understanding.

Experience indicates that programs which will be examined by another person, or which will be examined by the author of the program after some time has passed, need to be commented. Since your instructor will examine the programs you write, we suggest that you include comments, at least as thorough as those in the various examples in this text.

Case Study #1

To conclude this section, we develop another example similar to the one in the previous section. This case study will be added to in later sections.

1. *Statement of problem.* A class instructor needs a program to calculate the total of the scores on three tests for each of his students. The name should be printed along with the score.

2. *Preliminary analysis.* This program is probably going to be run on a terminal which creates a printed copy of the output, so that the resulting list of names and test totals can be saved.

In order to print the student's name, the program will have to obtain the name from the instructor (the user) as she runs the program. The other input will consist of the three test scores. Output will contain the student's name and the total of the three scores.

3. *Algorithm and variable list.* Based on the preliminary analysis, we can see the need for the following variables:

	Name	Type	Use	Comment
Input:	NAME	CHARACTER*12	Student name	Also printed
	SCORE1	INTEGER	Test scores	
	SCORE2	INTEGER		
	SCORE3	INTEGER		
Output:	TOTAL	INTEGER	Total of 3 scores	

The algorithm will involve a loop of the same general form as that in the previous example: obtain input, calculate answers, and print answers. We will choose to ask for the student's name first, then for the three test grades. In this way, we may use a dummy input of a blank name to terminate the loop. This planning leads to the following algorithm:

```
print instructions
loop
    prompt asking for name
    read NAME
    if NAME is blank then
        exit
    endif
    prompt asking for three scores
    read SCORE1, SCORE2, SCORE3
    TOTAL ← SCORE1 + SCORE 2 + SCORE3
    print NAME, TOTAL
endloop
stop
```

Compare this to the algorithm for the areas of rectangles. You will see that it is almost identical in form. The only difference is that the reading of the name is separated from the reading of the scores. This general form of algorithm will frequently be appropriate for the types of programs written in the early chapters of the text.

4. *Test plan.* At this point we might pause to plan our testing strategy. Recalling the discussion earlier in this section, we might include the following types of tests for the three scores (we are assuming that valid test scores are in the range from 0 to 100). It can be a good idea to jot down the expected result for each test, as shown here.

easy to check:	70, 70, 70	: 210	
	50, 100, 50	: 200	
more realistic:	87, 94, 78	: 259	
	68, 92, 75	: 235	
boundaries:	0, 0, 0	: 0	
	100, 100, 100	: 300	
bad data:	101, 103, 110	: 314	(program does not
	−1, −5, −10	: −16	detect bad data)

As we gain more sophistication in our testing, we will discover some other tests that might be important here. Notice that we have, for instance, included some bad data (101 and −1) on the boundary between being good and being bad.

In addition to these specific tests, we might include some randomly chosen input lines.

5. *Write program.* We now write the program, which is shown in finished form in Figure 1.9. We begin by declaring the variables, using the variable list (lines 1 and 2). This is followed by the header comments in lines 3 to 8. We then go through the algorithm one line at a time, writing the corresponding comment lines and code. Each line of the algorithm is listed in the following discussion, along with the lines of the program which correspond to it, and any especially noteworthy features of the program.

a. print instructions—lines 9–22. Notice that, in line 12, in order to print the word "student's," which includes an apostrophe, we must put the apostrophe in twice.
b. **loop**—lines 23–27. We put in the comment explaining the loop's purpose, and the labelled CONTINUE statement.
c. prompt asking for name—lines 28–29. We include a PRINT to print a blank line before the prompt.
d. read NAME—line 30.
e. **if** NAME is blank **then**—line 31. To see if the name is blank, we can simply compare it to the CHARACTER constant ' '.
f. **exit**—line 32.
g. **endif**—line 33.

```
      CHARACTER*12 NAME
      INTEGER SCORE1,SCORE2,SCORE3,TOTAL

C   WRITTEN BY *********, **/**/**

C   THIS PROGRAM CALCULATES THE TOTAL ON THREE TESTS, AND
C PRINTS THAT TOTAL WITH THE STUDENT'S NAME

C   BEFORE THE LOOP, PRINT INSTRUCTIONS

      PRINT *,'    This program totals test scores. For each'
      PRINT *,'student you will be asked to enter the student''s'
      PRINT *,'name. You must enclose that name in single'
      PRINT *,'quotes when you type it in. After that, you will'
      PRINT *,'be asked to type in three test scores, in the'
      PRINT *,'range from 0 to 100. Enter these all on one line,'
      PRINT *,'separated by commas or by blank spaces. Do not'
      PRINT *,'enclose them in quotes.'
      PRINT *,'    The program will then print the name and the'
      PRINT *,'total score, and repeat the whole process. When'
      PRINT *,'you wish to terminate the program, enter a totally'
      PRINT *,'blank name.'

C   IN THE LOOP, READ THE NAME AND SCORES AND CALCULATE THE
C TOTAL. QUIT WHEN THE NAME ENTERED IS BLANK.

   10 CONTINUE
         PRINT *,' '
         PRINT *,'Enter the name (blank to quit)'
         READ *, NAME
         IF (NAME.EQ.' ') THEN
            GO TO 500
         ENDIF
         PRINT *,'Now enter the three scores'
         READ *, SCORE1,SCORE2,SCORE3
         TOTAL = SCORE1 + SCORE2 + SCORE3
         PRINT *,'The total is ',TOTAL,' for ',NAME
         GO TO 10

C   AFTER THE LOOP, STOP THE PROGRAM.

  500 CONTINUE
      STOP
      END
```

Figure 1.9

h. prompt asking for three scores—line 34.
i. read SCORE1, SCORE2, SCORE3—line 35.
j. TOTAL ← SCORE1 + SCORE2 + SCORE3 – line 36. The next section has more details on the assignment statement in FORTRAN.
k. print NAME, TOTAL—line 37. Notice that we print a message, then the TOTAL variable, then another brief message, then the NAME variable. The resulting line printed will read like a sentence. Notice also the extra spaces around the word "for" to separate it from the total and from the name.
l. **endloop**—lines 38–42. We go back up to the top of the loop with a GO TO, and we also put the labelled CONTINUE for the exit step to branch to. In between, we place a comment about what happens after the loop is finished.
m. **stop**—lines 43–44. The STOP stops the program, and the END is always the last line in any program.

```
    This program totals test scores. For each
student you will be asked to enter the student's
name. You must enclose that name in single
quotes when you type it in. After that, you will
be asked to type in three test scores, in the
range from 0 to 100. Enter these all on one line,
separated by commas or by blank spaces. Do not
enclose them in quotes.
    The program will then print the name and the
total score, and repeat the whole process. When
you wish to terminate the program, enter a totally
blank name.

Enter the name (blank to quit)
>'John Jones'
Now enter the three scores
>70,70,70
The total is     210 for John Jones

Enter the name (blank to quit)
>'Sue Smith'
Now enter the three scores
>50,100,50
The total is     200 for Sue Smith

Enter the name (blank to quit)
>'Ab Simpson'
Now enter the three scores
>87,94,78
The total is     259 for Ab Simpson

Enter the name (blank to quit)
>' '
```

Figure 1.10

6. *Run program.* The results of a short sample run are given in Figure 1.10. Only a portion of the actual run is shown. The total run tested all the planned test items (from step 4 above), along with some other randomly chosen input. Notice that the word "student's" is printed by the program with just the one apostrophe.

One thing to observe about the run is that, when we use free format input for CHARACTER variables, the person running the program must remember to place apostrophes (') around the input. This is somewhat bothersome. (In fact, your author, in testing this program, forgot to include the apostrophes.) Because this is not very "user-friendly," we will soon be learning an alternate form of input which avoids the need for the apostrophes. However, for right now, we will choose program simplicity over user ease.

REVIEW

FORTRAN Syntax

No new FORTRAN syntax

Program Testing

Three phases:

1. hand testing algorithm
2. removing syntax errors
3. running program with test data

Test data:

1. some easy to check (but all should be checked, perhaps using calculator)
2. test near boundaries and away from boundaries
3. test bad data

Internal documentation (comment lines)

Header comments:

1. who wrote program
2. date written
3. what the program does

Signpost comments (convey program structure):

1. before loop
2. in loop
3. after loop

EXERCISES

1. Using the procedures for your particular computer, type in and run the first sample program (Figure 1.6).

2. Using the procedures for your particular computer, type in and run the second sample program (Figure 1.9).

3. Using the procedures for your particular computer, type in and run the programs from Exercise 1 of Section 1.3.
4. Determine appropriate comment lines for each of the programs for exercise 1 of Section 1.3.
5. Determine an appropriate set of test data for each of the programs from Exercise 1 of Section 1.3. Be sure to include some that are easy to check, some that are near any boundaries, some that are not near the boundaries, and some bad data (if applicable).
6. By following the method used in the example in the subsection titled "A CASE STUDY," write programs for the following.
   (a) The perimeter of a triangle is the sum of its three sides. Write a program to find perimeters of triangles.
   (b) The distance travelled in miles may be calculated as the product of the speed in miles per hour and the number of hours travelled. Write a program which reads appropriate input, and calculates the distance travelled, for a number of different inputs.
   (c) If we have a number which represents the number of inches, we can convert this to centimeters by multiplying by 2.54 (approximately). Write a program which does so for different values of inches read from the user.
   (d) Write a program which, for each employee in a company, prints the name and the weekly pay. The weekly pay is calculated as the hours worked times the hourly pay rate. (No overtime is calculated by this program.)
   (e) Write a program which updates the amount owned by each customer of a company, based on the following rule: The new amount owed should be calculated as 1.015 times the old amount owed. The program should, for each customer, print the customer name and the new amount owed.
7. Tell how to modify the first example (Figure 1.6) so that, just before it stops, it prints a message "Have a nice day," preceded by a blank line.
8. Tell how to modify the first example (Figure 1.6) to read the user's name at the beginning of the run, then print a message similar to the following at the end: "Have a nice day, John." Here we are assuming that John is the user's name.
9. Tell how to modify the second example (Figure 1.9) to read the date as a string of characters, and print the date prior to obtaining the lists of names and grades. It should simply print the date exactly as the user inputs it.

2

FUNDAMENTALS OF FORTRAN PROGRAM DESIGN

2.1 THE ASSIGNMENT STATEMENT

The first chapter introduced enough about program writing and about FORTRAN to enable you to start writing short programs. In this chapter, we will add to this foundation. Part of what we learn will have to do with program design and part will cover the FORTRAN language in more detail. By the end of this chapter you will have used examples of each of the four techniques of program design: sequencing, looping, decisions, and subprograms.

We begin our study in this chapter with a more complete description of the assignment statement which was introduced in a limited form in the example of the previous chapter.

The assignment statement is used to assign a new value to a variable. The basic form of the statement is

variable = expression

When the statement is executed, the computer evaluates the expression and assigns the value to the variable on the left of the equals sign. The equals sign between the variable and the expression is sometimes called an "assignment operator," to emphasize its purpose of assigning a value to the variable to its left. The expression on the right may be simple, or it may be very complicated. It may involve a mixture of constants and variables. For any variable in the expression, the current value of the variable is used in calculating the value represented by the expression. We shall first look at numeric assignment statements and then at a few very simple character assignments.

Numeric Assignment Statements

Numeric assignment statements are those in which the value of the expression on the right side of the equals sign and the variable on the left are numeric (that is, at this point, either real or integer). For example, the following are numeric assignment statements (all variables are REAL):

```
Y = 3.5
T = -14.0
X = R + 14.7
X = S - 13.15
X = Y
```

The first gives Y the value 3.5, the second assigns the value −14.0 to T, and the last three assign assorted values to the variable X. For the third, X = R + 14.7, the variable X is assigned the current value of R plus 14.7. Likewise, in the fourth example X will be given a value which is 13.15 less than the present value of S. In the last example the value of the expression is merely the current value of Y, and this value will be placed in the variable X. (The variables used in the expression part of the assignments—R, S, and Y—are not changed by the execution of the assignment statement. Only the variable on the left side is given a new value.)

Precedence

As you may see in the above examples, the assignment statement looks a lot like a formula. For example, the formula

$$d = rt$$

tells us how to calculate the distance d for a given value of r (rate) and t (time). In a formula such as this, just as in an assignment statement, the quantity on the left is the quantity we wish to calculate, using the formula or expression on the right side.

Formulas typically involve combinations of variables and constants, using such operations as addition, subtraction, multiplication, and division. For example, the familiar formula

$$F = 9/5C + 32$$

(for determining the Fahrenheit temperature corresponding to a given Centigrade reading) involves division (9 divided by 5), multiplication, and addition. The companion formula

$$C = 5/9(F - 32)$$

involves division, multiplication, and subtraction. It also introduces parentheses to control the order in which the operations are performed.

The following rules determine the order of operation in algebraic formulas. They are the same rules which are used in finding the value of FORTRAN expressions. Since they tell which operations precede which other operations, they are sometimes called **precedence** rules.

1. Multiplication and division are performed before addition and subtraction. If more than one multiplication/division is present, they are performed from left to right.

2. Addition and subtraction are then performed, again from left to right.
3. Grouping symbols, such as parentheses, may be used to group portions of an expression. Within the grouping symbols, the rules given above apply. For example:

$$3 + 4 \cdot 7 = 3 + 28 = 31$$
$$(3 + 4) \cdot 7 = 7 \cdot 7 = 49$$
$$7 \cdot 3 \cdot 2 = 21 \cdot 2 = 42$$
$$8/4 \cdot 2 = 2 \cdot 2 = 4 \text{ (not } 8/8 = 1\text{—go left to right)}$$
$$8/(4 \cdot 2) = 1$$
$$7 - 4 - 2 = 3 - 2 = 1$$
$$7 - (4 - 2) = 7 - 2 = 5$$
$$6 \cdot (5 - (2 + 1)) = 6 \cdot (5 - 3) = 6 \cdot 2 = 12$$

Observe, as in the last example, that when there is more than one set of parentheses present, the operations inside the innermost set of parentheses are performed first.

We can also express powers such as x^2 and $(y + 4)^5$ by using an exponentiation operator. Exponentiations are performed before multiplications and divisions but, unlike the rest of the numeric operations, are performed from right to left. The FORTRAN symbols for these operations are given below.

**	exponentiation
+	addition
−	subtraction
*	multiplication
/	division

In algebra, you may recall, a dot was used to indicate multiplication, as in the formula

$$y = a \cdot b$$

Later, you were allowed to drop the use of the dot, writing

$$y = ab$$

Consider, however, the corresponding FORTRAN assignment statement

```
Y = AB
```

Since FORTRAN variable names are allowed to be more than one letter long, we cannot be sure whether the right side refers to a single variable named AB or to a variable A times a variable B. To clarify the situation, we must include a symbol for multiplication. The asterisk symbol was chosen by the designers of the FORTRAN language (and by the designers of many other languages, as well). Many computer input and output devices do not permit the use of superscripts or subscripts. On such devices all information in a single line must appear at the same level. Therefore, FORTRAN and most other programming languages introduce special notations to replace superscripts and subscripts. The double asterisk (**) is the FORTRAN notation for the exponentiation operation indicated in normal algebra by a superscript power.

The precedence rules, as described above, are as follows:

1. ** first, right to left
2. * and / next, left to right
3. + and − next, left to right
4. parentheses may be used to group operations

Because the precedence rules are the same as those for algebraic formulas, most algebraic formulas can be rewritten as FORTRAN assignment statements with little difficulty. We must, however, remember to use the asterisk (*) for multiplication and the double asterisk (**) for exponentiation.

The following table illustrates the correspondence between algebraic formulas and FORTRAN assignment statements. All variables are taken to be REAL.

Algebraic formula	FORTRAN assignment
$y = x + t$	`Y = X + T`
$w = a - b + r$	`W = A - B + R`
$w = a - (b + r)$	`W = A - (B + R)`
$x = y/z + r$	`X = Y/Z + R`
$r = d/t$	`R = D/T`
$d = rt$	`D = R*T`
$y = ax + b$	`Y = A*X + B`
$y = x/(b + r)$	`Y = X/(B + R)`
$a = x(t + w)$	`A + X*(T + W)`
$b = a^c$	`B = A**C`

There are a few types of algebraic formulas which can present problems. One type of formula involves grouping by placement within a fraction. For example, in the expression.

$$y = \frac{b}{ac}$$

the *ac* is grouped as one term by its placement in the denominator of the fraction. Thus the multiplication (*a* times *c*) should be performed first, then the result divided into *b*. If we write a FORTRAN assignment statement

```
Y = B/A*C
```

the precedence rules will cause the division to be performed before the multiplication, giving the wrong answer. For example, if B is 6, A is 3, and C is 2, the result should be 6/6 = 1, but we would get 6/3 * 2 = 2*2 = 4. The solution to this dilemma is easy—use parentheses to obtain the correct grouping:

```
Y = B/(A*C)
```

A similar example is

$$y = \frac{x + t}{w}$$

where the placement of $x + t$ in the numerator groups these symbols together. Again, we must use parentheses to obtain the desired grouping:

```
Y = (X + T)/W
```

A similar type of implied grouping can occur in expressions containing exponentiations. For example the expression

$$(a + b)^{c-d} + e$$

would be written in FORTRAN as (A + B)**(C − D) + E.

> **NOTE.** It is permissible to include extra parentheses, if desired, to emphasize the meaning of an expression. For example, we may write
>
> ```
> Y = (B*A)/C
> ```
>
> for
>
> ```
> Y = B*A/C
> ```
>
> to emphasize that the multiplication comes before the division.

Pitfalls

For the most part, assignment statements in FORTRAN are very straightforward. If we know what formula, or expression, is needed to calculate a new value for a variable, we merely place the expression to the right of the equals sign and the variable to the left. There are, however, five points which deserve special emphasis.

The first two points have already been mentioned. First, the * symbol is used for multiplication, and the ** for exponentiation. One of the most common mistakes made by beginning programmers is omitting these symbols. Second, extra parentheses may be required to group numerators or denominators of fractions or exponents.

The third point concerns integer division. When two INTEGER variables or constants are divided, the result is an INTEGER. Suppose, then, that I, J, and K are INTEGER variables. These three assignment statements cause no difficulty:

```
I = 8/4
J = 27/3
K = (-145)/5
```

since the numbers divide evenly; however, the following three do cause problems:

```
I = 16/5
J = 1/4
K = (-14)/4
```

The results *"should be"* 3.2, 0.25, and −3.5, respectively. These are not integers, and the results the computer actually gives will be integers. In each case, the computer will simply omit the fractional part of the answer, obtaining the results 3, 0, and −3, respectively.

The formula for converting Fahrenheit to Centigrade is

```
C = 5/9(F - 32)
```

If we use REAL variables C and F in our program, we might write

```
C = (5/9) * (F - 32)
```

Unfortunately, this will always give an answer of 0, no matter what value F has. The reason is that the numbers 5 and 9 are integer constants, and therefore the division 5/9 will be done using integer arithmetic, giving an answer of 0.

Generally when a division occurs in an expression which has real variables or constants, the operands for the division should be real. If the operands are constants, then you can make them real by including a decimal point, as for example:

```
C = (5.0/9.0) * (F - 32)
```

If the operands are variables, their values may be converted to real by using a special conversion operation written as

```
REAL (integer variable)
```

For example, consider the assignment below, where AVG and SUM are REAL variables and N is an INTEGER variable.

```
AVG = SUM / REAL(N)
```

In this statement the variable N retains its integer nature and the original value. A copy of its value is converted to real and the copy is used in the division. Actually, it is enough for one of the operands to be real. If an operation of addition, subtraction, multiplication, or division has one real and one integer operand, the integer operand is converted to real and the operation is done as a real operation. We recommend, however, for division that one should explicitly write both operands as real to make it clearer to a person reading the program that real division is being used.

Even with addition, subtraction, and multiplication, we may wish to use real constants with real variables. For example, in the above assignment statement for temperature conversion, we might write

```
C = (5.0/9.0) * (F - 32.0)
```

subtracting the real constant 32.0 from the real variable F. However, this is not as vital as it can be when division is involved.

Exponentiation raises a related, but somewhat different, issue. FORTRAN systems sometimes use different methods for computing the value of expressions with exponentiations, depending on the type of the exponent. Frequently expressions with integer exponents are computed by multiplication, while expressions with real exponents are computed using logarithms. If this is done, an expression such as

$$x^2$$

where x is negative or zero could be computed, while the similar expression

$$x^{2.0}$$

would fail when the computer attempts to compute the logarithm of x. For this reason one should use integer exponents if possible, and, if not, then the expression being raised to a power should be positive.

The final point to be made is that, although an assignment statement looks very similar to an equation in algebra, it is not really the same. For example, the algebraic equations

$$j = i + 7 \text{ and } i + 7 = j$$

are the same. However, in an assignment statement we must place the variable whose new value is being assigned to the left of the equals sign. We may not write

```
I + 7 = J
```

This will lead to error messages.

An even more important example of the distinction is illustrated by the assignment statement

```
I = I + 1
```

where I is an INTEGER variable. If this were an algebraic equation, it would have no solution. However, it is a perfectly acceptable assignment statement, since an assignment statement

1. calculates the value of the expression (formula) on the right side of the equals sign, using the present value of any variable contained in the expression; and then,
2. places the resulting value into the variable on the left side.

For example, if I has the value 16, the value of the expression I + 1 will be 16 + 1, or 17. This result will then be placed into I, and the net effect is that the value of I will be increased by 1. (As we will see in Chapter 3, this type of assignment statement will be useful in determining how many times certain conditions occur.)

Once again, assignment statements are relatively simple to write and use. The precedence is the same as that in algebra, but we may need to add extra parentheses to group numerators or denominators of fractions. Other points to remember can be stated briefly as

1. ** for exponentiation
2. * for multiplication
3. caution on INTEGER division
4. not the same as an equation

Character Assignment Statements

Character assignment statements follow the same pattern as numeric assignments except that the expression on the right of the equals sign yields a character value and the variable on the left is a character variable. Like numeric expressions, character expressions may consist of a constant or a variable, or they may involve operators. At present we will only look at one character operator, the concatenation operator (//). If S1 is a CHARACTER*4 variable with the value 'ABCD', then the expression

```
S1 // 'EFG'
```

has the seven-character value 'ABCDEFG'. As you can see, the result of concatenating two character values is a new value composed of the two original values written one after the other. As another example, suppose A is a CHARACTER*4 variable with the value 'MATH' and B is a CHARACTER*2 variable with the value 'ED'. Then the expression

```
A // '-' // B
```

would have the value 'MATH-ED' and would be seven characters long.

Either of the expressions we used above can be used in an assignment statement. If D is a CHARACTER*7 variable, then the assignments

```
D = S1 // 'EFG'
```

or

```
D = A // '-' // B
```

would assign the seven character values of the expressions to D. However, D does not have to match the length of the expression. If the length of D is less than the length of the expression, the characters will be removed (truncated) from the right of the expression. For example, if D is a CHARACTER*3 variable, then

```
D = A // '-' // B
```

will assign the value 'MAT' to D. If the length of D is greater than the length of the expression, then extra blanks are added at the right of the value. For example, if D is a character*10 variable, then the assignment

```
D = A // '-' // B
```

will assign 'MATH-EDbbb' to D. Note that we have used three b's to represent the three blanks following the characters ED. These rules are summarized by saying that the length of the expression is matched to the length of the variable by right truncation or by right padding with blanks.

REVIEW

Terms and Concepts

assignment
precedence
truncation
padding with blanks

FORTRAN Syntax (the Assignment Statement)

variable = expression

"expression" consists of one or more variables or constants, combined by the following operations, together with parentheses:

\+ addition
− subtraction
* multiplication
/ division
** exponentiation

for numeric assignments and with the operation // (Concatenation) for character assignments

Action

The value of the expression on the right side is calculated, using the present value of any variables involved. The answer obtained is then placed into the variable on the left side. The rules of precedence apply:

1. ** first, right to left
2. * and / come next, left to right
3. + and − come last, left to right
4. If parentheses are present, work from the innermost set of parentheses out.

In the following examples assume variables beginning with I are INTEGER, all others are REAL.

```
Y = 2.0 * X + 5.3
CENT = (5.0/9.0) * (FAHR - 32.0)
I = I + 1
W = (3.5 + A)/4.2
A = B ** (C + D)
```

With character assignments, the length of the value of the expression is adjusted to match the length of the variable on the left by truncating or padding with blanks on the right.

Pitfalls

1. May have to use parentheses to group numerators or denominators of fractions, or powers
2. Use * for multiplication, ** for exponentiation
3. INTEGER division gives only the integer part of the answer.
4. An assignment statement is not like an algebraic equation. It is more like a formula for calculating the value of a particular variable (which must be to the left of the equals sign).

EXERCISES

1. Give the value of the following FORTRAN expressions.

(a) `3 * 2 + 7`
(b) `4/3`
(c) `6.5/2.0`
(d) `3.0/2.0 + 1.0`
(e) `3 * (2 + 5)`
(f) `3 - 7 + 2`
(g) `3 - (7 + 2)`
(h) `'A' // 'B'`
(i) `4 * 3/2`
(j) `4* (3/2)`
(k) `4.0 * (3.0/2.0)`
(l) `'X4*6' // '5 *3'`

2. Assume that A, B, and C are REAL, and I, J, and K are INTEGER. Also, assume that at the time the assignment statement is executed, the variables have these values:

```
A 3.2     B 6.0     C 1.5
I 4       J 63      K 17
```

What value is given to the variable on the left side of each assignment statement?

(a) `A = .5 * A`
(b) `I = I + 1`
(c) `K = J + I/2`
(d) `K + J/I`
(e) `C = A + B * C`
(f) `A = 16.03`
(g) `K = I ** 2`
(h) `K = 5.0 ** (B - I)`
(i) `A = 4.0 ** C`

3. Convert the following algebraic expressions to FORTRAN expressions. Assume all variables are REAL, except for J and K.

(a) $y = ax + b$

(b) $t = \frac{1}{2}a + r$

(c) $w = \frac{x + y}{2}$

(d) $j = k + 5$

(e) $s = t + 5$

(f) $r = \frac{x}{y + 3}$

(g) $w = \frac{x + 3y}{r + a - 3}$

(h) $j = (k + 3)j$

(i) $b = P\left(1 + \frac{r}{k}\right)^{ky}$

(j) $x = y^{3+5k}$

(k) $a = \frac{j + 2k}{3}$

4. For the following assignment statements determine what value is assigned to the variable on the left. Assume that all variables are character variables and that the length of A3 is 3, A5 is 5 and A7 is 7. Suppose B has the value 'BBB' and C has the value 'CCCC'

(a) `A3 = B`
(b) `A5 = B`
(c) `A3 = C`
(d) `A7 = 'B' // B // C`
(e) `A3 = 'B' // B // C`
(f) `A7 = 'B' // C`
(g) `A7 = '''B''//C'`
(h) `A3 = 'A3'`
(i) `A3 = 'cBc'`

5. Write FORTRAN expressions to perform each of the following calculations. Make up meaningful variable names and give declarations for your variables.

(a) Calculate the area of a rectangle, given the length and width.

(b) Convert inches to centimeters (1 inch = 2.54 centimeters).

(c) Find the average of three real numbers.

(d) Find a person's age in months, given his age in years and months (for example, 3 years, 4 months would yield 40 months as the answer).

(e) Find the local tax, given the income. The rule is: 5% of the portion of the income in excess of $1000. (Assume that the income is at least $1000.)

(f) Calculate batting average, given times at bat and number of hits.

(g) Find the percentage of mutated ants in an ant colony, given the number of mutated ants and the total number of ants in the colony.

6. Using the assignment statements you wrote in Exercise 5, plan and write complete programs which calculate the indicated values for a number of input lines.

2.2 INTRODUCTION TO SUBROUTINES

In Section 1.3, we listed four techniques used in developing programs:

1. sequencing
2. looping
3. decisions
4. subprograms

The examples in Sections 1.3 through 2.1 have made use of the first three techniques. Sequencing is implicitly used in any program, when we write down the steps in the order we wish the computer to perform them. Looping has been used in these examples to perform the activities repeatedly until the user indicates (by a dummy entry) that the process should terminate. Decisions have been used in the examples to detect the dummy entry and exit from the loop. In this section we present one possible use of subprograms. (In the process, we will see another use of decisions.)

An Example Subroutine

We will modify Case Study #1 (Section 1.4), reproduced in Figure 2.1, to illustrate the use of subroutines. Lines 11 through 22 of that program are all a result of the single "print instructions" step in the algorithm. We may think of the task of printing instructions as a subtask that the program needs to perform as one small part of its overall task. Although this subtask is important, the specific details of how it is performed do not affect the overall logic of the program. We could change the instructions by adding blank lines, by rewriting the PRINT statements to limit each line to 25 characters, or by adding additional sentences to make the instructions clearer. None of these changes would in any way modify the logic of the loop which is the main structure of the program.

As we will see as we progress through the text, this type of situation may lead us to consider using a subprogram. We have a task to be performed as a part of the

```
      CHARACTER*12 NAME
      INTEGER SCORE1,SCORE2,SCORE3,TOTAL

C   WRITTEN BY *********, **/**/**

C   THIS PROGRAM CALCULATES THE TOTAL ON THREE TESTS, AND
C PRINTS THAT TOTAL WITH THE STUDENT'S NAME

C   BEFORE THE LOOP, PRINT INSTRUCTIONS

      PRINT *,'     This program totals test scores. For each'
      PRINT *,'student you will be asked to enter the student''s'
      PRINT *,'name. You must enclose that name in single'
      PRINT *,'quotes when you type it in. After that, you will'
      PRINT *,'be asked to type in the three test scores, in the'
      PRINT *,'range from 0 to 100. Enter these all on one line,'
      PRINT *,'separated by commas or by blank spaces. Do not'
      PRINT *,'enclose them in quotes,'
      PRINT *,'     The program will then print the name and the'
      PRINT *,'total score, and repeat the whole process. When'
      PRINT *,'you wish to terminate the program, enter a totally'
      PRINT *,'blank name.'

C   IN THE LOOP, READ THE NAME AND SCORES AND CALCULATE THE
C TOTAL. QUIT WHEN THE NAME ENTERED IS BLANK.

   10 CONTINUE
         PRINT *,' '
         PRINT *,'Enter the name (blank to quit)'
         READ *, NAME
         IF (NAME.EQ.' ') THEN
            GO TO 500
         ENDIF
         PRINT *,'Now enter the three scores'
         READ *, SCORE1,SCORE2,SCORE3
         TOTAL = SCORE1 + SCORE2 + SCORE3
         PRINT *,'The total is ',TOTAL,' for ',NAME
         GO TO 10

C   AFTER THE LOOP, STOP THE PROGRAM.

  500 CONTINUE
      STOP
      END
```

Figure 2.1

overall program. That task can be easily stated ("print instructions"), but the details of the task can become fairly significant. (In the sample, the 12 lines which print the instructions are exactly as long as the loop itself!) This type of situation lends itself well to placing the subtask in a subprogram, separated from the rest of the program.

The result of splitting our sample program may be seen in Figure 2.2, which is numbered for easy reference. The program now consists of two smaller pieces, in place of the original single piece. The first piece consists of lines 1–36, the second of lines 39–58. For easier readability, we have placed two blank lines between the pieces. We will discuss each portion in turn.

The first piece is referred to as the **main** program. It is almost identical to the original version of the program. The differences are shaded. First, it includes a brief comment documenting the fact that a subprogram is used to do part of the task at hand (lines 9–10). In addition, instead of having twelve PRINT statements which print the directions, it contains the single statement

```
CALL INSTR
```

in line 14. The rest of the main program is unchanged.

The meaning of the CALL INSTR step may be summarized as "do the task in the INSTR subprogram, then continue with the main program steps." When this step is reached, the computer will temporarily go down to the INSTR subprogram and perform whatever steps are called for there. When those steps are finished, it will return to this same point in the main program and continue processing from there. Since the INSTR subprogram prints directions, those directions will have been printed by the time the CALL INSTR line of the program been completed.

The second piece of our program begins at line 39. It is a **subroutine**, one of the two possible types of subprograms in FORTRAN. (The other is the **function** subprogram, introduced in Section 2.6.) This subroutine prints the directions. It begins with the line

```
SUBROUTINE INSTR
```

This line identifies it as a subroutine whose name is INSTR. Notice that this name appears in the statement CALL INSTR in the main program. The rules for naming

```
1         CHARACTER*12 NAME
2         INTEGER SCORE1,SCORE2,SCORE3,TOTAL
3
4   C   WRITTEN BY *********, **/**/**
5
6   C   THIS PROGRAM CALCULATES THE TOTAL ON THREE TESTS, AND
7   C PRINTS THAT TOTAL WITH THE STUDENT'S NAME
8
```

Figure 2.2 *(continued)*

```
C   ONE SUBPROGRAM IS USED:
C        INSTR-A SUBROUTINE TO PRINT INSTRUCTIONS

C   BEFORE THE LOOP, PRINT INSTRUCTIONS

      CALL INSTR

C   IN THE LOOP, READ THE NAME AND SCORES AND CALCULATE THE
C TOTAL.  QUIT WHEN THE NAME ENTERED IS BLANK.

   10 CONTINUE
         PRINT *,' '
         PRINT *,'Enter the name (blank to quit)'
         READ *, NAME
         IF (NAME.EQ.' ') THEN
            GO TO 500
         ENDIF
         PRINT *,'Now enter the three scores'
         READ *, SCORE1,SCORE2,SCORE3
         TOTAL = SCORE1 + SCORE2 + SCORE3
         PRINT *,'The total is ',TOTAL,' for ',NAME
         GO TO 10

C   AFTER THE LOOP, STOP THE PROGRAM.

  500 CONTINUE
      STOP
      END


      SUBROUTINE INSTR

C   WRITTEN BY ********, **/**/**

C   THIS SUBROUTINE PRINTS INSTRUCTIONS

      PRINT *,'     This program totals test scores. For each'
      PRINT *,'student you will be asked to enter the student''s'
      PRINT *,'name. You must enclose that name in single'
      PRINT *,'quotes when you type it in. After that, you will'
      PRINT *,'be asked to type in the three test scores, in the'
      PRINT *,'range from 0 to 100. Enter these all on one line,'
      PRINT *,'separated by commas or by blank spaces. Do not'
      PRINT *,'enclose them in quotes.'
      PRINT *,'     The program will then print the name and the'
      PRINT *,'total score, and repeat the whole process. When'
      PRINT *,'you wish to terminate the program, enter a totally'
      PRINT *,'blank name.'
      RETURN
      END
```

Figure 2.2 *(continued from p. 57)*

subroutines are precisely the same as for naming variables: one to six letters or digits, with the first character a letter.

Lines 41–43 are the header comments for the subroutine. In this text, we adopt the documentation convention of including header comments for each subprogram we write. This can be useful when, in a large project, the different pieces are written by different individuals over a long span of time.

Lines 44–56 are the PRINT statements which were originally in the single main program. They now form the **body** of the INSTR subroutine.

Line 57 is a RETURN statement. Its purpose is somewhat similar to the STOP statement in the main program. It signals that the task of the subprogram is finished. However, we do not want the program to stop, rather we want it to continue with whatever it was about to do when it called the INSTR subroutine. The line

```
RETURN
```

means just that—return to the step which called the subroutine and continue from there.

Finally, line 58 is an END statement. The END statement in FORTRAN simply marks the boundary between the different pieces of the program. Notice that the main program has its own END statement in line 36. Each main program and each subprogram in FORTRAN has an END statement as its last line.

Writing and Using Subroutines

The subroutine developed in the example illustrates a few general ideas on writing and using subroutines which will be applicable for any subroutines we use.

1. A subroutine is frequently used to perform some task which forms a cohesive part of the entire job performed by the program. In this case, the task is printing instructions for the user.

2. When a program contains both a main program and a subroutine, we simply type in the main program first, followed by the subroutine. The main program's last line is the END line, which separates the main program from the following subroutine.

3. The form of a subroutine follows this pattern:

```
SUBROUTINE sname
any needed declarations of variables
     :
     :
body of subroutine, consisting of steps to
perform the desired task
     :
     :
RETURN
END
```

Here "sname" stands for "subroutine name," the name given to the subroutine.

4. The last two lines of the subroutine indicate the logical and physical end of the subroutine. The RETURN marks the logical end; the subroutine has finished its assigned task and is returning control to the main program. The END marks the physical end; it is the last line of the subroutine.

5. The main program uses a subroutine by including a statement of the form

```
CALL sname
```

where "sname" is again the name of the subroutine. This step causes the program to perform all the steps within the subroutine, then return (via the RETURN step of the subroutine) to the step following the CALL step in the main program.

In addition to these concepts illustrated by the sample program, there are two additional concepts we should describe briefly at this point. The concepts are discussed in more detail as we learn more about subprograms.

6. It is possible for a subroutine to declare and use variables. If it does, those variables will be distinct from the ones used in the calling program, even if they happen to have the same name. For example, suppose a main program and a subprogram both declare a variable called NAME. Any reference to NAME in the main program refers to the main program's NAME variable, and does not automatically affect the NAME variable in the subroutine. Similarly, using the NAME variable in the subroutine does not affect the main program. We say that the variables are **local**; they are used locally within one piece of the program.

7. A main program can use (CALL) any number of subroutines to perform different tasks. In fact, these subroutines could in turn use other subroutines to split their tasks up into still smaller pieces. In this case, the program as a whole would consist of the main program followed by the subroutines in any order. Each program unit (main or subprogram) would end with an END line.

We close this subsection with some additional terminology. We have seen what a main program and a subroutine are. The general term *program unit* is used to refer to either a main program or a subprogram. The term *module* has the same meaning.

Because of the word "CALL" in the FORTRAN statement to use a subroutine, we say that the main program **calls** the subprogram, and we might refer to the main program as the **calling program**. The word **invoke** is also used as a synonym for **call** in this setting.

Enhancing the Example

The INSTR subroutine may now be modified, if we wish, without in any way changing the main program portion of our program. This is one of the advantages of using subprograms in our program design. We may concentrate our attention, during development and during modification, on relatively small portions of the overall program. In this subsection, we present one possible enhancement of the subroutine, and we outline another whose details are left as an exercise.

If the program we are writing is used over and over by the same user, he may soon tire of seeing the instructions. By the third or fourth time he runs the program, he may feel pretty comfortable with just beginning to enter data. However, we do not want to remove the lines which print instructions from the program. Some other person may wish to use the program, or this user at some time in the future may again need to see the instructions.

A common solution to this problem is to ask the user whether or not he wishes to receive instructions. If he answers yes, we will print the instructions; otherwise, we will not. Although we have not yet studied this type of decision situation in great detail, we have seen how to use the **if** statement in connection with leaving a loop. The same statement may be used here, as shown in the algorithm below:

```
print 'do you want directions (Y or N)'
read ANSWER
if ANSWER = 'Y' then
  print directions
endif
```

If we use this as the algorithm for the INSTR subroutine, we will allow the user to control whether or not directions are printed.

Notice that this algorithm uses a variable, ANSWER, to hold the user's response. This variable should be of type CHARACTER*1, since the response will be a single letter (Y or N).

Figure 2.3 contains the modified subroutine. The modifications are shaded.

COMMENT. As we mentioned in point #6 of the previous subsection, subroutines in FORTRAN do not, in general, automatically share any variables with the program which calls them. Some of what this implies for a specific subroutine may be seen outlined in Figure 2.3. Notice that the variable ANSWER is declared in the INSTR subroutine where it is used. All the other variables are declared in the main program where they are used. Each program unit declares and uses its own list of "local" variables. When we write our INSTR subroutine, we do not need to worry about what variables the main program might be using, since the variables are totally independent.

We will have more to say on this issue in future sections, as we learn more about subprograms.

NOTE. If we run this version of the program, there is a minor inconvenience for the user. Because ANSWER is a CHARACTER variable, and because we are using free format, the user has to place the value in single quotes. Thus, in answer to the prompt

```
Do you want directions (Y or N)?
```

```
      SUBROUTINE INSTR
      CHARACTER*1 ANSWER

C    WRITTEN BY ********, **/**/**

C    THIS SUBROUTINE PRINTS INSTRUCTIONS, IF THE USER WISHES THEM

      PRINT *,' '
      PRINT *,'Do you want directions (Y or N)?'
      READ *, ANSWER
      IF (ANSWER.EQ.'Y') THEN
         PRINT *,'    This program totals test scores. For each'
         PRINT *,'student you will be asked to enter the student''s'
         PRINT *,'name. You must enclose that name in single'
         PRINT *,'quotes when you type it in. After that, you will'
         PRINT *,'be asked to type in the three test scores, in the'
         PRINT *,'range from 0 to 100. Enter these all on one line,'
         PRINT *,'separated by commas or by blank spaces. Do not'
         PRINT *,'enclose them in quotes.'
         PRINT *,'    The program will then print the name and the'
         PRINT *,'total score, and repeat the whole process. When'
         PRINT *,'you wish to terminate the program, enter a totally'
         PRINT *,'blank name.'
      ENDIF
      RETURN
      END
```

Figure 2.3

the user must respond either

```
'Y'
```

to answer "yes," or

```
'N'
```

to answer "no." Methods to make the program more "user-friendly" in this regard will be covered later.

We now consider a second possible modification to this or other similar instruction-printing subroutines. Suppose that the instructions consisted of 35 lines. On most terminals, this many lines would not fit on the screen. By the time the last line had printed, the first would have "scrolled" up off the top of the screen. To avoid this, we might print part of the instructions, then wait for user input before printing the rest. This could be accomplished by printing about 18 lines, then printing a message asking the user to enter a character when she is ready to see the rest of the instructions. A READ to read this character would cause the program to pause and wait for the input, prior to going on to the steps which print the rest of the directions. The details are left as an exercise.

Pitfalls

There are a few points to keep in mind when writing and using subprograms, and in particular subroutines of the type presented in this section. The first several all have to do with naming variables.

1. The main program and the subroutine are independent. This means that they do not automatically share any variables. The variables that are declared in the subroutine may not be referred to in the main program, and vice versa.
2. However, it is permissible to have duplicate names of variables. For example, both the main program and the subroutine could use variables called ANSWER. The thing to keep in mind is that the two, although they look the same, are actually different variables. Changing the value of the main program's ANSWER variable would not change the value of the subroutine's ANSWER variable, and vice versa.
3. Each main program and subroutine should declare those variables, and only those variables, which it uses itself.
4. It is necessary to have an END statement at the end of the main program, just prior to the beginning of any subroutine. The subroutine also ends with its own END statement.
5. The subroutine should not generally include a STOP statement, since this would stop the entire program. Rather, a RETURN statement returns to the main program when the subroutine's task is finished.
6. Finally, when running the program, recall that any character data entered must be placed inside single quotes.

A Quick Recap of Program Design

Following are the algorithm and variable list for the latest version of our case study example.

For the main program:

	Name	Type	Use	Comment
Input:	NAME	CHARACTER*12	Student name	Also printed
	SCORE1	INTEGER	Test Scores	
	SCORE2	INTEGER		
	SCORE3	INTEGER		
Output:	TOTAL	INTEGER	Total of 3 scores	

```
call INSTR
loop
   prompt for name
   read NAME
   if NAME is blank then
       exit
   endif
   prompt for scores
   read SCORE1,SCORE2,SCORE3
   TOTAL ← SCORE1 + SCORE2 + SCORE3
   print TOTAL,NAME
endloop
stop
```

For the INSTR subroutine:

Name	Type	Use	Comment
Input: ANSWER	CHARACTER*1	User answer	'Y' or 'N'

```
print 'do you want directions (Y or N)?'
read ANSWER
if ANSWER = 'Y' then
   print directions
endif
return
```

This example contains instances of the four ingredients for program design: sequencing, looping, decisions, and subprograms. We will discuss each in turn.

As stated earlier, **sequencing** refers to the idea that a computer program is executed one step at a time, from top to bottom. Thus, in a program with no loops or decisions, we would merely have a sequence of steps listed in the order they should be performed. The same thing is true in a program which does involve decisions or looping; within the loop the steps are listed in the order they are to be performed. Likewise, if there are several steps to be performed if a certain condition is true, they will be executed in the order they are listed.

The simplest steps in an algorithm, then, will not involve loops or decisions. This example contains three types of simple steps:

1. The assignment statement. We use the symbol "←" as our assignment operator, as in the step

   ```
   TOTAL ← SCORE1 + SCORE2 + SCORE3
   ```

2. I/O statements. We use "read" for input, and either "write" or "print" for output. Examples in the algorithm above include the steps

   ```
   print 'do you want directions (Y or N)?'
   read ANSWER
   ```

3. Stop and return. The main program includes a **stop** statement, and any subroutines include a **return** statement.

With a program involving only sequencing, we must run the program over and over to get the answer for different input values. The **looping** concept is a very natural solution to this problem. Using a loop, we can have the computer automatically repeat all or part of a program. When we write a loop, the following considerations are important:

1. Which portion of the program do we want to repeat? In more detail, what steps should be done before the loop, what steps in the loop, and what steps after the loop?
2. How do we get out of the loop? At this point we have considered only loops which terminate when the user indicates she is finished. However, there are many other ways to terminate loops, as we will see in Chapters 3 and 5.
3. Where should we place the test for leaving the loop? With our simple loops which terminate using a dummy entry, this question is easy to answer: the test comes right after the "read" step.

The algorithm language we use utilizes three statements for looping and leaving loops: **loop**, **endloop**, and **exit**. The first two, **loop** and **endloop**, are used to set off the steps we wish to have repeated. These steps are generally called the **body** of the loop. For increased clarity, we will also indent the body of the loop. The **exit** step describes when we will leave the loop. At this point, all the loops we write leave the loop when a dummy entry is supplied by the user; however, we want to emphasize that this will later be broadened to include more general types of loop exits. The **exit** step means "leave the loop," and when we leave the loop we proceed to the first step after the body of the loop.

In our example, the main program contains a loop which reads, calculates, and prints answers for a number of input values. The steps to be repeated are placed between the **loop** and **endloop** lines, indented to stand out better. Before the loop we place anything which must be done exactly once, before beginning the repetition. In this case, we want to call the INSTR subroutine to print directions. (What would happen if this step were placed in the body of the loop?) Finally, after the loop we place those steps to be performed once after we have completed all our repetitions of the steps in the loop. In this case we simply stop the program. Notice that the **exit** from the loop will take us to this step, since it is the first step following the body of the loop.

As is usual in the types of loops we are presently writing, we will leave the loop when there is no more data to be processed, and the test for exiting the loop comes right after a read step.

The program contains two instances of **decisions**. Each is an example of an **if-then** structure, which is patterned after our English language use of the word "if."

The main program contains the lines

```
if NAME is blank then
   exit
endif
```

and the subroutine, contains the lines

```
if ANSWER = 'Y' then
   print directions
endif
```

In each case, we are saying that, **if** the stated condition is true, **then** we want to perform the following steps. We use the **endif** in a way similar to the English use of a period to end a sentence—it marks the end of the list of things to be done if the condition is true.

Finally, the example uses a **subprogram** to perform the subtask of printing instructions if the user wants them. This leaves the main program less "cluttered"; the details of the PRINT statements, as well as the logic involved in determining whether or not the user wants instructions, are "hidden" in the subroutine. The main program's logic can concentrate on the major task of the program: obtaining total scores for the students in the class.

As we learn more about subprograms (both subroutines and function subprograms), we will observe this same type of situation. In performing a subtask for the calling program, the subprogram hides some details from the calling program. Thus, the calling program may concentrate on its own job. The overall complexity of the process is decreased by dividing it up into smaller pieces.

REVIEW

Terms

main program
subroutine
function subprogram
body of subroutine
program unit
module
call
invoke
calling program
local variable
body of loop

FORTRAN Syntax

The SUBROUTINE statement: SUBROUTINE sname

"sname" is the subroutine name, consisting of one to six letters or digits, the first a letter.

The CALL statement: CALL sname

This is used to invoke the subroutine from the program unit which uses it.

The RETURN statement: RETURN

This statement returns control back to the point where the subroutine was invoked.

Writing and Using a Subroutine

1. Algorithm for subroutine is the algorithm for performing the subtask.
2. The main program simply calls the subroutine to perform the subtask at the proper place.
3. The subroutine form is:

```
SUBROUTINE sname
declarations for subroutine
body of subroutine, code implementing its algorithm
RETURN
END
```

4. The program consists of the main program, followed by any subprograms which are used.

Pitfalls

1. The main program and subprogram do not automatically share any variables.
2. Each program unit declares its own variables. Duplicate names are allowed.
3. The main program must have an END statement as its last statement. The subroutine(s) used also end with an END statement.
4. Subroutines generally use RETURN, not STOP. (Using STOP would stop the whole program.)

EXAMPLE. See Figure 2.2 for a complete program consisting of a main program and one subroutine.

EXERCISES

1. Consider the programs written in Exercise 1 of Section 1.3. What difference would it make to the main program to use an instruction-printing subroutine to print the instructions? (Note: The name of the subroutine could be INSTR, if you wish, for each individual program.)
2. Rewrite the program of Figure 1.6 (Section 1.3) to utilize an instruction-printing subroutine.
3. Run the revised program from Exercise 2. Is there any difference in what appears on the screen as the program is running? Could a user tell whether or not the program uses a subroutine?

4. Choose one of the parts (a–e) of Exercise 6, Section 1.4. Rewrite and run the program, using an INSTR subroutine which asks if the user wishes to see instructions.
5. Consider the enhanced version of the INSTR subroutine (Figure 2.3). What will happen if the user accidentally enters 'y' instead of 'Y' when asked if she wishes instructions? Can you suggest any possible solutions? (Note: At this point you have not covered enough FORTRAN to code some of the possible solutions; however, you should be able to describe in words what you might do).
6. Complete the second suggested enhancement of the INSTR subroutine. More specifically, suppose that there are 25 line of instructions. Your subroutine should print the first 15 lines, then pause until the user inputs a character, then print the remaining ten lines.
7. Make the INSTR subroutine in Figure 2.3 "fancier" by having it print a pattern similar to this prior to asking if the user wishes instructions:

```
 SS        CCC       000       RRRR    EEEEE    SS
S  S      CC  C     0   0      R   R   E       S  S
S        CC        00    00    R   R   E       S
 S       CC        00    00    R RR    EEEE     S
  S      CC        00    00    RR      E         S
   S     CC        00    00    R R     E          S
S  S      CC  C     0   0      R  R    E       S  S
 SS        CCC       000       R   R   EEEEE    SS
```

2.3 DECISION STRUCTURES

One of the four main tools for programming in FORTRAN and other computer languages is the decision-making ability. This allows the choice of alternative actions to depend on some condition. As the program is running the computer is able to evaluate the condition, determine whether it is true or false, and choose the appropriate sequence based on this evaluation. In our examples up to this point, we have used simple decision making to leave the loop and also to determine whether or not to print instructions. This section will go into more detail on the types of algorithms one frequently encounters involving decisions, and will explain the FORTRAN language elements used.

It is possible to identify at least the following three different types of decision making in our daily lives:

1. Is some condition true? If so, do one set of actions; if not, do some other set of actions.
2. Is some condition true? If so, do some set of actions; if not, do nothing.
3. Which of the following conditions is true? If the first is true, do one set of actions. If the second is true, do a second set of actions. If the third is true, do a third set of actions, and so on.

Exactly these same decision types arise in the algorithms we write to solve problems on the computer. In this section we will concentrate on the first two general types listed above. Later we will come back to the somewhat more complicated situation where any one of a number of possible conditions may be true.

If-Then-Else

Let us consider the first type of decision making listed above. In this situation, we have a condition, some steps to be performed when the condition is true, and some steps to be performed when the condition is not true. Because we will perform one of two possible sets of steps, we sometimes refer to this as a "two-way branch."

The pseudocode description of such a two-way branch will follow the form:

```
if condition then
    code for case where condition is true
else
    code for case where condition is false
endif
```

In general, this **if-then-else** construction, as we will refer to it, has these three major components:

1. A condition. This is an expression whose value will be either true or false. The condition determines which of the two branches is to be performed.
2. A "true" branch. This sequence of steps follows the word **then** in the construction. It consists of the step or steps which should be performed if the condition is true.
3. A "false" branch. This sequence of one or more steps, which follows the **else** in the construction, tells what should be done if the condition is false.

Notice the use of indentation to make the two branches stand out at a glance. It is a good idea to use this as a reinforcement of the **if**, **then**, **else**, and **endif**.

The meaning of the pseudocode is as follows. When the **if** step is reached, the condition will be examined. If it is true, the steps following the **then** (but before the **else**) will be performed. On the other hand, if the condition is false, the steps following the **else** will be performed. In either case, the computer will then proceed to the step immediately following the **endif**. This, by the way, is the purpose of the **endif**. It marks the point where the two paths rejoin.

For example, consider the following segment of pseudocode.

```
read X,Y
if X>Y then
   Z ← 7
   W ← 3*X
else
   Z ← 5
   W ← X+Y
endif
T ← 2*Z
```

In order to further clarify the meaning of the **if-then-else**, we will hand-trace this algorithm segment. By this, we mean to make up some sample input values and work our way by hand through the steps that would be taken for those values. For example, suppose the numbers which the user will input are 5 and 3. We will execute these steps, with the indicated results:

1. Read X,Y. X gets the value 5, Y the value 3.
2. X>Y? Since X has the value 5 and Y the value 3, the answer is yes. We therefore follow the **then** branch of the algorithm.
3. Z ← 7. Z gets the value 7.
4. W ← 3*X. Since X is currently 5, W gets the value 15.
5. T ← 2*Z. In the third step, Z was given the value 7. Hence, T gets the value 2*7, or 14.

Now suppose the numbers supplied by the user had been 6 and 8. Again we will trace the execution:

1. Read X,Y. This time X gets the value 6, Y the value 8.
2. X>Y? For these values, the answer to the question is no. Hence we follow the **else** branch of the algorithm.
3. Z ← 5. Z gets the value 5.
4. W ← X + Y. W gets the value 6 + 8, or 14.
5. T ← 2*Z. Again, the step following the point where the branches rejoin sets T to twice the value of Z. Since Z was given the value 5 in the third step, this step sets T to 10.

NOTES.

1. If the two branches are both very short, we may write the entire construction on one line:

```
if X>5 then Y ← 17 else Y ← 14 endif
```

2. You might be wondering about the need for the **endif**. Its purpose is to make it completely unambiguous where the "false" branch ends. For example, suppose we left the **endif** off in our example:

```
read X, Y
if X>Y then
   Z ← 7
   W ← 3 * X
else
   Z ← 5
   W ← X + Y
T ← 2 * Z
```

The indentation pattern suggests that the step T ← 2 * Z is not part of the **else** branch. However, we cannot be perfectly sure this is true. Although in practice there may be some understanding of what the program does which will clarify the issue, it is generally better to avoid ambiguity whenever possible. The **endif** helps us accomplish this goal.

Following are several examples which utilize this two-way branch, or **if-then-else**, construction.

Taxes in a certain state are calculated by the following scheme: If the income is less than $10,000, the tax is 2 percent of income; if the income is $10,000 or more, the tax is $200 plus 3 percent of the amount of income over $10,000.

Notice that this is indeed a two-way branch, or **if-then-else** type of problem. Although at first glance it looks as if there are two different conditions to be examined, actually there is only one. Once we have answered the question, "Is the income less than $10,000?" we do not need to ask the question, "Is the income $10,000 or more?" If the answer to the first question is no, we automatically know that the income must be $10,000 or more.

For this problem we need two variables, INCOME and TAX, each REAL. The variable TAX will be calculated by one of these two formulas:

```
TAX ← .02*INCOME
```

or

```
TAX ← 200.0 + 0.3*(INCOME-10000.0)
```

Which formula we use depends, of course, on the amount of income. The pseudo-code for this tax calculation is given by

```
if INCOME≥10000 then
   TAX ← 200.0 + .03*(INCOME-10000.0)
else
   TAX ← .02 * INCOME
endif
```

(Notice that this is only a *segment* of code, not an entire algorithm. An entire algorithm would, at the very least, include some steps for input and output.)

Each line of input has a salesperson number and a weekly sales figure. Commission is calculated as the sales amount times the commission rate, where the commission rate is .02 if the sales amount is less than $100, otherwise .05. Write an algorithm to print a table of salesperson numbers, sales amounts, rates, and commissions.

There are a number of ways to do this, one of which follows. (Here, as elsewhere in the text, we call an INSTR routine to print instructions. The details of the subroutine are omitted.)

```
call INSTR
loop
   prompt
   read IDNO,SALES
   if IDNO<0 then
      exit
   endif
   if SALES < 100 then
      RATE ← .02
      COMM ← SALES * .02
   else
      RATE ← .05
      COMM ← SALES * .05
   endif
   print IDNO,SALES,RATE,COMM
endloop
stop
```

However, we might observe that in both branches of the **if-then-else** construction the last step performed is multiplying the rate times the sale to obtain the commission. Since this is done as the *last* step of *each* branch, we could very well perform it after the branches rejoin. We could thus write the following algorithm:

```
call INSTR
loop
   prompt
   read IDNO,SALES
   if IDNO < 0 then
      exit
   endif
   if SALES<100 then RATE ← .02 else RATE ← .05 endif
   COMM ← SALES * RATE
   print IDNO,SALES,RATE,COMM
endloop
stop
```

We have obtained an algorithm which is somewhat shorter and is at least a understandable.

Sometimes it is useful to find the larger and smaller of two given integer values, I and J. To do so, we will use two more integer variables, LARGER and SMALLR, for the larger and smaller of the two. Obviously, if I is greater than J, then the larger is I and the smaller is J; otherwise the larger must be J and the smaller I. The pseudocode description will be:

```
if I>J then
   LARGER ← I
   SMALLR ← J
else
   LARGER ← J
   SMALLR ← I
endif
```

Actually, you may be concerned about the possibility that the two could be equal. You should convince yourself that the algorithm given does work in this case, and that therefore we need not consider this possibility as a separate case.

If-Then

We now take up the second general type of decision making, namely the situation where if some condition is true we wish to perform a sequence of steps, but if it is false we wish to do nothing. In this case we do not need the **else** portion of the pseudocode, so we merely omit it. The general form is

```
if condition then
   code for case where condition is true
endif
```

We use this type of pseudocode for exiting from a loop when a dummy entry is entered, as in:

```
if  NAME is blank then exit endif
```

There are many other types of applications for the **if-then** construction. Some of the most useful occur in using a loop for counting, which is described in the next chapter.

A typical use of an **if-then** construction occurred in our INSTR subroutine. This type of construction was appropriate there because we either wanted to print instructions, or else do nothing. Let us discuss two additional examples.

First, suppose we want to allow a discount for large orders. More specifically, suppose the variable QUANT represents the number of items the customer has ordered, and that COST is the amount of the order. If the quantity is over 500, we want to calculate a variable DISCNT as a 10 percent discount, and subtract that amount from the cost. We may write

```
if QUANT > 500 then
   DISCNT ← 0.1 * COST
   COST ← COST - DISCNT
endif
```

The first step in the **then** branch calculates the discount. The second subtracts that discount from the current value of the COST variable, and then places the answer back into the COST variable. If the quantity is not over 500, we do nothing, so the COST variable retains its original value.

As a final example, we will write a segment of code for the following situation. Given variables A and B containing real numbers, we want to do nothing if they are equal; otherwise we want to add A to S and subtract B from T.

At first glance this does not seem to fit into the pattern we are discussing. Here if some condition is true, we want to do nothing; the actions to be performed are to be done when the condition is *false*. However, suppose we turn the statement of the problem around: if A and B are unequal, add A to S and subtract B from T (otherwise do nothing). Now the problem is recognizable as an **if-then** type of problem, and we can easily write the algorithm for the program segment.

```
if A ≠ B then
   S ← S+A
   T ← T-B
endif
```

Decisions in FORTRAN

We now consider how to implement, that is, code in FORTRAN, the **if-then-else** and **if-then** constructions. FORTRAN has language elements specifically designed to deal with both of these constructions. In fact, the language elements involved look almost exactly like the pseudocode we have been using. Specifically, there are three FORTRAN statements which we will use in coding two-way branches. They are the following:

1. IF(condition) THEN
2. ELSE
3. ENDIF

These three language elements are used in much the same way as we have used the corresponding pseudocode elements. If we have a program with a two-way branch, the FORTRAN coding for this two-way branch will be

```
IF(condition) THEN
    code for case where condition is true
ELSE
    code for case where condition is false
ENDIF
```

As in the algorithm, we will use indentation to emphasize the fact that the first block of code is to be performed in one case, the second in the other case. The indentation is not required by the compiler, but it does make the code easier to read and understand. Unlike the pseudocode, we may not write the entire IF-THEN-ELSE-ENDIF on a single line. The only allowable form is that given above.

The "condition" placed inside the parentheses in the IF-THEN step can be very complicated. We are allowed to place in the parentheses any so-called **logical expression**. Simply put, a logical expression is an expression whose value is either

"TRUE" or "FALSE." There are specific rules for forming logical expressions. For now, we will use only simple forms of logical expressions. In later chapters we will learn to use more complicated logical expressions.

The simplest form of logical expression compares two numerical, or arithmetic, quantities. Its general form will consist of two expressions separated by what is called a **relational operator**. The relational operator must be one of the following six operators:

```
.EQ.    equals
.NE.    is not equal to
.GT.    is greater than
.LT.    is less than
.GE.    is greater than or equal to
.LE.    is less than or equal to
```

The meaning of each of the relational operators is listed beside the operator. Notice that each of the operators begins and ends with a period. It is absolutely necessary to include these periods; they inform the compiler that the letters in between represent an operator.

The expressions may be any expressions at all. Any expression we could write on the right side of an assignment statement can be placed in a condition of this type. For example, the following are valid:

```
5       J+7           'Sam'
5.0     (X+Y)/3.5     ' '
X       (T+23.0)      'DORSET'
```

The expression may be as simple as a single variable or constant, but it may also be more complex, even utilizing parentheses.

In our "condition," which is placed inside the parentheses of the IF-THEN statement, we compare two expressions using one of the six relational operators. We can thus compare in six different ways. For example, in comparing the quantity presently in the variable I to the number 5, we can write any one of the following six conditions:

```
I.EQ.5    I.LT.5
I.NE.5    I.GE.5
I.GT.5    I.LE.5
```

Of course, we could also write 5.GT.I if we wished to; however, this would have the same effect as writing I.LT.5.

There are a couple of points worth noting in performing CHARACTER comparisons. First, if one expression is shorter than the other, the shorter expression is padded on the right with blanks in making the comparison. Thus, to see if the

CHARACTER*20 variable NAME is totally blank, we may simply write

```
IF (NAME.EQ.' ') THEN
```

We do not need to use 20 blanks.

Another point is that the comparison is an "alphabetical" comparison, with the letter 'A' preceding 'B', and so on. Thus, the condition 'ABC' .LT. 'ACB' would be true. However, there are no set rules concerning how special characters such as '$' will enter into the ordering scheme. For most of our examples, we will be using either .EQ. or .NE. as our relational operator when working with character values.

CAUTION. It does not make any sense to try to compare a character value with an integer or real value.

Here are some examples of valid conditions for an IF-THEN statement:

```
X.GT.4.7
T.NE.R
L+5.GT.MIN
(L+5).GT.MIN
SALARY.GT.10000.0
NAME.EQ.' '
STATE.NE.'VIRGINIA'
```

Figure 2.4 contains the FORTRAN code for two of the algorithm segments written in the subsection on the **if-then-else** construction. As you can see, the IF-THEN-ELSE-ENDIF construction in FORTRAN is almost identical to what we use in our algorithm. (Notice that we have included declarations for the variables the algorithm segment uses. We have not attempted to guess what other variables would be involved if this segment were included in a complete program.)

Once we have learned how to write the **if-then-else** in FORTRAN, the **if-then** follows easily. We simply leave out the ELSE branch, just as we do in the pseudocode. For example, we would code the algorithm segment

```
if A ≠ B then
   S ← S + A
   T ← T - B
endif
```

as the FORTRAN segment

```
IF (A.NE.B) THEN
   S = S + A
   T = T - B
ENDIF
```

Similarly, we would translate

```
if I is not less than 6 then X ← W + 4 endif
```

```
if INCOME>10000 then
   TAX ← 200.0 + .03*(INCOME-10000.0)
else
   TAX ← .02*INCOME
endif

   REAL INCOME,TAX
        .
        .
        .
   IF(INCOME.GT.10000.0) THEN
     TAX = 200.0 + .03 * (INCOME-10000.0)
   ELSE
      TAX = .02 * INCOME
   ENDIF

if I>J then
   LARGER ← I
   SMALLR ← J
else
   LARGER ← J
   SMALLR ← I
endif

   INTEGER I,J,LARGER,SMALLR
        .
        .
   IF(I.GT.J) THEN
      LARGER = I
      SMALLR = J
   ELSE
      LARGER = J
      SMALLR = I
   ENDIF
```

Figure 2.4

to the FORTRAN

```
IF (I.GE.6) THEN
    X = W + 4
ENDIF
```

Notice the following two points:

1. We may not, in FORTRAN, place the entire IF-THEN-ENDIF construction on a single line.
2. The condition "I not less than 6" is the same as the condition "I greater than or equal to 6." This is a simple example of forming the **negation** of a condition. The condition we have negated, or found the opposite of, is the condition "I

less than 6." Negation is generally indicated by the use of the word "not" in the description of a condition.

To negate our simple conditions, which use a single relational operator, we need only observe the following relationship between an operator and the opposite or negated operator.

```
.EQ. - .NE.
.NE. - .EQ.
.GT. - .LE.
.LT. - .GE.
.GE. - .LT.
.LE. - .GT.
```

Pitfalls

There are a number of relatively minor pitfalls to be avoided when using the techniques of this section.

1. One possible problem is forgetting the ENDIF statement. Although the compiler will likely detect that an ENDIF is missing, it will be unable to tell you where it should have gone.

   A worse problem would be placing the ENDIF in the wrong place. If you have fewer (or more) steps in the decision structure than you should, your program may run. However, it will not produce correct answers.

   Writing your algorithms carefully will reduce the likelihood of this happening.
2. We should remember that, for example, the negation of "less than" is "greater than or equal." There is a tendency to use "greater than," which is of course incorrect.
3. Comparing two quantities to see if they are equal is not the same as assignment. In FORTRAN, we use .EQ. in IF statements to check for equality, *not* in assignment statements. For example,

```
IF(I.EQ.6) THEN
   J = 17
ENDIF
```

Adding to Case Study #1

In this subsection, we consider further modifications to Case Study #1 begun in Section 1.4. In Section 2.2, we added a subroutine to handle the printing of instructions for the user. (The latest version of the main program appears in Figure 2.2, with the latest version of the subroutine in Figure 2.3.) The program is one which, for each student, calculates the total score on three tests.

We now consider two possible enhancements. First, we could modify the algorithm to also print an indication of whether the student is passing or failing. If we assume that a total score of 210 is a passing grade, then we might reason as follows:

> If the TOTAL is 210 or higher, then the student's
> result is "passing," otherwise it is "failing."

We may add a CHARACTER*7 variable to our list of variables, which we will call RESULT. This variable will be assigned either the word "passing" or the word "failing" based on the total score. Thus we have this segment of pseudocode:

```
if TOTAL ≥ 210 then
   RESULT ← 'passing'
else
   RESULT ← 'failing'
endif
```

We will place this immediately after the step which calculates the TOTAL on which it is based, and modify the print statement to include this variable in its list of items to print.

Our second modification will, in addition, print a message identifying those students who are exempted from the final exam (total score 290 or above). We would like the output to look something like this for such a student:

```
The total is 298 for JOHN SMITH      - passing
********* EXEMPT FROM FINAL *********
```

Since the message appears after the line with the total, name, and result, we will place the steps to do this after the print statement in the algorithm.

Notice that this is an **if-then** situation; no message is desired for those who are not exempt. Thus we will write

```
if TOTAL ≥ 290 then
   print exemption message
endif
```

Figure 2.5 contains the modified algorithm, variable list, and FORTRAN code for the main program. The changes are shaded. Notice that these change do not directly affect the INSTR subroutine, although we should probably modify it to reflect the changes. This is left as an exercise.

Testing

In Section 1.4 we introduced some of the concepts involved in program testing. At this point we are concerned with testing after we have obtained a "clean compile." By this we mean that the compiler is not listing any syntax errors. The program is running, and we want to see whether it is generating correct answers. In that section, we listed three principles:

1. Check all answers. Include some data that is easy to check.
2. Test near boundaries; also test a random sampling away from the boundaries.
3. Include some erroneous input, especially if the program is designed to detect and warn about such errors.

In this subsection we will look at the second of these principles in more detail.

When a program includes branching, boundary testing becomes especially

	Name	Type	Use	Comment
Input:	NAME	CHARACTER*12	Student name	Also printed
	SCORE1	INTEGER	Test scores	
	SCORE2	INTEGER		
	SCORE3	INTEGER		
Output:	TOTAL	INTEGER	Total of 3 scores	
	RESULT	CHARACTER*7	Pass/fail indication	

```
call INSTR
loop
    prompt
    read NAME
    if NAME is blank then exit endif
    prompt
    read SCORE1, SCORE2, SCORE3
    TOTAL ← SCORE1 + SCORE2 + SCORE3
    if TOTAL ≥ 210 then
      RESULT ← 'passing'
    else
      RESULT ← 'failing'
    endif
    print TOTAL, NAME, RESULT
    if TOTAL ≥ 290 then
      print exemption message
    endif
endloop
stop
      CHARACTER*12 NAME
      CHARACTER*7 RESULT
      INTEGER SCORE1,SCORE2,SCORE3,TOTAL

C   WRITTEN BY ********, **/**/**

C   THIS PROGRAM CALCULATES THE TOTAL ON THREE TESTS, AND
C PRINTS THAT TOTAL WITH THE STUDENT'S NAME

C   BEFORE THE LOOP, PRINT INSTRUCTIONS

      CALL INSTR

C   IN THE LOOP, READ THE NAME AND SCORES AND CALCULATE THE
C TOTAL AND RESULT. MARK EXAM EXEMPTIONS. QUIT WHEN THE
C NAME ENTERED IS BLANK.

   10 CONTINUE
         PRINT *,' '
         PRINT *,'Enter the name (blank to quit)'
         READ *, NAME
         IF (NAME.EQ.' ') THEN
            GO TO 500
         ENDIF
         PRINT *,'Now enter the three scores'
```

Figure 2.5 *(continued)*

```
      READ *,SCORE1,SCORE2,SCORE3
      TOTAL = SCORE1 + SCORE2 + SCORE3
      IF (TOTAL.GE.210) THEN
         RESULT = 'passing'
      ELSE
         RESULT = 'failing'
      ENDIF
      PRINT *,'The total is ',TOTAL,' for ',NAME,' - ',RESULT
      IF (TOTAL.GE.290) THEN
         PRINT *,'********** EXEMPT FROM FINAL **********'
      ENDIF
      GO TO 10

C   AFTER THE LOOP, STOP THE PROGRAM.

  500 CONTINUE
      STOP
      END
```

Figure 2.5 *(continued from p. 80)*

important. By a "boundary" we mean a point at which the rule for determining the answer changes. Experience has shown that programs are more likely to contain errors at or near boundary points. As a result, we want to include special tests to make sure that the program works at and near the boundary points.

For example, consider our case study program. There are now a number of different boundary points. Of course, there are still the boundaries of 0 and 100 for each individual score, which we included in our original test plan in Section 1.4. In addition, we now have two more boundaries, based on the total score. They are 210 and 290. At 210 the rule for determining pass or fail changes, and at 290 the rule for telling whether or not the student is exempt from the final exam changes. It is a good idea to include test cases which result in value exactly on the boundary, just below the boundary, and just above the boundary. Hence, in our test plan we might write:

Boundary on passing:

70, 69, 70—total 209, fail
65, 76, 69—total 210, pass
100, 50, 61—total 211, pass

Boundary on exempting final:

100, 90, 99—total 289, not exempt
95, 97, 98—total 290, exempt
99, 96, 96—total 291, exempt

In addition to these boundary values, we would also include other passing and failing grades chosen randomly, and other exempting and nonexempting grades chosen randomly.

COMMENT. Of the three tests listed for the boundary on passing, the first two are the most vital: 209 is the highest failing grade, and 210 the lowest passing grade. A similar comment applies for the second list.

In general, in testing a program involving branching, we will choose some test cases which exercise the boundary points, as well as others chosen more randomly within the different branches.

REVIEW

Terms and Concepts

two-way branch

hand-trace an algorithm

Selection of test data

Choose values at and near all boundary points

Algorithms (pseudocode)

Branching (decision making)

if-then-else

```
if condition then
  steps for 'condition true' case
else
  steps for 'condition false' case
endif
```

if-then

```
if condition then
  steps for 'condition true' case
endif
```

Examples

```
if I>J then
    LARGER ← I
    SMALLR ← J
else
    LARGER ← J
    SMALLR ← I
endif

if A ≠ B then
    S ← S+A
    T ← T-B
endif
```

FORTRAN Syntax

The IF-THEN-ELSE-ENDIF

```
IF(condition) THEN
    one or more statements
ELSE
    one or more statements
ENDIF
```

The IF-THEN-ENDIF:

```
IF(condition) THEN
   one or more statements
ENDIF
```

In each of the IF statements given above, the "condition" may be any logical expression. In particular, it may be:

expression   relational operator   expression

"expression" refers to any type of arithmetic or character expression. "Relational operator" refers to one of the following:

```
.EQ.   .NE.   .GT.
.LT.   .GE.   .LE.
```

Examples

The IF-THEN-ELSE-ENDIF

```
IF(I.GT.J) THEN
   LARGER = I
   SMALLR = J
ELSE
   LARGER = J
   SMALLR = I
ENDIF
```

The IF-THEN-ENDIF:

```
IF(A.NE.B) THEN
   S = S + A
   T = T - B
ENDIF
```

EXERCISES

1. Give an appropriate decision structure (**if-then-else** or **if-then**) for each of these situations. Use appropriate variables, and give both an algorithm segment and the corresponding segment of FORTRAN for the decision.

(a)

Income	Tax rate
less than $8000.00	2%
$8000.00 or higher	4.5%

(b) If the blood type is "O", print the identification number; otherwise do nothing.
(c) If the income is over $15000.00, add one to a variable CTR and add the income to a variable TOTAL; otherwise do nothing.
(d) If the sex code is "M," add 1 to the variable MALE, otherwise add 1 to the variable FEMALE.
(e) The value of X should be doubled if X is greater than 5, otherwise it should be tripled.
(f) The commission rate is 3 percent if the sales amount is less than $150. If the sales amount is $150 or more, the commission rate should be 5 percent.
(g) Sales tax is 6 percent on any purchase $500 or less but only 3.5 percent for a purchase over $500.
(h) If TAX is greater than $550 a penalty of 6 percent should be added to the tax.
(i) If T is currently 0, do nothing, otherwise add 1 to the value of T.
(j) Calculate the bonus based on the current value of YEARS and SALES. If YEARS is 5 or less then the bonus is nothing, otherwise it is 1 percent of the SALES.
(k) If the average of the three test scores is greater than 59.5, print "passed."
(l) If the ratio of two integers I and J is above 4.7, then calculate K as the sum of I and J; if not, K is the difference.

2. For each algorithm segment of Exercise 1, determine all boundary values and come up with a minimum set of test cases to test each branch at and near each boundary value.
3. Add appropriate input, output, and looping steps to create an entire algorithm built around the situations described in Exercise 1(a),(e),(f),(g), and (j). Where it makes sense, add names to the list of data input by the user.
4. Modify the Case Study example (Figure 2.5) to print "IMPROVING" for those students whose third grade is better than the average of the first two grades. What additions would be needed in the test plan?

For each of Exercises 5–9, do the following: (a) Determine the input and output and give a variable list; (b) write an algorithm; (c) create a test plan; (d) write the program in FORTRAN; (e) run the program, utilizing your test plan to help locate errors.

5. Each line of data has three integers A, B, C. These form a "Pythagorean triple" if A*A + B*B = C*C. Write an algorithm to read each input line, print the values of A, B, and C, and a message—either "IS A PYTHAGOREAN TRIPLE" or "IS NOT A PYTHAGOREAN TRIPLE."
6. Amount of the sale is quantity times price. The discount is 1 percent of the sales amount if the quantity is over 100, otherwise 0. The net price is the sales amount minus the discount. The commission is 3 percent of the net price if the net price is less than $250; 5 percent for $250 or more. The program should input quantity and price, then calculate and print the sales amount, discount, net price, commission rate, and commission.
7. The first input line contains the beginning balance of a savings account for a year. Each of the remaining lines represents one transaction for the account. Each such line has a

transaction code ('W'=withdrawal, 'D'=deposit) and an amount. Write an algorithm to determine the final balance at the end of the year, by adding and subtracting from the running balance based on each transaction. (You may assume that the code is either a 'W' or a 'D'.)

Revise the algorithm to print a running account of the transactions for the account, including the beginning and ending balance for each transaction.

8. Each data line has an employee name, an incentive factor (.01−.15), weekly base salary, and the number of units produced during the week. Write an algorithm to print a payroll for the company. A person's actual salary is computed from the base salary as follows: If the number of units produced is less than 500, then 10 cents is deducted from the person's pay for each unit by which he missed the quota of 500. If he produced 500 or more units, then the base salary is increased by an amount consisting of the incentive factor times the number of units produced.

Modify the algorithm to print a message "AT OR ABOVE QUOTA" or "BELOW QUOTA" for each employee.

9. The data lines are the same as in Exercise 8. However, this time the salary is computed as follows: If the number of units produced is less than 750, the salary is merely the base salary; if 750 or more units were produced, the incentive factor is treated as a percentage, and this percent of the base salary is added to the base salary to obtain the actual salary.

2.4 ADDITIONAL FORTRAN TOPICS

In this section we will discuss two important FORTRAN topics: library functions and FORMAT statements. In addition, we give a brief discussion of batch processing and file concepts.

Square Roots and Absolute Value

We can now write FORTRAN assignment statements corresponding to most algebraic expressions. There are, however, a few common algebraic formulas we would have some difficulty with, such as the following:

$$y = 3\sqrt{x}$$

$$y = |r - 5|$$

These involve the algebraic operations known as square root and absolute value, respectively. Fortunately, the FORTRAN programming language provides a simple approach to coding this type of expression, as well as many others.

FORTRAN has **library functions** which are designed to perform operations such as taking square roots or finding absolute values. (We will sometimes refer to these as "built-in" functions.) We begin our discussion of the library functions with the square root function.

Consider the following simple algebraic formula:

$$y = \sqrt{x}$$

The corresponding FORTRAN assignment statement would be

```
Y = SQRT(X)
```

The "SQRT" in this assignment statement stands for the built-in square root function. The variable we wish to take the square root of is placed within parentheses following the "SQRT." In this example, SQRT is the **function name**, and X is referred to as the **argument**, or **parameter**, of the function.

A library function is a special kind of FORTRAN subprogram. It consists of a predefined group of steps for the computer to perform. When the computer reaches the assignment statement "Y = SQRT(X)" in our program, it will temporarily interrupt the processing of our program. It will calculate the value of the argument, then proceed to the predefined group of steps making up the library function named SQRT. These steps will cause it to calculate the square root of the argument. When the computer resumes processing our program, it will place this square root into the variable Y.

Using a built-in function is sometimes referred to as "invoking" or "calling" the function. To invoke the SQRT function, the general form we will use is

```
SQRT(argument)
```

That is, we write the name of the function (SQRT), followed by the quantity we wish to take the square root of (the argument), enclosed in parentheses.

The argument for the SQRT function can be any expression, whatsoever, subject to the following two restrictions:

1. The expression must represent a REAL number (not an INTEGER).
2. The value of that expression, at the time the computer reaches the step which invokes the SQRT function, must not be a negative number. (Recall that the square root of a negative number does not exist as a real number.)

As was indicated above, the value of the argument will be calculated to obtain a single REAL value, then the SQRT function will be invoked to determine the square root of that value. We say that the SQRT function **returns** the square root of its argument. The value returned by the SQRT function will always be a REAL number. For this reason, the SQRT function is called a "REAL function." For example, if the value of the variable X is 4.0 when we perform the step "Y = SQRT(X)," then the value returned by the SQRT function will be the REAL number 2.0.

Consider now the algebraic formula

$$y = t + 3\sqrt{x - 42}$$

Can we write this formula as a FORTRAN assignment statement? The answer is yes. In general, we can write any algebraic expression involving square roots in FORTRAN by replacing the square root sign by the SQRT function, and placing the expression, whose square root is to be found, in parentheses as the argument of the function. We must, however, remember that the argument should be a REAL quantity. We therefore assume that X, Y, and T are REAL variables, and write

```
Y = T + 3.0*SQRT(X-42.0)
```

The table below lists several other examples of algebraic expressions and the corresponding FORTRAN expression.

Algebraic expression	FORTRAN expression
$x + \sqrt{x}$	`X + SQRT(X)`
$\sqrt{3/4}$	`SQRT(3.0/4.0) or` `SQRT(0.75)`
$3/\sqrt{x + 17}$	`3.0/SQRT(X+17.0)`
$\sqrt{x - 5 + y} - z$	`SQRT(X-5.0+Y) -Z`
$\sqrt{x + \sqrt{t}}$	`SQRT(X+SQRT(T))`

Of course, we are assuming that all variables have been declared to be REAL, and that the values of the arguments will turn out to be nonnegative when the SQRT function is invoked.

Notice especially the last example in the table. We have said that the argument of the SQRT function may be any expression whatsoever. That expression may itself involve taking a square root using the SQRT function!

These examples once again raise the question of precedence. When we have a function in a FORTRAN expression, in what order are the various operations performed? The answer is given by the following summary of precedence rules:

1. functions in the expression are evaluated first
2. ** comes next, right to left
3. * and / are next, left to right
4. + and − are last, left to right

Of course, in order to evaluate a function reference such as "SQRT(3.0*X−Y/4.5)," it is first necessary to determine what number we are to take the square root of. This will mean that the computer will first have to find the value of the argument "3.0*X−Y/4.5." It is therefore understood that when we say "functions in the expression are evaluated first," we mean that the arguments of the functions are evaluated (using the normal precedence rules), then the functions are invoked to return their value. For example, in evaluating the expression

```
4.2 + 5.0*SQRT(6.4-4.8/2.0)
```

the computer would perform the following steps in the order indicated:

```
4.2 + 5.0*SQRT(6.4-2.4)
4.2 + 5.0*SQRT(4.0)
4.2 + 5.0*2.0
4.2 + 10.0
14.2
```

Two important points about the SQRT function are illustrated by these two lines of code:

```
ROOT = SQRT(X)
PRINT *, 'The square root of ', X, ' is ', ROOT
```

First, we need a different variable into which the result of the function may be placed. We cannot use the name SQRT both as a function name and as a variable name in the same program. Thus, we cannot write

```
SQRT = SQRT(X)
```

Observe also that in the PRINT statement we print the variable ROOT, not the function name SQRT. If we are using the SQRT name as a function, we cannot use it as a variable name.

The same rule will apply to functions we write ourselves (Section 2.6).

COMMENT. As you may recall from algebra, the expression $x^{1/2}$ denotes the square root of x. In place of

```
Y = SQRT(X)
```

we could therefore write

```
Y = X ** 0.5
```

As a matter of fact, this method has more general application, since roots of any kind correspond to fractional exponents. For example, to find the fourth root of X, we would write "X**0.25," and so on.

However, the SQRT function, since it has been designed specifically to take square roots, is generally more accurate than raising to the one-half power. In addition, using the SQRT function is probably faster on most computers. Therefore, we will use the built-in function rather than the exponential form.

We now consider taking absolute values in FORTRAN. To do so we will need to use the built-in absolute value function ABS. This function can calculate the absolute value of a REAL expression or of an INTEGER expression. If it is given a REAL argument, it returns a REAL answer. On the other hand, if it is given an INTEGER argument, it returns an INTEGER answer. Let us suppose that the variables R, S, and T are REAL, and that J and K are INTEGER. Here are some algebraic expressions and the corresponding FORTRAN expressions.

Algebraic expression	FORTRAN expression	Algebraic expression	FORTRAN expression
$\lvert r - 5 \rvert$	`ABS(R - 5.0)`	$\dfrac{\lvert 5k \rvert - 3}{4}$	`(ABS(5*K) - 3)/4`
$\lvert j - 5 \rvert$	`ABS(J - 5)`		
$\lvert r + s \rvert - t$	`ABS(R+S) - T`	$\left\lvert \dfrac{s}{2r} \right\rvert$	`ABS(S/(2.0*R))`
$\lvert r + s - t \rvert$	`ABS(R+S-T)`		

Notice again that the expression which is the argument of the function can be complicated. It can even involve parentheses.

COMMENT. One important use of the absolute value function has to do with comparisons of REAL numbers. Because of the way the computer stores REAL numbers, it is possible for the number within the computer to be slightly more than or less than the number it represents. To understand the problem, suppose you had to represent 1/3 as a decimal fraction with three digits. You would write .333, which is slightly less than 1/3. If you added 1/3 to itself three times, you would get .999 when the answer "should be" 1.0. The computer has similar problems due to its finite storage area for REAL numbers.

As a result, we should not in general compare two REAL quantities using .EQ.. Instead, we should use the ABS function to see if the values are so close that they should be considered "equal for all practical purposes." For example, rather than

```
IF(A.EQ.B) THEN
```

we might write

```
IF(ABS(A-B).LT.0.0001) THEN
```

How close is "close enough?" That is something you, the programmer, will have to determine. It will depend on what types of numbers your particular program is dealing with.

Before we describe more functions, we would like to summarize the important characteristics which apply for any library function you may want to use.

1. Each function has one or more arguments, separated by commas. Each of the functions we have seen so far has exactly one argument. However, there are functions with several arguments, of which we will soon see an example (the MOD function).
2. Each of the arguments is of a certain type (INTEGER, REAL, and so forth). When we use the function, we must be sure to supply the proper type of expression for each argument.

   For some functions, there may be further restrictions to be met by the arguments in order for the function to work properly. (For example, the SQRT function does not work for negative numbers.)
3. When we use the function, we supply a value for each of its arguments. The value we supply can be in the form of any arbitrary expression, provided it satisfies Rule 2 above.
4. A function is invoked by including it in an expression. This expression may consist entirely of the function itself, or it may be very complex.
5. When we use a function, its name cannot be used for any other purpose in that program. In particular, it cannot be used as an ordinary variable.

If you find yourself writing the function name without including any arguments, you are probably violating this rule. For example, if you are using the SQRT function in a program, each of the following is invalid:

```
SQRT = SQRT(X)
PRINT *, SQRT
```

The MOD Function

The next function we will examine is the MOD function. We can summarize the MOD function as follows:

1. It has two arguments.
2. Both arguments are of type INTEGER.
3. It returns an INTEGER answer.
4. The answer returned by the MOD function is the **remainder**, when the first argument is divided by the second.

In elementary school, before you learned about fractions, you probably labeled the remainder when you divided two whole numbers. For example, consider the following:

```
     8          6           5          0
  6)50       7)43       12)60      17) 4
    48         42          60          0
     2=R        1=R         0=R        4=R
```

In each case, we have labeled the remainder with "=R." Notice that it is possible to have a remainder of zero; in fact, when this happens we sometimes say that the numbers "divide evenly."

The following table has four examples, each corresponding to one of the above division problems. For example, MOD(50,6) has the value 2, because when we divide 6 into 50 we get a remainder of 2.

Expression	Value
MOD(50,6)	2
MOD(43,7)	1
MOD(60,12)	0
MOD(4,17)	4

For each example, the first number is divided by the second, not the other way around. A comma is placed between the two arguments.

Perhaps the most common use of the MOD function is to see if one INTEGER number divides evenly into another. This can be done easily by seeing if the result of applying the MOD function is zero, since the remainder is zero precisely when the number divides evenly.

Let's try applying this new concept of MOD. Write a program which will read data lines, each containing an integer number. For each number, print a message telling whether the number is even or odd.

We will start with the following rough algorithm, where the only variable needed is the INTEGER variable NUMBER, which represents the number on the input line.

```
print instructions
loop
    prompt
    read NUMBER
    if NUMBER=0 then exit endif
    print proper message
endloop
stop
```

We now refine the step "print proper message."

What is required to refine this step? Hopefully, you will realize the answer: Print either the message "EVEN NUMBER" or the message "ODD NUMBER", depending on whether the number is even or odd. This should suggest a decision structure. In fact, you should realize that we need an **if-then-else**; there are two cases (even or odd), and we want to perform some actions for each case.

The proper refinement, then, is

```
if the number is even then
  print 'EVEN NUMBER'
else
  print 'ODD NUMBER'
endif
```

In this algorithm, we have written the condition as "the number is even," an English-language description. Before we can code this into FORTRAN, we will have to write this condition in terms of comparing two quantities.

The key to the solution is that the even numbers are those (such as 2, 4, 6, and 8) which are evenly divisible by 2. Consequently, we can use the expression MOD (NUMBER,2) to get the remainder when the input number is divided by 2. If this remainder is 0, then the number is even, otherwise it is odd. We can rewrite

```
if the number is even then
```

as

```
if MOD(NUMBER,2) = 0 then
```

Our smooth algorithm, with all the refinements included, looks like this:

```
print instructions
loop
   read NUMBER
   if NUMBER=0 then exit endif
   if MOD(NUMBER,2) = 0 then
     print 'EVEN NUMBER'
   else
     print 'ODD NUMBER'
   endif
endloop
stop
```

The **if-then** structure would be written as follows in FORTRAN

```
IF(MOD(NUMBER,2).EQ.0)THEN
   PRINT *, 'EVEN NUMBER'
ELSE
   PRINT *,'ODD NUMBER'
ENDIF
```

Functions can appear in expressions in IF conditions, as well as in assignment statements.

Data Conversion and Rounding

The two remaining functions we will consider are the INT and REAL functions. The REAL function is used to convert from INTEGER to REAL, the INT function to convert from REAL to INTEGER. We begin with the INT function. The INT function removes the fractional part of the real number that is its argument. The following table gives the value of INT(X) for various values of the REAL variable X. (Of course, X must have been declared REAL for the function to work.)

X	INT(X)
4.7	4
4.3	4
16.0	16
−7.5	−7
0.0	0

This function does not round to the nearest integer; it simply **truncates** (removes) the fractional part of the argument.

Suppose we do want to round a given real number to the nearest INTEGER. We will assume that the given number is positive. Recall that rounding means that if the fractional part is less than .5, we merely truncate the fractional part. On the other hand, if the fractional part is .5 or more, our answer is the next larger integer.

At first glance, this looks like we will need an **if-then-else** decision structure. However, we may use the INT function in a single assignment statement that works for either case, as indicated by the table below:

X	X+5	INT(X+5)
6.2	6.7	6
6.4	6.9	6
6.5	7.0	7
6.6	7.1	7
6.9	7.4	7

Observe that INT(X+.5) gives precisely the desired result.

We now discuss the REAL function, which was described briefly in Section 2.1. Given an INTEGER argument, it converts that integer to the corresponding real number. See the table below where I is assumed to be an INTEGER variable.

I	REAL(I)
6	6.0
0	0.0
−11	−11.0

As we briefly mentioned earlier, the primary use for the REAL function is to convert integers to real numbers, in order to avoid unwanted integer division. For example, suppose we wish to find the average of two integers A and B. The algorithm step would be

```
AVERAG ← (A+B)/2
```

Now we give declarations and code this step into FORTRAN.

There are actually two different solutions to the problem, depending on what type of result we want. First, we could do this:

```
INTEGER A, B,AVERAG
         .
         .
         .
AVERAG = (A+B)/2
```

The answer will be the integer average of the two numbers, with the fractional part (if any) truncated. For example, if A is 97 and B is 88, the average will be

(97+88)/2 = 185/2 = 92, since INTEGER division is performed. If this is what we want, fine. If, on the other hand, we want to get the "proper" answer 92.5 for this example, then AVERAG must be a REAL variable, and we must do REAL division. To change the numerator (A+B) to a REAL number, we merely apply the REAL function. We also write the denominator as the REAL number 2.0 rather than the INTEGER number 2. The solution in this case is

```
REAL AVERAG
INTEGER A,B
      *
      *
      *
AVERAG = REAL(A+B)/2.0
```

NOTE. There is no need to use the REAL function to convert the number 2 to a real number. Simply use the real number 2.0.

CAUTION. The expression

```
AVERAG = REAL((A+B)/2)
```

will not work. Why not?

Here are two more examples of the use of the REAL function:

```
REAL AVE                            REAL E
INTEGER TOTAL,N                     INTEGER N
    .                                   .
    .                                   .
    .                                   .
AVE = REAL(TOTAL)/REAL(N)           E = (1.0+1.0/REAL(N))**N
```

This completes our discussion of library functions. We have looked at the SQRT and ABS functions which are used in coding standard algebraic operations. In addition, we have looked at the MOD function, which is useful in determining whether or not a given integer divides evenly into another. Finally, we have considered the data conversion functions INT and REAL.

COMMENT. Those who are familiar with the trigonometric functions sin, cos, and so on will be interested in knowing that a number of trigonometric functions are available in FORTRAN. We note that these functions require one REAL argument which represents the angle in radians, not degrees.

In addition, there are many other useful functions which we will not cover in detail, including logarithmic and exponential functions. A list of the functions available on your particular system may be found in the FORTRAN manual for your computer (perhaps as an appendix). Table 2.1 lists and briefly explains several of the most frequently used standard library functions.

TABLE 2.1

Function name	Example[1]	Answer type	Definition	Argument type
SQRT	Y = SQRT(X)	REAL	Square root	1 Real, ≥0
ABS	Y = ABS(X)	REAL	Absolute value	1 Real
	J = ABS(I)	INTEGER	Absolute value	1 Integer
MOD	K = MOD(I,J)	INTEGER	Remainder of I/J	2 Integer
REAL	Y = REAL(I)	REAL	Convert to REAL	1 Integer
INT	J = INT(X)	INTEGER	Truncation	1 Real
SIN	Y = SIN(X)	REAL	Sine	1 Real in radians
COS	Y = COS(X)	REAL	Cosine	1 Real in radians
ATAN	Y = ATAN(X)	REAL	Arctangent	1 Real
ALOG	Y = ALOG(X)	REAL	Natural log (ln)	1 Real, >0
ALOG10	Y = ALOG10(X)	REAL	Log base 10	1 Real, >0
EXP	Y = EXP(X)	REAL	e^x	1 Real
TANH	Y = TANH(X)	REAL	Hyperbolic tangent $(e^x-e^{-x})/(e^x+e^{-x})$	1 Real

[1]In the examples, I, J, and K are INTEGER variables; X and Y are REAL variables.

Formatted Output

Consider the following portion of a FORTRAN program:

```
      INTEGER I,J
      REAL QUOT
          :
          :
      QUOT = REAL(I) / REAL(J)
      PRINT *, I,' divided by ',J,' = ',QUOT
```

Output from this program fragment might look something like this.

```
19 divided by                5 = 0.38000000 E+01
```

How much better it might be to have output more like this!

```
19 divided by   5 = 3.8
```

When we use free format output, the computer chooses the exact form the output will take. It may allow many spaces for the integer numbers, and it may print the real numbers using the scientific E notation.

It is possible, on the other hand, to write the program in such a way that we as programmers control the form of the output. For example, we may replace the print statement in the fragment by the following:

```
      WRITE (*,1000) I,' divided by ',J,' = ',QUOT
 1000 FORMAT(' ',I4,A,I4,A,F5.1)
```

This uses the general form of a WRITE statement which refers to a FORMAT statement. In general, the WRITE statement has the form

```
WRITE(*,format label) list to be written
```

and the FORMAT statement the form

```
label   FORMAT(list of individual format specifications)
```

In our specific example, the label in the WRITE statement and on the associated FORMAT statement was 1000. Within the FORMAT statement, the list of individual format specifications included six things: a *carriage control*, written as `' '`; an I4 format for the variable I; an A format for the message; an I4 format for the variable J; an A format for the message; and an F5.1 format for the variable QUOT. These are explained in more detail below. Between them, they specify the precise form in which the items in the WRITE statement should be printed.

Let us go into more detail on the individual format specifications. Together, these individual formats will determine the layout of the entire line of output.

1. The carriage control. This is designed to control output to a printer. For some terminals it is not needed when doing conversational output. However, other terminals do require it. In this text we will consistently use carriage controls when doing formatted output.

The carriage control character instructs the computer how many lines below the previous line of output to place this line. We will use the following three forms of carriage control:

`'1'` will cause the printer to advance the paper to the top of a new page.

`'0'` will cause the printer to double space, leaving one blank line between the previous line and this line.

`' '` will cause single spacing, with this line immediately below the previous line.

In addition, there is a '+' carriage control which suppresses spacing, staying on the same line.

If the carriage control character is omitted, the printer will take the first character from the line it is to print and use this as its carriage control. Not only can this cause erratic spacing, but it will also cause the first character of the output line to be missing.

2. The X format. The X format element is used to place spaces between the numbers being printed. Its general form is

```
nX
```

where the "n" specifies how many blank spaces are to be placed in the output line.

3. The I format used for printing INTEGER variables. For each INTEGER

variable listed in the WRITE statement, our FORMAT statement will contain an I format element. The general form of the I format is

```
Iw
```

where "w" specifies the number of columns allotted for printing the specific variable. The number itself will be printed right justified within the allotted columns. For example, suppose I has the value 15. The following table shows how I might appear with several different formats (the small b indicates a blank column).

Format	Result
I2	15
I3	b15
I4	bb15
I9	bbbbbbb15

4. The A format used for printing characters. This can be used to print CHARACTER variables or, as in our example, messages (character constants). It has a more flexible form than the I format. We need not specify the number of columns. The number used will exactly match the number of characters to be printed. For example, suppose a CHARACTER*5 variable INIT contains the value 'C. A.' and a CHARACTER*12 variable LAST contains the value 'Dickinson   '. The output from this WRITE and FORMAT

```
      WRITE(*,3000) 'Name:',INIT,LAST
 3000 FORMAT(' ',30X,A,2X,A,A)
```

would be (placed on the right side of the terminal by the 30X format):

```
Name: C. A. Dickinson
```

COMMENT. There are two distinct ways to print messages along with the values being printed. The one we have been using includes the messages in the PRINT or WRITE statement. It is also possible to include the messages in the FORMAT statement. For example, these are equivalent:

```
      WRITE(*,1000) 'Total grade: ',TOTAL
 1000 FORMAT(' ',A,I4)
```

and

```
      WRITE(*,1000) TOTAL
 1000 FORMAT(' ','Total grade: ',I4)
```

The text string in the FORMAT is called a **literal format**.) In this text we generally use the former approach. However, if the messages involved get lengthy, it is sometimes useful to adopt the second method.

5. The F format used for printing REAL variables. This format will print REAL variables much the way we are used to writing them. For example, output using this format might look like any of the following:

```
   7.25
   0.10
   1.52
2147.93
  -3.62
```

In the I and X formats we have to specify how many columns are to be used in printing the number (I format) or how many columns are to be left blank (X format). In printing a REAL number, however, we need to specify both how many columns to use and how many places to have after the decimal point. Thus we will have formats such as

```
F7.2, or F4.2, or F13.5, or F15.6
```

In each of these, the first number represents the number of columns used, and the second tells how many numbers will be placed after the decimal point. For example, suppose X has the value 3.9172. The following table shows how X might appear with several different formats (the small b indicates a blank column).

Format	Result
F8.4	bb3.9172
F7.4	b3.9172
F6.3	b3.917
F5.2	b3.92
F4.1	b3.9
F6.1	bbb3.9

NOTES

1. The number 3.9172 is printed as accurately as possible, within the number of spaces allocated after the decimal point. If two places are allocated, the fractional part is printed as .92. However, the number itself, in the variable, remains unchanged.
2. The first number is the total number of columns, NOT the number of columns preceding the decimal point. The number is printed right justified in the allotted columns.

   In setting aside the number of columns we need, we should observe that the decimal point takes up a column. In addition, the minus sign (if the number is negative) will also take a column. Finally, fractions such as .57 will be printed as 0.57, with a column containing a zero in front of the decimal point. Thus each number will have at least one digit, and possibly a minus sign, in front of the decimal point.

The person planning the layout of a printed line has a great deal of freedom in deciding how many columns to allot for each number. Decisions will be based on some knowledge of how large the numbers will be and on how many columns are available on the particular terminal or printer being used. (Two common widths are 80 and 132 columns.) Once these decisions are made, the proper formats must be determined. In the following examples, we will describe a line layout, then come up with an appropriate WRITE and FORMAT.

Give a WRITE and FORMAT to print the variables BASE, HEIGHT, and AREA in the following form (include declarations):

BASE = xxx.xx   HEIGHT = xxx.xx   AREA = xxxxx.xx

We will assume single spacing is desired. The decimal places in the output tell us that the variables are REAL. One possible solution is

```
      REAL BASE,HEIGHT,AREA
           .
           .
      WRITE(*,4000) 'BASE = ',BASE,'   HEIGHT = ',HEIGHT,'   AREA = ',AREA
 4000 FORMAT(' ',F6.2,F6.2,F8.2)
```

Notice that one way to achieve blanks in the output is to include them with our messages inside the quotes. Of course, we could also use the X format to achieve the same effect.

The following program illustrates the effect of formats and also illustrates again the difference between REAL and INTEGER division.

```
      INTEGER I,J,AVE1
      REAL X,Y,AVE2

C   WRITTEN BY ********, **/**/**
C   THIS  PROGRAM ILLUSTRATES FORMATS AND INTEGER
C AND REAL DIVISION.
C   GIVE I, J, X, AND Y SIMILAR INTEGER AND REAL VALUES.

      I = 2
      J = 7
      X = 2.0
      Y = 7.0
C
C   CALCULATE AVERAGES
C
      AVE1 = (I + J) / 2
      AVE2 = (X + Y) / 2.0
C
C   PRINT RESULTS AND STOP
C
      WRITE(*,1000) I,J,AVE1
      WRITE(*,2000) X,Y,AVE2
      STOP
C
C   FORMATS
C
 1000 FORMAT('1',I4,2X,I4,2X,I4)
 2000 FORMAT(' ',F6.1,F6.1,F6.1)
      END
```

NOTE. The FORMAT statement may be placed anywhere in the program. There are at least three popular schemes for the placement. Some people place each FORMAT immediately after the WRITE (or READ) which uses it. Others place all FORMAT statements together at the beginning of the program, and still others place all FORMAT statements together at the end of the program. We will generally follow this last practice, as in the program above.

The two output lines will be at the top of a page, due to the carriage control '1'. They will look like this.

```
2         7         4
2.0       7.0       4.5
```

CAUTION. One disadvantage that comes with formatted output is that we may underestimate the size of the numbers we are printing. If we do so, the computer will not print the number but rather will fill the allotted space with asterisks. For example, suppose that GRADE is an INTEGER variable with the value 100, and that PCT is a real variable with value 93.27. If we use

```
      WRITE(*,2000) 'Test grade ',GRADE,' - overall % ',PCT
 2000 FORMAT(' ',A,I2,A,F4.2)
```

we will get this output:

```
Test grade ** - overall % ****
```

Formatted Input

It is also possible to use a formatted version of the READ statement. It looks very much like the WRITE statement. It has the following form:

```
READ(*,format label) list of variables
```

The corresponding format statement will use a combination of I, F, A, and X formats describing the layout of the values on the card. THERE IS NO CARRIAGE CONTROL, since no printer must be controlled.

The four types of FORMAT (I, F, A, and X) are used in the following way:

1. Iw is used for reading an INTEGER number which is right justified in w columns.
2. nX is used for skipping n columns on the input line.
3. A is used to read a CHARACTER variable. The number of columns is precisely the size of the variable.
4. Fw.d is used to read a REAL number which is right justified in w columns, with d digits to the right of the decimal point.

For example, an input line has values for the variables A, B, C, and D, in the indicated form. Write declarations and a READ and FORMAT to read the line.

(A and C are REAL, B is INTEGER, and D is CHARACTER*4. The b's represent blank spaces, the x's columns with data.)

xx.xxxbbxxbxxxxx.xbbbxxxx

The solution is similar to those we used in printing variables, but there is no carriage control:

```
      INTEGER B
      REAL A,C
      CHARACTER*4 D
          .
          .
      READ(*,1000) A,B,C,D
 1000 FORMAT (F6.3,2X,I2,1X,F7.1,3X,A)
```

COMMENT. One difficulty with using format for a READ statement is that the input must precisely match the prescribed format. For example, a typical input line matching the layout given would, in general, follow the layout very closely, as shown in this example.

```
xx.xxxbbxxbxxxxx.xbbbxxxx     layout
14.367  14 14732.1    John    sample lines
 3.501   7       1.5    Barb
```

However, with the F format, some latitude is allowed in the placement of the data. If the decimal point is included, the number may be placed anywhere in the field. If no decimal point is typed in, an assumed decimal is taken to be in the space between two digits, as indicated by the format. For example, with an F5.2 format any of these is allowed:

```
xx.xx     layout
 1.50     sample lines—value 1.5
1.5
  150
```

Having to get the input in exactly the right columns can be very clumsy in a conversational program. For the most part, therefore, we will continue to use free format reads. The one exception has to do with character input. Using a formatted read allows the user to enter the character string without the enclosing quotes. We may therefore frequently use combinations such as this:

```
      PRINT *,'Do you want instructions?'
      READ(*,1000) ANSWER
 1000 FORMAT(A)
```

The user could enter the Y or N answer as a single character.

Notice, however, that if we use format for part of a line of input, the entire line must match the format. For example, to read NAME, AGE, and SALARY, we have four options:

1. Have the user place the name in quotes
2. Have the user enter a line with no quotes around the name, but with the age and salary values aligned precisely in the proper columns to match a FORMAT statement
3. Use two separate reads—a formatted read for the name, an unformatted one for the other data
4. Write a sophisticated input subroutine to combine the good features of free format and formatted input—unhappily a task beyond our capabilities at this point.

File Terminology

In Section 1.1 we described two common ways to obtain input for computer programs. One method frequently used for batch operations involves placing the input data on lines which are included with the program. In conversational computing, the program obtains data directly from the user at a computer terminal as the program is running.

Another common way to obtain input, used both in the batch mode and in the conversational mode, is to read the data from a file located on the file system of the computer. This method is especially useful when the data involved is of a permanent nature. For example, such things as name, address, telephone number, educational background, pay rate, and so on, might be maintained on a master employee file. Some of these items might change occasionally, but not on a daily or weekly basis. It would be wasteful to have to retype the data for every program using that particular information on the company's employees.

In addition, many programs write information onto files instead of, or in addition to, printing listings on a printer. In this way the data which is output from one program can easily be used as input for some other program.

Our purpose here is not to cover the use of files for I/O. Your instructor may give you a brief introduction if she wishes to have you run your program using data she has previously placed on a file. All we will do at the present is mention some of the terms associated with files. From time to time we will use these terms in describing examples throughout this text. In Chapter 5 we will discuss file operations in some detail.

A **record** is a collection of information that logically belongs together. For example, an employee master file might have one record for each employee. Each record might have a number of **fields**, such as name, address, social security number, and so on. The information in these fields logically belongs together because it is all information about one particular employee. This is a common situation: we have a file consisting of a large number of records; each record has the information for one person or other entity; and the information on the record is organized into a number of different fields.

This file terminology is frequently used even when the I/O medium being used is not a file. For example, when we are obtaining input from a terminal, we may use the term *record* as a synonym for input line. Likewise, a line of information being sent to a printer is frequently referred to as a record. The individual entries on an input line or a print line are referred to as fields.

In the remainder of this text, we will feel free to use the terminology of files whether we are doing our I/O operations with files or with terminal input or output.

Before we leave the topic of files, we have two comments to make. First, a READ statement which reads from a file is more likely to be a formatted read than is a conversational READ statement. This is especially true when the file was created by some previous program. If the records were placed on the file by a formatted write, they can easily be read by a formatted read.

Second, some programs only really make sense in a batch or file processing environment. For example, consider the following: "Read records containing name, age, sex, and salary, and print the names of all the females earning over $40,000." As a conversational program obtaining the records from the user, this makes no sense at all. As a program which extracts information from a file, it is typical of a large class of programs in common use.

Even though programs such as this do not make sense in the conversational setting, we will nevertheless sometimes write such programs and run them conversationally. There are two reasons for this. First, we do not want to omit an important type of program just because we have not yet learned how to work with files. Second, and perhaps more important, programs such as this might very well be debugged in a conversational mode prior to running them in the file processing mode.

Pitfalls

We have already described most of the commonly encountered pitfalls for this section. For convenience, we will list them here.
For library functions:

1. In a program which uses a function, we cannot also use the function name for a regular variable. Instead of

   ```
   SQRT = SQRT(X)
   PRINT *, SQRT
   ```

   we should use

   ```
   ROOT = SQRT(X)
   PRINT *, ROOT
   ```

   In particular, we use the variable name (not the function name) in the PRINT or WRITE statement.
2. In using the REAL function along with division, we generally want to convert both numerator and denominator to real numbers, in order to achieve real division. For example,

   ```
   REAL(I/10)
   ```

is probably not what we want. To achieve the desired answer, we should write

```
REAL(I)/10.0
```

3. The trigonometric functions require radian measure arguments, not degree measure arguments.

For formatted I/O:

4. A carriage control may be needed in a FORMAT used with a WRITE statement (and should not be used with a READ statement).
5. We must use the proper combination of I, F, and A formats for the particular variables being read or written. Never use an I format with a REAL variable or an F format with an INTEGER variable.
6. We should be sure to use a "large enough" format for the numbers we print. For example, an I5 format cannot be used to print the number 763942. If we attempt to do so, the entire five columns will be filled with asterisks.

   For REAL numbers, the situation is somewhat more complicated. We must allow enough columns before the decimal point to print the whole number portion of the number, including a minus sign if the number is negative. We must also remember that the decimal point occupies a column.

   NOTE. Before the decimal point, we must allow enough columns. However, after the decimal point any number of columns is acceptable. The computer will simply print the fraction rounded to the number of digits to be printed.

7. A literal format, like a carriage control, makes sense only for FORMAT statements used with WRITE statements.

REVIEW

Terms and Concepts

library function
function name
argument, parameter
invoke a function
function returns a value
truncate
carriage control

FORTRAN Syntax

Functions

Form—function name (list of arguments separated by commas)

Examples

SQRT(X) finds the square root of REAL argument X

ABS(X) finds the absolute value of REAL or INTEGER argument X

REAL(I) converts INTEGER argument I to REAL value

MOD(I,J) finds the remainder when INTEGER argument I is divided by INTEGER argument J

INT(X) truncates fractional part of REAL argument X

Notes

Must have one or more arguments.

Must supply proper type of argument (INTEGER, REAL).

Argument can be any expression of the appropriate type.

Function can be used in any expression.

Cannot use function name as regular variable name in same program.

Precedence

functions are evaluated

**, right to left

* and /, left to right

+ and −, left to right

Formatted I/O

Read—READ(*,format #) list of variables separated by commas

Print—WRITE(*,format #) list of values separated by commas

Format—label FORMAT (list of individual formats)

Individual formats:

Iw to read or print an INTEGER variable, w columns wide, right justified

Fw.d to read or print a REAL variable, w columns wide, d columns after the decimal point

nX to skip n columns on input or print line

carriage controls (for WRITE only)

`'1'`—top of page

`'0'`—double

`' '`—single space

Literal format

Form—`'message to be printed verbatim'`

Miscellaneous Notes

MOD(I,J) is zero precisely when J divides evenly into I.

INT(X+.5) rounds X to the nearest integer.

Pitfalls

1. Cannot also use function name as a regular variable name.
2. Convert both numerator and denominator to REAL to avoid INTEGER division.

3. SIN and COS require radians, not degrees, for the arguments.
4. May need carriage control for printing.
5. Use I format for INTEGER variables, F for REAL, A for CHARACTER.
6. Allow enough columns to print the number being printed. For REAL numbers, allow for a possible minus sign, the decimal point, and at least one digit before the decimal.
7. Literal formats only with WRITE statements.

EXERCISES

1. Give FORTRAN expressions corresponding to the following algebraic expressions. Assume that all variables are REAL.

(a) $1 + \sqrt{x}$
(b) $\sqrt{1 + x}$
(c) $|x - y|$
(d) $|3 - 2x| + y$
(e) x^{3+5y}
(f) $|x^3| - 16$
(g) $\sqrt{b^2 - 4ac}$
(h) $\dfrac{\sqrt{r + s} - 5}{5 - y}$

2. Give FORTRAN expressions for the following. Assume that variables beginning with the letters I–N are INTEGER, all others are REAL. State what the proper declarations would be for each problem.

(a) x^n
(b) $|3k| - 5$
(c) $|3x - 5|$
(d) $\dfrac{i + j}{k}$
(e) $\sqrt{j}$
(f) $\sqrt{\dfrac{x - y + |z|}{2k - m}}$

3. A variable X contains a real number which is supposed to represent a money figure. Find a formula to round the value in X to the nearest cent. (For example, X could be the balance in an account after calculating interest. The figure could be something like 100.557; this should be rounded to 100.56.)

4. Give the value of the following expressions.

(a) `MOD(5,2)`
(b) `MOD(2,5)`
(c) `MOD(53,4)`
(d) `MOD(180,10)`
(e) `ABS(16-11)`
(f) `SQRT(3.0*(4.0+8.0))`
(g) `ABS(3.4-6.2/2.0)`
(h) `ABS((3.4-6.2)/2.0)`

5. Give smooth algorithms for the following:

(a) Read a number of integers, one per data line. Print a message for each number, telling whether or not the number is evenly divisible by 10.
(b) Each record has two integers on it. For each record, tell whether or not the first number divides evenly into the second.
(c) Each record has an integer and a real number. Print a message telling whether or not the real number is less than the square root of the integer number.

6. Give FORTRAN code for the decision structures in Exercise 5.

7. Write a segment of FORTRAN for the following situations:

(a) If K divides evenly into L, then let M be 1, otherwise let M be the remainder when K is divided into L.

(b) If the absolute value of X is greater than 5, print a message saying J is being incremented by 1, and add 1 to J.

(c) If XOLD is within .001 of XNEW, then subtract 3 from T. (*Hint*: Use absolute value.)

8. Give appropriate declarations and a READ and FORMAT for reading each of the following records. (bb ·· represents blank columns).

(a) xxbbxxxxxxxxbbxxxxxxxxxxxxxxx

state # population capital

(b) xxxxxxxbbxxbxxbbbxxxx.xxbbxxxx.xxbbxxxx.xx

account # # deposits total of checks

checks beginning balance total of deposits

(c) xxxxxxxbxxxxxbxxxxxx

sample size # mutation B

mutation A

(d) xxxxxxxxxxxxxxbbxxxbxx

student name # hours taken this semester

previous credit hours

(e) xxxxxxbbxxbbbxxxbxxbxxxx.xxbxxx

i.d. # age weight height(″) monthly salary dept. abbreviation

9. Give appropriate WRITE and FORMAT statements to print out the variables read in Exercise 8.

10. For each of the following, make up reasonable variable names, give declarations, and give appropriate WRITE and FORMAT statements to print the indicated line or lines of output.

(a) The area of the triangle is xxxxxx.xx

(b) xxxx is not an even number

(c) Error made in data card—retype

(d) The side of the square is xxx the area is xxxxxx

(e) Employee #xxxx earned a total of $xxxx.xx for xx.xx hours worked

(f) Out of a total population of xxxxxxxx, xx.xx percent were faulty. This represents xxxxxxxx faulty items.

11. Repeat exercise 10, but include the message in the FORMAT rather than in the WRITE.

2.5 MORE DECISION STRUCTURES

In this section we will explore decisions in more depth. For one thing, we will learn how to write more complicated conditions involving more than one comparison. We will also learn the techniques for implementing decisions involving more than two branches. Finally, we will look at decisions within decisions **(nested decisions)**.

Logical Expressions

Up to this point the only conditions used in our IF statements have been simple ones which compared two arithmetic expressions. We would like to be able to write programs involving more complicated conditions.

For example, suppose we write a program which reads records containing name, age, and sex. We want to print the name of each female over age 21. Here is the relevant decision structure.

```
if female over 21 then
   print NAME,AGE
endif
```

If we can figure out how to code the condition in the **if** statement in FORTRAN, we should be able to complete the program.

How can we determine if a person is in the category we are interested in? Since we want people who are female over age 21, we want to combine two conditions: SEX = 'F' and AGE > 21.

So far all our IF statements have been of this form:

```
IF(expression relation expression) THEN
```

where "relation" is either .EQ., .NE., .LE., .LT., .GE., or .GT.. We have used the condition inside the parentheses to compare two expressions (either two INTEGER quantities, two REAL quantities, or two CHARACTER quantities).

More generally,we are allowed to place within the parentheses any **logical expression**. There are a number of ways to create logical expressions. The simplest, perhaps, is the form we have just described. Each of the following is a simple logical expression of this type:

```
X.GE.5.0
T.NE. (A+B)
MOD(I,J).EQ.0
```

The second method of building logical expressions is by combining simple expressions of the type above. To combine them we generally use the **logical operators** .AND.,.OR., and .NOT.. In the simplest cases we will have one of these two forms:

1. Two or more simple logical expressions, joined by the use of one or more .AND. operators. In this case the resulting condition is true when ALL the individual conditions are true. For example, "X.GT.4.9 .AND. Y.LE.7.2 .AND.Z. NE.5.0" is true if all three of the conditions are separately true.
2. Two or more simple logical expressions, joined by the use of one or more .OR. operators. In this case the combined condition is true if any one (or more) of the individual conditions are true. For example, "Y.NE.17.0 .OR. AGE.EQ.45" can be true if either $Y \neq 17$, or AGE = 45, or both.

For example, we can now see that the solution to our original problem is relatively simple. The condition "female over age 21" is the same as saying that sex is 'F' AND age is greater than 21; in FORTRAN we write the condition as

```
SEX.EQ. 'F' .AND. AGE.GT.21
```

> **NOTE.** The periods in the .AND., .OR., and .NOT. are necessary parts of the operator. This is similar to the periods in the comparison operators such as .GT..

As further examples, let us give FORTRAN logical expressions for each of the following conditions.

single male

X is between 15 and 17

either widowed or divorced

either earning less than $5000, or more than $25000, or in one of the departments WHSE or SALE

We will assume that X and INCOME are REAL variables, and all others are CHARACTER variables of the appropriate length. The solutions are:

```
STATUS.EQ. 'S' .AND. SEX.EQ. 'M'
X.GT.15.0 .AND. X.LT.17.0
STATUS.EQ.'W' .OR. STATUS.EQ. 'D'
INCOME.LT.5000.0 .OR. INCOME.GT.25000.0 .OR. DEPT.EQ.'WHSE'
     .OR. DEPT.EQ.'SALE'
```

This last condition raises a problem, since if we were to use it in an IF statement, the statement would extend past column 72. We will need to use continuation cards. Here is one possible way to space the cards for readability:

```
  IF(INCOME.LT.5000.0
$    .OR. INCOME.GT.25000.0
$    .OR. DEPT.EQ. 'WHSE'
$    .OR. DEPT.EQ. 'SALE') THEN
```

We now consider some more complex combinations of conditions. In order to write these correctly, we must realize that the operators have a precedence similar to that for the arithmetic operators. The order of operations is:

```
.NOT.     first
.AND.     second
.OR.      last
```

Within each level, the operation is from left to right.

When we write complex conditions we may, if necessary, use parentheses to group the conditions. This is similar to our use of parentheses with arithmetic expressions. To illustrate these ideas, we will write FORTRAN logical expressions for a number of conditions expressed in English.

1. not a female over age 21—This is an example of the concept of **negation**. To negate a logical expression is to form a new logical expression which represents the opposite condition. One common way we negate conditions in everyday speech is by using the word "not."

   In this example, the condition to be negated is

   ```
   SEX.EQ.'F' .AND. AGE.GT.21
   ```

   One way to accomplish this is to place the .NOT. operator in front of the condition:

   ```
   NOT. (SEX.EQ.'F' .AND. AGE.GT.21)
   ```

   The parentheses are necessary; without them only the SEX.EQ.'F' would be negated.

   There is another way to form the negation of a condition which contains either one or more .AND. operators or one or more .OR. operators. To see how this works, we reason as follows: There are two ways a person could fail to be in the category "female over age 21." The person could either not be a female or be age 21 or less (or both). Therefore the condition can be rephrased as

   ```
   (not female) or (age 21 or less)
   ```

   This is easily translated to the FORTRAN condition

   ```
   SEX.NE.'F' .OR. AGE.LE.21
   ```

2. I is either between 15 and 20 or over 50—In this example we combine two conditions with an "or": "between 15 and 20," "over 50." The "between 15 and 20" condition is similar to one we did earlier, and can be expressed as I.GT.15 .AND. I.LT.20. The entire condition, then, is

   ```
   (I.GT.15 .AND. I.LT.20) .OR. I.GT.50
   ```

   In this case we have included parentheses for clarity. Because .AND. has higher precedence than .OR., the parentheses are optional.

3. neither widowed nor divorced—One way to look at this is as the opposite (negation) of the example we did earlier: either widowed or divorced. We could therefore write:

   ```
   .NOT. (STATUS.EQ.'W' .OR. STATUS.EQ.'D')
   ```

   Another possible way to approach this "neither/nor" type of situation is to reason about what exactly the neither/nor means. When we say a person is "neither this nor that," we mean that they are not "this" and that they are furthermore not "that" either. In our present situation, we are saying "not widowed" and also "not divorced." We may write

   ```
   STATUS.NE.'W' .AND. STATUS.NE.'D'
   ```

   The two solutions are equivalent.

4. "good" data, defined as "CODE is 'I' and VAL is either below 0 or greater than 500"—This example combines both .AND. and .OR. as shown below:

```
CODE.EQ.'I' .AND. (VAL.LT.0 .OR. VAL.GT.500)
```

   In this case the parentheses are needed; otherwise the .AND. would be performed first, distorting the intended meaning.

5. "bad" data (see #4)—Since "bad" is the negation of "good," the easiest way to handle this is to place a .NOT. before the entire condition, with the condition in parentheses:

```
.NOT. (CODE.EQ.'I' .AND. (VAL.LT.0 .OR. VAL.GT.500))
```

NOTES

1. Although it is possible to negate conditions involving both .AND. and .OR. in other ways, the recommended approach is to simply use .NOT. as in the last example.
2. When we place the conditions in an IF statement, there will be an extra set of parentheses which are part of the IF. For example, the final condition might appear as follows:

```
IF (.NOT. (CODE.EQ.'I' .AND. (VAL.LT.0 .OR. VAL.GT.500))) THEN
```

Three Way Branches

Frequently, programming problems arise in which it is either obvious that there are several possible cases, or a little thought reveals that this is true. In our earlier discussion of decisions, all our examples dealt with situations where there were exactly two cases. (In some of the examples, only one case had steps to be performed.) Some of the same ideas we used in those sections can be applied to the more complex problems involving three or more cases. We will begin with an example with three cases. As you will see, once you know how to write FORTRAN programs with three cases, it will be relatively easy to work with problems involving four or more cases as well.

The following is a simplified form of tax table. It is similar to that used by the federal government.

If taxable income is	Tax is
not over 3200	0
over 3200 but not over 5600	15% of amount over 3200
over 5600	360.00 plus 25% of amount over 5600

Write a program segment which, given taxable income, calculates federal income tax.

Although the problem is not specifically stated in terms of the word "case," it is reasonably clear that there are 3 possible cases:

1. not over 3200
2. over 3200 but not over 5600
3. over 5600

This type of situation arises so frequently that we use a special form of pseudocode to describe it. We refer to the structure obtained as the **case** structure, emphasizing the fact that it should be used when any one of a number of possible cases can arise. For the particular instance with three possible cases, the **case** structure will have this form:

```
case
   1 (condition for case 1)
      code for case 1
   2 (condition for case 2)
      code for case 2
   3 (condition for case 3)
      code for case 3
endcase
```

We can describe the meaning of this **case** structure as follows: the computer will go down through the conditions describing the three cases, in order from top to bottom, until it finds a condition that is true. At that time it will perform the steps for that particular case, and then proceed *directly* to the step following the **endcase** step. It will not check any further conditions after that point. If none of the conditions are true, it will proceed to the step after the **endcase**. Step by step, then, here is the logic:

1. If the condition for case 1 is true, the computer will perform the steps listed for case 1 and proceed to the step after the **endcase**.
2. If the condition is not true for case 1, the computer will move on to the condition for case 2. If that condition is true, the steps listed for case 2 will be performed, followed by the step after the **endcase**.
3. If the condition for case 2 is false, the condition for case 3 will be examined. If true, the steps for case 3 will be performed, then on to the step following the **endcase**. If this last condition is also false, then the computer proceeds directly to the step after the **endcase**.

For obvious reasons, a structure such as this is sometimes referred to as a **three way branch**.

The algorithm segment for our particular problem would follow the general form given above:

```
case
   1 (INCOME < 3200) TAX ← 0
   2 (3200 < INCOME ≤ 5600) TAX ← .15*(INCOME–3200)
   3 (INCOME > 5600) TAX ← 360.00 + .25*(INCOME–5600)
endcase
```

In this example the three cases are **exhaustive**. By this we mean that every INCOME figure is certain to satisfy one of the three conditions. We could replace the third condition by a phrase such as "any other."

Coding the **case** structure with three cases, where the final case consists of "all others," is fairly straightforward. We will use these four statement types:

```
IF(condition) THEN
ELSE IF  (condition) THEN
ELSE
ENDIF
```

You will recognize that the only new statement is the "ELSE IF(condition) THEN" statement.

The IF/THEN statement will be used to describe the first case. In the two-way branch the second case was the only one remaining, and we were able to use the statement ELSE to describe the second case. However, in the three-way branch, we have two remaining cases to consider. We still need the word ELSE (meaning "if case 1 is not true"), but in addition we will need the word IF to further distinguish between case 2 and case 3. The ELSE IF/THEN is precisely what we need to describe case 2. When we get to case 3 (*provided* the cases are exhaustive), we may use the ELSE to mean "if cases 1 and 2 do not hold." Thus the FORTRAN implementation will be

```
IF(condition for case 1) THEN
   code for case 1
ELSE IF(condition for case 2) THEN
   code for case 2
ELSE
   code for case 3
ENDIF
```

Using the REAL variables INCOME and TAX, the only obstacle to writing a program segment implementing the **case** algorithm for our example is knowing how to describe the conditions in FORTRAN. The first condition "not over 3200" is easily written as

```
IF (INCOME.LE.3200.0) THEN
```

The second condition, "over 3200 but not over 5600," requires more thought. We could combine two conditions in one IF statement; however, since this will appear in an "ELSE IF(condition) THEN" we may simplify the condition somewhat.

The ELSE in the "ELSE IF" will ensure that, if case 1 was true, nothing from here on will be executed. People falling into the first category have been completely taken care of. If we get to the point of testing our condition for the second case, we already know we are dealing with a person whose INCOME is over $3200.00; those whose incomes are not over $3200.00 have been handled in the code for case 1. Thus, we already know that half our condition ("over 3200") is true. To see if the whole condition is true, we only need to examine the second part, "not over 5600." We may write

```
ELSE IF(INCOME.LE.5600.0) THEN
```

The entire **case** structure can be written as shown below, with declarations included for the variables.

```
REAL INCOME TAX
      .
      .

IF(INCOME.LE.3200.0) THEN
   TAX = 0.0
ELSE IF(INCOME.LE.5600.0) THEN
   TAX = .15*(INCOME-3200.0)
ELSE
   TAX = 360.0 + .25*(INCOME-5600.0)
ENDIF
```

Notice that this is only a program segment. A complete program would contain appropriate I/O and perhaps other steps as well.

The General Case Structure

We next consider the more general **case** structure. That for four or more cases looks the same as that for three cases. The logic implied is also the same: We want the computer to evaluate the conditions one at a time until it locates a condition which is true. It should then perform the step or steps listed for that condition, and proceed directly to the step following the **endcase**. Here is the general form:

```
case
   1(condition #1) code for case 1
   2(condition #2) code for case 2
                   .
                   .
                   .

   n(last condition) code for last case
endcase
```

We hope that it is reasonably clear how to write this general **case** structure in FORTRAN, assuming that the list of conditions is exhaustive. We use the same general pattern as before.

```
IF(case 1 condition) THEN
   case 1 code
ELSE IF(Case 2 condition) THEN
   case 2 code
                .
                .
                .

ELSE IF(next-to-last-case condition) THEN
   next-to-last-case code
ELSE
   last case code
ENDIF
```

To illustrate, we write a segment of code to determine the corresponding letter grade for a given numerical test grade. Letter grades are determined as follows: 90–100 A, 80–89 B, 70–79 C, 0–69 F.

Notice that this is a multiple (four-way) branch. The algorithm follows:

```
case
   1(GRADE ≥ 90) LETTER ← 'A'
   2(GRADE ≥ 80) LETTER ← 'B'
   3(GRADE ≥ 70) LETTER ← 'C'
   4(all others) LETTER ← 'F'
endcase
```

Following the pattern described above, we generate this segment of FORTRAN. (Once again, a complete program would also contain I/O and perhaps other steps.)

```
INTEGER GRADE
CHARACTER*1 LETTER
IF(GRADE.GE.90) THEN
   LETTER = 'A'
ELSE IF (GRADE.GE.80) THEN
   LETTER = 'B'
ELSE IF (GRADE.GE.70) THEN
   LETTER = 'C'
ELSE
   LETTER = 'F'
ENDIF
```

Notice that we are tacitly assuming that the grade on the line lies in the range 0–100. This allows us to write the question "Is this grade in the 90–100 range?" as IF(GRADE.GE.90).

Once again, if we get to the second IF statement, we know GRADE is not 90 or above. Hence, to ask "Is it 80–89?" we need only ask "Is it 80 or above?" or, in FORTRAN, IF(GRADE.GE.80).

In some situations, the conditions listed in a **case** structure are not exhaustive. In a way, this is similar to the **if-then** construction. In the **if-then**, there was an implicit second condition for which we wanted to do nothing. As a simple example, suppose that the input for a program includes, among other things, a code for the department an employee works in. A portion of the program is to add a bonus if the person works in either department 'TRA' ($100 bonus) or department 'SHP' ($500 bonus). An appropriate pseudocode segment might be

```
case
   1(DEPT = 'TRA') PAY ← PAY + 100
   2(DEPT = 'SHP') PAY ← PAY + 500
endcase
```

We cannot replace the final condition by the phrase "any other." Notice that, although we have only two cases listed, this is not an **if-then-else** situation. There is an implicit third case

```
3(any other) do nothing
```

which we may or may not explicitly include in the written algorithm.

Coding this type of algorithm is easy if we keep in mind that there is actually an "any other" case for which we do nothing. We write

```
CHARACTER*3 DEPT
REAL PAY
      .
      .
IF(DEPT .EQ. 'TRA') THEN
   PAY = PAY + 100.0
ELSE IF (DEPT .EQ. 'SHP') THEN
   PAY = PAY + 500.0
ENDIF
```

We merely omit the final ELSE for the implicitly present third case, since for this "any other" case there is nothing to be done. This is entirely analogous to leaving off the **else** in the **if-then** construction. In general, a **case** statement with nonexhaustive cases uses only the IF(condition) THEN, the ELSE IF(condition) THEN, and the ENDIF statements—never the ELSE statement.

Nested Decisions

Sometimes the steps to be performed in one or more of the branches of a decision structure involve other decisions. In such a problem we have what we might consider as subcases of one or more of the cases. These situations generally arise quite naturally, and our coding will merely combine the techniques used for the simpler problems.

For example, let us write a segment of code which, given a checking account balance and the type and amount of a transaction for that account, will process the transaction. A transaction can be either a check or a deposit. Moreover, a check may either be good or bounce, and we would like to print a message for those that bounce.

We may view our situation in this form:

Case 1: deposit   Case 2: check
                              Subcase 2a: good
                              Subcase 2b: bad

COMMENT. Since the decision concerning whether or not a check bounces is "nested" within Case 2 of the outer decision, we refer to this as a **nested decision** structure.

The rough algorithm follows this "subcase" structure. We assume that BALANC (previous balance), TYPE (either "C"—check or "D"—deposit), and AMOUNT (amount of the transaction) have been obtained previously, perhaps by means of a

READ statement. We calculate the new value of BALANC, and print an "overdraft" message if necessary.

```
case
   1(TYPE = 'D') code for deposit
   2(any other)
      case
         1(BALANC ≥ AMOUNT) code for good check
         2(any other) code for bad check
      endcase
endcase
```

Since each of these case structures has exactly two cases, we could write the algorithm using **if-then-else** constructions. However, we feel that the case structure is clearer when we have subcases for one or more of the original cases.

In this algorithm, we have a **case** structure, and within the second case we have another **case** structure. We code the first one as follows:

```
IF(TYPE.EQ.'D') THEN
   code for deposit
ELSE
   code for check
ENDIF
```

Now "code for deposit" is easy, but the code for a check is itself the following two-way branch:

```
IF(BALANC.GE.AMOUNT) THEN
   code for good check
ELSE
   code for bad check
ENDIF
```

Putting this in place of "code for check," the step it refines, we obtain the following program segment.

```
      CHARACTER*1 TYPE
      REAL AMOUNT,BALANC
         .
         .
      IF(TYPE.EQ. 'D') THEN
         BALANC = BALANC + AMOUNT
      ELSE
         IF(BALANC.GE.AMOUNT) THEN
            BALANC = BALANC - AMOUNT
         ELSE
            WRITE(*,2000) 'BAD CHECK ',AMOUNT,' - BALANCE IS ',BALANC
         ENDIF
      ENDIF
         .
         .
 2000 FORMAT ('0',A,F8.2,A,F8.2)
```

We have a two-way branch, and "nested" within the second branch of the structure another two-way branch.

> **COMMENT.** We could think of this as a three-way branch: good check, bad check, deposit. If we did, our code might be somewhat different from that given above. However, as presented, the problem seemed to fit naturally into the nested decision structure, and the coding of such a structure is relatively easy if viewed as a combination of simpler decision structures.
>
> Frequently different ways of viewing a problem lead to different solution structures.

Let us consider another example. Every salesman at XYZ Company is given a Christmas bonus. The bonus for people with ten years or more at the company is calculated based on the number of sales for the year: less than 500 earns a bonus of \$100; 500–1000 earns \$150; and over 1000 earns \$250. For those with less than ten years, the rules are as follows: 0–4 years, \$20; 5–7 years, \$50; 8–9 years, \$70 plus \$1 for each unit sold in excess of 1000, if any. Write an algorithm which, given YEARS and NUMSAL (number of years and sales, respectively), calculates BONUS.

This is a fairly complex problem, made more so by the fact that the information has been presented in a somewhat disorganized fashion. Our first task is to organize the rules given above.

First, notice that the rules are based on the number of years with the company. Thus, our outer decision structure will be a **case**, based on the variable YEARS (which we assume is an INTEGER):

```
case
   1(YEARS ≤ 4) ...
   2(4<YEARS ≤ 7) ...
   3(7<YEARS ≤ 9) ...
   4(YEARS ≥ 10) ...
endcase
```

Now for each of the four basic cases we will fill in the desired calculations. Cases 1 and 2 are very simple. Case 3 (8–9 years) is somewhat more difficult. We may set BONUS to \$70, then modify it if necessary.

```
BONUS ← 70.0
if NUMSAL > 1000 then
   BONUS ← BONUS + (NUMSAL−1000)
endif
```

Finally, for Case 4 (ten years or more), we have a full subcase structure, based on NUMSAL.

```
case
   1(NUMSAL<500) BONUS ← 100.0
   2(500≤NUMSAL≤1000) BONUS ← 150.0
   3(any other) BONUS ← 250.0
endcase
```

The complete algorithm is given below. The FORTRAN segment is left as an exercise.

```
case
   1(YEARS≤4)
      BONUS ← 20.0
   2(4<YEARS≤7)
      BONUS ← 50.0
   3(7<YEARS≤9)
      BONUS ← 70.0
      if NUMSAL > 1000 then
         BONUS ← BONUS + (NUMSAL-1000)
      endif
   4(YEARS≥10)
      case
         1(NUMSAL<500) BONUS ← 100.0
         2(500≤NUMSAL≤1000) BONUS ← 150.0
         3(any other) BONUS ← 250.0
      endcase
endcase
```

Case Study #2

In this case study we take a look at some error-handling concepts. In the process, we introduce the pseudocode statement **next iteration**.

1. *Statement of problem.* We need a program which inputs two one- to five-digit positive integer numbers and an operation code. The operation code is either a plus sign or a minus sign. The program should print output similar to the samples given below:

```
11111 + 20004 =  31115
12345 - 54321 = -41976
```

2. *Preliminary analysis.* The output form is specified; we need to determine an appropriate input form. There are several possibilities. We choose to use a free format read, with input lines of the form

```
11111,'+',20004
```

We will use a dummy entry consisting of both numbers being 0 to terminate the process.

3. *Algorithm and variable list.* Based on the problem description, we come up with the following variable list.

Name		Type	Use	Comment
Input:	NO1, NO2	INTEGER	The two numbers	Also printed
	OP	CHARACTER*1	Operation	Also printed
Output:	ANSWER	INTEGER	Sum or difference	

Our algorithm will involve a similar structure to those used in previous examples. We will use a loop terminated by dummy entry, and we will invoke a subroutine called INSTR to handle the details of printing instructions for the program. This INSTR subroutine is left as an exercise.

At first glance this looks like a problem from an earlier section. There appear to be only two cases. However, these two cases are not exhaustive. Between them they do not exhaust all the possibilities, unless we assume that the input will always be correct—a potentially dangerous assumption. In the input for the operation we could have a plus sign, or we could have a minus sign, or we could have something else. As an illustration of what we might do with faulty data, we will print an error message for an invalid operation. It might be helpful to list these cases in a table.

Operator	Action
+	Calculate answer as sum
−	Calculate answer as difference
Any other	Error message

It is fairly easy to write an algorithm and variable list for this example. However, as we will discuss below, our first attempt at an algorithm has a minor flaw.

```
call INSTR
loop
   issue prompt
   read NO1, OP, NO2
   if both NO1 and NO2 are 0 then exit endif
   case
      1(OP = '+') ANSWER ← NO1 + NO2
      2(OP = '-') ANSWER ← NO1 - NO2
      3(all other) print error message
   endcase
   print NO1, OP, NO2, ANSWER
endloop
stop
```

The problem with the algorithm given is that for faulty input the printing of the error message is followed by the step after the endcase. Thus we will print an error message followed by a line of output claiming to print an answer. There are several possible approaches to this problem:

1. We could ignore it, on the principle that the person reading the output has been warned by the error message something strange is happening.
2. We could, as part of the case 3 code, set ANSWER to 0. The 0 answer would then reinforce the error message.
3. We could move the print step up into cases 1 and 2:

```
call instr
loop
    .
    .
    case
       1(OP = '+') ANSWER ← NO1 + NO2
                   print NO1,OP,NO2,ANSWER
       2(OP = '-') ANSWER ← NO1 - NO2
                   print NO1,OP,NO2,ANSWER
       3(all other)print error message
    endcase
endloop
```

   This is a relatively easy solution for this problem, but becomes unwieldy when we have more than one step following the **endcase**.
4. We could recognize the need for a special facility in our pseudocode to handle this type of problem.

We will take the last approach. There are many instances when, after discovering that we have faulty input, we want to bypass all further processing for that card. We will express this in our pseudocode algorithm by the expression **next iteration**. This means "bypass the remainder of the loop body, proceeding directly to the next iteration of the loop."

When we include this step, we obtain the following revised algorithm:

```
call instr
loop
   issue prompt
   read NO1, OP, NO2
   if both NO1 and NO2 are 0 then exit endif
   case
      1(OP = '+') ANSWER ← NO1 + NO2
      2(OP = '-') ANSWER ← NO1 - NO2
      3(all other) print error message
                   next iteration
   endcase
   print NO1, OP, NO2, ANSWER
endloop
stop
```

4. *Test plan.* The test plan is fairly simple. We want to exercise all possible paths for the decision structure, especially including the possibility of a faulty operation code. In fact, we might include several different faulty codes.

If we reread the statement of the problem, we see that the input is to consist of one- to five-digit integers. This implies a range of 1 to 99999. We will want to include test data which exercises both boundaries (1,99999) for each number. In addition, we should include some numbers in between.

These considerations raise an important question. What happens if the numbers are not in the correct range? Ideally, the program should perform error checking here; this is the subject of one of the exercises. As the program stands, there are several possibilities:

1. We could get strange looking but correct output such as

```
-5 + -4000 = -4005
```

2. The numbers or the answer could be too large for the planned FORMAT, resulting in output similar to

```
***** - ***** =  50000
***** +    35 = ******
```

3. The numbers could be so large that the answer is too large for the computer to handle, resulting in a run-time error message.

In our test plan, we might include some input in the first two categories. However, the test plan does point out the need for further work on the algorithm, as indicated in the exercises.

One final test might involve entering a zero for exactly one of the two numbers. The looping process should not terminate unless *both* are zero.

5. *Write program.* We now write the program. Our output FORMAT will use an X format to place the answers on the right side of the terminal, separated from the input.

The **next iteration** is written in FORTRAN as a GO TO which skips over the remainder of the loop body.

You should try to write this program yourself before looking at Figure 2.6.

NOTE. It may strike you as strange that we have written a GO TO 200 which branches to a step GO TO 10. As a matter of fact, the **next iteration** may be coded as a direct branch back to the top of the loop in this type of problem. However, for some loops (DO loops—Chapter 3) it is important to code the **next iteration** as a branch to the bottom of the loop.

```
      INTEGER NO1,NO2,ANSWER
      CHARACTER*1 OP

C   WRITTEN BY ******, **/**/**

C   THIS PROGRAM ADDS OR SUBTRACTS TWO NUMBERS
C DEPENDING ON THE OPERATOR PRESENT ON THE INPUT

C   IT CALLS AN INSTR SUBROUTINE TO PRINT INSTRUCTIONS

C   PRINT INSTRUCTIONS BEFORE LOOP

      CALL INSTR

C   IN LOOP, READ DATA AND CALCULATE ANSWER; FOR A
C FAULTY OPERATOR, PRINT A MESSAGE

   10 CONTINUE
         PRINT *,'Enter number,operation,number'
         READ *,NO1,OP,NO2
         IF(NO1.EQ.0 .AND. NO2.EQ.0)THEN
            GO TO 500
         ENDIF
         IF(OP.EQ. '+') THEN
            ANSWER = NO1 + NO2
         ELSE IF(OP.EQ. '-') THEN
            ANSWER = NO1 - NO2
         ELSE
            PRINT*,'BAD CODE:',OP
            GO TO 200
         ENDIF
         WRITE (*,1000) NO1,OP,NO2, ' = ', ANSWER
  200    GO TO 10

C  AFTER LOOP,STOP

  500 CONTINUE
      STOP

C  FORMATS

1000  FORMAT(' ',40X,I5,1X,A1,1X,I5,A,I6)
      END
```

Figure 2.6

6. *An alternate solution.* As frequently happens, there is another approach to this problem. We present the algorithm below.

```
call INSTR
loop
   issue prompt
   read NO1, OP, NO2
   if NO1 and NO2 are both 0 then exit endif
   if OP is bad then
      print error message
      next iteration
   endif
   case
      1(OP = '+') ANSWER ← NO1 + NO2
      2(OP = '-') ANSWER ← NO1 - NO2
   endcase
   print NO1, OP, NO2, ANSWER
endloop
stop
```

The differences are in the placement of the steps which detect an erroneous operation code. As soon as the code is entered it is checked. In some programs, this placement is preferable. It can avoid additional input or processing prior to discovering that the original input was faulty after all. However, in some programs it is difficult or impossible to detect input errors until some further processing has been performed. It is useful to have several alternate ways to handle errors. (In fact, we will examine other alternatives from time to time in the remainder of the text.)

Testing

The test plan for the case study illustrates three testing concepts. The first two are expansions of concepts we have considered before.

1. Test all branches, both near the borders and away from the borders. If a five-way branch is involved, for example, then test all five branches.

2. Test bad input. Examine the statement of the problem for limitations on the input. Include data which violates those limitations (including borderlines if appropriate). Notice that this part of the test planning may suggest enhancements to the algorithm.

3. Test parts of combinations. When a decision is based on a combination of comparisons, it is a good idea to include some test data which satisfies some of the parts, some which satisfies all of the parts, and some which satisfies none of the parts. For example, if a decision in the program relates to the concept "single female," we might include these tests:

single female
single, but not female

female, but not single
not female or single (married, male)

Pitfalls

You have already been cautioned concerning many of the potential pitfalls. However, for easy reference we list them here.

1. Some care must be exercised in writing complex conditions. This is especially true if both .AND. and .OR. are involved. In addition, we must be careful in coding a neither/nor condition.

   It is a good idea, when working with complex conditions, to "hand trace" the conditions, by taking a number of sample values for the variables involved and seeing if the conditions are true or false.

   For example, suppose we have

   ```
   CODE.NE.'M' .OR. CODE.NE.'S'
   ```

   If we try code M, we see that the condition is true, since the second half is true. If we try code S, the first half is true, so the condition is true. For any other code (W,D,A,X, etc.), both halves are true so the condition is true. The condition is always true! Surely this is not what we meant to write.

   A little time spent hand tracing these complex conditions to see if they do what we meant can save countless hours of debugging time.
2. We must be sure to use parentheses when using .NOT. to negate complex expressions. In a condition involving both .AND. and .OR., parentheses may be required to obtain the desired meaning.
3. The proper form for a branch includes one IF-THEN at the beginning and one ENDIF at the end. In between we may have one or more ELSE-IF-THEN statements for the cases other than the first. If the conditions are exhaustive, we may have one ELSE for the final condition.

   We must not use the IF-THEN for the second or subsequent cases; the ELSE-IF-THEN is required. An IF-THEN where an ELSE-IF-THEN is needed will cause the compiler to view the structure as nested IF's, with the second ENDIF missing.

   Notice that the ELSE-IF-THEN statements do not have matching ENDIF statements. They are considered a continuation of the beginning IF THEN. The whole structure is ended using one ENDIF.

REVIEW

Terms

logical expression
logical operator
negation
exhaustive vs. nonexhaustive conditions

FORTRAN Syntax

Logical operators

```
.AND.
.OR.
```

Use—to combine two or more simple logical expressions (as condition in IF or ELSE IF)

Precedence:

```
.NOT.
.AND.
.OR.
```

may use parentheses to group

The ELSE-IF statement

Form—ELSE IF(condition) THEN

Use—in implementing multiple way branches **(case)**

Pseudocode and its implementation

case

```
   1(condition #1) code for case 1
   2(condition #2) code for case 2
         .
         .

   n(last condition) code for last case
```

endcase

```
IF(case 1 condition) THEN
   case 1 code
ELSE IF (case 2 condition) THEN
   case 2 code
      .
      .
      .
ELSE IF(next-to-last-case condition) THEN
   next-to-last-case code
ELSE                       ** may be omitted if cases **
   last case code          **   are not exhaustive    **
ENDIF
```

Nested decisions

Arise naturally in problems having "subcases"

Coded by nesting the FORTRAN implementation of the decision structures

```
IF(TYPE.EQ. 'D') THEN
   BALANC = BALANC + AMOUNT
ELSE
   IF (BALANCE.GE.AMOUNT) THEN
      BALANC = BALANC - AMOUNT
   ELSE
      WRITE(*,2000) 'BAD CHECK', AMOUNT,' - BALANCE IS ', BALANC
   ENDIF
ENDIF
```

EXERCISES

1. For each of the following, give appropriate variable declarations and write FORTRAN logical expressions for the given conditions. (Where variable names are explicitly given in the conditions, assume that variables beginning with the letters I–N are INTEGER variables and all others are REAL.)

(a) single female
(b) not a single female
(c) neither single nor female
(d) either a freshman ('FR') or a sophomore ('SO')
(e) neither a freshman nor a sophomore
(f) either a freshman with a QPA of 4.0, a sophomore with QPA of 3.7 or higher, or a junior or senior with QPA of 3.5 or higher.
(g) I divides evenly into both J and K
(h) one of I, J, or K is even
(i) all of I, J, and K are multiples of ten
(j) J is between 15 and 17
(k) J is not between 15 and 17
(l) made a passing grade (A, B, or C)
(m) X and Y are both positive
(n) X and Y are not both positive
(o) exactly one of X and Y is positive
(p) neither X nor Y is positive
(q) either I is negative, or both X and Y are greater than 5
(r) Y is greater than 5, and either I is negative or X is greater than 5

2. INTEGER variables I, J, K, and L have the values 4, 7, 12, and 19, respectively. What is the value of each of these logical expressions?

(a) I.GT.J.AND.K.GT.L
(b) J.LT.10.OR.K.EQ.7.AND.L.GT.10
(c) (J.LT.10.OR.K.EQ.7).AND.L.GT.10
(d) .NOT.I.LT.J.OR.I.NE.K.AND.K.NE.L
(e) .NOT.(I.LT.J.OR.I.NE.K).AND.K.NE.L
(f) (.NOT.I.LT.J.OR.I.NE.K).AND.K.NE.L

3. Negate the following logical expressions:

(a) X.EQ.4.5
(b) I.LT.J

(c) CLASS.NE.'SR'
(d) Y.LT.Z.OR.Y.GE.Z+4.0
(e) CLASS.EQ.'FR'.AND.SEX.EQ.'M'.AND.QPA.LT.3.2
(f) MOD(I,J).EQ.0.OR.MOD(I,K).EQ.0
(g) PCT.GT.0.49.AND.YEARS.LT.4.AND.BONUS.GT.5.53
(h) CLASS.EQ.'FR' .OR. CLASS.EQ. 'SO' .AND. HOURS.LT.35
(i) (CLASS.EQ.'FR' .OR. CLASS.EQ.'SO') .AND. HOURS.LT.35

4. Give declarations and FORTRAN code for the following algorithm segments. Assume that any variables which begin with the letters I–N are INTEGER, all others are REAL (or CHARACTER where appropriate).

(a)

```
case
     1(X<5)Y ← 72
     2(5≤X≤20)Y ← 74
     3(X>20)Y ← 76
endcase
```

(b)

```
case
     1(I = 15) P ← 17.54
               I3 ← I3 + 1
               print X
     2(I = 17) P ← 16.5
               T ← T + 4
               A ← 4*A-3*I
endcase
```

(c)

```
case
     1(R = 'PA') T ← .02*P
     2(R = 'MO') T ← .025*P
                 print 'out of state-Missouri'
     3(any other) do nothing
endcase
```

(d)

```
if I does not divide evenly into J then
   I ← I + 1
else
   I ← I - 1
   case
      1(I < 5) print I,J
      2(any other) I ← I - 5
   endcase
   print I,J
endif
```

5. Give an appropriate variable list and algorithm segment for each of the following situations.

(a) Football players are being marked on their performance in the preceding game. A grade above 93 percent is considered excellent, below 75 percent poor. Your algorithm segment should, given the grades, print the names, grade, and an appropriate message for those marked excellent and for those marked poor.

(b) Given three test grades, print "improving" if the third test score is greater than the average of the first two tests; print "declining" if it is five or more points less than that average.

(c) Tax rate is based on city codes as given in the following table:

City code	Tax rate
'MUR'	.005
'MORR'	.01
'JCY'	.03
'BSTA'	.005
Others	.0

Compute taxes for a given annual wage.

(d) Write an algorithm to calculate charges for a checking account. For "regular" accounts, the charge is $5.00 unless the lowest monthly balance is $500.00 or more, in which case there is no charge. For "special" accounts, the charge is 20 cents per check, and for "VIP" accounts there is no charge.

(e) Taxes in a certain state are based on taxable income, and are calculated differently depending on whether the person is single or married. The taxable income is either 0 or the income minus $13 for each dependent, whichever is more. The taxes are given by the following tables.

Taxable income	Tax (married)
less than 145.00	1% of income
145.00–293.00	2% of income
Over 293.00	$50.00, plus 3% of amount over 293.00

Taxable income	Tax (single)
less than 130.00	1% of income
130.00–250.00	2% of income
250.01–350.00	$60.00, plus 3% of amount over 250.00
Over 350.00	100.00

Write an algorithm segment to calculate taxable income and tax for a taxpayer, given the needed information.

(f) A certain small company manufactures five items. The prices are given below. Write an algorithm segment which, given a valid item number, will calculate the price.

Item No.	Price
34927	100.50
62178	3000.00
32111	14.97
61137	143.50
11342	2550.00

(g) Revise the algorithm of part (f) to print an error message if the item number is invalid.

6. For each of the variable lists and algorithms in Exercise 5, give appropriate declarations and a segment of FORTRAN code to implement the decision structure.

7. Write a segment of FORTRAN code for the algorithm on page 119 which calculates the BONUS earned.

8. Write complete algorithms for the the following, then implement the algorithms as FORTRAN programs.

(a) Each input line has this form:

```
ID , gross   , code for county
     income          P = Pembroke
                     R = Richland
                     T = Tioga
```

The three counties have different tax rates: Pembroke County 2 percent; Richland County 1.5 percent; Tioga County 3 percent. Write a program to print a listing of ID number, county code, gross income, tax rate, and tax. Print an error message for any lines containing an invalid county code.

(b) A salesperson's commission is based on two factors: the sales amount and the number of years with the company. The basic commission rate is found by using this table:

Sales amount	Rate
Less than 500.00	5%
500.00–1000.00	7%
1000.01–1499.99	8%
1500.00 on up	10%

In addition, the commission is doubled if the person has worked over seven years with the company. If over 15 years of employment, it is doubled and $5 is added for each year over 15. Write a program to calculate commission rate and commission for each employee.

(c) Calculate a customer's bill for an order of some quantity of a single item. We assume there are only four items available, as shown in the following table:

Item Number	Unit Price
100	24.03
247	105.00
16	10.35
240	16.00

A discount is allowed for large orders: If the total bill is $1000.00 or over, a 2 percent discount is given; from $800–$999.99 earns a 1 percent discount.

(d) The first input line contains a number indicating a beginning inventory (the number of items presently in stock). Each subsequent line has a code (P = purchase, S = sale) and a quantity. For a sale, the quantity should be subtracted from the current inventory; for a purchase, added to the inventory. Write the algorithm for a complete program to maintain the running status of the inventory.

If there is insufficient inventory to cover a sale, print a message and reject the sale. If after a sale the resulting inventory is below 750, issue a "time to reorder" message; if it is below 250, issue an "URGENT—time to reorder" message.

9. Indicate some tests that should be in a test plan for each of the following exercises. (If the the exercise is a complete program, write a test plan for the complete program. If it is only an algorithm segment, write a test plan for that specific segment.)

(a) Exercise 4a
(b) Exercise 4c
(c) Exercise 5a
(d) Exercise 5b
(e) Exercise 5d
(f) Exercise 5e
(g) Exercise 7
(h) Exercise 8b
(i) Exercise 8c
(j) Exercise 8d

10. The algorithm segment given in this section for calculating a letter grade given a numerical test grade (p. 115) tacitly assumes that the grade is in the proper 0–100 range. Write a complete algorithm to read numerical grades and calculate corresponding letter grades using this algorithm segment. Then show how to modify that algorithm to detect and warn the user of faulty input.

Exercises 11–14 refer to Case Study #2.

11. Write the necessary INSTR subroutine.

12. In the alternate solution, indicate how you should code the "OP is bad" condition in the step which checks the input.

13. Modify either the original or the alternate algorithm to detect and warn of bad numerical input (that is, NO1 or NO2 not in the prescribed 1–99999 range).

14. Modify either algorithm to handle three additional types of operations: *, /, and % (multiplication, integer division, and real division, respectively).

2.6 INTRODUCTION TO FUNCTION SUBPROGRAMS

In a previous section we began our study of subprograms in FORTRAN by considering a particular type of subroutine. This subroutine was used to perform a task, namely that of printing instructions, for the main program. In this section we study the second type of subprogram available in FORTRAN. This is the **function subprogram**, frequently referred to as simply a function.

The primary purpose of using subprograms in developing a program is to achieve **modularity**. This refers to the situation where the program as a whole consists of a number of pieces, or **modules**. This allows us to concentrate our attention, both during development and also during any later modifications, on relatively small pieces of the program. With an INSTR subroutine available to print instructions, we have concentrated our attention in our examples on the logic of the main program.

A function, or function subprogram, has many things in common with a subroutine. Most importantly, it is a piece of a program designed to perform some specific task. The type of task performed by a function is a very specialized one: A function is always used to calculate some single value. For example, the library functions you studied in Section 2.4 each calculate a single value. The SQRT function calculates the square root of a given number; the MOD function calculates the remainder when one number is divided by another; and so on. As we will see, much of what we learned about using the library functions will apply to using functions which we write ourselves. In this section we will study two major items: how to use functions which we write, and how to write those functions.

Using Function Subprograms

As we indicated in the introduction, functions are generally used when we can identify a subtask consisting of calculating some value. Some functions, such as SQRT, MOD, ABS, and so on, are supplied with the FORTRAN language. Any program which involves calculating a square root may use the SQRT function.

In this subsection, we will consider an example involving a calculation subtask, where the desired function is not supplied with the computer. We will see that the program which uses such a function is very similar to one which uses a library function. In the next section, we will learn how to write the function.

Suppose that we wish to write a program which calculates areas of triangles given input consisting of the lengths of the three sides. A rough variable list and algorithm might be

Name	Type	Use	Comment
Input: A, B, C	REAL	Sides of triangle	Assumed valid
Output: AREA	REAL	Area of the triangle	

```
print instructions
loop
   issue prompt
   read A, B, C
   if A = 0 then exit endif
   calculate AREA based on A, B, and C
   print AREA
endloop
stop
```

As usual, we will use a subroutine to perform the subtask "print instructions." In addition, we choose to use a function to perform the subtask "calculate AREA based on A, B, and C."

Prior to presenting the complete main program, let us do some more work on the step which calculates the AREA. Since we plan to use a function which we will write ourselves, we must choose a name for that function. We may not use A, B, C, or AREA, since those variables already are in use. We choose AREAF, where by the "F" we are conveying that this is a function to calculate area. We add this name to our variable list, obtaining:

	Name	Type	Use	Comment
Input:	A, B, C	REAL	Sides of triangle	Assumed valid
Output:	AREA	REAL	Area of the triangle	
Other:	AREAF	REAL		Function

When we use a library function, we supply as parameters the values on which the function value is based. (For example, we may write MOD(I,10) if we wish the remainder when the variable I is divided by 10.) Similarly, we will supply the three sides of the triangle as parameters to the AREAF function, since that is what the answer is based on. Thus this step may be refined to read:

```
AREA ← AREAF(A,B,C)
```

Notice that, as with library functions, the AREAF function may be invoked by including it in an expression as part of an assignment statement.

The main program is given in Figure 2.7. There are three points to be observed. First, notice that the AREAF function is included in the REAL declarations. Second, this function is listed in the comments along with the INSTR subroutine. Finally, the PRINT statement does not print the function name, but rather the variable AREA into which the value from the function has been placed.

A Sample Function

Before we can write function subprograms, we must know what they look like. Every function in FORTRAN follows the same general form (see Figure 2.8). We can divide the function into three parts: the setup portion, the body, and the ending portion. In the setup portion, we include the declaration of the parameters and other variables used within the function. The actual calculation of the function value is performed in the body of the function. The ending portion returns control to the calling program and marks the physical end of the function subprogram.

The first statement in any function is always the FUNCTION statement. Its form is:

```
type FUNCTION fname(par1,par2,...)
```

```
      REAL A,B,C,AREA,AREAF

C   WRITTEN BY ********, **/**/**

C   THIS PROGRAM CALCULATES AREAS OF TRIANGLES BASED ON THE THREE
C SIDES OF THE TRIANGLE.

C   IT USES THESE SUBPROGRAMS:
C       INSTR - A SUBROUTINE TO PRINT INSTRUCTIONS
C       AREAF - A FUNCTION TO CALCULATE THE AREA

C   BEFORE THE LOOP, PRINT INSTRUCTIONS

      CALL INSTR

C   IN THE LOOP, READ THE SIDES AND USE THE FUNCTION TO FIND THE AREA

   10 CONTINUE
           PRINT *,'Enter the three sides (0 to quit)'
           READ *, A,B,C
           IF (A.EQ. 0) THEN
              GO TO 500
           ENDIF
           AREA = AREAF(A,B,C)
           PRINT *, 'The area is ',AREA
           GO TO 10

C   AFTER THE LOOP, STOP

  500 CONTINUE
      STOP
      END
```

Figure 2.7

```
set up  {  type FUNCTION fname(par1,par2,...)
        {  declarations


 body   {  fname=expression (one or more)


ending  {  RETURN
        {  END
```

Figure 2.8

Here type declares the type of variable (REAL, INTEGER, CHARACTER*1, and so on) for the function name, and hence for the value calculated by the function. The name of the function is represented by fname; it must adhere to the usual rules for the names of variables. Inside the parentheses we place the names of the parameters or arguments. They are separated by commas.

The rest of the setup portion of the function is essentially the same as that for the main program. We must declare each of the variables used in the function. The following two points are worth noting:

1. The parameters are variables, and hence must be included in the declaration, along with any local variables.
2. On the other hand, we do not include the function name, since its type has already been declared in the FUNCTION statement.

As we will see in later chapters, the setup portion may also include DATA statements, COMMON statements, DIMENSION statements, and various other FORTRAN statements.

In the body of the function we include the necessary steps to calculate the function value. This may be fairly simple or it may be complicated. In fact, it may even include calls to other subprograms. Since the purpose of the body is to calculate the function value, and since the function value is passed back to the calling program by way of the function name, fname, there will generally be at least one step which assigns a value to fname:

fname = expression

Of course, there may be more than one such step (for example, for an algorithm involving branching).

Finally, the ending portion of the function represents both the logical end and the physical end of the program. The logical end is indicated by the RETURN step, which returns control to the calling program. The END statement signals the compiler that this is the physical end of the subprogram. Every main program and every subprogram must have an END statement as its last statement.

As an example of the form, consider the AREAF function presented in Figure 2.9. The lines are numbered for reference.

Lines 1–2 are the setup portion. The first line declares that AREAF is a REAL function with three parameters. Within the function, these parameters will be referred to as A, B, and C. (For convenience, we have chosen to use the same names that the main program used, although that was not required. The three parameters in the main program's call to the AREAF function will "match up" with the three parameters in the function itself even if the names are different. We will have more to say about this later.) Line 2 declares the three parameters, and also a local variable S which will be used in doing the calculations. Recall from our discussion of subroutines that this variable has nothing to do with the main program. Its use is limited to the AREAF function.

Lines 3–10 illustrate a possible form of commenting for functions. Since it is possible that the function was written at a different time and by a different person

```
1          REAL FUNCTION AREAF(A,B,C)
2          REAL A,B,C,S
3
4   C   WRITTEN BY ********, **/**/**
5
6   C   THIS FUNCTION FINDS THE AREA OF A TRIANGLE BASED ON THE SIDES
7
8   C   THE PARAMETERS ARE:
9   C        A, B, C-INPUT, REAL-THE THREE SIDES
10
11         S = (A + B + C) / 2.0
12         AREAF = SQRT(S*(S-A)*(S-B)*(S-C))
13         RETURN
14         END
```

Figure 2.9

than the main program, we indicate author and date. We give a brief discussion of what the function does, followed by a description of the parameters.

> **COMMENT.** The word "INPUT" used in describing the parameters means that the calling program must supply values for the parameters. It does **not** mean that the function will READ the values. All parameters for functions will be input parameters.

Lines 11–12 code the algorithm for finding the area given the three sides. This algorithm (formula) was found in a mathematics book. The variable S represents the "semiperimeter" (half the perimeter) of the triangle. Notice that functions may calculate intermediate values in the process of calculating the value for which they were intended. Notice also that a function may in turn call another function, in this case the SQRT function.) The final answer is placed in the AREAF variable which is the name of the function. This is FORTRAN's way of passing answers from functions back to the calling program.

Finally, lines 13–14 from the ending portion of the function.

> **COMMENT.** The whole program would consist of the three pieces, one after the other: the main program (presented in the previous subsection); the INSTR subroutine (left to the reader); and the AREAF function (presented above).

Communication and Parameters

One of the important things to understand about the use of subprograms in FORTRAN is that each subprogram is an independent program. This means that the variable names and statement labels in the subprogram are not in any way related to those in the main program or in any other subprogram. This has a number of advantages. For example, in performing branching in the subprogram, we can include a statement label 10 and a GO TO 10 statement without having to worry about whether or not we have used the label 10 in the main program or in some other subprogram. We can also use a variable name such as HOURS in a subprogram without worrying about whether the name is used, perhaps for a different purpose, in the main program or in some other subprogram. This is especially advantageous if different members of a team are writing the various subprograms. It keeps us from having to keep track of all the labels and variable names used in all the subprograms. This allows us to concentrate our attention on the portion we are working on at any given time.

This raises the question of just how the various subprograms communicate. How does the called program get the information it needs to do its job (in our example, the three sides of the triangle)? How does the calling program get the answer back (in our example, the area of the triangle)?

There are two answers. Most of the communication between calling program and called program takes place through the **parameters**, or **arguments**. In addition, there is some communication between a function subprogram and the calling program which does not take place through the parameters; function values (that is, answers) are passed back to the calling program through the **name** of the function. Thus by naming our function "AREAF" and placing the desired answer into the variable AREA using the statement

```
AREAF = SQRT(S*(S-A)*(S-B)*(S-C))
```

the function will automatically pass the answer back to the main program.

The use of A, B, and C in the main program and the AREAF function of the previous example points out four important facts about parameters:

1. They must match in **purpose**. The parameters in the call to the function and the parameters in the function itself both represent the three sides of the triangle in which we are interested.
2. They must match in **type**. The function expects the values passed through the parameters to be REAL values. Therefore the variables which are passed must be REAL variables.
3. They must match in **number**. The function expects exactly three parameters, so the calling program must supply exactly three parameters.
4. They need not match in **name**. In our example we chose to use the same names, but this was not necessary. The main program writer might have called the three sides SIDE1, SIDE2, and SIDE3. If so, the step calculating the area would have read

   ```
   AREA = AREAF(SIDE1,SIDE2,SIDE3)
   ```

   The values in these variables would be passed in to the function through its corresponding parameters A, B, and C. There would be no need to change the names in the subprogram.

If we think about our use of the library functions, we will realize that these principles are ones we have used with arguments for the library functions. For example, the MOD function requires two INTEGER parameters, the first of which is to be divided by the second. The actual names we give to the parameters is immaterial. (In fact, they may even be INTEGER constants or expressions.)

Writing Functions

In writing a function, it is helpful to observe that there are generally no I/O steps involved. The algorithm is a refinement of a step "perform calculations." There will be no read step; instead, the required information will be supplied by the calling program through the input parameters. Likewise, there will be no print step; the answers will be passed back to the calling program through the function name.

There are four major steps involved in writing a function subprogram.

1. Decide to use a function. The choice to use a subprogram is based on identifying a subtask. If this subtask calculates one value, a function is appropriate. At this point we also choose a name and type (INTEGER, and so on) for the function. Our choice is based on what we are to calculate.
2. Decide on parameters. For a function, the parameters will be input parameters. We need a variable name for each value which must be supplied by the calling program in order for the function to calculate its answer.
3. Write an algorithm and variable list. The variable list will include the parameters, plus any local variables used within the subprogram for intermediate calculations. The algorithm will consist of the steps needed to calculate the answer.

   This algorithm will generally be similar to the "calculate" portion of our previous algorithms.
4. Code the function in FORTRAN. The function name and type and the list of parameters together give the information needed to write the first line. In the declarations we declare all the variables in our variable list, including the parameters. The body of the function is the FORTRAN code for the algorithm we have written, and the ending portion includes the usual RETURN and END steps.

Any step in an algorithm which may be phrased as "calculate a value" is a candidate for implementation as a function. Many of the examples and exercises of the previous section could have involved the use of functions. As an example of the steps listed above, we consider Exercise 8(c) of Section 2.5. The statement of the problem is reproduced here:

Calculate a customer's bill for an order of some quantity of a single item. We assume there are only four items available, as shown below:

Item	Unit Price
100	24.03
247	105.00
16	10.35
240	16.00

A discount is allowed for large orders. If the total bill is $1000.00 or over, a 2 percent discount is given; from $800–$999.99 earns a 1 percent discount.

Step 1. Decide to use a function. Since one of the steps in solving the problem may be written as "calculate the bill," it would make sense to use a function for that step. It will be a REAL function, which we will name BILLF.

Step 2. Decide on parameters. For a function, the parameters consist of those variables on which the value being calculated depends. It is clear that the bill depends on what the item is, and on how many of the item are being purchased. Thus we begin our variable list:

	Name	Type	Use	Comment
Parameters (Input):	ITEMNO	INTEGER	Item number	
	QUANT	INTEGER	Quantity purchased	

Step 3. Write an algorithm, and decide on local variables. The algorithm consists of three steps: Calculate the price; calculate the total cost before discount; and deduct the discount if applicable. A smooth algorithm follows, along with local variables to be added to the variable list. Notice that the last step places the answer into the function name (BILLF). Also notice that we are assuming that ITEMNO is valid. Perhaps it has been checked in the main program.

	Name	Type	Use	Comment
Local:	PRICE	REAL	Price of item	From table
	TOTAL	REAL	Total cost	Before discount

```
case
   1(ITEMNO = 100) PRICE ← 24.03
   2(ITEMNO = 247) PRICE ← 105.00
   3(ITEMNO = 16)  PRICE ← 10.35
   4(any other)    PRICE ← 16.00
endcase
TOTAL ← PRICE * QUANT
case
   1(TOTAL ≥ 1000.00) TOTAL ← TOTAL − .02 * TOTAL
   2(TOTAL ≥ 800.00)  TOTAL ← TOTAL − .01 * TOTAL
endcase
BILLF ← TOTAL
```

Step 4. Code the function in FORTRAN. This consists of writing the FUNCTION line, declaring the parameters and local variable, coding the algorithm, and including the necessary RETURN and END.

```
      REAL FUNCTION BILLF(ITEMNO,QUANT)
      INTEGER ITEMNO,QUANT
      REAL PRICE,TOTAL

C     WRITTEN BY *********, **/**/**

C     THIS FUNCTION CALCULATES A BILL

C     THESE ARE THE PARAMETERS:
C        ITEMNO–INTEGER, INPUT–THE ITEM NUMBER PURCHASED
C        QUANT–INTEGER, INPUT–THE QUANTITY PURCHASED

      IF (ITEMNO.EQ.100) THEN
         PRICE = 24.03
      ELSE IF (ITEMNO.EQ.247) THEN
         PRICE = 105.00
      ELSE IF (ITEMNO.EQ.16) THEN
         PRICE = 10.35
      ELSE
         PRICE = 16.00
      ENDIF
      TOTAL = PRICE * QUANT
      IF (TOTAL.GE.1000.00) THEN
         TOTAL = TOTAL - 0.02 * TOTAL
      ELSE IF (TOTAL.GE.800.00) THEN
         TOTAL = TOTAL - 0.01 * TOTAL
      ENDIF
      BILLIF = TOTAL
      RETURN
      END
```

Testing

We have several options for testing a program which contains subprograms. For example, with a main program and one subroutine, there are four possibilities:

1. We could write the entire program, then start testing the whole program as a single unit.
2. We could make sure the main program works, test the subroutine separately, then put them together and see if they work together.
3. We could make sure the main program works, then add the untested subroutine and make sure the package works.
4. We could make sure the subroutine works, then add it to the untested main program and make sure the package works.

Of course, with two subprograms the possibilities increase.

The third and fourth alternatives are examples of what is called "incremental" testing. For programs containing large numbers of subprograms, incremental testing has been found to work better than the other two methods. The first method has the disadvantage that, when an error occurs, it can be difficult to determine which subprogram caused the error. The second method is an improvement, but it has been found that pieces that work perfectly well separately sometimes do not work well when they are combined. If we combine them all at once, it can be difficult to see which particular combinations are causing the problems.

Method #3 is an example of **top down testing**. The top level (main) module is tested first, then the lower level modules are added, one at a time, and the program is tested again. In this form of testing, so-called **stubs** are needed for the subprograms which have not yet been written and tested. We would test the main program with the stub versions of the subroutines. When we get this running properly, we would replace one of the stubs by the actual subprogram and perform more testing of the final program. This would be followed by replacing another stub by the actual subprogram, with the program as a whole tested again. This continues until the entire program has been tested.

Method #4 is an example of **bottom up testing**. The lowest level modules are tested; when they are running correctly, the program unit which calls them is added, and the combination is tested. This form of testing requires a **driver** main program, a substitute for the actual main program which is used to "drive" the subprograms being tested.

We will have more to say about incremental testing in general, and about top down and bottom up testing, in other TESTING sections later in the text. In the case study which follows, we illustrate simple instances of both top down testing with stubs and bottom up testing with drivers.

Case Study #3

This case study develops a complete program which uses a number of subprograms. It is a simplified payroll program. Part of the case study describes some strategies for testing a program which includes subprograms.

1. *Statement of problem.* Write a program which calculates weekly pay and the amount of state tax to be withheld from the paycheck. The pay is the hourly rate times the number of hours, except that hours over 40 earn "time and a half." The

state tax is based on the following rules. First, $12 is deducted from the income for each dependent. Then the tax is determined by the following table.

Resulting income	Tax
Less than 0	0
0–300	2% of resulting income
over 300	$15 plus 2.5% of amount over $300

2. *Preliminary analysis.* The problem is not well described, since it does not specify the necessary input. We will have to discover what the input records will look like by analyzing the problem. It is clear that we need at least the hourly rate and the number of hours in order to calculate the weekly pay. The tax is based on the pay (which we calculate) and the number of dependents, another part of the input record. Finally, we assume that the input will contain an integer clock number.

For output,we will print the clock number, weekly pay, and state tax withholding.

We will not do complete error checking on the input; that will be left as an exercise. However, we will check for one possible error—hours less than 0.

One final note: "Time and a half" means that if a person works over 40 hours, then the first 40 are paid at the normal rate; all other hours are paid at 1.5 times the normal rate.

3. *Algorithm and variable list.*

a. *Main program.* For the main program, we have the following input and output variables, based on our analysis:

	Name	Type	Use	Comment
Input:	CLOCK	INTEGER	Employee clock #	Also printed
	HOURS	REAL	Hours worked in week	
	RATE	REAL	Normal hourly rate	
	DEPEN	INTEGER	# of dependents	
Output:	PAY	REAL	Weekly pay	
	STATAX	REAL	State tax withholding	

The algorithm is quite similar to ones we have written before:

```
print instructions
loop
   issue prompt
   read CLOCK, HOURS, RATE, DEPEN
   if CLOCK ≤ 0 then exit endif
   if HOURS < 0 then
      print HOURS, error message
```

```
        next iteration
     endif
     calculate PAY
     calculate STATAX
     print CLOCK, PAY, STATAX
  endloop
  stop
```

We choose to use a subroutine called INSTR for the subtask "print instructions" and functions called PAYF and TAXF for the "calculate PAY" and "calculate STATAX" subtasks. We refine those three steps as follows:

```
print instructions:    call INSTR
calculate PAY:         PAY ← PAYF(HOURS,RATE)
calculate STATAX;      STATAX ← TAXF(PAY,DEPEN)
```

In doing so we have supplied as parameters the values on which the calculations are based. We add PAYF and TAXF to our variable list:

	Name	Type	Use	Comment
Other:	PAYF	REAL		Function
	TAXF	REAL		Function

NOTE. Given below is a **hierarchy chart** for the program. This is a visual description of the fact that it contains four modules, and that the main module calls the other three. Along with the diagram, we give a short description of the task each module performs.

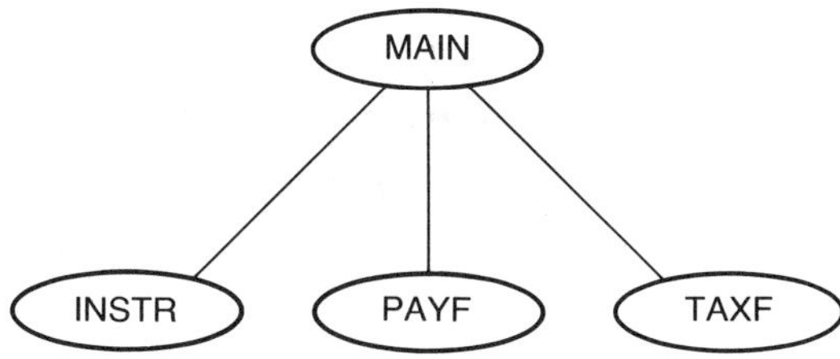

MAIN: reads data (some minor checking), calls functions, and prints answers in loop
INSTR: subroutine which prints instructions
PAYF: function which calculates weeky pay
TAXF: function which calculates state tax withholding

b. *PAYF function.* This completes the design for the main program. Next we design the PAYF function. We have already decided that it should be a REAL function with two parameters (hours, rate). No other variables are needed. We choose the names HOURS, RATE; these are the same as the main program, which is allowed.

	Name	Type	Use	Comment
Parameters (Input):	HOURS	REAL	Hours worked	
	RATE	REAL	Hourly rate	

The next step is to write an algorithm for the desired calculation. This algorithm is one possible solution.

```
if hours > 40 then
   PAYF ← 40.0*RATE + 1.5*RATE*(HOURS-40.0)
else
    PAYF ← HOURS*RATE
endif
```

c. *TAXF function.* We now design the TAXF function. It is a REAL function with parameters representing the pay (a REAL quantity) and the number of dependents (an INTEGER quantity). We choose names different from those in the main program; again, this is also allowed. In addition to the parameters, we need a local variable for the taxable income.

	Name	Type	Use	Comment
Parameters (Input):	INCOME	REAL	Week's pay	
	NDEP	INTEGER	# of dependents	
Other:	TAXINC	REAL	Taxable income	

The algorithm, based on the verbal description, is given below.

```
TAXINC ← INCOME - 12 * NDEP
case
   1(TAXINC < 0) TAXF ← 0
   2(TAXINC ≤ 300)  TAXF ← .02 * TAXINC
   3(any other)  TAXF ← 15.00 + .025 * (TAXINC - 300)
endcase
```

CAUTION. We must have the local variable TAXINC. If, instead, we change the parameter INCOME, the corresponding parameter PAY in the main program will also get changed. This will make it look like the pay function was wrong. NEVER CHANGE THE PARAMETERS OF A FUNCTION.

d. *INSTR subroutine.* The plan for the INSTR subroutine we leave to the reader.

NOTE. In working with subprograms, what we did above was typical. We developed and presented each module's plan as a separate piece, starting with the main program and working our way to the subprograms. This is part of what is meant by **top down design**.

4. *Test plan.* We now develop the test plan. This consists of two parts: a planned order to write and test the modules, and a set of test data for each module. We choose this order: PAYF, TAXF, MAIN, INSTR. Notice that this is "bottom up" in the sense that PAYF and TAXF are developed before the main program which uses them. On the other hand, it is "top down" in the sense that the main program is developed before its subroutine INSTR. Quite frequently in large projects a mixture of the two methods is used.

When we write a test plan for each separate module, this is sometimes referred to as **unit testing**. We will outline a plan for each of the modules.

Main: Branches and borderlines on bad hours:

hours = −0.1	hours = −5
hours = 0	hours = 30
hours = 0.1	

NOTE. There are other possible "bad data" situations, to be explored in the exercises.

(In testing the main program, we will also wind up repeating some of the branch tests we have done for the pay and tax functions.)

PAYF: Branches and borderlines on hours:

hours = 39.9	hours = 25
hours = 40.0	hours = 50
hours = 40.1	

TAXF: Branches and borderlines on number of dependents:

# dependents = 0	# dependents = 5
# dependents = 1	

Branches and borderlines on taxable income. For each test, we show the desired taxable income and also how it will be achieved. Notice that we use a variety of values for the number of dependents.

tax. inc. = −1	(income 23 #dep 2)
tax. inc. = 0	(income 12 #dep 1)
tax. inc. = 1	(income 1 #dep 0)
tax. inc. = 299	(income 299 #dep 0)
tax. inc. = 300	(income 360 #dep 5)

tax. inc. = 301	(income 337 #dep 3)
tax. inc. = −50	(income 10 #dep 5)
tax. inc. = 100	(income 148 #dep 4)
tax. inc. = 400	(income 400 #dep 0)

COMMENT. We have chosen to test our borderlines one dollar below and above rather than one cent below and above. At a 2 percent tax rate, a one cent difference in income would lead to only a very small change in the tax.

INSTR: Since the design of the INSTR subroutine has been left to the exercises, we also leave the details of the test plan to be completed by the student. It should include tests of branches based on whether or not instructions are wanted.

5. *Write program.* We write the program, following the order indicated in our test plan. First, the PAYF function:

```
      REAL FUNCTION TAXF(HOURS,RATE)
      REAL HOURS,RATE

C   WRITTEN BY *******, **/**/**

C   THIS FUNCTION CALCULATES PAY, GIVEN HOURS AND RATE.
C OVERTIME IS PAID FOR HOURS OVER 40.

C   THESE ARE THE PARAMETERS:
C        HOURS - INPUT, REAL - NUMBER OF HOURS WORKED
C        RATE - INPUT, REAL - HOURLY WAGE
C
      IF (HOURS.GT.40.0) THEN
         PAYF = 40.0 * RATE + 1.5 * RATE * (HOURS - 40.0)
      ELSE
         PAYF = HOURS * RATE
      ENDIF
      RETURN
      END
```

In order to test the function, we need a **driver** main program. This is a temporary main program written for the sole purpose of testing the function. Since it is temporary, we do not include comments or complicated instructions, and we use unformatted output. A possible driver is given below.

```
      REAL PAY,PAYF,HOURS,RATE
   10 CONTINUE
         PRINT *,'ENTER HOURS, RATE (0,0 to stop)'
         READ *,HOURS,RATE
         IF (HOURS.EQ.0 .AND. RATE.EQ.0)THEN
            GO TO 500
         ENDIF
```

(continued)

```
          PAY = PAYF(HOURS,RATE)
          PRINT *,'Pay is ',PAY
          GO TO 10
  500 CONTINUE
      STOP
      END
```

We place the driver with the PAYF function and run our planned tests. If there are any errors in the function, we correct them. When it seems correct, we proceed to the next step.

In the next step, we do exactly the same thing for the TAXF function. The details are left as an exercise.

We are now ready to write the main program, given in Figure 2.10. We will test the main program together with the two functions which we have already written and tested. However, notice that the main program also calls a subroutine which has not yet been written. In order to test the main program, we write a **stub** for the INSTR subroutine. This stub can be very simple, for example

```
SUBROUTINE INSTR
PRINT *,'INSTR subroutine successfully called'
RETURN
END
```

When we run the main program, this message will be printed prior to entering the loop. The actual subroutine will be added later.

The final step is to replace the stub with the actual INSTR subroutine and run our tests for this subroutine. At this point, we have a complete program. It is probably advisable to do some more testing, similar to what we did for the individual pieces, to try to make sure that the program as a whole is working properly.

6. *Modifications.* One of the advantages of modularity is that it makes modifications easier. For example, we will develop some additions to our program in the next chapter. Those additions will not affect any of the subprograms, so we will not have to retest them. As another example, if we modify the pay function, we will retest this function and the program as a whole. The exercises suggest some modifications to the case study.

Pitfalls

Subprograms, including function subprograms, are not difficult to write or use. We should remember the following points.

1. Functions are written to accomplish calculations. There will generally be no read or write steps.

   Input is obtained by input parameters from the calling program, not by reading. Answers are passed back to the calling program rather than being printed in the function.

```
      REAL HOURS,RATE,PAY,STATAX,PAYF,TAXF
      INTEGER CLOCK, DEPEN

C   WRITTEN BY **********, **/**/**

C   THIS PROGRAM CALCULATES WEEKLY PAY AND STATE WITHHOLDING

C   IT USES THESE SUBPROGRAMS:
C       INSTR - A SUBROUTINE TO PRINT DIRECTIONS
C       PAYF - FUNCTION TO CALCULATE PAY
C       TAXF - FUNCTION TO CALCULATE WITHHOLDING

C   BEFORE THE LOOP, PRINT INSTRUCTIONS

      CALL INSTR

C   IN THE LOOP, READ THE DATA, USE THE FUNCTIONS TO CALCULATE PAY
C AND WITHHOLDING, AND PRINT THE ANSWERS

   10 CONTINUE
         PRINT *,'Enter clock #, hours, rate, # dependents'
         READ *, CLOCK, HOURS, RATE, DEPEN
         IF (CLOCK.LT.0) THEN
            GO TO 500
         ENDIF
         IF (HOURS.LT.0) THEN
            PRINT *,'Bad hours - ',HOURS,' - reenter data'
            GO TO 200
         ENDIF
         PAY = PAYF(HOURS,RATE)
         STATAX = TAXF(PAY,DEPEN)
         WRITE(*,1000) 'Clock # ',CLOCK,': pay = ', PAY,
     $                 ', tax = ',STATAX
  200    GO TO 10

C   AFTER LOOP, STOP

  500 CONTINUE
      STOP

C   FORMATS

 1000 FORMAT(' ',20X,A,I5,A,F7.2,A,F7.2)
      END
```

Figure 2.10

2. Subprograms are independent. Each main program and subprogram should declare only those variables within its boundaries.
3. Within a function, the function name is used as a variable. For example, in the function PAYF we write

```
PAYF = HOURS * RATE
```

   However, in the calling program, the function name cannot be used as a variable name. We write

```
PAY = PAYF(HOURS,RATE)
```

   using the variable PAY to store the answer from the function.
4. In using a function, the calling program supplies constants, variables, or expressions which represent the parameter quantities in the calling program. These will not necessarily be the same names that the function uses for the parameters.

REVIEW

Terms

parameter
argument
function name
input parameter
stub
driver
top down testing
bottom up testing
incremental testing
unit test

Communication by Parameters

Parameters in calling and called program must match in number, type, and use.

They may or may not match by name.

Values of parameters are passed to the function from the calling program when it is invoked.

Answers are passed back, through the function name, when it RETURNs.

Program Layout

Main program is followed immediately by the subprogram or subprograms.

Declarations

Each main program and subprogram declares *its own variables*. The calling program also declares the function names for any functions it invokes.

FORTRAN Syntax

FUNCTION statement:

type FUNCTION fname(par1,par2,...)

"type" can be REAL, INTEGER, CHARACTER*1, and so forth.

"fname" must be 1–6 letters or digits, first a letter.

There may be one or more parameters, separated by commas.

RETURN statement:

RETURN

Used to return to calling program.

Writing a Function

1. Decide to use a function (for a subtask which calculates a value). Determine type and choose function name.
2. Determine input parameters needed and give them names.
3. Determine other variables needed and write algorithm. This step is similar to the "calculate" portions of algorithms considered earlier.
4. Code. Use function and parameter names to write the first line. Declare parameters and other variables. Code the algorithm, with RETURN and END steps.

Using a Function

1. Declare function name in calling program.
2. Include function name in an expression (assignment statement or condition in IF statement).
3. Supply parameters, expressions representing the desired quantities in terms of variables (or constants) *in the calling program*.

Testing

1. Use incremental approach (top down, bottom up, or a mixture).
2. Develop a unit test plan for each module.
3. Use drivers and stubs where needed.

EXERCISES

1. Write a function to find the smaller of two real numbers.

2. Write a function to find the largest of three integer numbers.

3. Write a function to find the smallest of three integer numbers.

4. Write a function to calculate the total surface area of a cone. The formula is $V = \pi r\sqrt{r^2 + h^2} + \pi r^2$

5. Write a function to determine the letter grade for a given numerical average. Use the usual 90–80–70–60 scale.

6. Write a function to calculate final average, based on homework average, test average, and final exam percentage. If the homework average is 0.70 or higher, the final average is the higher of the test average and the final exam percentage; otherwise, the final average is 0.3 times the homework average, plus .4 times the test average, plus 0.3 times the final exam percentage.

7. **(a)** Vacation days per year are based on employee type and years experience by the following rules. All type A employees get seven days; all type E employees get 21 days. Type S employees earn ten days if they have six or fewer years of experience, otherwise 15 days. All other types get zero days.

   Design a function to calculate the vacation days, up to the point of FORTRAN coding.

   (b) Code the function.

8. **(a)** Write a function to find the larger of two integer numbers.

   (b) Use the function you wrote in part (a) in an assignment statement to accomplish this task: The variable TRY should be given an initial value which is the larger of M and N.

   (c) Use the function you wrote in part (a) in an assignment statement to accomplish this task: The final grade for the course is to be the exam grade, or the average of the two test grades, whichever is larger.

9. **(a)** One function we might frequently use, but which is not a FORTRAN library function, is a ROUND function which rounds a given real number to the nearest integer. Using a parameter named X for the real number, write a function which does this.

   (b) Use the function you wrote in part (a) in an assignment statement to accomplish this task: Calculate the variable BPDAY ("baskets produced per day"). This is to be the number of baskets, divided by the number of days, rounded to the nearest integer.

   (c) Use the function you wrote in part (a) in an assignment statement to accomplish this task: Calculate the average score on three tests, rounded to the nearest integer.

10. Write functions for the algorithms from each of the following exercises from Section 2.5. If the exercise involves a complete program, then determine a portion which might be suitable as a function and write that function. For each function, describe a unit test plan.

    (a) Exercise 5c
    (b) Exercise 5d
    (c) Exercise 5e (tax only)
    (d) Exercise 5f
    (e) Exercise 8a
    (f) Exercise 8b
    (g) Exercise 8c

11. Describe a unit test plan for these exercises in this section.

    (a) Exercise 1
    (b) Exercise 2
    (c) Exercise 3
    (d) Exercise 5
    (e) Exercise 7
    (f) Exercise 9

12. Write a complete program to calculate wages and state taxes for a number of employees. Input consists of name, clock number, marital status, number of dependents, and job code. Wages are based on department and job code. If we let DEPT be the first digit of the clock number, the wages are as indicated in the table below (any entry not appearing indicates an error):

DEPT=1		DEPT=2		DEPT=3		DEPT=4	
Job	Wages	Job	Wages	Job	Wages	Job	Wages
A	157.00	A	345.00	A	264.00	A	130.00
B	171.00	B	415.00	B	289.00	B	175.00
C	306.00	any other	653.00	C	315.00	C	210.00
D	339.00			D	347.00	any other	239.00
				E	389.00		

State taxes are based on the algorithm given in Exercise 5(e) of Section 2.5.

Exercises 13–18 refer to CASE STUDY #3.

13. Give an algorithm and a test plan for the INSTR subroutine. The person should be able to get instructions by either entering a lower case or a capital Y. (How would you code the read statement to allow the entry not enclosed in quotes?)

14. Code the TAXF function and write a driver program for it.

15. Run the driver program and TAXF function to test the function.

16. Modify the PAYF function to allow "double time" for all hours in excess of 50. Give a revised test plan.

17. Modify the TAXF function to deduct 10 percent of the original income from the taxable income prior to calculating the tax. Give a revised test plan.

18. Modify the main program to check for other input errors. Note: Some errors violate "reasonableness" standards. For example, an hourly rate of $1000 would be unreasonable.

3

USING LOOPS: PART 1

3.1 COMMON APPLICATIONS OF LOOPS

The primary topic of this chapter is loops. In the first section we will examine some frequently used applications of looping. We will then study loop control in some detail. We begin with a general discussion of loops.

Loop Control

Whenever we write a loop in a program, we must incorporate some way to get out of (exit) the loop. We will refer to the portions of the loop which determine when we exit the loop as the **loop control**. One of the most common techniques of loop control is going until the user indicates the process should terminate by entering a dummy value. In our pseudocode algorithm description, we have used the following type of algorithm:

```
print instructions
loop
    read variables
    if dummy value then exit endif
    rest of loop body
endloop
```

It is possible to identify four frequently used methods of loop control. We might list these as follows:

1. Dummy entry.
2. Go until end-of-file.
3. Go until some condition is met.
4. Know in advance exactly how many times to go through the loop.

All our programs so far have utilized the first form of loop control.

When we work with files, or in a batch processing mode, we frequently write loops which read from the file, terminating the loop when the end of the file is reached. This technique will be discussed in Section 5.1.

We might phrase a sample problem of the third type as follows: "repeatedly draw a card from a deck of playing cards, counting the number of draws until an ace is obtained." In this problem we definitely would *not* keep going through the loop (that is, drawing cards) until we run out of cards. We want to exit from the loop as soon as we draw an ace. This is an example of going until some condition is met (the condition that the card drawn is an ace). This type of control will be discussed in Section 3.2.

As an example of a problem utilizing the last type of loop control, suppose we wanted to find the sum of the salaries for the first 27 employees in a file. In this case we would know that we should work with exactly 27 records, and that therefore we should go through our loop exactly 27 times. In Section 3.3 we consider the problem of writing FORTRAN loops using this type of control.

Planning a Loop

When we write a program which involves looping, it is essential to identify at the outset which type of loop control is needed. (If the answer is "go until a condition is met," we should also identify that condition.) In addition, it will be necessary to identify what must be done *before* the loop, what must be done *in* the loop, and what must be done *after* the loop. Finally, the placement of the exit step for the loop will be an important consideration.

Before the loop we frequently find steps which print instructions. In addition, many applications of loops require steps which may be generally classified as **initialization** steps. For example, programs which accumulate totals generally give the total an initial value of 0 before the loop. As you will see later in this section, initialization of one kind or another is a common ingredient in problems involving looping.

In the loop it is possible to identify two separate components. First, we have the actual steps which we wish to have performed repeatedly. This is frequently referred to as the **body** of the loop. In many of our examples, we have done these steps repeatedly: 1) read data; 2) calculate answers; and, 3) print a line of output. These steps form the body of the loop. In addition, there are some steps which might be thought of as **control** steps. They do not do any actual processing, but rather they control the sequence of steps in the program. In particular, these are the steps which cause the body of the loop to be repeated the proper number of times.

After the loop we frequently find steps which print summary information, or which use the information gathered in the loop for further calculations.

In conclusion, then, there are three things a programmer must ask himself when he knows he will need a loop. First, what type of loop control is appropriate? Second, what steps must come before the loop, in the loop, and after the loop? And finally, where should the **exit** step be placed? (For the time being, the exit will always immediately follow the read step.) These questions should be answered *before* the program itself is written; the answers will be incorporated in the algorithm.

In this section we examine three specific applications of loops. For each, we identify the required initialization steps, the steps which are performed in the loop body, and the summary steps performed after the loop.

Counting

Consider the following algorithm and variable list. The program is to read a series of positive numbers (terminated by a dummy entry of 0). For each number it is to print a message telling whether the number is even or odd.

	Name	Type	Use	Comment
Input:	NUMBER	INTEGER	Number to test	Must be positive

```
print instructions
loop
   prompt for number
   if NUMBER = 0 then exit endif
   if NUMBER < 0 then
      print error message
      next iteration
   endif
   if MOD(NUMBER,2) = 0 then
      print 'even'
   else
      print 'odd'
   endif
endloop
stop
```

We would like to modify the algorithm so that, after all the numbers are processed, it will tell us how many were even.

Writing programs which count how many times certain conditions occur is relatively easy, especially when the counting is done as a modification to an existing program. There are, in general, four things to keep in mind:

1. We will need a **counter**, a variable to do the actual counting (CTR). It should be an INTEGER variable.
2. This variable must be initialized to 0 before we begin counting. Typically, this is done before we enter some loop in which the actual counting is performed.

3. Within the loop, each time we encounter one of the things we are counting, we add 1 to our counter variable, using a step such as "CTR = CTR + 1".
4. After leaving the loop we either print the answer by printing the value of the counter variable, or use the answer in further calculations.

For our particular example, the variable list and algorithm will be changed to the following:

	Name	Type	Use	Comment
Input:	NUMBER	INTEGER	Number to test	Must be positive
Other:	CTR	INTEGER	Even counter	Printed at end

```
CTR ← 0
print instructions
loop
   prompt for number
   if NUMBER = 0 then exit endif
   if NUMBER < 0 then
      print error message
      next iteration
   endif
   if MOD(NUMBER,2) = 0 then
      print 'even'
      CTR ← CTR + 1
   else
    print 'odd'
   endif
endloop
print 'There were ',CTR,' even numbers'
stop
```

The changes in each are shaded. Notice that the changes correspond to the four considerations listed above.

The steps involved in coding this algorithm as a FORTRAN program are, of course, the same as those for any algorithm. Counting is an algorithmic concept; no new FORTRAN concepts are involved.

It is possible, of course, to have a program which does no processing other than the counting. The next example illustrates this.

Each record contains an identification number and an age. Write a program to determine what percentage of the people represented are age 30 or older.

Here we need two counters, since in order to calculate the percentage we must determine how many are 30 or older and also how many there are all together. Here is the resulting variable list.

	Name	Type	Use	Comment
Input:	IDNO	INTEGER	Identification number	
	AGE	INTEGER	Age	
Other:	OLDCTR	INTEGER	Number 30 or older	Counter
	TOTCTR	INTEGER	All together	Counter
	PCT	REAL	Percent 30 or older	

Once again, we must initialize both counters at 0 before entering our loop which reads records and does the counting. Each time through the loop we will add 1 to the OLDCTR variable if the AGE is 30 or above. This is similar to the previous example. Notice, however, that this time we must also add 1 to TOTCTR, whether or not AGE is 30 or above. After the loop, we use our counters to calculate PCT, then print the answer. We come up with the following algorithm:

```
print instructions
OLDCTR, TOTCTR ← 0
loop
   read IDNO, AGE
   if IDNO = 0 then exit endif
   TOTCTR ← TOTCTR + 1
   if AGE≥30 then OLDCTR ← OLDCTR +1 endif
endloop
PCT ← (OLDCTR/TOTCTR) * 100
print PCT
stop
```

You should write the program yourself, then refer to Figure 3.1 to see if your program appears to be correct. (As usual, we leave the INSTR subroutine to the reader.)

Perhaps the only step of the program which needs to be emphasized is the step which calculates the percentage:

```
PCT = (REAL(OLDCTR) / REAL(TOTCTR) ) * 100.0
```

First of all, this makes the assumption that TOTCTR is not 0. For this problem that is probably a fairly reasonable assumption; however, there are instances where a count of 0 is very possible, and in those instances we would want to guard against the possibility of dividing by 0.

Second, we use the REAL function to obtain real division. There are two common errors made by beginning programmers in coding this step. Neither of the following will work:

```
PCT = (OLDCTR/TOTCTR) * 100

PCT = (REAL(OLDCTR/TOTCTR) ) * 100.0
```

```
      INTEGER IDNO,AGE,OLDCTR,TOTCTR
      REAL PCT

C   WRITTEN BY ******, **/**/**

C   THIS PROGRAM DETERMINES THE PERCENTAGE OF PEOPLE
C AGE 30 OR OVER IN A PARTICULAR SET OF INPUT
C   IT USES ONE SUBPROGRAM:
C      INSTR—A SUBROUTINE TO PRINT INSTRUCTIONS

C   BEFORE THE LOOP, PRINT INSTRUCTIONS AND INITIALIZE COUNTERS

      CALL INSTR
      OLDCTR = 0
      TOTCTR = 0

C   IN THE LOOP READ A LINE, ADD TO TOTAL COUNTER, AND ADD
C TO OVER 30 COUNTER IF APPROPRIATE

   10 CONTINUE
        PRINT *,'Enter I.D. and age'
        READ *,IDNO,AGE
        IF (IDNO.EQ.0)THEN
           GO TO 500
        ENDIF
        TOTCTR = TOTCTR + 1
        IF(AGE.GE.30) THEN
          OLDCTR = OLDCTR + 1
        ENDIF
        GO TO 10

C   AFTER THE LOOP, CALCULATE AND PRINT PERCENTAGE

  500 CONTINUE
      PCT = (REAL(OLDCTR)/REAL(TOTCTR)) * 100.0
      WRITE(*,1000) 'Percentage of people age 30 or older is ',PCT
      STOP
C
C   FORMATS
C
 1000 FORMAT(' ',A,F6.2)
      END
```

Figure 3.1

In each case, the division will be performed using integer division. For example, if there were 25 persons age 30 or older out of a total of 55, then the expression OLDCTR/TOTCTR would have the value 25/55. Using integer division, this gives an answer of 0. Applying the REAL function and multiplying by 100.0 gives 0.0, certainly the wrong answer. The solution is that we need to use real division, where answers are not truncated to the next lower integer. To do so, we need to apply the REAL function to each of the two counters, *then* do the division.

Accumulation

We now consider the accumulation process. This process is designed to find the total of all the values in a list. For example, we may have an input list with ID numbers and net pay and want to write a program to determine the total payroll for the pay period. Or we may have a file with names and test scores and wish to determine the average score on the test (notice that to find the average, we must add all the scores up and divide by the number of students). The procedures used in accumulation problems are similar to those used in counting problems. First of all, we will need a variable, sometimes called an **accumulator**, to keep track of the running total. We will perform the required steps before, during, and after the loop as indicated here:

1. Before the loop we initialize our accumulator to 0.
2. In the loop, we read a record, perhaps do some calculations, and add the appropriate value to our accumulator (assuming the record read is of the type being accumulated).
3. After the loop we typically either print the total obtained or use it in further calculations.

The steps involved are analogous to what happens in a cash register when we check out at the grocery store. In the cash register, the accumulator is generally a piece of hardware within the machine. As each new grocery item is encountered, its price is added to the total. In this way the accumulator maintains a running total. At any point in the process, it will contain the total up to that point (the subtotal), and when all the items have been processed, it will contain the final total.

Let us assume that each record contains a salesperson number, a department number, a basic commission rate, and a sales amount for the week. Write a program to determine the total sales by all salespersons during the week.

This is a typical accumulation problem. We wish to accumulate, or add up, the week's sales amount for all the salespersons. To do this, we will use an accumulator. (Because it is accumulating REAL quantities, it will be REAL.) We will initialize the accumulator to 0 prior to entering the loop, add each salesperson's sales amount to it in the body of the loop, and print the answer after the loop. In addition to the accumulator, we will need variables for the quantities represented on the records.

	Name	Type	Use	Comment
Input:	IDNO	INTEGER	Salesperson number	
	DEPTNO	INTEGER	Department number	
	RATE	REAL	Commission rate	
	SALES	REAL	Sales for week	
Other:	TOTAL	REAL	Total sales	Printed at end

The algorithm merely incorporates what we have already decided should be done before, in, and after the loop. The loop is controlled by a dummy entry.

```
print instructions
TOTAL ← 0
loop
   prompt
   read IDNO, DEPTNO, RATE, SALES
   if IDNO = 0 then exit endif
   TOTAL ← TOTAL + SALES
endloop
print TOTAL
stop
```

The corresponding program is a straightforward coding of this algorithm, and is left as an exercise.

We now consider two modifications to this algorithm. First, suppose that we want to print the average sales instead of the total sales. Since the average is given by dividing the total by the number of persons involved, we will need a counter (CTR) to count the number of salespersons we have. Before the loop we will initialize CTR to 0; in the loop we will increment CTR by 1; after the loop we will divide TOTAL by CTR to obtain an average AVE. In addition to the variables in the previous variable list, we need CTR (an integer variable) for the counter and AVE (a real variable) for the average. We will also use the library function REAL in calculating the average.

The revised algorithm, with the changes highlighted, is found in Figure 3.2.

For our second revision, we consider a slightly more complicated problem. In

```
print instructions
TOTAL ← 0
CTR ← 0
loop
   prompt
   read IDNO,DEPTNO,RATE,SALES
   if IDNO=0 then exit endif
   TOTAL ← TOTAL + SALES
   CTR ← CTR + 1
endloop
if CTR = 0 then
   print 'no data entered'
else
   AVE ← TOTAL / REAL(CTR)
   print AVE
endif
stop
```

Figure 3.2

addition to the accumulation, we will perform other processing in the loop, and not every record will be included in the total.

For the same set of records used in the previous example, this time we want to write a program to print a report of commissions earned and to find the total commission earned by department 100.

In this problem, we will once again need an accumulator, this time to be used to calculate the total commission earned by department 100. As before, we will initialize this accumulator to 0 before the loop and print it after the loop. However, this time we do not want to include all the commissions, but only those for one particular department number. In addition, in the body of the loop we will need to calculate the commission for each salesperson regardless of the department number.

Here is the algorithm.

```
print instructions
TOTAL ← 0
loop
   prompt
   read IDNO,DEPTNO,RATE,SALES
   if IDNO = 0 then exit endif
   calculate commission (COMM)
   print IDNO, COMM
   if DEPTNO = 100 then
      TOTAL ← TOTAL + COMM
   endif
endloop
print TOTAL
stop
```

Notice that, in the loop we have a step specified as "calculate commission." At this time, we have not even specified how this commission is to be calculated. Let us use a function (named COMMF) to calculate the commission, and assume that the commission is based on the commission rate and the sales amount. The step "calculate commission" may then be refined as

```
COMM ← COMMF(RATE,SALES)
```

We have two variables which were not present in the first example. The first is the variable COMM. It is a REAL variable used for the commission. The second, COMMF, is the function which calculates the commission. (In addition, the variable TOTAL is now being used to accumulate the total commission in department 100 instead of the total sales.)

Now let us plan the function COMMF. We have already named it and identified its parameters as the commission rate and the sales amount. We have this list:

	Name	Type	Use	Comment
Parameters (Input):	RATE	REAL	Commission rate	First parameter
	SALES	REAL	Sales amount	Second parameter

Suppose the commission is merely rate times sales if sales is less than $250, otherwise it is 1.2 times rate times sales. Then the algorithm for the function is

```
if SALES < 250.0 then
   COMMF ← RATE * SALES
else
   COMMF ← 1.2 * RATE * SALES
endif
```

The complete program is given in Figure 3.3.

> **NOTE.** Either top down or bottom up testing could be used in this example. We could write a driver to test the COMMF function, then add the tested function to the untested main program. On the other hand, we could use the following simple stub for testing the main program's accumulation logic:
>
> ```
> REAL FUNCTION COMMF(RATE,SALES)
> REAL RATE,SALES
> PRINT *, 'COMMF called with RATE, SALES =',RATE,SALES
> COMMF = 100
> RETURN
> END
> ```
>
> Since the branching in the main program does not depend on having a "correct" answer from the COMMF function, this stub would work fine. When the main program is correct, we would replace the stub by the actual COMMF function.

To summarize, when we have a problem involving accumulation, we will need a special accumulator variable. *Before* the loop we will initialize the accumulator to

```
      INTEGER IDNO,DEPTNO
      REAL RATE,SALES,COMM,COMMF,TOTAL

C   WRITTEN BY *******, **/**/**

C   THIS PROGRAM PRINTS A LIST OF COMMISSIONS. IT ALSO DETERMINES
C THE TOTAL COMMISSION FOR DEPARTMENT 100.

C   IT USES TWO SUBPROGRAMS:
C       INSTR—A SUBROUTINE TO PRINT INSTRUCTIONS
C       COMMF—A FUNCTION TO CALCULATE THE COMMISSION

C   BEFORE THE LOOP, PRINT INSTRUCTIONS AND INITIALIZE

      CALL INSTR
      TOTAL = 0
```

(continued)

```
C   IN THE LOOP, READ DATA AND USE COMMF FUNCTION; ADD TO TOTAL IF
C DEPT #100

   10 CONTINUE
         PRINT *,'Enter i.d., department #, rate, sales'
         READ *,IDNO,DEPTNO,RATE,SALES
         IF (IDNO.EQ.0) THEN
            GO TO 500
         ENDIF
         COMM = COMMF(RATE,SALES)
         WRITE(*,1000) 'Commission for ',IDNO,' is ', COMM
         IF (DEPTNO.EQ.100) THEN
            TOTAL = TOTAL + COMM
         ENDIF
         GO TO 10

C   AFTER THE LOOP, PRINT THE TOTAL

  500 CONTINUE
      WRITE(*,2000) 'The total commission for department 100 is ', TOTAL
      STOP

C   FORMATS

 1000 FORMAT(' ',A,I5,A,F9.2)
 2000 FORMAT('0',A,F11.2)
      END

      SUBROUTINE INSTR
          (Left to the reader)
      RETURN
      END

      REAL FUNCTION COMMF(RATE,SALES)
      REAL RATE,SALES

C   WRITTEN BY *******, **/**/**

C   THIS FUNCTION CALCULATES THE COMMISSION

C   THERE ARE TWO PARAMETERS:
C      RATE—INPUT,REAL—THE COMMISSION RATE
C      SALES—INPUT,REAL—THE SALES AMOUNT

       IF(SALES.LT.250) THEN
          COMMF = RATE * SALES
       ELSE
          COMMF = 1.2 * RATE * SALES
       ENDIF
       RETURN
       END
```

Figure 3.3

0; *in* the loop we will add to the accumulator, if appropriate; *after* the loop we will either print the total or use the total in further calculations.

Largest and Smallest

We now discuss using a loop to determine the largest of a number of values. As a simple example, not directly related to the computer, consider the following problem. You (as a person) are given a large stack of cards each containing a number. You are asked to determine the largest number on any of the cards. You are told that the numbers could be positive, negative, or zero. How would you solve this problem?

Before reading on, stop a moment and consider exactly how you would find the largest number if someone handed you such a deck of cards and you had to sequence through the deck one card at a time. Try to be as detailed as you can in describing your solution.

There are a number of possible solutions to this problem. Perhaps your solution was similar to the following: "Pick up the first card in my left hand. Then repeatedly pick up one card in my right hand until I run out of cards; anytime that the card in my right hand is larger than the one in my left hand, I will replace the card in my left hand. At the end, the card in my left hand will be the one with the largest number on it."

If your algorithm was similar to this one, you have described a method for using a loop to determine the largest item in a list. We know a loop is involved, because you will repeat the steps of picking up a card and perhaps replacing the card in your left hand. You are using your left hand as a storage location for the largest value you have encountered so far and your right hand as a storage location for each of the other cards in succession. Before the loop, when you pick up the first card in your left hand, you are giving an initial (default) value to the largest value; if no other cards have a larger value, then at the end this one will be the largest.

It might be helpful to write this algorithm in the slightly more formal style we have been using for our other algorithms.

```
LARGE ← first value
loop
   NEXT ← next value (next card)
   if no more cards then exit endif
   if NEXT > LARGE then LARGE ← NEXT endif
endloop
print LARGE
stop
```

This is precisely the form of algorithm we will use whenever we wish to find the largest using a loop. The following example will illustrate this.

Each record contains a name and a yearly salary. Write a program to determine the largest yearly salary.

We will need the following variables:

	Name	Type	Use	Comment
Input:	NAME	CHARACTER*10	Employee name	
	SALARY	REAL	Yearly salary	
Other:	LARGE	REAL	Largest salary	Largest found so far, while looping; printed at end

The algorithm will be a special version of the general algorithm we used above to describe how we would find the largest number by hand.

```
print instructions
prompt
read NAME,SALARY
LARGE ← SALARY
loop
   prompt
   read NAME,SALARY
   if NAME = ' ' then exit endif
   if SALARY > LARGE then LARGE ← SALARY endif
endloop
print LARGE
stop
```

Observe how similar the process of finding the largest is to that of counting or accumulating. All three processes involve these properties:

1. A special variable is used to obtain the summary type information (count, or total, or largest value).
2. This variable is initialized prior to the loop.
3. In the loop, this variable is modified based on the values read. This may involve comparisons of various types.
4. After the loop, the summary value is either printed or used to determine other values (for example, an average).

COMMENT. We might notice that the two steps before the loop, which read the first record and give LARGE its default value, could actually be done in a single step

read NAME,LARGE

in which the first salary is read directly into the variable LARGE. Since this combination of steps can be confusing, we will leave the two steps separated at this time; in writing your programs you may, of course, wish to combine the steps.

In the preceding example, the quantity whose largest value we wished to find happened to be one of the fields on our input records. Of course, this need not be the case. For example, our record might contain the hourly rate and number of hours, and we might wish to find the largest gross pay. To do so we would have to calculate the pay for each person (perhaps using a function) and compare this pay with the largest we had found so far.

Another point which may very well have struck you as you read through the previous example is that it would be nice to know, in addition to the value of the largest salary, the name of that employee who has the largest salary.

This next example includes some of these features. Each record contains a student number and four test scores. We will write an algorithm to print a list of the class, consisting of student numbers and averages on the four tests. In addition, the program will print the student number and average of the person with the highest average.

In a problem of this type, in addition to having a variable for the largest average, we will need a variable for the number of the person with that largest average. We will call this variable LIDNO, but we must keep in mind that this does *not* stand for "largest ID" but rather for "ID of person with largest average." The complete variable list is given below.

	Name	Type	Use	Comment
Input:	IDNO	INTEGER	Student number	
	GRADE1	INTEGER	Test scores	
	GRADE2			
	GRADE3			
	GRADE4			
Output:	AVE	REAL	Average of four tests	
Others:	LARGE	REAL	Largest average	
	LIDNO	INTEGER	ID of person with largest average	

Before we write the algorithm, we should discuss the use of the variable LIDNO a little further. We already know that we will want to give LARGE a default value prior to the loop, and that in the loop if we encounter a larger average than LARGE we will change LARGE. Since at the end of the loop LIDNO should contain the ID number of the person with the largest average, it follows that as the program runs it should at all times contain the ID number of the person with the largest average so far. Thus, whenever we give a new value to LARGE, we should at the same time give LIDNO a new value. With this in mind, we realize that we should give LIDNO an initial value before the loop, and that in the loop we should change LIDNO precisely when we change LARGE. The algorithm can now be written. We must, of course, include the necessary steps for calculating the average from the four test scores and for printing the class list.

```
print instructions
prompt
read IDNO,GRADE1,GRADE2,GRADE3,GRADE4
AVE ← (GRADE1+GRADE2+GRADE3+GRADE4)/4
print IDNO,AVE
LIDNO ← IDNO
LARGE ← AVE
loop
   prompt
   read IDNO,GRADE1,GRADE2,GRADE3,GRADE4;
   if IDNO = 0 then exit endif
   AVE ← (GRADE1+GRADE2+GRADE3+GRADE4)/4
   print IDNO,AVE
   if AVE > LARGE then
      LIDNO ← IDNO
      LARGE ← AVE
   endif
endloop
print LIDNO,LARGE
stop
```

There are two further topics we need to discuss concerning the preceding example. The first is the matter of ties. Suppose there are two people in the class with the same largest average. Our algorithm will identify only the first person. (Why?) Although this can be fixed, it is relatively difficult to do, especially prior to studying arrays (Chapter 6). We will therefore ignore the possibility of ties.

The second topic is an alternate method which can sometimes be used in giving LARGE its initial value. To see its usefulness, consider the following two versions of an algorithm. We are calculating the net pay of our employees, and we wish to determine the person with the largest net pay.

```
read IDNO, other data
calculate NET
LIDNO ← IDNO
LARGE ← NET
loop
   read IDNO, other data
   if dummy entry then exit endif
   calculate NET
   if NET > LARGE then
      LIDNO ← IDNO
      LARGE ← NET
   endif
endloop
print LIDNO,LARGE
stop
```

```
LARGE ← -1
loop
   read IDNO, other data
   if dummy entry then exit endif
   calculate NET
   if NET > LARGE then
      LIDNO ← IDNO
      LARGE ← NET
   endif
endloop
print LIDNO,LARGE
stop
```

In the first version, we read and process the first record prior to entering the loop. In the second version, *all* the records are read and processed within the loop. If we think about what will happen in the second version, we realize that, since LARGE is given an initial value of −1, the first person's NET will be larger than this value. Therefore, during the first pass the LIDNO and LARGE variables will be given the values from the first data card.

In other words, since we are finding the largest of a number of *positive* values, we may give an initial value of −1 to LARGE. No initial value for LIDNO is needed, since this variable will not be used in any calculations prior to the point where it is given the value from the first card. On the other hand, the variable LARGE has to have a value when it is compared to the NET from the first data card.

> **CAUTION.** Giving LARGE an initial value of −1 works only because the very first NET calculated will be larger than −1. When we are working with negative numbers, or when we are finding the smallest in some list, we must use a different initial value.
>
> The general rule for determining an appropriate initial value will be based on the possible range of values in the list of numbers involved. Our initial value should be chosen to be smaller than the smallest number in this possible range. In this way, the first value in the list will be larger than the initial value, and LARGE will be changed to this first number.

Up until now, all our examples have dealt with finding the largest value in a list. Finding the smallest value is similar, with only two differences:

1. When we initialize our variable (perhaps called SMALL), we start either with the first value or with a number larger than the possible range of values.
2. In the loop, we change SMALL when we find a smaller value than the current smallest.

For example, this algorithm reads name, age, and sex code, and finds the name, age, and sex of the youngest person.

```
print instructions
SMALL ← 200
loop
   prompt
   read NAME,AGE,SEX
   if AGE < 0 then exit endif
   if AGE < SMALL then
      SMALL ← AGE
      SMNAME ← NAME
      SMSEX ← SEX
   endif
endloop
print SMNAME, SMALL, SMSEX
stop
```

Keep in mind that for a problem in which we are to find the largest of some value, and perhaps other information concerning the record possessing that largest value, we will need special variables for the largest value (say LARGE) and for all the other information we need concerning the record with the largest value. *Before* the loop we will either initialize LARGE to a suitable small value or we will initialize LARGE and all the other variables based on the first data record. *In* the loop we will change LARGE and all the associated special variables whenever we find a record with a larger value than that currently stored in LARGE. *After* the loop, we will either print the answers or use them in further calculations.

Finding the smallest value is similar.

Case Study #3 (Continued)

As a comprehensive illustration of the topics discussed in this section, we will modify the program written in Section 2.6 as Case Study #3. The main program for that case study appears in Figure 2.10, on page 148.

1. *Statement of problem.* Case study #3 calculated wages and state tax withholding for a number of employees. We wish to modify that program to report how many employees had tax withholding of $10 or less, who had the largest amount of tax and what that amount was, and what the average pay was.

2. *Preliminary analysis.* One of the advantages of modularity is that modifications may be restricted to only portions of the program as a whole. That is the case here. Our modifications do not change the methods for calculating the wages or the tax withholding, so those two functions will remain entirely unchanged. The only changes will involve the main program. (You might want to consider minor changes in the INSTR subroutine, but those will not be presented here.)

3. *Algorithm and variable list.* In a problem of this type, we need to plan for the additional variables needed. All the variables originally used in the main program will still be used. Here is a list:

	Name	Type	Use	Comment
Others:	LOWCTR	INTEGER	# with tax ≤ 10	Counter
	LARGE	REAL	largest tax	
	LCLOCK	INTEGER	clock # for person with largest tax	
	TOTPAY	REAL	total pay	Accumulator
	CTR	INTEGER	# of employees	Counter
	AVERAG	REAL	average pay	

The rest of our planning involves inserting the proper steps before the loop, in the loop, and after the loop, using our original algorithm.

4. *Test plan.* When a program is modified, it should be run again using the original test plan that was used when it was developed. This ensures that those things that worked previously still do work. In addition, we would want to devise additional tests relating to the steps we have added. Details of the types of tests needed will be covered in the next subsection.

5. *Write program.* The complete modified main program is in Figure 3.4. Again, note that the functions would not be modified.

```
      REAL HOURS,RATE,PAY,STATAX,PAYF,TAXF,LARGE,TOTPAY,AVERAG
      INTEGER CLOCK,DEPEN,LOWCTR,LCLOCK,CTR

C   WRITTEN BY **********, **/**/**

C   THIS PROGRAM CALCULATES WEEKLY PAY AND STATE WITHHOLDING
C IT ALSO FINDS SOME SUMMARY INFORMATION: NUMBER WITH TAX $10
C OR LOWER; WHO HAD THE LARGEST TAX AND WHAT THAT AMOUNT WAS;
C AND WHAT THE AVERAGE PAY WAS

C   IT USES THESE SUBPROGRAMS:
C       INSTR—SUBROUTINE TO PRINT DIRECTIONS
C       PAYF—FUNCTION TO CALCULATE PAY
C       TAXF—FUNCTION TO CALCULATE WITHHOLDING

C   BEFORE THE LOOP, PRINT INSTRUCTIONS AND INITIALIZE

      CALL INSTR
      LOWCTR = 0
      LARGE = 0
      TOTPAY = 0
      CTR = 0
```

(continued)

```
C   IN THE LOOP, READ THE DATA, USE THE FUNCTIONS TO CALCULATE PAY
C AND WITHHOLDING, AND PRINT THE ANSWERS

   10 CONTINUE
         PRINT *,'Enter clock #, hours, rate, # dependents'
         READ *, CLOCK, HOURS, RATE, DEPEN
         IF (CLOCK.LT.0) THEN
            GO TO 500
         ENDIF
         IF (HOURS.LT.0) THEN
            PRINT *,'Bad hours- ',HOURS,' -reenter data'
            GO TO 200
         ENDIF
         PAY = PAYF(HOURS,RATE)
         STATAX = TAXF(PAY,DEPEN)
         WRITE(*,1000) 'Clock # ',CLOCK,': pay = ', PAY,
     $                 ', tax = ',STATAX

C   ALSO IN THE LOOP, PERFORM STEPS TO COUNT PERSONS WITH TAX
C UNDER $10, TO FIND THE LARGEST TAX, AND TO FIND THE TOTAL
C PAY AND COUNT THE EMPLOYEES

         IF (STATAX.LE.10) THEN
            LOWCTR = LOWCTR + 1
         ENDIF
         IF (STATAX.GT.LARGE) THEN
            LARGE = STATAX
            LCLOCK = CLOCK
         ENDIF
         TOTPAY = TOTPAY + PAY
         CTR = CTR + 1
  200    GO TO 10

C   AFTER LOOP, PRINT SUMMARY INFORMATION

  500 CONTINUE
      AVERAG = TOTPAY / REAL(CTR)
      WRITE(*,2000) LOWCTR,' had tax $10 or less.'
      WRITE(*,2001) 'The highest tax was ',LARGE,' by clock #',
     $              LCLOCK
      WRITE(*,2002) 'The average pay was ',AVERAG
      STOP

C   FORMATS

 1000 FORMAT(' ',20X,A,I5,A,F7.2,A,F7.2)
 2000 FORMAT('0',I5,A)
 2001 FORMAT(' ',A,F7.2,A,I5)
 2002 FORMAT(' ',A,F7.2)
      END
```

Figure 3.4

Testing

It may require several runs of the program to adequately test a program involving counting, accumulation, or finding the largest/smallest value. Among the most important types of tests are these:

Finding the largest:
1. largest first (no ties)
2. largest last (no ties)
3. largest in middle (no ties)
4. all the same value

Counting:
1. no data input at all
2. data input, but count is still 0 for what is being counted
3. everything in the input list is in the category being counted

Accumulation: this is similar to counting.

It may help you understand these tests if you view them as the boundary answers to questions such as: 1. Where in the list is the largest found? 2. How many ties are there? 3. How many items are in the list of data? 4. How many items are in the category being counted or accumulated?

As we mentioned earlier, boundary situations are those which are most likely to yield errors in our programs. Hence, these types of tests are the most fruitful, since they are the most likely to uncover the errors that may be in the program.

Pitfalls

The most frequently encountered pitfalls in writing algorithms and programs using the methods of this section may be briefly described as follows:

1. Forgetting to initialize counters and accumulators.
2. Improper use of REAL in calculating averages. If a real average is desired, then REAL should be used to ensure real division.
3. Improper initialization of "LARGE" or "SMALL" variables. There are two choices. We may give the variable a value based on the first record. In this case we must be sure to also initialize any associated variables (for example, LIDNO) being used to maintain additional information concerning the record with the highest value.

   On the other hand, we may initialize based on the known range of values. If we do so, we should initialize LARGE (or SMALL) in such a way that the first record is certain to contain a larger (or smaller) value. If we choose this approach, the associated variables such as LIDNO need not be initialized.
4. Improper assignment statements. A typical error of this type is

```
if SALARY > LARGE then
   SALARY ← LARGE
   IDNO ← LIDNO
endif
```

The two assignment statements are both reversed. Remember that the variable to be changed should be on the left-hand side. Since we want to change LARGE and LIDNO, we should write

```
if SALARY > LARGE then
   LARGE ←SALARY
   LIDNO ← IDNO
endif
```

REVIEW

FORTRAN Syntax

No new syntax

Algorithms

Counting:
- Before loop—initialize to 0
- In loop—add 1 to counter, if appropriate
- After loop—print or use answer

Accumulation:
- Before loop—initialize to 0
- In loop—add to accumulator, if appropriate
- After loop—print or use answer

Finding largest
- Before loop—initialize to a "small" value or value from first record
- In loop—change LARGE and associated variables when new value is larger
- After loop—print or use answer

EXERCISES

NOTE. For any exercise which calls for a calculation without giving details of the rules to be used, do the following. Make reasonable assumptions concerning the parameters needed, and use a function call to do the assignment. In such cases, you need not actually write the function.

1. Code the first example in the ACCUMULATION subsection as a FORTRAN program.

2. For each of the following, determine appropriate initial values for LARGE for an algorithm to find the largest of the quantity indicated. Then determine appropriate initial values for SMALL for an algorithm to find the smallest.
(a) age
(b) age of elementary school children
(c) IQ

(d) salary of managers in a small company
(e) number of children in family
(f) numbers ranging from −53000 to +1700
(g) balances in checking accounts which just had an overdraft
(h) balances in checking accounts

3. Each record has a name and a letter grade (A,B,C,D, or F). Write a program to count the number who passed and the number who failed.

4. Each record has a name and a numerical average. Write a program which, for each record, will calculate the variable RESULT as follows: if the numerical average is 60.0 or higher, the variable should be given the value 'PASS', otherwise the value 'FAIL'. The program should print the name, numerical average, and RESULT for each person, and tell how many passed.

5. In a certain company, a bonus is based on the number of years worked and a skill code (a one character code). For skill level 'E', the bonus is $15 for each year worked. Write a program to read a set of records, each with name, years worked, and skill code, and print a list of the bonuses for persons with skill level 'E'. Also print the total of those bonuses.

6. Each record has an ID number, sex code, age, and number of children.
(a) Write an algorithm to count the number of females under age 21.
(b) Write an algorithm to find the average number of children for persons under age 25.
(c) Write an algorithm to find the age and ID number of the oldest person with no children. (Assume that there is such a person.)
(d) Revise part (c) to find the age and ID number of the youngest person who has children.

7. Each record has an ID number, yearly income, number of years worked for the company, and a four letter department code.
(a) Write an algorithm to find the ID number and yearly income of the person who earned the most during the year.
(b) Modify this algorithm to print how many years this person has worked for the company and his department code (this will require two more special variables).
(c) Write an algorithm to find the average number of years worked by persons in department 'TRNG'.
(d) Write an algorithm to find the ID number and income of the person who earned the least during the year.

8. Each record contains, for a single course, the number of credits and a letter grade (A, B, C, D, or F). There is one record for each course taken by John Smith during his college career. Write a program to calculate his grade point average. (A—4 quality points per semester hour; B—3 per semester hour; C—2 per semester hour; and D—1 per semester hour).

9. Write a program to handle all the transactions on a single checking account during a month. Input will consist of a single record with an account number, account type, and a beginning balance, followed by a number of transaction records, each containing a code (C—check, D—deposit) and an amount.

Output should be a table with each transaction and the resulting balance, as illustrated below:

```
ACCOUNT # 12345   BEGINNING BALANCE = 123.14   TYPE = R

    CODE                AMOUNT                BALANCE
    ----                ------                -------

     C                  150.00                 -26.86
    *** OVERDRAFT -- $5.00 CHARGE ***          -31.86
     D                   30.00                  -1.86
     C                    1.00                  -2.86
    *** OVERDRAFT -- $5.00 CHARGE ***           -7.86
     D                  100.00                  92.14
     C                   10.05                  82.09

                                  CLOSING BALANCE = 82.09
```

The following summary information should be given: number of bad checks, service charge for month (based on minimum balance and type), total of the checks not including the bad checks.

10. Each record contains name, four test scores, final exam, and quiz grade. Give an algorithm to print final average and resulting letter grade for each student. Also, tell who had the highest and lowest scores on the final exam, which of the four tests had the highest class average, and how many received an A for the course.

3.2 LOOP CONTROL: COUNT-CONTROLLED LOOPS

In this section we will consider mechanisms for counting the number of times the computer executes the body of a loop, and exiting from the loop after a certain number of executions. The basic approach is to use a counter variable similar to the one used earlier in counting the number of males, and similar problems. However, in this case we increase the counter by one for every trip through the loop, and we exit from the loop when the counter reaches some particular value.

We shall consider a few ways to organize our algorithms. Since such algorithms are quite common in practice, most programming languages provide a convenient method for coding them. In FORTRAN a special statement, the DO statement, can be used. We shall consider some special cases of the DO statement. The DO statement is actually fairly complex, and we defer a full discussion of it until Chapter 7.

Simple Loops with Count Control

We wish to write an algorithm to determine the number of rabbits that would be present in a given area after 15 years, if the number of rabbits doubles each year and there are 2 rabbits to start with.

Suppose we count the rabbits in a variable RABBIT and the years in a variable

YEAR. At the start we would have RABBIT = 2. After the first year RABBIT would be 4 and YEAR would be 1. After the second year RABBIT would be 8 and YEAR would be 2. This process would continue until we reached the end of the 15th year, and then we would want to stop. Here are three algorithms which we could write to carry out the calculations (other algorithms are possible).

```
RABBIT ← 2
YEAR ← 0
loop
   YEAR ← YEAR + 1
   if YEAR > 15 then exit endif
   RABBIT ← 2 * RABBIT
endloop
print RABBIT
```

```
RABBIT ← 2
YEAR ← 1
loop
   RABBIT ← 2 * RABBIT
   YEAR ← YEAR + 1
   if YEAR > 15 then exit endif
endloop
print RABBIT
```

```
RABBIT ← 2
YEAR ← 1
loop
   RABBIT ← 2 * RABBIT
   if YEAR ≥ 15 then exit endif
   YEAR ← YEAR + 1
endloop
print RABBIT
```

You should trace through each of these three algorithms and make sure you understand why they each work correctly. To make the tracing easier you might replace the 15 by a smaller value such as 3 or 4.

Notice each algorithm has a step before the loop in which YEAR is assigned an initial value. In the first algorithm the value is 0 and in the last two it is 1. They each have a step of the form YEAR ← YEAR + 1; this is usually called the **increment step** and the value 1 is called the **increment**. Finally, they each have a step of the form

```
if condition involving YEARS then exit endif
```

Note that the condition is different in the last algorithm. The placement of the exit step, the condition in that step, and the initialization steps are closely related. This fact is illustrated by the three different solutions to the rabbit population problem.

Each of the loops given above was a **count-controlled loop**. The decision on when to exit from the loop was controlled by the counting variable YEAR. It is possible to construct our own count-controlled loops, in forms similar to the three given for the sample problem. However, as we indicated earlier, most programming languages have a feature to automatically implement count-controlled loops. We will use the following construction in our psuedocode for such a loop.

```
loop for index = first to last
  .
  .
  .
endloop
```

Index is the name of the variable to be used for counting the number of executions of the loop. "First" and "last" are the extreme values the index variable will assume. In terms of this construction our rabbit algorithm becomes:

```
RABBIT ← 2
loop for YEAR = 1 to 15
   RABBIT ← 2 * RABBIT
endloop
print RABBIT
```

The meaning of the **loop for** YEAR = 1 **to** 15 is as follows: the first time through the loop YEAR will have the value 1; the second time through the loop YEAR will have the value 2; and so on. The final time through the loop, YEAR will have the value 15. As a result, the body of the loop will be executed exactly 15 times. Notice that:

1. there is no initialization step for YEAR;
2. there is no increment step for YEAR; and,
3. there is no **exit** step for the loop.

All of these will be taken care of automatically by the computer. In languages such as FORTRAN which contain this type of automatic count-controlled loop structure, we need only indicate what first and last values we want our **index** variable to assume. Everything else is taken care of automatically.

The DO Loop

The FORTRAN translation of the **loop for** construction is the DO statement. The statements

```
      DO 10 YEAR = 1,15
        .
        .
        .
10    CONTINUE
```

cause the statements between the DO statement and statement 10 (including statement 10) to be executed with YEAR taking on the values 1,2,3, ... 15.

The general form of the DO statement illustrated above is

```
DO label index = first,last
```

The meaning is, "Repeatedly perform the steps down to and including the one with the given label. The index variable should have the value "first" the first time through the loop. Each time through the loop the index value should be one larger, until its value is "last" on the final pass through the loop."

We generally place a CONTINUE step at the bottom of the loop, with the label indicated in the DO statement:

```
label    CONTINUE
```

The FORTRAN steps between the DO and its corresponding CONTINUE contain the code for the body of the loop.

For now, the index will always be an INTEGER variable. The first and last values will be INTEGER expressions (constants, variables, or more complex expressions).

> **COMMENT.** The DO loop looks more like our algorithm language than the other FORTRAN loops. We do not place a GO TO at the bottom of the loop. The repetition is implied in the statement DO label index = first,last itself. When the step with the given label has been performed, the computer system itself automatically:
>
> 1. increments the index;
> 2. tests for the exit condition; and,
> 3. branches back to the top of the loop if it is not yet time to exit.

Using the DO statement, we can write the following program to solve our rabbit problem.

```
      INTEGER RABBIT, YEAR

C   WRITTEN BY *******, **/**/**

C   PROGRAM TO PRINT NUMBER OF RABBITS IN AN AREA
C AFTER 15 YEARS IF WE START WITH 2 RABBITS AND
C THE NUMBER DOUBLES EVERY YEAR.

      RABBIT = 2

      DO 10 YEAR = 1,15
         RABBIT = 2 * RABBIT
   10    CONTINUE

      WRITE(*,1000)'After 15 years there are ',RABBIT,' rabbits.'
      STOP

 1000 FORMAT(' ',A,I10,A)
      END
```

Random Numbers

We pause momentarily in our study of the count-controlled loop to introduce the notion of random numbers. These give us many interesting applications where count-controlled loops are appropriate. They will also prove useful for examples and exercises in Section 3.3.

Many computer languages include functions which generate "random" numbers. What this means is that every time the function is used a value results in what looks like a random pattern. For example, the following algorithm might print the sequence of values 3, 2, 7, 4, 3, 10, 6, 8.

```
loop for I = 1 to 8
   VALUE ← RND(10)
   print VALUE
endloop
```

The numbers printed are all in the range from 1 to 10, and they might well be the result of spinning a spinner with 10 possible, equally likely values on it.

> **COMMENT.** These functions are sometimes called "pseudorandom number generators." This refers to the fact that the output looks random, but it actually follows a set (but complicated) rule.

The FORTRAN language does not contain a random number function. However, it is possible to write one, and many computers do supply similar functions or subroutines which can be called from a FORTRAN program. Throughout the rest of the text, we will imagine that such a function does exist, with the following form (see the previous example). Its name is RND, it is of type INTEGER, and it has a single integer parameter N. The value it returns is an (apparently) random integer in the range from 1 to N. Each of the possible values is equally likely to occur. Thus, the assignment statement

```
VALUE ← RND(10)
```

assigns VALUE a randomly chosen integer from 1 to 10, inclusive, and each value is equally likely.

Random functions such as this can be used to perform a variety of **simulations** of events in the real world that occur with randomness. For example, we may simulate rolling a pair of dice by the assignment

```
DICE ← RND(6) + RND(6)
```

Each RND(6) gives a value from 1 to 6, and represents one of the dice. The total on the two dice is placed into the variable DICE.

> **CAUTION.** For the simulation to be valid, each outcome must be equally likely. This is the reason for simulating each die by a separate call to the function.

For example, the following algorithm simulates an experiment in which we roll a pair of dice 1200 times, counting the number of 7's that occur.

```
COUNT7 ← 0
loop for I = 1 to 1200
   DICE ← RND(6) + RND(6)
   if DICE = 7 then COUNT7 ← COUNT7 + 1 endif
endloop
print COUNT7
```

When we write the corresponding program and run it, of course, we or someone else must write the RND function. However, we can write algorithms to solve problems which use random numbers even if there is no RND function on our computer.

Tables of Output; Headings

One possible application of the DO loop is to print tables. As a simple example, let us print a table showing the square, cube, and square root for each integer from 1 to 25.

In order to do this problem, it will be useful to know that we are allowed to use the loop index within the body of the DO loop (the algorithm's **loop for**). In our present problem, it is clear that a count-controlled loop would be appropriate. If we write

```
loop for I = 1 to 25
```

then the variable I will take on the values 1, 2, 3, and so on, up to 25, on the successive passes through the loop. As a result, this algorithm will work:

```
loop for I = 1 to 25
   SQUARE ← I*I
   CUBE ← I**3
   ROOT ← SQRT(REAL(I))
   print I, SQUARE, CUBE, ROOT
endloop
```

The first time through the loop I will be 1, and the program will print the number 1 and its square, cube, and square root. On the next pass, I is 2, so the number 2, its square, its cube, and its square root are printed.

> **CAUTION.** We are allowed to use the index in any way we wish: using it in calculations, passing it as a parameter to a function, printing it, and so on. However, we must **not** modify it within the loop body.

The FORTRAN code for this program is given in Figure 3.5. Figure 3.6 shows the output from running that program.

In a program such as this, which prints many lines of data, we might wish to modify our approach somewhat. As you can see in Figure 3.6, the repetitious messages can obscure the data. In this case, we might be well advised to change to a table form of output, where we label the columns once at the top of the page, rather

```
      INTEGER I,SQUARE,CUBE
      REAL ROOT

C    WRITTEN BY ********, **/**/**

C    THIS PROGRAM PRINTS A TABLE OF SQUARES, CUBES, AND SQUARE ROOTS

      DO 10 I = 1,25
         SQUARE = I * I
         CUBE = I ** 3
         ROOT = SQRT(REAL(I))
         WRITE(*,1000) 'Number = ',I,'. Its square is ',SQUARE,
     $           '. Its cube is ',CUBE,'. Its square root is ',ROOT,'.'
   10    CONTINUE
      STOP

C    FORMATS

 1000 FORMAT(' ',A,I2,A,I4,A,I6,A,F8.4,A)
      END
```

Figure 3.5

```
Number =  1. Its square is   1. Its cube is     1. Its square root is 1.0000.
Number =  2. Its square is   4. Its cube is    16. Its square root is 1.4142.
Number =  3. Its square is   9. Its cube is    27. Its square root is 1.7321.
Number =  4. Its square is  16. Its cube is    64. Its square root is 2.0000.
Number =  5. Its square is  25. Its cube is   125. Its square root is 2.2361.
Number =  6. Its square is  36. Its cube is   216. Its square root is 2.4495.
Number =  7. Its square is  49. Its cube is   343. Its square root is 2.6458.
Number =  8. Its square is  64. Its cube is   512. Its square root is 2.8284.
Number =  9. Its square is  81. Its cube is   729. Its square root is 3.0000.
Number = 10. Its square is 100. Its cube is  1000. Its square root is 3.1623.
Number = 11. Its square is 121. Its cube is  1331. Its square root is 3.3166.
Number = 12. Its square is 144. Its cube is  1728. Its square root is 3.4641.
Number = 13. Its square is 169. Its cube is  2197. Its square root is 3.6056.
Number = 14. Its square is 196. Its cube is  2744. Its square root is 3.7417.
Number = 15. Its square is 225. Its cube is  3375. Its square root is 3.8730.
Number = 16. Its square is 256. Its cube is  4096. Its square root is 4.0000.
Number = 17. Its square is 289. Its cube is  4913. Its square root is 4.1231.
Number = 18. Its square is 324. Its cube is  5832. Its square root is 4.2426.
Number = 19. Its square is 361. Its cube is  6859. Its square root is 4.3589.
Number = 20. Its square is 400. Its cube is  8000. Its square root is 4.4721.
Number = 21. Its square is 441. Its cube is  9261. Its square root is 4.5826.
Number = 22. Its square is 484. Its cube is 10648. Its square root is 4.6904.
Number = 23. Its square is 529. Its cube is 12167. Its square root is 4.7958.
Number = 24. Its square is 576. Its cube is 13824. Its square root is 4.8990.
Number = 25. Its square is 625. Its cube is 15625. Its square root is 5.0000.
```

Figure 3.6

than over and over with each line printed. We might obtain output something like that given in Figure 3.7.

What changes to the program are required to accomplish this? We will have to change the WRITE statement in the loop to print only the variables (with no messages). In addition, we will need to include WRITE statements to print the various lines of the heading, one WRITE statement per line. We will also include a PRINT statement to print a blank line after the headings. Naturally, all these steps to print the heading must come prior to the body of the loop.

A reasonable approach to printing headings is to treat this as a subtask, and to use a subroutine. We might call this subroutine HEADER. The revised program, complete with the HEADER subroutine, may be seen in Figure 3.8.

A few comments are in order concerning the HEADER subroutine. First, we use a row of dashes (minus signs) on the next line of output to achieve underlining. On many printers this is more attractive than using the underline character.

```
                     POWERS AND ROOTS
                     ------ --- -----

Number        Square        Cube        Square root
------        ------        ----        ------ ----

     1             1           1           1.0000
     2             4          16           1.4142
     3             9          27           1.7321
     4            16          64           2.0000
     5            25         125           2.2361
     6            36         216           2.4495
     7            49         343           2.6458
     8            64         512           2.8284
     9            81         729           3.0000
    10           100        1000           3.1623
    11           121        1331           3.3166
    12           144        1728           3.4641
    13           169        2197           3.6056
    14           196        2744           3.7417
    15           225        3375           3.8730
    16           256        4096           4.0000
    17           289        4913           4.1231
    18           324        5832           4.2426
    19           361        6859           4.3589
    20           400        8000           4.4721
    21           441        9261           4.5826
    22           484       10648           4.6904
    23           529       12167           4.7958
    24           576       13824           4.8990
    25           625       15625           5.0000
```

Figure 3.7

```
      INTEGER I,SQUARE,CUBE
      REAL ROOT

C   WRITTEN BY ********, **/**/**

C   THIS PROGRAM PRINTS A TABLE OF SQUARES, CUBES, AND SQUARE ROOTS

C   IT USES THIS SUBPROGRAM
C       HEADER—A SUBROUTINE TO PRINT HEADINGS AT THE BEGINNING

      CALL HEADER
      DO 10 I = 1,25
         SQUARE = I * I
         CUBE = I ** 3
         ROOT = SQRT(REAL(I))
         WRITE(*,1000) I,SQUARE,CUBE,ROOT
   10    CONTINUE
      STOP

C   FORMATS

 1000 FORMAT(' ',2X,I2,6X,I4,5X,I6,6X,F8.4)
      END

      SUBROUTINE HEADER

C   WRITTEN BY ********, **/**/**

C   THIS SUBROUTINE PRINTS HEADINGS AT THE TOP OF A NEW PAGE OF OUTPUT

      WRITE (*,1000) 'POWERS AND ROOTS'
      WRITE (*,1001) '------ --- -----'
      WRITE (*,1002) 'Number','Square','Cube','Square root'
      WRITE (*,1003) '------','------','----','------ ----'
      PRINT *,' '
      RETURN

C   FORMATS

 1000 FORMAT('1',15X,A)
 1001 FORMAT(' ',15X,A)
 1002 FORMAT('0',A,3X,A,7X,A,4X,A)
 1003 FORMAT(' ',A,3X,A,7X,A,4X,A)
      END
```

Figure 3.8

Second, we use a carriage control of '1' to advance to the top of a new page of output. This assumes that the output is going to a device which handles carriage controls properly (a printer, or a terminal which acts like a printer). The next case study, later in this section, examines some possible modifications for output going to a video type terminal.

Third, the subroutine is independent of the main program in the sense that any variables and labels it uses are independent of those in the main program. Thus it is permissible to use the format label 1000 in both the main and the subprogram, with no confusion to the compiler.

Fourth, we have chosen to include the column headers in the WRITE statements themselves, using X format to achieve reasonable spacing. Alternatively, we could have, for example, used

```
      WRITE(*,1000)
 1000 FORMAT('1',15X,'POWERS AND ROOTS')
```

placing the text string in the format statement. Which you do is a matter of your personal programming style.

Finally, we will routinely use HEADER subroutines in our examples throughout the rest of the text, without always presenting the code for the subroutine.

More Complex Examples

In this subsection we present a series of examples illustrating the versatility of the count-control (DO) loop. In many programs, the index of the DO loop is used strictly for count control. It does not appear in any statement of the program other than the DO statement itself. However, as we have seen in the previous example, the index may be used (not modified) within the loop body.

Suppose that in the previous example we had wanted the table of powers and roots for the numbers 101 to 125 rather than 1 to 25. As we plan the loop for the problem, we probably realize that the term "count control" is being used somewhat loosely. What is most important to us is not the actual number of times we need to go through the loop (25). Instead, we need a variable to take on the successive values 101, 102, 103, . . ., 123, 126, 125. However, the "count control" type of loop is exactly what we need since the index in a count-control loop does successively take on every value from the "first" value to the "last" value. We would want

loop for I = 101 **to** 125

for this example. Otherwise the algorithm remains the same.

In fact, we can let the user decide on the values in the table, as illustrated by this algorithm:

```
call INSTR
read LOW,HIGH
call HEADER
loop for I = LOW to HIGH
   SQUARE ← I * I
   CUBE ← I ** 3
   ROOT ← SQRT (REAL(I))
   print I,SQUARE,CUBE,ROOT
endloop
stop
```

COMMENTS

1. If the ending value is less than the starting value, the loop body is executed zero times. If the user chooses 50 to 20 as the limits, the table will be empty.
2. If the user chooses 1 to 100 as the limits, the output will span more than one page (or screen) of output. Techniques for handling this situation will be discussed in the next case study, later in this section.
3. The starting and ending values of the **loop for** may be constants, they may be variables, or they may be more complicated expressions. For example, these are allowed:

```
loop for I = 1 to N-1
loop for J = I+1 to N/2
loop for K = 1 to J+2-N
```

In FORTRAN, these might be written as

```
DO 15 I = 1,N-1
DO 100 J = I+1,N/2
DO 35 K = 1,J+2-N
```

Sometimes we would like the index of the **loop for** construction to take on successive values which do not differ by 1. For example, we might want it to take on all the even values from 2 to 48. If we write

```
loop for I = 2 to 48
```

I will be 2, 3, . . ., 47, 48, so this will not work. We would like I to "count by 2's." To accomplish this, we introduce the **step size**, or **increment**, portion of the **loop for** construction. By writing

```
loop for I = 2 to 48 by 2
```

we imply that I should increase by 2 for each new iteration of the loop.

In general, the **loop for** construction has the form

```
loop for index = starting value to ending value by step size
   body of loop
endloop
```

The "**by** step size" portion indicates the amount by which the index variable should be incremented each pass through the loop. If the step size is 1, as it has been for all our algorithms to this point, we generally omit this portion of the **loop for** statement.

The corresponding FORTRAN DO statement has the form

```
DO label index = starting value, ending value, step size
```

As in the algorithm, the step size may be omitted if it is 1.

Now let us consider a few examples of this concept. Using the **loop for** construction, find the sum of the numbers indicated:

$$3 + 7 + 11 + 15 + \ldots + 439 + 443$$

We want the index I to take on the successive values 3, 7, 11, 15, . . ., 439, 443. The starting value should be 3, the ending value 443, and the step size 4. We therefore write an accumulation loop, where the index I takes on these values and is the quantity being accumulated.

```
SUM ← 0
loop for I = 3 to 443 by 4
   SUM ← SUM + I
endloop
```

The FORTRAN code is easy to write.

```
      INTEGER I,SUM
      SUM = 0
      DO 50 I = 3,443,4
         SUM = SUM+I
   50    CONTINUE
```

Similarly, the following algorithm finds the sum of the odd integers (1, 3, 5, etc.) between 1 and 200.

```
SUM ← 0
loop for I = 1 to 199 by 2
  SUM ← SUM + I
endloop
```

COMMENT. In this algorithm, we chose an ending value of 199. To do so, we had to reason that 199 was the last value less than or equal to 200 which the index should assume.

However, we could have used an ending value of 200 instead. The index I would still assume the values 1, 3, . . ., 195, 197, 199. Since the next value for I would be 201, which is larger than the ending value 200, the loop would terminate.

To see how this may be useful, suppose the upper bound given above were a variable N. We may write

```
SUM ← 0
loop for I = 1 to N by 2
   SUM ← SUM+I
endloop
```

We need not worry whether or not N is even. In either case, the index will take on the proper values.

The preceding example illustrates the fact that, in working with step sizes other than 1, it becomes important for us to know more about how the count-control loop actually operates. The **loop for** construction's basic meaning is given by

```
index ← starting value
loop
   if index > ending value then exit endif
   perform body of loop
   index ← index + step size
endloop
```

Three consequences are:

1. The index might not actually attain the "ending" value. The term "ending value" actually indicates a boundary value. When the index passes this boundary value, the loop terminates.
2. If the starting value is larger than the ending value, the loop terminates prior to the first pass.
3. The value of the index, after leaving the loop, is the value it would have had on the next pass. For example, I has the value 17 after a loop beginning with "**loop for** I = 1 **to** 16."

To illustrate this, let us list the values taken on by the index for each of the following, assuming no early exit is taken. Also, tell what value the index has after the loop terminates.

```
loop for I = 1 to 17 by 3
loop for I = 16 to 24 by 2
loop for I = 11 to 33 by 7
loop for I = 14 to 10 by 5
```

The solutions are

for the passes:	value after loop:
1,4,7,10,13,16	19
16,18,20,22,24	26
11,18,25,32	39
there are no passes	14

COMMENT. The step size may be any variable or any expression. It need not be a constant. It may be either positive or negative, as indicated in the next example.

Sometimes it is convenient to count down rather than to count up. In this case we would like to have a negative step size. For example, to go from 100 down to 1, we might write

```
loop for I = 100 to 1 by -1
```

The index I will start at 100; each time through the loop its value will be decreased by 1. (Notice that, with a negative step size, the ending value becomes a boundary below which the index may not go; that is, when the index is less than the ending value, the loop terminates.)

Again, let us list the successive values assumed by the index for the following and tell what value it has after the loop terminates.

```
loop for I = 10 to 1 by -1
loop for I = 16 to 4 by -2
loop for I = 35 to 7 by -8
loop for I = 14 to 10 by -5
loop for I = 1 to 10 by -1
```

The solutions are

for the passes:	value after loop:
10,9,8,7,6,5,4,3,2,1	0
16,14,12,10,8,6,4	2
35,27,19,11	3
14	9
no passes	1

To illustrate the negative step size, we write an algorithm to print a table of feet and inches for values of feet running from 25 down to 10. We use a **loop for** with the variable FEET as index. For each successive value of FEET, we calculate the corresponding value of a variable INCHES.

```
call HEADER
loop for FEET = 25 to 10 by -1
   INCHES ← 12 * FEET
   print FEET,INCHES
endloop
```

As our final example in this subsection, we write a function whose algorithm involves a **loop for** construction. The function is to determine how many divisors a given integer has. The input parameter will be N, the given integer. The value calculated (NODIV) is the function name. It is of type integer. We will use a local variable COUNT to count the divisors.

The algorithm is simple. We will check each number from 1 to N to see if it divides evenly into N. This implies a count-controlled loop, since we want a variable to take on the values from 1 to N.

```
COUNT ← 0
loop for I = 1 to N
   if MOD (N, I) = 0 then
      COUNT ←COUNT + 1
   endif
endloop
NODIV ← COUNT
return
```

When the index I is a divisor of N, we increase the counter by 1.

This algorithm is easily coded in FORTRAN.

```
      INTEGER FUNCTION NODIV(N)
      INTEGER N,I,COUNT

C     WRITTEN BY *******, **/**/**.

C     THIS FUNCTION DETERMINES HOW MANY DIVISORS A GIVEN
C   INTEGER HAS.

C     THESE ARE THE PARAMETERS:
C         N-INPUT, INTEGER-INTEGER NUMBER

C     INITIALIZE

      COUNT = 0

C     COUNT CONTROLLED LOOP; CHECK EACH I FROM 1 TO N

      DO 100 I = 1,N
         IF (MOD(N,I).EQ.0)THEN
           COUNT = COUNT + 1
         ENDIF
  100    CONTINUE
      NODIV = COUNT
      RETURN
      END
```

Case Study #4

This case study illustrates another type of application of count-controlled loops. In addition, it explores additional possibilities involved with a heading printing subroutine. The case study will be modified and expanded upon in Section 3.3

1. *Statement of problem.* In its simplest form, we may state the problem as follows. A man deposits $100 in a savings account which pays 5 percent interest, compounded annually. We wish to print a statement showing the amount in the account at the end of each year for 20 years.

2. *Preliminary analysis.* The phase "compounded annually" means this: at the end of the first year, he will have the original $100 plus 5 percent of $100 ($5), for a total of $105. During the second year he will be earning interest on the entire $105 at 5 percent, so his interest will be 105 times .05, or $5.25. At the end of two years, he will have $105 + 5.25 = $110.25. Each year, his 5 percent interest will be calculated on the total amount in his account. We are assuming that he never withdraws any money from the account or adds any additional money to the account.

We are actually going to solve a more general problem. Instead of solving the problem for the fixed figures of $100.00, 5 percent interest, and 20 years, we will allow the user to input those values at the start of the program. For this case study we will assume that the numbers supplied are correct; in the next section (Section 3.3) we will modify the case study to detect errors in the input.

The form of the output table has not been specified in detail. We will use headings, with four columns of information: year number, balance at the start of the year, interest for the year, and balance at the end of the year. The beginning of the table might look something like this:

```
     Balances for interest rate = 0.05
Year      Start      Interest       End
----      -----      --------       ---
   1     100.00        5.00      105.00
   2     105.00        5.25      110.25
```

3. *Algorithm and variable list.*

a. *Main program* Our preliminary analysis suggests a subroutine to print headings; it also leads to the following list of possible variables.

	Name	Type	Use	Comment
Input:	BEGBAL	REAL	Beginning balance	
	RATE	REAL	Interest rate	0.05 for 5%, etc.
	N	INTEGER	Number of years	
Output:	YEAR	INTEGER	Year number	1, 2, etc.
	START	REAL	Starting balance for year	
	INTRST	REAL	Interest for year	
	ENDING	REAL	Ending balance for year	

Before the loop, we must read the input data. We will then call the HEADER subroutine to print the headings. Since the rate is to be included in the headings, it must be passed to the subroutine as an input parameter. (This is the same concept as an input parameter for a function, which we have previously seen.) We will also have to initialize START for the first year.

In the loop (which will be a count-controlled loop), we calculate the interest, add it to the starting balance to obtain the ending balance, and print the output line. The only subtle point is that we must then include a step

```
START ← ENDING
```

to assign the proper starting balance for the next year. Each year's starting balance is the same as the previous year's ending balance.

After the loop, we will print a line indicating "end of list."

The algorithm follows:

```
read BEGBAL,RATE,N
call HEADER(RATE)
START ← RATE
loop for YEAR = 1 to N
   INTRST ← RATE * START
   ENDING ← START + INTRST
   print YEAR,START,INTRST,ENDING
   START ← ENDING
endloop
print 'end of list'
stop
```

b. *HEADER subroutine.* The variable list and algorithm are very straightforward. The parameter, which we will call RATE, is a REAL variable. The algorithm consists of a series of print statements, printing the headings indicated in our preliminary analysis.

4. *Test plan.* We omit the test plan at this point. In Section 3.3, where we enhance the case study, we will discuss a test plan.

5. *Write program.* The main program is left as an exercise. The HEADER subroutine is given below. Notice that the techniques for using input parameters in a subroutine are identical to those in a function.

```
      SUBROUTINE HEADER(RATE)
      REAL RATE

C   WRITTEN BY *********, **/**/**

C   THIS SUBROUTINE PRINTS HEADERS, INCLUDING AN INTEREST RATE

C   THERE IS ONE PARAMETER:
C      RATE - INPUT, REAL - THE INTEREST RATE

      WRITE(*,1000) 'Balances for interest rate = ',RATE
      WRITE(*,1001) 'Year     Start     Interest     End'
      WRITE(*,1002) '----     -----     --------     ---'
      PRINT *,' '
      RETURN

C   FORMATS

 1000 FORMAT('1',A,F4.2)
 1001 FORMAT('0',A)
 1002 FORMAT(' ',A)
      END
```

6. *Modifications.* We briefly consider three possible modifications to the program. Some of the details will be left as exercises.

When the bank adds interest to an account balance, that interest is calculated to the nearest cent. The algorithm just given does not do so.

If we were merely printing the interest, we would not have to worry about this. A format such as F9.2 will automatically cause the number printed to appear rounded to two decimal places. However, since this interest is used in further calculations as we continue looping, we must also round the value in the INTRST variable. Failure to do so will gradually introduce errors into the calculation.

As a general rule, our programs should ensure that REAL variables representing money amounts which will be used in further calculations are rounded to the nearest cent. We therefore write a function (see the exercises) called ROUND which, given a real number representing dollars and cents, returns the value rounded to the nearest cent. The calculation of interest becomes:

```
INTRST ← ROUND(RATE * START)
```

If the value of N is large, the table we print will not fit on a single printed page. We therefore indicate some possible modifications to print a maximum of 40 lines of output per page, with headings on each new page. We also wish to print the page number on each new page.

To do so, we add a second parameter, PAGENO, to the header subroutine. We must call the HEADER routine several times while the program runs. There are a number of ways to determine when the routine should be called. We use the following approach and observe that we want headings when we are about to print the 1st, 41st, 81st, 121st, etc., line of output. Using the MOD function, we may express this pattern by observing that MOD(YEAR,40) has the value 1 for each of these lines. The modified algorithm is as follows, with the differences shaded:

```
read BEGBAL,RATE,N
PAGENO ← 1
START ← RATE
loop for YEAR = 1 to N
   INTRST ← ROUND(RATE * START)
   ENDING ← START + INTRST
   if MOD(YEAR,40) = 1 then
      call HEADER(RATE,PAGENO)
      PAGENO ← PAGENO + 1
   endif
   print YEAR,START,INTRST,ENDING
   START ← ENDING
endloop
print 'end of list'
stop
```

Since MOD(1,40) is 1, the first headings are handled automatically, so we no longer call HEADER prior to the loop. Notice how PAGENO is initialized to 1, then incremented each time HEADER is called.

As our final modification, we consider the possibility that our output is going to a video terminal. This would imply that we need headers every 15 lines or so, rather than every 40 lines. This change is easy to accomplish; simply change MOD(YEAR,40) to MOD(YEAR,15) in the algorithm above.

In addition, we modify the HEADER subroutine itself to wait until the user indicates he is ready before printing the headings for the next page. To do so, we use a local CHARACTER*1 variable READY, and we place the following code in the subroutine:

```
      PRINT *,'Enter any character to continue'
      READ(*,1000) READY
 1000 FORMAT(A)
```

Pitfalls

The major pitfall to avoid in writing count-controlled loops is misuse of the loop index. We are allowed to print its value, or to use it in calculating values for other variables. However, we should never change the index value within the loop. We should leave it to the computer system to make sure the index takes on the appropriate values.

In addition, we should not modify any variable used in calculating the "starting" and "ending" value for the loop. For example, in the loop which begins

```
DO 100 J = I+1,N/2
```

we should not change J, I, or N.

Two other pitfalls are related to coding the count-control loop in FORTRAN. First, there is a tendency to incorrectly place a GO TO at the bottom of a DO loop. Since other loops in FORTRAN use this explicit GO TO to branch back to the top of the loop, this is a natural inclination. We must remember that this, along with the initialization, the increment, and the **exit** from the loop, is automatic with a DO loop.

The second pitfall in coding involves the use of the **next iteration** feature. Consider this sample algorithm segment and its corresponding FORTRAN code:

```
loop for I = 1 to N
       .
       .
       .
   if K>5 then next iteration endif
       .
       .
       .
endloop
```

```
      DO 110 I = 1,N
         .
         .
         IF (K.GT.5) THEN
            GO TO 110
         ENDIF
         .
         .
110      CONTINUE
```

It is vital that we branch to the *bottom* of the loop. If our GO TO sends us to the top of the loop, we will miss the automatic incrementing and testing of the index.

Finally, there is a tendency, once DO loops have been studied, to use them for every type of looping situation. Keep in mind that the DO loop is designed for a special type of looping situation and is not appropriate for other situations. We should reserve its use for loops which use count control.

REVIEW

Terms

count-controlled loop
increment
increment step
index
random number generator (RND function)
headings

Algorithm Form

```
loop for construction
     loop for index = starting value to ending value by step size
```

index: a variable which will assume the values from "starting value" to "ending value"

starting value: the first value of the index

ending value: a boundary point; the loop terminates when the index passes beyond this boundary

step size: the amount by which the index will be changed for each successive pass through the loop

1. The starting value, ending value, and step size may be any integer constant, variable, or expression.
2. The number of passes through the loop is determined by the value of the starting value, ending value, and step size *when the loop begins.*
3. It is possible to have zero passes through the loop.
4. The step size is optional.

FORTRAN Syntax:

```
The DO statement

            DO label index = starting value, ending value, step size
                 .
                 .
                 .
      label   CONTINUE
    The step size is optional.

Input parameters for subroutine—same syntax as for functions
```

Pitfalls

1. Within the loop, do not change the values of the index or of any variables involved in the starting value, ending value, or step size expressions.
2. Loop not coded with GO TO at bottom.
3. **Next iteration** branches to CONTINUE step.
4. Use only where appropriate.

EXERCISES

1. For each of the following, list the values assumed by the index on each pass of the loop. Also tell what value the index has after the loop terminates.

(a) **loop for** I = −5 **to** 3
(b) **loop for** I = 1 **to** 7 **by** 3
(c) **loop for** I = 1 **to** 8 **by** 3
(d) **loop for** I = 7 **to** 2 **by** 2

(e) **loop for** I = 7 **to** 2 **by** −2
(f) **loop for** I = 17 **to** −4 **by** −3

2. Write algorithms for the following.
   (a) Find the sum of the first 87 integers.
   (b) Find the sum 2 + 4 + 6 + ⋯ + 2444.
   (c) Find the sum 1 + 3 + 5 + ⋯ + 211.
   (d) Find the sum of the first 200 even integers.
   (e) Find the sum of the first 200 odd integers.
   (f) Find the sum of the first 737 odd integers.
   (g) Find the sum of the integers between 100 and 500, inclusive.
3. (a) Write a function to find the sum of the integers between (and including) two given integers. Assume the first is less than or equal to the second.
   (b) Each data line contains two INTEGER numbers FIRST and LAST. For each such line, calculate and print the sum of the numbers between FIRST and LAST, inclusive. You may assume FIRST≤LAST. Use the function from part (a).
   (c) Each data line contains FIRST and N. For each line, find the sum of the N numbers beginning at FIRST. (For example, if FIRST is 17 and N is 5, the answer is 17+18+19+20+21 = 95.) Use part (a).
4. Write a function to find the sum of the first N even integers.
5. Write FORTRAN program segments for each of the following algorithm segments:

(a)

```
Y ← 0.0
F ← 1.0
loop for I = 1 to N
  Y ← Y + F
  F ← F * X/I
endloop
stop
```

(b)

```
read N
SUM ← 0
SUMSQ ← 0
loop for I = 1 to N
   read X
   SUM ← SUM + X
   SUMSQ ← SUMSQ + X * X
endloop
AVE ← SUM/N
```

$$STD \leftarrow \sqrt{\frac{SUMSQ}{N} - AVE^2}$$

```
print N,AVE,STD
```

The algorithm given in (a) computes the sum of the first N terms of an expression for Y = e^X. That given in (b) is a common method for computing the average and the standard deviation of a series of numbers.

6. Code the algorithm of Exercise 5(a) as a function.
7. Write a function which, given an integer N and a real number X, computes X raised to the

Nth power by multiplying X by itself the proper number of times. (It should be able to perform if N is 0, 1, or a negative number.)

8. Write an algorithm to print a table of feet and inches for:
 (a) feet from 1 to 30;
 (b) feet from 30 back to 1;
 (c) feet from 1 to N;
 (d) feet from N back to 1;

9. **(a)** Using the NODIV function developed in this section, write an algorithm for a main program which reads two numbers M and N and prints a table showing, for each number from M to N, the number of divisors.
 (b) Modify (a) to also determine which number had the most divisors.
 (c) Using the NODIV function print a list of all the prime numbers between 100 and 200.

10. Mathematicians have shown that the sum

$$1 - 1/3 + 1/5 - 1/7 + 1/9 - 1/11 + \cdots$$

gets close to $\pi/4$ as more and more terms are added.
 (a) Write an algorithm to calculate this sum out to the term 1/401; out to the term 1/4001.
 (b) Write an algorithm to perform the summation in the opposite order.

11. Write an algorithm to calculate $n!$ for a given n. ($n!$ is $n*(n-1)*(n-2)*...*2*1$)
 [*Hint:* Finding the product of the first n integers is very similar to finding their sum.]

12. **(a)** For an angle X in radian measure, we may calculate sin X by the sum

$$X - X^3/3! + X^5/5! - X^7/7! + \cdots$$

 Write an algorithm which, given X and an odd number N, calculates the sum out to the term involving X^N.
 (b) Notice that, in (a), we may reduce the amount of computation by calculating each successive term from the previous term. For example,

$$X^9/9! = (-X^7/7!) * (-X^2/(9*8)),$$

 and a similar pattern exists for each term.
 Modify your algorithm to incorporate this improvement.

13. **(a)** Write an algorithm for a function to calculate the "number of combinations of n items taken k at a time," whose value is given by

$$\frac{n!}{k!(n - k)!} \quad (n! \text{ is } n*(n - 1)*...*2*1)$$

 (b) The $k!$ in the above formula "cancels with" with last k factors in the $n!$, leaving

$$\frac{n(n - 1)(n - 2)\ ...\ (k + 1)}{(n - k)!}$$

 Revise your algorithm to take advantage of this fact.

14. **(a)** In this section we wrote a function NODIV which calculated the number of divisors of a given integer N. In this exercise you are to write a subroutine which, for a given N, prints a table listing its divisors.
 (b) Write a main program which reads a series of records each containing an integer. For each such integer, it should use the subroutine from part (a) to print a table of divisors of the integer.

15. Write HEADER subroutines for each of the following indicated sets of headings. Each line of the heading should be underlined, there should be a blank line between lines of the heading, and the last line of the heading should be followed by the indicated number of blank lines.

(a) First line—COMMISSIONS, in column 50.
Next line—idno, sales, low rate, high rate, actual rate, amount, spaced appropriately.
Two blank lines.

(b) First line—GRADE REPORT, in column 25.
Next line—name, section, average, grade, spaced appropriately.
One blank line.

(c) First line—ALPHABETICAL LIST OF EMPLOYEES.
Two blank lines.

(d) First line—THE HIGHEST TEN SCORES.
Next line—name, school, class, score, spaced appropriately.
One blank line.

Exercises 16–20 use the hypothetical RND function discussed in this section.

16. **(a)** Write a program to simulate generating 1000 random numbers in the range 1 to 10000 and to print the largest number generated.

(b) Write a program to simulate generating 1000 random numbers in the range 1 to 1000 and to count how many times the number generated matches the loop index.

17. **(a)** How could RND be used to simulate the toss of a coin?

(b) Simulate tossing a coin 1000 times and counting the number of heads.

(c) Simulate tossing a coin 1000 times and counting the number of times the toss does not match the previous toss.

(d) Simulate tossing a coin 1000 times and determining the longest streak of consecutive heads.

18. **(a)** How could RND be used to simulate a situation with equally likely outcomes varying from 5 to 15?

(b) How could RND be used to simulate a roulette wheel with numbers from 1 to 36, plus two other positions marked as 0 and 00?

(c) How could RND be used to simulate a situation with equally likely outcomes 3, 6, 9, 12, 15, and 18?

19. We can estimate the probability of a particular outcome occurring in a random experiment by performing the experiment a large number of times and finding for what percentage the outcome occurs. For example, if we roll a pair of dice 12000 times, and there are COUNT7 7's, then the probability of getting a 7 is approximated by COUNT7/12000. Using this idea, write algorithms for the following.

(Note: These can also be solved mathematically.)

(a) What is the probability that the roll on a pair of dice is between 4 and 8?

(b) If two people each roll a pair of dice, what is the probability that their rolls will be identical?

(c) If I toss three coins simultaneously, what is the probability that exactly one is a head?

(d) If you draw a card at random from a set of 10 cards numbered 1 to 10, what is the probability that it is an even number?

(e) If you draw two cards from the set of cards, replacing the first before drawing the second, what is the probability that both are even numbers?

(f) For the situation in part (e), what is the probability that the sum of the cards is at least 15?

20. Simulate an election in which candidate A is expected to receive 60 percent of the vote, and candidate B 40 percent. There are 100000 votes, and your loop should simulate each vote. (*Hint:* generate a random number from 1 to 10, with 1–6 indicating a vote for A, 7–10 a vote for B.)

Your algorithm should indicate three things: at how many times in the counting the vote was tied; what was the last time the vote was tied; and the largest lead candidate A ever had. Output might be similar to this:

The vote was tied 100 times.
The last tie occurred when counting the 917th ballot.
At ballot 93417 A was ahead by 21013 votes, his largest lead.

21. In this exercise we describe an example of a technique sometimes known as the "Monte Carlo" method. Consider the following diagram, with a quarter of a circle of radius 1 in a square of side 1.

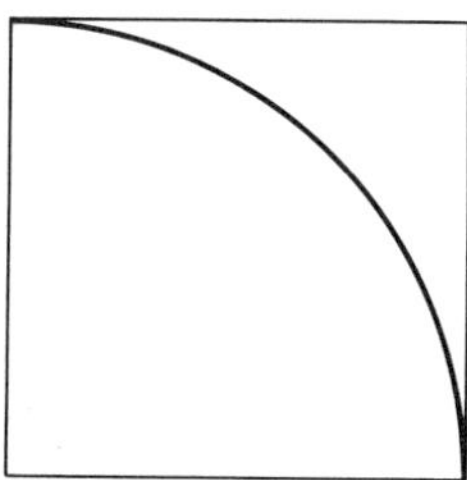

If we randomly dropped a large number of darts onto the figure, we would expect that the following ratio would be approximately true:

$$\frac{\text{\# in quarter circle}}{\text{total \# dropped}} = \frac{\text{area of quarter circle}}{\text{area of square}}$$

Since the area of the quarter circle is $\pi/4$, and the area of the square is 1, we get an estimate for π given by

$$\pi = 4\left(\frac{\text{\# in quarter circle}}{\text{total \# dropped}}\right)$$

We can simulate this situation by generating a large number of pairs of number (x,y) in the range from 0 to 1. If $x^2 + y^2 \leq 1$, then the point is inside the quarter circle. Write a program to estimate π using this technique. *Hint:* The formula

```
REAL ((RND(10001) - 1)) / 10000.0
```

will generate a real number between 0 and 1, inclusive.

Exercises 22–26 relate to Case Study #4.

22. Fill in the missing details (for example, write the main program code) and run the case study with all its modifications.

23. Modify the algorithm to print, at the end, the total interest earned.

24. Modify the algorithm to place an asterisk in the left margin for the first year (if any) in which the ending balance exceeds twice the original balance.

25. Modify the algorithm as follows. Instead of the number of years, the input record contains the beginning and ending years. It still contains beginning balance and rate. For example, a sample record might contain the values

1986, 2015, 1000.00, 0.06

The output should print the year (such as 1986) as part of its output line.

26. Modify the algorithm as follows (see exercise 25). The input record contains the beginning year and the number of years. It still contains beginning balance and rate. In addition, it contains an amount which will be deposited at the end of each year, after interest is calculated but before printing. Output should be as in exercise 25.

3.3 LOOP CONTROL: GENERAL CONDITION LOOPS

In this section we will examine some loops which use the "general condition" type of loop control, repeating the loop until some condition is met. We will explore further the use of a pseudocode description of a loop as an aid in the planning and writing of bug-free programs. Recall that the key ingredients of the pseudocode description of a loop are:

1. **loop** and **endloop** to surround the body of the loop.
2. **exit** to describe the loop control.

In general, the placement of the **exit** step will be in one of three locations: at the top of the loop, at the bottom of the loop, or somewhere in the middle of the loop. Many languages have a special form of loop command for the situation where the exit is from the top of the loop. This type of loop is frequently referred to as a **while** loop. In addition, some languages have a special construction for loops where the test is at the bottom of the loop, sometimes referred to as **repeat until** loops. There is no commonly accepted name for the type of loop where the exit takes place somewhere in the middle of the loop.

In FORTRAN, we do not have a special command for the **while** type of loop or for the **repeat until** type of loop. At first glance this might seem to be a disadvantage, and in some ways it is. As a general rule, commands which automatically incorporate complex logic make programming easier. We have seen an example of this in Section 3.2, where the DO loop of FORTRAN made count-control loops easier to code than they are without this structure.

However, there are also some advantages to be gained from this apparent shortcoming of the FORTRAN language. First of all, we do not have to remember which of the phrases "do while" and "repeat until" refers to which of the situations they describe. Secondly, all our general condition loops can be coded in identically the same fashion, even those where the exit is from the middle of the loop. Finally, loops with multiple exit conditions will be easier to handle as we will see in Chapter 5.

Our approach will be to use the pseudocode description of a loop, with the controlled flexibility it allows, in planning our loops. We will give a great deal of thought to the questions of what is done before, during, and after the loop; of what condition indicates that the loop process should terminate; and of where the **exit** based on this condition should be placed.

In this section we examine three important instances of the general condition loop: dummy entry, searching, and validating input. In addition, other examples using this type of loop control are presented.

Dummy Entry

We have, of course, been using dummy entry loop control throughout the text. Observe that this is indeed a special instance of general condition loop control, with the condition being that the dummy value has been supplied by the user. In this type of loop the placement of the **exit** step is usually obvious—it comes right after the value has been read.

A dummy entry can be used to indicate the end of one portion of the input rather than the end of the entire input. In the following example we have data consisting of two parts. The first is a list of scores on a test for one class, the second a list of scores for another class. How many people in the second class exceed the average score of the first class? Assume that a dummy score of −1 indicates the end of each class.

Here we will have two loops. The first will find the average of the first class; the second will count those people in the second class who exceed that average. Each loop will use a dummy entry exit.

```
TOTAL ← 0
CLASS1 ← 0
loop
   read SCORE
   if SCORE < 0 then exit endif
   TOTAL ← TOTAL + SCORE
   CLASS1 ← CLASS1 + 1
endloop
AVE ← TOTAL/CLASS1
HICTR ← 0
loop
   read SCORE
   if SCORE < 0 then exit endif
   if SCORE > AVE then HICTR ← HICTR + 1 endif
endloop
print HICTR,AVE
stop
```

Searching

We have previously seen examples of the use of loops for counting, for accumulating totals, and for finding the largest or smallest item in a group of data items. Another important application of looping is for what might be described as a searching process. For example, we might wish to locate a record in a file with an identification number of 3917, or the first record in the file having type O blood, or the smallest divisor of a particular number. In general, the body of a loop to perform a search will contain a step designed to obtain the next item to be examined, and a step to see if the item being examined is the one being searched for. If we know that there is only one item of the type we are looking for, or if we are interested only in the first such item, then this "step to see if the item being examined is the one being searched for" will be the step used to exit the loop.

Searching in a file or in an array will be an extremely important application. Both files and arrays will be covered in detail later in the text. We illustrate the nature of the searching technique by considering the problem in the context of a conversational program; however, the technique illustrated is much more applicable for files or batch processing, or for arrays.

> **NOTE.** Some of the examples in the subsection titled "Other Examples" may be viewed as searching problems of a slightly different nature.

For example, consider the difference between the following two situations. In each we have a set of data for potential blood donors to be entered, consisting of name, phone number, and blood type. In the first example, we want to obtain a list of all the donors with type O blood. We have a loop of the type considered in earlier sections:

```
loop
   read NAME,PHONE,TYPE
   if NAME = ' ' then exit endif
   if TYPE = 'O' then print NAME,PHONE endif
endloop
stop
```

This simple loop merely processes each data record in the entire set of data. If, on the other hand, we want to print only the name and phone number of the first type O donor in the data, we do not want to process the entire set of data; when we find the first O type donor, we will leave the loop. Here is the pseudocode for this second situation:

```
loop
   read NAME,PHONE,TYPE
   if TYPE = 'O' then exit endif
endloop
print NAME,PHONE
stop
```

Observe that, after we exit from the loop, we print the name and phone number of the donor we have located. Since the printing logically occurs only once— after we have stopped the searching process—this physical placement of the print step after the body of the loop is desirable.

> **NOTE.** In the example above, we have ignored the possibility that there is no record with type O blood. Strictly speaking, our loop should have another exit in case the data ends before we locate a type O donor. Thus we really need a loop with "multiple exits," that is, with more than one exit. **Multiple exit** loops and the techniques for implementing them are examined in detail in Chapter 5.

For the sake of simplicity, we will assume for the time being that what we are searching for does exist, so that our loop will eventually take the exit.

Validating Input

Perhaps you have heard the phrase "garbage in, garbage out." This is a rather cynical reaction to shortcomings that are often found in programs. The phrase indicates that if you supply the program with invalid data, you may very well get answers which are not to be trusted.

Unfortunately, that is an accurate observation for many programs in current use. There are many programs which make no effort to check if the data being supplied makes sense. While there is some excuse for this with beginning programmers, and while it is not always possible to anticipate every possible error in input, it is certainly possible to make an effort to avoid this type of lazy programming.

Already in this text we have indicated some techniques involved in "editing" the input—that is, making sure that it has an appropriate value. In this subsection, we examine some commonly used methods for examining the input as soon as it is read, and not proceeding any further unless it is valid. While this is not *always* possible to do (the validity of a code, for example, may depend on some calculation not yet performed), it is frequently possible.

If we consider an algorithm which contains a step such as

```
read LENGTH, WIDTH
```

we might replace this step by the step

```
read valid LENGTH, WIDTH
```

If we do so, it is apparent that we may view the task of obtaining the length and width and making sure that it is valid as a subtask. We might choose to write a subroutine to perform the task. This is a frequently used method for reading and validating input: place the steps involved in a subprogram. We will present our example in this context.

We begin with an algorithm for obtaining a valid length and width for a rectangle. To do so, we must decide (or be told) what constitutes valid data. For our example, we will assume that the length and width must lie between 0 and 9999, inclusive (0 is used as a dummy entry by the main program).

The fact that a loop is involved in this algorithm may be seen by considering that we want to keep reading the data until the user inputs valid data. When the data is valid, we will leave the loop. If it is not valid, we will print an error message and repeat the read. This analysis leads to the following algorithm:

```
loop
   prompt
   read LENGTH, WIDTH
   if data is valid then exit endif
   print 'invalid, please try again'
endloop
```

To write this as a subprogram, we need to learn about **output parameters**. A subroutine can pass information back to the calling program by using parameters. These parameters are called output parameters to convey the idea that information is flowing out of the subroutine back to the calling program. In our example, there are two pieces of information the calling program needs—the length and the width. Thus these variables will be output parameters.

The complete subroutine may be seen in Figure 3.9. There are several things to observe about that subroutine. First, the syntax for dealing with output parameters for a subroutine is identical to that for input parameters. (In fact, the FORTRAN compiler does not know which type they are. The terms input and output parameters are terms we humans use in describing how we are using the parameters.)

When the data is invalid, the subroutine prints the values that the user entered prior to printing an error message. Although this was not required by the problem description (or even the algorithm), it is a good idea.

The subroutine could be improved by having it tell exactly which rule (or rules) of the input was not followed. This is left as an exercise. In general, it is also a good idea to supply the user with printed or written material explaining what the input

```
      SUBROUTINE INPUT(LENGTH,WIDTH)
      REAL LENGTH,WIDTH

C   WRITTEN BY ********, **/**/**

C   THIS SUBROUTINE READS AND VALIDATES A LENGTH AND A WIDTH. EACH
C MUST LIE BETWEEN 0 AND 9999, INCLUSIVE.

C   THESE ARE THE PARAMETERS:
C      LENGTH-REAL, OUTPUT-THE LENGTH
C      WIDTH-REAL, OUTPUT-THE WIDTH

C   THE LOOP READS THE VALUES, EXITING WHEN THEY ARE BOTH VALID

   10 CONTINUE
         PRINT *,'Enter length and width (0-9999 inclusive)'
         READ *,LENGTH, WIDTH
         IF (LENGTH.GE.0 .AND. LENGTH.LE.9999 .AND.
     $               WIDTH.GE.0 .AND. WIDTH.LE.9999) THEN
            GO TO 500
         ENDIF
         PRINT *,'You entered these values:',LENGTH,WIDTH
         PRINT *,'Data was not valid, try again'
         GO TO 10
  500 CONTINUE
      RETURN
      END
```

Figure 3.9

rules are, and what the program will do if those rules are violated. This may be part of what is sometimes called a "user's guide" for the program.

We now consider what changes would be made to the main program as a result of writing the subroutine to **edit** (validate) the input. Actually, the changes are minor. In our example, we might have had an algorithm

```
print instructions
loop
   read LENGTH,WIDTH
   if LENGTH = 0 then exit endif
   AREA ← LENGTH * WIDTH
   print AREA
endloop
stop
```

The only step we would change is the read step, which would now become

call INPUT(LENGTH,WIDTH)

> **NOTE.** As is frequently the case, the main program and the subroutine are using the same names (LENGTH, WIDTH) for the two parameters. We remind you, however, that this is not a requirement of the language. If the person writing the subroutine had chosen different variable names, the program would still have worked the same. The parameter correspondence is by position in the list of parameters, not by name.

Other Examples

Write an algorithm segment to find the smallest integer (greater than 1) which divides evenly into N, where N is a positive integer greater than 1. For example, if N is 15, our answer is 3; if N is 36, our answer is 2; and if N is 17, our answer is 17.

If you were asked to do this by hand, you might come up with this solution: starting at 2, keep trying larger and larger numbers until you find one that works. Observe that you would have described a loop and the condition for exiting from the loop. In addition, you would have described an initialization step, with the words "starting at 2." To complete our algorithm, we must decide on variable names, and on what to do before the loop, in the loop, and after the loop.

We will use the following variables:

	Name	Type	Use	Comment
Input:	N	INTEGER	The given number	
Other:	TRY	INTEGER	The numbers we try, starting at 2	When we are done, it will be the answer

Before the loop, we must initialize TRY to 2. In the loop, we must perform the test for exiting from the loop and increase TRY by one for the next attempt. After the loop TRY will contain the answer.

There is one further matter we must consider; namely, the placement of the test for exiting the loop. In this example, *since we initialize TRY to* 2, we must place the test at the top of the loop, prior to increasing TRY by one for the next attempt. (This is true because 2 may divide evenly into N.) The placement of the test depends on the chosen method of initialization. This relationship between initialization and the placement of the loop control occurs frequently.

We now know the type of loop control we will use [loop until TRY divides evenly into N, that is, MOD(N,TRY) is 0] and its placement (at the top of the loop). We are therefore ready to write our algorithm.

```
TRY ← 2
loop
   if MOD(N,TRY) = 0 then exit endif
   TRY ← TRY + 1
endloop
```

This is an appropriate segment to code as a FORTRAN function. We will name the function LOWDIV; it is INTEGER. After the loop, we copy the answer from TRY into the function name. Coding the function is a relatively easy process once we have written a good algorithm. We must add the proper declarations as well as coding the loop in the standard manner.

```
      INTEGER FUNCTION LOWDIV(N)
      INTEGER TRY,N
C
C    WRITTEN BY ********, **/**/**
C
C    THIS FUNCTION FINDS THE LEAST DIVISOR OF A GIVEN INTEGER

C    THERE IS ONE PARAMETER:
C      N-INPUT,INTEGER-THE GIVEN NUMBER

C    INITIALIZE TRY TO LOW VALUE

      TRY = 2

C    LOOP UNTIL TRY DIVIDES N EVENLY

   10 CONTINUE
        IF(MOD(N,TRY).EQ.0) THEN
           GO TO 100
        ENDIF
        TRY = TRY + 1
        GO TO 10

C    AFTER THE LOOP, MOVE THE ANSWER TO THE FUNCTION NAME

  100 CONTINUE
      LOWDIV = TRY
      RETURN
      END
```

NOTE. We may view this example as a "search" loop, since it is searching for a divisor of N and leaves the loop when the first one is found. Compare this to the NODIV function in the previous section, which found all the divisors of N.

It might be instructive to look at the general form of search loops. We will consider only those where the test is either at the top of the loop or at the bottom of the loop. If the test is at the top of the loop, as in the previous example, we have a **while** loop of the following general form:

```
obtain the first item to be examined
loop
   if this is the desired item then exit endif
   obtain the next item to be examined
endloop
```

If, on the other hand, the test is at the bottom of the loop, we will have a **repeat until** loop of the following form:

```
initialization steps, if needed
loop
   obtain the next item to be examined
   if this is the desired item then exit endif
endloop
```

Some explanation of the "initialization steps, if needed" may be in order. The purpose of these steps is to ensure that the actual steps used to "obtain the next item to be examined" will, the first time through the loop, cause the first item to be obtained. In the example where we were searching for the ID number 11457, the next item was obtained by using a READ statement, and no initialization steps were needed. However, as the following example illustrates, we occasionally do need some such initialization steps.

Let us reconsider the problem of finding the least divisor of a number N. If we write the loop with the test at the bottom, we have the following loop:

```
loop
   TRY ← TRY + 1
   if MOD(N,TRY) = 0 then exit endif
endloop
```

In this case, the next value to be examined is obtained by the step TRY ← TRY + 1. To cause this step to obtain the first number to be examined (the number 2) on the first pass through the loop, we must initialize TRY to 1 prior to the loop. Here is the entire algorithm:

```
TRY ← 1
loop
   TRY ← TRY + 1
   if MOD(N,TRY) = 0 then exit endif
endloop
LOWDIV ← TRY
```

As another example, consider the following. We wish to use the RND function (introduced in the previous section) to simulate a game of chance. In this game, a pair of dice is rolled once to establish a "goal." The dice are then rolled repeatedly until the goal is matched on a future roll. The player pays $10 to play the game, and wins $1 for each successful roll that does not match the goal. Our algorithm will simulate one play of the game, printing the net results for the player.

The word "until" in the description of the game indicates that we need a general condition loop. Let us write the condition immediately, since we know what it is:

```
if ROLL = GOAL then exit endif
```

The game is over when a later roll matches the goal.

We now consider what must be done before, in, and after the loop. Before the loop we must set the goal variable, and set the player's money to −10 (to indicate he has paid $10 to play). In the loop we roll, add $1 to the player's money, and check for the exit. After the loop we print the results.

This analysis leads to the following algorithm:

```
MONEY ← −10
GOAL ← RND(6) + RND(6)
loop
   ROLL ← RND(6) + RND(6)
   MONEY ← MONEY + 1
endloop
print results
```

where we have omitted the exit step. We now consider where to place that step. Notice that the rules say that the person does not get paid for the roll which matches the goal. Thus, the exit step must be placed between the step which calculates ROLL and that which increments MONEY. A refined algorithm follows:

```
MONEY ← −10
GOAL ← RND(6) + RND(6)
loop
   ROLL ← RND(6) + RND(6)
   if ROLL = GOAL then exit endif
   MONEY ← MONEY + 1
endloop
case
   1(MONEY < 0) print 'you lost', ABS(MONEY)
   2(MONEY = 0) print 'you broke even'
   3(MONEY > 0) print 'you won', MONEY
endcase
```

Observe that some thought, plus a re-examination of the statement of the problem, was required in order to properly place the exit step.

Testing

In programs involving general condition loops, one type of test which is useful may be classified as an "error guessing" test. What this refers to is that we may guess (based on our own experience or perhaps that of others) that a particular type of input will cause an error. In this context, the type of input frequently used is input which causes the loop to exit on the first pass. For a "while" type of loop, with the exit test at the top, this input will cause the loop to exit before performing any steps.

Experience has shown that this type of input is likely to uncover errors in the program. For example, some value may have been initialized incorrectly.

To illustrate this, we might examine the function to find the smallest divisor of a number. When we look at the loop exit condition, MOD(N,TRY) = 0, we might suspect that having N with a value of 2 would be a good test. (As matter of fact, this would detect the possible error of writing an algorithm which initialized TRY to 2, then incremented TRY in the loop prior to testing divisibility.)

A similar type of testing is frequently used with count-controlled loops: choose data which causes the loop to execute zero times. In Case Study #4 of the previous section, we might test the program with an input of N (number of years to be printed) equal to 0.

In some cases it also makes sense to have test data which causes the loop exit to occur on the last possible pass. For example, if we search for a specific name in a file, we might run a test with that name the last in the file.

It may be useful to observe that this type of test may also be considered a "boundary" test in answer to the question, "How many times will the program execute the loop body?" The answer is "zero or more," and a test to cause it to execute the body zero times is a boundary test. If there are a maximum number of passes possible, a test of this condition is also a boundary test.

Case Study #4 (Continued)

W now consider two possible modifications to Case Study #4, based on material in this section. First, we will use a subroutine to read and edit the data. Second, we will print a table containing the balance for every year up to and including the year in which the balance first exceeds twice the original balance. Observe that this implies that the data contains only an initial balance and an interest rate.

We consider first the main program. The original algorithm and variable list are reproduced in Figure 3.10. We will make the following changes:

1. We no longer need the variable N.

2. The read statement will be replaced by a call to a subroutine we will name INPUT. There will be two parameters—the beginning balance and the interest rate.

3. The loop control will no longer be count control. However, we do need to print the year number, so we will use the variable YEAR as a counter which we will handle ourselves.

	Name	Type	Use	Comment
Input:	BEGBAL	REAL	Beginning balance	
	RATE	REAL	Interest rate	0.05 for 5 percent, etc.
	N	INTEGER	Number of years	
Output:	YEAR	INTEGER	Year number	1, 2, etc.
	START	REAL	Starting balance for year	
	INTRST	REAL	Interest for year	
	ENDING	REAL	Ending balance for year	

```
read BEGBAL,RATE,N
PAGENO ← 1
START ← RATE
loop for YEAR = 1 to N
   INTRST ← ROUND(RATE * START)
   ENDING ← START + INTRST
   if MOD(YEAR,40) = 1 then
      call HEADER(RATE,PAGENO)
      PAGENO ← PAGENO + 1
   endif
   print YEAR,START,INTRST,ENDING
   START ← ENDING
endloop
print 'end of list'
stop
```

Figure 3.10

4. The loop control will use an exit step.

```
if ENDING > 2*BEGBAL then exit endif
```

Because we are to print up to and including the year in which this occurs, we place this step right after the print step.

The algorithm and variable list in Figure 3.11 reflect these changes.

We now consider the design of the INPUT subroutine. It has two output parameters—the beginning balance and the interest rate. We choose variables called BALANC and RATE to represent these two quantities. (Notice that these names may or may not be the same as what the main program calls the same quantities.) We will assume that the beginning balance for this program must be at least $10.00 and no more than $10,000.00. (Even this latter figure is likely to lead to accuracy problems on some computers for which real numbers are limited to about 6 digits of

	Name	Type	Use	Comment
Input:	BEGBAL	REAL	Beginning balance	
	RATE	REAL	Interest rate	0.05 for 5 percent, etc.
Output:	YEAR	INTEGER	Year number	Counter
	START	REAL	Starting balance for year	
	INTRST	REAL	Interest for year	
	ENDING	REAL	Ending balance for year	

```
call INPUT(BEGBAL,RATE)
PAGENO ← 1
START ← RATE
YEAR ← 0
loop
   YEAR ← YEAR + 1
   INTRST ← ROUND(RATE * START)
   ENDING ← START + INTRST
   if MOD(YEAR,40) = 1 then
      call HEADER(RATE,PAGENO)
      PAGENO ← PAGENO + 1
   endif
   print YEAR,START,INTRST,ENDING
   if ENDING > 2*BEGBAL then exit endif
   START ← ENDING
endloop
print 'end of list'
stop
```

Figure 3.11

accuracy.) The interest rate must lie between 4 percent and 20 percent. In general form, the algorithm is similar to that of the earlier input routine.

```
loop
   prompt
   read BALANC,RATE
   if all data is valid then exit endif
   print error message
endloop
return
```

In this case, we will print a precise message telling what is wrong with the input. The subroutine is in Figure 3.12.

```
      SUBROUTINE INPUT(BALANC,RATE)
      REAL BALANC,RATE

C   WRITTEN BY ********, **/**/**

C   THIS SUBROUTINE READS AND VALIDATES A BEGINNING BALANCE AND
C AN INTEREST RATE,

C   THERE ARE TWO PARAMETERS:
C        BALANC-REAL, OUTPUT-THE BEGINNING BALANCE
C        RATE  -REAL, OUTPUT-THE RATE

C   ISSUE PROMPT AND READ DATA. IF VALID, LEAVE LOOP.

   10 CONTINUE
         PRINT *,'Enter balance ($10-$10,000) and rate (4-20%)'
         READ *,BALANC,RATE
         IF (BALANC.GE.10 .AND. BALANC .LE.10000 .AND.
     $          RATE.GE.0.04 .AND. RATE.LE.0.20) THEN
            GO TO 500
         ENDIF

C   ISSUE ERROR MESSAGE FOR BALANCE, IF BAD

         IF (BALANC.LT.10) THEN
            PRINT *,'Balance must be at least $10.00. You ',
     $              'entered ',BALANC
         ELSE IF (BALANC.GT.10000) THEN
            PRINT *,'Balance must not exceed $10000.00. You ',
     $             'entered ', BALANC
         ENDIF

C   ISSUE ERROR MESSAGE FOR RATE, IF BAD

         IF (RATE.LT.0.04) THEN
            PRINT *,'Rate must be at least 0.04. You ',
     $              'entered ',RATE
         ELSE IF (RATE.GT.0.20) THEN
            PRINT *,'Rate must not exceed 0.20. You ',
     $              'entered ',RATE
         ENDIF
         GO TO 10

C   RETURN WHEN GOOD

  500 CONTINUE
      RETURN
      END
```

Figure 3.12

Finally, we consider a test plan for the revised program. We will not present a complete test plan; however, we will discuss some pertinent issues.

This program would lend itself quite well to top down testing. The hierarchy chart has this appearance:

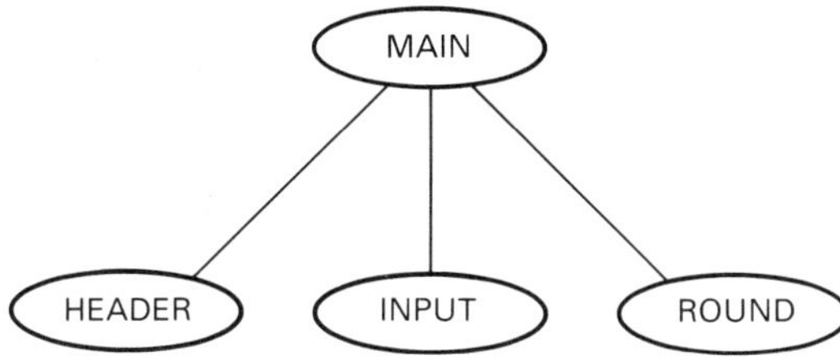

Each of the subprograms can be written as a stub. For example, the INPUT subroutine stub might include only the read, without the data editing features. The ROUND function stub could simply return the value of the parameter.

In testing the main program logic, there are a number of boundary conditions. For example, it would be good to run a test where exactly one page (40 lines) is printed, and another where exactly one extra line (41 lines in all) is printed. This may be difficult to achieve in this program—it would be easy to achieve in the original Case Study #4 (Figure 3.10).

A second boundary condition concerns the number of passes through the loop. By entering a rate of over 100 percent (possible using the stub INPUT routine), we can cause the exit to occur during the first pass.

Another boundary condition involves the exit condition. We would like one test where the balance is just less than twice the original balance, one where it is just more than twice, and one where it is exactly twice. Again, this would be difficult to do with the actual INPUT routine, but it is possible (by entering rates of 99 percent, 100 percent, and 101 percent) with the stub routine.

There are a number of important tests for the input routine itself. Obviously, there are four boundaries to be tested. In addition, it would be good to test various combinations, such as:

good balance, bad rate
bad balance, good rate
both bad
both good

Finally, at least one of our tests should enter good data when first asked, since this causes the loop exit to occur during the first pass through the loop.

Pitfalls

We have now seen three of the four general classes of loop control listed in Section 3.1: loop until dummy entry, count control, and loop until some general condition is met. For each of these situations it is vital to decide which type of loop control to use, and also to determine those steps which come before, within, and after the loop. The placement of the test for exit is also an important consideration. It is probable that in many problems the natural placement of the test will be at the top of the loop (a **while** loop) or at the bottom of the loop (a **repeat until** loop). (In some instances the choice of placement is dependent on initial values given to variables.) However, there are occasions where the natural and proper placement of the test is in the middle of the loop.

To summarize briefly, these are some important considerations in planning a loop in a program:

1. type of loop control;
2. what steps come before, in the body of, and after the loop;
3. placement of the test for leaving the loop

The pitfalls encountered in working with loops, especially general condition loops, generally arise from insufficient consideration of the three points listed above. In particular, we must be very careful in placing the exit from a general condition loop. This exit placement can depend on the initialization steps used, and it can affect the order in which steps in the body are performed. A careful rereading of the statement of the problem may be in order when deciding on the placement of the exit step. The most common results of incorrect placement are:

1. Execution of the loop body once too few or once too many times.
2. Performing some steps which should not have been performed on the last pass through the loop.

REVIEW

Terms

while
repeat until
output parameter

FORTRAN Syntax

No new syntax (NOTE: Output parameter syntax is the same as that for input parameters.)

Algorithms

Validating input (in a subroutine, frequently)

```
loop
   read data
   if data is O.K. then exit endif
   print error message(s)
endloop
```

Search loops

```
obtain the first item to be examined
loop
   if this is the desired item then exit endif
   obtain the next item to be examined
endloop

initialization steps, if needed
loop
   obtain the next item to be examined
   if this is the desired item then exit endif
endloop
```

Sample algorithm

```
loop
   read NAME,PHONE,TYPE
   if TYPE = '0' then exit endif
endloop
print NAME,PHONE
stop
```

EXERCISES

1. Each record contains an ID number and a numerical IQ score. The records are divided into two groups, with each group terminated by an appropriate dummy entry record.
   (a) Write an algorithm to count how many in the second group have an IQ higher than the highest IQ in the first group.
   (b) Revise the algorithm to also count how many in the second group have an IQ within 10 points on either side of the lowest IQ in the first group.
2. Write FORTRAN program segments for each algorithm segment. All variables are REAL.

(a)

```
Y ← 0
loop
   read X
   if X < 0 then exit endif
   Y ← X + Y
endloop
print Y
```

(b)

```
loop
   read A,B,C
   Y ← A * B * C
   if Y < 0 then exit endif
   print Y
endloop
W ← 0
```

(c)

```
T ← 500
C ← 1
loop
    print C,T
    C ← C + 1
    T ← T * 1.1
    if T > 775 then exit endif
endloop
print C,T
```

3. Each record contains ID, number of dependents, and marital status. Is employee number 645 married? Write an algorithm and program to answer "yes" or "no." Assume that employee 645 is present.
4. (a) Write an algorithm to print all multiples of 19 which are less than 642 (19, 38, 57, and so on).
   (b) Extend part (a) to write a subroutine which prints all multiples of M which are less than N.
5. I deposit $200 at 5 percent compounded annually. Write algorithms (and code into FORTRAN) to do the following:
   (a) Tell how many years it takes for the amount in the account to exceed $600.
   (b) Print the amount in the account at the end of each year until the amount exceeds $475.
   (c) Print the amount in the account at the end of each year for 9 years.
6. Modify each part of Exercise 5 to reflect a deposit of $25 made at the end of each year.
7. I deposit $10,000 at 8 percent compounded annually. At the end of each year, after the interest has been added, I plan to withdraw $1000 from the account.
   (a) Write an algorithm which prints the balance in the account every year up to, but not including, the year in which I am unable to withdraw my $1000.
   (b) Modify the algorithm to tell how many $1000 withdrawals I was able to make and also the amount that I could withdraw the final year.
8. Refer to Exercise 5a. Quite likely the amount will go over $600 during the final year. Modify the algorithm to tell how many years and days it takes for the amount to reach $600.

   Note: Assume a year contains 360 days, and that 1/360 of the interest earned during that final year is earned each day of that year.
9. Write INPUT subroutines to input each of the following lists of variables with the indicated restrictions. For this exercise, the error message handling may simply print a single error message "invalid data."
   (a) Name and sex code, where the sex code must be either 'M' or 'F'.
   (b) Four test scores, each of which must be in the range 0–100, inclusive.
   (c) A single integer which must be larger than 2 and no more than 10000.
   (d) Two integers which must both be positive and even.
   (e) A color code (3 characters) which must be either 'RED', 'GRE', 'BLU', 'BLA', 'WHI', or 'ORA'.
   (f) Three real numbers which must be in order from lowest to highest.
10. Modify the subroutines in exercises 9(b), 9(d), and 9(f) to have the error message tell exactly what is wrong with the input data.
11. Hand trace the following algorithm segment for the indicated input values for the variables I and J. Tell what values are printed by the print statement.

```
read I,J
loop
   I ← 2 * I
   if I>J then exit endif
endloop
print I
```

(a) 2, 4 **(c)** 0, 12
(b) 3, 14 **(d)** −1, 0

12. Each of these algorithms is supposed to print a table of powers of 2 which are less than or equal to N, where N is known to be at least 2. By hand tracing with different values of N, determine whether or not they are correct.

(a)
```
read N
I ← 0
P ← 1
loop
   print I, P
   if P > N then exit endif
   I ← I + 1
   P ← P * 2
endloop
```

(b)
```
read N
I ← 0
P ← 1
loop
   if P > N then exit endif
   print I, P
   I ← I + 1
   P ← P * 2
endloop
```

(c)
```
read N
I ← 0
P ← 1
S ← 0
loop
   if P > N then exit endif
   print I, P
   I ← I + 1
   S ← S + P
   P ← S + 1
endloop
```

13. Write an algorithm which generates a series of random numbers in the range 1 to 10, counting how many numbers must be generated until two consecutive numbers are the same.

14. Write an algorithm which simulates rolling a pair of dice until a 5, 6, or 7 is rolled. If it took an even number of rolls and a 5 or 7 occurred, it should print a message "you win"; otherwise it should print a message "you lose."

15. (a) Write a function with two parameters N and TOTAL. The function should count how many random numbers in the range 1 to N must be generated to obtain a sum of the numbers generated which is greater than TOTAL.

(b) By placing the call to the function in part (a) in a loop which is executed 15000 times, calculate the average number of random numbers which must be generated in the range 1 to 100 to obtain a sum greater than 500.

16. Write an algorithm for a program which generates a random number in the range 1 to 1000, then asks the user to guess the number. The program should terminate with a message telling how many tries it took the user to guess the number. For incorrect guesses, it should print a message "too high" or "too low."

17. By thinking about your guessing strategy for exercise 16, write an algorithm for a program in which the computer tries to guess what number the user is thinking of. *HINT:* The program might want to keep track of a range in which it knows the answer lies.

18. In this section we wrote a function LOWDIV(N), which found the smallest divisor (other than 1) of a number N. Using a similar idea, write a function HIDIV(N) which finds the largest divisor (other than N itself) of a number N. *HINT:* Start high and work your way down; then the first divisor found will be the largest.

19. Using an idea similar to that in the LOWDIV function of this section, write a function GCD(M,N). The input parameters are positive integers. The answer is the "greatest common divisor" of M and N. That is, it is the largest number which divides evenly into both M and N. *HINT:* Start at the smaller of M and N, and work your way down.

20. (See exercise 19.) Write a function LCM(M,N) which finds the "least common multiple" of M and N. This is the smallest number into which both M and N divide evenly.

21. The algorithm suggested in exercise 19 for the greatest common divisor of M and N runs very slowly for large values of M and N. There are a number of better algorithms. Probably the most popular and fastest algorithm for calculating the GCD of two positive integers is an algorithm credited to Euclid. One form of Euclid's algorithm is

```
if M > N then
   BIG ← M
   SMALL ← N
else
   BIG ← N
   SMALL ← M
endif
loop
   R ← MOD(BIG,SMALL)
   if R = 0 then exit endif
   BIG ← SMALL
   SMALL ← R
endloop
GCD ← SMALL
```

(a) Hand trace this algorithm for the following pairs of numbers:

i. 45, 10	**iv.** 105, 32
ii. 10, 45	**v.** 10000, 4994
iii. 100, 48	**vi.** 500, 735

(b) Code the algorithm as a function.

(c) Temporarily modify each of the functions in exercises 19 and 21(b) to count and print the number of assignment statements executed. Write a main program which inputs a series of pairs of numbers and calls each function. Compare the speed of the two functions in terms of the number of assignment statements.

22. Give test plans for the following exercises.

(a) Exercise 1a	**(f)** Exercise 9e
(b) Exercise 3	**(g)** Exercise 9f
(c) Exercise 4b	**(h)** Exercise 17

(d) Exercise 9b **(i)** Exercise 18
(e) Exercise 9d **(j)** Exercise 19 (or 21)

23. Do the following for Case Study #4, as modified in this section.
   (a) Print the line of output for every year up to, but not including, the year in which the balance first exceeds twice the original balance.
   (b) Modify the input record to contain a beginning balance, an interest rate, and an ending balance. The output should print information up to and including the year in which the balance exceeds the ending balance indicated on the input record.
   (c) Give a test plan for part (b).

3.4 ANTIBUGGING, DEBUGGING, AND TESTING

Many sections of a textbook represent material to be mastered, perhaps through memorization, preferably through concentrated practice and understanding. In the view of the authors, many sections in this book fall into that category. For example, we believe that you should come to thoroughly understand counting applications; if you are asked to do any problem which involves counting, the techniques involved should be fairly automatic.

This section has a somewhat different flavor. In it we attempt to gather together some ideas which will aid you in writing correct programs and in feeling confident that they are correct. The section does not cover any new algorithmic techniques as such. We will not be learning how to search through a file or how to find the largest of a set of numbers. However, the section does contain some techniques and ideas which can form a part of your program development style, no matter what the specific program is designed to accomplish.

In some of your early programs, the program logic was relatively simple. On the other hand, all the rules about how to write the FORTRAN statements were new and perhaps confusing. As a result, your programs may have generated many "compiler" error messages. (This type of error includes, for example, such things as forgetting the final parenthesis in a FORMAT statement, leaving out the continuation indicator on a continuation line, or misspelling the word INTEGER in a declaration.) It is possible that, once you got past the list of errors generated by the compiler and your misunderstandings about the FORTRAN language, your programs ran correctly.

By this time, on the other hand, your programs are becoming more complex, but you are becoming familiar with the FORTRAN language. It is possible that you are able to resolve compiler-generated errors with little difficulty. However, you may be discovering that, even with "no errors" (that is, no compiler-detected errors), the program just is not doing what it should. In the first subsection, we discuss antibugging and debugging, two related techniques which seek to avoid this situation, or to allow you to correct this situation as easily as possible.

The second subsection is on program testing. We have included sections on this topic from time to time in the text, and we will continue to do so. Here we attempt to organize some of the ideas into a single summary discussion of program testing.

Antibugging and Debugging

We begin with two related concepts: antibugging and debugging. Both terms come from the common use of the word **bug** to describe an error in a computer program. They tend to relate to the types of errors which occur after you have obtained a "clean compile." That is, errors which the compiler detects are not the primary subject of this section. Those errors can generally be fixed by careful examination of the subject line of code, comparing it to the required syntax (form) for that type of statement. The errors we are discussing are the more subtle errors, which frequently require more work to uncover.

The purpose of antibugging is to avoid bugs, and the purpose of debugging is to help you uncover and remove those bugs which do occur. The two concepts are closely related. Of course, if the antibugging is done sufficiently well, then no debugging is necessary! In a way, debugging may be thought of as adding more antibugging to the system to flush out those bugs which the original antibugging was not sufficient to prevent.

We will cover these concepts by presenting a list of ideas which may be useful, either in antibugging or in debugging. Where it is appropriate, we will indicate differences between using the ideas for antibugging and using them for debugging. Following the list, we discuss a few issues which arise when using these ideas.

1. *Awareness of pitfalls.* This is emphasized throughout the text. By being aware of what some common errors are, we can avoid making those errors. This is a form of antibugging. On the other hand, if errors do occur, we may review the known pitfalls to see if we have made any of the common errors and to see if the particular pitfall accounts for the observed behavior of the program. This is a form of debugging.

2. *Hand tracing.* This refers to "playing computer" and executing the algorithm by hand. It is especially useful for general condition loops, to determine the proper spot to place the exit step. However, it can be useful in almost any algorithm.

Deciding on the data to hand trace is in some ways similar to deciding on test data. We want to use that data which is most likely to uncover any errors, just as we do in testing.

It is sometimes useful to hand trace a slightly modified form of an algorithm. For example, if an output table is to contain 40 lines per page, it could take a long time to hand trace enough to make sure that exactly 40 lines are printed prior to moving to a new page. We might want to write and hand trace the same algorithm, but modified to print 3 lines per page. If the modified algorithm works correctly, we can expect that the original algorithm will also work.

3. *Echo printing of input.* This is especially pertinent for a program which uses formatted reads. For example, we might enter

40 50

as two test scores for a student, expecting a final grade of 'F'. If the final grade is 'A' instead, we could spend quite a bit of time examining the section of the program which calculates the letter grade. The error, however, might simply be that our input data has not matched the required format, and the computer has read the values as 400 and 500. (In formatted reads, blanks are treated as zeros if they are in the field being read.) To avoid this type of problem, we could always echo print all input into the program. This would be antibugging. Alternatively, we could insert such echo prints when errors do occur. This would be debugging.

4. *Edit (validate) input.* This topic was discussed in Section 3.3. If we check all input for correctness and reasonableness, we can avoid many problems. For example, the error described in the previous paragraph would be uncovered by an input subroutine which made sure that the grades were in the proper 0 to 100 range.

In our discussion of testing, we have indicated that input routines might initially be written as stubs which do not yet perform the error checking. It would probably be a good idea for those stubs to at least echo print the input.

5. *Diagnostic prints (trace prints).* This idea expands upon the idea of echo printing the input. Trace prints are print statements which trace the execution of the program. A few examples are as follows:

a. If the program does many complex calculations, it might be desirable to print the partial answers as they are calculated. For example, in a function which calculates the total taxes for an individual, each specific tax could be printed as soon as it is calculated. The print statement could use a variable name, as in

```
PRINT *,'STATAX = ',STATAX
```

or a more meaningful message as in

```
PRINT *,'State tax = ',STATAX
```

Which you use is up to you; the output from these print statements will not be seen by the final user of the program.

b. Trace prints can be useful in examining the progress of a loop. For example, if the only output in Case Study #4 had been an indication of how many years it took for the money in the savings account to double, we might put a trace print within the loop body to print the balance as it grows. Similarly, a program to locate a particular name in a file might print each name that it reads within the search loop.

c. Trace prints are frequently used in programs which involve a number of subprograms. They might consist of a print statement at the beginning of each subprogram and one at the end of each. The one at the beginning might print a message saying "entering subprogram xxxxx", where xxxxx is the subprogram name. This trace print might also print the value of all input parameters. (This is similar to echo printing all user input.) The print statement at the end could print a message "leaving subprogram xxxxx" and print the input parameters and the output parameters. (Printing the input parameters verifies that they have not been distorted by the subprogram.)

For the trace prints to aid our error detection, we would compare the output to that we expect to obtain. This implies that we are hand tracing the program or algorithm to determine what to expect. By seeing exactly where the output begins to differ from what we expect, we can focus in on the portion of the program which is causing the error.

The term "diagnostic prints" which is frequently used to describe trace prints conveys the idea of using these prints as a debugging tool, to "diagnose" errors. Many people, however, do not wait until errors occur; they routinely include trace prints in all their programs.

> **NOTE.** Programs which involve random numbers may need trace prints even to know if the answer is correct. For example, if the program is supposed to count the number of 7's rolled in a dice simulation, we should print each dice roll to check the answer. (Of course, we might temporarily modify the program to perform the simulation only 10-20 times rather than 12000 times.)

The various prints (echo prints of input, trace prints) raise an important issue. There may very well be differences between the program during development and the program as delivered. The extra prints are useful in uncovering and fixing bugs, but the person who is running the finished program certainly does not want to see them. She is interested only in the final answer, not in all the details on how the program reached that answer. Thus, the final version must not print the trace messages.

There are several ways to remove the extra print statements. The simplest way is to delete them. However, this is disadvantageous in that if they are needed later (for example, when modifications are made to the program) they must be done over. Another alternative frequently used is to "comment them out." This means to change the first character of the line to a 'C' to make the line into a comment line. If the prints are needed again, the 'C' can be changed back to a space to reactivate the print statement. A variation of this might involve changing the first several characters to 'C', as illustrated here:

```
CCCCCCC     PRINT *,'AREA=',AREA
```

This makes them stand out more, and thus they are easier to locate when they need to be reactivated. In addition, they appear different from ordinary comments.

Other possibilities for handling this problem exist; some will be discussed in later sections.

> **COMMENT.** If the print statements are going to be left in the program as comments, they should not interrupt the indentation pattern of the program.

Testing

In this subsection we summarize a number of testing concepts, most of which have been presented in more detail earlier in the text. Since whole textbooks have been written on the subject, our treatment here will obviously be on an elementary level. By the time you finish the course which uses this text, you will not be an expert tester. (Of course, neither will you be an expert programmer. Each skill will require further development in later courses and experience.) However, you can be aware of the need for testing and have some ability to come up with a reasonable test plan for the types of programs you are writing.

We should emphasize that the purpose of testing is to find bugs. For some (perhaps most) people, testing is psychologically difficult—they do not really want to find bugs in the program they have just developed so carefully. For that reason, many companies which develop computer software have groups whose primary job is to test the programs written by other people. In the context of a programming course, however, you will generally be doing your own testing. It may help to adopt the attitude, when a test case indicates a problem, that the bug was there and would probably have been noticed by the person grading the program. The fact that your test uncovered the bug is therefore a benefit, not something to get upset about.

We begin with some general testing concepts. This is followed by a few specific pointers for testing programs which use some of the "standard" algorithmic concepts we study, such as counting and searching. Finally, top down and bottom up testing are discussed. Further explanations of all these topics may be found in the various TESTING subsections throughout the text.

1. *Check your answers.* Some of the test cases should contain data for which the correct answer is easily determined, preferably without using a calculator. This will allow you to see at a glance whether there are obvious bugs in the program. However, this does not imply that you should ignore the other test cases. After you have verified that the program is working correctly for those cases which are easy to check, you should check all the answers. NEVER STOP WORK ON A PROGRAM FOR WHICH THERE ARE KNOWN ERRORS. Some of the techniques described in the previous subsection may be helpful in tracking down and removing the bugs.

2. *Class testing.* This is sometimes referred to as branch testing, since it frequently relates to branching in the program. For example, when a program contains a decision structure

```
case
   1(VALUE < 1000) RATE ← .04
   2(VALUE < 5000) RATE ← .07
   3(any other) RATE ← .10
endcase
```

we may identify three branches or classes for the variable VALUE: under 1000; 1000 or greater but less than 5000; 5000 or greater.

However, we generally should base our analysis of what classes there are on the problem description in addition to, or instead of, the actual algorithm. Even if the programmer found some way to calculate the RATE without using a decision structure, the testing should treat the calculation of RATE as one involving three classes for VALUE. As a simple example, in rounding a real number to the nearest integer, we may identify two classes of input: input with fractions less than .5 and input with fractions .5 or greater. The rounding process treats these two classes of input differently, so we want to test both classes. The fact that the formula INT(X+.5) is used rather than a decision structure does not change the need for that testing.

Class testing frequently involves ranges of values, as in the previous example. It sometimes involves specific values rather than ranges. For example, if the price of a window depends upon its color, we might identify these classes for the color: white; brown; cream; etc.

In class testing, we want to include test cases which exercise each identifiable class. In fact, if the class consists of a range of values, we should generally include a number of realistic, randomly chosen values within that class.

3. *Bad data.* In the previous example which calculated the variable RATE, we actually missed at least one important class: VALUE less than 0. This represents an error class for which the program should ideally generate some sort of error message. In addition, the problem statement or analysis may indicate that values larger than 100000 are considered unreasonable and probably indicate a data entry error. If so, then another class of bad data (larger than 100,000) exists and should be tested.

Just as we generate test cases for each class of good data, we generate test cases for each error class. It is important to note here that each error should be tested separately. For example, if the sex code must be 'M' or 'F', and the grade must lie between 0 and 100, we identify three classes of bad data:

sex code incorrect
grade less than 0
grade greater than 100

Each should be tested by itself. A single record with an incorrect sex code and a grade less than 0 is not adequate.

4. *Boundary values.* Experience has shown that errors are more likely to occur for boundary values than for any other values. Thus, test cases which exercise the boundaries are likely to be more valuable in uncovering bugs.

Boundary values are frequently related to class testing. If a class consists of a range of values, then there are boundaries at each end of the range. For example, in the calculation of RATE based on VALUE (described above) we may identify these boundaries:

0	(between good data and bad data)
1000	
5000	
1000000	(between good data and bad data)

Since 1000 is the lowest number in the class for which the RATE is to be .07, we include a test case with VALUE equal to 1000. We also want to test the upper boundary of the class where the RATE is .04, so we include a value just below 1000, perhaps 999, or 999.99, or even both. A similar discussion holds for the other boundaries.

Some comments may help here. First, we might wish to test both just below and just above the boundary. In the previous example, we would add test case 1000.01, or 1001, or both. Second, the actions for the two classes are sometimes not distinguishable for numbers very close to the boundary. For example, consider this decision structure:

```
if AMOUNT ≤ 500 then
   TAX ← 50
else
   TAX ← 50 + .10 * (AMOUNT − 500)
endif
```

If AMOUNT is 500.01, then TAX would be 50.001, which would appear as 50.00 if printed as a dollars and cents figure (with an F7.2 format, perhaps). Since this cannot be distinguished from the answer for 500.00, we might include a test case a little further from the boundary (for example, 500.10).

Finally, we should note that some boundaries are related to output rather than input. For example, if we are supposed to print exactly 45 lines per page, we should include a test where the output ends on the 45th line of a page and a test where it ends on the first line of the following page.

5. *Special cases.* This type of testing is closely related to boundary testing, and in fact you may wish to view them as the same thing. An example of a special case test might involve a program finding the average check amount for a month in a checking account. We would want to include a test where there were no checks at all.

For many, if not all, "special case" tests, we may view the test as a boundary test in connection with a "how many?" or a "where?" question. For example, if we ask, "How many of the transactions for the month were checks?" the answer would be, "Anywhere from no checks to all checks." Our special case where there were no checks is one of the two boundaries on the possible range of answers to the question. Similarly, in looking for the largest of a set of numbers, we could ask, "Where in the list could the answer occur?" The answer is, "Anywhere from first to last," and we have two boundaries (first, last) on that range.

6. *Combinations.* Consider the following verbal description of who gets a bonus: "Any employee who has an attendance record of 95 percent, or who sold more than 500 units, or who recruited at least one new customer receives a bonus." This can be coded as a simple if-then construction. However, in testing the program it is not really sufficient to just test both branches. We should test various combinations of the three conditions involved. As you can see in the following table, there are eight possible combinations.

attendance > 95%	sold > 500	recruited
no	no	no
no	no	yes
no	yes	no
no	yes	yes
yes	no	no
yes	no	yes
yes	yes	no
yes	yes	yes

Ideally, we should check all combinations in a situation like this. We should at least check the "boundaries" (all no, all yes, exactly one no, exactly one yes) and some randomly chosen other possibilities.

A particularly important example of combinations occurs in validating input data. To be valid, the data typically must meet a number of criteria. This implies a number of combinations, similar to those for the preceding example. Experience has shown that for each way in which the data could fail to be acceptable, there should be a test case which is correct except for that one particular way.

7. *Loop exits.* In Section 5.3 we will study loops with more than one exit condition. For this type of loop, we should include at least one test case for each possible exit condition. As a simple example, consider a search loop which is looking for the name 'John Jones' in a data file. In Section 3.3 we ignored the possibility that he might not be in the file. In Section 5.3 we will deal with that possibility. This would lead to a loop with two conditions for exiting: either we find John Jones, or we reach the end of the file and therefore know he is not in the file. Both possibilities should be tested for in our test plan.

We now consider how some of the general concepts listed above apply to specific types of algorithms. We are especially interested here in "special case" tests. For example, for a counting problem we might identify the following tests:

no data input
data input, but count is 0
everything input is in the class being counted

A similar list would apply for accumulation. For finding the largest (or smallest) value, we could list tests such as:

no data input
exactly one data item (would be both largest and smallest)
first is largest (no ties)
last is largest (no ties)
largest in middle (no ties)
all values the same

In a program which searches for a particular value in a file we can list tests:

not found
found, only one in file
found, first one in file (others there also)
found, last one in file (others there also)
found, somewhere in middle of file

Similar tests would apply to searching in an array (Chapter 6).

Generalizing this last situation just a little, we can come up with the following types of tests for algorithms which use either count-control or general condition loops:

exit on first pass through loop
exit on last possible pass through loop

We now turn to a brief resume of the topics of top-down and bottom-up testing. To illustrate the difference, consider the following hierarchy chart of modules:

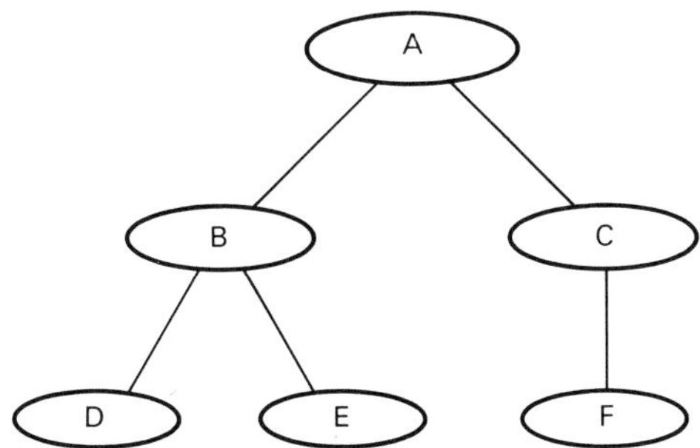

In both types of testing, we test one module at a time in the context of modules which are already tested. For example, one possible order for top-down testing would be:

A (stubs for B and C)
B (using the tested A, and stubs for D, E, and C)
D (using the existing A and B, and stubs for E and C)
E (using the existing A, B, and D, and a stub for C)
C (using the existing A, B, D, and E, and a stub for F)
F (using the existing A, B, D, E, and C)

Other orders are also possible, such as: A, B, C, D, E, F.

In bottom-up testing, on the other hand, we would start with the lowest level modules, perhaps in this order:

D (using a driver)
E (using a driver)

B (using a driver to call it, and the existing D and E)
F (using a driver)
C (using a driver, and the existing F)
A (using the existing B, C, D, E, and F)

Again, other orders are possible, such as: F, D, E, C, B, A.

Sometimes it is helpful to combine the two techniques. For example, suppose that the logic of the main program (A) depends heavily on output parameters from B, and that output cannot be easily imitated by a stub. We might first develop the subsystem consisting of B, D, and E. The resulting order might be: B, D, E, A, C, F.

Summary

This concludes our discussion of antibugging, debugging, and testing. We remind you that this section, in contrast with many others in the text, may be most useful as a reference to be applied to your programming projects. It, together with PITFALLS and TESTING subsections throughout the text, can be useful in writing programs which avoid bugs and in discovering, uncovering, and removing those bugs which do occur.

4

MORE ON SUBPROGRAMS

4.1 COMMUNICATION AND PARAMETERS

This chapter consolidates what we have learned so far about subprograms. The previous two chapters have already given us a good deal of information about them. In Section 2.2, we introduced the concept of a subroutine with no parameters, which was used to print instructions. Functions, with their input parameters, were first used in Section 2.6. Sections 3.2 and 3.3 supplied a few more details about subroutines. In Section 3.2, we wrote some subroutines which used input parameters, and in Section 3.3 we used output parameters in a subroutine for the first time.

The purpose of this chapter is twofold: (1) to review and summarize the material covered in these earlier sections, and (2) to add some further details concerning writing and using functions and subroutines.

The first section reviews and extends our knowledge of the parameter mechanism in FORTRAN. In the second section, we look in detail at both functions and subroutines. The third section introduces a new type of variable, the LOGICAL type, and covers LOGICAL functions.

Before we begin, let us briefly review some terminology. First, we have the concept of a **main program**. A program with no subprograms is a main program; it can be run as an independent program. A main program can use one or more **subprograms** to perform subtasks. The term **program unit** is used to denote either a main program or a subprogram.

In FORTRAN, there are two types of subprograms, the **function subprogram** (or, more simply, just **function**) and the **subroutine**. "Subprogram" is a generic term which includes both types. The procedures for writing these two types of subprograms are very similar. On the other hand, the techniques for using them are completely different. A function is used by including it in an expression (in an assignment statement or a comparison). A subroutine is used by writing a CALL statement.

A subprogram cannot be run by itself; it is run when our main program **invokes** or **calls** the function or subroutine. Thus a subprogram is a program unit which is invoked by some other program unit.

It is possible for the main program to call a subprogram which in turn calls a second subprogram, and so on. Suppose the main program calls subprogram A, which in turn calls subprogram B. From the point of view of subprogram B, subprogram A is the main program. However, the term "main program" is generally reserved for the one program which is not invoked by any other program. Hence the terms **calling program** and **called program** are frequently used in place of "main program" and "subprogram" in describing which program is doing the calling. In our example above, we have two calls.

1. The main program invokes subprogram A. Here the main program is the calling program, and subprogram A is the called program.
2. Subprogram A invokes subprogram B. Here subprogram A is the calling program, and subprogram B is the called program.

Reasons for Subprograms

There are at least four reasons for using subprograms. We mention them here briefly. However, these themes, especially the third, will be expanded upon in the further development of the text.

1. **Repetition.** Suppose that, in writing a program, you find that there are four different places in the program where you need to perform exactly the same operations, perhaps using different data each time. A subprogram which, given the appropriate data, performs these operations, may be desirable. This approach will prevent having to repeat the same sequence of code at each of the four locations in the program. This is especially useful if the code involved is rather long or complicated.
2. **Universal use.** There are some procedures which might be needed in more than one program. Perhaps a large group of programmers all need the same procedure. By writing a subprogram and making it available to an entire group, we can avoid duplication of effort (not only the effort required to copy the code, but also the effort required to create the code in the first place).
3. **Modularity.** As the types of things we do in our programs become more complicated, the programs themselves become longer and more complicated. Before long, they become too complex for us to comprehend easily. By using subprograms, we can break the program up into more manageable pieces or modules. This practice has the added advantage that it can simplify the process of maintaining and modifying the program in later years.

4. **Teamwork.** A large percentage of programming in the real world is done by programming teams. Rather than having the whole team work on the whole program, the program is generally divided into subprograms. Each subprogram will be written by one or two members of the team.

Of these four reasons, in our view the most important is the third. As we have seen in some of our examples involving subprograms, it is extremely useful to be able to allocate subtasks to either functions or subroutines. This aids in the **top down design** of our program. As we design the main program, we identify various tasks or calculations which we allocate to subroutines or functions. This allows us to complete the design of the overall solution to our problem without getting bogged down in the details of the subtasks. We then come back and design the various subprograms for each identified subtask. Of course, if the subtask is complex, we may in turn identify further subtasks. This would lead to one subprogram in turn invoking another subprogram. We continue in this fashion until we have designed the entire program to solve our particular problem. Because we start with the main program and work our way down to successively more and more detailed pieces, we refer to this as "top down" design and refinement.

> **NOTE.** Top down design is similar to but different from top down testing. In coding and testing a program which has already been designed, it may make sense to use top down testing, or bottom up testing, or some suitable combination. However, the design process should always be top down.

Two Simple Subprograms

The primary purpose of this first section is to discuss the use of parameters to achieve communication between a calling program and the subprogram it calls. Recall that, in FORTRAN, each subprogram is an independent unit. This means that the variable names and statement labels in the called program unit are not in any way related to those in the calling program unit, or in fact to those in any other program unit within the entire program. The advantages of this are obvious, especially when a program is being developed as a team effort. The team member writing a particular subprogram does not need to be concerned that using a particular variable name will somehow interfere with what some other member of the team is doing. We do not have to keep track of all the labels and variables that are used in all the subprograms. This allows us to concentrate our attention on the particular subtask at hand.

On the other hand, this does mean that we must use some mechanism to allow the various program units to communicate those values which are needed. In FORTRAN, this is achieved by two mechanisms. Most of the communication between calling program and called program takes place through **parameters** (sometimes called **arguments**). In addition, functions pass their answer back to the calling program through the **name** of the function.

In working with parameters, there are four principles to remember:

1. The parameter in the called program and that in the step of the calling program which invokes the subprogram must match in **purpose**. For example, if the

subprogram expects the parameter to be the height of a triangle, it must indeed be the height, not the side of the triangle.

2. They must also match in **type**. For example, if the parameter is declared REAL in the subprogram, then a REAL value must be supplied.
3. They must match in **number**. For example, if the subprogram has two parameters, the calling program must supply two corresponding parameters.
4. They may (but need not) match in **name**. For example, if the subprogram is using the variable HEIGHT for the parameter which is the height of the triangle, the calling program must supply a value which represents the height of the triangle. If the calling program's variable list indicates that height is called HEIGHT in the calling program, then the parameters would match by name. However, if the person writing the calling program used HT to stand for the height, then the parameter supplied in the call would be HT.

We illustrate these concepts with two simple examples. First, consider the program in Figure 4.1, consisting of a main program and a function.

There are several points worth mentioning here. First, this function has two parameters, each of which is an input parameter. The function expects the calling program to supply values to these parameters. The values supplied must be REAL, and they must be in the order specified—first the radius, then the height.

Second, we have chosen in the example to use the same names for the parameters in the main program and in the function. This is permissible, but again we emphasize that it is not necessary. The communication between the programs is based on the order of the parameters, not the names of the parameters. The first parameter of the calling program corresponds to the first parameter of the called program, and so on. Our calling program could just as well have read as follows:

```
      REAL A,B,V,VOLUME
   10 CONTINUE
         PRINT *,'Enter radius and height (0 to quit)'
         READ *,A,B
         IF (A.EQ.0) THEN
            GO TO 500
         ENDIF
         V = VOLUME(A,B)
         WRITE(*,1000) 'Volume is ',V
         GO TO 10
  500 CONTINUE
      STOP
 1000 FORMAT(' ',A,F10.2)
      END
```

The parameters *must* match in number, type, and purpose; they *may* match in name.

A third point is that the number of parameters must match. The function expects two values, radius and height. Obviously, if the calling program only passes one value, the function will be unable to calculate the volume. On the other hand, it would not make sense to have V = VOLUME(RADIUS,HEIGHT,X), since the X

```
      REAL RADIUS,HEIGHT,VOLUME,V

C   WRITTEN BY *******, **/**/**

C   THIS PROGRAM IS DESIGNED TO TEST THE VOLUME FUNCTION.
C IT CALLS THIS FUNCTION.

   10 CONTINUE
         PRINT *, 'Enter radius and height (0 to quit)'
         READ *,RADIUS,HEIGHT
         IF (RADIUS.EQ.0) THEN
            GO TO 500
         ENDIF
         V = VOLUME(RADIUS,HEIGHT)
         WRITE(*,1000) 'Volume is ', V
         GO TO 10
  500 CONTINUE
      STOP
 1000 FORMAT (' ',A,F10.2)
      END
      REAL FUNCTION VOLUME(RADIUS,HEIGHT)
      REAL RADIUS, HEIGHT

C   WRITTEN BY *******, **/**/**

C   THIS FUNCTION CALCULATES THE VOLUME OF A CONE

C   THESE ARE THE PARAMETERS:
C      RADIUS - INPUT, REAL - RADIUS OF THE BASE
C      HEIGHT - INPUT, REAL - HEIGHT OF THE CONE

      VOLUME = (1.0 / 3.0) * 3.1416 * RADIUS ** 2 * HEIGHT
      RETURN
      END
```

Figure 4.1

would not correspond to any parameter in the function. The calling program must provide exactly two parameters.

A fourth point concerns the use of the VOLUME subprogram in the calling program. Since it is a function, it is placed in an assignment statement, which places the answer into the variable named V. This variable is the one which is then printed.

We now consider a simple subroutine (see Figure 4.2). This subroutine has both input and output parameters. The input parameters are two integers which the subprogram calls DIVDND and DIVISR. The output parameters are the quotient and the remainder, respectively, when DIVDND is divided by DIVISR. These output parameters are named QUOT and REM.

The main program in Figure 4.2 is an extremely simple one, which we have

```
      INTEGER I,J,K,L
      I = 5
      J = 3
      CALL QUOREM (I,J,K,L)
      WRITE(*,1000) I,J,K,L
      STOP
 1000 FORMAT(' ', 4I5)
      END
      SUBROUTINE QUOREM(DIVDND,DIVISR,QUOT,REM)
      INTEGER DIVDND,DIVISR,QUOT,REM

C    WRITTEN BY *******, **/**/**

C    THIS SUBROUTINE CALCULATES THE QUOTIENT OF TWO INTEGERS
C   AND THE REMAINDER FROM THE DIVISION

C   THESE ARE THE PARAMETERS:
C      DIVDND - INPUT,   INTEGER - THE DIVIDEND
C      DIVISR - INPUT,   INTEGER - THE DIVISOR
C      QUOT   - OUTPUT,  INTEGER - THE QUOTIENT
C      REM    - OUTPUT,  INTEGER - THE REMAINDER


      QUOT = DIVDND/DIVISR
      REM = DIVDND - DIVISR*QUOT
      RETURN
      END
```

Figure 4.2

written to illustrate a few more ideas on parameters. We want to examine exactly how input and output parameters work.

First, the terms *input parameter* and *output parameter* are merely a technique to remind the programmer of the purpose of each parameter. There is no distinction in FORTRAN between the types of parameters. All parameters are treated the same, from the standpoint of what happens as the program runs. We will now describe how communication is actually achieved. (The procedure used will in fact vary from machine to machine. We will describe one common method that should help us think about the use of parameters.)

In Chapter 1 we described how the FORTRAN compiler sets aside space for each variable used. This is true in the main program and for most variables in subprograms. However, space is not assigned to parameters of subprograms. (These parameters are sometimes referred to as **dummy arguments** to emphasize this point.) When the subprogram is invoked by a main program, this main program will supply values for the parameters (these values are sometimes called **actual parameters** or **actual arguments** as opposed to dummy arguments.) The main program will of course have these values in certain storage locations. It tells the subprogram the location of these actual arguments, and the subprogram works directly with the numbers in their locations in the main program.

For example, for the program in Figure 4.2, the compiler will set aside locations for I, J, K, and L. When the program is run, the number 5 will be placed in the I location, and the number 3 in the J location. The step "CALL QUOREM(I,J,K,L)" invokes the QUOREM subroutine written at the beginning of this section, with the following parameter matchups:

I—DIVDND
J—DIVISR
K—QUOT
L—REM

Since the subprogram works directly with the corresponding variables in the main program, we may view the locations as temporarily having two names:

In main		In subroutine
I	5	DIVDND
J	3	DIVISR
K		QUOT
L		REM

As QUOREM runs, it works directly with the locations provided in the main program. Thus the step

```
QUOT = DIVDND/DIVISR
```

causes this to occur:

```
I   5   DIVDND
J   3   DIVISR
K   1   QUOT
L       REM
```

and likewise after the step

```
REM = DIVDND - DIVISR*QUOT
```

we have:

```
I   5   DIVDND
J   3   DIVISR
K   1   QUOT
L   2   REM
```

When we reach the RETURN step, control is returned to the calling program. Notice that the values of the answers K and L have been passed back automatically because the subprogram works directly with the memory locations in the main program.

This method of communication is sometimes referred to as **call by location** because the subprogram is told the locations of the actual parameters, and it uses these locations in its calculations.

Consider now the following possible calling program for the QUOREM subroutine:

```
INTEGER Q,R
CALL QUOREM(17,5,Q,R)
PRINT *,Q,R
STOP
END
```

In this main program, we have supplied actual numbers for the two values whose quotient and remainder are to be found. This is allowed for input parameters. In fact, for an input parameter we may supply any expression of the proper type (INTEGER, etc.). We have already done so in connection with library functions when we have written, for example, Y = SQRT(2.5*(X−W)). On the other hand, it would not make any sense to supply either a number or an expression to match an output parameter. We must supply a variable into which the subroutine may place the calculated answer.

Another Example

It may be useful to consider one further example. This example is taken from Section 3.2. In that section we wrote a function NODIV which found the number of divisors of a given integer. In Exercise 9(a) of that section, you were asked to use that function to write an algorithm for a main program which reads two numbers, M and N, and prints a table showing, for each number from M to N, the number of divisors of that number. Reproduced in Figures 4.3 and 4.4, respectively, are the NODIV function and the answer to the exercise, taken from the answer key in the back of the text. Although these two program units were written by the same person, the main program was written several months after the function.

Close examination of the variables used in the two program units reveals some interesting things. First, notice that the parameter is called N (for "number") in the function. The function finds the number of divisors of the number it refers to as N. In the main program, however, the value passed is the loop index variable I. This is done because that index is the variable for which the main program wishes to count the divisors. This again illustrates the concept that the parameters need not match by name.

Other ideas may be explored by listing the variables used in the main program and in the subprogram side by side. We include the function name as a variable in both lists. The only correspondences are those indicated by the dashed lines, arising from either the function name or the parameter correspondence.

```
Main program                          Function
  NODIV  -----------------            NODIV
  I      -----------------            N
  M                                   I
  N                                   COUNT
  PAGENO
  DIVCTR
```

```
      INTEGER FUNCTION NODIV(N)
      INTEGER N,I,COUNT

C   WRITTEN BY *******, **/**/**

C   THIS FUNCTION DETERMINES HOW MANY DIVISORS A GIVEN
C INTEGER HAS.

C   THESE ARE THE PARAMETERS:
C    N - INPUT, INTEGER - INTEGER NUMBER

C   INITIALIZE

      COUNT = 0

C   COUNT CONTROLLED LOOP; CHECK EACH I FROM 1 TO N

      DO 100 I = 1,N
         IF(MOD(N,I.EQ.0) THEN
            COUNT = COUNT + 1
         ENDIF
  100    CONTINUE
      NODIV = COUNT
      RETURN
      END
```

Figure 4.3

```
call INSTR
prompt
read M,N
PAGENO ← 1
loop for I = M to N
   DIVCTR ← NODIV(I)
   if time for new page then
      call HEADER(PAGENO)
      PAGENO ← PAGENO + 1
   endif
   print I,DIVCTR
endloop
stop
```

Figure 4.4

It turns out that both program units use the variable I. This is understandable, since each unit has a count-controlled loop and the variable I is frequently used in such a situation. Fortunately, this is allowed in FORTRAN. The use of I in the function does not interfere with the loop index I in the calling program.

Notice that this is true even though the main program variable I is passed as a parameter to the function! Within the function, that parameter is referred to by the name N. This can be a difficult point to comprehend. However, we can deal with any confusion we may have by simply remembering this: When we write one program unit, we do not need to worry at all about the variable names used by another program unit. Our local variables have nothing to do with the local variables in other units. And because parameters do not have to match by name, even our parameter names are not affected by what variable name some other program unit may use. The program units are independent in this sense.

We summarize some of the points concerning communication between calling program and called program as follows:

1. The primary means of communication is the parameters.
2. The names of the parameters in calling and called programs need not match.
3. The number, type, and purpose of the parameters must match.
4. At the time the subprogram is invoked, a correspondence is established between the parameters in the subprogram and those in the calling program.
5. In the case of a function subprogram, the answer is also passed back to the calling program by way of the name of the function.
6. Each program and subprogram must have its own declaration statements (REAL, INTEGER, and so forth). Function names must be declared in the calling program.

Pitfalls

In using subprograms in FORTRAN, we must avoid confusion on two points. First, we must remember that FORTRAN subprograms are independent entities. Each subprogram must declare the variables that are used within that subprogram. The fact that a variable with the same name has already been declared in the main program or some other subprogram is irrelevant, since each subprogram is independent.

Along the same lines, each main program and subprogram should declare only those variables it actually uses. It is not necessary or desirable to declare all the variables used by all the other subprograms which form the entire program.

A second major pitfall involves the use of a subprogram. When we use a subprogram, we frequently know what names it uses for its parameters. In invoking the subprogram, however, we must use the variable or expression which represents that same quantity in the calling program.

REVIEW

Terms

main program
subprogram
function subprogram

subroutine
calling program
called program
invoke(call)
parameter
argument
function name
input parameter
output parameter

Reasons for Using Subprograms

Repetition
Universal use
Modularity
Teamwork

Communication by Parameters

Parameters in calling and called program must match in number, type, and use.

They may or may not match by name.

For input parameters, constants or expressions may be used in the calling program.

When a subprogram is invoked, a correspondence is set up between the parameter in the subprogram and the calling program.

Declarations. Each main and subprogram declares *its own variables.* The calling program also declares the function names for any functions it invokes.

EXERCISES

For each exercise you are given a portion of a calling program and the beginning portion of a subprogram. You are to indicate whether or not the correspondence of the parameters is legal.

1.

```
INTEGER A,G,W                  SUBROUTINE TEST(M,N,I)
REAL X                         INTEGER M,N,T,Z,
  .                            REAL I,J
  .
  .
CALL TEST(A,G,X)
```

2.

```
INTEGER A,B,C                  SUBROUTINE MAXMIN(I,J,K)
  .                            INTEGER I,J,K
  .
  .
CALL MAXMIN(A,B,C)
```

3.
```
INTEGER A,B,C, TFUNC
REAL X,Y
   .
   .
   .
A = TFUNC(B,C)
```
```
INTEGER FUNCTION TFUNC(B,C)
REAL B,C
```

4.
```
INTEGER I,J,K
REAL X,Y,Z,ZVAL
   .
   .
   .
Z = ZVAL(X,Y)
```
```
REAL FUNCTION ZVAL(X,Y)
REAL X,Y
```

5.
```
INTEGER IDNO, WKPAY
REAL PAY, HOURS, RATE
   .
   .
   .
PAY = WKPAY(HOURS,RATE)
```
```
REAL FUNCTION WKPAY (HOURS, RATE)
REAL HOURS, RATE
```

4.2 FUNCTIONS AND SUBROUTINES

There are two different types of subprograms in FORTRAN—the subroutine and the function subprogram, frequently referred to simply as "function." There are many similarities between the two types of subprograms. The major difference is that with a function a single value is passed back to the main program by way of the function name. Because of this, the function is generally chosen when we want to calculate exactly one thing. For example, in the VOLUME function of the previous section, we were interested in calculating one thing: the volume of a cone. Each of the parameters in the example was an input parameter; that is, the function expected to receive values for those parameters, and it used those values to calculate the desired quantity. This is typical of the most common use of function subprograms. We wish to calculate one quantity, and that quantity depends on one or more variables which become the input parameters. A subroutine, on the other hand, is used to accomplish a more general subtask. This might involve calculating more than one value, or it might involve a task which does not calculate any answers.

For a function, the answer is communicated to the calling program by the function name. In addition, there is communication with the calling program by means of the parameters, which are generally input parameters. For a subroutine, on the other hand, all the communication is through the parameters. This means that, if we want to calculate three quantities in the subroutine, then these three quantities must be among the parameters for the subroutine. These parameters will be **output** parameters, since the subroutine will use them to pass answers back to the calling program.

COMMENT. Less frequently, a subroutine has parameters which act as both input and output parameters. For example, for a subroutine which updates the balance in a checking account, the variable BALANC might be such a parameter. When the subroutine is invoked, the current balance is passed as input to the subroutine. The subroutine updates this balance and passes the result back as output to the calling program.

Such a parameter we will call an **update** parameter.

Form of a FORTRAN Subprogram

In general form, there are more similarities than differences between a function and a subroutine. The following table summarizes and compares the form of the two types of subprograms. Notice that in each case we can distinguish a "setup" portion, a "body" portion, and an "ending" portion. A subprogram consists essentially of a segment of FORTRAN code (the body) which accomplishes some task, surrounded by the necessary setup and ending statements. We discuss the specific form of functions and of subroutines briefly in the following paragraphs.

COMPARISON OF FORM

	FUNCTION	SUBROUTINE
setup	type FUNCTION fname(par1,par2,...) declarations (INTEGER, REAL, etc.)	SUBROUTINE sname(par1,par2,...) declarations (INTEGER, REAL, etc.)
body	code to calculate the function value. Generally includes one or more steps of the form fname = expressions	code to perform the required procedures/calculations. If some of the parameters are output parameters, they must be calculated here.
ending	RETURN END	RETURN END

COMPARISON OF USE

FUNCTION	SUBROUTINE
Use in expression involving function name (in assignment statement, IF statement, etc.) e.g. Y = SQRT(X)	Invoke by CALL statement e.g. CALL SPLIT (NO,T,H,U)

The first statement in any function is always the FUNCTION statement. Its form is:

```
type FUNCTION fname(par1,par2,...)
```

Here type declares the type of variable (REAL,INTEGER,CHARACTER*1, and so on) for the function name and hence for the value calculated by the function. The name of the function is represented by fname; it must adhere to the usual rules for the names of variables. Inside the parentheses we place the names of the parameters or arguments, as they are used within the function. They are separated by commas.

1. The parameters are variables and hence must be included in the declarations.
2. On the other hand, we do not include the function name, since its type has already been declared in the FUNCTION statement.

In the body of the function we include the necessary steps to calculate the function value. Since the function value is passed back to the calling program by way of the function name fname, there will generally be at least one step which assigns a value to fname:

```
fname = expression
```

Of course, there may be more than one such step.

Finally, the ending portion of the function represents both the logical end and the physical end of the program. The logical end is indicated by the RETURN step, which returns control to the calling program. The END statement signals the compiler that this is the physical end of the subprogram. Every main program and every subprogram must have an END statement as its last statement.

Likewise, a subroutine begins with a setup portion, which includes the name of the subroutine, the list of parameters, and all needed declarations.Every variable used in the subroutine, including the parameters and the names of any functions invoked by the subroutine should be declared.

The subroutine will begin with the FORTRAN statement

```
SUBROUTINE sname(par1,par2,...)
```

As usual, this begins in column 7 or beyond. The subroutine name "sname" follows the usual FORTRAN naming rules: one to six letters or digits, with the first character a letter. The list of parameters is placed in parentheses, with commas between the individual parameters. It is possible for a subroutine not to have any parameters at all. In this case the list of parameters, including the parentheses, is omitted:

```
SUBROUTINE sname
```

The body of the subroutine contains the FORTRAN code which performs the desired tasks or calculations. This is similar to the body of a function. However, the name of the subroutine does not represent a quantity to be calculated. It may not be used in any calculations within the body of the subroutine. On the other hand, some of the parameters may represent quantities to be calculated by the subroutine. If so, they will naturally be calculated within the body of the subroutine.

Finally, the ending portion consists of the steps

```
RETURN
END
```

just as in the function subprogram.

There is an important fact about the parameter list which we should reemphasize at this point. The compiler makes no distinction between input parameters, output parameters, and update parameters in the parameter list. The distinction is one which we will make as programmers to remind outselves of the purpose of the parameters. In our example, the first two parameters happen to be input parameters, the second two, output parameters. This ordering is a matter of convenience only.

****
W A R N I N G
****

CAUTION. Typically a calling program expects that the update and output parameters of a subprogram will be changed. This is the mechanism used for passing back answers. It does *not* expect the input parameters to be modified. If they are, this may cause problems in the calling program. We will give some examples in the PITFALLS section below.

NEVER CHANGE THE VALUE OF AN INPUT PARAMETER WITHIN A SUBPROGRAM.

****
W A R N I N G
****

The following table summarizes some of the important differences between a function and a subroutine.

	Function	Subroutine
Name	Has a type (INTEGER, and so on)	Does not have a type
	Function name is given a value	Subroutine name does not get a value
	Function name declared in calling program	Subroutine name not declared
Use	Used to calculate a single value	Used to perform a task; or to calculate two or more values
	Invoked by using in an expression	Invoked by CALL statement
Parameters	Has at least one parameter	May have zero or more parameters
	Parameters are input parameters	Parameters may be input, output, or update

Writing a Subprogram

In writing any type of subprogram, it is important to identify precisely the task to be performed. It is frequently the case that that task will be to perform certain calculations. Many of our early algorithms have been of the form

```
loop
    read input data
    if dummy entry then exit endif
    perform calculations
    print answers
endloop
```

Typically, subprograms which refine the step "perform calculations" in this type of algorithm do not involve any I/O (except perhaps temporary trace prints). Input is obtained from input parameters, and output is passed back to the calling program either through a function name or through output parameters. This is especially true of functions—they will almost never involve any I/O operations.

On the other hand, some subroutines do specifically involve I/O. In fact, we have seen three major examples of this type of subroutine: input subroutines, header-printing subroutines, and instruction-printing subroutines.

The key to proper design is determining exactly what task the subprogram is supposed to accomplish.

The steps involved in writing a subprogram may be summarized as follows:

1. Identify the task to be performed. Determine whether to use a function or a subroutine (use a function when the task is the calculation of a single value). Choose a name for the subprogram, and determine the type (for example, REAL or INTEGER) if a function is being written.
2. Decide on parameters (input, output, update). The output parameters represent the values the subroutine will calculate. The input parameters are the values needed in order to calculate those answers. Any variable which is used as input and whose value is then modified will be an update parameter. Notice that all parameters for a function should be input parameters.
3. Write an algorithm and variable list. This algorithm will consist of the steps needed to perform the desired subtask. If there are output or update parameters, the algorithm will include steps to give values to those parameters. Similarly, for a function there will be steps which give a value to the function name.

   A parameter which has been identified as an input parameter must not be modified by this algorithm.
4. Code the subprogram in FORTRAN. The first line is written using the function or subroutine name and the list of parameters we have already chosen. All variables are declared, and the algorithm is coded. The body of the subprogram is followed by the RETURN and END statements.

Examples—Calculations

Now let us write a number of fairly simple subprograms, both functions and subroutines.

Let us write a subprogram to calculate commission for a salesperson. In order to know how to proceed with this calculation, we need to know how commission is calculated. For this example, suppose we have a monthly commission calculation based on the sales for that month. Each salesperson has a basic rate; the rate used to calculate the commission is obtained from the basic rate according to the following table:

Sales amount	Rate used
less than 3,000.00	Basic rate
3000.00 – 5499.99	1.3* (basic rate)
5500.00 – 7999.99	1.5* (basic rate)
8000.00 on up	1.7* (basic rate)

It is appropriate to write a function because we are calculating one thing: commission. We will use MTHPAY (for "monthly pay") as the function name, and we observe that this will be a REAL function.

What parameters (input information) do we need to calculate the commission? Obviously we will need the sales amount. We might think we need the rate to be used, but a little thought will tell us that we really need the basic rate. Our algorithm will determine the rate actually used based on the sales amount. Are any other parameters needed? No, because the amount of commission depends only on the sales amount and the basic rate.

The variable list is as follows:

Name	Type	Use	Comment
MTHPAY	REAL	Commission	Function name
SALES	REAL	Sales amount	Input parameter 1
BASIC	REAL	Basic rate	Input parameter 2
RATE	REAL	Rate used	

The setup portion, based on the preceding discussion, is:

```
REAL FUNCTION MTHPAY (SALES, BASIC)
REAL SALES, BASIC, RATE
```

The rule for determine the proper value for RATE is a typical four-way branch whose algorithm may be given as:

```
case
   1 (SALES < 3000) RATE ← BASIC
   2 (SALES < 5500) RATE ← 1.3* BASIC
   3 (SALES < 8000) RATE ← 1.5* BASIC
   4 (any other) RATE ← 1.7 * BASIC
endcase
```

(As usual, in writing our conditions we take advantage of the fact that if the sales amount is not less than $3000.00, it must be $3000.00 or more, and so on.) From this point, completing the function will be a relatively straightforward procedure. The body of the function consists of the code for this four-way branch. See Figure 4.5 for the entire function.

```
      REAL FUNCTION MTHPAY(SALES,BASIC)
      REAL SALES,BASIC,RATE

C   WRITTEN BY *******, **/**/**

C   THIS FUNCTION CALCULATES MONTHLY COMMISSIONS. THE RATE
C USED IS A MULTIPLE OF THE BASIC RATE (BASED ON SALES AMOUNT)

C   THESE ARE THE PARAMETERS
C     SALES - INPUT, REAL - MONTHLY SALES AMOUNT
C     BASIC - INPUT, REAL - BASIC RATE


C   CALCULATE RATE USED (4-WAY BRANCH)

      IF(SALES.LT.3000.0) THEN
         RATE = BASIC
      ELSE IF(SALES.LT.5500.0) THEN
         RATE = 1.3 * BASIC
      ELSE IF(SALES.LT.8000.0) THEN
         RATE = 1.5 * BASIC
      ELSE
         RATE = 1.7 * BASIC
      ENDIF

C   CALCULATE COMMISSION

      MTHPAY = SALES * RATE
      RETURN
      END
```

Figure 4.5

This example illustrates the fact that a subprogram may use variables which are neither parameters nor the function name. In this function we calculate RATE as an intermediate step in the calculation of MTHPAY. However, since the calling program does not need to know the actual rate used (only the final commission), we use RATE only within the function itself, as a local variable.

As our second example, let us write a subprogram to find the largest and smallest of three real numbers. Since we are calculating two quantities, we will use a subroutine called MAXMIN. We will need three input parameters (the three numbers) and two output parameters (the largest and the smallest). We will use our standard procedure for determining the largest and the smallest. (We give LARGE the value of the first number, then change it whenever we find a larger number; and similarly for SMALL.)

Name	Type	Use	Comment
A,B,C	REAL	Three numbers	Input parameters 1, 2, and 3
LARGE	REAL	Largest	Output parameter 4
SMALL	REAL	Smallest	Output parameter 5

Here is the algorithm.

```
LARGE ← A
SMALL ← A
if B > LARGE then
   LARGE ← B
endif
if B < SMALL then
   SMALL ← B
endif
if C > LARGE then
   LARGE ← C
endif
if C < SMALL then
   SMALL ← C
endif
return
```

To complete the subprogram, we need only convert this algorithm to FORTRAN and include the appropriate setup and ending portions.

```
      SUBROUTINE MAXMIN(A,B,C,LARGE,SMALL)
      REAL A, B, C, LARGE, SMALL

C   WRITTEN BY *******, **/**/**

C   THIS SUBROUTINE FINDS BOTH THE LARGEST AND THE SMALLEST
C OF THREE REAL NUMBERS

C   THESE ARE THE PARAMETERS:
C     A,B,C - INPUT, REAL   - THE THREE NUMBERS
C     LARGE - OUTPUT, REAL - THE LARGEST
C     SMALL - OUTPUT, REAL - THE SMALLEST


C   INITIALIZE LARGE, SMALL

      LARGE = A
      SMALL = A
```

(continued)

```
C    COMPARE TO B, CHANGE IF NECESSARY

       IF (B.GT.LARGE) THEN
          LARGE = B
       ENDIF
       IF (B.LT.SMALL) THEN
          SMALL = B
       ENDIF

C    COMPARE TO C, CHANGE IF NECESSARY

       IF (C.GT.LARGE) THEN
          LARGE = C
       ENDIF
       IF (C.LT.SMALL) THEN
          SMALL = C
       ENDIF
       RETURN
       END
```

Now let us write a subprogram to calculate the least common multiple (LCM) of two positive integers A and B. (This could be used in finding a least common denominator if A and B were denominators of fractions.) For example, if A = 4 and B = 6, then our answer should be 12 since both 4 and 6 divide evenly into 12, and 12 is the smallest number which is evenly divisible by both 4 and 6.

In this example the easiest part is planning the setup portion. Since we are calculating exactly one value, we will use a function. The input parameters will be the integers A and B, and the answer will be an integer we will name LCMF. Thus the tentative setup portion is

```
INTEGER FUNCTION LCMF(A,B)
INTEGER A,B
```

We may have to add other variables to our declarations if we need more variables to solve the problem.

What about an algorithm for solving the problem? There are a number of possible approaches. We will choose what is perhaps the easiest conceptually, since it is an example of a searching process.

Our algorithm is this: we try first 1, then 2, and 3, and so on, looking for a number which is evenly divisible by both A and B. As soon as we find one, that number will be the smallest (since we start looking at 1 and work our way up). Thus we need a variable TRY which will take on the successive values 1, 2, 3, and so on, until it is finally divisible by both A and B.

This algorithm will involve a loop, since we want to do the same thing repeatedly (see if the latest value of TRY is divisible by both A and B). Our loop control will be of the form "go until some condition is met" (in particular, the condition that TRY is evenly divisible by A and B). Before the loop we initialize TRY; in the loop we see if this value works, and if not go to the next value of

TRY; after the loop we place the value of TRY that does work into the LCMF function-name variable.

Here is the smooth algorithm. (Notice that this is not an infinite loop, since we are certain to leave the loop when TRY is equal to A*B, if not earlier.)

```
TRY ← 1
loop
   if both A and B divide evenly into TRY then exit endif
   TRY ← TRY + 1
endloop
LCMF ← TRY
return
```

The FORTRAN code is relatively simple to write. As usual, we will use the MOD function to determine whether one number divides evenly into another. The condition "both A and B divide evenly into TRY" may be written as

```
MOD(TRY,A).EQ.0 .AND. MOD(TRY,B).EQ.0
```

since both remainders must be 0.

```
      INTEGER FUNCTION LCMF(A,B)
      INTEGER A,B,TRY

C   WRITTEN BY *******, **/**/**

C   THIS FUNCTION FINDS THE LEAST COMMON MULTIPLE OF
C TWO POSITIVE INTEGERS.

C   THESE ARE THE PARAMETERS:
C     A,B - INPUT, INTEGER - THE TWO POSITIVE INTEGERS


C   FIRST NUMBER TO TRY IS 1

      TRY = 1

C   SEE IF COMMON MULTIPLE. IF SO, DONE. IF NOT, INCREMENT.

    5 CONTINUE
         IF (MOD(TRY,A).EQ.0.AND.MOD(TRY,B).EQ.0) THEN
            GO TO 10
         ENDIF
         TRY = TRY + 1
         GO TO 5

C   ASSIGN ANSWER TO FUNCTION NAME

   10 CONTINUE
      LCMF = TRY
      RETURN
      END
```

In the following example let us write a tax calculation routine which will calculate federal withholding, social security, state, and local tax.

To do this problem we must be told how each of these taxes is calculated. We will assume the following procedures, which are in some cases simplifications of the procedures used for an actual payroll.

1. Federal withholding. Subtract $10.50 from gross pay for each dependent. Use the withholding rate given by the following table.

Net pay after deductions for dependents	Rate
less than $80.00	0%
$80.00 to $99.99	12%
$100.00 to $249.99	16%
$250.00 on up	19%

2. Social security. Take 7.43 percent of gross pay, except that social security is not deducted for any amount over $41,000 in the given year.
3. State and local. Take 2.5 percent of gross pay for state tax, 1 percent for local.

We first observe that a subroutine is needed, since we calculate four different tax figures. We name the subroutine TAXES. Our output parameters are the various taxes calculated. To decide on the input parameters, we must determine what information is needed in the calculation of the various taxes.

1. The federal withholding calculation uses the gross pay and the number of dependents.
2. For social security, we need to know the gross pay. In addition, since taxes are not deducted after the yearly pay reaches $41,000, we need to know the total yearly pay prior to this check.
3. State and local taxes are based on the gross pay only.

Thus our input parameters will be gross pay, number of dependents, and year-to-date pay prior to this pay period.

The logic for social security, state tax, and local tax is fairly simple. The logic for withholding tax, even with the simplifications we have made, is somewhat more difficult. For this reason we choose to write a separate subprogram FEDRAL to calculate this tax. (This would make it easier to revise our tax routine to actually work without any simplifications.)

Since the FEDRAL routine calculates a single REAL answer (the federal withholding), we will use a REAL function. In the variable list below, notice the use of the variable FEDWH to store the answer from this function. We also use another variable, NETSS, to calculate the amount actually subject to social security tax.

	Name	Type	Use	Comment
Parameters				
Input:	GROSS	REAL	Gross pay	
	NUMDEP	INTEGER	Number of dependents	
	YTDGR	REAL	Year-to-date gross	
Output:	FEDWH	REAL	Federal tax	
	SOCSEC	REAL	Social Security	
	STATE	REAL	State tax	
	LOCAL	REAL	Local tax	
Local var.:	NETSS	REAL	Amount on which social security is deducted	
	FEDRAL	REAL		Function—parameters are gross pay, dependents

The logic for the social security calculation may be seen to be a typical three-way branch, as shown by the following table.

Situation	Amount taxable (NETSS)
Previously over 41,000	0
Goes over 41,000 on this check	41,000—previous year-to-date
Still under 41,000	gross for this period

A rough algorithm for the calculations might be

```
use FEDRAL function to calculate FEDWH
calculate NETSS
SOCSEC ← .0743 * NETSS
STATE ← .025 * GROSS
LOCAL ← .01 * GROSS
```

The refinement of the step "calculate NETSS" is a **case** structure based on the table given above.

```
case
   1 (YTDGR > 41,000) NETSS ← 0
   2 (YTDGR + GROSS > 41,000) NETSS ← 41,000 - YTDGR
   3 (any other) NETSS ← GROSS
endcase
```

Notice that the order in which the cases are listed is important. (Why?)

To refine the step which calculates FEDWH, we will write an assignment statement which invokes the FEDRAL function. As we pointed out in the earlier discussion, this function will require two input parameters: the gross pay and the number of dependents. When we invoke the function, we supply as actual parameters the variables which represent gross pay and number of dependents in *our own* subprogram.

```
FEDWH ← FEDRAL(GROSS,NUMDEP)
```

(We do not even need to know what names the author of the FEDRAL function will give to these parameters.)

The program is given in Figure 4.6. We leave the FEDRAL function as a reasonably simple exercise. (This is an example of the "teamwork" reason for using subprograms.)

We now consider some examples which use subroutines to perform tasks other than calculations.

Examples—Other Subtasks

We have previously examined three important classes of subroutines which perform subtasks involving things other than calculations. These are: printing instructions, printing headings, and obtaining valid input. In this section, we want to expand slightly on some of the ideas involved in printing headings for tabular output.

Following is a sample header printing subroutine developed in Section 3.2 (Case Study #4). If we want to have the page number printed along with the heading on each page of output, there are two possible approaches.

```
      SUBROUTINE HEADER(RATE)
      REAL RATE

C     WRITTEN BY ********, **/**/**

C     THIS SUBROUTINE PRINTS HEADERS, INCLUDING AN INTEREST RATE

C     THERE IS ONE PARAMETER:
C       RATE - INPUT, REAL - THE INTEREST RATE

      WRITE(*,1000) 'Balances for interest rate = ',RATE
      WRITE(*,1001) 'Year   Start   Interest   End'
      WRITE(*,1002) '----   -----   --------   ---'
      PRINT *,' '
      RETURN

C     FORMATS

 1000 FORMAT('1',A,F4.2)
 1001 FORMAT('0',A)
 1002 FORMAT(' ',A)
      END
```

First, we could modify our main program to keep track of the page number, and have it pass the page number as an input parameter to the HEADER subroutine.

```
      SUBROUTINE TAXES(GROSS,NUMDEP,YTDGR,FEDWH,SOCSEC,STATE,LOCAL)
      REAL GROSS,YTDGR,FEDWH,SOCSEC,STATE,LOCAL,NETSS,FEDRAL
      INTEGER NUMDEP

C   WRITTEN BY *******, **/**/**

C   THIS SUBROUTINE CALCULATES TAXES TO BE WITHHELD FROM A
C WEEKLY PAY CHECK

C   THESE ARE THE PARAMETERS
C      GROSS  - INPUT, REAL    - GROSS PAY THIS PERIOD
C      NUMDEP - INPUT, INTEGER - NUMBER OF DEPENDENTS
C      YTDGR  - INPUT, REAL    - YEAR-TO-DATE GROSS PRIOR
C                                TO THIS WEEK
C      FEDWH  - OUTPUT, REAL   - FEDERAL WITHHOLDING
C      SOCSEC - OUTPUT, REAL   - SOCIAL SECURITY
C      STATE  - OUTPUT, REAL   - STATE TAX
C      LOCAL  - OUTPUT, REAL   - LOCAL TAX


C   FEDERAL

      FEDWH = FEDRAL(GROSS,NUMDEP)

C   SOCIAL SECURITY - FIND TAXABLE AMOUNT

      IF(YTDGR.GE.41000.0) THEN
         NETSS = 0.0
      ELSE IF(YTDGR+GROSS.GT.41000.0) THEN
         NETSS = 41000.0 - YTDGR
      ELSE
         NETSS = GROSS
      ENDIF

C   SOCIAL SECURITY - FIND TAX

      SOCSEC = .0743 * NETSS

C   STATE AND LOCAL

      STATE = .025 * GROSS
      LOCAL = .01 * GROSS
      RETURN
      END
```

Figure 4.6

(We have used this approach in Section 3.2.) Second, we could have the subroutine keep track of the page number. This second approach seems more reasonable, since it avoids cluttering the main program with details involving the printing of the answers.

Thus, our sample main program will not be changed. We will change the subroutine HEADER to maintain a counter, PAGENO. This counter will have an initial value of 1 and will be increased by 1 each time the subroutine is called.

If we use an assignment statement PAGENO = 1 to initialize PAGENO in the HEADER subroutine, we will have trouble. Each time we invoke the subroutine this statement will be performed, and every page will be labelled PAGE 1. What we desire is a single initialization to 1 at compile time (prior to running the program), not a new initialization at each successive call of the subroutine. We need to use two new statements—DATA and SAVE—as shown in Figure 4.7.

The following two subsections will indicate how the DATA and SAVE statements work together to make sure PAGENO always has the correct value. Observe that, after writing the headings including the page number, the counter PAGENO is incremented by 1 so that it will have the proper value when HEADER is called again.

```
      SUBROUTINE HEADER(RATE)
      REAL RATE
      INTEGER PAGENO
      SAVE PAGENO
      DATA PAGENO/1/

C   WRITTEN BY *******, **/**/**
C   MODIFIED BY *******, **/**/**, TO PRINT PAGE NUMBERS

C   THIS SUBROUTINE PRINTS HEADERS, INCLUDING AN INTEREST RATE

C   THERE IS ONE PARAMETER:
C     RATE - INPUT, REAL - THE INTEREST RATE

      WRITE(*,1000) 'Balances for interest rate = ',RATE, 'page', PAGENO
      PAGENO = PAGENO + 1
      WRITE(*,1001) 'Year   Start    Interest    End'
      WRITE(*,1002) '----   -----    --------    ---'
      PRINT *'  '
      RETURN

C   FORMATS

 1000 FORMAT('1',A,F4.2,25X,A,I3)
 1001 FORMAT('0',A)
 1002 FORMAT(' ',A)
      END
```

Figure 4.7

The DATA Statement

The preceding example illustrates a method which is frequently used when we wish to initialize and maintain the value of a variable within a subprogram. In a main program we can use an assignment statement to initialize a variable. By never branching back up to that assignment statement, we can be sure that the initialization occurs only once. However, if we place an assignment statement at the beginning of a subprogram, that assignment statement will be performed again each time the subprogram is invoked.

The DATA statement provides an alternative method of initializing a variable. Because the DATA statement is a **declaration** statement rather than an **executable** statement, its use avoids the problem we have with an assignment statement.

Consider the following two declarations:

```
INTEGER I
DATA I/5/
```

These tell the compiler that the variable I is an INTEGER variable. In addition, they tell the compiler that, when the program starts to run, the variable I should contain the value 5. The compiler will place the number 5 in the variable I. This happens before the program starts to run.

Once the program begins, the INTEGER and DATA statements have been discarded; they do not become a part of the machine-language version of the program. As a result, the DATA statement is not **executable**; it will never be executed once the program begins. Its effect is achieved at **compile time**, prior to running the program.

As the program is running, it may use an assignment statement such as I = I + 7 or I = 5 to modify the value of the variable I. However, the value of I will never again be set to 5 by the DATA statement.

The DATA statement may be used in either main programs or subprograms. In FORTRAN main programs, the tendency is to use the assignment statement instead. However, the DATA statement has a very valuable use in subprograms, as we have just shown.

The form of the DATA statement is

```
DATA variable / value /
```

It is possible to have more than one DATA statement in a program:

```
INTEGER I,J,K
REAL X,Y
CHARACTER*1 VAL
DATA I/5/
DATA J/7/
DATA X/3.5/
DATA VAL/'T'/
```

Any data statement present must appear after all other declarations (including the SAVE statement).

Rather than writing the four DATA statements separately, we may combine them in either of the following two ways.

```
DATA I/5,J/7/,X/3.5/,VAL/'T'/
```

or

```
DATA I,J,X,VAL/5,7,3.5,'T'/
```

NOTE. Observe that INTEGER variables are given integer values, REAL variables are given real values, and CHARACTER variables are given character values of the appropriate length.

The general form of the DATA statement is either of the following:

```
DATA variable1/value1/,variable2/value2/,...
DATA variable1/variable2,.../value1,value2,.../
```

Of course, in the second form the number of variables and the number of values must match.

The SAVE Statement

The subroutine for printing headings given earlier also illustrates the use of the SAVE statement. This statement is also a declaration statement. It informs the compiler that the value of the given variable should be saved between calls to the subprogram.

For example, our subroutine includes the following:

```
INTEGER PAGENO
SAVE PAGENO
DATA PAGENO/1/
     .
     .
     .
PAGENO = PAGENO + 1
```

The first time we call this subroutine, PAGENO will have the value 1. This value will have been placed in the PAGENO variable by the compiler, prior to running the program. After printing the headings, we increment PAGENO to get ready for the second page. When we RETURN to the calling program, PAGENO has the value 2. We would like PAGENO to retain this value, so that its value will still be 2 when the subroutine is called again later. The inclusion of the SAVE statement guarantees that this will happen.

The general form of the SAVE statement is

```
SAVE variable1,variable2,...
```

Since it is a declaration, we place it in the setup portion of our subprogram, along with the INTEGER, REAL, CHARACTER, and DATA declarations.

> **COMMENT.** On some computer systems, the value of PAGENO will automatically be retained even if we forget to include the SAVE statement. However, it is not wise to count on this happening.

Using Subprograms

The rules for using functions and subroutines are similar. A function is used by including it in an expression. On the other hand, we use the CALL statement to invoke the subroutine. We write one of the following forms:

CALL sname
CALL sname (list of actual parameters)

For a subroutine with no parameters, we merely CALL the subroutine by name. If, however, the subroutine has one or more parameters, we must supply a list of parameters in the CALL statement.

> **CAUTION.** Remember that the parameters supplied in the function invocation or in the CALL statement must be the variables or expressions which represent the desired quantities **in the calling program.**
>
> The names used will not necessarily match those which were used in the subprogram itself.

In writing our list of parameters, we must of course adhere to the usual rules concerning actual parameter lists:

1. The number of parameters must be correct.
2. The parameters in the call *must* match the subprogram parameters by type (INTEGER, REAL, and so forth) and by use.
3. The parameters in the call *may* match those in the subprogram by name. The correspondence is based on position in the parameter list rather than on matching names. We use the names which represent the appropriate quantities in our calling program.

For example, for the subroutine QUOREM of Section 4.1, we have this set up portion:

```
SUBROUTINE QUOREM(DIVDND,DIVISR,QUOT,REM)
INTEGER DIVDND,DIVISR,QUOT,REM
```

Each of the following represents a valid call of this subroutine:

1. ```
   INTEGER A,B,QUOT,R
   CALL QUOREM(A,B,QUOT,R)
   ```
2. ```
   INTEGER DIVDND,DIVISR,QUOT,REM
   CALL QUOREM(DIVDND,DIVISR,QUOT,REM)
   ```
3. ```
   INTEGER Q,R
   CALL QUOREM(5,3,Q,R)
   ```
4. ```
   INTEGER X,Y,Q,R
   CALL QUOREM(X+Y,X-Y,Q,R)
   ```

On the other hand, the following are not valid, for the reasons indicated:

5. ```
   INTEGER I,J,K,L
   CALL QUOREM(I,J,K)
   ```
   (Need four parameters)
6. ```
   INTEGER A,B,X,Y
   REAL Q,R
   CALL QUOREM(A,B,Q,R)
   ```
   (Types do not match for Q, R)
7. ```
   REAL DIVDND,DIVISR,QUOT,REM
   CALL QUOREM(DIVIDND,DIVISR,QUOT,REM)
   ```
   (Types do not match)
8. ```
   INTEGER DIVIDND,DIVISR,QUOT,REM
   CALL QUOREM
   ```
   (No parameter list in call)
9. ```
   INTEGER I,J
   CALL QUOREM(I,J,5,3)
   ```
   (Use of parameters does not match. In particular, the third and fourth parameters are used by the subroutine to pass back answers (output parameters). The parameters in the call must be variables, not constants.)

This last example illustrates a rule about parameters which is really just a "common sense" rule. The programmer is allowed to use any expression as an input parameter when calling a subprogram. For example, the following calls are legal

```
Y = SQRT(X**2 + 2.0*X + 25.0)
A = SQRT(ABS (X))
CALL QUOREM (X+Y,X-Y,Q,R)
CALL QUOREM (5,3,Q,R)
```

provided the proper type declarations have been made so that the parameters match by type. The value of any constant or expression can be passed to a subprogram as an input parameter. However, common sense tells us that the same freedom cannot be allowed when the subprogram uses the parameter as an output (or update) parameter. In this case an answer will be passed back to the calling program by way of this parameter. The calling program must provide a variable into which this answer may be placed. A constant or expression as an output or update parameter makes no sense and can lead to very unpredictable results. (Many, but not all, compilers will create code which detects this type of difficulty and terminates the faulty program at that point.)

Pitfalls

There are a number of potential errors in the use of subprograms.

1. Many subprograms are written to accomplish calculations. Unless those calculations specifically require a loop or I/O, there will generally be no read, write, or looping steps.

   Input is generally obtained by input parameters from the calling program, not by reading. Answers are usually passed back to the calling program rather than being printed in the subprogram.
```

There are exceptions to these rules. However, before including I/O steps in a subprogram, we should make sure that is really part of the prescribed subtask.

2. Subprograms are independent. Each main program and subprogram should declare only those variables which are used within itself.
3. Within a function, the function name is used as a variable. For example, in the function VOLUME (Section 4.1) we write

```
VOLUME = (1.0/3.0) * 3.1416 *RADIUS**2 * HEIGHT
```

However, in the calling program, the function name cannot be used as a variable name. We write

```
V = VOLUME (RADIUS,HEIGHT)
```

using the variable V to store the answer from the function.

4. We must not forget, in a function, to place the answer into the function name variable. Calculating the value in some other variable will not in itself convey the answer back to the calling program.
5. The calling program must properly declare the function name. For example, in a calling program which uses a real function SALARY, we would include a declaration

```
REAL SALARY
```

If we do not declare the function, the compiler will choose a type for us, and this choice may be incorrect.

6. In using a subprogram, the calling program supplies constants, variables, or expressions which represent the parameter quantities in the calling program. These will not necessarily be the same names that the subprogram uses for the parameters.
7. A subroutine has no type. The subroutine name is never declared, either in the calling program or in the subroutine.
8. When calling a subroutine, care must be taken to supply variables (*not* constants or expressions) to match update or output parameters. Since the subroutine will be giving values to these parameters, we must supply a variable into which the answer may be placed.

   On the other hand, it makes perfectly good sense to supply constants or expressions to correspond to input parameters.
9. The DATA statement and the assignment statement both assign a value to a variable. The difference is that the DATA type assignment happens only once, before the program starts to run. This is useful within a subroutine, in connection with the SAVE statement, to give a local variable an initial value. For the present that is the only use we will make of the statement.
10. We must never, in a subprogram, change the value of a parameter which was assigned as an input parameter. (For a function, this typically includes all the

parameters.) We will explain the reason behind this warning in the next subsection.

Parameter Passing

In describing the QUOREM subroutine in Section 4.1 we described a parameter passing mechanism. In that example, all four parameters were treated the same. No distinction was made between input and output parameters. The following examples will illustrate what can happen if we are not careful.

Let us write a subroutine called SPLIT which, given a positive integer one to three digits long, will calculate these three digits (units, tens, and hundreds). The subroutine is given in Figure 4.8, together with a driver main program.

Let us trace the program with an input value of the number 739. We read NO, placing the value 739 into the variable NO. We then call the SPLIT subroutine with this resulting correspondence of parameters:

Main program		Subroutine
NO	739	NUM
H		HUND
T		TENS
U		UNITS

The step HUND=NUM/100 calculates HUND (and hence H in the main program):

NO	739	NUM
H	7	HUND
T		TENS
U		UNITS

The next step causes us problems, precisely because it modifies a parameter which was meant to be an input parameter. The computer calculates NUM = NUM − HUND*100 = 739 − 7*100 = 39. But since the dummy argument NUM refers to the actual parameter NO, the variable NO in the main program is changed at this instant.

NO	39	NUM
H	7	HUND
T		TENS
U		UNITS

The remaining steps calculate TENS = NUM/10 = 39/10 = 3, and UNITS = NUM − TENS*10 = 39 − 3*10 = 9.

NO	39	NUM
H	7	HUND
T	3	TENS
U	9	UNITS

We then return to the main program, where we print the answers, including the *modified* version of the original number.

```
      INTEGER NO,H,T,U
   10 CONTINUE
         PRINT *, 'Enter number (0 to stop)'
         READ *, NO
         IF(NO.EQ.0) THEN
            GO TO 500
         ENDIF
         CALL SPLIT(NO,H,T,U)
         PRINT *, NO,H,T,U
         GO TO 10
  500 CONTINUE
      STOP
      END
      SUBROUTINE SPLIT(NUM, HUND, TENS, UNITS)
      INTEGER NUM, HUND, TENS, UNITS

C   WRITTEN BY *******, **/**/**

C   THIS SUBROUTINE BREAKS A 1-3 DIGIT POSITIVE NUMBER INTO
C ITS THREE SEPARATE DIGITS.

C   THESE ARE THE PARAMETERS:
C    NUM   - INPUT, INTEGER  - THE 1-3 DIGIT POSITIVE INTEGER
C    HUND  - OUTPUT, INTEGER - HUNDRED'S DIGIT
C    TENS  - OUPUT, INTEGER  - TEN'S DIGIT
C    UNITS - OUPUT, INTEGER  - UNIT'S DIGIT


C   CALCULATE HUNDRED'S DIGIT

      HUND = NUM/100

C   NOW SUBTRACT THE NUMBER OF HUNDREDS, LEAVING A TWO DIGIT
C NUMBER; THEN GET TEN'S DIGIT

      NUM  = NUM - HUND*100
      TENS = NUM/10

C   FINALLY CALCULATE UNIT'S DIGIT

      UNITS = NUM - TENS*10
      RETURN
      END
```

Figure 4.8

The subroutine SPLIT will modify its first parameter to be a two-digit number. Consider what might happen if we call it with something like

```
CALL SPLIT(449,H,T,U)
```

The subroutine will try to change the constant 449 to 49. On some compilers this is detected, and an error message is generated. On others, the computer will actually allow the program to change the value of the constant. On systems such as these, any future reference to the constant 449 will actually refer to 49 instead!

As you can imagine, an error of this type can be very difficult to track down. It is much easier to avoid such problems by conscientiously identifying each parameter as input, output, or update, and not modifying any input parameter.

To solve this problem, we can rewrite the subroutine SPLIT, utilizing a variable LASTWO to contain the last two digits of NUM:

```
      SUBROUTINE SPLIT(NUM, HUND, TENS, UNITS)
      INTEGER NUM, HUND, TENS, UNITS, LASTWO

C   WRITTEN BY *******, **/**/**

C   THIS SUBROUTINE BREAKS A 1-3 DIGIT POSITIVE NUMBER INTO
C ITS THREE SEPARATE DIGITS.

C   THESE ARE THE PARAMETERS:
C     NUM   - INPUT, INTEGER   - THE 1-3 DIGIT POSITIVE INTEGER
C     HUND  - OUTPUT, INTEGER - HUNDRED'S DIGIT
C     TENS  - OUPUT, INTEGER   - TEN'S DIGIT
C     UNITS - OUPUT, INTEGER   - UNIT'S DIGIT


C   CALCULATE HUNDRED'S DIGIT

      HUND = NUM/100

C   NOW SUBTRACT THE NUMBER OF HUNDREDS, LEAVING A TWO DIGIT
C NUMBER; THEN GET TEN'S DIGIT

      LASTWO = NUM - HUND*100
      TENS = LASTWO/10

C   FINALLY CALCULATE UNIT'S DIGIT

      UNITS = LASTWO - TENS*10
      RETURN
      END
```

Now only the output parameters HUND, TENS, and UNITS, and the additional variable LASTWO, appear on the left side of an assignment statement. The input parameter NUM is no longer modified.

To summarize this discussion, we have three major points:

1. Arguments in subprograms do not have space reserved for them. When arguments are used in a subprogram, the subprogram works directly with the actual parameters in their memory locations as assigned within the calling program.
2. Statements which alter dummy arguments within a subprogram will alter the

corresponding actual arguments. This is the mechanism used to pass back answers from subroutines.

3. Unfortunate things occur when arguments which should not be changed are changed. When making up our list of parameters, we should specify which are input parameters, which are output parameters, and which are update parameters. Our code must never change an input parameter.

REVIEW

Terms

declaration

executable statement

dummy parameter/argument

actual parameter/argument

call by location

FORTRAN Syntax

FUNCTION statement:

```
type FUNCTION fname(par1,par2,...)
```

"type" can be REAL, INTEGER, CHARACTER*1, and so forth.

"fname" must be one to six letters or digits, the first a letter.

There may be one or more parameters, separated by commas.

RETURN statement:

```
RETURN
```

Used to return to calling program.

The SUBROUTINE statement

```
SUBROUTINE sname
SUBROUTINE sname(par1,par2,...)
```

"sname" must be one to six letters or digits, the first a letter.

There may be 0 or more parameters, separated by commas.

The CALL statement

```
CALL sname
CALL sname(par1,par2,...)
```

The DATA statement

```
DATA variable1/value1/,variable2/value2/,...
```

or

```
DATA variable1,variable2,.../value1,value2,.../
```

Values are INTEGER, REAL, or CHARACTER constants.

In the second form, the number of values must match the number of variables.

Places values in variables at compile time.

Appears following all other declaration statements.

The SAVE statement

SAVE variable1,variable2,...

Used in subprograms to cause value of variables to be retained between successive calls.

Writing a Subprogram

1. Decide on function or subroutine. Choose function name and type, or subroutine name.
2. Determine parameters and give them names. Classify as input (used to pass values from calling program to subprogram), output (used to pass answers back), or update (combination of input and output).
3. Determine other variables needed and write algorithm. Algorithm must not modify input parameters.
4. Code. Setup portion uses function or subroutine name, parameter list, and variable list. Body uses algorithm. Ending portion contains RETURN and END steps.

Using a Function

1. Declare function name in calling program.
2. Include function name in an expression (assignment statement, or condition in IF statement).
3. Supply parameters, expressions representing the desired quantities in terms of variables (or constants) *in the calling program*.

Using a Subroutine

1. Use CALL statement.
2. Supply parameters—any expression or variable for input parameters; must be variable for output/update parameters.

   These expressions represent the parameters in terms of variables (or constants) *in the calling program*.

Pitfalls

1. Identify subtask. Frequently no I/O or looping is involved (especially for function).
2. Each module declares its own local variables.
3. Do not use function name as a regular variable in calling program.
4. In a function, place the answer into the function name variable.

5. The calling program must properly declare the function name.
6. The calling program supplies parameters *based on its own list of variables.*
7. A subroutine name is never declared as REAL, etc.
8. Output or update parameters must be matched by variables (not constants or expressions) in the calling program.
9. Do not confuse the DATA statement and the assignment statement.
10. Never change the value of an input parameter.

EXERCISES

1. Modify the LCMF function given in this section so that, instead of beginning its search at 1, it begins at the larger of A and B. (Why does this work? Why is the resulting program better?)

2. Design and write the FEDRAL function invoked by the TAXES subroutine of this section.

3. Write a subprogram to calculate the volume and surface area of a sphere of radius R.

$$V = 4/3\ \pi R^3$$
$$S = 4\ \pi R^2$$

4. One way to approximate the square root of a real number X is by the method of iteration, as given by Newton. This consists of choosing a first approximation (perhaps X itself), then repeatedly getting a new (and better) approximation by using the following formula:

$$a_{new} = 1/2 \left[a_{old} + \frac{X}{a_{old}} \right]$$

Thus we have a loop involved. We will go until some condition is met, namely

$$| a_{new} - a_{old} | < 0.00001$$

Write a subprogram to approximate the square root of X in this manner. Then write a main program which invokes your program and also the built-in SQRT function. Print both answers and compare them. How good is your subprogram?

5. If P dollars is deposited in a savings account earning interest I compounded annually, then after N years the amount present is given by

$$A = P(1 + I)^N$$

Write a subprogram to calculate A and also the actual total interest earned, given P,I, and N.

6. Write a subprogram to determine state tax, based on the following rules. First, $500 is deducted from the income for each dependent. Then a standard deduction of 10 percent of the original income is subtracted. Finally, the tax is determined by the following table.

Resulting income	Tax
Less than 0	0
0–10,000	2% of resulting income
over 10,000	$200.00 plus 2.5% of amount over $10,000

7. Write a subprogram to find the largest and smallest of two integers I and J.
8. Write a subprogram to calculate the letter grade, given the number grade, based on the following table. (What type of variable is the answer?)

Number	Letter
90 up	H
75–89.999	C
Under 75	F

9. Write a subprogram with three REAL parameters NO1, NO2, and NO3. This subprogram will find the range of the numbers, that is, the difference between the largest of the three and the smallest of the three. Use the MAXMIN subroutine developed in this section.
10. **(a)** Write a subprogram which calculates the quarterly bonus for an employee. To earn a bonus, the employee must have had at least $2000.00 of sales in each of the three months in the quarter, and her average sales per month must be $4000.00 or more. If she qualifies for a bonus, it is calculated based on her total sales for the quarter as follows:

Total sales	Bonus
less than 15000.00	$ 50
15000.00–15999.99	$150
16000.00 on up	$200

(b) Write a main program which, using the subprogram from part (a) and the MTHPAY function written in this section, does the following: (1) reads a series of records containing name, three monthly sales figures, and a commission rate; (2) outputs the name, the total regular pay for the quarter, and the bonus pay for the quarter for each employee.

(c) Modify part (b) to find some summary information: name of the person with the largest regular pay, percentage whose bonus pay is not zero, and total bonus pay for the entire file.

11. Write a subprogram which, given an integer and a position, finds the digit in that place. For example, for the number 29867 we would have the following answers for various positions.

position:	answer:
1	7
2	6
3	8
4	9
5	2
6	0
.	.
.	.
.	.

12. **(a)** Write a subprogram which finds the largest of three integers.
    (b) Modify the subprogram to find the largest of four integers.
    (c) Modify the subprogram to find the largest of seven integers. (If this is difficult, you might want to reconsider your design.)

13. Write a subprogram to find both the least common multiple and the greatest common divisor of A and B. You may utilize any subprograms written previously in the examples or exercises.

14. The least common multiple of three numbers may be found by first finding the least common multiple of the first two (say LCM2). The answer is then the least common multiple of LCM2 and the third number.

    Write a subprogram which uses the LCMF function of this section to find the least common multiple of three INTEGER parameters I1, I2, and I3.

15. You have available three REAL functions ASALF, JSALF, and MSALF. These calculate salary for apprentice, journeyman, and master worker, respectively. Each requires a single input parameter—number of years of experience.

    Write a subroutine which, given a code for the type of employee ("APPR," "JOUR," or "MAST") and the number of years experience, will calculate the salary and annual vacation days for the individual.

    Note: Employees with eight years experience or less receive ten vacation days, all others receive 20 days. In addition, master employees receive three more days.

16. **(a)** You have a REAL function GRADEF(TESTS,QUIZT,EXAM). Given the total of the test scores, the total of the quiz scores, and the exam score, this function calculates the final numerical average. You also have available a CHARACTER*1 function LETTF(AVE) which, given the final numerical average, calculates the letter grade.

    Each data line has a name, three test scores, an exam score, and the quiz total. Refine this algorithm, by inserting the proper formulas for the needed calculations, using appropriate variable names.

```
print instructions
loop
   prompt
   read NAME,T1,T2,T3,EXAM,QUIZES
   if NAME = ' ' then exit endif
   calculate numerical average
   calculate letter grade
   print NAME, numerical average, letter grade
endloop
stop
```

    (b) Code the algorithm as a FORTRAN main program.

17. **(a)** You have available a function TUITF(HOURS) which calculates tuition based on how many hours a student is taking. You also have a function ROOMBD(TYPE, DORM) which calculates room and board charges based on a code (giving the "type" of student) and the dormitory number.

    Refine this algorithm, by including formulas for the calculations. Use appropriate variable names.

```
print instructions
loop
   prompt
   read SSN,NHOURS,TYPE,DORMNO
   if SSN = 0 then exit endif
   calculate total costs (tuition, room and board combined)
   print SSN,HOURS,TYPE,DORMNO,total costs
endloop
stop
```

(b) Code the algorithm as a FORTRAN main program.

18. Write the main program for the following situation. (You will want to decide on steps which might be done as subprograms, and what parameters would be required).

Each data line contains employee ID number, rank, number of units manufactured, basic bonus rate, and number of years experience. Your program should calculate and print basic pay and bonus pay for each employee. It should also print the ID of the person of rank 'A' with the most units produced and the average years of experience of the employees.

The basic pay consists of $200 for code 'A', $300 for code 'B', and $355 for code 'C', plus $5 for each year of experience.

The bonus pay is based on the number of units manufactured: 0 if under 100, basic bonus rate times basic pay if 100–150, 1.5 times as much if over 150.

19. Complete the program of Exercise 18 by designing and writing each of your planned subprograms.

20. Describe a unit test plan for these exercises in this section.

(a) Exercise 2
(b) Exercise 4
(c) Exercise 6
(d) Exercise 7
(e) Exercise 9
(f) Exercise 10a
(g) Exercise 11
(h) Exercise 12a
(i) Exercise 12b
(j) Exercise 14
(k) Exercise 21

21. Write input routines for each of the following situations. Give each a different name; they will be used in the next exercise.

(a) Read an ID number which is either 0, or between 10000 and 99999, inclusive.
(b) Read a daily hour figure between 0 and 12, inclusive.
(c) Read a department which is one of PUR, PRO, or PER.
(d) Read an employee code which is either M, S, or P.

22. By using the different input routines in the previous exercise, write a single input routine which accomplishes this job. It should read an ID, five daily hour figures, a department, and an employee code, using the validation criteria given. In addition, the total of the five daily hours figures should be between 20 and 50, inclusive. (If not, begin again, reading the daily hours figures.) Finally, if the employees code is P, it should read a percentage figure which is positive but less than 50 percent.

23. Another way to approach the previous problem is just to read a single record with all the data on it, including the percentage. Then, if any errors occur, they can be flagged and the read repeated. From the point of view of the user, which do you think is preferable? Why?

24. Exercise 21 in Section 3.3 presented an algorithm for a function GCD(M,N) which finds the greatest common divisor of two integers M and N. It uses an algorithm which we owe to Euclid. A slightly different form of the algorithm is given below:

```
loop
    R ← MOD(M,N)
    if R = 0 then exit endif
    M ← N
    N ← R
endloop
GCD ← N
```

Hand trace this algorithm for the following pairs of numbers:

a. 45, 10 **b.** 10, 45 **c.** 169, 101

Then comment on whether the algorithm is appropriate for coding as a FORTRAN function.

4.3. LOGICAL VARIABLES AND FUNCTIONS

In this section we introduce a fourth type of variable available in FORTRAN, the LOGICAL variable. This type of variable is of special value in situations in which we need to indicate whether or not some specific condition is true. We could use some sort of integer code to accomplish this (for example, use 1 to mean true and 0 to mean not true). However, the LOGICAL data type is specifically designed to handle this situation.

We begin with some details concerning this data type. This will be followed by some examples illustrating its use, including Case Study #5.

Logical Variables—Declaration and I/O

A variable is declared to be LOGICAL by the LOGICAL statement, which works just like the INTEGER and REAL declarations. For example, we could have

```
LOGICAL GOOD    or    LOGICAL X,Y,Z
```

A LOGICAL variable may take on only one of two possible values. Its value is either TRUE or FALSE. To assign a value to a logical variable X we use one of these two statements:

```
X = .TRUE.    or    X = .FALSE.
```

Notice that periods precede and follow the words TRUE and FALSE. This prevents the FORTRAN compiler from confusing the **LOGICAL constant** .TRUE. with an ordinary variable named TRUE.

Finally, determining whether a given LOGICAL variable presently has the value .TRUE. or not is easy to do. For example, the algorithm segment

if L3 is true **then** I ← I + 1 **endif**

where L3 is a LOGICAL variable, may be written

```
IF(L3) THEN
   I = I + 1
ENDIF
```

To understand this, notice that in the more familiar type of statement, IF(X.GT.Y) THEN, the expression X.GT.Y is a **logical expression** whose value is either .TRUE. or .FALSE.. In our example above, L3 does not need to be compared with anything to obtain a logical expression having either a .TRUE. or .FALSE. value. The variable by itself is such an expression. In fact, FORTRAN does not allow comparisons of logical quantities. The statement

```
IF(L3.EQ..TRUE.) THEN
```

although it seems reasonable, is just *not* allowed.

To implement the algorithm segment

if L3 is false **then** T ← 3 * T **endif**

we can write

```
IF(.NOT.L3) THEN
   T = 3 * T
ENDIF
```

Observe that L3 being false is the same as the expression .NOT.L3 being true.

We frequently choose LOGICAL variable names based on what a value of .TRUE. means. For example, if the variable is to indicate whether or not the user indicated a desire to terminate the program, we might declare the variable as

```
LOGICAL QUIT
```

with a value of .TRUE. meaning that the user does wish to quit, or a value of .FALSE. meaning that she does not.

One possible use of a LOGICAL variable occurs in validating input where several values are read from a single record. (This is perhaps more frequently encountered in a batch or file application than in a conversational one. It is not usually a good idea to make a user input five values over again just because the third one is faulty.)

To illustrate the technique, suppose we are reading a record with two test scores which should be between 0 and 100. We might be inclined to write a rough algorithm something like this:

```
loop
   read TEST1, TEST2
   check TEST1, error message if bad
   check TEST2, error message if bad
   if both were o.k. then exit endif
endloop
```

The problem occurs when we reach the exit step. If we wish to avoid performing the same checks over again, we need some way to "remember" what happened in the two individual checks. A LOGICAL variable is ideal for this purpose, since it is either true or false that the record was valid.

The following algorithm illustrates a helpful refinement. We set a LOGICAL variable GOOD to .FALSE. any time an error is detected. Since we initialize it to .TRUE. prior to the checking, we can see if everything was valid by seeing if it is still true.

```
loop
   read TEST1, TEST2
   GOOD ← .TRUE.
   if TEST1 < 0 OR TEST1 > 100 then
     print TEST1, 'bad'
     GOOD ← .FALSE.
   endif
   if TEST2 < 0 OR TEST2 > 100 then
     print TEST2, 'bad'
     GOOD ← .FALSE.
   endif
   if GOOD is still true then exit endif
endloop
```

In coding this algorithm in FORTRAN, the only step that needs particular explanation is the exit step. We write

```
IF (GOOD) THEN
   GO TO 500
ENDIF
```

Recall that saying GOOD in a logical expression conveys the concept "GOOD is true." (Saying .NOT.GOOD conveys the concept "GOOD is false.")

It is possible to read and write LOGICAL variables, using the L format. In its simplest form, we would use a format L1. As always, the "1" refers to the number of columns.

On input, using an L1 format, the column being read must contain either the letter "T" or the letter "F". Depending on which is present, the variable being read will receive the value .TRUE. or .FALSE., respectively.

Conversely, on output the value printed will be either a T or an F, depending on the value of the variable.

More generally, for a format of Lw, indicating a field w columns wide,

1. on input, the T or F may be anywhere within the w columns;
2. on output, the T or F will be printed right justified in the field.

COMMENT. The input rules are more flexible than indicated. For example, using an L7 format we could correctly read in the strings of characters '.TRUE. ' or '.FALSE.'. Unfortunately, however, on output only a T or an F will be printed, regardless of the size of the field.

Because the output of a single letter T or F is not likely to be of much meaning to the user of our program, we usually do not use L format except in trace prints. For a final answer, we might use a technique similar to that indicated by this example, where PASS indicates whether or not a person passed the course:

```
IF (PASS) THEN
   PRINT *,NAME,' passed'
ELSE
   PRINT *,NAME,' failed'
ENDIF
```

The output from this (for example, Sam Jones   passed) is much more meaningful than would be the output from using the L format (for example, Sam Jones   T).

LOGICAL Functions

Once we know about LOGICAL variables, it is quite easy to write LOGICAL functions. A LOGICAL function is written in exactly the same way as any other function, except that the answer is a logical value rather than a real, integer, or character value. We illustrate with an example.

To illustrate, let us write a function which, given three integer numbers A, B, and C, determines whether or not the average of A and B is larger than C.

The "whether or not" in the problem statement indicates the need for a logical function. We will name it BIGAVE, indicating a "big" average. The parameters are the three integers. For the algorithm, we calculate the average and determine the answer. The complete function is given in Figure 4.9.

We can illustrate the method for using a logical function by the following example. We want to print a message "declining" for a student whose average on the first two test grades (GRADE1, GRADE2) is greater than her third grade (GRADE3). We will present two possible solutions. In each, we will use the BIGAVE function illustrated in Figure 4.9.

First, we could place the answer from the BIGAVE function into a separate logical variable, then test that variable, as indicated in this segment of code:

```
LOGICAL DECL,BIGAVE
INTEGER GRADE1,GRADE2,GRADE3
     .
     .

DECL = BIGAVE(GRADE1,GRADE2,GRADE3)
IF (DECL) THEN
   PRINT *,'Declining'
ENDIF
```

```
      LOGICAL FUNCTION BIGAVE(A,B,C)
      INTEGER A,B,C
      REAL AVERAG

C   WRITTEN BY *******, **/**/**

C   THIS FUNCTION TELLS WHETHER OR NOT THE AVERAGE OF
C TWO GIVEN INTEGERS IS GREATER THAN A THIRD INTEGER.

C   THESE ARE THE PARAMETERS:
C    A, B, C - INPUT, INTEGER - THE THREE INTEGERS

      AVERAG = REAL(A+B) / 2.0
      IF (AVERAG.GT.C) THEN
         BIGAVE = .TRUE.
      ELSE
         BIGAVE = .FALSE.
      ENDIF
      RETURN
      END
```

Figure 4.9

Notice that we pass the three grades to match the function's parameters A, B, and C.

Another approach is indicated here:

```
LOGICAL BIGAVE
INTEGER GRADE1,GRADE2,GRADE3
    .
    .
IF (BIGAVE(GRADE1,GRADE2,GRADE3)) THEN
   PRINT *,'Declining'
ENDIF
```

In this solution, we place the function call right in the IF statement. Either solution is acceptable, although the first may take a small amount of extra time and computer memory space.

LOGICAL Expressions

We have used LOGICAL expressions of varying complexity in IF statements such as

```
IF (.NOT.GOOD) THEN
IF (A.LT.100.0 .OR. A.GT.250.0) THEN
IF (CODE.NE.'A' .AND. CODE.NE.'R' .AND. CODE.NE.'T') THEN
```

A LOGICAL expression is an expression whose value is either .TRUE. or .FALSE.. The simplest forms of LOGICAL expressions are:

a LOGICAL constant

a LOGICAL variable

a single comparison, such as A.LT.100.0

In addition, we may combine simple LOGICAL expressions using .AND.,.OR., and .NOT. to obtain more complex expressions.

Suppose GOOD, L1, and L2 are LOGICAL; CODE is CHARACTER*1; and I and J are INTEGER. These are permissible expressions:

```
.NOT. GOOD .OR. I.GT.J
I.LT.J .AND. I.GT.J-1
CODE.EQ.'A' .OR. CODE.EQ.'B' .AND. I.NE.0
L1 .OR. L2
L1 .AND. .NOT. L2
```

Observe that the simpler expressions being combined may be either LOGICAL variables or simple comparisons. The operators .AND. and .OR. each combine two logical quantities, while .NOT. negates a single quantity:

L1.AND.L2 is	true if both L1 and L2 are true false, otherwise
L1.OR.L2 is	true if either L1 or L2 (or both) is true false, otherwise
.NOT.L1 is	true if L1 is false false, otherwise

In combining these operators, we must recall the **precedence** of the three operators. Logical expressions are evaluated in much the same way that arithmetic expressions are, using these rules of precedence:

.NOT. is applied first
.AND. is applied next
.OR. is applied last

As with arithmetic expressions, parentheses may be used to alter the order.

For example, suppose that L1,L2, and L3 are LOGICAL variables whose present values are .TRUE., .TRUE., and .FALSE., respectively. Tell the value of these expressions.

```
.NOT.L1.OR.L2
.NOT.(L1.OR.L2)
L1.OR.L2.AND.L3
(L1.OR.L2).AND.L3
```

In the solutions, we use T and F to abbreviate .TRUE. and .FALSE..

```
.NOT.L1.OR.L2 = .NOT.T.OR.T = F.OR.T = T
.NOT.(L1.OR.L2) = .NOT.(T.OR.T) = .NOT.T = F
L1.OR.L2.AND.L3 = T.OR.T.AND.F = T.OR.F = T
(L1.OR.L2).AND.L3 = (T.OR.T).AND.F = T.AND.F = F
```

Assignment Statements

Logical expressions occur both in IF statements and in assignment statements. We have previously limited our assignment statements for LOGICAL variables to the form

variable = logical constant (either.TRUE. or .FALSE.)

However, any logical expression whatsoever may appear on the right side of the assignment statement. In particular, any expression which may appear as the condition in an IF statement may be used in a LOGICAL variable assignment statement.

Suppose PAIR and BIG are LOGICAL variables, and PRIME(A) is a LOGICAL function. These are possible assignment statements

```
BIG = .TRUE.
BIG = .NOT.(X.LT.Y .OR. X.LT.Z)
PAIR = PRIME(A) .AND. PRIME(A+2)
```

Now consider this two-way branch from the BIGAVE function of this section.

```
IF (AVERAG.GT.C) THEN
   BIGAVE = .TRUE.
ELSE
   BIGAVE = .FALSE.
ENDIF
```

Another way to accomplish the same thing is to write

```
BIGAVE = AVERAG.GT.C
```

The logical expression "AVERAG.GT.C" is either true or false. If it is true, we want BIGAVE to be true; if it is false, we want BIGAVE to be false. Thus BIGAVE's assigned value can be obtained by using the expression itself.

Other Uses of LOGICAL Variables

The uses of logical variables and functions are varied. We have considered their use as **flags**, such as GOOD. We describe briefly two somewhat different applications of these variables.

One common technique for debugging is to place what are sometimes called diagnostic prints in the program at appropriate spots. These print statements might indicate the value of strategic variables (such as parameters within a subprogram). They help us diagnose any bugs occurring in the program; hence their name.

One approach is to put the statements in as needed, then later remove them.

Another approach is to leave the prints in but disable them when they are no longer needed, as illustrated by this example:

```
LOGICAL DEBUG
DATA DEBUG/.TRUE./
    .
    .
    .
IF (DEBUG) THEN
   PRINT *,I,J,K
ENDIF
```

After the program has been successfully debugged, the DATA statement may be changed to

```
DATA DEBUG/.FALSE./
```

to disable the diagnostic prints. This approach has at least two advantages:

1. When changes are made to the program, the "debug prints" may easily be reactivated until the changes are completely debugged.
2. Even in "correct" programs, bugs may crop up after months or years of use. Once again, the diagnostic prints may be easily reactivated.

COMMENT. By using this technique in each subprogram, it is possible to selectively activate and deactivate the debug prints. By changing DEBUG to .FALSE. we may remove the messages for those subprograms which have been thoroughly checked out.

Another use of LOGICAL variables is as follows. Sometimes the same decision may be referenced at more than one point in a program. In this case, we may speed up program execution by storing the result of the decision in a logical variable. This type of simplification is especially important if the expression involves a function reference.

Case Study #5

This case study illustrates the use of a LOGICAL function in a natural setting.

1. *Statement of problem.* Write a program to print the first N primes, where N is an integer, greater than or equal to 1, supplied by the user.

2. *Preliminary analysis.* We recall that a number p is prime if its only divisors are 1 and p itself. For example, 2, 3, 5, and 17 are prime, but 4 is not (it is divisible by 2) nor is 35 (it is divisible by both 5 and 7).

We had better put an upper limit on N as well. We choose 300 as the limit.

3. *Algorithm and program.* We begin with a broad description of what we want to do.

> Read N
> Repeat the following until the number of primes is N:
> Test another integer; if prime, print it and count it.

Now we know that we will have a loop, controlled by the counter NOPRIM which counts the number of primes. We will leave the loop when some condition is met, namely that NOPRIM = N.

We will also need a variable to hold the integer we will test, say I. Then a slightly smoother version of the above algorithm would be:

```
read N
NOPRIM ← 0
I ← 2
loop
   if I is prime then
      print I
      NOPRIM ← NOPRIM + 1
   endif
   I ← I + 1
   if NOPRIM = N then exit endif
endloop
stop
```

For the step "read N" we will use a subroutine. For this case study we will not worry about headers. Thus the only step in the process which requires further refinement is the decision step.

How do we determine whether or not I is prime? There are a number of ways; suppose we merely stipulate that we will use a subprogram which, for a given integer A, determines whether or not that integer is prime. Since the given integer either is or is not prime, a LOGICAL function is appropriate. Thus, we will write a function PRIME(A) which, given an integer A, will return the value .TRUE. if A is prime, the value .FALSE. if not. Then we can proceed with the writing of our main program.

The hierarchy chart given below illustrates which program calls which other programs, for our example.

```
INPUT: subroutine which reads and edits a number.
PRIME: a LOGICAL function which determines whether or not a given
       integer is prime.
```

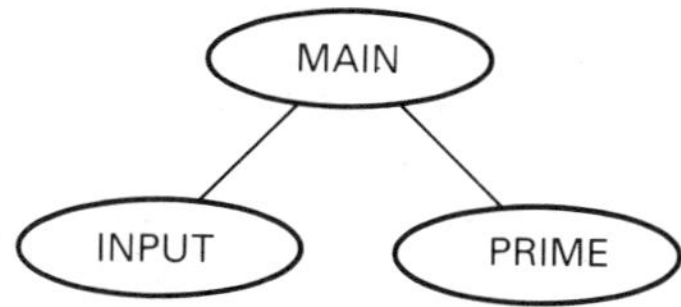

We can now write the complete main program, based on our algorithm and the accompanying discussion.

```
      INTEGER NOPRIM, I, N
      LOGICAL PRIME

C   WRITTEN BY *******, **/**/**

C   THIS PROGRAM INPUTS AN INTEGER N, THEN PRINTS
C THE FIRST N PRIMES. N MUST BE 300 OR LESS.

C   IT CALLS THE FOLLOWING SUBPROGRAMS:

C       INPUT - TO INPUT AND CHECK N
C       PRIME - TO DETERMINE WHETHER AN INTEGER IS PRIME

C   READ N AND INITIALIZE

      CALL INPUT(N)
      NOPRIM = 0
      I = 2

C   IN LOOP, CHECK FOR PRIME. REPEAT UNTIL NOPRIM = N

   10 CONTINUE
          IF(PRIME(I).EQ.1) THEN
              PRINT *,I
              NOPRIM = NOPRIM + 1
          ENDIF
          I = I + 1
          IF(NOPRIM.EQ.N) THEN
              GO TO 500
          ENDIF
          GO TO 10

C  AFTER LOOP, STOP

  500 CONTINUE
      STOP
      END
```

The INPUT routine follows the same procedure we have used several times. It is left as an exercise. We will discuss the PRIME function briefly, since it is a little more difficult.

Recall that an integer is prime if the only divisors it has are 1 and the number itself. One way, then, to determine if A is prime is to find the smallest divisor it has (other than 1) and see if that smallest divisor is A itself. Thus we have the following algorithm:

```
calculate SMDIV, the smallest divisor of A
if SMDIV = A then
   PRIME ← .TRUE.
else
   PRIME ← .FALSE.
endif
```

Now, how do we determine the smallest divisor of A? One thing we could do is write a function SMALL which, given an integer, returns its smallest divisor other than 1. However, since this is simply an example of a search loop, we might choose to implement that step without using a subprogram.

We have considered this problem before (Section 3.3). Here is an algorithm.

```
SMDIV ← 2
loop
   if SMDIV divides A then exit endif
   SMDIV ← SMDIV + 1
endloop
```

The corresponding subprogram is given below:

```
      LOGICAL FUNCTION PRIME(A)
      INTEGER A,SMDIV

C     WRITTEN BY *******, **/**/**

C     THIS FUNCTIONS RETURNS THE VALUE .TRUE. IF A IS PRIME, .FALSE. IF NOT

C     THIS IS THE PARAMETER:

C         A - INPUT, INTEGER - THE NUMBER TO BE TESTED

C     IN LOOP, SEARCH FOR SMALLEST DIVISOR OF A

      SMDIV = 2
   10 CONTINUE
        IF(MOD(A,SMDIV).EQ.0) THEN
           GO TO 20
        ENDIF
        SMDIV = SMDIV + 1
        GO TO 10

C     WHEN FOUND, SET 'PRIME' BASED ON VALUE OF SMALLEST
C DIVISOR OF A.

   20 CONTINUE
      IF(SMDIV.EQ.A) THEN
         PRIME = .TRUE.
      ELSE
         PRIME = .FALSE.
      ENDIF
      RETURN
      END
```

COMMENT. The parameter for the function PRIME is an integer whose "primeness" is to be checked. In the main program, we must supply as parameter the integer to be tested. Hence we write

```
IF(PRIME(I)) THEN
```

We do not let the fact that the subprogram itself calls this parameter "A" confuse us. As we have mentioned before, the calling program supplies parameters based on the names of variables as used in the *calling* program.

Notice that the top-down design process consisted of writing down our thoughts on how we might solve the problem, without worrying at first about the details of how to implement each step. We then came back to the individual steps and repeated the whole process. Notice also that the question of when to use a subprogram and when just to insert the necessary code into the program itself is at least partially a matter of individual preference. We could have written PRIME to use a function SMALL(I) which, given I, determines the smallest divisor of I. Our diagram of the relationship between modules would then take the form:

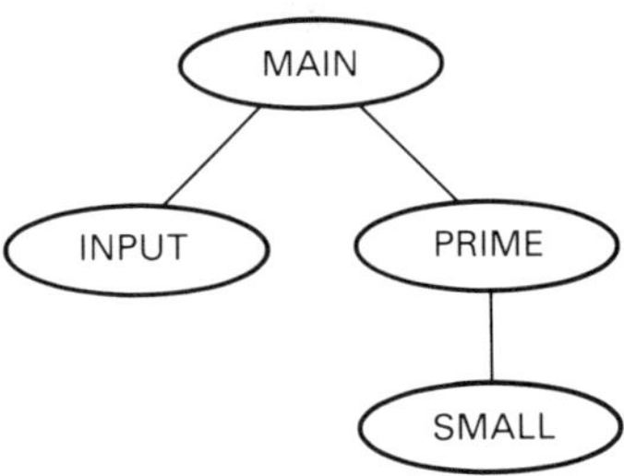

On the other hand, it would have been possible to incorporate the entire problem into one large program, with no subprograms.

Whether or not subprograms are used for a particular step, the process of top-down design is a valuable one. It helps us organize our thoughts and gives us more time to catch potential errors before we reach the programming phase. It tends to make our resulting program more modular, whether the module consist of blocks of code within a program or of separate subprograms.

4. *Test plan.* This program might use a combination of bottom up and top down testing. The key program unit seems to be the PRIME function, so it might be coded and tested first. Then the main program could be written and tested, using a stub for the input subroutine. Finally, the stub could be replaced by the actual subroutine.

We describe a few key tests for each program unit. For the input routine, there are some obvious boundaries at 1 and 300.

For the prime function, the test plan should include some numbers that are prime and some that are not. It might also include some perfect squares (such as 49), since these numbers have exactly one too many divisors. Some answers should be easy to check. A worthwhile test is to take two fairly large primes (for example, 29 and 53) and multiply them. The resulting number should not be indicated as being prime.

5. *Modifications*. We consider briefly two possible modifications. First, in the main program we wrote, the variable I takes on the values 2, 3, 4, 5, 6, 7, 8, 9, and so on. Since we know that, other than 2, there are no even primes, it is really a waste of time to check 4, 6, 8, and the other even numbers. We could save some computer time by following this algorithm:

```
read N
print 2 (2 is the first prime)
NOPRIME ← 1
I ← 3
loop
    if NOPRIM = N then exit endif
    if I is prime then
        print I
        NOPRIM = NOPRIM + 1
    endif
    I ← I + 2
endloop
stop
```

This has further implications for the PRIME function itself. Since that function now "knows" that its parameter is an odd number, it can itself be modified to take advantage of that fact. The details are left to the exercises.

Second, we have not considered the use of headers for the output. Again, the details of this modifiction are left to the exercises. Notice that this would add to our test plan. We would want to run a test that prints exactly one full page of output and a separate test that has one full page plus one additional line of output.

Pitfalls

The pitfalls in using a LOGICAL variable or function have been already mentioned. The two most common pitfalls are

1. writing IF (L1.EQ..TRUE.) rather than just IF (L1); or IF (L1.EQ..FALSE.) instead of IF (.NOT.L1); and
2. forgetting that in a function the answer must be placed into the function name variable.

REVIEW

FORTRAN Syntax

LOGICAL constants
  .TRUE.,.FALSE.

LOGICAL variables
  Declaration: LOGICAL var1,var2,...
  Use: Can assign .TRUE. or .FALSE.to a logical variable
  Comparisons in IF statements:
    To see if a LOGICAL variable L1 is true, write
      IF(L1)...
    To see if L1 is false, write
      IF(.NOT.L1)...

The LOGICAL function
  Definition: LOGICAL FUNCTION fname(par1,par2,...)
  In body: fname = .TRUE. and fname = .FALSE.
  Declaration in calling program: LOGICAL fname
  Use in calling program:
      L1 = fname(par1,par2,...) (L1 is a LOGICAL variable)
      IF(fname(par1,par2,...)) THEN
      IF(.NOT.fname(par1,par2,...)) THEN
  (Use is similar to use of normal LOGICAL variable.)

EXERCISES

1. L1, L2, and L3 are currently .TRUE.; L4 and L5 are .FALSE.. Give the value of each of these expressions.

(a) `L1.OR..NOT.L4`
(b) `L1.AND.L2.OR.L3.AND.L4`
(c) `.NOT.L1.OR..NOT.L2.AND..NOT.L3.OR..NOT.L4`
(d) `.NOT.L1.AND.L2.AND..NOT.L3.AND.L4`
(e) `.NOT.(L1.AND.L2).AND.L3`

2. Fill in the following table:

L1	L2	(L1.OR.L2).AND..NOT.(L1.AND.L2)
.TRUE.	.TRUE.	
.TRUE.	.FALSE.	
.FALSE.	.TRUE.	
.FALSE.	.FALSE.	

3. Although we are not allowed to directly compare two LOGICAL variables, we may write functions to accomplish the same thing, as described below.

(a) Write a LOGICAL function NOTEQ(L1,L2) which returns true if L1 is different from L2, otherwise false. Be careful; you may *not* compare L1 and L2. See Exercise 2 for a possible hint.

(b) Write a similar function EQUAL(L1,L2).

(c) Using these functions, write these conditions in FORTRAN:

```
L1 ≠ L2 or L3 = L4
L1,L2, and L3 are all the same
(L1 and L2) = (L3 and L4)
```

4. (a) Write a LOGICAL function PASSF which, given four test scores, tells whether or not the average score is at least 60.0

(b) Using this function, write a main program that, for a list of students, tells what percentage failed the course. Each student record contains a name and four test scores.

(c) Give a test plan for the PASSF function.

5. Write a LOGICAL function VOWEL(CHAR) which, given a CHARACTER*1 parameter, tells whether or not that character is a vowel.

6. (a) Write a LOGICAL function CLOSE(TEST,HOMEWK) to do the following. Input will consist of two REAL numbers between 0.0 and 1.00, representing a test percentage and a homework percentage. The function will return .TRUE. if the homework percentage is no more than one letter grade below the test percentage (using 90% = A, 80% = B, and so on); otherwise it will return .FALSE..

For example, for a test percentage of 0.958 and a homework percentage of 0.8012 the answer is .TRUE.. For 0.901 and 0.795 the answer is .FALSE..

(b) Write a main program which reads a series of data lines containing name, test percentage, and homework percentage. For each line it should calculate and print the final average and the corresponding letter grade. Use subprograms where appropriate. For any subprogram you use, describe its parameters and logic.

Note: The final average is

.7*test percentage + .3* homework percentage

However, for a person for whom the homework percentage is lower than the test percentage but "close" as defined in (a), the final average is just the test percentage.

(c) Give a test plan for the CLOSE function.

7. Two positive integers A and B are said to be **relatively prime** if the only number that divides evenly into both is 1. For example, 4 and 15 are relatively prime. The divisors of 4 are 1, 2, and 4. The divisors of 15 are 1, 3, 5, and 15. The only common divisor is 1.

(a) Write a LOGICAL function RELPR(A,B) which returns .TRUE. if A and B are relatively prime, .FALSE. otherwise. Use the GCD function developed earlier: GCD(A,B) is the greatest common divisor of A and B.

(b) Code this main program in FORTRAN, using the LOGICAL function of (a).

```
loop
   call INPUT(A,B)
   if A = 0 then exit endif
   if A and B are relatively prime then
      ANSWER ← 'YES'
   else
      ANSWER ← 'NO'
   endif
   print ANSWER
endloop
stop
```

(c) Give the logic of the INPUT routine for (b).
(d) Give a test plan for the RELPR function.

8. Write an input subroutine which has two parameters: a real value X, and a logical value QUIT. The real value should lie between 100 and 500, except that a value of 0 is used to indicate that the user wishes to quit. The parameter QUIT is passed back to the calling program as true if the user entered a 0 for X, false if he entered a legal value between 100 and 500.

9. **(a)** Write a logical function which is given three integer parameters VALUE, LOW, and HIGH. It should check to see if the given value lies between the low and the high, inclusive (true means yes, false means no).
(b) Using the function from part (a), write an input routine which reads three scores and checks to make sure that each lies between 0 and 100, inclusive.
(c) Using the function from part (a), write a segment of code which checks to see if at least one of the integers I and J is between 15 and 17.
(d) Using the function from part (a), write a segment of code which checks to see whether an integer A is at least one half of B, and no more than twice B.

10. **(a)** Write a logical function which, given integers X and Y, determines whether or not Y is within ten units of X.
(b) Give a unit test plan for the function.

11. **(a)** Write a logical function which checks a five-digit number to see if it is a "palindrome," that is, it reads the same from front to back as back to front. For example, 10401 and 89498 are palindromes.
(b) Give a unit test plan for the function.

12. **(a)** Write a logical function called INBOX which checks a point to see if it lies in the unit square from (0,0) to (1,1). Notice that a point is determined by both an x and a y coordinate.
(b) Give a unit test plan for the function.

13. Write a logical function called INCIRC which checks a given point to see if it lies within a circle centered at (0,0) and with a given radius.

14. Write a logical function which, given three points, determines whether or not they lie on a single straight line.

Exercises 15 to 19 relate to Case Study #5.

15. Write a program which reads an integer N, then prints all primes which are less than or equal to N.

16. Write a program which reads a series of data lines each containing a single number. The program should, for each data line, print "yes" or "no," depending on whether or not the number on the line is prime.

17. The PRIME(A) routine as originally written will work for any value of A bigger than or equal to 2. However, we later modified the main program to check only odd numbers.
    Revise the PRIME(A) function under the assumption that A is an odd number bigger than or equal to 3. [Hint: In calculating SMDIV, you need only check odd values. If A is odd, it cannot possibly have an even divisor.]
    Is this an improvement? Why?

18. Write the INPUT routine for the case study.

19. **(a)** Add steps to the main program to call a header routine to print headers every 40 output lines.
    (b) What additions to the test plan should you make because of this change?
    (c) In part (a), the logic of the main program had to be modified to keep track of how many lines of output were printed. An alternate approach involves writing a DETAIL subroutine to print the detail line. Using the techniques of DATA and SAVE, it can do the counting of the number of lines printed, thus removing that logic from the main program. Carry out the details of this modification.
    (d) What advantages do you see to the approach in part (c)? Are there any disadvantages?

Exercises 20 to 23 involve writing packages of subprograms, or complete projects, which may or may not involve the use of logical functions.

20. Using real numbers for dollars and cents operations can lead to accuracy problems. An alternate approach might be to keep each money value as two integer variables, representing the dollars and the cents, respectively. Write the following subprograms for this situation.
    (a) A subprogram to add two such figures. Notice that there are two answers. Given 101 and 50 representing $101.50, and 45 and 63 representing $45.63, the answers should be 147 and 13 representing $147.13. You may assume that the numbers are positive.
    (b) A subprogram to subtract two such figures. Assume that the first amount is larger than the second.
    (c) A subprogram similar to part (b), except that it does not assume that the first amount is larger than the second. Instead, it has another parameter which is used to report to the main program whether or not it was able to do the subtraction. If it is able to, it sets this parameter to true and does the subtraction; if not, it sets this parameter to false.
    (d) A subprogram to multiply two such figures. Assume that both are positive, and round the answer to the nearest cent. For example, 145.01 times 1.10 should be 159.51.
    (e) Modify part (d) to make the second figure represent a real number with three decimal places. (For example, 1 and 85 to represent 1.085.)
    (f) Subprograms to compare two such dollar and cents figures. One, called EQUAL, should tell whether or not they are equal. The second, called LARGER, should tell whether or not the first is larger than the second.

(g) If you write a program for Exercise 7(a) in Section 3.3, using real variables, you will almost certainly find that the answers you get are not quite accurate, due to the imprecision of real variables. Rewrite that program to use the subprograms developed in this exercise.

21. Write a program to find the roots of a quadratic equation, using the following general design.

Recall that, for a quadratic equation $ax^2 + bx + c = 0$, the roots are given by

$$\frac{-b + \sqrt{b^2 - 4ac}}{2a} \quad \text{and} \quad \frac{-b - \sqrt{b^2 - 4ac}}{2a}$$

There are three distinct possibilities:

(1) $b^2 - 4ac$ is positive. Then there are two distinct real roots. For example, if $b^2 - 4ac = 4$, we might have

$$\frac{-1 + \sqrt{4}}{2} = \frac{-1 + 2}{2} = .5$$

$$\frac{-1 - \sqrt{4}}{2} = \frac{-1 - 2}{2} = -1.5$$

(2) $b^2 - 4ac$ is zero. There there is a single real root. For example,

$$\frac{-2 + \sqrt{0}}{2} = -1.0 \text{ (other root is same).}$$

(3) $b^2 - 4ac$ is negative. Then there are two complex number solutions $m + ni$ and $m - ni$, where

$$m \text{ is } \frac{-b}{2a} \text{ and } n \text{ is } \frac{\sqrt{-(b^2 - 4ac)}}{2a}$$

For example, with $b^2 - 4ac = -4$, we might have

$$\frac{-1 + \sqrt{-4}}{2} = \frac{-1}{2} + \frac{2i}{2} = -.5 + 1.0i$$

$$\frac{-1 - \sqrt{-4}}{2} = \frac{-1}{2} - \frac{2i}{2} = -.5 - 1.0i$$

Note: The quantity $b^2 - 4ac$ is referred to as the **discriminant**, and the letter D is used to indicate it.

Your output should appear in a form similar to the following, with new headings on each page.

A	B	C	TYPE	ROOT1	ROOT2
1.00	-2.00	-3.00	2 REAL	3.00	-1.00
1.00	-2.00	10.00	2 COMPLEX	1.00 + 3.00 I	1.00 - 3.00 I
1.00	-2.00	1.00	1 REAL	1.00	

(a) Write a DETAIL routine to print the output line in the proper form. It should have six parameters: A, B, C, NO1, NO2, TYPE. A, B, and C are the coefficients of the original equation.

TYPE is an INTEGER which is either 1, 0, or −1, the "sign" of the discriminant (1 for positive, −1 for negative, 0 for zero). NO1 and NO2 are REAL; what they represent depends on the value of TYPE:

(1) If TYPE Is 1 (D is positive), then NO1 and NO2 are the two distinct real roots.

(2) If TYPE is 0 (D is 0), then NO1 is the single real root and NO2 is meaningless.

(3) If TYPE is −1 (D is negative), then NO1 and NO2 are the real and imaginary parts of the complex solutions (m and n above). You may assume that NO2 is positive. The answers are

```
NO1 + NO2 i
NO1 - NO2 i
```

(b) Write an INPUT routine which reads data records containing A, B, and C, the coefficients of a quadratic equation. We will insist that A must be a positive number; print an error message for faulty input.

(c) Write a routine which calculates three values. The first is the sign of the discriminant $D = b^2 - 4ac$. The second and third are

$$\frac{-b}{2a} \text{ and } \frac{\sqrt{|D|}}{2a}$$

(d) Using the routines developed in (a−c), write a program which reads a series of records each containing A, B, and C, and prints a table of solutions to the corresponding equations.

22. Modify the program of Exercise 21 to remove the restriction that A must be positive. (Notice that if A is 0, the equation is $bx + c = 0$, which has 1 real solution $x = -c/b$. However, if both A and B are 0, print an error message.)

23. Computers can be used to control physical devices, including such things as machine tools and laboratory apparatus. Let us assume that we wish to control a small laboratory furnace and that we have four subprograms available. The first, TEMP, is written as a real valued function with one real argument (which is ignored). The function TEMP returns the internal temperature of the furnace in degrees Celsius. The remaining subprograms are subroutines. Subroutine FURN has one integer argument. If the argument is 0, the furnace is turned off; if the argument is 1, the furnace is turned on. Subroutine WAIT has one integer argument, N. The action for WAIT is to cause the program to wait for N milliseconds before continuing with the statement following the CALL WAIT(N). (A millisecond is 1/1000 of a second.) The final subroutine is INTFRN with no arguments. This subroutine initializes the control circuitry, ensures that the furnace is off, prints a message on the user's terminal requesting the loading of the furnace, and waits until the user responds to the message. (Writing these subprograms would involve techniques beyond standard FORTRAN. However, we may use the subprograms as outlined below.)

Write a subroutine named RNFURN(TIME,SAMPLE,TMP,TOL) to run the furnace and control its temperature for a time of TIME minutes, to a temperature range of TMP − TOL to TMP + TOL, sampling the temperature every SAMPLE seconds. TIME and SAMPLE are integers, and TMP and TOL are real. The subroutine should print messages when the temperature reaches TMP − TOL, TIME minutes later and when the temperature has cooled to 50 degrees or lower.

As an example suppose we have the calling statement

```
CALL RNFURN(10, 5, 250.0, 5.0)
```

In this case, we want the furnace to run for ten minutes with a temperature of 250 ± 5.0 degrees. The temperature will be sampled every five seconds.

The furnace would go through a three-stage process. During the first phase, the furnace would be on and the temperature would rise to the operating temperature. During the second phase, the furnace would be cycled on and off to maintain the temperature within the desired limits. Finally in the last phase, the furnace would be off and the temperature would be decreasing to a safe value at which the furnace could be opened.

The basic operation of the subroutine will be to use INTFRN to initialize the furnace and FURN(1) to turn the furnace on. It will then test the temperature every five seconds until it reaches 250.0−5.0 = 245.0 degrees and write a message indicating the second phase has started. It will then continue sampling the temperature, using FURN(K) with K = 0 to turn off the furnace when the temperature exceeds the desired range, or with K = 1 to turn it on when the temperature falls below the desired range. After 10 minutes it will turn the furnace off and write a message indicating that the cooling down stage has started. At this point, it will continue testing the temperature every 5 seconds until the temperature falls below 50 degrees, writing a message when the cool down period is over.

An improvement on the preceding is to have the program determine actual minimum and maximum temperatures during the second phase above. An additional feature would be to compute the average temperature during that time.

5

USING LOOPS: PART 2

5.1 FILE AND BATCH PROCESSING CONCEPTS

Batch Processing

Up to now, we have concentrated our attention on conversational programs. In these programs, all input was obtained directly from the user as the program was running. All output was displayed at the user's terminal, again as the program was running. This mode of programming provides one of the easiest learning environments, partially due to the immediate feedback of the answers for a particular set of input. For similar reasons, it can be extremely useful for the development and debugging of programs and subprograms, even if the program will eventually not be run as a conversational program.

In this chapter, we will examine a few topics which relate specifically to programming environments other than the conversational environment. We begin with the topic of **batch processing**.

In many early computer systems, programs were written and run in an environment which used punched cards as the input medium and a line printer as the output medium. Thus, for example, to run a programming assignment, a student might prepare a deck of cards with the following general format:

1. job control language (JCL) to cause the program to be compiled
2. the program to be compiled
3. JCL to cause the compiled program to be run

4. data for the program to use as it runs
5. JCL indicating that the job is complete

This deck of cards would be read by a card reader and placed in a list of jobs waiting to be executed. At some point, the computer would execute the job. This would involve two major steps. First, the compiler would compile the program. Second, the program would run, reading the data which was present in the deck of cards. Output from both the compiler and the program itself would be sent to a line printer, where it would be printed.

Generally speaking, present-day batch processing techniques differ slightly from the scenario given above. The primary difference is that the original JCL, program, and data are not prepared as a deck of cards. Rather, the student would prepare (using a text editor) a file which has the same format as the one described for the cards. This file would be submitted to the operating system as a job to be placed in the list of jobs to be executed, rather than reading the cards with a card reader. However, the steps from this point on would be pretty much the same.

The key differences between a batch processing application and a conversational one to accomplish the same job may be summarized as follows:

1. The program will not use prompts in a batch processing job. There is no user waiting to put the data in; rather the data has been prepared in advance and submitted along with the program.
2. The output is much more likely to be in table form, with both the input and the resulting answers appearing in print. For example, a conversational program might ask for a length and a width, then tell the user the area of the rectangle. A batch program for the same task would print a table with three columns—length, width, and area.
3. A batch program is not as likely to use a dummy entry to terminate the input loop. A special end-of-file technique (described in the next subsection) is available and is generally used.
4. Error detection for the input may be handled differently. In a conversational program, if a user has entered six values, one of which is incorrect, the program might ask only for a new value for the one which was incorrect. In a batch program, any error detected in an input record is likely handled by skipping that record and proceeding to the next. If that doesn't make sense, the program may simply have to print a message and stop, since there is no user present from whom to seek guidance.

Loop Control: End of File

In the next subsection, we will examine some ideas involved with processing files of data. One of those ideas, however, relates specifically to the general batch processing environment. We will therefore address it in this subsection.

In the discussion of the preceding subsection, we indicated that the data is submitted along with the program in a batch processing program development situation. The compiled program reads that data, usually one card (that is, line or record) at a time. In such a situation, the FORTRAN language provides a mechanism for the program to determine that there is no data remaining to be read, thus controlling the loop which is reading the data. We do not need a dummy value as the last data value; instead we may write the program to take advantage of this capability to automatically discover that there is no more data. This makes the data preparations slightly easier for the user: He simply includes the actual data for the program to use.

The condition when there is no more data might be called "end of data." Because an identical technique is used when the data is being read from a data file, it is more commonly referred to as "end of file." The following simple algorithm indicates how we may write a loop which is controlled by "going until end of file." (The abbreviation "eof" stands for end of file.)

```
loop
   read LENGTH, WIDTH
   if eof then exit endif
   AREA ← LENGTH * WIDTH
   print LENGTH, WIDTH, AREA
endloop
```

COMMENT. Because the end-of-file condition is detected as part of the read step, we frequently combine the exit step with the read step, as indicated in this example:

```
read LENGTH, WIDTH; if eof then exit endif
```

There are two ways to code this type of loop exit in FORTRAN. Both make use of the following general form of the READ statement:

```
READ(*,format,other options) list of variables
```

At first glance this might seem to imply that we must use formatted reads to use this technique. However, the "format" indicated here may be either a format label such as 1000 or simply an asterisk (*) to indicate that we want to use free format. We will use the second approach in our example given below.

The first possible coding of the end of file uses the IOSTAT = option of the read statement. As a simple example of its use, consider this segment of code:

```
      INTEGER STATUS
      REAL LENGTH,WIDTH
        .
        .
   10 CONTINUE
         READ (*,*,IOSTAT=STATUS) LENGTH,WIDTH
         IF (STATUS.LT.0) THEN
            GO TO 500
         ENDIF
```

We use an INTEGER variable which we call STATUS to indicate the "status" of the read. By placing the option

```
IOSTAT = STATUS
```

in the read statement, we inform the computer of this use of STATUS. When the read is executed, the computer will *automatically* place a value of 0 into the variable STATUS if the read was successful. It will place a negative value into the variable if end of file was reached (that is, there was no data left to read). Thus, we can use the test IF (STATUS.LT.0) to determine if it is time to leave the loop.

An alternative approach is indicated by the following segment of code for the same program.

```
      REAL LENGTH,WIDTH
        .
        .
   10 CONTINUE
         READ (*,*,END=500) LENGTH,WIDTH
```

In this approach, we use the "END=label" option of the read statement. This option means, "If end of file is encountered, go directly to the indicated label (500 in our example)."

It is difficult to make a snap judgment as to which approach is better. The use of END= is, of course, briefer. However, the IOSTAT= approach is more consistent with our usual way of handling loop exits. One argument in favor of the END= approach is that it is more familiar, since it was available on many earlier versions of FORTRAN, whereas the IOSTAT= was not. Finally, as we will see in Section 5.3, the IOSTAT= approach adds some flexibility which we will find useful in certain types of problems. All in all, which to use may very well become a matter of personal preference or perhaps adherence to local programming standards.

As an example, we will develop a batch program to read a series of records, each containing a student number and a numerical test grade. The program should determine the corresponding pass/fail letter grade (70−100=P, 0−69=F). In addition, the program should count how many of each letter grade occurs. To simplify the problem in order to concentrate on the batch processing issues, we make two assumptions. First, we assume that the data is correct. Second, we assume that the output will all fit on a single printed page.

Figure 5.1 contains the algorithm and variable list. Figure 5.2 contains the main program, utilizing the IOSTAT= approach to coding the exit. Notice that, because the program is not conversational, there are no prompts. Similarly, the output is printed in table form, rather than simply printing a message to the user identifying the result for each student in turn. Finally, the READ contains an IOSTAT= option, and it could have contained an END= option. With the exception of these differences, the program looks pretty much the same as it would as a conversational program.

NOTE. Because we realized we were going to use the IOSTAT= option, we included STATUS in the variable list. In some cases, this choice may have been

	Name	Type	Use	Comment
Input:	IDNO	INTEGER	Student number	Also printed
	GRADE	INTEGER	Test grade	Also printed
Output:	LETTER	CHARACTER*1	Letter grade	
Others:	PCTR	INTEGER	Number of P's	Counter
	FCTR	INTEGER	Number of F's	Counter
	STATUS	INTEGER	Used for IOSTAT=	

```
call HEADER
PCTR, FCTR ← 0
loop
   read IDNO,GRADE; if eof then exit endif
   if GRADE ≥ 70 then
      LETTER ← 'P'
      PCTR ← PCTR + 1
   else
      LETTER ← 'F'
      FCTR ← FCTR + 1
   endif
   print IDNO,GRADE,LETTER
endloop
print PCTR,FCTR
stop
```

Figure 5.1

made after the original variable list had been created; thus, we may need to go back and add the read status variable to the list.

File Processing

Before we undertake a detailed study of the FORTRAN procedures for dealing with files, we will consider just a few of the many ways in which files may be used by a program.

By a **file** we are referring to a data file, that is, a collection of data which is stored for a relatively long time on the computer system. It exists beyond the time the particular program which uses it is running. It might exist before the program starts to run, or after the program stops running, or both.

You have already been using files extensively in the creation and storage of your programs themselves. However, this is not the use of files we have in mind here. What we have in mind is files which contain, not programs, but data which is used or created by the programs. For example, the file might consist of a set of student records, each containing a name, four test scores, and ten quiz scores for one student.

One possible scenario for using files is very closely related to the concepts introduced above for batch processing. For example, Figure 5.3 contains a slightly

```
      INTEGER IDNO,PCTR,FCTR,STATUS,GRADE
      CHARACTER*1 LETTER

C   WRITTEN BY *******, **/**/**

C   THIS PROGRAM ILLUSTRATES BATCH PROCESSING CONCEPTS. IT IS
C A PROGRAM TO CALCULATE PASS/FAIL GRADES, AND TO COUNT THE
C STUDENTS IN EACH CATEGORY.

C   IT CALLS A HEADER ROUTINE TO PRINT HEADINGS

C   BEFORE THE LOOP, PRINT HEADINGS AND INITIALIZE COUNTERS

      CALL HEADER
      PCTR = 0
      FCTR = 0

C   IN THE LOOP, CALCULATE AND COUNT THE LETTER GRADES

   10 CONTINUE
         READ(*,*,IOSTAT=STATUS) IDNO,GRADE
         IF (STATUS.LT.0) THEN
            GO TO 500
         ENDIF
         IF (GRADE.GE.70) THEN
            LETTER = 'P'
            PCTR = PCTR + 1
         ELSE
            LETTER = 'F'
            FCTR = FCTR + 1
         ENDIF
         WRITE(*,1000) IDNO,GRADE,LETTER
         GO TO 10

C   AFTER THE LOOP, PRINT THE COUNTS.

  500 CONTINUE
      WRITE(*,2000) PCTR,FCTR
      STOP

C   FORMATS

 1000 FORMAT(' ',2X,I4,6X,I3,8X,A1)
 2000 FORMAT('0','THERE WERE ',I2,' PASSING GRADES AND ',
     $       I2,' FAILING GRADES.')
      END
```

Figure 5.2

```
      INTEGER IDNO,PCTR,FCTR,STATUS
      CHARACTER*1 LETTER

C   WRITTEN BY ********, **/**/**

C   THIS PROGRAM ILLUSTRATES FILE PROCESSING CONCEPTS. IT IS
C A PROGRAM TO CALCULATE PASS/FAIL GRADES, AND TO COUNT THE
C STUDENTS IN EACH CATEGORY.

C   INPUT IS OBTAINED FROM A FILE STUDENT.FILE, AND OUTPUT IS
C SENT TO A FILE STUDENT.RESULTS.

C   IT CALLS A HEADER ROUTINE TO PRINT HEADINGS

C   BEFORE THE LOOP, OPEN THE FILES, PRINT HEADINGS, AND
C  INITIALIZE COUNTERS

      OPEN (10,FILE='STUDENT.FILE')
      REWIND (10)
      OPEN (20,FILE='STUDENT.RESULTS')
      REWIND (20)
      CALL HEADER
      PCTR = 0
      FCTR = 0

C   IN THE LOOP, CALCULATE AND COUNT THE LETTER GRADES

   10 CONTINUE
         READ(10,*,IOSTAT=STATUS) IDNO,GRADE
         IF (STATUS.LT.0) THEN
            GO TO 500
         ENDIF
         IF (GRADE.GE.70) THEN
            LETTER = 'P'
            PCTR = PCTR + 1
         ELSE
            LETTER = 'F'
            FCTR = FCTR + 1
         ENDIF
         WRITE(20,1000) IDNO,GRADE,LETTER
         GO TO 10

C   AFTER THE LOOP, PRINT THE COUNTS AND CLOSE THE FILES.

  500 CONTINUE
      WRITE(20,2000) PCTR,FCTR
      CLOSE (10)
      CLOSE (20)
      STOP

C   FORMATS

 1000 FORMAT(' ',2X,I4,6X,I3,8X,A1)
 2000 FORMAT('0','THERE WERE ',I2,' PASSING GRADES AND ',
     $       I2,' FAILING GRADES.')
      END
```

Figure 5.3

modified version of Figure 5.2. This new version reads its input from a file named STUDENT.FILE and sends its output to a file named STUDENT.RESULTS. The new version could be run either as a batch job or as a conversational job. In either case, all the input and output would involve the two files.

It may be instructive to examine the modified portions, indicated by shading in Figure 5.3. (Details on the FORTRAN statements used will be given in the next subsection.) First, we open and rewind the files at the beginning of the program. This makes sure that the files are properly available for the program to use. It also indicates a **logical unit number**, or just **unit number**, to be used when referring to the file. (In our example, the unit number is 10 for the STUDENT.FILE file, and 20 for the STUDENT.RESULTS file.) Second, we close the same files at the end of the program, using their associated unit numbers. Finally, we use the unit numbers associated with the files in all READ or WRITE statements having to do with the file. Thus, all our reads will have

```
READ (10, ...
```

rather than the usual

```
READ (*, ...
```

to indicate that we want to read from the file opened as logical unit number 10. Likewise, we use

```
WRITE (20, ...
```

to write to the output file. (The HEADER routine would also use unit number 20 in its WRITE statements.)

As it is written in Figure 5.3, the program creates what we will refer to as a **printer-destined** file. By this we mean the output file contains a report in a form suitable for printing. Each record is a line to be printed, and each record includes a carriage control character. At any time in the future, we may issue a suitable operating system command to print the file, interpreting the first character of each record as FORTRAN carriage controls.

An alternative approach might be simply to create a file containing the output records. There would be no headers, and the records would not contain carriage control characters. In addition, we would quite likely not include the counts. A commonly used approach involves creating both a printer-destined file and a similar file which contains only the output data. Although we could certainly print this second file, we will not refer to it as printer-destined. When we print it, we will not interpret the first character as a carriage control. A file such as this is more suitable for later reading by another program, since each record contains data on a single student.

There are many other possible ways in which a program could use a file or files, either as input or as output. The program could be either conversational or batch oriented. We will sketch a few fairly typical applications to indicate some of the possibilities.

In building a set of data to be used in a number of future applications, we might want to be especially sure that the data is correct. Thus, we might create the data by hand, using a text editor, then run it through an editing program. This editing program would use our original file as its input. It might have two output files. The first would be a file in exactly the same form as the input, but containing only the records with no errors. The second would be an error file which contains all the records which have errors, along with an indication of what the error was.

An instructor might use a conversational program to calculate final grades based on some complex grading scheme. This program might read student records from a student file. It could calculate the final numerical score, determine whether the student's performance is improving, declining, or remaining steady, and suggest a letter grade to the instructor. It could then obtain the instructor's choice of letter grade, along with an optional explanation if this is different from the suggested grade. Output could consist of three files: a printer-destined file for printing a grade report, a file to become a permanent record for the instructor, and a file to be sent to the registrar containing only the student identification number and final letter grade.

A conversational payroll program might read from an employee file whose records contain fields such as name, hourly rate, and year-to-date pay. It could, for each employee, input (conversationally) the number of hours worked for the current week. Using this plus the information on the employee record, it could calculate the pay for this week. The output might consist of two files: a printer-destined file which represents pay checks to be printed; and a new version of the employee file, with such things as year-to-date pay modified based on this week's paycheck.

In an engineering environment, an engineer might have a file which represents (in some complex way beyond the scope of this text) a bridge that is being designed. She might use a program which reads this information into the computer and permits modification. The program might also contain options to run various types of analysis subprograms on the design. For example, a stress analysis might be run to study the quality of the design. If any changes are made, the program might save a copy of the revised information on a separate output file.

> **COMMENT.** In many applications, as you can see, the output file created by a program may be used later as input either for the same or for a different program. Of course, the output from a program will be nicely lined up in columns based on the output format. As a result, READ statements which read from a file are frequently formatted reads. If the file has been created without a carriage control character, then the same FORMAT used in creating the file may be used to read the file.

FORTRAN Details

Chapter 13 will cover files in more detail. For now, we consider only a few of the possible options which are available. These options, however, will be sufficient to allow us to write many useful programs to work with data files.

The five file processing statements we will examine are the OPEN, REWIND,

READ, WRITE, and CLOSE statements. For some of these statements, it is useful to visualize a **file pointer** which the system uses to keep track of where the program is working within a given file.

The OPEN statement has the form

```
OPEN (unit,FILE=filename)
```

This serves to make the file available for use in the program. It also identifies the logical unit number which will be used within the program to refer to the file. The rules concerning what numbers may be used as logical unit numbers vary from computer to computer. In our examples, we will frequently use numbers in the range from 10 to 50.

The filename may be any character expression. For example, it may be a character constant such as 'STUDENT.FILE' or it may be a character variable whose value is obtained by a conversational read.

The REWIND statement has the form

```
REWIND (unit)
```

Its purpose is to ensure that the file pointer is at the first record of the file. We generally issue a REWIND statement immediately after opening a file.

The READ statement has the form

```
READ (unit,format,options) list of variables
```

Its meaning has been discussed throughout the text. In a file environment, the unit is that established by the OPEN for that file. The format is either a format label or an asterisk(*) to indicate free format. The options we have considered are the END= and the IOSTAT= options.

The WRITE statement has the form

```
WRITE (unit,format) list of expressions
```

The unit is that established by the OPEN for that file. The format is either a format label or an asterisk(*) to indicate free format. If the output is printer-destined, the first character of the output record should be a carriage control.

The CLOSE statement has the form

```
CLOSE (unit)
```

It disconnects the file from the indicated unit. This frees that unit for use in connection with another file, if necessary. However, we will generally restrict ourselves to simply closing all files as the last step of our program.

To illustrate these concepts, consider the program in Figure 5.4. This reads a file whose 100-column records contain several fields, including a major code in columns 10–12. It creates a partial file consisting of the history majors (major code = 'HIS'). Notice the use of two variables MISC1 and MISC2 to read the mis-

```
      INTEGER STATUS
      CHARACTER*9 MISC1
      CHARACTER*3 MAJOR
      CHARACTER*88 MISC2

C   WRITTEN BY *******, **/**/**

C   THIS PROGRAM CREATES A PARTIAL FILE OF HISTORY MAJORS.

C   BEFORE THE LOOP, OPEN AND REWIND FILES

      OPEN (10,FILE='STUDENT.MASTER')
      REWIND (10)
      OPEN (11,FILE='HISTORY.MAJORS')
      REWIND (11)

C   IN THE LOOP, READ THE MASTER AND CHECK FOR HISTORY MAJORS

   10 CONTINUE
         READ(10,1000,IOSTAT=STATUS) MISC1,MAJOR,MISC2
         IF (STATUS.LT.0) THEN
            GO TO 500
         ENDIF
         IF (MAJOR.EQ.'HIS') THEN
            WRITE (11,1000) MISC1,MAJOR,MISC2
         ENDIF
         GO TO 10

C   AFTER THE LOOP, CLOSE FILES AND STOP

  500 CONTINUE
      CLOSE (10)
      CLOSE (11)
      STOP

C   FORMATS

 1000 FORMAT(A,A,A)
      END
```

Figure 5.4

cellaneous characters on the input records. Notice also that both the READ and the WRITE use the format labelled 1000. This is appropriate because the output record is to be an exact copy of the input record, and the output file is not a printer-destined file. If we were creating a report listing the history majors, we would likely include headings and carriage controls with the output.

REVIEW

Terms

conversational

batch

data file

logical unit number

end of file

Algorithms

End of file exits: **if** eof **then exit endif**

FORTRAN Syntax

End of file exits:

`IOSTAT=variable`

option in read, sets indicated variable to indicate status of read:

0—o.k.

negative—end of file reached

variable must be INTGER

`END=label`

option in read, transfers directly to indicated label when end of file detected

File processing statements:

`OPEN (unit,FILE=filename)`

makes the file available for use and identifies its logical unit number

filename may be any character expression

`REWIND (unit)`

ensures that the file pointer is at the first record of the file

`READ (unit,format,options) list of variables`

unit is that established by the OPEN for that file

format is either a format label or an asterisk (*) to indicate free format

options are the END= and the IOSTAT= options

`WRITE (unit,format) list of expressions`

unit is that established by the OPEN for that file

format is either a format label or an asterisk (*) to indicate free format if the output is printer-destined, the first character of the output record should be a carriage control

`CLOSE (unit)`

disconnects the file from the indicated unit

EXERCISES

1. Each record contains a name, a sex code ('M' or 'F'), and an hourly wage.
  (a) Write an algorithm to find the average hourly wage.
  (b) Write an algorithm to count the number of males.
  (c) Write an algorithm to determine the number of females earning over $10.00 per hour. Modify the algorithm to also find the average hourly wage of the males.

2. Each record has a name, sex code, age, and number of children.
  (a) Write an algorithm to count the number of females under age 21.
  (b) Write an algorithm to find the average number of children for persons under age 25.
  (c) Write an algorithm to find the age and name of the oldest person with no children. (Assume that there is such a person.)
  (d) Revise part (c) to find the age and name of the youngest person who has children.

3. Each record has an ID number, yearly income, number of years worked for the company, and a four-letter department code.
  (a) Write an algorithm to find the ID number and yearly income of the person who earned the most during the year.
  (b) Modify this algorithm to print how many years this person has worked for the company and her department code (this will require two more special variables).
  (c) Write an algorithm to find the average number of years worked by persons in department 'TRNG'.
  (d) Write an algorithm to find the ID number and income of the person who earned the least during the year.

4. Each record contains ID number, name, age, zip code, year of marriage, number of children, salary, and blood type. Write algorithms to answer these questions. (If searching is involved, assume the record being sought is there.)
  (a) How many children does JOE JONES have?
  (b) How many people in the file were married prior to 1963?
  (c) What is the average salary of the people with zip code 14037?
  (d) Who is the first person on the file with blood type O+?
  (e) What is the salary of the person with ID number 1406?

5. Code the following as batch FORTRAN programs.
  (a) Exercise 1(a)
  (b) Exercise 1(a), modified to also print a list of names and hourly wages, 40 per page.
  (c) Exercise 2(c)
  (d) Exercise 3(c), modified to also print a list of the entire set of data, with 40 per page, and with the TRNG department lines "flagged" by placing an asterisk at the end of the line.

6. Code the following as FORTRAN programs which read their data from a data file.
   (a) Exercise 1(c)
   (b) Exercise 2(a)
   (c) Exercise 3(b)
   (d) Exercise 4(a)
   (e) Exercise 4(e)
7. Write a program to handle all the transactions on a single checking account during a month. Input will consist of a single record with an account number and a beginning balance, plus a number of transaction records, each containing a code (C—check, D—deposit) and an amount.

   Output should be a table with each transaction and the resulting balance, as illustrated below:

```
ACCOUNT # 12345          BEGINNING BALANCE = 123.14

                CODE              AMOUNT                BALANCE
                ----              ------                -------
                  C               150.00                 -26.86
                *** OVERDRAFT -    $5.00 CHARGE ***      -31.86
                  D                30.00                  -1.86
                  C                 1.00                  -2.86
                *** OVERDRAFT -    $5.00 CHARGE ***       -7.86
                  D               100.00                  92.14
                  C                10.05                  82.09
                                        CLOSING BALANCE = 82.09
```

8. **(a)** A master file contains 100-column records consisting of data for the employees in a company. Columns 1–9 contain the social security number, columns 10–29 the last name, and columns 49–50 the department code. Write a program to create an output file consisting of the records for those employees who are either in the purchasing department (code PURC) or in the accounting department (code ACCT).
   (b) Write a program, similar to that in part (a). This program creates two separate output files for the two indicated departments. Moreover, the output file records contain only the last name and social security number (in that order) for each person.
   (c) Modify the program in part (b) to also create two printer-destined files, one for each department. Each such file will contain a report for the department, listing the employees, 40 per page with suitable headings. *HINT*: It may be helpful to use subprograms to write the report lines. These subprograms could handle the line-counting tasks.
9. Each record of an input file contains a student name, a student number, and four test scores. Write a program to create two output files. The first is an exact copy of the input file, but with any faulty records removed. The second is a list of erroneous records, with an indication of what is wrong with each. The errors to check for: the name must not be blank, the student number must lie between 10000 and 19999, and the test scores must each lie between 0 and 100.

5.2 NESTED LOOPS

In Section 2.5 we discussed nested decision structures, and we have been using them where apropriate since then. The word "nested" in this context means "one within the other." We had one decision structure completely contained within another.

The same type of situation frequently occurs with looping. In the problems described in Section 2.5, we had a decision structure. As we analyzed the steps to be included in this decision structure, we realized that more decisions would be involved. Likewise, in the problems presented in this section we will have a loop. As we analyze the steps to be included in this loop we will realize that more looping will be involved.

Nesting

Suppose each record contains a positive integer larger than 1. For each record, determine the smallest divisor (other than 1) of the integer on the card. For example, if our data cards contained the numbers 15, 8, and 17, respectively, then our answers would be 3, 2, and 17 in that order.

We immediately realize that we will need a loop, since we are processing a number of data lines. This loop will terminate on encountering a dummy entry of 0.

```
loop
   read N
   if N = 0 then exit endif
   find smallest divisor of N
   print N and the smallest divisor of N
endloop
stop
```

For each data line we will find and print the smallest divisor. To complete the algorithm we need to **refine** the step "find smallest divisor of N." When we do so, we have two choices. We can write the step as a function, or we can include the refinement right in our main program. In this example, we choose the latter alternative.

Finding the smallest divisor of a single number N was one of our examples in Section 3.3. Our basic strategy is to look for a number which divides evenly into N, starting at 2 and working our way up until we succeed. Since we will try several numbers we need a loop to locate this smallest divisor. The algorithm segment for locating the smallest divisor involves a loop where we continue searching until MOD(N,TRY) is 0.

```
TRY ← 2
loop
   if MOD(N,TRY) = 0 then exit endif
   TRY ← TRY + 1
endloop
```

To complete our entire algorithm, we place this algorithm segment in the original algorithm in place of the step it refines, "find smallest divisor of N."

```
 1  loop
 2    read N
 3    if N=0 then exit endif
 4    TRY ← 2
 5    loop
 6      if MOD(N,TRY) = 0 then exit endif
 7      TRY ← TRY + 1
 8    endloop
 9    print N,TRY
10  endloop
11  stop
```

The algorithm segment for finding the smallest divisor forms lines 4–8 of the entire algorithm.

> **COMMENT.** We follow our usual indentation pattern for loops by indenting the body of the loop. Lines 2–9 form the body of the **outer loop**. This outer loop includes an **inner loop** (lines 5–8), whose body (lines 6 and 7) is indented still further.

As indicated in the comment, we frequently refer to the two loops as the outer loop and the inner loop. In addition, we say that the inner loop is nested within the outer loop.

A possible source of confusion is the fact that this algorithm has two different "exit" steps, lines 3 and 6. However, if we recall what we originally meant when we wrote these steps, we will have no problem. The exist in line 3 is taken because we have no more data; we must leave the loop which reads the data (the outer loop). On the other hand, the exit in step 6 indicates that we have found a divisor of N, and we want to leave the loop which looks for this divisor (the inner loop). In each case, we are exiting from the innermost loop which contains the given exit step. Almost always, when we use the term *exit* this will be our intention. We therefore adopt the following rule:

> The term **exit** means to leave the innermost loop containing the exit step.

COMMENTS.

1. Loops may be nested to any depth. In the above example, we had a "loop within a loop." It is possible to have a "loop within a loop within a loop," and so on. However, if we find ourselves needing such a structure, we might consider using subprograms to reduce the complexity. Even in this example, which only involves two nested loops, it would have been reasonable to use a subprogram to calculate the smallest divisor of N. If we had done so, the inner loop would have been in this subprogram. Neither the main program nor the subprogram would have contained nested loops.
2. Loops may be nested; they may not overlap. The inner loop must be completely contained within the outer loop.

Our second example of nested loops prints a multiplication table, from $1 \times 1 = 1$ to $12 \times 12 = 144$.

```
loop for I = 1 to 12
   loop for J = 1 to 12
     MULT ← I * J
     print I,J,MULT
   endloop
endloop
```

COMMENT. I is the index of the outer loop, J the index of the inner loop. For each value of I, J will take on the values from 1 to 12. We therefore obtain all the "1 times" answers, followed by all the "two times" answers, and so on.

We say that the inner loop index "varies more rapidly" than the outer loop index.

The next example illustrates a method of grouping data which is frequently encountered. The data file is organized as shown below:

```
employee record
   sale record
   sale record
      .
      .
      .
   dummy sale record
employee record
   sale record
      .
      .
      .
   dummy sale record
      .
      .
      .
and so on
```

Each employee record contains an employee number and a commission rate. Each sale record has the amount of one sale by the employee it is grouped under. A dummy entry record with a value of 0 for the sales amount indicates the end of the list of sales for each employee.

Write an algorithm which, for each employee, calculates and prints his total sales and commission. In addition, it should print the employee number and commission of the person earning the largest commission. (Commission is total sales times the commission rate for the salesperson, with a bonus of $100 if the total sales exceed $5000.00).

COMMENT. Notice the nested structure of the data. We have a pattern consisting of an employee record, plus a repetition of sales records. This pattern is in turn repeated. This type of data structuring frequently leads to a nested loop structure in the program.

From the description of the problem we see the need for the following variables. (We choose to use a function to calculate the commission. Since commission is based on total sales and commission rate, it will have these two values as input parameters.)

	Name	Type	Use	Comment
Input:	IDNO	INTEGER	Employee number	
	RATE	REAL	Commission rate	
	SALE	REAL	Amount of one sale	
Other:	TOTAL	REAL	Total sales for employee	Accumulator
	COMM	REAL	Commission	
	COMMF	REAL		Function to calculate commission
	LARGE	REAL	Largest commission	
	LIDNO	INTEGER	ID of person with largest commission	

This list was obtained by determining what values are to be printed as well as what values are to be read from the cards. We observe that TOTAL will be an accumulator, since we have to add SALE figures from a number of records. The algorithm will utilize the standard methods for finding the largest number in some list.

We know we need a loop because we are processing more than one employee. We will exit from this loop when there are no more employees to be processed. When we attempt to read an employee record and none remains, this condition will have occurred.

Before the loop we will initialize LARGE to 0, taking advantage of the fact that our commissions will be positive numbers. After the loop we will print LARGE and LIDNO. In the loop, in addition to processing and printing answers for one employee, we will change LARGE and LIDNO whenever a larger commission occurs. This planning leads to the following rough algorithm. (The INPUT subroutine reads and edits the employee record, setting a LOGICAL variable EOF to true if end of file occurs. The DETAIL subroutine prints a "detail line" and counts the lines printed to determine when headings are needed.)

```
LARGE ← 0
loop
   call INPUT(IDNO,RATE,EOF)
   if EOF is true then exit endif
   calculate TOTAL
   COMM ← COMMF(TOTAL,RATE)
   call DETAIL(IDNO,RATE,TOTAL,COMM)
```

```
        if COMM > LARGE then
           LARGE ← COMM
           LIDNO ← IDNO
        endif
    endloop
    print LIDNO,LARGE
    stop
```

(The step "calculate TOTAL" will involve reading all the cards between the employee card for this employee and the next employee card.)

We now refine the step which calculates TOTAL. When we reach this step, we have already read in the employee record for the employee in whom we are interested. The next few records each contain the amount of one sale, terminated by a dummy entry of 0. In order to calculate the TOTAL, we will have to read all these records, and this will require a loop.

The type of loop we have is one we have already encountered. It uses a dummy entry to terminate the loop, and it is an accumulation loop. Before the loop, we must initialize our accumulator. In the loop, we read a record and add to the accumulator. (After the loop, we will use the accumulator to calculate the commission.) The loop, including the initialization step, follows. (The INPUT2 subroutine reads and edits the sale record.)

```
TOTAL ← 0
loop
   call INPUT2(SALE)
   if SALE = 0 then exit endif
   TOTAL ← TOTAL + SALE
endloop
```

Notice the standard placement of the dummy entry exit immediately following the read.

The entire algorithm (Figure 5.5) is formed by inserting this refinement in place of the step it refines.

COMMENTS.

1. It is frequently useful to identify a "purpose" for each loop we write. By this we mean stating what one pass through the body of the loop is designed to accomplish.

   For this algorithm, each pass through the outer loop will "process one employee." Each pass through the inner loop will "process one sale."

   It may be helpful to label the loops, as indicated in Figure 5.5, with comments relating to the purpose of the loop. For one thing, this reinforces which **endloop** goes with which **loop**.

2. Until now, we have always been able to say things like "initialize accumulators before the loop." With nested loops we must be more careful. For example, the accumulator TOTAL is initialized within the body of the outer loop, but before the inner loop. During the process of top down design the proper

```
LARGE ← 0
loop (employees)
   call INPUT(IDNO,RATE,EOF)
   if EOF is true then exit endif
   TOTAL ← 0
   loop (sales)
      call INPUT2(SALE)
      if SALE = 0 then exit endif
      TOTAL ← TOTAL + SALE
   endloop (sales)
   COMM ← COMMF(TOTAL,RATE)
   call DETAIL(IDNO,RATE,TOTAL,COMM)
   if COMM > LARGE then
      LARGE ← COMM
      LIDNO ← IDNO
   endif
endloop (employees)
print LIDNO,LARGE
stop
```

Figure 5.5

placement happened automatically. However, we should observe that the placement is correct: We want to reinitialize TOTAL for each new employee, prior to starting the accumulation process for the employee.

Nested loop structures generally arise naturally during the top down design and refinement of algorithms. It is not necessary to see at a glance that a particular problem either will or will not involve nested loops. However, as in our previous example, a data structure with nested repetitions may indicate a nested loop structure.

Implementation

As the above examples illustrate, we may have loops of any type nested within other loops of any type. Writing a FORTRAN program for an algorithm which contains nested loops does not involve any new techniques or concepts. We simply write the code needed for each loop separately. For example, the algorithm for the multiplication table may be coded as this segment:

```
      INTEGER I,J,MULT
      DO 100 I = 1,12
         DO 50 J = 1,12
            MULT = I * J
            WRITE(*,1000)I,J,MULT
 50         CONTINUE
100      CONTINUE
```

We continue our practice of indenting the body of a loop, as in the algorithms themselves. The FORTRAN program corresponding to our first algorithm is given in Figure 5.6; the lines are numbered to correspond to the line numbers in the algorithm, which is also reproduced in the figure.

The FORTRAN program for the second algorithm is left as an exercise.

```
 1      loop
 2         call INPUT(N,EOF)
 3         if EOF is true then exit endif
 4         TRY  2
 5         loop
 6           if MOD(N,TRY) = 0 then exit endif
 7           TRY  TRY + 1
 8         endloop
 9         print N,TRY
10      endloop
11      stop

           INTEGER N,TRY,MOD
           LOGICAL EOF

      C   WRITTEN BY *******, **/**/**

      C   THIS PROGRAM FINDS THE SMALLEST DIVISOR OF NUMBERS

      C   OUTER LOOP-READ NUMBER, FIND SMALLEST DIVISOR, PRINT

 1         10 CONTINUE
 2              CALL INPUT(N,EOF)
 3              IF (EOF) THEN
                  GO TO 500
                ENDIF

      C   INNER LOOP-SEARCH FOR A DIVISOR

 4              TRY = 2
 5         20   CONTINUE
 6                 IF(MOD(N,TRY).EQ.0) THEN
                      GO TO 100
                   ENDIF
 7                 TRY = TRY + 1
 8                 GO TO 20
          100   CONTINUE
 9              PRINT *,N,TRY
10              GO TO 10
          500 CONTINUE
11            STOP
              END
```

Figure 5.6

Pitfalls

The error most commonly made in working with nested loops is improper placement of initialization and print steps. The process of top down design helps avoid this problem. However, it is a good idea to specifically examine the placement of these steps.

For example, the placement of the step TOTAL ← 0 in our second example was prior to the inner loop, within the body of the outer loop. This was correct, since we wanted to calculate a new total for each employee. For each new employee we must reinitialize TOTAL to 0.

On the other hand, the step LARGE ← 0 occurs prior to the outer loop, since we are looking for the largest commission overall. If we were looking for the largest sale for *each* employee, the placement would be different. Similar comments apply to the print steps in that example.

REVIEW

Programming Technique: Nested Loops

Use when one of the steps being repeated in a loop itself requires a loop. Algorithm form:

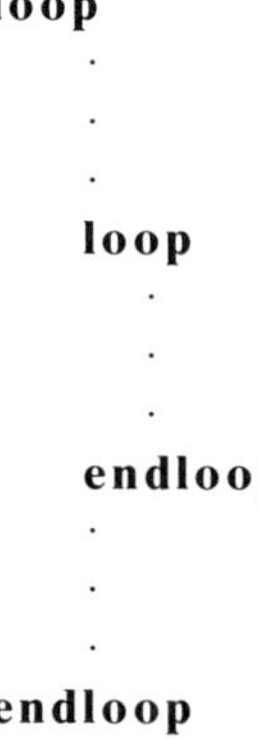

FORTRAN implementation: Write code for each loop using standard techniques.

EXERCISES

1. (a) Write algorithms for the INPUT routine of the first example in this section. What editing is needed?

(b) Do the same for the third example. For any error in input, your INPUT or INPUT2 routines should skip directly to the next employee (read and ignore down to the dummy sale card). This will require a nested loop. Also give an algorithm for the DETAIL routine.

2. Write a FORTRAN program for the third example of the section, after writing an algorithm for the COMMF function.
3. Write FORTRAN progams for the following. All variables are INTEGER. No FORMATS need be included.
   (a)

```
read I,J,K
print I,J,K
C ← 0
loop
   loop
     if I > J then exit endif
     I ← 2 * I
     C ← C + 1
   endloop
   if I > K then exit endif
   print I,J,K
   J ← J + 1000
endloop
print C
stop
```

   (b)

```
loop
   read X
   if X < 0 then exit endif
   print headings
   loop
     print X
     X ← X * 5
     if X > 500 then exit endif
   endloop
endloop
stop
```

4. Write an algorithm for each of the following situations.
   (a) Each record has a beginning balance and an interest rate. The interest is compounded annually: the balance after one year is the original balance plus the interest for that year, and the interest for the second year is based on this new balance (and so on). Write a program which, for each record, will tell how many years it takes for the balance in the account to be more than twice the starting balance.
   (b) The setup is the same as for (a). However, for each record the algorithm should print out a table showing the year number, the beginning balance for that year, the interest for the year, and the ending balance for the year, up through and including the year in which the balance exceeds twice the starting balance. (One new page per record.)
   (c) Modify (b) so it does not print a line of information for the final year, when the balance goes over twice the starting balance.

(d) Repeat (a), but with no data records. Instead, use a beginning balance of \$1000.00, and interest rates of 4 percent to 20 percent in steps of 0.25 percent (that is, 4%, 4.25%, 4.5%, and so on).

5. Write FORTRAN programs for the algorithms of Exercise 4.

6. Write algorithms for the following.

(a) Each record has two positive integers each greater than 1. For each record your algorithm should find the largest integer which divides evenly into both numbers.

(b) Each record has a single positive integer. For each record, print a complete list of the numbers which divide evenly into that number. Start a new page of output for each record.

7. Write FORTRAN programs for each of the algorithms of Exercise 6.

8. Find and print the smallest divisor of each odd number from 3 to 201.

9. The data file consists of repetitions of the following pattern:

student record
1 or more course records for this student
dummy course record

The student record contains name, ID, total semester hours attempted to date (prior to this semester), total semester hours earned to date, and total quality points earned to date. Each course record contains course department (3 characters), course number (3 digits), semester credit hours for the course, and letter grade (A, B, C, D, or F). The department is "XXX" on the dummy course record. The course records represent courses taken this semester.

Write an algorithm to generate a report containing the following columns

name

ID

hours attempted, earned, quality point average before this semester

same three figures for this semester's courses

same three figures after this semester

The quality points earned in a course are calculated by multiplying the semester hours for the course by 4 for an A, 3 for a B, 2 for a C, 1 for a D, 0 for an F. For an F grade, the hours are counted as attempted but not earned. The quality point average is the total quality points divided by the hours attempted.

10. Do the following for the data file of Exercise 9. For each student, generate a grade report on a new page. The report should include the following information in a suitable format: name, ID, list of courses (with department, number, semester hours, grade, and quality points earned in course), hours attempted, earned, and quality point average for the semester, same three figures after this semester.

11. The data file contains repetitions of this pattern:

account record for a checking account
0 or more transaction records for this account
dummy transaction record (code "L")

For each account, generate output similar to that illustrated in Exercise 7 of Section 5.1.

12. Modify Exercise 11 to do the following for each account.

(a) Count the checks and deposits.

(b) Determine the lowest and highest balance.

(c) Calculate the average check amount.

(d) Calculate the service charge for the month. The first record of each group will contain an account type (R, S, or V). For regular (R) accounts, the service charge is $3.00 unless the minimum balance is at or above $750, in which case it is 0. For special (S) accounts, the charge is $.20 per check. For V.I.P. (V) accounts, the charge is based on the *average* of the minimum and maximum balances. If this is less than $500, there is a $7.00 charge; $500–$1,000, a $5.00 charge; over $1,000, free.

13. The data file has this layout:

Number of departments
Record with three-character dept. code, number of professors in dept.
Professor records containing ID and salary (one for each professor)
Dept. record same as above
And so on

Write an algorithm to generate a list of professors in the following format:

```
DEPT.       ID       SALARY
-----       --       ------

 XXX       XXXX      XXXXX
           XXXX      XXXXX
           XXXX      XXXXX
 XXX       XXXX      XXXXX
           XXXX      XXXXX
      and so on
```

Then show how to modify the algorithm to add the following:

(a) Find and print the person with the highest salary in *each* department.

(b) Find and print the average salary in each department.

(c) Find and print the average salary in the whole school.

(d) Count the number earning over $18,000 in the whole school.

(e) Find the largest average salary for a department. For example, your algorithm might print a message such as

```
BIO DEPARTMENT HAS LARGEST AVERAGE SALARY - 15533.00.
```

14. Each row in a classroom contains 16 seats. There are six rows. Give an algorithm to create a seating chart with appearance similar to this:

```
ROW 1 SEAT  1----
      SEAT  2----
             .
             .
             .
      SEAT 16----
ROW 2 SEAT  1----
        and so on
```

15. For each number from 1 to 200, print a list of its divisors, in a format similar to this:

```
DIVISORS OF 1: 1
DIVISORS OF 2: 1
               2
```

(continued)

```
DIVISORS OF 3: 1
               3
DIVISORS OF 4: 1
               2
               4
    and so on
```

16. Write an algorithm to verify the correctness of the formula

$$1 + 2 + \cdots + N = \frac{N(N+1)}{2}$$

for each value of N from 1 to 75.

17. Suppose we generate random numbers in the range from 1 to 10. On the average, how many numbers would have to be generated until two consecutive numbers are the same? To answer the question, write a program to perform the experiment 1000 times.

18. A person offers you a game of chance that involves rolling a pair of dice until either a 2, or 7, or an 11 comes up. If a 2 or 11 comes up, you win $5, otherwise you lose $2. Should you play the game (assuming you are a betting person in the first place)? To answer the question, write a program to play the game 1000 times.

19. Some state lotteries operate on the following principle: You bet $1, choose a number in the range 0 to 999, and win $500 if your number is drawn in the lottery. One of the authors of this text overheard a person describing his sure-fire system to win: Bet on the same number every day, eventually it's bound to turn up. This exercise explores the wisdom of that system.

(a) Assume that the person has $1500 with which to play the lottery 300 times a year for five years (50 weeks a year, six days a week). Write a conversational program to allow the user to choose a number, then simulate five years' worth of play. At the end of the simulated five years, tell the person how much of the $1500 she started with is left.

(b) Suppose 1000 people all tried this system. What would be the average amount left after the five years? To answer the question, write a program to simulate the five years' play 1000 times, using a single chosen number.

(c) Modify part (b) to simulate each of the 1000 people choosing a different number to play for the five years.

5.3 LOOP CONTROL: MULTIPLE EXIT CONDITIONS

In Section 3.3 we used an algorithm to locate employee number 11457 in a file of employees:

```
loop
    read IDNO,AGE,WAGE,NUMDEP
    if IDNO = 11457 then exit endif
endloop
print IDNO,AGE,NUMDEP
stop
```

The algorithm as written works properly only if there is an employee with IDNO 11457 in the file. The problem with the algorithm is that we could reach the end of the file without locating the desired employee. What we need is another exit from the loop, on encountering end of file. The loop itself might be revised to read as follows:

```
loop
   read IDNO,AGE,WAGE,NUMDEP; if eof then exit endif
   if IDNO = 11457 then exit endif
endloop
```

As usual, after leaving the body of the loop we will proceed to the step immediately following the **endloop**. At this point we will need to make another minor change to the algorithm. If we did locate employee 11457 we want to print the IDNO, AGE, and NUMDEP variables. However, if no such employee existed we should instead print an error message. As you can see, we will need a decision structure (**if-then-else** or **case**). The revised algorithm might read:

```
loop
   read IDNO,AGE,WAGE,NUMDEP; if eof then exit endif
   if IDNO = 11457 then exit endif
endloop
if end of file was reached then
  print 'no employee #11457'
else
  print IDNO,AGE,NUMDEP
endif
```

The General Form

There are many types of problems for which there are two or more different conditions for leaving a loop. Generally, by the time an algorithm is written the program designer has thought about the loop in enough detail to realize that multiple exits are needed. At this point, the algorithm can be written. In general, we will have

```
initialization, if any
loop
   body of loop, including two or more exits
endloop
decision structure based on which exit was taken
```

For example, we can use our RND function to return an integer from 1 to 25 randomly chosen. Using this function we can write a program to simulate a game of chance with these rules: if the number is 1, 2, 3, or 4 you win $5; otherwise you lose $1. We will write an algorithm which, starting with $20, plays this game until either you are broke or your money has doubled. In planning this loop we realize we need a variable, MONEY, which must be initialized to 20. In the body of the loop we will use RND to generate a number and adjust our money supply accordingly. After the loop, we should print an appropriate message. From the very statement of the program it is clear that there are two different conditions for terminating the loop—we are broke or we have doubled our money. A possible solution is given below.

```
MONEY ← 20
loop
   NUM ← RND(25)
   case
     1(NUM < 5) MONEY ← MONEY + 5
       if MONEY ≥ 40 then exit endif
     2(any other) MONEY ← MONEY − 1
       if MONEY = 0 then exit endif
   endcase
endloop
if MONEY doubled then
   print 'you doubled your money to', MONEY
else
   print 'you are broke'
endif
```

We have placed the test for one of the exits following the step which adds $5 to our money supply, since at this point we may have doubled our money. Since we are going up by 5, we must use the test "greater than or equal to 40" rather than merely "equal to 40."

> **COMMENT.** Other approaches to this problem are possible, particularly if we do not wish to print the two different messages at the end. For example, we might write

```
MONEY ← 20
loop
   NUM ← RND(25)
   if NUM < 5 then
     MONEY ← MONEY + 5
   else
     MONEY ← MONEY − 1
   endif
   if MONEY = 0 or MONEY ≥ 40 then exit endif
endloop
print MONEY
stop
```

There can be more than two possible exit conditions for a loop. In addition, one of the possible exits may be the automatic exit from a **loop for**, or count-controlled, looping structure. For example, let us reconsider the preceding game of chance. The participant may have decided in advance to play the game no more than 30 times. Thus, the game would terminate when it had been played 30 times, when the player had doubled her money, or when she had gone broke, whichever occurred first. The algorithm describing this situation is similar to the previous one. The differences are shaded.

```
MONEY ← 20
loop for I = 1 to 30
   NUM ← RND(25)
   case
     1(NUM < 5) MONEY ← MONEY + 5
       if MONEY ≥ 40 then exit endif
     2(any other) MONEY ← MONEY - 1
       if MONEY = 0 then exit endif
   endcase
endloop
if played 30 times then
   print ''you played 30 times with money left'', MONEY
else if MONEY doubled then
   print 'you doubled your money to', MONEY
else
   print 'you are broke'
endif
```

Use of Multiple Exits

The examples just given are typical of many problems in which multiple exits from a loop are needed. In each example we could view the loop as performing a process which would either succeed or fail. When searching for some item, we may find it or we may not. In the wagering example, we might view doubling our money as success and going broke or running out of times as failure.

The following example illustrates another type of application; again it is possible to view the algorithm from a succeed/fail perspective. Suppose that the INTEGER variable N contains an odd positive integer greater than or equal to 3. We will write an algorithm segment to print a message telling whether or not the number N is prime.

By "prime" we mean that the number cannot be further factored. Thus the only divisor of N, if N is prime, will be N itself (and, of course, 1). Also, since N is odd, we know that whether it is prime or not its only possible divisors are the odd numbers 3, 5, 7, and so on.

To see if N is prime, then, we might just try dividing N by these odd numbers (3, 5, 7, ...). If one of the numbers divides evenly (remainder 0), then that number is a factor and N is thus not prime. Otherwise, N is prime.

So far, we have outlined a loop: Each pass through the loop we will calculate MOD(N,TRY) to see if the variable TRY divides evenly into N. TRY will successively take on the values 3, 5, 7, and so on. Since there are two possibilities—N is a prime (success) or N is not a prime (failure)—we might expect to have two exits from the loop. Before reading on, you should try to determine the conditions for these exits and their proper placement within the loop outline given below:

```
TRY ← 3
loop
   calculate MOD(N,TRY)
   TRY ← TRY + 2
endloop
```

The solution may be devised by analysis similar to the following. If MOD(N, TRY) is 0, then we have found a divisor and thus N is not prime. On the other hand, if TRY ever becomes equal to N itself, then we have a prime number since we have failed to find a divisor less than N. Moreover, we should check to see if TRY = N prior to calculating MOD(N,TRY). The complete algorithm segment follows.

```
TRY ← 3
loop
   if TRY = N then exit endif
   if MOD(N,TRY) = 0 then exit endif
   TRY ← TRY + 2
endloop
if no divisor found then
   print N, 'is prime'
else
   print N, 'is not prime'
endif
```

COMMENT. Although perhaps most algorithms involving multiple exits may be viewed in "succeed/fail" terms, we do not wish to imply that all such algorithms fit this pattern. For example, if we are simultaneously reading from two different files, the various exits may be based on which file reaches end-of-file first. Examples of this type will be discussed in Chapter 13.

Implementation

A loop with multiple exits is written in FORTRAN in much the same way as a loop with a single exit. This is especially true when all the exits are of the "general condition" form. As we will see, exits on end of file and the standard exit from a **loop for** construction will require special consideration.

COMMENT. The method we present here is one possible method. There are other, more "mechanical" methods possible. However, with a little care, this method is probably the simplest to use.

The only "problem" which occurs in implementing these types of algorithms is knowing exactly how to code the conditions which tell us which exit occurred. In our algorithms, we have used verbal descriptions such as "MONEY doubled" to convey these conditions. During the coding step (or during the algorithm step itself, if we prefer to refine the algorithm), we must clarify the conditions.

The simplest type of algorithm to code is that exemplified by our prime number example. We have neither a count-controlled loop exit nor an end-of-file exit. The corresponding program may be found in Figure 5.7. Notice that we simply base our condition on the conditions which led to the exit in the first place.

CAUTION. This example does illustrate one pitfall which we must avoid. Sometimes it is important which of the possible exit conditions we examine first when we leave the loop. This matter is examined further in the exercises.

```
Algorithm segment
  TRY ← 3
  loop
     if TRY = N then exit endif
     if MOD(N,TRY) = 0 then exit endif
     TRY ← TRY + 2
  endloop
  if no divisor found then
    print N, 'is prime'
  else
    print N, 'is not prime'
  endif
```

```
Program segment

      INTEGER N,TRY
          .
          .
          .
C     INITIALIZE

        TRY = 3

C     INCREMENT TRY UNTIL IT EQUALS N OR
C DIVIDES EVENLY INTO N

   10 CONTINUE
           IF(TRY.EQ.N) THEN
              GO TO 100
           ENDIF
           IF(MOD(N,TRY).EQ.0) THEN
              GO TO 100
           ENDIF
           TRY = TRY + 2
           GO TO 10

C     PRINT PROPER MESSAGE

  100 CONTINUE
        IF(TRY.EQ.N) THEN
           WRITE(*, 5000) N, ' is prime'
        ELSE
           WRITE(*, 6000) N, ' is not prime'
        ENDIF
```

Figure 5.7

A somewhat more difficult type of problem is that involving a **loop for** construction. However, to successfully handle this type of problem, we need only recall the meaning of the **loop for** construction (and the corresponding FORTRAN DO loop). If we take the normal exit from a DO loop, then the value of the loop index will be the value it would have been on the next pass through the loop. Thus, we can examine the loop index to determine whether we have taken the standard exit or have exited early with some other exit. It is suggested that this possibility always be checked first in a program involving a **loop for** with other exit steps. Figure 5.8 contains the FORTRAN code for the algorithm which involved count control.

A similar approach can be used in connection with loops which have an end-of-file exit. Recall from Section 5.1 that there are two common ways to code such loops in FORTRAN. The first uses the IOSTAT= option, the second the END= option. Although the END= option may be more convenient, the IOSTAT= option is better when multiple exit loops are involved. When we reach the decision structure following the loop body, we can use the condition of the IOSTAT= variable to determine whether or not end of file was reached. (Recall that this variable is automatically set to a negative value if the read statement detects end of file.) Figure 5.9 contains the algorithm and code for the program which searches for ID number 11457 in a file.

We recommend that the end of file condition be the first one checked in the decision structure following the loop.

> **NOTE.** If we use an INPUT routine to read and edit the data, it might well pass back a logical variable (perhaps called EOF) which indicates that end of file occurred in the subroutine. This variable may be used not only to exit the loop, but also in the decision structure following the loop to detect that end of file did occur.

Alternate Approaches

Before we leave the topic of implementation, we give a very brief description of two additional methods which are sometimes used. The first involves using various default values and giving values to variables as part of the exit step. In this way we can avoid the need for a decision structure after the loop. For example, here is an alternative to the algorithm for testing to see if a number is prime:

```
ANSWER ← 'YES'
loop for I = 3 to N-1 by 2
   if MOD(N,I) = 0 then
      ANSWER ← 'NO'
      exit
   endif
endloop
print N,ANSWER
```

We will use this approach from time to time in various examples in the remainder of the text. Notice that the decision to take this view of the problem probably occurs during algorithm design rather than during coding.

The second approach, which is almost never necessary, involves setting a variable to a different value as part of the different exit steps, then using that variable's value after the loop to see which exit occurred. In practice, it is almost

Algorithm segment:

```
MONEY ← 20
loop for I = 1 to 30
   NUM ← RND(25)
   case
     1(NUM < 5) MONEY ← MONEY + 5
       if MONEY ≥ 40 then exit endif
     2(any other) MONEY ← MONEY - 1
       if MONEY = 0 then exit endif
   endcase
endloop
if played 30 times then
   print 'you played 30 times with money left', MONEY
else if MONEY doubled then
   print 'you doubled your money to', MONEY
else
   print 'you are broke'
endif
```

Program segment:

```
      INTEGER MONEY,I,RND
          .
          .
      MONEY = 20
      DO 150 I = 1,30
         NUM = RND(25)
         IF (NUM.LT.5) THEN
            MONEY = MONEY + 5
            IF (MONEY.GE.40) THEN
              GO TO 200
            ENDIF
         ELSE
            MONEY = MONEY - 1
            IF (MONEY.EQ.0) THEN
              GO TO 200
            ENDIF
         ENDIF
  150    CONTINUE
  200 CONTINUE
      IF (I.GT.30) THEN
         PRINT *, 'You played 30 times with money left ', MONEY
      ELSE IF (MONEY.GE.40) THEN
         PRINT *, 'You doubled your money to ', MONEY
      ELSE
         PRINT *, 'You are broke'
      ENDIF
```

Figure 5.8

```
Algorithm segment:

    loop
       read IDNO,AGE,WAGE,NUMDEP; if eof then exit endif
       if IDNO = 11457 then exit endif
    endloop
    if end of file was reached then
       print 'no employee #11457'
    else
       print IDNO,AGE,NUMDEP
    endif
```

```
Program segment (OPEN and CLOSE steps are omitted)

      INTEGER IDNO,AGE,NUMDEP,STATUS
      REAL WAGE
         .
         .
   10 CONTINUE
         READ (10,1000,IOSTAT=STATUS) IDNO,AGE,WAGE,NUMDEP
         IF (STATUS.LT.0) THEN
            GO TO 500
         ENDIF
         IF (IDNO.EQ.11457) THEN
            GO TO 500
         ENDIF
         GO TO 10
  500 CONTINUE
      IF (STATUS.LT.0) THEN
         PRINT *, 'No employee #11457'
      ELSE
         WRITE(*,2000) 'EMPLOYEE #',IDNO, ' is ',AGE,' years old with ',
     $                 NUMDEP,' dependents'
      ENDIF
```

Figure 5.9

certainly possible to determine which condition caused the exit without resorting to this technique.

Testing

Loops with more than one exit condition raise a new issue in testing. The basic idea is similar to some of the other types of testing we have discussed. We want to be sure to cover all major categories of input and output in our testing.

Consider, for example, a search loop which, given a person's name, looks for that person in a file. There are two classes of people: those whose names are in the file and those whose names are not in the file. Our test plan should certainly include people in both categories. If we now think about the algorithm and program which carry out the search, we see that the two categories correspond to the two exit conditions—finding a name that matches the given name and reaching end of file without finding the name.

This type of reasoning is the basis for the following general rule for loops with more than one exit.

> The test plan for loops with more than one exit condition should include test cases for each possible exit condition.
>
> **NOTE.** This rule applies whether the exit conditions when we code the loop wind up in a single IF or in several IF statements.

Carrying our reasoning one step further, we realize that it would be good to check any boundary conditions to determine the pass during which the exits occur. For example, for an algorithm with this structure

```
loop for I = 1 to N
         .
         .
    if ... then exit endif
         .
         .
endloop
```

we can see these tests as important:

1. N = 0 (count-control exit on first pass);
2. other exit on first pass;
3. other exit on last possible pass (when I = N);
4. count-control exit with N not 0.

Pitfalls

Consider the following faulty algorithm, which is supposed to generate up to 30 random numbers and tell whether or not the number 15 was generated. The logical variable FOUND is to be true if 15 was generated, false if not.

```
loop for I = 1 to 30
    NUMBER ← RND(100)
    if NUMBER = 15 then
      FOUND ← .TRUE.
    else
      FOUND ← .FALSE.
    endif
endloop
```

This algorithm is typical of one of the most common pitfalls into which students fall. Notice that what the faulty algorithm actually does is tell whether or not the thirtieth number generated is a 15. The problem is that this type of "searching" problem is not symmetric. As soon as one 15 is found, the .TRUE. answer is known; but to know that the answer should be .FALSE., you must try all 30 numbers. Thus, as soon as a 15 is found, the loop should be terminated early. If it is not terminated early, then we know that no 15 occurred.

Here are two correct solutions to the problem.

```
loop for I = 1 to 30
   NUMBER ← RND(100)
   if NUMBER = 15 then exit endif
endloop
if I > 30 then
   FOUND ← .FALSE.
else
   FOUND ← .TRUE.
endif
```

```
FOUND ← .FALSE
loop for I = 1 to 30
   NUMBER ← RND(100)
   if NUMBER = 15 then
     FOUND ← .TRUE.
     exit
   endif
endloop
```

The first uses the fact that the index will be 31 if we took the standard exit from the loop. The second uses the notion of a default value: Assume that you will not find what you are looking for, and change the value if you do find it. The first approach may involve fewer subtleties.

There are three other pitfalls to be avoided:

1. In a search loop, we should generally leave the loop when we find what we are searching for. Although staying in the loop may not necessarily yield a wrong answer, it will certainly use additional computer time.

2. Sometimes we must be careful about the order in which we check the various conditions. The most subtle of these pitfalls can generally be avoided by first checking end-of-file conditions (for example, STATUS.LT.0) and count-control conditions (for example, I.GT.30). See Exercise 1.

3. A very subtle pitfall involves end of file. The FORTRAN standard says that, when end of file occurs, the variables in the READ statement become "undefined." For example, if the READ statement includes the variables IDNO and AGE, then both of these comparisons are "nonstandard" (read as "illegal") if end of file has occurred:

```
    IF (IDNO.EQ.4206) THEN
and IF (AGE.GT.30) THEN
```

Exactly what "nonstandard" means in this context depends upon the computer. Thus it is possible to write a program that violates this rule but works on one particular computer. When the program is transferred to another computer, perhaps years later, it might suddenly cease working.

This means that, for the program in Figure 5.9, we would be technically incorrect if we combined the two consecutive IF statements into the following:

```
If (STATUS.LT.0.OR. IDNO.EQ.11457) THEN
   GO TO 500
ENDIF
```

This seems to make good sense, but it causes us to make a comparison using IDNO after end of file has occurred if ID 11457 is not in the file.

REVIEW

Multiple exits

Common use: in search loops (find, no-find exits)

Other uses: any situation involving more than one way in which the loop may terminate

Implementation

Each exit branches to step immediately following loop

Decision structure following loop to determine which condition caused exit

For count-control loops, standard exit condition is "index variable > ending value"

For end-of-file loops, use IOSTAT= variable (see if negative)

Testing

Test each possible exit condition with separate test data

Test each possible exit condition at "boundaries" (first time through loop, last possible time through loop)

Pitfalls

Watch out for nonsymmetric nature of search process

Check conditions in proper order (especially check end of file and count control exits before others)

Do not use variables in read statement after end of file has occurred

EXERCISES

1. Each of the following is a faulty simplification of one of the samples in this section. For each, tell why the simplification is faulty and suggest a correct simplification.

(a) (Figure 5.7)

```
      INTEGER N,TRY,MOD
         .
         .
      TRY = 3
   10 CONTINUE
         IF(TRY.EQ.N) THEN
            GO TO 100
         ENDIF
         IF(MOD(N,TRY).EQ.0) THEN
            GO TO 100
         ENDIF
         TRY = TRY + 2
         GO TO 10
  100 CONTINUE
      IF(MOD(N,TRY).EQ.0) THEN
         WRITE(*,6000) N, ' is not prime'
      ELSE
         WRITE(*,5000) N, ' is prime'
      ENDIF
```

(b) (Figure 5.9)

```
      INTEGER IDNO,AGE,NUMDEP
      REAL WAGE

   10 CONTINUE
         READ(*,1000,END=500) IDNO,AGE,WAGE,NUMDEP
         IF(IDNO.EQ.11457) THEN
            GO TO 500
         ENDIF
         GO TO 10
  500 CONTINUE
      IF(IDNO.EQ.11457) THEN
         WRITE(*,2000) IDNO,AGE,NUMDEP
      ELSE
         PRINT *, 'No employee #11457'
      ENDIF
```

2. Each record in a file contains ID number, name, age, zip code, year of marriage, number of children, salary, and blood type. Write algorithms to answer these questions.
   (a) How many children does JOE JONES have?
   (b) How many people in the file were married prior to 1963?
   (c) What is the average salary of the people with zip code 14037?
   (d) Who is the first person on the file with blood type O+?
   (e) What is the salary of the person with ID number 1406?
3. Write a FORTRAN program for each algorithm in Exercise 2.
4. Write a test plan for each algorithm in Exercise 2.
5. **(a)** The file of Exercise 2 has been sorted in ascending order by age. List all the 21-year-olds.
   (b) The same file is in ascending order by ID number. How old is number 1425?
   (c) The same file is in ascending order by salary. List all people earning under $28,000.

6. The first record on a file contains a number N, telling the number of employee records the file is supposed to contain. Each employee record has name and salary. Write an algorithm to print each name and salary. At the end, it should report whether the number of employee records actually in the file was correct, too low, or too high.

7. Using the RND function to simulate the throw of a pair of dice, write algorithms for the following:

(a) Simulate rolling the dice 12,000 times, counting the number of times a 7 occurs.

(b) Simulate an experiment in which we roll the dice once, then attempt to match that number on future rolls. If we succeed in five or fewer rolls, print how many rolls it took, otherwise print a message reporting failure.

(c) Write an algorithm to repeat the experiment of (b) 10,000 times, reporting the percentage of successes and the average number of rolls for the successes. (For example, SUCCEEDED 75% OF THE TIME, WITH 3.72 AVERAGE ROLLS FOR EACH SUCCESSFUL EXPERIMENT.)

(d) Simulate a game in which two players will roll dice. Player A starts with $15, player B with $23. When they roll, the player with the higher number wins $1. They agree to go until one or the other is broke, or 100 rolls, whichever occurs first. Print an appropriate message at the end.

8. What is the probability that, if you are allowed no more than five rolls of the dice, you will roll a 7? To answer the question, repeat a simulation of the experiment many times and find what percentage of the time the desired result occurs.

9. Two individuals, in an election in which 10,000 votes are cast, agree that whoever gets ahead by at least 250 votes during the counting will be automatically declared the winner. Write a program to simulate this situation.

10. Suppose that 5000 people all decide to play the daily number lottery game until they either go broke or win once. Each person starts with $1000 dollars. Based on a simulation of the situation, answer these questions. What percentage will go broke? What percentage will quit with more than $1000? What percentage will quit with between 0 and 1000 dollars? (See Exercise 19 of Section 5.2 for a description of the lottery game.)

11. (a) Write a program to simulate the following version of the game of craps. The participant rolls a pair of dice. If a 7 is rolled, he wins; if a 2 or 11 is rolled, he loses. Other wise, the amount rolled becomes his "point." He then rolls the dice repeatedly, trying to match this point. If he does so, he wins. If he rolls a 7 or 11 first, he loses.

(b) Add "betting" to the program. That is, allow the user to play the game several times, betting on the outcome each time. The user should start with a set amount of money and no credit rating.

6

ONE DIMENSIONAL ARRAYS

6.1 INTRODUCTION

The algorithms we have worked with up to this point have been able to process a large number of records using only a few variables. For example, if each record contains a name, age, salary, and marital status for one person, we may use variables such as NAME, AGE, SALARY, and MARTAL to store the values in the computer.

In a typical algorithm to process these records, the variables NAME, AGE, SALARY, and MARTAL are given values by reading a record. We then perform some processes using the values of those variables, perhaps printing some answers or adding to accumulators or counters. When we finish these processes, we go back to the READ step to begin the loop body all over. As soon as the record is read, the variables assume the values as given on this record; the values from the first record are no longer stored in the computer.

This feature of variables, the ability to store only one value at any given time, has been perfectly acceptable in previous algorithms. The reason is that, within the body of the loop, we completely process the first record's values prior to reading the second. By the time we read the next record, we no longer need the values from the previous one. Because of this, one AGE variable may be used to store all the ages from all the records, one person's age at a time.

The Need for Arrays

For many applications of the computer, the above discussion will hold true. However, there are times when, for example, the salaries or ages of many people must be simultaneously stored in the computer. The following examples illustrate this point.

Each record contains one person's age. There are thirty records. How many people in the file are over age 17? This problem is the type of problem that we have previously solved. We can write the following simple algorithm:

```
CTR ← 0
loop for I = 1 to 30
   read AGE
   if AGE > 17 then
      CTR ← CTR + 1
   endif
endloop
print CTR
stop
```

The computer only needs to store one person's age at a time, so the single variable AGE will suffice. This variable will store each of the 30 different ages, one at a time.

For the same file, how many people are older than the average age? At first glance, this problem looks similar to the first one. However, there is a subtle difference. Before we can begin counting, we must know the average age. To calculate the average age we must read all the ages. Since the computer will need to know those ages again in order to count how many are above the average age, we will want to write a program which stores all 30 ages within the computer. The single variable AGE, which can store only one age at a time, will not be good enough.

This example is typical of many problems which require an **array**. The key feature is the need to have a large number of different ages simultaneously stored in the computer.

Before we can proceed with the example, we must learn something about arrays.

What an Array Is

In the preceding example we could, of course, think up 30 different variable names for the 30 different ages. However, this would be clumsy even for only 30 records; and if there were 3000 records this approach would be completely unworkable.

What we need is the ability to refer to 30 different storage locations by a single variable name. In connection with this, we need a systematic way of referring to each of the 30 different locations individually. Arrays provide precisely those desirable features.

We think of an array as a sequence of consecutive storage locations, as illustrated in Figure 6.1. The array illustrated in the figure has the name AGE, and this variable name refers to the entire 30 locations. However, we also need a way to refer to each of the 30 locations individually. For this we use a numbering scheme as illustrated in Figure 6.2. The AGE(1), AGE(3), and AGE(30) refer to the first, third, and thirtieth locations in the array, respectively. For any one of the 30 locations, we can refer to that location by placing its number in parentheses after the

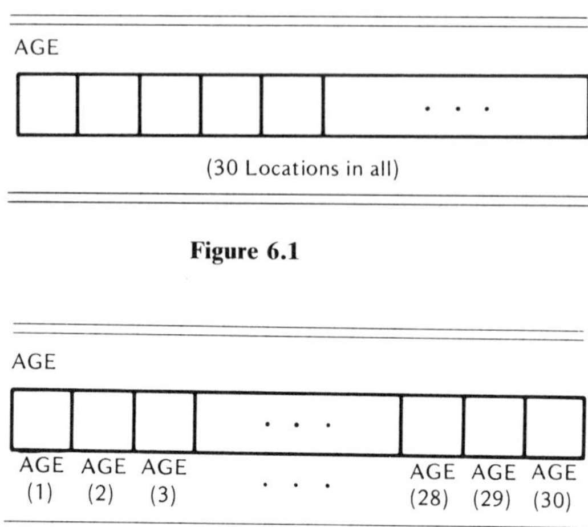

Figure 6.1

Figure 6.2

variable name AGE. For example, to refer to the twenty-sixth location in the array AGE, we write AGE(26).

> **COMMENT.** The number in parentheses is referred to as a **subscript**. In algebraic notation we might write x_1, x_2, and so on for subscripted variables. In our algorithms we could also put subscripts below the line: AGE_1, AGE_2, and so forth. However, we choose to use the notation AGE(1), AGE(2), ... This will be in keeping with the notation used in many programming languages (in particular, in FORTRAN).
>
> Because we use a subscript to refer to the individual storage locations within the array, arrays are frequently referred to as **subscripted variables**.

Arrays, or subscripted variables, would have little use if the subscript always had to be a constant. Fortunately, however, the subscript is allowed to be an expression. In our algorithm we may write the array reference as AGE(I). The value of the variable I at the time we reach the step containing AGE(I) will determine which of the 30 locations is referred to by the reference. If I is 16, the sixteenth location, AGE(16), will be the one referred to.

With this background, together with the assurance that the FORTRAN language does allow the use of arrays (see Section 6.3), we may proceed with the example presented earlier.

Recall that we have 30 records, each containing an age. We want to read the 30 records and calculate the average age. As we are reading the ages, we want to store them in an AGE array so that we can later go back and see how many are larger than the average.

We will first consider the portion of the algorithm which reads and stores the ages and finds the average. We need the following variables:

	Name	Type	Use	Comment
Input:	AGE	INTEGER	30 Ages	Array—size 30
Other:	I	INTEGER		**loop for** index
	TOTAL	INTEGER	Total age	Accumulator
	AVE	REAL	Average age	

A rough algorithm is fairly simple:

```
TOTAL ← 0
loop for I = 1 to 30
   read an age, store it in the AGE array, and
      add it to TOTAL
endloop
AVE ← TOTAL/30
```

The step "read an age, store it in the AGE array" can be written as

read AGE(??)

provided we can determine the proper subscript for the array. To do so, we reason as follows:

"The first time through the loop, we want to read AGE(1)."
"The second time through the loop, we want to read AGE(2)."
"The third time through the loop, we want to read AGE(3)."

.
.
.

"The twenty-sixth time through the loop, we want to read AGE (26)."

.
.
.

"The thirtieth time through the loop, we want to read AGE(30)."

We need a variable for the subscript. The variable should have the value 1 the first time through the loop, 2 the second time through, 3 the third time through, and so on. An appropriate variable is the loop index (I) itself. Hence we write:

```
TOTAL ← 0
loop for I = 1 to 30
   read AGE(I)
   TOTAL ← TOTAL + AGE(I)
endloop
AVE ← TOTAL/30
```

Notice that, just as I was the proper subscript for the AGE array in the read statement, so also I is the proper subscript in the step

```
TOTAL ← TOTAL + AGE(I)
```

As I takes on the values 1, 2, 3, and so on, we will read AGE(1), AGE(2), AGE(3), and so on; and we will add AGE(1), AGE(2), AGE(3), and so on, to the accumulator TOTAL.

Now for the second half of the algorithm, we wish to go back through those 30 ages that are stored in the AGE array, seeing how many are larger than AVE. Since we want to examine the individual locations within the AGE array, we will need a subscript for the array. Once again, the loop index itself provides an appropriate subscript.

```
CTR ← 0
loop for I = 1 to 30
   if AGE(I) > AVE then
      CTR ← CTR + 1
   endif
endloop
print CTR
stop
```

The first time through the loop, I has the value 1, and the algorithm compares AGE(1) to AVE. The second time through the loop, AGE(2) is compared to AVE. This process repeats until, on the thirtieth pass through the loop, we compare AGE(30) to AVE. Since the 30 ages which were originally on the records have been stored in the array locations AGE(1) through AGE(30), we will have compared each of those 30 ages to our average, counting how many are larger than the average. The complete algorithm is given in Figure 6.3.

```
TOTAL ← 0
loop for I = 1 to 30
   read AGE(I)
   TOTAL ← TOTAL + AGE(I)
endloop
AVE ← TOTAL/30
CTR ← 0
loop for I = 1 to 30
   if AGE(I) > AVE then
      CTR ← CTR + 1
   endif
endloop
print CTR
stop
```

Figure 6.3

NOTE. We may use the same loop index I for the two loops, since they are not nested loops.

Another Scenario

In the preceding example, we used an array because we had 30 different ages on 30 different records in the file. This illustrates a common application of arrays. Another common application is illustrated by the following example.

Each record contains a student name and 15 quiz scores. Print a list of names and total scores. To solve this problem, we will use an array (of size 15) for the quiz scores. A rough algorithm may be given as:

```
loop
   read NAME, QUIZ array; if eof then exit endif
   TOTAL ← sum of 15 scores in QUIZ array
   print NAME, TOTAL
endloop
```

In Section 6.3 we will learn how to read the entire QUIZ array at once. For now, let us simply observe that the step which calculates the total may be refined as follows:

```
TOTAL ← 0
loop for I = 1 to 15
   TOTAL ← TOTAL + QUIZ(I)
endloop
```

This is exactly the same type of loop which we used in processing the AGE array in the previous example.

To summarize briefly, we have seen two slightly different uses of arrays. In the first, we used an array AGE to store 30 different ages for different people, read from 30 different records. In the second, the array QUIZ was used to store 15 different quiz scores for a single individual, read from a single record. The I/O steps would vary slightly for the two different applications. However, once the array has been read, the techniques used to process the data are similar.

Working With Arrays

When we need to store a sequence of related data items in the computer, we will generally use an array. Assuming that the values have been read into the array by an earlier portion of our program, we may then perform any number of different procedures utilizing the information stored in the array.

We will find that we are led to use the **loop for** construction in working with arrays, with the number of times through the loop equal to the array size. In many of these problems, a reasoning process similar to the one given in the previous example will show that the proper subscript for the array reference in the loop body is the loop index itself. There are therefore numerous problems in which the solution will fit this general pattern:

```
initialization, if any
loop for I = 1 to array size
   process A(I)
endloop
final processing, if any
```

In Figure 6.3, "process A(I)" in the first loop is "read A(I) and add A(I) to TOTAL." In the second loop, "process A(I)" becomes "compare A(I) to AVE, adding 1 to CTR if it is greater than AVE." In general, the term *process* can refer to counting, accumulating, printing, assigning a value to, using in calculations, and so on. We will discuss this in more detail in the next section.

The examples and exercises in this and the following sections will be made clearer if you keep the following two points in mind.

1. When we use an array, we will make a comment in our variable list that that particular variable is an array. We will also list its size. (Section 6.3 tells how to convey this information to the compiler in the program itself.)
2. We will frequently assume that the values in the array have been obtained by some previous portion of our algorithm. When we say "given an array A, find the largest number in the array," we imply that the values in the array have already been assigned.

REVIEW

Terms

array
subscript
subscripted variable

Form of Array

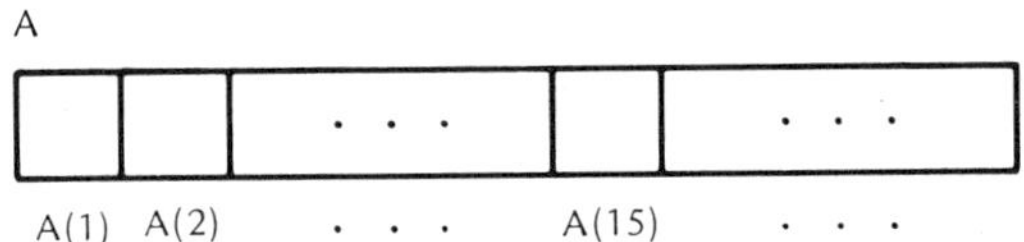

When to Use

When, for some reason, a large number of related values must be simultaneously stored in the computer.

Working with Arrays

Frequent algorithm form

```
initialization, if any
loop for I = 1 to array size
   process A(I)
endloop
final processing, if any
```

EXERCISES

1. Give two more examples of problems in which an array would be useful.
2. For these problems, assume that some earlier portion of your algorithm has assigned values to the arrays to which they refer. Write an algorithm segment to:
   (a) Count the number of salaries over $15,000 in any array SALARY of size 100.
   (b) Print each number which is positive in an array G of size 1400.
   (c) Find the sum of the numbers in an array LO of size 750.
   (d) Find the highest grade in an array GRADES of size 50.
3. Each of 30 records has ID number and age. Print the ID of each person who is older than the average age. [Hint: Use an array ID to store the ID numbers and an array AGE to store the ages.]

6.2 STANDARD ALGORITHMS USING ARRAYS

In this section we will study a few examples of the use of one-dimensional arrays. In most of our examples we assume that the array elements have already been assigned values in some manner, and we wish to obtain some information about the values in the arrays. We will consider several different types of problems: processing the entire array in some fashion, working with single elements of an array, and working simultaneously with several arrays.

Processing The Entire Array

In Section 6.1 we introduced the method used to process an entire array. The general form for the algorithm is:

```
initialization, if needed
loop for I = 1 to N
   process A(I)
endloop
final processing, if needed
```

where N is the number of elements in the array.

> **COMMENT.** In actual problems, N may be the size of the array, or it may be less. For example, we could have an array of size 30 which presently contains numbers only in the first 15 locations. For most applications involving this array, N would be 15 rather than 30.

For instance, let us find the largest value in an array A of size 100. The technique used to solve a problem of this type for an array is analogous to the technique used for a series of records. We will maintain a variable BIG which at all times contains the largest value encountered so far. We compare each value in the array with this largest value found up to the point in the array. Our "process A(I)" step is

```
if A(I)>BIG then BIG ← A(I) endif
```

The initialization step must assign some value to BIG so that BIG has a valid value when the index I is equal to 1. Just as when we were searching for the largest value in a set of records, we choose an initial value of BIG which will ensure that A(I)>BIG when I is 1. This requires that we know enough about the values in the array A to be able to pick an initial value smaller than any of the A(I) values.

If the A array contained ages, then of course all of the A(I) values would be positive and we could choose the initialization step

```
BIG ← 0
```

Thus if all the A values are positive an algorithm to print the largest value is

```
BIG ← 0
loop for I = 1 to 100
   if A(I)>BIG then BIG ← A(I) endif
endloop
print BIG
```

COMMENT. An alternative initialization step is

```
BIG ← A(1)
```

We are giving BIG a **default value**; if it turns out that no other element in A is larger than A(1), BIG will have the proper answer. Since this approach works even when we do not know if the array elements are positive, we will employ it frequently.

Consider now a slight modification to the algorithm just given. In the revised algorithm, we wish to know, in addition to the largest value, the **position** (that is, subscript) for which the largest value occurred. The algorithm appears as follows, with additional steps shaded.

```
BIG ← A(1)
IBIG ← 1
loop for I = 1 to 100
   if A(I) > BIG then
      BIG ← A(I)
      IBIG ← I
   endif
endloop
print BIG, IBIG
```

Notice that we have added another variable IBIG, to keep track of the value of the loop index I for which the largest value occurs. Every time we assign an array value to BIG, we assign a corresponding subscript value to IBIG.

As one final modification to this algorithm, we observe that we really no longer need the variable BIG. At all times in the algorithm, BIG may be seen to have the value A(IBIG). This is true because we are using IBIG to "remember" where (that is, for which subscript) BIG received its latest value. Removing BIG from the algorithm, we obtain the following algorithm, again with modifications shaded.

```
IBIG ← 1
loop for I = 1 to 100
   if A(I) > A(IBIG) then IBIG ← I endif
endloop
print A(IBIG),IBIG
```

The variable IBIG in this example is sometimes called a **pointer**. We may think of it as "pointing to" the largest value in the array A, as illustrated here:

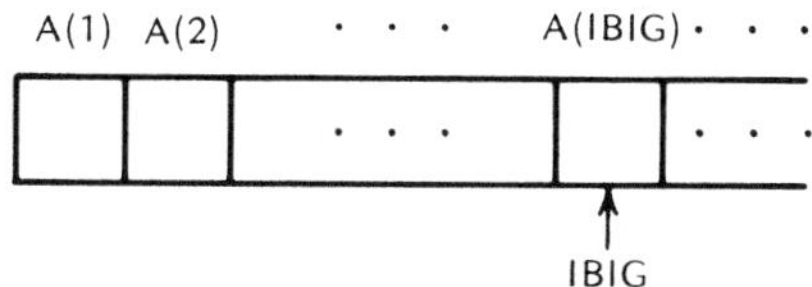

For example, if IBIG is 3, we think of it as pointing to the third element of A.

The concept of a subscript as a pointer is a very important one. Notice that, if we know the subscript, we can easily obtain the value from the array.

CAUTION. One of the most frequent errors made in working with an array is confusing a subscript with the array element it "points to." In the algorithm just given we do not write

```
if I>IBIG then IBIG ← I endif
```

We do not want to compare the subscripts I and IBIG, but rather the array elements A(I) and A(IBIG) corresponding to these subscripts.

On the other hand, notice that if A(I) is indeed larger than A(IBIG), we write IBIG←I. We do not write A(IBIG)←A(I).

```
if A(I)>A(IBIG)    then    IBIG ← I endif
   compare array elements  change pointer (subscript)
```

In working with arrays, one must always ask the question, "Do I want the subscript or do I want the array element itself for this step in the algorithm?"

If there are two or more elements of A with the same largest value, this algorithm will still work correctly. As it is written, IBIG will be the position of the first element with the largest value. If we want IBIG to be the position of the last such element we can rewrite the "if" statement as

```
if A(I) ≥ A(BIG) then IBIG ← I endif
```

Let us consider another problem. Write an algorithm to count the number of elements in an array ARR of size 500 whose value is between 1 and 10, inclusive. For this our "process" step is

```
if ARR(I) ≥ 1 and ARR(I) ≤ 10 then COUNT ← COUNT + 1 endif
```

We must initialize COUNT to zero before entering the loop.

A more complex example would be counting the number of entries in an array B (of size 50) equal to the largest entry. This problem can be solved in two steps. First we find the largest value, and second we count the number of values equal to this largest value.

```
IBIG ← 1
loop for I = 1 to 50
   if B(I) ≥ B(IBIG) then IBIG ← I endif
endloop
COUNT ← 0
loop for I = 1 to N
   if B(I) = B(IBIG) then COUNT ← COUNT + 1 endif
endloop
```

This algorithm follows the same form for finding the number of values greater than the average as discussed in Section 6.1. There is, however, a fundamental difference between the two problems. In the case of counting values greater than the average, the average is not known until after the entire array is scanned once. In the problem of counting the number of values equal to the largest value, we can be sure that, whenever we find the first true largest value, all the values equal to it will occur after it in the array. Therefore, we can find the largest and count the number of values equal to it in one scan of the array. In the algorithm which follows we will search for the largest value and also count the number of values equal to the largest in the variable COUNT. Whenever a new "largest value" is found we will set COUNT back to 1.

```
COUNT ← 0
IBIG ← 1
loop for I = 1 to 50
   if B(I) = B(IBIG) then COUNT ← COUNT + 1 endif
   if B(I) > B(IBIG) then
      IBIG ← I
      COUNT ← 1
   endif
endloop
print B(IBIG),COUNT
```

What would happen in the preceding algorithm if the two **if** statements were written in the opposite order? How can the algorithm be modified to give the correct value for COUNT with this rearrangement?

Initialization and Copying

We have considered a few examples of processing an entire array. These examples have been of the general type considered at length in earlier chapters: counting, accumulating, and finding largest or smallest. Searching is another important process which we will consider in detail later in this section.

We now consider some array processing methods which have no analogous procedure in earlier chapters. It is frequently necessary to initialize arrays to some known value. To initialize all elements of an array X with 100 elements to some value, for example Z, we would write

```
loop for I = 1 to 100
   X(I) ← Z
endloop
```

Of course, Z could be replaced by a constant such as 0, ' ', or other value, as might be needed.

Another common initialization is to place values equal to the index of the element into each element; for example, X(1)=1, X(2)=2, . . ., X(100)=100. This can be accomplished by

```
loop for I = 1 to 100
   X(I) ← I
endloop
```

In addition to initializing arrays, we frequently wish to copy one array or part of one array into another. Suppose we want to copy ten elements of an array B into the ten elements of an array A. A simple loop like

```
loop for I = 1 to 10
   A(I) ← B(I)
endloop
```

will suffice.

On the other hand, suppose we want to copy the elements 1−5 and 10−15 of B into the first 11 positions of A. One approach is to copy B(1)−B(5) to A(1)−A(5) as in the first example, then copy B(10)−B(15) to A(6)−A(11).

There are several approaches to writing a loop to move B(10)−B(15) to A(6)−A(11). We might make a table of subscripts, as follows:

A subscript	comes from	B subscript
6		10
7		11
8		12
9		13
10		14
11		15

After studying this table, we might write

```
loop for I = 1 to 5
   A(I) ← B(I)
endloop
loop for I = 1 to 6
  A(I+5) ← B(I+9)
endloop
```

The second loop was written by first noting that we wished to move six elements. This led to the **loop for** I = 1 **to** 6. Now we know we want our loop body to be of the form

```
A(??) ←B(??)
```

We must come up with proper formulas for the A subscript and the B subscript. To determine the formula for the A subscript, we note that

when I is 1, the subscript is 6
when I is 2, the subscript is 7
and so on

The subscript is always 5 more than I, and hence the proper formula is I+5. Similar reasoning leads to the formula I+9 for the B subscript.

NOTE. The second loop could be replaced by

```
loop for I = 6 to 11
   A(I) ← B(I+4)
endloop
```

In this case we have chosen the index range to match the destination subscripts. By having I take on the values 6−11, we avoid the need to determine a formula for the A subscript. The formula for the B subscript is found by observing that it is always 4 more than the A subscript.

If we do not wish to devise a formula for B's subscript, we might use this alternate approach:

```
J ← 10
loop for I = 6 to 11
   A(I) ← B(J)
   J ← J + 1
endloop
```

By initializing J to 10 prior to the loop and incrementing it each time through the loop, we have J take on the values 10−15.

Parallel Arrays

Frequently, arrays will be used to retain related information. For example, we might have a class of, say, 20 students. The ID numbers of the students might be stored in an array ID. Perhaps their test scores on the three tests would be stored in the three arrays, TEST1, TEST2, and TEST3, and their average scores in an array AVG. We could arrange to have the information for one student stored in the corresponding elements of each array.

Arrays used in this manner sometimes referred to as **parallel arrays**. As another example, consider parallel arrays ID, AGE, SEX, and SALARY, each of size 50. We may think of these arrays as the columns of a table, as illustrated below.

ID	AGE	SEX	SALARY
1149	25	M	12,500
1614	20	F	14,000
2319	35	F	17,250
1003	50	M	16,750
3914	39	M	22,000
.	.	.	.
.	.	.	.
.	.	.	.

Notice that, in this diagram, the arrays are parallel to each other.

A key feature of parallel arrays is that corresponding entries "belong together." For example, ID(5), AGE(5), SEX(5), and SALARY(5) all refer to the same individual. In order to find out any desired information about this individual, all we need to know is the person's subscript, 5. Thus a **pointer** for parallel arrays (that is, a subscript) can be thought of as "pointing to" the entire row of the table.

Any of the processing we do for single arrays can be done in a similar manner for parallel arrays.

For the parallel arrays ID, TEST1, TEST2, TEST3, and AVG, we might obtain information for the first four arrays using the algorithm

```
loop for I = 1 to 20
   read ID(I),TEST1(I),TEST2(I),TEST3(I)
endloop
```

To compute the average of the grades for each student, we might use:

```
loop for I = 1 to 20
   AVG(I) ← (TEST1(I)+TEST2(I)+TEST3(I))/3
endloop
```

Now suppose we want to print the ID number of the student with the highest average grade. This can be done by using an earlier algorithm to find the position of the maximum average and then printing the ID number corresponding to that largest average.

```
IBIG ← 1
loop for I = 1 to 20
   if AVG(I) > AVG(IBIG) then IBIG ← I endif
endloop
print ID(IBIG)
```

This idea of determining an index value (subscript) from one array and using that index to select an element of another array occurs frequently. For example, one might wish to print grade information for a student with a particular ID number. Let us suppose that the desired ID number is in the variable IDNUM. We would search the array ID for an element matching IDNUM:

```
loop for I = 1 to 20
   if ID(I) = IDNUM then exit endif
endloop
if I > 20 then
   print IDNUM, 'not found'
else
   print TEST1(I),TEST2(I),TEST3(I)
endif
```

When we print the answer in the preceding example, we know we want to print somebody's test scores. We therefore will print TEST1(??), TEST2(??), and TEST3(??). To determine the proper subscripts, we observe that when the "early" **exit** is taken, it is because we have found ID(I) = IDNUM. At this point the variable I is a **pointer** to the location in the ID array containing the desired ID number. By the nature of parallel arrays, the corresponding test scores for the individual are in the same relative location within the TEST1, TEST2, and TEST3 arrays. Hence, I is also the proper subscript to use in printing the three test scores.

One final comment about this example is in order. It is frequently unreasonable to try to make the arrays of precisely the "right" size. We are more likely to set the problem up with arrays of slightly larger size than we expect to need. We might set aside arrays of size 30 or 35. We would then have the program maintain a variable NSTUD (number of students) telling how many positions in the arrays actually contain data.

If we follow this practice, our loops will generally have the form

```
loop for I = 1 to NSTUD
```

since we do not wish to work with the unused portions of the parallel arrays.

Processing Single Elements

In the examples we have considered so far in this section, the subscripts of the array elements have been set by the index of a loop or have been obtained using a formula in terms of that index.

The loops are of the general form

```
loop for I = 1 to N
   process A(I)        [or A(formula involving I)]
endloop
```

Frequently, however, we need to work with a single element of an array. We will need a subscript, but since we are not in a loop, the subscript will not be a loop index.

It sometimes happens that, in reading values for an array, we do not read the entire array at once. Instead, each input record may contain a subscript along with the value to be placed in the array at that position. For example, the input

```
7,150.25
```

would indicate that the value 150.25 is to be placed into A(7).

It is possible to read such an input record using

```
read I,A(I)
```

This practice is dangerous, however, since it makes the program vulnerable to data entry errors. For example, we might have an array with ten elements in it, and the data value read for I might be 25. A reference to A(25) will either be recognized as an error (if we are fortunate) or be treated as a reference to some part of the computer memory outside of the array A. A much better approach is to read the array value into a temporary variable. We then check that the subscript is in the valid range before placing the value in the array. Thus the read statement above would be better written as

```
read I,TEMP
if I ≥ 1 and I ≤ 10 then
   A(I) ← TEMP
else
   print error message
endif
```

A second type of situation involving subscripts which are not loop indexes may be illustrated by the following problem. We are to simulate rolling a pair of dice 10,000 times, counting the number of times each possible number (2 through 12) occurs.

One approach would be to use 11 separate counters CT2, CT3, . . ., CT12. However, this would require a **case** structure to determine which counter to increment for each roll of the dice. By using an array with allowable subscripts from 2 to 12, we may reduce the complexity of the solution. We will first initialize the entire array to zeros:

```
loop for I = 2 to 12
   COUNT(I) ← 0
endloop
```

The basic algorithm is then

```
loop for I = 1 to 10000
   ROLL ← RND(6) + RND(6)
   COUNT(??) ← COUNT(??) + 1
endloop
```

Our only problem is determining the proper subscript. However, this problem is easily solved. If the roll is 2, we want to increment COUNT(2); if it is 3, we want to increment COUNT(3); and so on. The variable ROLL gives the desired subscript. Thus the counting step should be

```
COUNT(ROLL) ← COUNT(ROLL) + 1
```

As a final indication of the use of subscripts other than the loop index itself, consider the following situation. We have parallel arrays ID, AGE, SALARY, and GROUP. There are N entries at present. Each person's GROUP entry is a number from one to ten. Count how many are in each group.

We have an algorithm similar to the one involving dice rolls:

```
loop for I = 1 to N
   calculate subscript CSUB for COUNT array
   COUNT(CSUB) ← COUNT(CSUB) + 1
endloop
```

What is the proper value for CSUB? It is the person's group number, namely GROUP(I):

```
CSUB ← GROUP(I)
COUNT(CSUB) ← COUNT(CSUB) + 1
```

NOTE. We may combine the steps as

```
COUNT(GROUP(I)) ← COUNT(GROUP(I)) + 1
```

We have considered a few examples of the ways in which arrays can be used and a few algorithms for manipulating the arrays. The next section will consider the ways in which arrays are defined and referenced in FORTRAN programs.

Testing

In working with arrays, there are two natural boundaries: the first element in the array and the last element in the array. Moreover, in speaking of the last element in the array, we can mean two things: the last element in the array is capable of holding or the last element it actually holds. For example, consider an array NAMES of size 50, capable of holding names for a class of 50. For a given class, it might actually contain only 33 students. The "last" element of the array could be thought of as NAMES(33) or as NAMES(50).

Likewise, in an array such as the NAMES array, we have boundaries on how "full" the array is. Put another way, if NSTUD indicates the number of students in the class, then there are boundaries at NSTUD=0, NSTUD=1, and NSTUD=50.

Most testing involving arrays uses these considerations together with those for the specific problem. For example, in finding the largest grade in an array GRADE of size 50 which currently contains NSTUD grades, we can identify tests such as these.

Value of NSTUD: 0, 1, 50, in between, 51 (an error)

Location of largest (assuming no ties):
- position 1
- position NSTUD, with NSTUD = 1
- position NSTUD, with NSTUD > 1
- position NSTUD, with NSTUD = 50
- in between 1 and NSTUD

Number of ties for largest:
- none
- all scores the same
- in between none and all

Another type of testing situation, different from those we have studied before, arises when using parallel arrays as tables of information. For example, suppose we have name and salary in parallel arrays. We might have a program which allows us to add a name to the list, delete a name from the list, change the salary for a specific name, and so on. In this type of program, we might want to test the relationship of various steps performed in sequence. For example, these might be some important tests:

1. Delete a name, then try to delete the same name again
2. Delete a name, do some other steps, then add the same name
3. Try to add the same name twice in a row
4. Change the salary, then later change it again for the same person
5. Add a name, change the salary, and delete the name
6. Add enough names to "overflow" the array
7. With the array full, try to add a name that is already there

In this type of problem, the results of a specific step depend on what has come before. The rules for determining the important test sequences, in a context such as this, are not as precise as those for boundary or class testing considered earlier. Creating a good test plan for this type of problem becomes even more of a "creative" process than it usually is.

Pitfalls

The major pitfalls in working with arrays are as follows:

1. Using subscripts in place of array elements, and vice versa. In any reference to an array, we must ask, "Do we want the location (the subscript), or the value in that location of the array?" For example, in

   ```
   if A(I) > A(IBIG) then IBIG  I endif
   ```

   IBIG and I are *pointers* (subscripts). We compare the two *array elements* A(I) and A(IBIG). If we have found a new largest value, we change the *pointer* IBIG. We do *not* change A(IBIG).
2. Incorrect formula for subscripts. Because so many standard processes involve a reference A(I), we have a tendency to assume that all subscripts will always be a loop index I. In this section we have seen examples where the proper subscript is in fact
   a. a simple formula in terms of I, such as I+4
   b. a formula based on a dice roll
   c. a value obtained by a search loop
   d. a value read from a data card
   e. a group number obtained from another array of group numbers

   In any reference to an array, we must think carefully about what expression or calculation will give us the proper subscript.
3. Subscript out of range. This can be caused by the errors indicated in items 1 and 2. In addition, some common causes are:
   a. failure to edit input which indicates a subscript
   b. adding values to an array without checking to see if the array is full

REVIEW

Terms

pointer
parallel arrays

Algorithms

Standard algorithms working with "entire" array:

```
initialization, if needed
loop for I = 1 to N
   process A(I)
endloop
final processing, if needed
```

"Process" may include: counting, accumulation, largest, smallest, initialization, copying, searching.

Working with single element
    Subscript based on some action, such as searching, formula calculation, reading data.

Testing

Natural boundaries for arrays:
- First element
- Last possible element
- Last element actually present

Portion of array in use:
- None
- Completely in use
- In between

Special testing for table (parallel array) modification programs:
- Combinations such as: add, add
  add, delete
  delete, delete
- Add to overflow the table size

Pitfalls

1. Confusing subscript and corresponding array element.
2. Using wrong subscript.
3. Subscript out of range.

EXERCISES

NOTE. Unless the problem specifically involves reading or calculating array values, you may assume that all arrays described have been assigned values by some previous portion of the program.

1. Assume that we have an array A of N elements. Write algorithms to:
- **(a)** Find the value of the smallest element in A.
- **(b)** Find the location of the first element equal to the smallest.
- **(c)** Find the location of the last element equal to the smallest.
- **(d)** Count the number of elements equal to the smallest.
- **(e)** Find the value of both the largest and the smallest, using one loop.

2. Write algorithms for the following for an array ARR. Assume the array is of size 50, but presently contains only N values.
- **(a)** Find the average of the values.
- **(b)** Find what percentage of the values are positive.
- **(c)** Set a variable LOCAT to contain the subscript of the first negative value in the array (LOCAT is to be 0 if there are no negative values).
- **(d)** Set a logical variable NONZER to true if none of the array values are 0, otherwise to false.

(e) Add a new value to the end of the array. The variable NEWVAL contains the value to be added.

(f) Repeat part (e), but assume that if that value is already present in the array, it should not be added.

(g) Repeat part (f), but assume that the numbers in the array are in increasing order and that they should still be in increasing order after the new value is inserted.

3. The standard deviation of a group of N values A is defined as

$$\sqrt{\frac{1}{(N-1)}\sum_{i=1}^{N}(A_i - \bar{A})^2}$$

(The Σ notation indicates the sum of the indicated values, for i from 1 to N.)

(a) Write an algorithm which will compute $\bar{A}$, the average of the A values, then compute the sum of the values $(A_i - \bar{A})^2$, and finally compute the standard deviation.

(b) Modify the algorithm to also compute the largest and smallest A value without adding any more loops.

4. Data on grades for a class has been provided in a group of parallel arrays ID, G1, G2, G3, G4. ID(I) contains the ID number of the Ith student, G1(I) contains the grade (0–100) for the first test for the Ith student, and so on. The array AVE has been provided to contain each student's average score. Assume there are N students. Write algorithms to do the following.

(a) Compute the values of AVE.

(b) Print the ID number of all students who received the highest average. (Requires two loops.)

(c) Print the highest and lowest score on each test. (Can be done with one loop.)

(d) Compute the average score for each test.

(e) Suppose we also have an array LETTS which is to contain letter grades. The function LETTF will calculate a letter grade, given a numerical average. Write an algorithm to compute values for the LETTS array. (Assume that LETTF has already been written.)

5. Repeat Exercise 4 but assume that students may withdraw. When they do, their information remains in the arrays; however, their ID number is replaced by its negative.

(a–d) Repeat (a–d) of Exercise 4 but ignore all students who have withdrawn.

(e) Write an algorithm to count the number of students who have withdrawn and print the percentage of withdrawals.

(f) Write an algorithm which, given an ID number, will locate the entry for that student and mark it as a withdrawn student. If the student has already withdrawn or if the ID number is not present, print error messages.

6. Write algorithms for the following, assuming you have parallel arrays EMPNO, NAME, SALES, AGE, SEX, DEPT, NUMDEP, GROUP. At present, there are NEMPL entries in these arrays.

(a) Find the percentage of males.

(b) Print the information for all females in department 'ADJ' who have 0 dependents.

(c) There are ten groups. Find the total sales for each of the ten groups, placing the answers in an array of size 10. Then read an employee number and new sales amount; add this amount to that employee's SALES figure and to the total for her group.

(d) Suppose an array VALDEP of size 17 contains a list of all the valid department codes at present. Print the employee number of all employees whose DEPT entry is presently invalid.

(e) Add a new employee to the bottom of the list. First, check that the new employee number given is not already in use, and that the new department code given is valid [see (d)].
(f) Print the name of the employee with the largest SALES figure. Assume no ties.
(g) Rewrite (f) to handle ties.
(h) Count how many are in each of the following age groups: under 20, 20–29, 30–39, 40–49, 50–59, 60 or over. Do not use a **case** structure; use an array of counters.
(i) Count how many are in each department. [Hint: The VALDEP array of (d) may be used to convert a valid department name to a number from 1–17.]

7. Assume that we have arrays A and B, each containing 100 elements. Write algorithms for the following.
(a) Copy B to A.
(b) Copy the first 50 locations of B to the last 50 locations of A; that is, copy B(1–50) to A(51–100).
(c) Copy B(17–23) to A(1–7).
(d) Copy B(START) through B(END) to the first locations of A. Assume that START and END are variables containing numbers in the range 1–100, with START ≤ END.
(e) Copy the next six numbers, starting with the first nonzero number in B, into A(1–6). You may assume that there is a nonzero number in B, located prior to or at location 95.
(f) Repeat (e), but print an error message if there is no nonzero number in B, and move six numbers or fewer. For example if B(98) is the first nonzero number, you should move only three numbers—B(98), B(99), and B(100).

8. A large data file contains the SAT scores for all the students in an incoming freshman class. The scores can range from 200 to 800.
(a) Write an algorithm which counts how many students had each of the possible scores.
(b) Modify the algorithm to also tell which score occurred most frequently.
(c) Give two ways to find the average score.
(d) Modify part (a) to count scores in ranges of 10 points each: 200–209, 210–219, etc. *HINT:* Use integer division by 10.
(e) Modify part (a) to count scores in the ranges 200–300, 301–400, . . ., 701–800.

9. Write an algorithm to interchange the elements in positions I and J of an array A.

10. Write an algorithm to reverse the elements of an array A of the five elements. For example, if A=(2,4,6,8,10) then the algorithm should change A to (10,8,6,4,2). (Set this up so that elements 1 and 5 are interchanged followed by elements 2 and 4.)

11. Do exercise 10 except allow the number of elements to be N. Does N have to be odd? *Hint:* First do the specific cases where N = 51 and where N = 50.

12. (a) Write an algorithm for scanning an array A and, whenever A(I) > A(I+1), interchanging A(I) and A(I+1). If the array has N elements, how many comparisons should be made? What is the value of the last element of A after the algorithm has been performed?
(b) Enclose your solution to (a) in a loop which causes J to take on the values I through N–1. Trace this algorithm using N = 5 and A = (1,4,5,3,2)

13. Write an algorithm to compare two arrays A and B of N elements each to see if the arrays are identical. In other words, the algorithm should see if the Ith element of A is the same as the Ith element of B for all I from 1–N. If the arrays are identical print "yes," otherwise print "no."

14. Write an algorithm to check if each element of A occurs only once in A. Print "yes" if each does, and "no" if some element occurs more than once.

15. Write an algorithm to check if each element of A occurs at least once in an array B. Print "yes" if each element of A is equal to at least one element of B, otherwise print "no."

16. Suppose we have three arrays A, B, C, each with N elements. The elements of A and B are all either equal to 1 or equal to 0. Write algorithms to assign zeros or ones to the elements of the array C, where
    (a) C(I) ← 1 if A(I) is equal to 1 and B(I) is equal to 1.
    (b) C(I) ← 1 if at least one of A(I) or B(I) is equal to 1.
    (c) C(I) ← 1 if A(I) and B(I) are different.

17. We are given two arrays A and B of N elements each. Write an algorithm to compute

$$P = A_1{}^*B_1 + A_2{}^*B_2 + \cdots + A_N{}^*B_N$$

18. A is an array of N elements where N is larger than 7. Write an algorithm to locate the largest element in positions 7 through N and interchange it with the element in position 7.

19. **(a)** Redo Exercise 18 but, instead of using element 7, make that position variable, perhaps J.
    (b) Enclose your solution to (a) in a loop which causes J to take on the values 1 through N−1. Trace this algorithm using N = 5 and A = (1,4,5,3,2).

20. Each record contains an ID and 12 monthly take-home pay figures. Here is a rough algorithm to read and print the entire file. The INPUT subroutine reads and edits a record, setting EOF true on end of file. The DETAIL routine prints a line of data, printing headings when appropriate. PAY is an array of size 12 containing the 12 monthly take-home pay figures.

```
loop
    call INPUT(ID,PAY,EOF)
    if EOF then exit endif
    call DETAIL(ID,PAY)
endloop
```

Show how to modify the algorithm to do the following:
(a) Also print total yearly take-home pay for each person.
(b) Find and print the person who had the highest total take-home pay.
(c) Find the highest take-home pay for each of the 12 months. [*Hint:* Us an array LSAL of size 12.]
(d) Tell who had the highest take-home pay in each month:

```
IN MONTH 1 xxxxx HAD THE LARGEST PAY - xxxxx.xx.
```

(e) Modify (d) to print messages like

```
IN JANUARY xxxxx HAD THE LARGEST PAY - xxxxx.xx.
```

[*Hint:* Use a CHARACTER*9 array of size 12 with the names of the months.]

21. Give test plans for the following exercises in this section.

(a) Exercise 1	**(h)** Exercise 6c
(b) Exericse 2a	**(i)** Exercise 7d
(c) Exercise 2b	**(j)** Exericse 9

(d) Exercise 2c
(e) Exercise 2f
(f) Exercise 2g
(g) Exercise 4b
(k) Exercise 11
(l) Exercise 13
(m) Exercise 15

6.3 FORTRAN ARRAYS

In this section we will learn how to implement arrays in FORTRAN. There are two aspects to this study: we must learn how to declare arrays and how to use them in the body of our programs. Of particular importance is learning how to use arrays with functions and subroutines. In addition, we will study the DATA statements as it relates to arrays.

The DIMENSION Statement

In FORTRAN we may declare that a variable is to be an array by using a DIMENSION statement. Like other declaration statements, the DIMENSION statement conveys information to the compiler concerning the intended use of the variable. In addition to notifying the compiler that the variable will be used as an array, it tells the size of the array. More precisely, the DIMENSION statement gives the range of allowable subscripts for the array. The statement has the form

```
DIMENSION name1(range1),...,nameN(rangeN)
```

where name1 to nameN are the array names. The range1 to rangeN are each expressions of the form

```
num1:num2
```

The elements num1 and num2 are integer constants which give the minimum and maximum values for the array subscript. For example

```
DIMENSION X(-5:15),K(1:10)
```

defines X and K as arrays whose subscripts can be between −5 and 15 for X, and between 1 and 10 for K.

The DIMENSION statement by itself conveys only "size" information about the array; it does not fix the type of the array. Generally, arrays must be declared both as to type and as to size. We might have declarations such as

```
INTEGER IDS,SUM,I
REAL AVE,RATES
DIMENSION IDS(1:100),SUM(0:11),RATES(-5:55)
```

However, we are allowed to include the size information within the type declaration (INTEGER, and so on) itself, as in

```
INTEGER IDS(1:100),SUM(0:11),I
REAL AVE,RATES(-5:55)
```

NOTE. A given array may be typed in a type statement and its subscript range defined in a DIMENSION statement as

```
REAL X
DIMENSION (X-5:15)
```

or simply declared as

```
REAL X(-5:15)
```

However, the subscript range information may only be given once in a program unit. A construction such as

```
REAL X(-5:15)
DIMENSION X(-5:15)
```

is not permitted even though the subscript range information is identical.

Arrays whose lowest subscript value is 1 occur very frequently. Range information of the form 1:10 may be abbreviated as just the upper value, in this case 10. Thus

```
INTEGER K(1:10)
```

and

```
INTEGER K(10)
```

are completely equivalent.

Array References

Once we have declared the arrays for a program, using the DIMENSION statement or including the range information with the type declarations, we will code the algorithm which uses the array. With only a few exceptions, each reference to an array in FORTRAN will include a subscript. This subscript acts as a pointer to the particular member of the array to be used. It can be an INTEGER constant, an INTEGER variable, or any more complex expression whose value is an INTEGER.

An **array element** (array name with a subscript value) can be used in expressions and most other places that a simple (nonarray) variable could be used. The subscript expression will be enclosed in parentheses, as in these examples:

```
X(5) = A(I) + B(2*J+3)
T(I*J) = X(5+MOD(I,J))
SUM(GRP(I)) = SUM(GRP(I)) + VALUE(I)
```

The subscript expression may be any INTEGER expression; it may include function calls (for example, MOD(I,J)) or even references to other arrays (for example, GRP(I)).

The value of the subscript expression must, however, always be within the range specified in the DIMENSION or type statement declaring the array. When the array is declared, the FORTRAN compiler will reserve space for the elements of the array. If the subscript is outside the specified range, the program may modify information which should not be altered. Some FORTRAN compilers generate instructions to check for this condition, and the program will terminate with an error message if the condition occurs. Unfortunately, many compilers do not generate the checking instructions, and the results during execution can become quite bizarre, depending upon precisely what information is modified.

In writing our algorithm, we have generally determined what expression we need as the subscript. Because our notation for subscripts in the algorithms is the same as that used in FORTRAN, we will find that most array references in the algorithm translate verbatim into FORTRAN.

> **COMMENT.** The form of a reference to an array element is the same form as that used to call a function. Many FORTRAN compilers distinguish between the two cases by the fact that an array name must have been declared with a subscript range, in a type or DIMENSION statement. If the range information is not given, we may obtain error messages which pertain to functions and not arrays.

Let us code the following algorithm from Section 6.2, which prints the largest element of an array A and the number of elements equal to that value.

```
COUNT ← 0
IBIG ← 1
loop for I = 1 to N
   if A(I) = A(IBIG) then COUNT ← COUNT + 1 endif
   if A(I) > A(IBIG) then
      IBIG ← I
      COUNT ← 1
   endif
endloop
print A(IBIG),COUNT
```

Of course, this algorithm represents only a segment of a total program; we are assuming that the array A already contains some values.

We first declare all variables, remembering to include the size information for A. We may write either A(1:100) or A(100). The FORTRAN code for the algorithm itself is straightforward.

```
      REAL A(100)
      INTEGER IBIG,COUNT,N,I

C   PROGRAM SEGMENT TO PRINT LARGEST ELEMENT AND NUMBER
C OF OCCURRENCES.

C       A—ARRAY TO BE SEARCHED
C       IBIG—SUBSCRIPT OF LARGEST VALUE
C       COUNT—NUMBER OF OCCURRENCES
C       N—NUMBER OF ELEMENTS TO SEARCH. N MUST BE
C         POSITIVE AND NO MORE THAN 100
```

(*continued*)

```
      COUNT = 0
      IBIG = 1
      DO 10 I = 1,N
         IF(A(I).EQ.A(IBIG)) THEN
            COUNT = COUNT + 1
         ENDIF
         IF(A(I).GT.A(IBIG)) THEN
            IBIG = I
            COUNT = 1
         ENDIF
10       CONTINUE
      WRITE(*,1000) A(IBIG),COUNT
```

Arrays with Subprograms

Arrays may be used in subprograms, both subroutines and functions. Within a subprogram, we may have an array which is one of the parameters for the subprogram. It is thus possible for a calling program to pass a whole array as an argument to a subprogram. In addition, it is possible for a subprogram to declare arrays which are not among the parameters of the subprogram.

First of all, an array element may be used in a statement calling a subprogram to match a simple variable of the same type as the array. For example, a function AREA, which calculates the area of a circle, might be called with a statement of the form

```
A = AREA(X(I))
```

if X has been declared as a REAL array in the calling program. The AREA function expects a single REAL number as its input parameter. Since X is a REAL array, X(I) is a single REAL number, and is acceptable as a parameter. (Of course, the subscript I must lie within the proper range of subscripts for X.)

Likewise, an array element may be used to match an output or update parameter in a subroutine parameter list. The subroutine QUOREM of Chapter 4 can be called with a statement of the form

```
CALL QUOREM(A,B,C,D(K))
```

provided A, B, and C are declared as INTEGER variables, and D is an INTEGER array. The subroutine will place the result of dividing A by B into the simple variable C, with the remainder going into the array element D(K). Once again, the value of K must be within the valid subscript range.

These calls do not require any change in the definitions of the function AREA or subroutine QUOREM. However, it is important that we are passing a single array element to match the simple variable the subprogram expects. Leaving off the subscript in either of these examples would cause problems.

In addition to passing single array elements to match simple variable parameters, we may pass an entire array to a subprogram which expects an entire array as its parameter.

For example, the function which follows has an array as its first parameter.

```
      REAL FUNCTION SUM(X,N)
      REAL X(100)
      INTEGER I,N

      SUM = 0.0
      DO 10 I = 1,N
         SUM = SUM + X(I)
10       CONTINUE
      RETURN
      END
```

The name X is declared to be an array by the appearance of subscript range information in the REAL statement. Only the name of the array is used in the parameter list. FORTRAN does not permit the use of a name with range information or subscript information in the parameter list in a FUNCTION or SUBROUTINE statement. Earlier we saw that we could use an array element in a calling statement; however, that array element must match a simple variable in the FUNCTION or SUBROUTINE statement. When the subprogram parameter is an array name, it must be matched by an array name in the calling statement. For example, the function SUM might be called using statements of the form:

```
S1 = SUM(A,15)
S2 = SUM(B,30)
```

The arrays A and B must be declared as REAL and as having a subscript range from 1–100 in the calling program. The following statement would be one way of making a proper declaration in the calling program:

```
REAL A(100),B(100)
```

The rules for working with arrays in connection with subprograms are based on the fact that parameters must match by type. We can summarize these rules as follows:

1. When the subprogram parameter is a simple variable, the calling program may pass a single array element. This will be written as an array name with a subscript.
2. When the subprogram expects an array as a parameter, the calling program must pass an array. The array passed as a parameter must be declared in both the calling and the called program units. It must have the same type in both units, and also the same subscript range.

   Only the array name (without subscripts) appears in the parameter lists in both the call and the definition.

There are exceptions which will be considered later, but if you write your programs keeping these rules in mind, you will avoid many difficulties.

COMMENT. This is one of the few places where an array name appears in FORTRAN without an accompanying subscript. The reason for this is quite simple. With a subscript, an array reference refers to a single element of the array. Since we want to pass the *entire* array as a parameter, we use the array name without a subscript.

We now write a subprogram which will find the maximum value in the first N elements of an array A of size 100, and count the number of elements equal to the maximum. Since we are calculating two values, we choose to write a subroutine named CNTMAX. As input parameters we need the array and the number of elements the subroutine is to examine (A and N, respectively). Output parameters will be MAX, the largest element, and COUNT, the number of elements equal to this largest element.

We have already written this algorithm and coded it as a program segment earlier in this section. One minor modification is required. After the loop, we must assign the largest value, A(IBIG), to our output parameter MAX. (We do not print the answers in the subprogram; instead, we pass them back to the calling program as output parameters.)

```
      SUBROUTINE CNTMAX(A,N,MAX,COUNT)
      REAL A(100),MAX
      INTEGER N,COUNT,I,IBIG

C   WRITTEN BY *******, **/**/**

C   CNTMAX COUNTS THE NUMBER OF ELEMENTS IN THE FIRST N
C ELEMENTS OF AN ARRAY WHICH ARE EQUAL TO THE MAXIMUM VALUE
C IN THE FIRST N ELEMENTS.

C   THESE ARE THE PARAMETERS:

C         A-INTEGER ARRAY (SIZE 100), INPUT-ARRAY OF
C           NUMBERS
C         N-INTEGER, INPUT-NUMBER OF ELEMENTS TO SEARCH
C         MAX-INTEGER, OUTPUT-LARGEST VALUE
C         COUNT-INTEGER,OUTPUT-NUMBER OF ELEMENTS EQUAL
C              TO LARGEST VALUE

      COUNT = 0
      IBIG = 1
      DO 10 I = 1,N
         IF(A(I).EQ.A(IBIG)) THEN
            COUNT = COUNT + 1
         ENDIF
         IF(A(I).GT.A(IBIG)) THEN
            IBIG = I
            COUNT = 1
         ENDIF
   10    CONTINUE
      MAX = A(IBIG)
      RETURN
      END
```

A program segment to use this subroutine might contain steps similar to these:

```
REAL SALARY(100),LARGE
INTEGER NEMP,COUNT
         .
         .
         .
CALL CNTMAX(SALARY,NEMP,LARGE,COUNT)
```

(Keep in mind that parameters may or may not match by name. They must match in number, type, and purpose.)

Now let us consider another problem. Write a subprogram to copy the first N elements of an array A to an array B. Assume that A and B are CHARACTER*1 arrays of size 70, and that N is between 1 and 70, inclusive.

This requires a subroutine, since no single answer is being calculated. The array A is needed as an input parameter, as is the variable N. Since B is being modified, it will be an output parameter; however, notice that only the first N locations of B are changed.

```
      SUBROUTINE MOVE(A,B,N)
      CHARACTER*1 A(70),B(70)
      INTEGER N,I
          .
          .
          .
      DO 10 I = 1,N
         B(I) = A(I)
 10      CONTINUE
      RETURN
      END
```

COMMENT. Each of our examples illustrates an important idea which is sometimes used when we have an array parameter. In addition to specifying the array as a parameter, we have a parameter such as "N" which specifies how much of that array the subprogram is to use. (This parameter N is likely to be used as the ending value for a DO loop.)

This technique allows us to work with arrays which may be only partially filled with data at any given time.

As our final consideration, we examine a problem which occurs frequently, especially in working with parallel arrays. We will write a "lookup" routine which looks up a given key in an array. For this particular example, we assume that we are given an INTEGER array of size 1:100 and an INTEGER key for which to search.

When we look for a value in an array, we generally want to know two things—whether it is found and, if so, its location (subscript). By setting the location to an invalid subscript number if the value is not found, we may convey both pieces of information in one answer. We will therefore use a function named LOOKUP, which either returns the first location containing the given key or −1 if the key is not present. NUMENT will be an INTEGER variable indicating the number of entries used in the array. In addition to NUMENT, the input parameters are the given key and array, which we call KEY and TABLE.

The algorithm is a standard array search algorithm, as presented in Section 6.2. To simplify the exits, we give LOOKUP a *default* value of −1 prior to entering the loop. Thus it has the proper value whether the standard DO loop exit or the "early" exit is taken.

```
LOOKUP ← -1
loop for I = 1 to NUMENT
   if KEY = TABLE(I) then
      LOOKUP ← I
      exit
   endif
endloop
return
```

In addition, we check the validity of NUMENT, setting the answer to −2 if it is invalid. The FORTRAN code follows.

```
      INTEGER FUNCTION LOOKUP(KEY,TABLE,NUMENT)
      INTEGER KEY,TABLE(1:100)
      INTEGER NUMENT,I,TABSIZ
      SAVE TABSIZ
      DATA TABSIZ/100/

C   WRITTEN BY *******, **/**/**

C   THIS INTEGER FUNCTION RETURNS THE INDEX IN TABLE OF THE
C FIRST ELEMENT MATCHING KEY, -1 IF THERE ARE NO MATCHING
C ELEMENTS, -2 IF THERE IS AN ERROR.

C   THESE ARE THE PARAMETERS:

C       KEY-INTEGER, INPUT-VALUE TO LOOK FOR
C       TABLE-INTEGER ARRAY (SIZE 100), INPUT-TABLE OF
C             VALUES
C       NUMENT-INTEGER, INPUT-NUMBER OF ELEMENTS
C              IN TABLE WHICH ARE USED


      IF(NUMENT.LT.1 .OR. NUMENT.GT.TABSIZ) THEN
         LOOKUP = -2
         RETURN
      ENDIF
```

(*continued*)

```
C    IF NO ERROR, PERFORM SEARCH

        LOOKUP = -1
        DO 10 I = 1,NUMENT
           IF(KEY.EQ.TABLE(I)) THEN
              LOOKUP = I
              GO TO 100
           ENDIF
   10      CONTINUE
  100   CONTINUE
        RETURN
        END
```

The function LOOKUP can easily be modified to work with other types of keys and tables by modifying the declaration statement for KEY and TABLE. Moreover, we may easily change the table size by modifying the declaration for TABLE and the DATA statement.

As an example of the use of this LOOKUP function, suppose we have parallel arrays ID, SALARY, and GROUP, each of size 100. The following algorithm segment may be used to print the group number for employee number 1407.

```
I ← LOOKUP (1407,ID,100)
if I>0 then
   print GROUP(I)
endif
```

We could print error messages if I turns out to be −1 or −2.

Initialization of Arrays

Arrays can be initialized with executable code, and in many cases this is the best way to perform an initialization. However, arrays may also be initialized with DATA statements. We must remember that the initialization indicated in a DATA statement occurs only once, at compile time. The DATA statement is a *declaration*, not an *executable statement*.

For example, the following declaration statements give initial values to three arrays.

```
INTEGER CT(10)
REAL CUTS(7)
CHARACTER*1 C(5)
DATA CT/0,0,0,0,0,0,0,0,0,0/
DATA CUTS/53.5, 72.1, 86.4, 105.2, 171.5, 230.8, 502.0/
CATA C/'A', 'B', 'C', 'Y', 'Z'/
```

In each case we have declared the array first. Then, in the DATA statement, we list the values to be placed in the arrays by the compiler. Just as for simple variables, we place integer data in INTEGER variables, real data in REAL variables, and character data in CHARACTER variables. Notice that the array name in the DATA statement contains no subscript or range information.

The general form used above is

```
DATA array-name/value list/
```

The value list in a DATA statement can be abbreviated in many cases. For example, rather the writing ten zeroes in the DATA statement just given for CT, we may write

```
DATA CT/10*0/
```

(The asterisk here does not indicate multiplication, but rather "occurrences of.") This is especially useful for large arrays. For example, the sequence

```
REAL X(100)
DATA X/1.0,98*0.0,2.0/
```

declares X as an array of 100 REAL values and initializes X(1) to 1.0, X(2)–X(99) to 0.0, and X(100) to 2.0.

As an example, we write a program segment to replace each vowel in a CHARACTER*1 array LETTS of size 70 with an asterisk. One approach is to place the vowels in an array VOWELS of size 5. We could then write

```
loop for I = 1 to 70
   if LETTS(I) is in VOWELS array then
      LETTS(I) ← '*'
   endif
endloop
```

Suppose we have a LOOKUP function similar to that given earlier, but using CHARACTER*1 arrays of size 5 rather than INTEGER arrays of size 100. Then our condition is true precisely if that function returns a positive value, and we may code the algorithm segment as

```
      CHARACTER*1 LETTS(70),VOWELS(5),LOOKUP
      INTEGER I
      DATA VOWELS/'A', 'E', 'I', 'O', 'U'/
                     .
                     .
                     .
      DO 10 I = 1,70
         IF(LOOKUP(LETTS(I),VOWELS,5).GT.0) THEN
           LETTS(I) = '*'
         ENDIF
10       CONTINUE
```

We use the DATA statement to initialize the VOWELS array. We then pass to the LOOKUP routine the key LETTS(I) to be searched for, the array VOWELS to search in, and the number of elements of VOWELS to use, that is, 5.

Array I/O and Files

In many of our algorithms, we have assumed that all the arrays already contained data. Of course, that data did not simply materialize! In many cases, the values may be the results of calculations; however, it is likely that some of the data has been read.

This subsection does not give an exhaustive treatment of array input and output. Section 8.2 contains more a thorough coverage. At this time we simply cover enough material to be able to handle a few common situations. We begin with array input.

The first possibility we consider occurs when each input record contains precisely one value. For example, if each of 30 records contains the age for one person, we may write

```
loop for I = 1 to 30
   read AGE(I)
endloop
```

This is easily coded as a FORTRAN DO loop.

A simple extension of this idea involves parallel arrays, where each record contains all the information for one "row" of the parallel array table. It is also possible to indicate the number of records in the first data line. For example, we may use

```
read N
loop for I = 1 to N
   read NAME(I), AGE(I), SALARY(I), SEX(I)
endloop
```

to read the name, age, salary, and sex for each of N individuals.

It should be clear that similar looping structures may be used to print arrays or parallel arrays, with information on one entity for each line of output.

A scenario that is frequently used begins with a data file which contains the information of the preceding example. That is, the first line of the data file contains N, the number of records which follow; the remaining records each contain name, age, salary, and sex for one individual. We then write a program, either conversational or batch, to perform the following steps:

1. Read the information on the file into arrays
2. Do some processing, which perhaps changes the data in the arrays
3. Record the resulting information in a file

Such a program might use a subroutine (perhaps called INIT) for step 1, and a subroutine (perhaps called FINAL) for step 3. A sample FINAL subroutine follows.

Case study #6, in the next section, contains a complete example of this concept.

```
      SUBROUTINE FINAL(NAME,AGE,SALARY,SEX,N)
      CHARACTER*20 NAME(100)
      INTEGER AGE(100),N
      REAL SALARY(100)
      CHARACTER*1 SEX(100)
      INTEGER I

C   SAMPLE 'FINAL' SUBROUTINE

      OPEN (10,FILE='UPDATED.MASTER')
      WRITE (10,1000) N
      DO 100 I = 1,N
         WRITE (10,2000) NAME(I),AGE(I),SALARY(I),SEX(I)
  100    CONTINUE
      CLOSE (10)
      RETURN
 1000 FORMAT(13)
 2000 FORMAT(A,I3,F9.2,A)
      END
```

Notice that the subroutine uses a formatted WRITE with no carriage control. The output file is not printer destined. It will be copied to the master file and used as the input file the next time the program is run. The INIT routine which reads the file would use precisely the same FORMAT statement to ensure consistency of the data.

The final situation we wish to cover is the following. Occasionally, as indicated in Section 6.1, we use an array to hold a number of values for a single entity. For example, a GRADES array might be used to hold the 15 grades for a single person rather than the grades on a single test for a whole class. In such a case, the input or output record might contain the values for the entire array on one record. For example, suppose an input record contains a name and 15 grades. A sample record might have this appearance:

```
SAM JONES      100 98 69 89 .....
```

The following program segment could be used to read that record.

```
      CHARACTER*20 NAME
      INTEGER GRADES(15)
           .
           .
      READ (*,1000) NAME,GRADES
 1000 FORMAT(A,15I3)
```

The read statement says, "Read the name and the **entire** grades array." (This is another of the few instances in which we use the array name with no subscript.) The format statement indicates that the record consists of an alphanumeric field and 15 integer fields each three digits wide.

Alternatively, if the record is in free format, we could use a free format read:

```
      READ *,NAME,GRADES
```

CAUTION. There are two potential problems with the free format read here. First, the name on the input record would have to be enclosed in single quotes. Second, there would have to be 15 grades even if some were zero because the tests have not yet been taken. A possible input record would be

```
'SAM JONES',100,98,69,89,0,0,0,0,0,0,0,0,0,0,0
```

With formatted reads, blank spaces are automatically interpreted as zeros, so this is not a problem.

Pitfalls

Most of the pitfalls associated with array use relate to the subscript. In the previous section we discussed some pitfalls to avoid in writing the algorithm. When we code the algorithm, there are several other points at which we must be careful.

1. To let the compiler know that a variable is an array, we must declare the range of subscripts to be used. If we do not, the compiler will frequently not recognize that an array is being used. As a result, error messages will often not mention arrays at all. Frequently, error messages will refer to functions, or to an entity known as a "statement function."
2. The second problem occurs when a subscript is used which is outside the range of subscripts declared for the array. If the compiler does not check for this error (and many do not), it is possible to change the values of other variables, FORMAT statements, and even the translated machine code. Almost any type of error may be generated in this case.
3. A third problem relates to whether we should or should not use a subscript with an array name. The following notes summarize the use of range information and subscripts.
   a. In the declarations, range information must be given once (and only once). All other references, such as in a DATA statement, use the array name by itself. The range information is never indicated again.
   b. Most array references in the executable code use a subscript, since we are referring to one element of the array.
   c. In passing an array as a parameter to a function or subroutine, we use the array name alone, with no subscript, if the whole array is being passed to match an array in the subprogram.

      However, if one element of the array is being passed to match a simple variable in the subprogram, we must include a subscript. In this case we are referring to a single element of the array.
   d. In the FUNCTION or SUBROUTINE definition statement, we always use the array name with no subscript or range information.
   e. When reading an entire array from one record, we use the array name with no subscript. A similar comment applies to writing the entire array.
4. When reading an entire array with free format reads, values must be present for each element of the array.

REVIEW

Terms

subscript range declaration

FORTRAN Syntax

Array Declarations

DIMENSION var(lower:upper),. . .
type var(low:upper),. . .

"Var" is an array name; "lower" and "upper" are the lower and upper limits of a subscript range, expressed as integer constants; and "type" is one of REAL, INTEGER, or other type.

Alternate form

DIMENSION var(upper),. . .
type var(upper),. . .

Can be used if "lower" is equal to 1.

Array elements

var(subscript)

"Var" is an array name and "subscript" is an INTEGER expression.

Example

```
REAL MAXPAY(25:35)
REAL TAXRT(50),PAY(25:35),PRICE(100)
INTEGER STATE,PROD
IF (PAY(I).GT.MAXPAY) THEN
    MAXPAY=PAY(I)
ENDIF
COST=(1.0+TAXRT(STATE))*PRICE(PROD)
```

Using Arrays and Array Elements as Parameters in Subprograms

Elements of the parameter list in a SUBROUTINE or FUNCTION statement may be either array names or simple variable names, but may not be array elements.

Elements of a parameter list in a call of a subprogram must be arrays if the corresponding parameter in the subroutine or function is an array. Parameters in the call may be either simple variables or array elements (or in some cases expressions) if the corresponding parameter in the subroutine or function statement is a simple variable.

Array I/O

Can read/write one "entity" per record, using DO loop.

Can read/write **entire** array on one record, using array name in READ or WRITE statement.

EXERCISES

Each of Exercises 1–20 refers to the exercise with the same number in Section 6.2.

1–20. For each of the algorithms developed in the exercises of Section 6.2, do the following: [*Note:* Phrases such as "array A of size N" should be interpreted as using the first N locations in an array A of some fixed size, perhaps 100. The choice of the array's fixed size will be up to you in these problems.]

- **(a)** Code the algorithm as a program segment, including all necessary declarations.
- **(b)** Determine whether it would be appropriate to code the segment as a subprogram. If so, identify the parameters needed, and specify whether they are input, output, or update. Then write the SUBROUTINE or FUNCTION definition statement, and indicate any other changes in the code which would be required to transform the program segment into a subprogram.

21. Give two different ways to initialize a CHARACTER*1 array of size 50 to contain all blanks. What is the difference between the two methods? When would the use of DATA definitely not be appropriate?

22. **(a)** Give code to declare and initialize an array of size 26 which contains the letters of the alphabet in order.

- **(b)** Declare and initialize (use DATA) a REAL array SUMS of size 45 containing all zeroes.
- **(c)** Declare and initialize a REAL array X of size 100, where the first 25 locations contain 1.0, the next 59 the value 6.5, and the rest the value 17.2.

23. Write algorithms for the following.

- **(a)** Initialize an array of size 500 to contain the numbers 1, 2, . . ., 500.
- **(b)** Initialize an array of size 500 to contain the numbers 2, 3, 4, . . ., 501.
- **(c)** Initialize an array of size 250 to contain the numbers 0, 1, 0, 1, 0, 1, 0, 1, ...
- **(d)** Initialize an array of size 93 to contain the numbers 0, 1, 2, 0, 1, 2, 0, 1, 2, ...
- **(e)** Initialize an array of size 500 to contain random numbers in the range 1 to 1000.
- **(f)** Move all the zeroes in an array of size 150 to the end of the array. (For an array 0, 1, 6, 0, 3 of size 5 the result would be 1, 6, 3, 0, 0.)
- **(g)** Move all the zeroes in an array of size 150 to the front of the array.
- **(h)** Do a "right circular shift" of an array of size 100 by three places. (A(1) goes to A(4), A(2) to A(5),. . ., A(97) to A(100), A(98) to A(1), and so on.)

24. **(a)** Write an algorithm to calculate and print $n!$ for n from 1 to 15. ($n!$ is $n^*(n-1)^*\ (n-2)^*. . .^*2^*1$)

- **(b)** Repeat (a), but this time store the answers in an array called FACT of size 15. (Place 1! in FACT(1), 2! in FACT(2), and so on.)
- **(c)** Most likely your answer to (b) contains nested loops. Can you suggest an improvement which will be more time-efficient?
  [*Hint:* $n! = n(n-1)!$]

25. In case study #5, Section 4.3, we wrote a logical function PRIME(A) which tested A to see if it was prime. The method used was inefficient, since it checked A for divisibility by all the numbers less than or equal to A. It would suffice to check only for the primes which are less than or equal to the square root of A.

- **(a)** Modify the function to have three parameters: A, the number to check; PLIST, an array of size 300 containing all the primes less than A, and N, the number of items currently in the array PLIST.

(b) Modify the main program of the case study to use the modified function. Notice that primes, as they are found, must be placed into the array of primes as well as being printed. In fact, you could wait to print the list until all the primes are found.

26. Write a FORTRAN subprogram which builds a CHARACTER*1 array (size 70) of X's and blanks, based on a given integer number.

(a) Assume that the number N is in the range from 0 to 70. The array should consist of N X's with the rest of the array blank.

(b) Modify part (a) to handle values of N in the range 0 to 700, with one X for every ten units in N.

(c) Modify part (a) to handle values of N in the range 0 to 200, with one X for every three units in N.

27. Write a program to test the RND random number generator as follows. Generate 10000 random numbers in the range from 1 to 1000, counting how many fall in the range 1–20, how many in the range 21–40, and so on. Print a graph showing the relative frequencies of the various ranges. If the random number generator is good, the graph should be relatively "level." *Hint:* See Exercise 26 for some ideas for creating the graph.

6.4 CASE STUDIES

Case Study #6

1. *Statement of problem.* Write a batch program to handle customer orders for a company. The company keeps information concerning its customers and its products on two files. The following tables represent sample information from the two files.

Item number	Initial inventory	Price	Customer number	Base discount
101	249	3.89	34398	2%
247	1300	24.99	33898	1/2%
93	500	0.78	66756	1%
16	55	100.04	14528	1/2%
89	453	6.34		

This program will accept a sequence of input records, each containing a customer number, item number, and quantity ordered. For each such order it will determine the net cost, update the inventory, and print a line of information.

Each customer has a specific base discount. In addition, if the quantity ordered is 101–500, we add 1 percent to the discount. If it is over 500, we double this figure [that is 2 * (base discount + 1%)]. For records with faulty customer or item number, or for orders which we cannot fill due to insufficient stock, we will print an appropriate message and skip to the next order.

2. *Preliminary analysis.* We will use two sets of parallel arrays to maintain

information on the customers and on the products. As the first step of the program, we will read the information from the files into the arrays. At the end of the program, we will need to place the product information onto a modified product file, since the inventory amounts will have changed.

This program represents only one aspect of the total order-processing system for this company. For example, there must be ways to add customers to the customer file and to modify the prices for items in the product file. However, these are beyond the scope of this program.

We will need some limits on the number of customers and the number of products. We will assume that these limits are 150 and 250, respectively. Since we add neither products nor customers to the files, we will for simplicity assume that these limits are maintained. We also assume that the form of each file consists of an integer value indicating the number of customers (or products), followed by that number of records with the information for each customer (or product).

Error handling will use an error file, with the entire input record placed on the file for each error encountered.

Although the problem statement calls only for the final net cost as output, we will modify that somewhat. We will print all the input, plus the unit cost of the item, the cost before discount, the discount, and the net cost.

3. *Algorithms and variable lists.*

a. *Main program.* This is far from being a routine problem, but it is not really too difficult if we follow the principles of top down design. We begin with our first step, a very rough algorithm.

1. Input record.
2. See if quantity is available and update available amount. If not available, issue a "back order" message and go on to next order. If bad item number, issue error message and go on to next order.
3. Look up price of item.
4. Determine gross cost.
5. Look up customer number and determine the appropriate amount of discount. If bad customer number, issue error message and go on to next order.
6. Determine net cost.
7. Print a line with appropriate information.

We will of course repeat the seven steps for each record in a loop.

NOTE. Prior to the loop, we will initialize our customer and product information from the appropriate files. After the loop, we will place the modified product information on a file. Error messages will be placed on an error file, which we will open and close in the main program.

A very rough algorithm may therefore be given as follows:

```
open error file
initialize customer and product information
loop
   read record, exit on end of file
   update inventory (next iteration if bad item #)
   calculate unit price
   calculate gross
   calculate discount (next iteration if bad customer #)
   calculate net cost
   print a detail line
endloop
save updated product information
close error file
```

Before we continue developing the algorithm for the main program, let's consider what we know so far about the necessary data. Based on the description of the input, the output, and the various files, we have these general categories of data:

Customer information: number of customers, customer number array, base discount array

Product information: number of products, item number array, inventory array, price array

Input record: customer number, item number, quantity ordered

Output required: net cost

Other output: unit price, cost before discount, discount

As we develop the algorithm, we will discover the need for a few additional variables. The complete variable list is given in Figure 6.4.

It will be helpful to look at the steps we just outlined and begin to plan the subprograms to be used. (As it turns out, we will use subprograms for most of the steps.) The design will not be optimal, and the exercises will suggest some possible improvements.

open error file. This can be done with a single OPEN statement.

initialize customer and product information. We will write a subroutine INIT, whose output parameters will include all the customer and product information listed in our preliminary variable list.

read record, exit on end of file. We will write an INPUT subroutine with four output parameters—the three values on the input record and a logical variable indicating that end of file has occurred.

update inventory (next iteration if bad item #). We will write an UPDATE subroutine. The parameters needed include all the input record values (in case of an error, all the values must be placed on the error file.) This includes the item number to be looked up. Other parameters include the item number

	Name	Type	Use	Comments
Input:	CUSTNO	INTEGER	Customer number	
	ITEMNO	INTEGER	Item number	
	QUANT	INTEGER	Quantity desired	
Output:	UNITPR	REAL	Unit price	
	GROSS	REAL	Gross cost	
	DISCNT	REAL	Discount (in dollars)	
	NET	REAL	Net cost	
File data:	ITEMS	INTEGER array	List of items	Size 250
	PRICES	REAL array	Prices for items	Size 250
	INVENT	INTEGER array	Inventories of items	Size 250
	NITEMS	INTEGER	Number of items	Portion of above 3 arrays in use
	CUSTID	INTEGER array	List of customers	Size 150
	CUSPCT	REAL array	Discounts for customers	Size 150
	NCUST	INTEGER	Number of customers	Portion of above 2 arrays in use
Other:	EOF	LOGICAL	Indicate end-of-file	
	BAD	LOGICAL	Indicate bad input	
	PRICE	REAL		Function used to calculate UNITPR

Figure 6.4

array and inventory array, plus the number of items. Of these parameters, the inventory array is update; all others are input. We also need as output a logical variable which indicates whether or not the item number was bad (either not in the array, or insufficient inventory).

calculate unit price. We will write a PRICE function. This is a REAL function. The parameters are the item number being purchased, plus the number of items in the product arrays, the item number array, and the price array.

calculate gross. This can be done as an assignment statement: unit price times quantity.

calculate discount (next iteration if bad customer #). We will write a DISC subroutine to calculate the discount, along with a logical variable indicating if the customer number is bad.

calculate net cost. This can be done as an assignment statement: gross cost minus discount.

print a detail line. We will write a DETAIL subroutine with parameters consisting of those values which are to be printed.

save updated product information. We will write a FINAL subroutine with input parameters consisting of the product information.

close error file. This will be done with a single CLOSE statement.

We now turn to the design of the necessary subprograms. For convenience, we will use the same names for the parameters in the subprograms as we do in the main program.

b. *INIT subroutine.* The only local variable is I, a loop index. The algorithm is as follows:

```
open product file
read NITEMS
loop for I = 1 to NITEMS
   read ITEMS(I),INVENT(I),PRICE(I)
endloop
close product file
open customer file
read NCUST
loop for I = 1 to NCUST
   read CUSTID(I),CUSPCT(I)
endloop
close customer file
```

c. *INPUT subroutine.* The only local variable is STATUS, used in the IOSTAT= option. The algorithm is as follows:

```
loop
   read CUSTNO,ITEMNO,QUANT (setting STATUS)
   if STATUS < 0 then exit endif
   if data is valid then exit endif
   write input data, error message on error file
endloop
if STATUS < 0 then
   EOF ← .TRUE.
else
   EOF ← .FALSE.
endif
```

d. *UPDATE subroutine.* This is a straightforward application of a search loop in a set of parallel arrays. Once we locate the item in the item number array, we have access to the inventory in the parallel inventory array. We must check for two errors—item not present and insufficient inventory. We use the local variable I as a loop index.

```
loop for I = 1 to NITEMS
   if ITEMNO = ITEMS(I) then exit endif
endloop
case
   1(I>NITEMS)
      error message (not found)
      BAD ← .TRUE.
```

(*continued*)

```
    2(QUANT>INVENT(I))
       error message (insufficient inventory)
       BAD ← .TRUE.
    3(any other)
       INVENT(I) ← INVENT(I) - QUANT
       BAD ← .FALSE.
endcase
return
```

e. *PRICE function.* This is a standard use of parallel arrays; moreover, we are assured that the item number is valid, since invalid numbers have previously been detected by the UPDATE routine. We simply look up the given item in the array of valid item numbers and obtain the price from the corresponding entry in the array of prices.

```
loop for I = 1 to NITEMS
   if ITEMNO = ITEMS(I) then exit endif
endloop
PRICE ← PRICES(I)
return
```

f. *DISC subroutine.* This also involves looking up the customer number to obtain the base percent. The actual discount is then calculated based on the rules given in the problem description.

```
BAD ← .FALSE.
loop for I = 1 to NCUST
   if CUSTNO = CUSTID(I) then exit endif
endloop
if I > NCUST then
   error message
   BAD ← .TRUE.
   return
endif
PCT ← CUSPCT(I)
case
   1(100<QUANT≤500) PCT ← PCT + .01
   2(QUANT>500) PCT ← 2.0 * (PCT + .01)
endcase
DISCNT ← PCT * GROSS
return
```

g. *DETAIL subroutine.* This routine uses a local variable LINECT to keep track of how many lines have been printed since the last time headings were printed. When the value reaches or exceeds 45, a HEADER subroutine is called. A SAVE statement for the LINECT variable makes sure it maintains its value between successive calls to DETAIL. A DATA statement initializes the line count to a large value to force headings the first time DETAIL is called. The algorithm is as follows:

```
if LINECT ≥ 45 then
   call HEADER
   LINECT ← 0
endif
print detail line
LINECT ← LINECT + 1
```

h. *FINAL subroutine.* This is analogous to the INIT subroutine. The only local variable is I, a loop index.

```
open updated-product file
write NITEMS
loop for I = 1 to NITEMS
   write ITEMS(I),INVENT(I),PRICE(I)
endloop
close updated-product file
```

i. *HEADER subroutine.* This routine uses a local variable PAGENO to keep track of the page number. A SAVE statement for this variable makes sure it maintains its value between successive calls to HEADER. A DATA statement initializes the page number to 1. The algorithm is simple:

```
print headings (with PAGENO)
PAGENO ← PAGENO + 1
```

4. *Test plan.* We do not give a complete test plan, but we will indicate some important points. First, not too much can be done without the INIT routine, so it might be written and tested first. To test it, we will simply call it, then print the associated arrays and other values. Using the INIT and stubs, we might write a skeleton of the main program. This cannot be thoroughly tested, however, without either fairly sophisticated stubs or the actual subroutines. We therefore propose that the subroutines be added to the skeleton main program, in essence using this main program as a driver for each module in turn. Even though the final program is to be a batch program, the stub versions of the INPUT and detail routines might be written as conversational subroutines.

We now describe a few of the most important unit tests for the various program units.

a. *Main program.* There are two **next iteration** locations, both of which should be tested. Otherwise, there is not much complex logic in the main program.

b. *INIT subroutine.* Some borderlines: 0 customers, 0 items, 1 customer, 1 item, 150 customers, 250 items. For these last two tests, a modified version of the subroutine with lower limits might be used, although there are some risks involved in this simplification.

c. *INPUT subroutine.* There are borders involved with the various validity tests. A "combination" test might involve reaching end of file right after a bad record.

d. *UPDATE subroutine.* Borderlines: Item is first in array, last in array; quantity equals inventory, quantity one more than inventory. The "not found" condition should certainly be tested.

e. *PRICE function.* The same borderlines concerning the item as in the UPDATE subroutine also apply here.

f. *DISCNT subroutine.* This is similar to the UPDATE routine. In addition, there are borderline values of 100 and 500 for the quantity.

g. *DETAIL subroutine.* One run should print exactly 45 lines, another exactly 46. One run should cover several pages of output.

h. *FINAL subroutine.* This routine is not so much subject to testing as to verification that the output file is correct.

i. *HEADER subroutine.* The testing should include at least two pages in one of the tests to verify that the page numbering is working.

5. *Write program.* The main program and the DETAIL, INIT, and UPDATE subroutines are contained in Figures 6.5 through 6.8. The others are left as exercises.

6. *Modifications.* There are some shortcomings in the current design of the program. Some of these are discussed in the exercises. In addition, we want to consider the possibility of incorporating this into a comprehensive on-line (conversational) program.

To begin with, we could certainly just turn this program into a conversational one. The primary changes would occur in the INPUT and DETAIL routines. However, there might be other changes as well. For example, a faulty customer number might be handled by allowing the user to reenter the customer number at that point. If the customer is a new one, it might be desirable to allow an insertion into the customer arrays. (This might require a password, since setting the customer percentage discount is not something you would want just any clerk to be able to do.)

On a broader scale, processing a sale is just one part of what might be done in this context. To see how one might proceed, consider the following algorithm for a main program:

```
call INIT
loop
   call MENU
   obtain user input from menu
   if choice = code for quit then exit endif
   case
      1 (choice = code for sale) call SALE
      2 (choice = code for new item) call NEWITM
      3 (choice = code for price change) call NEWPRI
      .
      .
   endcase
endloop
call FINAL
```

```
      INTEGER NITEMS,ITEMS(250),INVENT(250),NCUST,CUSTID(150),
     $   CUSTNO,ITEMNO,QUANT
      REAL PRICES(250),CUSPCT(150),UNITPR,PRICE,GROSS,DISCNT,
     $   NET
      LOGICAL EOF,BAD

C   WRITTEN BY *******, **/**/**

C   THIS PROGRAM UPDATES AN INVENTORY AND CALCULATES COSTS
C FOR A SERIES OF PURCHASE ORDERS.

C   THESE SUBPROGRAMS ARE USED (ALL EXCEPT 'PRICE'
C ARE SUBROUTINES):

C        INIT—INITIALIZE DATA ON CUSTOMERS AND ITEMS
C        FINAL—REWRITE THE ITEM DATA
C        INPUT, DETAIL—STANDARD I/O ROUTINES
C        UPDATE—CHECK PROPER ITEM #, UPDATE INVENTORY
C        PRICE—CALCULATE UNIT PRICE
C        DISC—CHECK CUSTOMER #, CALCULATE DISCOUNT

C   THE LOGIC CONSISTS OF A STRAIGHTFORWARD LOOP TO
C READ DATA, UPDATE INVENTORY, CALCULATE COST, PRINT ANSWERS

      CALL INIT(NITEMS,ITEMS,PRICES,INVENT,NCUST,CUSTID,
     $   CUSPCT)

   10 CONTINUE

         CALL INPUT (CUSTNO,ITEMNO,QUANT,EOF)
         IF(EOF) THEN
            GO TO 500
         ENDIF
         CALL UPDATE(CUSTNO,ITEMNO,QUANT,BAD,NITEMS,ITEMS,
     $      INVENT)
         IF(BAD) THEN
            GO TO 20
         ENDIF
         UNITPR = PRICE(ITEMNO,NITEMS,ITEMS,PRICES)
         GROSS = UNITPR * QUANT
         CALL DISC(CUSTNO,ITEMNO,QUANT,GROSS,DISCNT,BAD,NCUST,
     $      CUSTID,CUSPCT)
         IF(BAD) THEN
            GO TO 20
         ENDIF
         NET = GROSS - DISCNT
         CALL DETAIL(CUSTNO,ITEMNO,QUANT,UNITPR,GROSS,
     $      DISCNT,NET)
   20    GO TO 10
  500 CONTINUE
      CALL FINAL(NITEMS,ITEMS,PRICES,INVENT)
         STOP
         END
```

Figure 6.5

```
      SUBROUTINE DETAIL(CUSTNO,ITEMNO,QUANT,UNITPR,GROSS,
     $   DISCNT,NET)
      INTEGER CUSTNO,ITEMNO,QUANT,LINECT
      REAL UNITPR,GROSS,DISCNT,NET
      SAVE LINECT
      DATA LINECT/45/

C   WRITTEN BY *******. **/**/**.

C   THIS SUBROUTINE PRINTS DETAIL LINES, WITH HEADINGS
C WHEN NEEDED. IT CALLS A HEADER SUBROUTINE.

C   THESE ARE THE PARAMETERS:

C        CUSTNO-INPUT, INTEGER-CUSTOMER NUMBER
C        ITEMNO-INPUT, INTEGER-ITEM NUMBER
C        QUANT-INPUT, INTEGER-QUANTITY ORDERED
C        UNITPR-INPUT, REAL-UNIT PRICE
C        GROSS-INPUT, REAL-GROSS COST
C        DISCNT-INPUT, REAL-DOLLAR DISCOUNT
C        NET-INPUT, REAL-NET PRICE


C   SEE IF HEADING NEEDED

      IF(LINECT.GE.45) THEN
         CALL HEADER
         LINECT = 0
      ENDIF

C   PRINT DETAIL LINE

      WRITE(*,1000) CUSTNO,ITEMNO,QUANT,UNITPR,GROSS,DISCNT,NET
      LINECT = LINECT + 1
      RETURN

C   FORMATS

 1000 FORMAT(' ',17X,I5,12X,I3,11X,I5,9X,F8.2,7X,F10.2,
     $       8X,F8.2,9X,F10.2)
      END
```

Figure 6.6

The MENU subroutine displays a set of menu choices for the user to choose from. Among these choices are those indicated in the **case** structure. For example, the SALE subroutine would include essentially the set of steps that are in the loop of our current version of the case study. Notice that, if some of the activities might change the customer data, then the FINAL subroutine would have to be modified to write that information out to an updated customer file.

```
      SUBROUTINE INIT(NITEMS,ITEMS,PRICES,INVENT,NCUST,CUSTID,
     $                CUSPCT)
      INTEGER NITEMS,ITEMS(250),INVENT(250),NCUST,CUSTID(150)
      REAL PRICES(250),CUSPCT(150)
      INTEGER I

C    WRITTEN BY ********, **/**/**

C    THIS SUBROUTINE INITIALIZES CUSTOMER AND PRODUCT
C  INFORMATION.

C    THESE ARE THE PARAMETERS (ALL OUTPUT)
C       NITEMS-INTEGER-NUMBER OF PRODUCT ITEMS
C       ITEMS-INTEGER ARRAY SIZE 250-ITEM #'S
C       PRICES-REAL ARRAY SIZE 250-PRICES
C       INVENT-INTEGER ARRAY SIZE 250-INVENTORY AMOUNTS

C       NCUST-INTEGER-NUMBER OF CUSTOMERS
C       CUSTID-INTEGER ARRAY SIZE 150-CUSTOMER NUMBERS
C       CUSPCT-REAL ARRAY SIZE 150-CUSTOMER DISCOUNT %'S

C    PRODUCT INFORMATION

      OPEN (10,FILE='PRODUCT.FILE')
      READ (10,1000) NITEMS
      DO 10 I = 1,NITEMS
         READ (10,2000) ITEMS(I),INVENT(I),PRICE(I)
   10    CONTINUE
      CLOSE (10)

C    CUSTOMER INFORMATION

      OPEN (11,FILE='CUSTOMER.FILE')
      READ (11,3000) NCUST
      DO 20 I = 1,NCUST
         READ (11,4000) CUSTID(I),CUSPCT(I)
   20    CONTINUE
      CLOSE (11)

C    FORMATS

 1000 FORMAT(I3)
 2000 FORMAT(I5,I7,F8.2)
 3000 FORMAT(I3)
 4000 FORMAT(I5,F5.3)
      END
```

Figure 6.7

```
      SUBROUTINE UPDATE(CUSTNO,ITEMNO,QUANT,BAD,NITEMS,ITEMS,INVENT)
      INTEGER CUSTNO,ITEMNO,QUANT,NITEMS,ITEMS(250),INVENT(250)
      LOGICAL BAD
      INTEGER I

C    WRITTEN BY ********, **/**/**

C    THIS SUBROUTINE UPDATES INVENTORY INFORMATION.

C    THESE ARE THE PARAMETERS
C       CUSTNO-INTEGER, INPUT-CUSTOMER #
C       ITEMNO-INTEGER, INPUT-ITEM # PURCHASED
C       QUANT -INTEGER, INPUT-QUANTITY PURCHASED
C       BAD   -LOGICAL, OUTPUT-FLAG FOR BAD ITEM #
C       NITEMS-INTEGER, INPUT-NUMBER OF PRODUCT ITEMS
C       ITEMS -INTEGER ARRAY SIZE 250, INPUT-ITEM #'S
C       INVENT-INTEGER ARRAY SIZE 250, UPDATE-INVENTORY AMOUNTS

C    SEARCH FOR GIVEN ITEM #

      DO 10 I = 1,NITEMS
         IF (ITEMNO.EQ.ITEMS(I)) THEN
            GO TO 100
         ENDIF
   10    CONTINUE

C    DETECT ERRORS, OR ADJUST INVENTORY

  100 CONTINUE
      IF (I.GT.NITEMS) THEN
         WRITE(20,*) CUSTNO,ITEMNO,QUANT,' No such customer'
         BAD = .TRUE.
      ELSE IF (QUANT.GT.INVENT(I)) THEN
         WRITE(20,*) CUSTNO,ITEMNO,QUANT,' Insufficient inventory'
         BAD = .TRUE.
      ELSE
         INVENT(I) = INVENT(I) - QUANT
         BAD = .FALSE.
      ENDIF
      RETURN
      END
```

Figure 6.8

Case Study #7

In this case study we will prepare a package of subprograms rather than a program. The subroutines will enable us to write programs that manipulate polynomials in a single variable. While we are writing such programs, we will be able to concentrate on the problem we wish to solve and not on the details of how to work with polynomials, since the package of subprograms will handle those details.

1. *Statement of Problem.* Polynomials of degree N or less in a single unknown, say *x*, can be written as

```
c(0) + c(1) * x ** 1 + c(2) * x ** 2 + ··· + c(N) * x ** N.
```

where the *c*'s are the coefficients of the individual powers of *x*, and we have used the FORTRAN notations for subscripts and powers.

Such a polynomial can be specified completely by giving the values for the coefficients and the name of the single unknown. We want to have a collection of subprograms for performing arithmetic and other operations on polynomials of a single unknown which we will call X. We will suppose that all of the polynomials are of degree N or less.

2. *Analysis.* The polynomials will be represented by real arrays containing their coefficients. For example, a polynomial C will be represented by an array C declared as (for some constant N)

```
REAL C(0 : N)
```

Note that we are taking advantage of the fact that we can specify the lower bound of an array subscript in FORTRAN. (This was not true in earlier versions of FORTRAN). Thus the coefficient of X**K in the polynomial is in the element of the array with subscript K.

We will next decide on the operations to be performed. We normally would like to provide addition, subtraction, multiplication, and division. Division turns out to be fairly difficult and therefore we will not do that in this example. Other operations that we can provide are the evaluation of a polynomial for a given value of X, and integration and differentiation by X. More computer-related operations would be reading and writing polynomials, finding the degree of a polynomial, comparing two polynomials to see if they are the same polynomial, and copying one polynomial into another. We shall also include some special cases of multiplication, namely by a constant, and by X. Refer to Table 6.1 for a summary of these operations.

TABLE 6.1 OPERATIONS TO BE PROVIDED BY POLYNOMIAL PACKAGE

a) Addition
b) Subtraction
c) Multiplication
d) Multiplication by a constant
e) Multiplication by X
f) Evaluate a polynomial
g) Integrate a polynomial
h) Differentiate a polynomial
i) Read a polynomial
j) Write a polynomial
k) Find degree of a polynomial
l) Compare two polynomials for equality
m) Copy a polynomial

We must next decide on the form our operations will take. Most of the operations will require a number of steps to complete, and so it seems reasonable to use subprograms for the operations. Most of the operations will have a polynomial for a result. In FORTRAN a function can only return a simple value as the function value, and the polynomials are represented by arrays. It seems reasonable to use subroutines for these operations. Operations (f), (k), and (l) do return single values and thus could be implemented using functions.

Let us name the subprograms with names that start with POL for polynomial and end with characters in some sense descriptive of the operation. Thus we will use names like POLADD, POLSUB, POLMUL, and POLVAL. By starting with the characters POL, the routines will usually be listed together in any automatically generated alphabetic lists of subprograms used in any program.

The arithmetic operations require two operands and one result. We could use another argument to indicate success or failure of the operation. However, to simplify the argument lists of the subprograms, we will adopt the following convention: Any error will cause an error message and the program will terminate.

The operation

```
R ← OP1 - OP2
```

could be represented with six different orderings of R, OP1, and OP2. However, it would be very confusing to the user of the routine to have OP1 follow OP2 or to have OP1 separated from OP2 by the result R. Therefore, the two reasonable choices for the ordering of these three seem to be (R, OP1, OP2) and (OP1, OP2, R). Since in FORTRAN the result of an assignment is placed on the left of an equals sign, it seems that the first choice would be more natural. Therefore, we shall adopt the policy that results, if any, will be the first arguments and operands the remaining arguments.

The first three routines then should be:

```
SUBROUTINE POLADD(R, P, Q)
SUBROUTINE POLSUB(R, P, Q)
SUBROUTINE POLMUL(R, P, Q)
```

where R is the array representing the result polynomial, and P and Q are the arrays representing the operand polynomials.

One remaining question is the size of the arrays to be used. We will simply pick 50 as the maximum degree, N, of the polynomials. Therefore a polynomial P will be declared as

```
REAL P(0:50)
```

in every subprogram that uses it.

3. *Algorithms and programs.* Most of the algorithms are very simple and short, so in many cases we will omit the variable lists. Also since we have many short programs we will show them right after the discussion of the algorithm.

Addition of two polynomials is performed by adding the coefficients of the same power of X. The sum of

$$5X^5 - 4X^2 + 6$$

and

$$6X^5 + 2X^3 + 3$$

is

$$11X^5 + 2X^3 - 4X^2 + 9$$

The first and second polynomials are represented by arrays containing

6, 0, −4, 0, 0, 5

and

3, 0, 0, 2, 0, 6

as their first six elements (in positions 0 through 5). The result is represented by the array

9, 0, −4, 2, 0, 11

The algorithm would be:

```
loop for I = 0 to N
   R(I) ← P(I) + Q(I)
endloop
```

Coding the algorithm in FORTRAN gives us the following subroutine.

```
      SUBROUTINE POLADD(R, P, Q)
      REAL R(0:50), P(0:50), Q(0:50)

C     WRITTEN BY ***************, **/**/**

C     THIS ROUTINE FORMS THE SUM OF TWO POLYNOMIALS
C     REPRESENTED BY THE ARRAYS P AND Q. THE RESULT
C     IS PLACED IN THE ARRAY R

C     PARAMETERS:
C     R-OUTPUT, REAL ARRAY CONTAINING THE COEFFICIENTS
C               OF THE RESULT.
C     P-INPUT,  REAL ARRAY CONTAINING THE COEFFICIENTS
C               OF THE FIRST OPERAND.
C     Q-INPUT,  REAL ARRAY CONTAINING THE COEFFICIENTS
C               OF THE SECOND OPERAND.

      INTEGER I

      DO 10 I = 0, 50
          R(I) = P(I) + Q(I)
   10     CONTINUE

      RETURN
      END
```

The subtraction routine is very similar to the addition routine. Multiplication, on the other hand, is much more complex. The product of two polynomials

$$p0 + p1\,x + p2\,x^2$$

and

$$q0 + q1\,x + q2\,x^2 + q3\,x^3$$

is

$$\begin{aligned} &p0\,q0 + (p0\,q1 + p1\,q0)\,x + \\ &(p0\,q2 + p1\,q1 + p2\,q0)\,x^2 + \\ &(p0\,q3 + p1\,q2 + p2\,q1)\,x^3 + \\ &(p1\,q3 + p2\,q2)\,x^4 + p2\,q3\,x^5 \end{aligned}$$

The first polynomial has three terms and the second, four terms. The product has 12 individual terms, each a product of one p term and one q term. In other words each p coefficient is multiplied by each q coefficient. The power of x in the product associated with the term $(pi\ qj)$ is just $(i + j)$.

The degree of the product polynomial is the sum of the degrees of the two factors. This is one place where it will be convenient to have a routine to compute the degree of a polynomial. Let us define that routine as an integer function named

POLDEG(P)

and write it later.

In order to multiply each term of polynomial P by each term of polynomial Q, we will need a nested loop structure. We will use the variables IP and IQ as indices for the loops. For the degrees of P and Q we will use the variables NP and NQ, similarly, IR and NR for the index and degree associated with the resultant polynomial R.

The rough algorithm for the multiplication routine would be

Compute degree of R and check for legal value
Initialize coefficients of R to zero
Compute all products of terms of P and Q, adding into appropriate terms of R

The first step becomes:

```
NP ← POLDEG(P)
NQ ← POLDEG(Q)
NR ← NP + NQ
if NR > 50 then
   write error message
   stop
endif
```

The second step becomes:

```
loop for IR = 0 to 50
   R(IR) ← 0.0
endloop
```

Note that we initialize all elements of R to zero and not just the elements from 0 to NR. This is done so that later we can calculate the degree of R correctly. The main part of the algorithm will be the nested loops multiplying the individual terms and adding to the proper terms in R.

```
loop for IP = 0 to NP
  loop for IQ = 0 to NQ
    IR ← IP + IQ
    R(IR) ← R(IR) + P(IP) * Q(IQ)
  endloop
endloop
```

Writing the FORTRAN code gives us the following subroutine:

```
      SUBROUTINE POLMUL(R, P, Q)
      REAL R(0:50), P(0:50), Q(0:50)

C  WRITTEN BY *************, **/**/**

C  THIS ROUTINE FORMS THE PRODUCT OF TWO POLYNOMIALS
C  REPRESENTED BY THE ARRAYS P AND Q. THE RESULT IS
C  PLACED IN THE ARRAY R.

C  PARAMETERS
C  R  OUTPUT, REAL ARRAY CONTAINING THE COEFFICIENTS OF
C             THE RESULT.
C  P  INPUT,  REAL ARRAY CONTAINING THE COEFFICIENTS OF
C             THE FIRST FACTOR.
C  Q  INPUT,  REAL ARRAY CONTAINING THE COEFFICIENTS OF
C             THE SECOND FACTOR.

C  OTHER VARIABLES
C  IR, NR INTEGER, INDEX AND DEGREE OR POLYNOMIAL R.
C  IP, NP INTEGER, INDEX AND DEGREE OF POLYNOMIAL P.
C  IQ, NQ INTEGER, INDEX AND DEGREE OF POLYNOMIAL Q.

C OTHER ROUTINES
C POLDEG   INTEGER FUNCTION RETURNING ACTUAL DEGREE OF
C          POLYNOMIAL.

      INTEGER IR, NR, IP, NP, IQ, NQ, POLDEG

      NP = POLDEG(P)
      NQ = POLDEG(Q)
      NR = NP + NQ
      IF( NR .GT. 50 ) THEN
        PRINT *, 'RESULT TOO LARGE IN POLMUL'
        STOP
      ENDIF

      DO 10 IR = 0, 50
        R(IR) = 0.0
   10   CONTINUE
```

(continued)

```
      DO 20 IP = 0, NP
        DO 30 IQ = 0, NQ
          IR = IP + IQ
          R(IR) = R(IR) + P(IP) * Q(IQ)
30        CONTINUE
20      CONTINUE

      RETURN
      END
```

Let us now work on the POLDEG function used in POLMUL. The degree of a polynomial, P, is the highest power of X that appears in the polynomial. This corresponds to the subscript of the last nonzero element in the array representing the polynomial. A simple way to find that element is to search the array from the last term forward until we find a nonzero element. Note that if all the elements are zero then the polynomial represents the constant zero and the degree is zero. One possible algorithm is the following:

```
POLDEG ← 50
loop
   if P(POLDEG) ≠ 0 or POLDEG = 0 then exit endif
   POLDEG ← POLDEG - 1
endloop
```

A segment of FORTRAN code corresponding to this algorithm would be:

```
      POLDEG = 50
10    CONTINUE
        IF(P(POLDEG) .NE. 0.0 .OR.
     $     POLDEG .EQ. 0 ) THEN
          GO TO 20
        ENDIF
        POLDEG = POLDEG - 1
        GO TO 10
20    CONTINUE
      RETURN
```

A possible modification would be to remove statement 20 and the RETURN and replace the GO TO 20 by a RETURN.

We could also use a DO loop as in the following segment:

```
      DO 10 POLDEG = 50, 1, -1
        IF(P(POLDEG) .NE. 0) THEN
          RETURN
        ENDIF
10      CONTINUE
      POLDEG = 0
      RETURN
```

Now let us consider the routine for evaluating a polynomial. This routine will require two arguments—the array of coefficients and the value of X. The routine will return only a single value and therefore can be a function. Let us call the function POLVAL, with arguments P and X.

A first rough algorithm might look like the following:

```
PD ← POLDEG(P)
POLVAL ← P(0)
loop for I = 1 to PD
   compute XI ← Ith power of X
   POLVAL ← POLVAL + P(I) * XI
endloop
```

The step compute XI can be expanded to:

```
XI ← X
loop for J = 2 to I
   XI ← XI * X
endloop
```

To compute XI would require I − 1 multiplications. To compute the value of a polynomial of degree N would require N multiplications of coefficients by powers of X plus

$$(N-1) + (N-2) + (N-3) + \cdots + 2 + 1$$

additional multiplications to compute the various powers of X. The expression $(N-1) + \cdots + 2 + 1$ is equal to

$$\frac{n(n-1)}{2}$$

and so the total number of multiplications needed is

$$\frac{n^2}{2} - \frac{n}{2} + n = \frac{n^2}{2} + \frac{n}{2}$$

If N were 50 this would require 1275 multiplications. This number can be reduced considerably. Notice first that the powers of X are needed in sequence. Rather than compute the Ith power of X starting from scratch we can compute it from the (I − 1)st power. This leads to the following algorithm:

```
PD ← POLDEG(P)
XI ← 1
POLVAL ← P(0)
loop for I = 1 to PD
  XI ← XI * X
  POLVAL ← POLVAL + P(I) * XI
endloop
```

For this algorithm the number of multiplications for a polynomial of degree N is just $2n$. Note that for N = 50 this is a reduction by a factor of almost 13.

There is still a better method, commonly called Horner's method. A polynomial such as

$$p0 + p1 * X + p2 * X^2 + p3 * X^3 + p4 * X^4$$

can be rewritten in a nested form as

$$p0 + X * (p1 + X * (p\ 2 + X * (p3 + X * (p4)))).$$

This can be evaluated in the order

```
val ← p4
val ← p3 + X * val
val ← p2 + X * val
val ← p1 + X * val
val ← p0 + X * val
```

When we are finished *val* will be the value of the polynomial, but we will have used, in this case, only four multiplications. In general the algorithm would be:

```
PD ← POLDEG(P)
POLVAL ← P(PD)
loop for I = PD - 1 to 0 by -1
  POLVAL ← P(I) + X * POLVAL
endloop
```

Of course here a polynomial of degree N requires N multiplications. Notice that in this situation the fastest of our three algorithms is also the shortest to write. One should not assume that this last procedure will be twice as fast as the second procedure, since there are other operations, such as additions and loop control involved. Still this should be faster than the others on most conventional computer systems.

The routines for integration and differentiation use similar methods. If you have not yet studied calculus, you can skip this material without its affecting your understanding of the other routines in the package. The integral of a polynomial is the sum of the integrals of each of the terms plus an arbitrary constant. The integral of the term

$$P(I) * X^I$$

is

$$P(I) * X^{(I+1)}/(I + 1).$$

The result is a new polynomial, say Q, with the (I + 1)st coefficient of Q being the Ith coefficient of P divided by (I + 1). For the degree of Q to be less than or equal to 50 the degree of P must be less than or equal to 49.

Let us call our routine POLITG and use arguments Q, P, and C, where P is the original polynomial, C is the arbitary constant, and Q is the resultant polynomial.

The algorithm would be:

```
PD ← POLDEG(P)
if PD > 49 then
  print 'Degree of polynomial too large in POLITG'
  stop
endif
Q(0) ← C
loop for I = 1 to PD + 1
  Q(I) ← P(I - 1) / REAL(I)
endloop
loop for I = PD + 2 to 50
  Q(I) ← 0
endloop
```

For our final example we will write the output routine. This should be a subroutine since it returns no value. It needs only the one argument, the polynomial to be printed. Let us call the routine POLOUT. Suppose we print all coefficients except the constant term as

```
(dddddd.ddddd) * X ** (dd)
```

where the d's stand for digits, and the constant term as

```
(dddddd.ddddd)
```

Let us also not print any terms with a zero coefficient; however, we should be sure to print at least one term. We will use a logical variable ANYPRT to indicate whether any terms have been printed. Our algorithm would be:

```
ANYPRT ← false
loop for I = 50 to 1 by -1
  if P(I) ≠ 0 then
    print P(I), I
    ANYPRT ← true
  endif
endloop
if P(0) ≠ 0 or ANYPRT is still false then
  print P(0)
endif
```

The program would be:

```
      SUBROUTINE POLOUT(P)
      REAL P(0:50)

C   ROUTINE PRINTS THE POLYNOMIAL P.

C   PARAMETERS
C   P,       INPUT, REAL ARRAY, COEFFICIENTS OF THE
C            POLYNOMIAL TO BE PRINTED.
```

(continued)

```
C    OTHER VARIABLES
C    ANYPRT, LOGICAL, FLAG TO INDICATE WHETHER ANY
C            COEFFICIENTS HAVE BEEN PRINTED.

         LOGICAL ANYPRT
         INTEGER I

         ANYPRT = .FALSE.

         DO 10 I = 50, 1, -1
           IF(P(I) .NE. 0.0) THEN
             WRITE(*,100) P(I), I
             ANYPRT = .TRUE.
           ENDIF
 10        CONTINUE

         IF(P(0) .NE. 0.0 .OR.
        $    .NOT. ANYPRT) THEN
           WRITE(*,110) P(0)
         ENDIF

         RETURN

100      FORMAT(' (', F12.5, ') * X ** (', I2, ')' )
110      FORMAT(' (', F12.5, ')' )

         END
```

4. *Testing.* Testing a package of subprograms differs from testing a program in several ways. First, the individual subprograms cannot stand alone and so you must write programs to call the subprograms. These programs are commonly called drivers. Second, the individual routines tend to be fairly simple and so tests can sometimes be fairly simple also.

Probably the input and output subroutines should be tested first so that you can use those routines to test the others. A simple way to test these routines is to use a driver program that calls the POLIN (the input routine) and POLOUT in a loop. You can then check the output to see if it matches your input. The driver should also print the array corresponding to the polynomial which has been read by POLIN, to guard against errors in POLOUT and POLIN which might cancel each other. An example of such an error would be if POLIN placed the coefficients in the wrong elements of the array and POLOUT picked up the elements in same wrong manner. The test data for the driver should include polynomials of degree 0, 1, 49, 50, and some over 50. Some of the polynomials should consist of just a few nonzero terms, while others should have all nonzero terms. The constant 0 should be one of the test values since that will cause a special action in the POLOUT routine.

Once POLIN and POLOUT are tested and appear to be correct you can begin testing the others. A driver which reads two polynomials and computes their degrees (POLDEG), adds them (POLADD), subtracts them (POLSUB), differentiates them, compares for equality, and multiplies by X would be a natural next step, and would test a large number of the routines. These operations have been grouped together since they each require one or two input polynomials but do not require any additional data. In addition separate drivers should be used to provide each of the routines that have error checks built in with invalid data to check the error handling.

The copy routine can be tested after the routine for comparing for equality. Finally the last group to be tested could be the routines for evaluating a polynomial (POLVAL), multiplication by a constant, and integration (POLITG). This group requires both a polynomial and a real value as inputs for each routine.

The detailed unit test plans for the various modules are left as an exercise. To get you started, we list a few possible tests for two of the modules.

For POLDEG:	degree 50
	degree 1
	degree 0 (not zero polynomial)
	degree 0 (zero polynomial)
For POLADD:	both polynomials zero
	first polynomial zero
	second polynomial zero
	neither polynomial zero, result not zero
	neither polynomial zero, result zero.

5. *Documentation.* The documentation for such a package would normally include a description of what operations are provided, how the polynomials are represented, how the user has to define the data arrays which hold the polynomials, and finally a detailed description of each routine in the package. The detailed description should include precise descriptions of how to call each routine and precise descriptions of each argument. It would be desirable to include examples of the use of each routine. You can use FORTRAN terminology, if convenient, to describe these routines, since anybody using the package is going to have to know FORTRAN to write a program calling the routines. Notice that the user documentation for a package such as this differs from that for a program. For a program, FORTRAN terminology would not be appropriate for the user's guide.

Case Study #8

In this brief case study we will examine the concept of **sorting**. By this we mean arranging the elements in an array in some predetermined order. We will assume that our array elements are numerical, and we will arrange them in numerical order from largest to smallest. Easy modifications to the algorithm we develop will allow the elements to be arranged from smallest to largest. In addition, the concepts developed apply equally well to alphabetical sorting of character arrays.

The algorithm we develop is sometimes referred to as a **selection sort**. The underlying idea is to select the number which should be in the first position in the array and put it there. We then select the number which belongs in the second position in the array and put it there. We continue in this fashion until the proper numbers have been selected for each position and placed in the array.

The selection sort is not a very efficient sort; for reasonable sized arrays it can take an unreasonable amount of time to perform. There are many other, more sophisticated sorting mechanisms which have been developed to work much faster. However, the selection sort remains one of the easier to understand.

1. *Statement of problem.* We will, for the time being, assume that we have an array of ten numbers to sort into *descending order* (largest to smallest). We will call this array A.

2. *Preliminary analysis.* In order to understand the selection sort algorithm, we begin with some preliminary examples.

Write an algorithm segment to determine the subscript LSUB of the largest element in A. We have written algorithms of this type before. We use a **loop for** indexed by the variable J. (The reason for the use of J rather than I will become apparent later.)

```
LSUB ← 1
loop for J = 1 to 10
    if A(J)>A(LSUB) then LSUB ← J endif
endloop
```

Now write an algorithm segment to exchange A(1) and A(LSUB). For example, if LSUB is 7, this will exchange A(1) and A(7).

The idea is to set aside a temporary location to store the value of A(1). We move data as indicated by the diagram, in the order indicated.

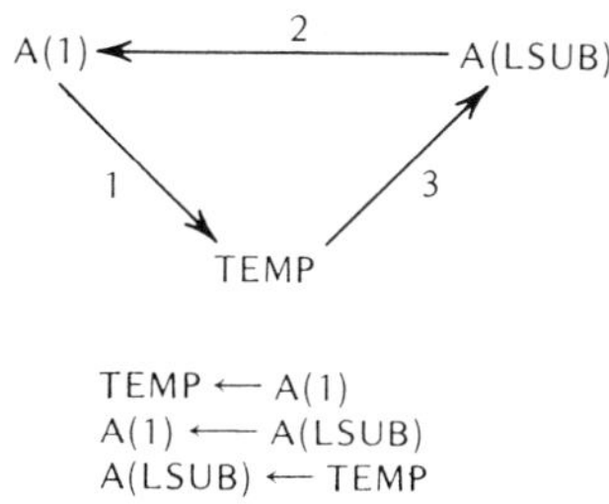

We now write an algorithm segment to determine the subscript LSUB of the largest element in A(I) through A(10), and then exchange A(I) with A(LSUB). For example, if A is the array pictured below and I is 4, then LSUB will be 7.

```
16 12 11 3 0 4 9 6 1 2
```

After swapping A(4) and A(7) we will have A as follows:

```
16 12 11 9 0 4 3 6 1 2
```

The algorithm is a combination of the preceding algorithms, slightly generalized. We start at position I, rather than 1, and we swap position I with position LSUB.

```
LSUB ← I
loop for J = I to 10
   if A(J)>A(LSUB) then LSUB ← J endif
endloop
TEMP ← A(I)
A(I) ← A(LSUB)
A(LSUB) ← TEMP
```

3. *Algorithm and modifications.* The selection sort method consists of applying this algorithm segment repeatedly. Starting with an array A which is not sorted, we determine the subscript LSUB of the largest number in A(1) through A(10), then exchange A(1) with A(LSUB). For example, if A is

3 7 20 1 6 4 13 9 5 8

then after this first swap we have:

20 7 3 1 6 4 13 9 5 8

We now determine the subscript LSUB of the largest number in A(2) through A(10), and exchange A(2) with A(LSUB) with the results shown:

20 7 3 1 6 4 13 9 5 8

20 13 3 1 6 4 7 9 5 8

As you can see, the first exchange located and placed into A(1) the largest number in A. The second placed the proper number (the largest of the remaining numbers) into A(2). A third exchange will determine the subscript LSUB (it turns out to be subscript 8) of the largest number in A(3) through A(10), exchanging A(3) with A(LSUB):

20 13 9 1 6 4 7 3 5 8

After each such exchange, one more number is in its correct location. After nine exchanges, nine numbers will be correct, and the tenth will therefore also be correct. Our algorithm is

```
loop for I = 1 to 9
   determine the subscript LSUB of the largest
      element in A(I) through A(10), then exchange A(I)
      with A(LSUB)
endloop
```

To obtain a smooth algorithm, we replace the body of the loop with the algorithm segment written earlier which accomplishes the required task.

```
loop for I = 1 to 9
   LSUB ← I
   loop for J = I to 10
      if A(J)>A(LSUB) then LSUB ← J endif
   endloop
   TEMP ← A(I)
   A(I) ← A(LSUB)
   A(LSUB) ← TEMP
endloop
```

Modifying the algorithm to work with different size arrays is easy. For example, in an algorithm to sort an array A of size 75 in descending order, only the loop controls change:

```
loop for I = 1 to 74
   LSUB ← I
   loop for J = I to 75
```

To complete the case study, we will write a subprogram to sort an INTEGER array A of size 100 in descending order. By now this should be relatively easy to write. To make it slightly more general, we add a parameter N which tells how much of the array is in use (See Section 8.3, Adjustable Dimensions, for other generalizing methods.) A possible solution follows:

```
      SUBROUTINE SORT(A,N)
      INTEGER A(100),N,I,J

C   WRITTEN BY *******, **/**/**

C   THIS SUBROUTINE SORTS AN INTEGER ARRAY OF SIZE 100

C   THE PARAMETERS USED ARE:

C        A—UPDATE, INTEGER(100)—THE ARRAY TO BE SORTED
C        N—INPUT, INTEGER—PORTION IN USE

C   EACH PASS THROUGH OUTER LOOP: (A.) FINDS THE LARGEST
C NUMBER AMONG A(I) TO A(N); THEN (B.) EXCHANGES IT WITH A(I)


      DO 100 I = 1,N-1

C   (A.) FIND

         LSUB = I
         DO 50 J = I,N
            IF(A(J).GT.A(LSUB)) THEN
               LSUB = J
            ENDIF
   50       CONTINUE
C
```

(continued)

```
C    (B.) EXCHANGE

              TEMP = A(I)
              A(I) = A(LSUB)
              A(LSUB) = TEMP
     100      CONTINUE
          RETURN
          END
```

EXERCISES

Exercises 1–6 refer to Case Study #6.

1. Write FORTRAN subprograms for the following:
   (a) INPUT
   (b) PRICE
   (c) DISC
   (d) FINAL
   (e) HEADER
2. Both PRICE and UPDATE do an array lookup of ITEMNO in the ITEMS array. Modify the algorithms to use a function ITLOOK (ITEMNO,ITEMS,NITEMS) to perform the lookup. ITLOOK should return the subscript where the item number was located, or −1 if not present.
3. The outright rejection of an invalid customer number is perhaps unreasonable. Rewrite the DISC algorithm to give a PCT of 0.0 to customers not present in the CUSTID array. What changes would this make in the main program? (You might want to retain the error message as a warning message, but not reject the order.)
4. Even if both the PRICE and UPDATE routines use a lookup routine to look up the item (as suggested in Exercise 2), this involves extra computer time. It would be better to have the UPDATE routine pass back to the main program the subscript where the item number was located. This would do away with the need for the PRICE function. Make the necessary changes to the UPDATE routine and the main program.
5. **(a)** It would be nice (at least, consistent with earlier programs) to do all error checking in the INPUT routine, including checking for faulty item number or customer number and insufficient inventory. Modify the INPUT routine to do so.
   (b) The problem with the straightforward solution to (a) is that it will be necessary to do array searches later to again look up the customer and item numbers.
   By having INPUT pass the item subscript rather than the item number itself to the main program (and similarly the customer subscript), we can avoid this duplication of effect. Make the needed changes to carry out these suggestions.
6. Carry out the modifications to make the system a menu-driven conversational system. What other desirable activities can you think of?

Exercises 7–13 refer to Case Study #7.

7. Design the algorithm and write the routine POLIN(P,EOF) to read a polynomial. The input records should be formatted like those produced by POLOUT. Thus the first two characters on an input line containing a term are a blank and a left parenthesis. The end of a polynomial is indicated by a line containing only the characters EP, for End Polynomial.

The argument EOF is a logical value set to .TRUE. by POLIN if an end of file has been reached or if the user types ED, for End Data, when POLIN starts to read a new polynomial. If the package is going to be used interactively, it would be reasonable to have POLIN prompt for its input.

8. Complete the routines POLVAL, POLSUB, POLITG (if you have studied calculus), and POLDEG.

9. Design and write the routines POLMLC and POLMLX for multiplication of a polynomial by a constant or by X.

10. If you have studied calculus, design and write the routine POLDIF for differentiation.

11. Design and write the routines POLEQU and POLCPY for comparing for equality and copying polynomials.

12. Test all of the routines written in Exercises 7 to 11.

13. The family of polynomials known as the Chebyshev polynomials is used in several different areas of mathematics. These polynomials are denoted by

$$T_N(x)$$

where N is the degree of the individual polynomial. The first few of these are defined as:

$$T_0(x) = 1$$
$$T_1(x) = x$$
$$T_2(x) = 2x^2 - 1$$

and

$$T_{10}(x) = 512x^{10} - 1280x^8 + 1120x^6 - 400x^4 + 50x^2 - 1$$

The polynomial of degree N can be calculated from those of degree $(N - 1)$ and degree $(N - 2)$ by the equation

$$T_N(x) = 2x\,T_{N-1}(x) - T_{N-2}(x)$$

Write a program, using the polynomial package, to compute and print the Chebyshev polynomials of $N = 0$ through $N = 15$. How would you have to modify the package for N greater than 15?

Exercises 14 and 15 refer to Case Study #8.

14. Suppose we have parallel arrays IDNO and AGE. If we sort these based on IDNO, then whenever we swap two IDNO entries we must also swap the corresponding AGE entries.

(a) Write an algorithm to sort the ID-age combinations in descending order by ID.

(b) Write an algorithm to sort the ID-age combinations in ascending order by age.

15. Parallel arrays NAME, G1, G2, G3, G4, and LETTER contain information on students—last name, four test grades, and letter grade.

(a) Sort the information in alphabetical order by last name. *Note:* CHARACTER comparisons such as .GT. are allowed, and give alphabetical order comparisons.

(b) Sort the information in descending order by total of the four test grades.

Exercises 16–20 suggest packages of subprograms which could be developed to aid in working with certain types of problems.

16. Integers of long length may be stored in the computer as arrays, one digit per array element. For example, a 15-digit number could be represented as an INTEGER array NUMBER of size 15. NUMBER(1) would contain the first digit of the number, NUMBER(15) the last digit.

(a) Write a subroutine to add two such numbers. It should give an indication of whether or not the answer will fit in the array which represents the answer.
(b) Subtract two such numbers, indicating whether it is possible to do so.
(c) Compare two such numbers to see whether the first is greater than the second. (This might be a LOGICAL function.)
(d) Multiply two such numbers.
(e) Use this package to find the sum

$$1 + 2 + 4 + 8 + \cdots + 2^{1} + \cdots + 2^{63}$$

(The answer is fewer than 30 digits long.)

17. Numbers in base 10 may be represented as arrays, each array element having one digit, whose value is 0–9 (see Exercise 16). If we limit our digits to 0–7, we have a "base 8" number instead of a base 10 number.

For example, in base 8, the array

0, 0, 0, 0, 1, 5, 3

would represent $1 * 8^2 + 5 * 8 + 3 = 107$.

(a) Given an array and a base, calculate the value of the number represented by the array in that base.
(b) Given a value, convert it to an array in a given base.
(c) Write a subroutine to print the number represented by an array, given the array and the base.

For example:

array	base	result
0,0,8,0,3	10	803
0,1,5,1,0	8	1510
0,15,10,1,9	16	FA19

[*Hint:* Convert the given array to an array of characters, with leading zeroes converted to blanks.]

(d–g) Revise (a–d) of Exercise 16 to work for arrays representing numbers in any given base.

18. We may represent a nonvertical straight line by an array LINE of size 2, where LINE(1) is the slope m, LINE(2) is the y-intercept b of the line

$$y = mx + b$$

Write routines to perform the following:

(a) Given two lines, tell whether or not they are parallel. (It may be advisable to use a LOGICAL function.)
(b) Tell whether or not two lines are perpendicular.
(c) Tell whether or not two lines are the same.
(d) Given a line and an x value, determine the corresponding y value.
(e) Given a line and a y value, determine the x value.
(f) Given a line and a point (x,y), tell whether the point is on the line.
(g) Given a line and two points, tell whether or not the points are on the same side of the line.

19. We may represent a line by an array of size 4, containing the (x,y) coordinates of two points on the line. The array is (X1,Y1,X2,Y2).

(a–g) Repeat (a–g) of Exercise 18, using this representation.
(h) Write routines to convert between the two representation forms.

20. The REAL variables in FORTRAN are, of course, approximations. As a result, we have difficulties such as 1.0/3.0*3.0 possibly not being exactly equal to one. This type of approximation is not sufficient for some applications. In this exercise we consider the design and implementation of a package of subprograms to provide exact arithmetic for a subset of rational numbers.

As you know, **rational numbers** are those numbers whose value is given as the ratio of two integers. For example, 1/2, 3/562813, 5/3, 15/25, and −15/17 are all rational numbers. Integers are also rational numbers, since any integer can be represented as the ratio of itself and one. For example, 5 may be written as 5/1.

There are an infinite number of representations for a given rational number. For example, 1/2, 5/10, 25/50, −7/−14, and so on, all represent the same rational number. However, there is a unique preferred representation, namely the one in which the numerator and denominator have no common factors and the denominator is positive.

Since the mathematical representation of a rational number contains two integer numbers, it is natural to choose a computer representation which uses two FORTRAN integers. In our case, we will use a one-dimensional INTEGER array of length 2 to represent a single rational number. To represent the rational number Q, we will use an array declared as

```
INTEGER Q(2)
```

We will use the element Q(1) as the numerator, and Q(2) as the denominator.

(a) Table 6.2 contains a list of operations to be provided in your package. Output parameters which are rational numbers should be in the "preferred" form described above.

TABLE 6.2 OPERATIONS TO BE PROVIDED BY RATIONAL ARITHMETIC PACKAGE

a. Addition
b. Subtraction
c. Multiplication
d. Division
e. Input
f. Output
g. Convert rational to REAL
h. Convert rational to INTEGER
i. Convert INTEGER to rational
j. Compare

(b) Write a program using the rational arithmetic package to read three rational numbers A, B, C, and compute and print D1 = (A+B)/C and D2 = (A−B)/C.

(c) Write a program to read rational numbers A, B, and C and an integer number X. Calculate and print $P = A * X^2 + B * X + C$. The answer should be printed as an integer if possible.

(d) Repeat (c), but print the answer as a real number.

(e) Repeat (d), also calculating the answer by first converting A, B, C, and X to real numbers. Compare the two answers obtained.

Exercises 21–26 suggest other "case study" type applications.

21. (a) A simple encryption ("secret code") method is to jumble the alphabet, replacing (perhaps) A by D, B by X, C by M, and so on. One way to implement this uses two parallel arrays. The first contains the letters in order, the second contains the letters in the desired jumbled order (perhaps D, X, M, . . .). Give the declarations and DATA statements to create these arrays.

(b) Write an algorithm segment to encode a single character. Assume that characters which are not letters are replaced by themselves (CAB$ might become MDX$).

(c) Write a FORTRAN main program which codes or decodes lines of text. It will read a series of records, each 65 columns long. The first column of each should contain either a C or D, to indicate whether the remaining 64 columns should be coded or decoded. *Hint:* Use a CHARACTER*1 array of size 64 to read the remaining columns.

22. (a) Modify Exercise 21 to use the following different encryption method: A is replaced by G, B by H, C by I, and so on. Each letter is replaced by the sixth letter further along in the alphabet. Some care is required to properly handle the letters near the end; for example, Z is replaced by F. Use only a single array containing the letters in order.

(b) Modify Exercise 21 to replace A by Z, B by Y, C by X, D by W, and so on. Use only a single array containing the letters in order.

23. Write algorithms for the following actions which deal with parallel arrays EMPID, SALES, RATE of size 200. There are presently NEMP employees represented in these arrays. *Hint:* Write a LOOKUP routine first.

(a) Inquire. Given an ID number, print the sales amont and rate for that employee, or print an error message if the given ID is faulty.

(b) New sale. Given a sales amount and ID, add the amount to the SALES figure for that ID (or print an error message). Also calculate commission as sales amount times rate.

(c) Change rate. Given a new rate and an ID, change the RATE for that employee to the given new rate, or print an error message.

(d) Find largest. Print the ID, rate, and sales amount of the salesperson with the largest sales amount.

(e) New employee. Given a new employee ID and rate, add that employee to the end of the list. If the ID is already in use, print an error message.

(f) INIT and FINAL. Write routines similar to those of Case Study #6.

(g) Sort. Sort the data in order by sales (highest to lowest).

24. Repeat Exercise 23 under the assumption that the EMPID array is maintained in increasing numerical order. Notice that, for (e), the new employee goes at the proper place based on ID number, not necessarily at the end of the list. (For part (g), create a separate sorted table.)

Hint: Rewrite the LOOKUP routine so it returns the subscript of the first table element bigger than or equal to the given key. This will simplify (e), but it will also require some changes in (a–c).

25. (a) Write a general-purpose COPY routine to copy a portion of the array B to the array A. Assume A and B are INTEGER arrays each of size 200.

The routine will be given A, APOS, B, BPOS, and LENGTH. APOS and BPOS represent the starting positions in the A and B arrays, respectively. LENGTH is the number of items to be copied. You may assume that LENGTH is valid; that is, copying that many items will not run past the end of either A or B.

(b) Rewrite (a) to handle the possibility that LENGTH may be "too long." The routine should copy up to LENGTH items, taking care to start within the bounds of both arrays. For example, APOS = 199, BPOS = 3, LENGTH = 14. Only two items are copied, to A(199) and A(200).

26. An efficient method for determining all the primes less than some given value N is the so-called sieve of Eratosthenes, which consists of two major phases. The first is to write down the positive integers from 2 to N. The second phase is a nested search and marking process. Starting with the first unmarked number, say K, in the list (at the start all the numbers are unmarked), go through the list and mark off all multiples of K.

The result of applying this process three times to the numbers from 2–34 is shown in the listing that follows. The marks are shown above the numbers so that we can indicate at which time the markings occurred. Notice some numbers are marked more than once. The first marking marked all numbers divisible by 2 except for 2. The second marking marked all values divisible by 3 except for 3. The third marking marked multiples of 5 (4 was already marked since it is a multiple of 2). Upon completion of the entire marking process all numbers divisible by some smaller number other than 1 have been marked. The unmarked values thus are primes.

3rd									X		
2nd					X			X			X
2st			X		X		X		X		X
	2	3	4	5	6	7	8	9	10	11	12

3rd			X					X			
2nd			X			X			X		
1st		X		X		X		X		X	
	13	14	15	16	17	18	19	20	21	22	23

3rd		X					X				
2nd	X			X			X			X	
1st	X		X		X		X		X		X
	24	25	26	27	28	29	30	31	32	33	34

The key to the efficiency of this process is that the marking process does not require any checking of divisibility. Also, notice that only values up to $K = \sqrt{N}$ need to be processed.

(a) Write an algorithm for initializing an integer array NUM, with subscript range 2 to 2000, to the values 2, 3, . . ., 2000.

(b) Write an algorithm which, given the array NUM initialized as in (a), carries out the marking process described for the sieve of Eratosthenes. One way of marking the numbers is to set the number equal to zero.

(c) The values of the numbers do not actually have to be used since the position of the number can indicate its value in this algorithm. Rewrite the algorithms in (a) and (b) using a logical array MARKED with 1999 elements. Initialize the elements to .FALSE. and indicate marking by setting an element to .TRUE.. After marking, we may determine if a value J where $2 \leq J \leq 2000$ is prime by checking to see if MARKED(J) is true or false.

(d) Write an algorithm to produce a printed table of primes up to 2000 with ten primes printed on each line. One way of doing this is to use an array of length 10 and insert primes into the array until it is full, print the array, and restart the insertion process. What happens at the end when you have processed all of the primes and the array may not have been filled with ten numbers?

7

MORE ON DO LOOPS

7.1 MORE ON DO LOOPS

Chapter 3 introduced the notion of a count-controlled loop. In that chapter we examined the **loop for** algorithm construction and the FORTRAN DO loop. We have used these constructions extensively, especially in working with arrays in Chapter 6.

The general form for a count-controlled loop in a pseudocode algorithm is the following:

```
loop for index = starting value to ending value by step size
   body of loop
endloop
```

The algorithms we have used to this point have all utilized an INTEGER variable as the loop index. In this chapter, we explore the use of REAL variables as the loop index. We also examine the DO loop "semantics" (exactly how it works) more thoroughly.

Form of the DO Statement

The FORTRAN DO statement is of the form

DO label, variable = expression 1, expression 2, expression 3

The comma following the label is optional. The third expression and the comma preceding it are also optional; if they are omitted the value is taken to be 1. The variable is used as the **index** of the loop. The three expressions are the **starting**

value of the index, the **ending value**, and the **step value**, respectively. The index variable and the expressions may be of either REAL or INTEGER types. (They may also be of DOUBLE PRECISION type, which is discussed further in Chapter 11.) They do not have to be of the same type (the expressions will be converted to the same type as the index variable), but for clarity we suggest using the same type.

Some sample legal DO statements are shown below:

```
DO 10,  I = 1, 5, 2
DO 10   I = 1, 5, 2
DO 20   INDEX = FIRST, LAST, STEP
DO 15   X = .5, 3.
DO 20   X = 5.0, END, END/25.0
DO 15   J = 5, -3, -2
```

There are a number of restrictions involving the use of the DO statement in FORTRAN. These are briefly discussed below. For the most part, the restrictions are very reasonable. If you follow the techniques presented in the earlier discussion of the DO loop, you should have no problems.

The statements following the DO, down to and including the statement whose label appears in the DO statement, are called the **range** of the DO. There are a number of statements which are not allowed as the last or **terminal statement** of the range. A list of the statements which are not permitted is given in Table 7.1. If we always end a DO loop with a CONTINUE statement as was suggested in Section 3.2, we will avoid any problems with these restrictions.

If the ranges of two DO statements overlap at all, then the range of one of the DO's must be completely within the range of the other. Furthermore, if an IF THEN appears within the range of a DO, the corresponding ENDIF must also be within the range of the DO. If the DO appears between an IF THEN and an ELSE,ELSE IF, or ENDIF—or between an ELSE or ELSE IF and the following ELSE IF or ENDIF—then the terminal statement of the range must also appear between the same two statements.

In brief, the range of a DO cannot partially overlap the range of another DO or

TABLE 7.1 STATEMENTS WHICH CANNOT BE USED AS THE LAST STATEMENT IN A DO RANGE

GO TO	END
assigned GO TO[1]	DO
arithmetic IF[1]	logical IF containing:
IF THEN	DO
ELSE IF	IF THEN
ELSE	ELSE IF
ENDIF	ELSE
RETURN	ENDIF
STOP	END

[1]Discussed briefly in Chapter 14.

one of the blocks of an IF THEN ELSE type construction. In terms of program structures, this says that a decision structure cannot be half in and half out of a loop. On the other hand, a loop cannot be half in and half out of one branch of a decision structure. Nor can a loop be half in and half out of another loop. If you think about the algorithms you have written to this point, you will realize that these are very reasonable rules. We have had decision and looping structures nested within one another, but never overlapping.

The following segments show some permitted DO ranges:

a.
```
      DO 10 I = 1,5
         DO 10 J = 2,7
            .
            .
10          CONTINUE
```
b.
```
      DO 10 I = 1,5
         DO 15 J = 2,7
            .
15          CONTINUE
10       CONTINUE
```
c.
```
      IF(X.LT.Y) THEN
         DO 10 I = 1,10
            .
10          CONTINUE
      ENDIF
```
d.
```
      DO 15 K = 1,5
         IF(X.GT.Y) THEN
            .
            .
         ELSE
            .
            .
         ENDIF
         .
         .
15       CONTINUE
```

The range of a DO statement may only be executed by executing the DO statement. One may not use a GO TO or any other mechanism to enter the range of the DO from outside the DO. (However, it is permissible to use a GO TO to leave the range of the DO. This technique may be used to implement the algorithm's **exit** step.)

REAL Loop Index

Generally speaking, the index for a count-controlled loop should be an INTEGER variable if there is no strong reason to choose a REAL variable. We prefer to write

loop for I = 1 **to** 5

rather than

```
loop for X = 1.0 to 5.0
```

However, there are situations where it is natural to use a REAL index. As an example, let us write an algorithm to print a table of values of x and y, where $y = x^2 + 2x - 5$, for x ranging from -4.5 to 3.0 in steps of 0.1.

This is a fairly simple problem, since a **loop for** construction may use any appropriate starting value, ending value, and step size. We write

```
loop for X = -4.5 to 3.0 by 0.1
   Y ← X ** 2 + 2 * X - 5
   call DETAIL(X,Y)
endloop
```

COMMENT. If we want the table to contain X values in decreasing order, we need only change the first line of the algorithm to

```
loop for X = 3.0 to -4.5 by -0.1
```

To further examine these ideas, let us list the values assumed by the REAL index X for each pass of the following loop, as well as the value after the loop is terminated.

```
loop for X = 1.5 to 3.3 by  0.25
loop for X = 1.7 to 1.5 by  0.1
loop for X = 1.7 to 1.5 by -0.1
```

The solutions would be:

1.5,1.75,2.0,2.25,2.5,2.75,3.0,3.25	3.5 after
no passes	1.7 after
1.7,1.6,1.5	1.4 after

For reasons discussed later in this section, we sometimes avoid using a REAL index when we code these algorithms in FORTRAN. However, for the algorithm itself we never hesitate to use a REAL index when appropriate.

Iteration Count

For any given **loop for** construction it is possible to calculate, in advance, the number of times the body of the loop will be executed (barring any nonstandard exits from the loop). For example, in the construction

```
loop for I = 2 to 7 by 2
```

we see that I will take on the values 2, 4, 6. Thus the body of the loop will be executed three times. Similarly in

```
loop for X = 1.6 to 2.3 by .3
```

X will take on the values 1.6, 1.9, 2.2. Again we have the body being executed three times.

Notice in the first case we have $(7 - 2 + 2)/2 = 3.5$ and in the second $(2.3 - 1.6 + .3)/.3 = 3\ 1/3$. In each case the number of iterations will be the integer part of the expression

```
(M2 - M1 + M3)/M3
```

where M1, M2, and M3 are the parameters of the construction

loop for I = M1 **to** M2 **by** M3

Since we cannot execute a loop a negative number of times, we modify our expression for the iteration count to be

```
IC = MAX(0,INT((M2-M1+M3)/M3))
```

Table 7.2 shows a few sample values of the parameters M1, M2, and M3, the iteration count, the values of the index, and the value upon normal exit.

Action of the DO

The action of the DO statement consists of several steps. The first step is to evaluate the three parameter expressions to obtain values M1, M2, and M3 for the initial, final, and increment values, respectively. M1 is then assigned as the initial value of the DO index. The next step is to compute the iteration count using this formula developed in the previous subsection:

```
IC ← MAX(INT((M2-M1+M3)/M3),0)
```

NOTE. If M3 is positive, the iteration count will be zero if M2<M1; and if M3 is negative, then the iteration count will be zero if M2>M1. For example, consider these DO statements:

```
DO 10 I = 5,3,2
DO 20 X = 7.2,8.3,-.1
```

In the first, we are to go from 5, going up by 2, until I is greater than 3. Since I starts out greater than 3, the iteration count is 0.

TABLE 7.2

M1	M2	M3	IC	Index Values	Final Value
1.5	1.5	.5	1	1.5	2.0
4.0	2.0	−.5	5	4.0,3.5,3.0,2.5,2.0	1.5
4.0	2.0	.5	0		4.0
1.5	1.5	−.5	1	1.5	1.0
1.5	1.75	.5	1	1.5	2.0

Similarly, to go "down" from 7.2 by −.1 until we are below 8.3, we need an iteration count of 0.

Observe that this is the same meaning given to the **loop for** structure in our algorithms, under similar circumstances.

If the IC is not zero, the statements in the range of the DO are next executed. If the last statement does not cause a transfer of control (and it will not if you use a CONTINUE), then the value of the index variable is incremented by the M3 value, and the IC count is decreased by 1. At this point, if the value of the iteration count is not zero, the statements in the range are reexecuted.

When the iteration count reaches zero, or if a transfer occurs to a point outside the range, or if a RETURN is executed, the DO index retains the value which was last assigned to it.

The entire sequence may be summarized in algorithmic form as shown in Figure 7.1. We emphasize that all these actions occur automatically. We do not have specifically to program them.

There are several implications of this sequence of operations. First note that the index variable is always defined upon an exit from the loop. If the exit is caused by a transfer from the range to a statement outside the range or by a RETURN, the index value is the same as the value during the last partial execution of the range. If the loop terminates normally (the iteration count reaches zero), the index variable value is the same as it would have been on the next execution of the range. Finally, if any of the variables used in the parameter expressions are changed within the loop, the changed values will have no effect on the number of times the loop is executed or on the values the index variable assumes.

```
M1 ← value of expression 1 (starting value)
M2 ← value of expression 2 (ending value)
M3 ← value of expression 3 (step value)
index ← M1
IC ← MAX(INT((M2−M1+M3)/M3),0)
loop
   if IC = 0 then exit ('standard' exit) endif
       .
       . (range of DO)
       .
   INDEX ← INDEX + M3
   IC ← IC − 1
endloop
```

Figure 7.1

Examples

For our first example, we write an algorithm segment to form the sum

$$\frac{1}{1^2} + \frac{1}{2^2} + \frac{1}{3^2} + \cdots + \frac{1}{N^2}$$

where N is given.

In a problem like this, there are definite advantages to adding the terms up from right to left (that is, from smallest to largest). In this way, we are never adding a very small term to a very large accumulator value.

> **COMMENT.** To see why this is desirable, consider the following. If we add .0000002 to 1.5 on a machine which has only six significant digits, we "should" get 1.5000002. However, this has eight significant digits, and the result we would get might be 1.50000, with the .0000002 lost. By adding from right to left our terms get larger as our accumulator grows, and we reduce the likelihood of this type of error.

A rough algorithm might be

```
SUM ← 0
loop for I = N to 1 by -1
   SUM ← SUM + term #I
endloop
```

To complete the problem, we must determine the proper formula for term I. This is a matter of recognizing a pattern. In this type of problem you may find it helpful to construct a table similar to the following.

I	Term #I
1	1/(1**2)
2	1/(2**2)
3	1/(3**2)
.	.
.	.
.	.
N	1/(*N***2)

As we study the table, we realize that the general formula for term I is 1/(I**2). To complete the algorithm we merely replace the phrase "term I" by this expression. The corresponding FORTRAN segment is easy to code:

```
      REAL SUM
      INTEGER I,N

      SUM = 0
      DO 50 I = N,1,-1
         SUM = SUM + 1.0/REAL(I**2)
50       CONTINUE
```

When money is borrowed from a bank on an installment loan, the total amount of interest paid depends on both the interest rate and the number of years taken to repay the loan. This example will investigate this dependence for various values of the interest rate and for various numbers of years to repay. We will assume monthly payments are made.

If money (amount B) is borrowed for Y years at an annual interest rate of R, the formula for the monthly payment P is

$$P = B\left[\frac{\frac{R}{12}}{1-\left(1+\frac{R}{12}\right)^{-12Y}}\right]$$

($R/12$ is the monthly interest rate, and $12Y$ represents the total number of payments). We would like to generate output as indicated here:

```
                 PAYMENTS ON LOAN OF XXXXX.XX

              MONTHLY        TOTAL        INTEREST
RATE          PAYMENT        PAID           PAID

                   PAID BACK IN 1 YEAR

0.09          XXXX.XX      XXXXX.XX     XXXXX.XX
0.10          XXXX.XX      XXXXX.XX     XXXXX.XX
 .               .             .             .
 .               .             .             .
 .               .             .             .
0.24          XXXX.XX      XXXXX.XX     XXXXX.XX

*****************************************

                   PAID BACK IN 2 YEARS

0.09          XXXX.XX      XXXXX.XX     XXXXX.XX
0.10          XXXX.XX      XXXXX.XX     XXXXX.XX
 .               .             .             .
 .               .             .             .
 .               .             .             .
0.24          XXXX.XX      XXXXX.XX     XXXXX.XX
```

This general pattern should be reproduced for the number of years varying from one to 25.

As a tentative variable list, we have the following.

	Name	Type	Use	Comment
Input:	BORROW	REAL	Amount borrowed	
Output:	PAYMNT	REAL	Monthly payment	
	TOTAL	REAL	Total amount paid	
	INTRST	REAL	Amount of interest paid	
Other:	RATE	REAL	Annual interest rate	
	YEARS	INTEGER	Number of years to pay back	

We can now write a rough algorithm.

```
read BORROW
loop for YEARS = 1 to 25
   generate a table for this value of YEARS
     (interest rate ranging from 0.09 to 0.24)
endloop
stop
```

To refine the algorithm, we determine that printing the table will itself involve a loop. Since the interest rate varies from 0.09 to 0.24, this loop may be a count-control loop of this form:

```
loop for RATE = 0.09 to 0.24 by 0.01
```

Before the loop, we must print the heading, including the variable YEARS; in the loop we calculate and print PAYMNT, TOTAL, and INTRST; after the loop we will print the row of asterisks which separates the tables for the different values of YEARS.

> **NOTE.** We will use a DETAIL routine to print the heading containing the YEARS variable; it will determine when new overall headings on a new page are needed. Since these overall headings print the variable BORROW, it will need parameters YEARS and BORROW.

Based on this discussion, we refine the algorithm as shown in Figure 7.2. The corresponding program is in Figure 7.3

The FORTRAN DO permits the use of real indices. There are times, however, when it may be better to use integer indices with proper scaling of values. The reason for this is that most real numbers are not represented quite precisely in the computer. For many applications the slight inaccuracy is acceptable, but there are times when it is not.

```
read BORROW
loop for YEARS = 1 to 25
   call DETAIL(YEARS,BORROW)
   loop for RATE = 0.09 to 0.24 by 0.01
      PAYMNT ← formula given earlier
      TOTAL ← PAYMNT * 12 * YEARS
      INTRST ← TOTAL - BORROW
      print RATE,PAYMNT,TOTAL,INTRST
   endloop
   print row of asterisks
endloop
stop
```

Figure 7.2

```
      REAL BORROW,RATE,PAYMNT,TOTAL,INTRST
      INTEGER YEARS
        .
        .
      READ(*,1000) BORROW
      DO 60 YEARS = 1,25
         CALL DETAIL(YEARS,BORROW)
         DO 50 RATE = 0.09,0.24,0.01
            PAYMNT = BORROW*(RATE/12.0)/(1 - (1+RATE/12.0)**(-12*YEARS)))
            TOTAL = PAYMNT * 12 * YEARS
            INTRST = TOTAL - BORROW
            WRITE(*,2000) RATE,PAYMNT,TOTAL,INTRST
50          CONTINUE
         WRITE(*,3000)
60    CONTINUE
         .
         .
```

Figure 7.3

Consider, for example, the program of Figure 7.3, which contains the statement

```
DO 50 RATE = 0.09,0.24,0.01
```

The step size 0.01 will not have a precise representation in the computer. Hence, each time it is added to the index an additional small discrepancy is introduced.

However, since we go through this loop only 16 times, the problem is relatively minor.

On the other hand, consider this program segment. (F is the name of some REAL function.)

```
      DO 100 X = 1.0,10.0,0.01
         Y = F(X)
         CALL DETAIL(X,Y)
100      CONTINUE
```

Here the index will be incremented by 0.01 nine hundred times! Each time, a small error is made. By the time we reach the larger X values, the accumulated error can be significant. On the other hand, the statements

```
      DO 10 I = 100,1000,1
         X = REAL(I)/100.0
         Y = F(X)
         CALL DETAIL(X,Y)
10       CONTINUE
```

provide the same theoretical X values. With this segment, only one small error is made for each X value, with no accumulation of errors from the preceding values. As a result, the computations will be more accurate.

Notice that, to determine the values for the I loop, we have simply "cleared the X loop in the algorithm step of fractions." We have multiplied each parameter in

loop for X = 1.0 **to** 10.0 **by** 0.01

by 100 to obtain

```
DO 10 I = 100,1000,1
```

Thus I takes on values 100 times as large as those desired for X, and hence we obtain X by dividing I by 100.0. Similar techniques may be used for other situations.

Here are two more algorithm **loop** steps and corresponding code:

loop for X = 1.4 **to** 352.2 **by** .4	DO 10 I = 14,3522,4 X = REAL(I)/10.0
loop for X = 152.15 **to** 0 **by** −.1	DO 10 I = 15215,0,−10 X = REAL(I)/100.0

Efficiency

The question of what makes one program run faster than another which does the same task is a very complex one. However, the program of Figure 7.2 can be modified to illustrate two techniques which are easy to use and which can speed up a program.

Consider the calculation of the variable PAYMNT, whose formula is

```
PAYMNT = BORROW*((RATE/12.0)/(1 - (1+RATE/12.0)**(-12*YEARS)))
```

It is wasteful to have the computer calculate RATE/12.0 twice. We might add a REAL variable MNRATE ("monthly rate") to our declarations, and write

```
MNRATE = RATE/12.0
PAYMNT = BORROW*(MNRATE/(1 - (1+MNRATE)**(-12*YEARS)))
```

Similarly, the expression 12* YEARS, which occurs in both this formula and the one for TOTAL, can be calculated and stored in an INTEGER variable MONTHS, with these formulas resulting:

```
PAYMNT = BORROW*(MNRATE/(1 - (1+MNRATE)**(-MONTHS)))
TOTAL  = PAYMNT*MONTHS
```

In this case, moreover, we may go one step further. Since the value of YEARS does not vary within the inner loop, the calculation of MONTHS may be placed before this inner loop. To see what savings result from this, observe that statements within the inner loop are executed $25 \times 16 = 400$ times, compared with only 25 times for those inside only the outer loop. This simplification would have been advisable even if MONTHS were used for only one calculation in the inner loop.

COMMENTS.

1. It might even be worthwhile to perform the negation of MONTHS prior to the loop, writing MINMON = −MONTHS. Then we would use MINMON in the PAYMNT formula.
2. As indicated above, simplifications made within nested loops are the most valuable ones, since the steps inside the nested loops are executed more frequently than the rest of the program.
3. Some compilers, called "optimizing" compilers, are designed to automatically detect and carry out this type of improvement.

REVIEW

Pseudocode

loop for index = starting value **to** ending value **by** step size

Form of DO

DO label, variable = expression 1, expression 2, expression 3.

variable—index
expression 1—starting value
" 2—ending value
" 3—ending value
Comma after label and ",expression3" part are optional.

Notes

1. Variable and expressions may be INTEGER or REAL

2. Value of expressions may be positive or negative.
3. "Iteration count" may be zero.
4. Index value is defined after exit from loop:
   standard exit: value it would have on next iteration;
   other exits: value at point exit occurs.
5. Loops and decisions may be nested, may not overlap.
6. INTEGER index generally preferable to REAL, due to possible accumulated errors with REAL index.

Action of DO. See Figure 7.1.

EXERCISES

1. For each of the following, list the values assumed by the index on each pass of the loop, and calculate the iteration count, IC, using the formula given in this section. Also tell what value the index has after the loop terminates.
   (a) **loop for** 1 = −5 **to** 3
   (b) **loop for** 1 = 1 **to** 7 **by** 3
   (c) **loop for** 1 = 1 **to** 8 **by** 3
   (d) **loop for** 1 = 7 **to** 2 **by** 2
   (e) **loop for** 1 = 7 **to** 2 **by** −2
   (f) **loop for** 1 = 17 **to** −4 **by** −3
   (g) **loop for** X = 17.25 **to** 19.5 **by** 0.5
   (h) **loop for** X = 1.5 **to** −3.5 **by** −1.0

2. For each of the following, indicate a segment of code which uses an integer loop index to accomplish the desired action.
   (a) Exercise 1(g)
   (b) Exercise 1(h)
   (c) **loop for** X = 3.619 **to** 7.234 **by** 0.001
   (d) **loop for** X = 3.724 **to** 6.864 **by** 0.01
   (e) **loop for** X = 19 **to** 1 **by** −0.25

3. Write algorithms for the following.
   (a) Find the sum of the first 87 integers.
   (b) Find the sum 2 + 4 + 6 + ··· + 2444.
   (c) Find the sum of the first 200 even integers.
   (d) Find the sum of the first 200 odd integers.
   (e) Add up an array of size 900, in reverse order.

4. Write an algorithm to print a table of feet and inches for:
   (a) feet from 1 to 30;
   (b) feet from 30 back to 1;
   (c) feet from 1 to N;
   (d) feet from N back to 1; and
   (e) feet from 1 to 20 in steps of 1/2 foot.

5. Write an algorithm to determine how many years it takes for the balance in a savings account to double at 5.25% interest compounded annually.

6. Mathematicians have shown that the sum

$$1 - 1/3 + 1/5 - 1/7 + 1/9 - 1/11 + \cdots$$

gets close to $\pi/4$ as more and more terms are added.

(a) Write an algorithm to calculate this sum out to the term 1/401; out to the term 1/4001.

(b) Repeat part (a), but add up the terms from right to left as indicated in this section.

(c) Give a FORTRAN segment for part (b).

7. (a) For an angle X in radian measure, we may calculate sin X by the sum

$$X - X^3/3! + X^5/5! - X^7/7! + \cdots$$

Write an algorithm which, given X and an odd number N, calculates the sum out to the term involving X^N.

(b) Notice that, in (a), we may reduce the amount of computation by calculating each successive term from the previous term. For example, $X^9/9! = (-X^7/7!) * (-X^2/(9*8))$, and a similar pattern exists for each term.

Modify your algorithm to incorporate this improvement.

(c) To use the idea of part (b), we want to generate the terms from left to right. However, as discussed in this section, it may be advantageous to add them up from right to left.

Modify the algorithm of (c) to place the generated terms into an array called TERMS, then come back to add them up in reverse order.

8. (a) Write an algorithm to calculate and print $n!$ for n from 1 to 15.
($n!$ is $n*(n-1)*(n-2)*...*2*1$)

Hint: Finding the product of the first n integers is very similar to finding their sum.

(b) Repeat (a), but this time store the answers in an array called FACT of size 15. (Place 1! in FACT(1), 2! in FACT(2), and so on.)

(c) Most likely your answer to (b) contains nested loops. Can you suggest an improvement which will be more time-efficient?

Hint: $n! = n(n-1)!$

9. Modify the algorithm of Figure 7.2 to produce one table for each interest rate with the years varying.

10. Write an algorithm to verify the correctness of the formula

$$1 + 2 + \ldots + N = N(N + 1)/2$$

For each value of N from 1 to 75.

11. For a function $y = f(x)$ which is positive between $x = a$ and $x = b$, we may approximate the area under the curve from a to b by the formula

$$A = \frac{h}{3}\left[f(a) + 4f(a + h) + 2f(a + 2h) + 4f(a + 3h) + \ldots + 4f(a + (n - 1)h) + f(a + nh) \right]$$

where n is an even integer, and h is $(b-a)/n$.

Assuming that F is a given FORTRAN function, write an algorithm and program segment to calculate this sum.

12. If a projectile is fired with a velocity V at an angle A, the distance the projectile will travel is given as

```
RANGE = (V² /32) * (SIN(2A))
```

For each velocity 100, 200, 300,..., 1400, print a table of ranges for angles from 0 radians (=0 degrees) to 1.5 radians (almost 90 degrees) in steps of 0.1 radians.

13. **(a)** Write an algorithm and program which prints a list of mortgage payments, given:

AMT—initial mortgage amount
RATE—annual interest rate
PAYMNT—amount of monthly payment
YEARS—number of years to repay

The table should contain five columns: payment number, amount of payment, amount of payment going for interest, amount of payment going for principal, and remaining balance on mortgage.

Begin a new page of output for each year; the headings on each new page should list the initial amount, rate, monthly payment, number of years, and balance remaining.

(b) Revise (a) to print only one summary line per year, instead of the complete table. This line should contain year number, balance at the start of year, total interest paid during the year, total paid on principal during the year, and balance at the end of the year.

8

MORE ON ARRAYS

8.1 INPUT AND OUTPUT OF ARRAYS

In Chapter 6 we introduced simple array I/O concepts. The techniques covered there were quite simple, but they were sufficient for the applications we had in mind. The two techniques are typified by these two FORTRAN segments.

```
      INTEGER ITEMNO(100),I,N
      REAL PRICE(100)
          .
          .
      READ (10,1000) N
      DO 10 I = 1,N
         READ (10,2000) ITEMNO(I),PRICE(I)
10       CONTINUE
```

```
      CHARACTER*12 NAME
      INTEGER GRADES(10)
          .
          .
10    CONTINUE
         READ (10,1000) NAME,GRADES
```

In the first example, we use a DO loop to fill parallel arrays of item numbers and prices, where each record in the file contains a single item number and price. In the second example, each record contains a name and ten grades. We use an array to hold the ten grades, and we read the entire GRADES array along with the name.

In this section, we explore the subject of input and output of arrays in greater depth. With the techniques covered here, we should be able to write READ statements to match any given record structure and WRITE statements to supply any desired output. We will explore three topics: using a simple DO loop, total array I/O, and the implied DO loop. Only the last of these will be totally new to us.

Using a Simple DO Loop

The first of the two FORTRAN segments given above is an example of this method. As another example, suppose we have an INTEGER array A of size 1000, each containing a number between 2 and 12. We wish to print the entire array.

A simple solution would be

```
          INTEGER A(1000)
             .
             .
          DO 50 I = 1,1000
                WRITE(*,1000) A(I)
       50       CONTINUE
                   .
                   .
     1000 FORMAT(' ',I4)
```

How many lines of output are printed by this program segment? The answer is 1000. With the WRITE statement inside the body of the loop, we will get a new line of output each time through the loop. Each line will contain precisely one of the 1000 different numbers to be printed.

These examples illustrate the major limitation of using a simple DO loop for array I/O. When we are reading data, each pass through the loop will reexecute the READ or WRITE statement. Thus, in general, each input record must have one group of information (perhaps the information for one person). Similarly, when we are writing, each line of output will contain one group of information.

In the remainder of this section we will explore ways to overcome this "one number per line" limitation.

Total Array I/O

As we have discussed in earlier chapters, most references to an array in FORTRAN must include a subscript. However, there are a few places where we wish to refer to the entire array rather than merely a single element in the array. For example, we have seen that to pass an array to a subprogram we list the array name (with no subscript) as the parameter.

Another place where it is possible to use the array name with no subscript is in a READ or WRITE statement. This use of the array name will mean READ (or WRITE) the *entire* array. This type of I/O is therefore referred to as **total array I/O**.

The second FORTRAN segment in the introductory remarks was an example of this method. We may also use total array output to print the entire integer array A of the preceding subsection, as shown here:

```
INTEGER A (1000)
      .
      .
      .
WRITE(*,1000) A
```

We simply list the array name "A" as the variable to be printed.

In FORTRAN input and output, the "what" is separated from the "how." In the READ or WRITE statement we tell what is to be read or printed by giving a list of variables. The FORMAT statement tells how the information appears on the input lines or is to appear on the output lines. Writing FORMAT statements for total array I/O is not hard if we keep in mind the following principle:

> **RULE.** In general, the FORMAT for a total array READ statement describes the layout of *one* typical input record. The FORMAT for a total array WRITE describes the layout of *one* typical line of output.

We have written the appropriate WRITE statement to print the 1000 numbers of the INTEGER array A. We will now give a number of possible FORMAT statements, depending on how we would like the output to appear.

First, we could print one number per line by using

```
1000 FORMAT(' ',I4)
```

However, if we do this we will have 1000 lines of output. To reduce this to 100 lines each containing ten numbers we could use the format

```
1000 FORMAT(' ',10I4)
```

> **NOTE.** The format 10I4 used here is simply shorthand for I4,I4,I4,I4,I4,I4, I4,I4,I4,I4.

Another possibility is

```
1000 FORMAT(' ',20I4)
```

which would cause 20 numbers to be printed per line for a total of 50 lines.

> **COMMENT.** The WRITE and FORMAT work together like this. The WRITE statement contains a list of values to be printed using the given FORMAT. The computer will keep printing values until it has printed all the variables in the list. (Leaving a portion of the FORMAT statement unused causes no problems.)
>
> Suppose the computer runs out of FORMAT codes before all the values are printed. In this case it will "reuse the FORMAT." It will go to a new line

of output and continue printing values using the FORMAT over again from left to right. This process is repeated as long as values remain to be printed.

Similarly, when a READ statement runs out of FORMAT codes it will go to a new input record and continue reading variables, reusing the FORMAT from left to right.

This is the reason for the RULE given earlier that the FORMAT should describe one input record or one output line.

As a final example of a FORMAT we could use to print the array A, consider the following:

```
1000 FORMAT(' ',30I4)
```

This will print 30 numbers per line for 33 lines, for a total of 990 numbers. At this point, there will be ten numbers left to print. The computer will use the first ten of the 30 individual I4 formats to print these numbers. (Recall that 30I4 is shorthand for writing I4 down 30 times.) The last line will have only ten numbers; all the others will have 30 per line.

Let us consider another example where we give an appropriate declaration, READ, and FORMAT to read a REAL array X of size 90. The numbers are given three per record as illustrated here:

```
xxx.xxxbbxxx.xxxbbxxx.xxx
```

The solution is fairly simple. The READ statement lists the variable we want to read, and the format describes one record.

```
     REAL X(90)
         .
         .
         .
     READ(*,1000) X
         .
         .
         .
1000 FORMAT(F7.3,2X,F7.3,2X,F7.3)
```

If there were four numbers per card instead of three, only the FORMAT would change.

Just as there are limitations to using a simple DO loop for array I/O, so there are limitations to total array I/O. The most obvious is implied by the name itself: It cannot be used to read or print a portion of the array. Since we frequently have arrays which are purposefully made large with the idea of using some variable portion of the array, this limitation can be a problem.

In addition, total array I/O does not work well with parallel arrays, as illustrated by the following example.

Consider parallel arrays ID,AGE, and SALARY each of size 50. We want to read the arrays assuming that each data record has information for two people:

ID age salary ID age salary

The fact that each record has information for more than one person makes using a simple DO loop clumsy. We might be inclined to write

```
READ(*,1000) ID,AGE,SALARY
```

using total array input. Unfortunately, this tells the computer to read the entire ID array,then the AGE array, then the SALARY array. For this to work, the data would have to have the 50 ID numbers prior to the 50 ages, and these prior to the 50 salaries. Since the data is not set up in this way, total array input will not work.

What we need here is the logic of the DO loop:

```
      DO 10 I = 1,50
         READ(*,1000) ID(I),AGE(I),SALARY(I)
10       CONTINUE
```

without the limitation of one person per record.

The Implied DO

FORTRAN supplies a feature, known as the **implied DO loop**, that fulfills our needs precisely. When we have a READ within a loop as above, then for each new value of I the READ statement is executed again. On the other hand, with the implied DO, the desired looping is buried within the READ statement. With the implied DO loop we can easily work with parallel arrays or with portions of arrays, and we are not restricted to "one number per record."

For the previous example, the simple DO loop solution would be

```
      DO 10 I = 1,50
         READ(*,1000) ID(I),AGE(I),SALARY(I)
10       CONTINUE
```

but this would require one person per record (no matter what the FORMAT looks like).

The implied DO solution for this example would be

```
READ(*,1000) (ID(I),AGE(I),SALARY(I),I=1,50)
```

Notice that the list of variables to be read looks the same in the implied DO loop form as in the regular DO loop above. The loop control "I=1,50" has been buried within the READ statement, immediately following the list of variables, and the whole thing has been placed in parentheses.

The logic of the implied DO is the same as the usual DO loop construction. The two solutions given above (the regular DO loop and the implied DO loop) read exactly the same sequence of variables: ID(1), AGE(1), SALARY(1),ID(2), AGE(2), SALARY(2),..., ID(49), AGE(49), SALARY(49), ID(50), AGE(50),

SALARY(50). However, with the implied DO loop, the READ statement is executed only once. In this respect it is similar to total array input.

The implied DO in a READ or WRITE statement interacts with the corresponding FORMAT statement in the same manner as for total array I/O; when the computer runs out of format it will go to a new record and continue, reusing the format from left to right. Thus, we will write our FORMAT statement to describe one typical input or output record.

The precise form of an implied DO loop is as follows:

```
(list, index=starting value,ending value)
```

The index should be an INTEGER variable. The starting and ending values may be any INTEGER expressions. The entire implied DO structure consists of a list of items to be read or written, followed by the count control of a DO loop, all placed within parentheses. The entire construction may be placed in a READ or WRITE statement in the same place a regular variable might appear.

The following examples will illustrate the possible uses of the implied DO loop construction. In each example, the FORMAT statement describes one typical record.

It can be used to read or write an entire array.

```
      INTEGER ARR(700)
       .
      READ(*,1000) (ARR(I),I=1,700)
       .
 1000 FORMAT(10I5)
```

This is equivalent to using total array input or output.

It can be used to read or print a portion of an array.

```
      REAL ARR(75)
      INTEGER I,N
       .
       .
      WRITE(*,1000) (ARR(I),I=4,15)
       .
       .
      WRITE(*,1000) (ARR(I),I=1,N)
       .
       .
 1000 FORMAT(' ',7F15.3)
```

It can be used to print or read parallel arrays.

```
      INTEGER AGES(160),I,N
      CHARACTER*20 NAMES(160)
       .
      READ(*,1000) N
      READ(*,2000) (NAMES(I),AGES(I),I=1,N)
       .
 1000 FORMAT(I2)
 2000 FORMAT(A20,I2,3X,A20,I2,3X,A20,I2)
```

We can print the subscript along with the array element.

```
      INTEGER VAL(35)
            .
      WRITE(*,2000) (I,VAL(I),I=1,35)
            .
 2000 FORMAT(' ',4X,I2,8X,I8)
```

Notice that, since we only want one I and VAL(I) per line, we could have used a regular DO loop in this example:

```
      DO 20 I=1,35
         WRITE(*,2000) I,VAL(I)
20       CONTINUE
```

Once we are accustomed to implied DO loops, however, we will generally be inclined to use them even in situations where the normal DO loop would also work.

We can use an implied DO along with other variables, if we like.

```
      INTEGER I
      CHARACTER *11 STATE
      REAL RAIN(12)
            .
      READ(*,1000) (STATE, RAIN(I),I=1,12)
            .
 1000 FORMAT(A11,3X,12F5.2)
```

In this example each record contains a state's name and the twelve monthly rainfall figures for that state.

COMMENT. In addition to its use in array I/O, the implied DO may be used in the DATA statement (Section 11.4).

Summary

In addition to the techniques discussed in Sections 6.2 and 6.3 for reading and printing individual elements of an array, there are three commonly used methods of array I/O in FORTRAN.

The first method, placing a READ or WRITE within a DO loop, is easy to use. However, it requires that there be one number or group of related information per input or output record.

Total array I/O is handy to use when we want to read or print the entire array. To use it we place the array name (without subscripts) in the READ or WRITE statement. The FORMAT generally describes the layout of one typical record. Total array I/O cannot be used when working with portions of arrays or with parallel arrays whose values are interspersed with each other.

The most generally applicable method is the implied DO loop. In this method the loop control is placed within the READ or WRITE statement right after the list of items to be read of printed. Once again the FORMAT generally describes one record. This method works very well with either all or part of an array and with parallel arrays. In addition, it is easy to print the subscripts along with the values being printed.

Pitfalls

In performing input and output with arrays, the most common pitfall has to do with the use of subscripts. Because some forms of I/O use subscripts and some do not, the compiler will not be able to warn us if we use subscripts which should be omitted or omit subscripts which are needed.

There are three ways to refer to an array:

array name
array name(subscript)
array name(size)

For example, for an array A of size 415 we might write A, A(1), A(25), A(I), or A(415). The reference "A(415)" refers to the last element in the array (that is, 415 is a subscript), except in the declaration of the array's dimension.

The most common errors in array I/O are these:

1. Using array name(size). Because A is size 415, it is easy to think of A(415) as the name of the array. It is not. If we write

   ```
   WRITE(*,1000) A(415)
   ```

   only one value will be written; the 415 will be taken as a subscript. Likewise, if we write

   ```
   WRITE(*,1000) (A(415),I=1,415)
   ```

   the value of A(415) will be printed 415 times.
2. Using the array name with no subscript where a subscript is needed. If we write

   ```
   WRITE(*,1000) (A,I=1,100)
   ```

   the computer wil print all 415 items in A, and it will do so 100 times. We probably meant to write

   ```
   WRITE(*,1000) (A(I),I=1,100)
   ```

   (A similar error is writing (A(1),I=1,100).)
3. Using the array name with a subscript where total array I/O was intended. We sometimes get so used to seeing a subscript I used with an array that we include it without thinking. It is easy to write

   ```
   WRITE(*,1000) A(I)
   ```

   when we meant to write

   ```
   WRITE(*,1000) A
   ```

To avoid these pitfalls, we should remember that in doing I/O we will have either the array name or the array name with a subscript. When we write the array name down, we should ask, "Is a subscript required, or am I doing total array I/O?" If a subscript is required, we should determine which subscript (constant or variable) is appropriate. Generally speaking, in an implied DO loop or an explicit DO loop, the subscript is likely to be the same as the loop index.

REVIEW

Forms of Array I/O

1. READ or WRITE within DO loop—"one number per record"
2. Total array I/O—whole array at once
3. Implied DO

   Total array I/O

```
INTEGER A(1000)
WRITE(6,2000) A
```

   Format describes one record

   Implied DO

   Syntax: (List to be read/written, index=start, end)
   Logic: Same as explicit DO loop; each pass writes the items in the list
   Use: Generally, the items in the list refer to the loop index (for example, as a subscript)
   Implied DO is placed as one of the list of things in the READ or WRITE
   Format describes one record

   Examples

```
READ(*,1000) (ARR(I),I=1,700)
WRITE(*,2000) (ARR(I),I=100,251)
WRITE(*,3000) (ARR(I),I=1,N)
READ(*,4000) (NAMES(I),AGES(I),I=1,N)
WRITE(*,5000) (I,VAL(I),I=1,35)
READ(*,6000) STATE,(RAIN(I),I=1,12)
```

Pitfalls

1. Using array size, e.g., A(415 where A is size 415
2. Leaving off subscript in implied DO
   Using constant subscript in implied DO
3. Using subscript when total array I/O is intended

EXERCISES

1. An input record has ten test grades on it, each in I4 format. Write a segment of code to find and print the average of these ten scores (use F6.1 format for the average).

2. Give appropriate declarations, READ, and FORMAT to read the following.
   (a) Each record has seven integers, each five columns wide. There are 500 numbers in all.
   (b) Each record has 11 real numbers, each six columns with three places after the decimal. There are 553 numbers in all.
3. Give declarations, WRITE, and FORMAT to print a real array A of size 800:
   (a) one number per line;
   (b) ten numbers per line; and
   (c) thirteen numbers per line;
4. Each record has an ID, an age, and an hourly wage. All 60 records are to be read to fill the parallel arrays IDNO, AGE, and WAGE.
5. The parallel arrays EMPNO(100) and SALARY(100) contain the employee numbers and salaries of our employees. At present only the first N spaces are filled (we have N employees). Print the list of employee numbers and their salaries.
6. Give declarations, READ, and FORMAT to fill the parallel arrays ID, AGE, SEX, and SALARY each of size 100, where:
   (a) There are 100 records, each with one person's information.
   (b) There are 50 records, each with two persons' information.
   (c) Each record has three persons' information.
   (d) The first record contains NOEMP, the number of employees represented in the rest of the file. Each additional record has information on three people. (*Note*: The last record may have only one or two people.) Fill the first NOEMP locations of the parallel arrays.
7. **(a)** A character array of size 80 contains one character for each element. Print the entire array on one line, one column per character.
   (b) This time print only the first 35 characters, one column per character.
   (c) This time print only up to (and not including) the first blank in the array. Assume there is at least one blank and at least one nonblank character before that blank.
8. Using the RND random number generator, described in Chapter 3, write a program to simulate rolling the dice 1200 times. Use an array CTRS of counters to count how many times each number occurs, and print the answers in this form.

```
THE NUMBER 2 OCCURRED xxxx TIMES.
THE NUMBER 3 OCCURRED xxxx TIMES.
```

   and so on.
9. **(a)** In Exercise 6(d) you wrote code to read NOEMP (the number of employees), and to fill the first NOEMP spaces in the parallel arrays ID, AGE, SEX, and SALARY. Place this code in a subroutine INIT which reads from a file (unit 10).
   (b) Write a subroutine FINAL which writes out the same information in exactly the same form it was read in, to a file on unit 11.

8.2 TWO-DIMENSIONAL ARRAYS

In one of the examples of the previous section we had input records each containing a state name and 12 monthly rainfall figures for that state. To read these records we used a variable STATE and an array RAIN of size 12. As long as the process we are performing allows us to process data for each state completely prior to reading the data for the next, these variables will work nicely.

Suppose, however, that our program requires the data for all 50 states to be stored in the computer simultaneously. We would immediately change the variable STATE to an array of size 50 (and perhaps change the name to STATES, as well). For the rainfall, we are already using an array to store the information for a single state. To store the information for 50 states we need something which will somehow represent 12 different rainfall figures for each of 50 different states. In FORTRAN (and many other languages) the **two-dimensional array** provides this facility.

The Two-Dimensional Array

To represent the rainfall data on paper, we might create a table containing 50 rows (one for each state) and 12 columns (one for each month). The entry in the fifth row and seventh column would be the rainfall in state 5 during the seventh month (July). This is the basic idea behind the two-dimensional array. To save space, we will discuss these arrays with a smaller example:

```
6.2  -3.5  0.0  4.5
0.0  16.5  1.0  0.0
3.1  -1.4  7.2  6.0
```

This array has three rows and four columns. We will say it is a 3 × 4 array (read as "3 by 4").

> **COMMENT.** You may have worked with arrays like this in some of your math courses. If so, you probably referred to them as **matrices** (singular is **matrix**). "Matrix" and "two-dimensional array" are synonymous.
>
> Matrices have important mathematical applications in addition to the data storage uses indicated by our example above.

To refer to the numbers in arrays we use subscripts. In the arrays we used in Chapter 6 (**one-dimensional arrays**) a single subscript was used. However, to locate a position in a two-dimensional array we need to know both the row and the column. Any reference to an element of a two-dimensional array will therefore contain two subscripts, separated by commas. The first subscript tells the row number, the second the column number.

For example, consider the 3 × 4 real array named A; for convenience we have labeled the rows and columns:

	Col. 1	Col. 2	Col. 3	Col. 4
Row 1:	6.2	-3.5	0.0	4.5
Row 2	0.0	16.5	1.0	0.0
Row 3:	3.1	-1.4	7.2	6.0

(These values have been read in or assigned earlier in the program.)

If we write A(2,3) we are referring to row 2 and column 3; at present A(2,3) has the value 1.0. Likewise A(3,2) has the value -1.4, A(3,4) has the value 6.0, and A(4,3) does not exist (there is no row 4).

We can also refer to entire rows and columns. For example, the sum of row 2 is 17.5, and the largest number in column 4 is 6.0

It is possible to use INTEGER variables as subscripts. Just as for one-dimensional arrays, the value of the variables will determine which location is being referred to. In fact, any INTEGER expression can be used as an array subscript. If I, J, STATNO, and MONTH are INTEGER variables, the following are valid array references.

```
A(I,J)
A(I,5)
B(16,J)
B(I+J,I-J)
RAIN(STATNO,MONTH)
```

Of course, the row number and column number indicated by the subscript must exist in the array in order for the array reference to make sense.

> **NOTE.** The variable I is commonly used as a row subscript, and the variable J as a column subscript. This is consistent with the mathematical notation generally used with matrices. However, other variables or expressions may be used. In the 50 × 12 array RAIN, for example, the rows represent state numbers, and the columns month number. Thus STATNO and MONTH would be more meaningful subscripts than I and J.

Processing

Processing two-dimensional arrays is similar in many ways to working with one-dimensional arrays. This processing can include such things as initializing, finding the largest and smallest, finding an average, and so on. For the examples in this subsection, we assume that we have a 17 × 22 INTEGER array named ARR, and that this array already has values in it.

First, we can process a single row of the array. For example, we might process row 9 of our 17 × 22 matrix ARR:

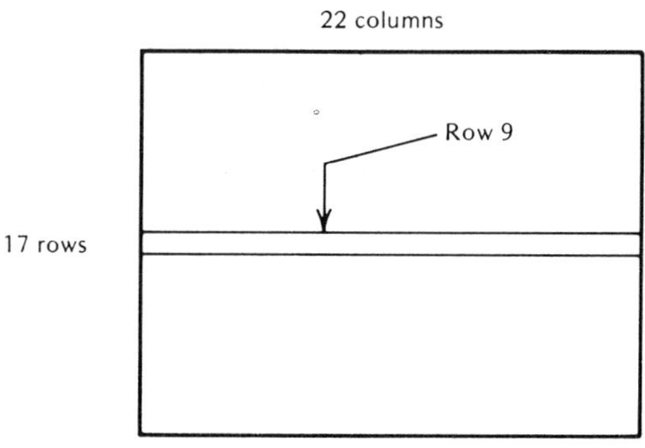

As you can see from the diagram, row 9 will have 22 elements in it. We might expect to use a count-control loop with exactly 22 iterations.

The elements we will process are

```
ARR(9,1) ARR(9,2) ARR(9,3)...ARR(9,21) ARR(9,22)
```

The column subscript varies from element to element, and the row subscript is always 9. Since J is commonly used as a variable column subscript, we will use J as our loop index, and write

```
loop for J = 1 to 22
   process A(9,J)
endloop
```

The row subscript is a constant, since every element in the row has the same row number. The column subscript varies from 1 to 22, and is the loop index.

For example, let us find the sum of row 4 of ARR. Prior to the loop, we must initialize. In this problem, "process" means "add to the accumulator."

```
SUM ← 0
loop for J = 1 to 22
   SUM ← SUM + ARR(4,J)
endloop
```

Now let us double each number in row 17 of ARR.

```
loop for J = 1 to 22
   ARR(17,J) ← 2 * ARR(17,J)
endloop
```

The general form is

```
loop for J = 1 to '# of columns'
   process array ('row #',J)
endloop
```

The row number itself may, of course, be a variable whose value will not change while we are processing the row. (As a simple example, we may have user input which told the program which row to process.)

We can also process a single column of the array. This time the row subscript varies from 1 to 17 and the column subscript remains the same:

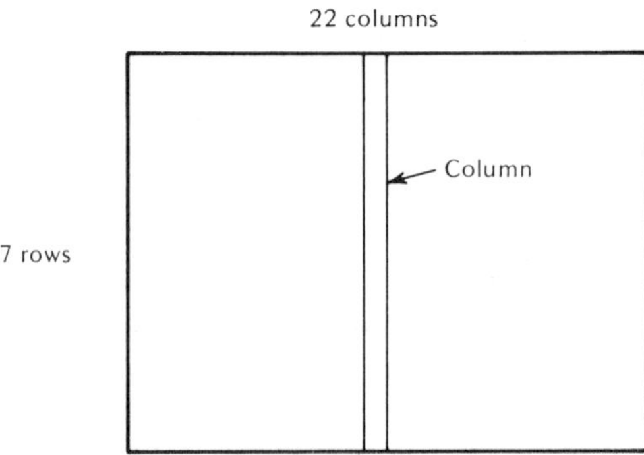

We will use I as our loop index, since the row number is changing. In general, the form is

```
loop for I = 1 to '# of rows'
   process array (I,'column #')
endloop
```

We can also process the entire array, one row at a time. That is, we will process row 1, then row 2, and so on. This yields an algorithm

```
loop for I = 1 to '# of rows'
   process row #I
endloop
```

However, the phrase "process row #I" can be refined, using the general form for processing a single row, as given above. Thus the entire refined algorithm yields the following nested loop pattern:

```
loop for I = 1 to '# of rows'
   loop for J = 1 to '# of columns'
     process ARR(I,J)
   endloop
endloop
```

Study the differences between the following two examples.

1. Find and print the sum of the entire 16 × 25 INTEGER array named SCORES.

```
SUM ← 0
loop for I = 1 to 16
   loop for J = 1 to 25
     SUM ← SUM + SCORES(I,J)
   endloop
endloop
print SUM
```

2. Find and print the sum of each row of the same array.

```
loop for I = 1 to 16
   SUM ← 0
   loop for J = 1 to 25
     SUM ← SUM + SCORES(I,J)
   endloop
   print SUM
endloop
```

In each example we process the entire array, one row at a time. However, the placement of the initialization and print steps depends on whether or not our sum is to be reinitialized and printed for each new row of the matrix.

Using reasoning similar to that for processing the array by rows, we come up with the following algorithm for processing the entire array, one column at at time:

```
loop for J = 1 to '# of columns'
    loop for I = 1 to '# of rows'
      process ARR(I,J)
    endloop
endloop
```

COMMENT. Notice that when we process "by rows," the outer loop index is the row subscript. When we process "by columns," the column subscript becomes the index of the outer loop.

Provided we have a **square matrix** (the number of rows and columns are the same), we can process what is known as the **main diagonal** of the matrix. For example, for a 5 × 5 matrix A, the main diagonal consists of the elements A(1,1), A(2,2), A(3,3), A(4,4), and A(5,5) shaded in the diagram below.

```
A(1,1) A(1,2) A(1,3) A(1,4) A(1,5)
A(2,1) A(2,2) A(2,3) A(2,4) A(2,5)
A(3,1) A(3,2) A(3,3) A(3,4) A(3,5)
A(4,1) A(4,2) A(4,3) A(4,4) A(4,5)
A(5,1) A(5,2) A(5,3) A(5,4) A(5,5)
```

Since the row and column subscripts are related to each other (they are the same), we do not need nested loops. We may write

```
loop for I = 1 to 5
    process A(I,I)
endloop
```

As I takes on the values 1 to 5, we process precisely the desired elements of the array.

As another example, we write an algorithm to initialize each element of the main diagonal of the 18 × 18 REAL array IDEN to the value 1. The solution is

```
loop for I = 1 to 18
    IDEN(I,I) ← 1.0
endloop
```

The general form for procesing the main diagonal of a square matrix ARR is

```
loop for I = 1 to '# of rows'
    process ARR(I,I)
endloop
```

(In the exercises we explore other techniques used with square arrays.)

Examples

The preceding discussion has been "generic," that is, not making specific reference to the meaning of the data in the arrays. In actual practice, of course, we are using the methods to extract useful information from the data in the arrays.

For the first few examples of this subsection, we will assume that we have a CHARACTER*12 array STATES of size 50 containing the states' names in no specific order. We also have a 50 × 12 REAL array RAIN, where row I corresponds to the state given by STATES(I), and each column represents one month. (Each of these arrays already contains information.)

What was the average monthly rainfall for the 50 states during the month of November?

Since November is the eleventh month, this requires us to find the average of column 11:

```
SUM ← 0
loop for STATNO = 1 to 50
   SUM ← SUM + RAIN(STATNO,11)
endloop
AVE ← SUM/50
```

Notice that we use STATNO ("state number") as the row subscript. The column subscript is constant.

Now suppose user input indicates a particular state number. Read the state number and print the total rainfall for that state.

This time we want to sum a row, the row number being given by the number on the data line. (Although STATNO is a "variable," notice that it remains constant as the sum is being calculated.)

```
read STATNO
SUM ← 0
loop for MONTH = 1 to 12
   SUM ← SUM + RAIN(STATNO,MONTH)
endloop
print SUM
```

This time the user supplies not a state number but a state name. To determine the appropriate row number we look this state up in our STATES array.

```
read STNAME
loop for I = 1 to 50
   if STNAME = STATES(I) then exit endif
endloop
STATNO ← I
SUM ← 0
loop for MONTH = 1 to 12
   SUM ← SUM + RAIN(STATNO,MONTH)
endloop
print SUM,STNAME
```

COMMENTS.

1. Each of the last two examples assume valid input. The exercises will ask you to modify them to print error messages for faulty input.
2. In the last example, we could have used a subprogram to perform the array lookup, as discussed in Section 6.3.

In this final example, we have two REAL arrays A and B, each 4 × 9. We wish to calculate C, the sum of the two.

The matrix C is a 4 × 9 REAL array, each of whose elements is calculated by adding the corresponding elements from A and B. Thus, we need to process the entire C array. Whether we do so by rows or by columns is up to us. We write

```
loop for I = 1 to 4
   loop for J = 1 to 9
      process C(I,J)
   endloop
endloop
```

(In the absence of meaningful names for row and column subscripts, we use the standard I and J.)

By "process C(I,J)," we mean "calculate C(I,J) as the sum of the corresponding elements from A and B." The smooth algorithm is therefore

```
loop for I = 1 to 4
   loop for J = 1 to 9
      C(I,J) ← A(I,J) + B(I,J)
   endloop
endloop
```

Use In FORTRAN Main Programs

Using two-dimensional arrays in FORTRAN programs is not difficult. Just as for one-dimensional arrays, we must include information on the size of the array in our declarations. This can be done using a DIMENSION statement as in this example:

```
INTEGER A,B,I
REAL C
DIMENSION A(20),B(15,21),C(7,9)
```

Here I is a scalar (nonarray) variable, A is a one-dimensional array of size 20, and B and C are two-dimensional arrays. The form of the DIMENSION statement illustrated by this example is

```
DIMENSION array-name(# of rows, # of columns)
```

Observe that we may include several arrays of different sizes within our DIMENSION statement.

Alternatively, we may include the dimension information with the type declaration:

```
INTEGER A(20),B(15,21)I
REAL C(7,9)
```

COMMENT. The numbers in the DIMENSION statement for a two-dimensional array represent the maximum permissible subscripts for the row and column, respectively. As with one-dimensional arrays, the lowest permissible subscripts are assumed to be 1, unless we say otherwise. It is possible to use the **range form** of dimension declaration for either the row or column or both subscripts. (Most of our applications will use the simpler form indicated earlier.)

The following declarations yield the indicated range of permissible subscripts for row and column:

DIMENSION	Row subscripts	Column subscripts
A(3,4)	1 – 3	1 – 4
A(−5:7,6)	−5 – 7	1 – 6
A(5,3:10)	1 – 5	3 – 10
A(−2:4,0:3)	−2 – 4	0 – 3

As an example illustrating the use of two-dimensional arrays in a FORTRAN program, let us write a FORTRAN segment corresponding to the algorithm segment which, given a state name, prints the total rainfall for that state.

```
      CHARACTER*12 STNAME,STATES(50)
      INTEGER I,STATNO,MONTH
      REAL RAIN(50,12),SUM
          .
          .
      PRINT *,'Enter a state name'
      READ(*,1000) STNAME
      DO 10 I = 1,50
         IF(STNAME.EQ.STATES(I)) THEN
            GO TO 100
         ENDIF
 10      CONTINUE
100   CONTINUE
      STATNO = I
      SUM = 0.0
      DO 150 MONTH = 1,12
        SUM = SUM + RAIN(STATNO,MONTH)
150     CONTINUE
      WRITE(*,2000) SUM,STNAME
          .
          .
1000  FORMAT(A)
2000  FORMAT(' ','THERE WERE ',F7.2,'INCHES OF RAIN IN ',A)
```

Use in Subprograms

When we pass a two-dimensional array to a subprogram (as input, output, or update parameter), we will generally use one of two methods. Both will involve the subprogram's declaring the array size to be the same as its declaration in the main program. The alternatives are:

1. We will declare the array the same in main and subprogram, and pass the array as a parameter.
2. We will, in addition, pass either a value indicating how many rows are actually in use, or a value indicating how many columns are actually in use, or both.

Now, write a subprogram which, given a month number, finds the average rainfall in the 50 states for that month.

Since we are calculating just one value, we will use a function, named AVEF. These variables are used:

	Name	Type	Use	Comment
Parameters:				
Input:	MONTH	INTEGER	Month number	
	RAIN	REAL(50,12)	Rain array	
Local:	STATNO	INTEGER	Index for DO	
	SUM	REAL	Total in 50 states	Accumulator

The algorithm has been (essentially) written earlier. The complete function, based on the variable list given above and that algorithm, appears in Figure 8.1

A similar application would be to write a subprogram which finds the average rainfall for each of the 12 months. This time we are calculating 12 answers, so we need a subroutine. For convenience, we will use an array AVES for the 12 averages.

The variable list will be essentially the same as for the previous example. The array RAIN will be an input parameter, the array AVES an output parameter. We will use MONTH as a loop index going from 1 to 12. (Since we are doing the calculation for each month, this is no longer an input parameter.)

As a rough algorithm we have

```
loop for MONTH = 1 to 12
   calculate the average for month #MONTH,
      placing the result in AVES(MONTH)
endloop
return
```

```
      REAL FUNCTION AVEF(MONTH,RAIN)
      INTEGER MONTH,STATNO
      REAL RAIN(50,12),SUM

C   WRITTEN BY *******, **/**/**.

C   THIS FUNCTION FINDS THE AVERAGE RAIN FOR
C THE 50 STATES IN A GIVEN MONTH.

C   THESE ARE THE PARAMETERS:

C    MONTH-INPUT, INTEGER-THE PARTICULAR MONTH
C    RAIN-INPUT, REAL(50,12)-ARRAY OF RAINFALL
                                FIGURES

      SUM = 0
      DO 10 STATNO = 1,50
       SUM = SUM + RAIN(STATNO,MONTH)
  10   CONTINUE
      AVEF = SUM/50.0
      RETURN
      END
```

Figure 8.1

Now to refine the body of this loop, we could write a typical accumulation loop. On the other hand, we could use the function (AVEF) we have already written. If we pass it the RAIN array and a particular month number, it will calculate the average for us. Thus the refinement leads to a step

```
AVES(MONTH)   AVEF(MONTH,RAIN)
```

The complete program is in Figure 8.2. Notice that the AVEF function is included in the declarations.

Write a subprogram which will add two REAL matrices of a size up to 10×10.

To solve this type of problem, we will assume that the arrays involved are 10×10 arrays in the calling program, and that the calling program will let us know how many rows and columns are in actual use.

```
      SUBROUTINE AVERAG(RAIN,AVES)
      INTEGER MONTH
      REAL RAIN(50,12),AVES(12),AVEF

C   WRITTEN BY *******, **/**/**.

C   THIS SUBROUTINE CALCULATES THE AVERAGE RAINFALL
C FOR EACH OF THE 12 MONTHS.

C   THE PAREMETERS ARE:

C    RAIN-INPUT, REAL(50,12)-THE RAINFALL ARRAY
C    AVES-OUTPUT, REAL(12)-THE 12 AVERAGES

C   THIS FUNCTION IS CALLED

C    AVEF-TO CALCULATE ONE AVERAGE

      DO 10 MONTH = 1,12
         AVES(MONTH) = AVEF(MONTH,RAIN)
   10    CONTINUE
      RETURN
      END
```

Figure 8.2

Because we are calculating an array answer, we use a subprogram with these variables.

	Name	Type	Use	Comment
Parameters:	A	REAL(10,10)	First array	Input parameter 1
	B	REAL(10,10)	Second array	Input parameter 2
	C	REAL(10,10)	Answer	Output parameter 3
	M	INTEGER	Number of rows in use	Input parameter 4
	N	INTEGER	Number of columns in use	Input parameter 4
Local:	I	INTEGER	Row subscript	
	J	INTEGER	Column subscript	

We will process the entire array by rows using this algorithm:

```
loop for I = 1 to M
   loop for J = 1 to N
      C(I,J) ← A(I,J) + B(I,J)
   endloop
endloop
return
```

The program is written using the variable list and algorithm just cited (see Figure 8.3). A sample call might look like

```
CALL ARRSUM(X,Y,Z,5,7)
```

or

```
CALL ARRSUM(ARR1,ARR2,SUM,NROW,NCOL)
```

Array I/O

For two-dimensional arrays, we will generally use nested implied DO loops. Recall the general form of an implied DO:

(list,index=start,end)

The list may include variables, array references, or even other implied DO's.

For example, in order to print out a 7 × 10 INTEGER array named A, we can use

```
WRITE(*,2000) ((A(I,J),J=1,10),I=1,7)
```

The implied DO here is in the form

(list,I=1,7)

```
      SUBROUTINE ARRSUM(A,B,C,M,N)
      INTEGER M,N,I,J
      REAL A(10,10),B(10,10),C(10,10)

C   WRITTEN BY *******, **/**/**.

C   THIS SUBROUTINE ADDS TWO M X N ARRAYS (UP TO
C SIZE 10 X 10)

C   THE PARAMETERS ARE:

C     A,B-INPUT, REAL(10,10)-THE MATRICES TO ADD
C     C-OUTPUT, REAL(10,10)-THE SUM
C     M,N-INPUT, INTEGER-THE PORTION IN USE (M X N)


      DO 100 I = 1,M
         DO 50 J = 1,N
            C(I,J) = A(I,J) + B(I,J)
   50       CONTINUE
  100    CONTINUE
      RETURN
      END
```

Figure 8.3

The "list" is shaded in the WRITE statement. It consists of an inner implied DO

```
(A(I,J),J=1,10)
```

Notice that if we wrote this as normal nested DO loops we would have

```
      DO 20 I = 1,7
         DO 10 J = 1,10
            WRITE(6,3000) A(I,J)
10          CONTINUE
20       CONTINUE
```

Having the outer loop indexed by the row subscript is consistent with our other algorithms which process the array by rows.

The general form given may be used to read or print any array in its entirety one row at a time. As for previous uses of the implied DO, the FORMAT will describe one record of the input or output. Let us now look at several examples using implied DO's.

Each record contains one row of a 6 × 9 REAL array SAL. Give appropriate declarations, READ, and FORMAT.

```
      INTEGER I,J
      REAL SAL(6,9)
      READ(*,1000) ((SAL(I,J),J=1,9),I=1,6)
1000  FORMAT(9F8.2)
```

Each record has a state name and 12 monthly rainfall figures. To read the STATES and RAIN arrays we may use the following.

```
      CHARACTER*12 STATES(50)
      INTEGER I,J
      REAL RAIN(50,12)
      READ(*,1000) (STATES(I),(RAIN(I,J),J=1,12),I=1,50)
1000  FORMAT(A12,3X,12F5.2)
```

The "list" for the I-indexed implied DO is

```
STATES(I),(RAIN(I,J),J=1,12)
```

It contains an array reference (similar to those in Section 8.1) and a nested implied DO, as discussed in this section. For each I, we read one state into STATES(I) and 12 rainfall figures into row I of the RAIN array.

CAUTION. Sometimes we must have the outer (I) loop as a regular DO loop, with the inner (J) loop as an implied DO, as illustrated by the following example.

The REAL array C is 10 × 10; however, only M rows and N columns are in use. If we write

```
WRITE(*,4000) ((C(I,J),J=1,N),I=1,M)
```

we will be unable to write the required FORMAT. In an implied DO of this type—since the computer goes to a new line when it runs out of FORMAT—we need to have "N" individual FORMATS. This is not possible. Consider what will happen if we make the outer (I-indexed) loop an explicit DO loop:

```
      DO 45 I = 1,M
         WRITE(*,4000) (C(I,J),J=1,N)
45       CONTINUE
```

Now each new I will be a new pass through an explicit DO loop and will re-execute the WRITE statement. Thus, we will get a new line for each new I, that is, for each new row. With this approach our FORMAT can be written to handle the largest number of columns we can have in use (10).

```
4000 FORMAT(' ',10F12.3)
```

For each row, the portion of the FORMAT needed for that row will be used.

To summarize, we will generally use nested implied DO loops

((array(I,J),J=1,#col),I=1,#rows)

with the FORMAT describing one record or line. However, when printing a variable portion of the array we may make the outer loop an explicit DO loop. In this case the FORMAT describes the number of columns in the actual array.

Pitfalls

Most pitfalls in using two-dimensional arrays are the same as those in using one-dimensional arrays and are related to subscripts.

The declarations contain the array size (dimensions); all other references will either use the array name alone or with two subscripts. To write the subscripts correctly we must determine what variable or constant (or more complex expression) represents the row number we are interested in, and likewise for the column number.

There are three other pitfalls peculiar to two-dimensional arrays.

1. We do not use total array output for a two-dimensional array. The reason is that we will get the output by column. For example, consider the 3×4 array A given below:

```
1 4 7 6
3 9 8 4
6 7 1 3
```

if we write

```
     WRITE(*,2000) A
2000 FORMAT(' ',4I5)
```

we will get the numbers printed by columns: 1, 3, 6, 4, 9, 7, 8, 1, 6, 4, and 3. The 4I5 will place four numbers per line, and we will get:

```
1 3 6 4
9 7 7 8
1 6 4 3
```

This is not at all what we hoped to get.

2. The same output will result if we indavertently exchange the I and J loop control in the implied DO:

```
WRITE(6,2000) ((A(I,J),I=1,3),J=1,4)
```

To read or print by rows, the row subscript should be the index of the outer loop.

3. Not all processes dealing with two-dimensional arrays use nested loops. As a general guideline, nested loops should be used for processing portions of the array which have an "area." Portions which do not (e.g., a row or a diagonal) will generally use only one loop.

REVIEW

FORTRAN Syntax

Array size declaration: DIMENSION array name(#rows,#cols.)

1. "#rows" may be replaced by

   lowest row subscript:highest row subscript

2. "#columns" may be replaced in the same way.
3. Array size declaration may combine with type declaration.
4. It should be the same size in main and subprograms.

Array reference: array name(row subscript, column subscript)
row subscript, column subscript may be any INTEGER expressions

Array I/O with implied DO

((array-name(I,J),J=1,#cols),I=1,#rows)

1. Outer (I) loop may be explicit DO loop.
2. Other variables and array references may be used along with the implied DO.

Processing

1. One row:

```
loop for J = 1 to #cols
   process ARR(row#,J)
endloop
```

2. One column:similar to #1
3. Entire array by rows:

```
loop for I = 1 to #rows
   loop for J = 1 to #cols
      process ARR(I,J)
   endloop
endloop
```

4. Entire array by columns: similar to #3
5. Main diagonal of square array:

```
loop for I = 1 to #rows
   process ARR(I,I)
endloop
```

EXERCISES

1. You have an INTEGER array A, size 30 × 47. Write algorithms to perform the following.
   (a) Initialize the entire array to 0.
   (b) Double each element in row 17.
   (c) Find the average of the array, at the same time counting the positive numbers in each column.
   (d) Find the largest number in column 3.

2. Write FORTRAN subprograms for each of the algorithms in Exercise 1. Where appropriate, make the problem more general. [For example, your subprogram in (a) should be able to initialize the entire array to any given constant.]

3. For each part of Exercise 2, identify each parameter as input, output, or update.

4. What changes would you have to make to the subprograms of Exercise 2 in order to handle the situation where only M rows and N columns of the array are actually in use?

5. You have a 21 × 28 REAL array ARR. Write algorithms for the following.
   (a) Find the largest number in the entire array.
   (b) Modify the algorithm of (a) to also tell in which row and column that largest number will occur. Assume there are no ties.
   (c) Modify (b) to handle ties.
   (d) Find the largest number in each row, placing the results in an array LARGE; also place the column numbers of the largest numbers in an array COLS.
   (e) Find and print, with row number, the sum of each row.
   (f) For row 5, locate and print the column number of the first positive number, assuming there is a positive number in that row.
   (g) Exchange rows 14 and 19.

6. Give algorithms for the following for a square array of size 15 × 15.
   (a) Count the positive numbers on the main diagonal.
   (b) Find the smallest number on the main diagonal.
   (c) Triple each number on the main diagonal.
   (d) Find the sum of the diagonal which runs from lower left to upper right.

(e) Find the largest number on or below the main diagonal:

(f) Find the average of the numbers on or below the diagonal from lower left to upper right.

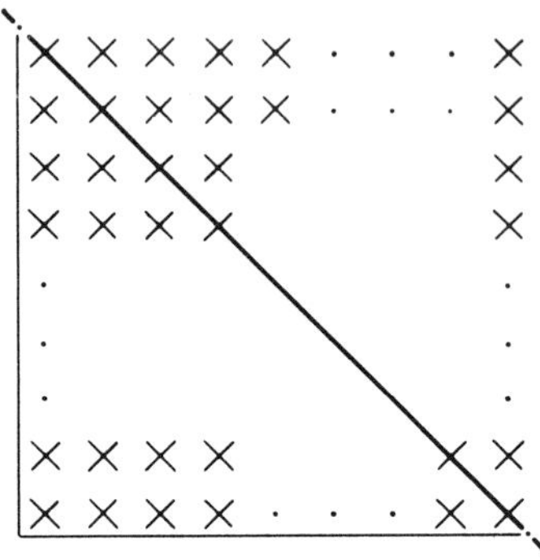

(g) Tell whether or not the matrix is "symmetric." It is symmetric if each element equals the one in the same position on the other side of the main diagonal. This matrix is symmetric:

```
6 7 3 4
7 5 1 2
3 1 8 9
4 2 9 4
```

7. Give appropriate declarations, READ or WRITE, and FORMAT for the following.

(a) Each of 24 input records represents one row of a matrix. Each record has 14 integer numbers on it. Fill the matrix.

(b) There are 17 records, each with 12 real numbers. Each record is one row of a matrix. Fill the matrix.

(c) Print out the array of (a).

(d) Repeat (c), including the row number with each row in this form:

```
ROW 1:
ROW 2:
and so on
```

(e) Print the array of (b), with both row and column labels.

8. Follow the directions of Exercise 7.

(a) The first record contains M and N, the number of rows and columns (up to 10 × 10). Each successive record has N integer numbers, and there are M lines, one for each row. Read the matrix.

(b) Print out the array of (a).

(c) The first record contains NOEMP and indicates how many employee records follow (up to 35). Each employee record contains employee number, age, and six semi-monthly pay figures for the quarter. Read the records into appropriate arrays.

(d) Write the data from (c) in exactly the same format as it was read in.

(e) Print row 7 of a 14 × 23 integer array ARR.

(f) Print column 17 of the same array (horizontally, not vertically).

9. Follow the directions of Exercise 7.

(a) Print the main diagonal of a 15 × 15 real array (on one line).

(b) Print the diagonal which runs from lower left to upper right for the same array.

(c) Print those elements on or below the main diagonal for the same array.

10. Write subroutines for the following matrix operations; they should work for arrays up to 10 × 10. You may use the addition subroutine in Figure 8.3 as an example.

(a) Multiply a matrix by a scalar (by multiplying each element in the array by that scalar).

(b) Subtract two matrices (each the same size).

(c) See if two matrices are equal.

11. Suppose we have a 4 × 5 INTEGER array A and a 5 × 7 INTEGER array B. Then each row of A contains five numbers and each column of B contains five numbers. The **inner product** of a row of A with a column of B is found by multiplying each of the five numbers in the row of A by the corresponding five numbers in the column of B, and adding up the result.

For example, the inner product of

```
1 3 4 2 7 and 6
              7
              3
              4
              2
```

is $1 \times 6 + 3 \times 7 + 4 \times 3 + 2 \times 4 + 7 \times 2 = 6 + 21 + 12 + 8 + 14 = 61$.

(a) Write a count-controlled loop to form the inner product of row 2 of A with column 6 of B.

(b) Write a count-controlled loop to form the inner product of row 1 of A with column 3 of B.

(c) Write a subprogram which, given a row number for A and a column number for B, finds the inner product. What type of subprogram do you need? What parameters are needed?

12. (See Exercise 11.) Since the number of columns in A is equal to the number of rows in B, we can form inner products of rows of A and columns of B. Therefore we can form the **matrix product** A × B.

A × B is a matrix with as many rows as A(four) and as many columns as B(seven). If we call this matrix C, then

C(I,J) = the inner product of row I of A
with column J of B

Write a subprogram to calculate C. [*Hint*: Use Exercise 11.]

13. Give algorithms for the following.

(a) Each record contains a person's birthday in the form: month (1−12), day (1−31). Read these records and keep track of how many people in the file were born on each day. At end of file, print a list of all days on which two or more people in the file were born. [*Hint*: You might use a 12 × 31 arrays of counters.]

(b) Instead of reading data records with birthdays, imagine you have a subroutine BIRTH(MONTH,DAY) which generates random birthdays (such a subroutine could be written using RND.) Using this subroutine, generate and count 30 birthdays. Print a message telling whether or not there were any duplicates.

(c) Repeat the process of (b) 1000 times, and print how many times out of the 1000 there was a duplicate.

14. In this exercise we will work with the STATES and RAIN arrays used in several examples in this section.

(a) Write an algorithm which reads the name of a month and finds the average rainfall for that month. [*Hint*: You will need an array of month names. Give the DATA statement used to initialize that array.]

(b) One of the examples was a subroutine which calculated an array of 12 monthly averages. Write a segment of FORTRAN which, using that subroutine, prints a table containing month name and average rainfall for the month.

(c) Write a lookup routine which looks up a given state name in the array of state names. It should return the subscript where the state was found, or 0 if not found.

(d) Using the routine of (c), write an algorithm segment which reads a state name and finds the total rainfall for that state. It should print an error message if the state name is invalid.

15. For this exercise you have arrays NAMES(50) and GRADES(50,10). Each element of the NAMES array, and each row of the GRADES array, represents one student. The columns of the GRADES array represent ten tests.

A variable NUMBER tells how many students there actually are, and a variable TESTS tells how many tests have already been taken by the class. (Any tests not taken have a score of −1 in them.) You are to write FORTRAN subprograms which perform each of the following actions. *Note*: You may wish to have these subprograms call other subprograms.

(a) Write an INIT subroutine to read the data from a file into the arrays. Also write a RESTOR subroutine which writes the data out to a file in precisely the form it was read in.

(b) Given a name, calculate a student's average on tests taken so far. (Any tests which should have been taken but still have a −1 should be counted as 0.)

(c) Record the scores on the next test taken by the class. To do so, read a series of records each containing name and grade, checking for reasonable data. Place the grade in the proper spot in the GRADES array.

(d) Add a student to the bottom of the list, given his name.

(e) For a given test, list and count the people who have not yet taken the test.

(f) Calculate an array of letter grades for the students, based on 90–100 A, 80–89.99 B, and so on.

(g) Swap the data for two students, given their positions in the names array.

(h) Sort the data in alphabetical order by name.

16. For this exercise you have parallel arrays IDS(100), GROUPS(100), and SALES(100). Each person has an ID number, a group number (1–7), and a monthly-to-date sales figure. There are NOEMP employees at present.

You also have a 7 × 12 array SUMMRY, where SUMMRY(I,J) represents the dollar amount of sales by group I in product line J. These variables all have appropriate data. You are to write FORTRAN subprograms for each of the following.

(a) Calculate an array GRPSUM of size 7, containing the total sales for each of the seven groups.

(b) Calculate an array PRDSUM of size 12 with totals for the 12 products.

(c) Add a given employee, with her group number, to the list of employees.

(d) Given an employee ID, a sales amount, and a product line number, make appropriate modifications to the SALES and SUMMRY arrays. (Print an error message if the employee does not exist.)

(e) Print a summary page showing the SUMMRY array with all groups and product line entries well labelled. It should also print group and product line totals.

(f) Find the group with the lowest total sales.

(g) Find the employee with the highest total sales. Print the employee's ID and group number along with her sales figure.

(h) Get ready for a new month by resetting all appropriate entries to 0.

17. (a) Write the algorithm for a function to calculate the "number of combinations of n items taken k at a time," whose value is given by

$$\frac{n!}{k!(n-k)!} \quad (n! \text{ is } n^*(n-1)^*\ldots{}^*2^*1)$$

(b) The $k!$ in the above formula "cancels with" the last k factors in the $n!$, leaving

$$\frac{n(n-1)(n-2)\ldots(k+1)}{(n-k)!}$$

Revise your algorithm to take advantage of this fact.

(c) By using an array, we can calculate a number of these values more efficiently. Suppose we set up a two-dimensional array COMB(0:10,0:10); COMB(N,K) will be the "number of combinations of N items taken K at a time." Then it is known that a formula for COMB(N,K) is

$$\text{COMB(N,K)} = \begin{cases} 1, \text{ if K} = 0 \text{ or N} = \text{K} \\ \text{COMB(N}-1,\text{K}-1)+\text{COMB(N}-1,\text{K}), \textit{ otherwise} \end{cases}$$

Use this fact to write an efficient algorithm to fill the array.

[*Note*: Only the "lower triangle" of the array will be filled (see the diagram); K must be ≤N.]

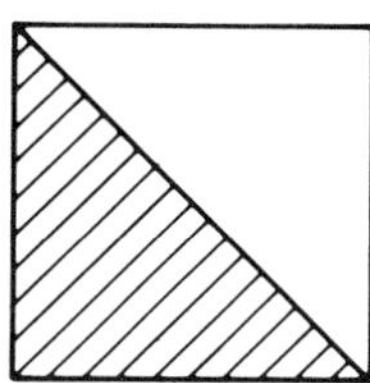

18. Write a program to play the Game of Life. On an infinite checkerboard, each square has eight neighbors:

1	2	3
4		5
6	7	8

This game simulates growth and decay in a collection of interacting organisms, where cells (squares) are born, survive, or die based on how "crowded" things are. The cycle occurs in "generations" by these rules (each square is either *dead*—empty—or *alive*).

1. Birth. If an empty (dead) square has exactly three live neighboring squares, it will be alive the next generation.
2. Survival. If a live square has either two or three live neighbors, it will still be alive the next generation.
3. Death. Any live square that does not survive dies, either from overcrowding (≥4 neighbors) or isolation (≤1 neighbor).

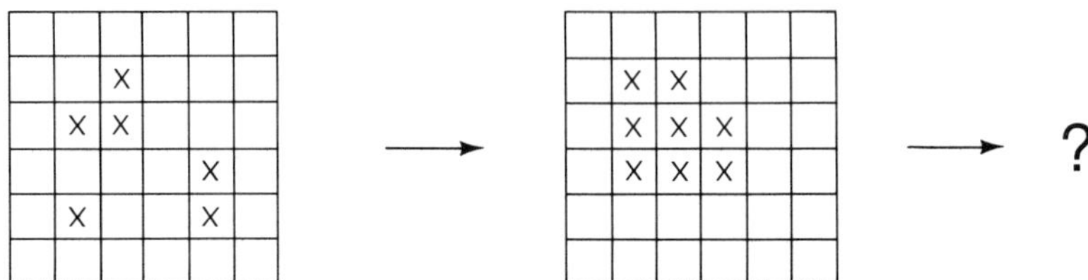

Example

Input to the program will include an initial configuration and an indication of how many generations to print. Output will be one page per generation (starting with the initial configuration).

Since programming an infinite array is tough (not to mention printing it), we will restrict ourselves to a 50 × 50 array. We will use 'X' to denote live, and ' ' (space) to denote dead. Moreover, we will assume that rows 1 and 50 and columns 1 and 50 are infertile regions where nothing is ever born. [*Note*: Develop separate input and print routines for this program. The input routine should obtain an initial configuration with at least 15 live squares. Do so by inputting I,J coordinates for each live square. Be sure to edit (2 ≤ I ≤ 49, 2 ≤ J ≤ 49). This routine also obtains and edits how many generations are desired. Its parameters are (1) the 50 × 50 board with 'X' and ' ' as required; (2) the number of generations desired. The print routine prints the entire 50 × 50 board in suitable format, with good labelling including the generation number.]

8.3 ADJUSTABLE DIMENSIONS

Consider the following function which finds the sum of an integer array:

```
      INTEGER FUNCTION SUM(A)
      INTEGER A(100)
      INTEGER I

      SUM = 0
      DO 10 I = 1,100
         SUM = SUM + A(I)
10       CONTINUE
      RETURN
      END
```

This program is "general purpose" in a limited sense. It can be used to find the sum of any integer array of size 100. If a program we write this week requires the sum of 100 test grades contained in an array, we could use this function. Then, in the same or a later program, we could use the same function to find the sum of 100 IQ's contained in a different array. However, there are at least two ways in which we could make the function even more generally applicable. Our goal is to write a function which can be used to sum any integer array of any size.

In previous examples, we have considered the possibility that the entire array might not be in use. We could use this idea for the SUM function. We would add a parameter N indicating how many elements of A are actually present, with the following changes to the function:

```
      INTEGER FUNCTION SUM(A,N)
      INTEGER A(100),N
      INTEGER I

      SUM = 0
      DO 10 I = 1,N
         SUM = SUM + A(I)
10       CONTINUE
      RETURN
      END
```

This is a valuable technique. At first glance, this might seem to solve our problem. However, in this instance we need even more. The main program could use the modified subroutine to sum the first 50 locations of an array AGES of size 100:

```
      INTEGER AGES(100),SUM,AGESUM
              .
              .
      AGESUM = SUM(AGES,50)
```

However, it could not sum an array SCORES of size 50. We need the concept of **adjustable dimensions**.

One-Dimensional Arrays

In a main program, the dimension of an array must be a constant. In a subprogram, however, the dimension may be a variable provided:

1. the array is a parameter of the subprogram, and
2. the variable representing the dimension is also a parameter of the subprogram.

(This works properly because the computer does not set aside space in the subprogram for the array parameter but works with the actual array from the calling program.)

We may therefore pass in another parameter which indicates the size of the array A:

```
      INTEGER FUNCTION SUM(A,ASIZE,N)
      INTEGER ASIZE,N
      INTEGER A(ASIZE)
      INTEGER I

      SUM = 0
      DO 10 I = 1,N
         SUM = SUM + A(I)
10       CONTINUE
      RETURN
      END
```

We still use the parameter N which tells how many elements of A are in use.

> **CAUTION.** The variable ASIZE must be declared *before* it is used in declaring the size of A. Switching the first two INTEGER statements would cause errors.

We may now use this routine to sum the first 50 locations of AGES and also to sum the entire array SCORES referred to earlier.

```
INTEGER AGES(100),SCORES(50),AGESUM,SCSUM,SUM
          .
          .
AGESUM = SUM(AGES,100,50)
          .
          .
SCSUM = SUM(SCORES,50,50)
```

The first number will be used by the function to correctly declare the dimension of the array being summed. The second, which indicates how much of the array is actually in use, controls the DO loop in the program logic itself.

Two-Dimensional Arrays

The concept of adjustable dimensions may be applied to two-dimensional arrays as well. To illustrate the method, we write a general-purpose matrix addition routine to calculate

$$C \leftarrow A + B$$

where A, B, and C are REAL matrices of the same size.

We have already developed (in Section 8.2) a routine which works provided the arrays are 10 × 10. We now remove this restriction on the array sizes.

The idea is similar to that of the previous example. Among our parameters we must include NROWS and NCOLS, which tell the actual size of the arrays being passed as parameters. We then declare

```
INTEGER NROWS,NCOLS
REAL A(NROWS,NCOLS),B(NROWS,NCOLS),C(NROWS,NCOLS)
```

In addition, we want parameters which indicate how many rows and columns of the matrices are presently in use. We will name these parameters M and N.

We thus have two distinct pairs of parameters:

1. NROWS, NCOLS. This pair gives the actual physical size of the arrays, which is used in the delcaration.
2. M, N. This pair gives the portion of the arrays presently in use. This information is used in the program logic.

See Figure 8.4 for the subroutine.

CAUTION. DO NOT use the M and N in the dimensioning of the array. This pair tells the portion in use, NOT the actual size. Failure to abide by this warning can lead to extremely puzzling results.

```
      SUBROUTINE ADD(A,B,C,NROWS,NCOLS,M,N)
      INTEGER NROWS,NCOLS,M,N,I,J
      REAL A(NROWS,NCOLS),B(NROWS,NCOLS),C(NROWS,NCOLS)

C    WRITTEN BY *******, **/**/**

C    THIS IS A GENERAL-PURPOSE MATRIX ADDER:
C           C <- A + B

C    THESE PARAMETERS ARE USED:

C       A,B-INPUT, REAL-MATRICES TO ADD
C       C-OUTPUT, REAL-MATRIX SUM
C       NROWS, NCOLS-INPUT, INTEGER-SIZE OF A,B,C
C       M,N-INPUT, INTEGER-PORTION OF A,B,C IN USE


      DO 100 I = 1,M
         DO 50 J = 1,N
            C(I,J) = A(I,J) + B(I,J)
   50       CONTINUE
  100    CONTINUE
      RETURN
      END
```

Figure 8.4

COMMENT. A sample calling program might include the following:

```
      REAL ARR1 (10,15),ARR2(10,15),ARR3(10,15)
      REAL X(20,20),Y(20,20),Z(20,20)
      INTEGER M,N
        .
        .
C ARR3 <- ARR1 + ARR2. ENTIRE ARRAYS ARE IN USE.

       CALL ADD(ARR1,ARR2,ARR3,10,15,10,15)
        .
        .
C Z <- X + Y. ONLY M ROWS AND N COLUMNS ARE IN USE.

      CALL ADD(X,Y,Z,20,20,M,N)
```

An Alternate Approach

The latest version of FORTRAN, on which this textbook is based, has added a feature which enables some simplifications in the adjustable dimension procedures. The simplification is extremely useful for one-dimensional arrays, since it completely avoids the need for passing in the actual array size. For the two-dimensional case, however, it is still necessary to have a parameter which indicates the actual number of rows. The parameter for the actual number of columns may be omitted.

COMMENT. We would, in any case, want to keep the parameters which indicate how much of the array is in use.

To utilize this alternate method, we simply place an asterisk as the size of the one-dimensional array, as in this declaration:

```
INTEGER A(*)
```

For a two-dimensional array, we use an asterisk as the final dimension (that is, the number of columns). The number of rows must either be a constant or a variable included as a parameter, as in these two declarations:

```
INTEGER B(20,*)
INTEGER C(NROWS,*)
```

To illustrate the alternate method, Figure 8.5 contains modified versions of the two subprograms developed in this section, with differences shaded.

Which technique you choose to use is a matter of individual programming style. Notice that the first method presented is more consistent, but the second method is simpler.

```
      INTEGER FUNCTION SUM(A,N)
      INTEGER A(*),N
      INTEGER I

      SUM =0
      DO 10 I = 1,N
         SUM = SUM + A(I)
10      CONTINUE
      RETURN
      END


      SUBROUTINE ADD(A,B,C,NROWS,M,N)
      INTEGER NROWS,M,N,I,J
      REAL A(NROWS,*), B(NROWS,*), C(NROWS,*)

      DO 100 I = 1,M
         DO 50 J = I,N
            C(I,J) = A(I,J) + B(I,J)
50          CONTINUE
100      CONTINUE
      RETURN
      END
```

Figure 8.5

REVIEW

FORTRAN Syntax

Adjustable dimensions

Method 1: Include parameters which indicate actual size of array being passed. Use these parameters to declare the array.

Method 2: Same as Method 1, except that no parameter is needed for a one-dimensional array, or for number of columns in a two-dimensional array. Instead, an * is used in the declaration in the subprogram.

Caution: The "actual size" concept is distinct from the "portion in use" concept.

Terminology

General-purpose subprogram: One which uses both the "adjustable dimension" ("actual size") concept and the "portion in use" concept for arrays which are parameters.

EXERCISES

Note: The phrase "general purpose" in the exercises implies the use of adjustable dimensions.

1. Write general-purpose FORTRAN subprograms for the algorithms in the following exercises from Section 6.2.
- **(a)** Exercise 1(a)
- **(b)** Exercise 1(e)
- **(c)** Exercise 7(d)
- **(d)** Exercise 7(e)
- **(e)** Exercise 9
- **(f)** Exercise 11
- **(g)** Exercise 12(b)
- **(h)** Exercise 13
- **(i)** Exercise 16

2. Write general-purpose FORTRAN subprograms for the algorithms in the following exercises from Section 8.2.
- **(a)** Exercise 1(a)
- **(b)** Exercise 1(b)
- **(c)** Exercise 1(d)
- **(d)** Exercise 5(b)
- **(e)** Exercise 5(d)
- **(f)** Exercise 6(e)
- **(g)** Exercise 6(g)
- **(h)** Exercise 11(c)

3. Modify the SORT subroutine in Case Study #8 (Section 6.4) to use the concept of adjustable dimension.

4. Write a general-purpose array lookup function to locate a given value in a given array. Both the value and the array are integer. The answer is the subscript where the value was found, or 0 if it is not present in the array.

5. Write a general-purpose SWAP routine which will exchange rows I and J of a matrix A.

6. Write a general-purpose ROWSUM routine to find the sum of row I of a matrix A.

7. Write an algorithm to sort the rows of the array A into descending order based on the sums of the rows.

```
           1 3 1 4                  0 6 2 5
If A is    0 6 2 5    A becomes     3 1 3 3
           3 1 3 3                  1 3 1 4
```

[*Hint*: Use Exercises 5 and 6.]

8. We have parallel INTEGER arrays IDNO and GRADES. The GRADES array is two-dimensional; row I represents the grades of the student whose ID is in IDNO(I).
- **(a)** Write a general purpose routine to sort these parallel arrays into ascending order based on the ID.
- **(b)** Write a general purpose routine to sort these arrays into descending order based on the sum of the grades for each student. (See the hint for Exercise 7.)

9. Write general-purpose matrix routines for the following. A,B, and C are REAL matrices.
- **(a)** C ← A − B.
- **(b)** B ← R*A (R is a single REAL number).
- **(c)** C ← A*B. (*Hint*: See Section 8.2, Exercise 12.)
- **(d)** C gets the value of A with all entries above the main diagonal set to 0.0

9

Simple Control Breaks

9.1 SIMPLE CONTROL BREAKS

There are many instances, especially in business applications of the computer, where the data to be processed occurs in groups. If there are special tasks to be performed when one group ends and another begins, we have a structure frequently referred to as a **control break** structure. In this type of application, information contained within the data itself is generally used to determine when we move from one group to another.

An important consideration for this type of problem is that the records being processed must be prearranged into the groups involved. Usually that data is on a file, and the programs process it in batch mode. Our examples in this chapter will be written to run in batch mode. Therefore there will be no prompts. We will assume that the file of data is being accessed as the standard input.

An Example

Each data record contains a department number, salesperson number, and expense amount, as illustrated here. The records are arranged with the salespersons for each department grouped together in the file.

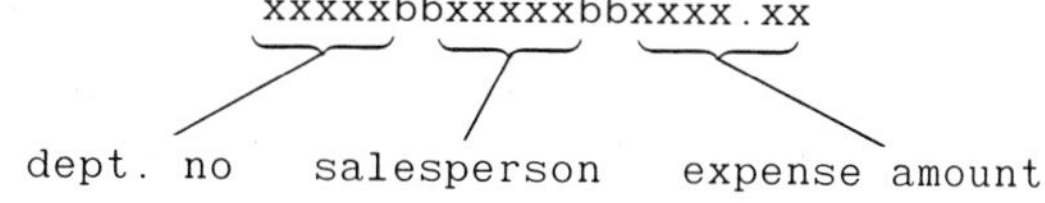

Write a program to create a summary listing as illustrated in Figure 9.1.

```
                    EXPENSE TOTALS
                    ------- ------

DEPARTMENT          SALESPERSON          EXPENSES
----------          -----------          --------

       100                10000           1000.00
       100                10001           1000.00

               DEPARTMENT TOTAL:          2000.00


       200                38907            500.00
       200                43798           1603.45
       200                44359           1000.75

               DEPARTMENT TOTAL:          3104.20


       300                32987            984.50

               DEPARTMENT TOTAL:           984.50


      1800                43871           1500.00
      1800                78340            390.25
      1800                38469             50.75
      1800                78307            500.00

               DEPARTMENT TOTAL:          2441.00


     12050                33498             35.50

               DEPARTMENT TOTAL:            35.50


                    GRAND TOTAL:          8565.20
```

Figure 9.1

Suppose we start with the realization that a loop will be needed to process the data. We will need at least the following variables:

	Name	Type	Use	Comment
Input:	DEPT	INTEGER	Department number	
	ID	INTEGER	Salesperson number	
	EXPENS	REAL	Expense amount	
Output:	TOTAL	REAL	Department total	Accumulator
	GRAND	REAL	Grand total	Accumulator

Many file processing problems follow this general pattern:

```
initialization
loop
   read; if eof then exit endif
   process & print
endloop
summary
stop
```

However, the control break logic will require a somewhat more complex algorithm, since there are special tasks to be performed when we finish one group and start another. Somewhere after the read step we will insert a step something like this:

```
if this is a new department then
    perform 'change of department' steps
endif
```

The "change of department" steps will include, among other things, printing the total for the previous department. In general we must perform some "cleanup" steps for the old department and some "setup" steps to get ready for the new department. These general categories may overlap somewhat.

> **NOTE.** In many programs the test to check whether we have a new group will come immediately after the read step. However, there are instances when some preliminary processing must be done prior to determining whether a new group has occurred.

If we ask, "how can we tell if this is a new department?" the answer might be to compare the department number just read with the previous department number; we might therefore make an addition to our variable list:

	Name	Type	Use	Comment
Other:	OLDEPT	INTEGER	Previous department number	

With a little more thought, we might conclude that the first data record should be treated separately, since there is no "old department number" with which to compare the first department number. We might be led to read and process that first record before we enter the loop, since it will be treated differently from the rest. If so, we would come up with a rough algorithm something like this:

```
print headings
GRAND ← 0
read DEPT,ID,EXPENS
do 'setup' steps for first department
print DEPT,ID,EXPENS
TOTAL ← TOTAL + EXPENS
loop
   read DEPT,ID,EXPENS; if eof then exit endif
   if OLDEPT ≠ DEPT then
      perform 'change of department' steps
     ('cleanup' and 'setup')
   endif
   print DEPT,ID,EXPENS
   TOTAL ← TOTAL + EXPENS
endloop
perform 'cleanup' steps for last department
print GRAND
stop
```

We "setup" for the first department prior to the loop. This is sometimes referred to as **priming**. In addition, we must perform the "cleanup" for the last department after the loop, when we have run out of data.

To complete the algorithm, we must determine what will be involved in setting up for a new department and cleaning up after an old department. To do so, we should review the required output. If we concentrate on the "department change," we should be able to determine most of what will be required. Each step will be labeled as "cleanup" or "setup."

This step should be obvious:

1. Print TOTAL (clean up).

Some others are not quite as obvious:

2. Set TOTAL back to 0, to get ready to accumulate a new total for the new department (setup).
3. Give OLDEPT the value of DEPT (setup).
4. Add TOTAL to GRAND (before setting TOTAL back to 0). GRAND represents the sum of the individual department totals (cleanup).

NOTE. As "cleanup" for the last department, we must perform the steps numbered 1 and 4. The "setup" for the first department will consist of steps 2 and 3.

Adding these refinements to our algorithm, we obtain the following:

```
print headings
GRAND ← 0
read DEPT,ID,EXPENS
TOTAL ← 0
OLDEPT ← DEPT
print DEPT,ID,EXPENS
TOTAL ← TOTAL + EXPENS
loop
   read DEPT,ID,EXPENS; if eof then exit endif
   if OLDEPT ≠ DEPT then
      print TOTAL
      GRAND ← GRAND + TOTAL
      TOTAL ← 0
      OLDEPT ← DEPT
   endif
   print DEPT,ID,EXPENS
   TOTAL ← TOTAL + EXPENS
endloop
PRINT TOTAL
GRAND ← GRAND + TOTAL
print GRAND
stop
```

Control Breaks: General

The preceding example illustrates the control break concept. There are some general comments we can make about planning this type of algorithm. The algorithm will usually involve a loop which terminates on end of file. We will discuss in some detail what types of steps will generally appear before, in the body of, and after this loop.

Keep in mind that the underlying feature of the control break structure is that the data is arranged in groups based on some field of the individual records. In addition to the usual analysis of the steps to be performed for each individual data record, we must determine the steps required due to the grouping. As a general rule, these steps fall into two categories:

1. Those steps used in starting a new group, such as initializing (or reinitializing) counters or accumulators or printing special lines of information.
2. Those steps used in finishing up an old group, such as printing summary information.

Whenever we encounter a new group, we must perform all these steps.

The principal features of the algorithm will be:

1. Before the loop:
   a. Initialize for the entire file (for example, GRAND ← 0).
   b. Read first record.
   c. Set up for first group.
   d. Process first record.
2. In the loop:
   a. Read new record.
   b. If a new group, finish up previous group and set up for new group.
   c. Process the record.
3. After the loop:
   a. Finish up last group.
   b. Print summary information for entire file.

Most control break problems fit fairly well into this general outline. For some applications steps 2b and 2c must be modified slightly, since the first record of each new group is processed slightly differently from the subsequent records in that group. However, this outline should help us obtain a good algorithm for any control break problem we may encounter.

Using Subprograms With Control Breaks

In the preceding discussion we have not indicated how subprograms fit into the control break program logic. We have at least these four possibilities.

1. We can use an INPUT routine for reading and editing the data, as explained in Section 3.3.
2. We can use a DETAIL routine for printing detail lines. In this way we can proceed to a new page of output when we reach the bottom of each page.
   It will frequently be helpful to pass, as an input parameter for this subroutine, a logical flag indicating whether or not this is the first record in a new group. We might use LOGICAL variable NEWGRP for this purpose. (The first record in each group is frequently handled differently in the DETAIL routine.)
3. The processing of the record may very well involve complicated logic which will warrant one or more subprograms.
4. The "setup" and "cleanup" steps themselves may be placed in the subprograms. We discuss this possibility further.

There are several possible reasons for placing the setup and the cleanup steps in subprograms. First of all, each one is generally used twice. For example, the setup steps are performed before the loop for the first record, and in the loop whenever a new group is encountered. In addition, these steps could be fairly complex. The more complex they become, the more likely it becomes that we will choose to place them in subprograms. Finally, using subprograms emphasizes the similar structure of the various control break programs we write.

We will reexamine our sample control break algorithm to illustrate these ideas. For that example, the algorithm for a SETUP subprogram is

```
TOTAL ← 0
OLDEPT ← DEPT
return
```

This will require a subroutine; the parameters are TOTAL (output), DEPT (input), and OLDEPT (output).

For a CLENUP subprogram, we have

```
print TOTAL line, plus three blank lines
GRAND ← GRAND + TOTAL
return
```

TOTAL is an input parameter and GRAND an update parameter for this subroutine.

For the DETAIL routine we will have input parameters DEPT, ID, and EXPENS, together with the logical variable NEWGRP discussed earlier. We write

```
if NEWGRP is true then LINECT ← LINECT + 5 endif
if LINECT ≥ 45 then
   print headings
   LINECT ← 6
endif
print DEPT,ID,EXPENS
LINECT ← LINECT + 1
```

COMMENT. This subroutine is somewhat different from some earlier ones in its handling of the LINECT variable. This is to adjust to the fact that lines other than detail lines are being printed by this program. If we simply count detail lines, we will be unable to judge when we are near the bottom of the page. Rather than merely counting detail lines, we count all lines of output. As a result, LINECT is set to 6 after printing headings. In addition, for a new group we add 5 to LINECT. This counts the DEPARTMENT TOTAL line we have printed, plus the one blank line before and three blank lines after that line.

The INPUT routine is standard; we do not discuss it. Our main program becomes

```
GRAND ← 0
call INPUT(DEPT,ID,EXPENS,EOF)
call SETUP(TOTAL,DEPT,OLDEPT)
call DETAIL(DEPT,ID,EXPENS,.TRUE.)
TOTAL ← TOTAL + EXPENS
loop
   call INPUT(DEPT,ID,EXPENS,EOF)
   if EOF is true then exit endif
   NEWGRP ← .FALSE.
   if DEPT ≠ OLDEPT then
      NEWGRP ← .TRUE.
      call CLENUP(TOTAL,GRAND)
      call SETUP(TOTAL,DEPT,OLDEPT)
   endif
   call DETAIL(DEPT,ID,EXPENS,NEWGRP)
   TOTAL ← TOTAL + EXPENS
endloop
call CLENUP(TOTAL,GRAND)
print GRAND
stop
```

NEWGRP is given a default value of .FALSE. prior to comparing DEPT with OLDEPT, then changed to .TRUE. if appropriate. Coding this algorithm involves no new FORTRAN; the program is left as an exercise.

Now suppose each record contains a customer name, item number, and cost of purchases. All orders for each customer are grouped together. Write a program to create a listing as illustrated in Figure 9.2.

> **NOTE.** This output is **group indicated** by name. By this we mean that the records with the same name are grouped together. Moreover, the name itself is printed only for the first record of the group.

For this program we need the following variables:

	Name	Type	Use	Comment
Input:	NAME	CHARACTER*20	Customer name	
	ITEM	INTEGER	Item number	
	COST	REAL	Item cost	
Output:	BILL	REAL	Customer total	Accumulator
	AVE	REAL	Average bill	
Other:	OLDNAM	CHARACTER*20	Previous customer name	
	TOTAL	REAL	Grand total	Accumulator
	CTR	INTEGER	Number of customers	Counter
	EOF	LOGICAL	End-of-file indicator	

```
        NAME              ITEM       COST
        ----              ----       ----
xxxxxxxxxxxxxxxxxxxx      xxxxx      xxxx.xx
                          xxxxx      xxxx.xx
                          xxxxx      xxxx.xx
                          xxxxx      xxxx.xx
                                   ----------
                                   xxxxxx.xx TOTAL FOR xxx...xxxx

xxxxxxxxxxxxxxxxxxxx      xxxxx      xxxx.xx
                                   ----------
                                   xxxxxx.xx TOTAL FOR xxx...xxxx

xxxxxxxxxxxxxxxxxxxx      xxxxx      xxxx.xx
                          xxxxx      xxxx.xx
                          xxxxx      xxxx.xx
                                   ----------
                                   xxxxxx.xx TOTAL FOR xxx...xxxx

                         (and so on)
          AVERAGE BILL FOR xxx CUSTOMERS IS xxxxxx.xx
```

Figure 9.2

The algorithm generally follows the outline given earlier. You should determine which steps are due to considerations 1a, 1b, and so forth, as listed in the subsection "Control Breaks: General."

```
TOTAL ← 0
call INPUT(NAME,ITEM,COST,EOF)
BILL ← 0
OLDNAM ← NAME
call DETAIL(NAME,ITEM,COST,.TRUE.)
BILL ← BILL + COST
loop
   call INPUT(NAME,ITEM,COST,EOF)
   if EOF is true then exit endif
   NEWGRP ← .FALSE.
   if NAME ≠ OLDNAM then
      NEWGRP ← .TRUE.
      print BILL,OLDNAM,followed by 2 blank lines
      TOTAL ← TOTAL + BILL
      CTR ← CTR + 1
      BILL ← 0
      OLDNAM ← NAME
   endif
```

(continued)

```
        call DETAIL(NAME,ITEM,COST,NEWGRP)
        BILL ← BILL + COST
    endloop
    print BILL,OLDNAM,followed by 2 blank lines
    TOTAL ← TOTAL + BILL
    CTR ← CTR + 1
    AVE ← TOTAL/CTR
    print CTR,AVE
    stop
```

COMMENTS

1. Since the first record in each group is printed differently from the rest, we need the NEWGRP parameter for the DETAIL routine.
2. Each time we have a new name, that ends one customer. We add 1 to our customer counter and add this bill to the total.
3. Similarly, reaching end of file ends the last customer. We add 1 to our customer counter and add this bill to the total.

It is possible to carry this idea of control breaks further, by dividing each group into subgroups and performing special processing whenever we reach a new subgroup as well as when we start a new group. This possibility will be explored in the exercises.

REVIEW

Terms

control break
group indicated
priming

Program Logic: Control Break

1. Before the loop:
   a. Initialize for the entire file (for example, GRAND ← 0).
   b. Read first record.
   c. Set up for first group.
   d. Process first record.
2. In the loop:
   a. Read new record.
   b. If a new group, finish up previous group and set up for new group.
   c. Process the record.
3. After the loop:
   a. Finish up last group.
   b. Print summary information for entire file.

EXERCISES

1. Write a FORTRAN program for the example on page 455.
2. There are several possible revisions to the output indicated in Figure 9.1. In general, it should be possible to make these revisions by modifying only the DETAIL routine, provided the totals are still printed in the same manner. Make the necessary changes in DETAIL for each of the following:
   (a) Group indicate the data, by department.
   (b) Group indicate by department; when a page break occurs in the middle of a department, the first line on the next page should look something like this:

   ```
   4157 (CONTINUED)    16141 945.30
   ```

   (c) Repeat (b), but also begin a new page for each new group.
   (d) Obtain output in the format illustrated in Figure 9.3.

```
                         EXPENSE TOTALS
                         ------- ------
DEPARTMENT NUMBER 100             SALESPERSON        EXPENSES
                                     10000            1000.00
                                     10001            1000.00

                               DEPARTMENT TOTAL:      2000.00


DEPARTMENT NUMBER 200             SALESPERSON        EXPENSES
                                     38907             500.00
                                     43798            1603.45
                                     44359            1000.75

                               DEPARTMENT TOTAL:      3104.20


DEPARTMENT NUMBER 300             SALESPERSON        EXPENSES
                                     32987             984.50

                               DEPARTMENT TOTAL:       984.50


DEPARTMENT NUMBER 12050           SALESPERSON        EXPENSES
                                     33498              35.50

                               DEPARTMENT TOTAL:        35.50


                                  GRAND TOTAL:        8565.20
```

Figure 9.3

3. Do the following for the example on page 458.
   (a) Give the algorithm for the DETAIL subroutine.
   (b) Modify the DETAIL algorithm so that no customer's order appears split over two pages. You may assume that each order is limited (by the size of the order form, perhaps) to seven items.
   (c) Which steps in the main program algorithm are "setup" steps? Which are "cleanup?" Which are "process record?" Which are initialization and summary for the entire file?
   (d) Modify the main program so that only the total bills are printed (without the list of individual items).
4. Give algorithms and variable lists for each of the following:
   (a) Each data record has name, course number, and letter grade. Records are grouped by name. Output should be group indicated by name (similar to Figure 9.2). For each person, print number of courses taken and number of courses failed.
   (b) Each data record has department (6 characters), name, rank (4 characters), and salary. Records are grouped by department. Output should be similar to that in Figure 9.1. For each department, print the number of full professors (rank = 'PROF') and the average salary. Also count the departments.
   (c) Modify the algorithm of (b) to also find the department with the highest average salary.
   (d) Each record contains a state abbreviation (2 characters), a city name (20 characters), and a population figure. Records are grouped by state. Output should be similar to that of Figure 9.3. For each state, print the total population of the cities given, and count the cities with population over 500,000.
   (e) Modify the algorithm of (d) to also find the total number of cities listed with population over 500,000 and the average population of all the cities listed (for the entire file).
   (f) Each data record has department number, employee number, and hourly wage. Use output similar to that in Figure 9.2. For each department, print the number of the person with the lowest hourly wage; also print the number of the employee in the entire company with the lowest hourly wage.
5. Give FORTRAN programs for each of the algorithms of Exercise 4.
6. Each record contains a numerical grade, a course number, and a name. The records are in ascending order based on the numerical grade.

   The letter grade is calculated by the rule: 0–59.99 F, 60–69.99 D, 70–79.99 C, 80–89.99 B, and 90–100 A. Give an algorithm to generate the report illustrated in Figure 9.4.

   [*Hint:* Some preliminary processing of the data may be needed prior to determining if you have a new group.]
7. Write the program for the algorithm of Exercise 6.
8. Each data record contains an ID number for a sample steel rod and the measured length of that particular sample. The records are arranged in ascending order based on the length of the samples. The report format of Figure 9.5 groups the samples; for example, the heading "1–2 inches" means "between 1 and 2 but not including 2." Give an algorithm to generate this report.

   See the hint of Exercise 6. Notice that there may be "gaps" in the groups. After "16–17 inches" might come "23–24 inches."
9. Write the program for the algorithm of Exercise 8.
10. Student records contain social security number, name, section number, course name,

```
GRADE     NAME             COURSE
-----     ----             ------
  F       XXXX...X          XXX
          XXXX...X          XXX
              .
              .
              .
  D       XXXX...X          XXX
              .
              .
              .
          (and so on)
```

Figure 9.4

```
   GROUP        SAMPLE #      LENGTH
   -----        --------      ------
1-2 INCHES        XXXX        XXX.XXX
                  XXXX        XXX.XXX
                    .            .
                    .            .
                    .            .
     xxx SAMPLES IN THIS GROUP

2-3 INCHES        XXXX        XXX.XXX
                    .            .
                    .            .
                    .            .
            (and so on)
```

Figure 9.5

credit hours, sex, class (FR, SO, JR, or SR), school (1 digit), major code (3 digits), and grade (A, B, C, D, F, W, or P).

(a) The records are grouped by section number. Print a report which lists the students (social security number, name, and grade) in each section. It should begin each new section on a new page, with section number, course name, and hours of credit at the top of the page, and with pages numbered from 1 on up in each section. Put 24 students on a page, double spaced. At the bottom of the last page for each section print a count of the students in that section.

(b) The records are grouped by social security number. Print a grade report, "group indicated" by student. Each line contains course name, grade, credit hours, and total quality points (earned credit hours times 4.0 for A, 3.0 for B, 2.0 for C, 1.0 for D, 0.0 for F, W, or P). After each student's list, print her grade point average. This is the total quality points divided by the total credit hours, with W and P grades ignored.

Use a subprogram to calculate quality points earned and to tell whether or not the course should be included in the grade point average.

(c) The records are grouped by course name. Print a report with lines containing course name, number of A's, number of B's (and so on), and total number of students. Notice that there is only one line of output per course name.

11. Each data record contains division number, department number, and employee number. The records are grouped by division, and within each division by department. Give an algorithm to generate the report illustrated in Figure 9.6. This an example of what is called a multiple level control break.

[*Hint:* Each new record could be the start of a new division; in addition, it could be the first record of a new department within the same division.]

12. Each of these exercises refers to Exercise 4. State what assumptions you make on the order of the data.

```
DIVISION   DEPARTMENT           EMPLOYEE
--------   ----------           --------
  xxxx       xxxx                 xxxxx
                                  xxxxx
                                  xxxxx
                                  xxxxx

                       xxx EMPLOYEES IN DEPT xxxx

             xxxx                 xxxxx
                                  xxxxx
                                  xxxxx

                       xxx EMPLOYEES IN DEPT xxxx

xxxx EMPLOYEES IN xxx DEPARTMENTS IN DIVISION xxx

 xxxx        xxxx                 xxxxx
                                  xxxxx
                .
                .
                .
           (and so on)
```

Figure 9.6

(a) Modify 4(b) to print a report group indicated by department, and by rank within departments.

(b) For 4(d) create a report group indicated by state, which lists cities group indicated by size, as shown here

```
xx          0- 49999 xxxxx....xxx
        50000-100000 xxxxx....xxx


   (and so on, in steps of 50,000)
```

13. Suppose the records of Exercise 10 are grouped by course name and within each course name by section.

(a) Print a report group indicated by course name and section, similar to Figure 9.6. No summary information is desired.

(b) Print a report group indicated by course name, which for each section prints how many of each grade (A, B, and so on) were earned. For each course name, print a message telling how many sections of that course there were.

10

MORE ON FORMAT

10.1 THE SLASH (/) FORMAT CODE

This chapter fills in some details concerning formats. In this section we examine the slash (/) format code. In the next we examine how the FORMAT statement interacts with READ and WRITE statements. This interaction matches variables to individual formats within the overall FORMAT statement.

In Section 10.3 we detail the basic form of various types of individual formats allowed, such as I, F, and X.

The slash format is used to let a single READ read a number of records, or to let a single WRITE or PRINT statement write a number of lines. As an example, consider writing a heading on a page using five WRITE statements referring to the following formats:

```
2000 FORMAT('1',20X,'PAYROLL')
2001 FORMAT(' ',20X,'-------')
2002 FORMAT('0','EMP. NO.',4X,'HOURS',5X,'RATE',9X,'PAY')
2003 FORMAT(' ','---- ---',4X,'-----',5X,'----',9X,'---')
2004 FORMAT('0')
```

These WRITEs will produce the following actions with each format:

2000—Print the word PAYROLL, centered.

2001—Underline the word PAYROLL.

2002—Print column headings.

2003—Underline the column headings.

2004—Skip two lines prior to detail lines.

The slash code (/) allows us to combine the five WRITE and FORMAT statements into the following single WRITE and FORMAT

```
      WRITE(*,2000)
 2000 FORMAT('1',20X,'PAYROLL'/
     $        ' ',20X,'-------'/
     $        '0','EMP. NO.',4X,'HOURS',5X,'RATE',9X,'PAY'/
     $        ' ','---- ---',4X,'-----',5X,'----',9X,'---'//)
```

In essence, we have taken the first four FORMAT statements and combined them into a single statement with slashes between them; the last FORMAT has been replaced by the two slashes at the end of our new FORMAT. The action of the slashes between portions of the FORMAT causes the printer to go to the next line. After the slash, we place the portion of the FORMAT describing that next line, *including the carriage control for that line*. (For easy readability, we have placed the format for that next line on the next line of our program, so that each line of the FORMAT corresponds to one line of the heading. The indentation pattern in the FORMAT statement also makes the FORMAT more readable.)

Placing a slash between two portions of a FORMAT statement will always cause the printer to go to the next line on the page. If we place two slashes between portions of the statement, the printer will go to the next line twice, with the result that there will be a blank line in the output. Thus, a slash followed by a double space carriage control (/'0') could be replaced by two slashes followed by a single space carriage control (//' '). As a general rule, if we place N slashes between portions of our FORMAT statement, this will result in N−1 blank lines. Any blank lines caused by carriage control will be in addition to these.

If we place a slash at the *end* of the FORMAT statement, the printer will again go to the next line, but then it will have nothing to print on that line. This will cause a blank line. Likewise, two slashes at the end of the FORMAT will cause two blank lines. In general, N slashes at the end of the FORMAT will cause N blank lines to appear on the output. In our example we have two slashes at the end of the FORMAT, which will give us two blank lines in our output.

In summary, then:

1. N slashes between two portions of a FORMAT statement will cause N−1 blank lines in the output (one slash causes 0 blank lines, placing the printer on the very next line).
2. N slashes at the end of a FORMAT statement will cause N blank lines in the output.
3. It happens that N slashes at the *beginning* of the FORMAT also cause N blank lines.

All these rules apply to FORMAT statements used for output. There are similar rules for a FORMAT statement used with a READ.

1. N slashes between two portions of the FORMAT cause N−1 records to be skipped (one slash causes 0 records to be skipped, thus moving to the very next record).
2. N slashes at the beginning or the end of the FORMAT statement cause N records to be skipped.

The slash is more commonly used in FORMATs associated with WRITE statements than in FORMATs for READ statements.

One additional item concerning the slash code is that it is considered a separator like the comma; therefore, one does not have to use commas with the slash code.

REVIEW

Slash (/)

1. On input, the remainder of the current record is skipped, and I/O control passes to the beginning of the next input record.
2. On output, the current record is complete; a new record is initiated, and I/O control proceeds to the beginning of that new record.

EXERCISES

1. Write a WRITE statement and a FORMAT to skip a blank line, print the value of I in ten columns, skip three lines, print the values of J and K in five columns each, and then skip six lines. (Assume I, J, K are all integers.)

2. Write a WRITE statement and a FORMAT to advance to a new page, print PAGE in columns 1−4 and the value of PAGENO in columns 6−8, then skip two lines, print equal signs in columns 5−20, and finally skip two more lines.

3. Write a READ statement and a FORMAT to read the values of I, J, K (all integers) from columns 1−10 of three successive input records.

4. Give a WRITE statement and a FORMAT to print the following output, where XXXX's show where the variables should be printed.

```
XXXXX CUSTOMERS HAD A TOTAL BILL OF XXXXXXXX.XX
THE AVERAGE BILL WAS XXXXX.XX
```

10.2 REPETITION FACTORS, GROUPING, AND REUSE

Repetition Factors and Grouping

It is convenient mentally to divide the individual types of format into two categories:

1. The first category consists of formats which relate to a variable in the **I/O list** (the list of variables in the corresponding READ or WRITE statement).

Of the formats we have studied, the following are in this first category.

```
I
F
A
```

Let us refer to these as **variable-related** formats.

2. The second category consists of formats which do not process variables. Included are these types of format:

```
literal (including carriage control)
X
/
```

These formats either cause messages to be printed or else control where the next variable is read or written. We will refer to these as **control** formats.

NOTE. The terms "variable-related" and "control" are not standard terminology. We will use them only for this chapter, to distinguish between the two types. (The standard terms are "repeatable" and "nonrepeatable," respectively.)

As we have already learned, the "variable-related" formats I, F, and A may be preceded by **repetition factors**. We may have a FORMAT such as

```
1000 FORMAT(A5,3I4,F7.2,2F7.1,2X,12A1)
```

This FORMAT has the same effect as writing

```
1000 FORMAT(A5,I4,I4,I4,F7.2,F7.1,F7.1,2X,A1,A1,A1,
   $       A1,A1,A1,A1,A1,A1,A1,A1,A1)
```

The "repetition factors" are:

```
 3 in 3I4
 2 in 2F7.1
12 in 12A1
```

These repetition factors must be nonzero, unsigned integer constants. Repetition factors such as −3, 0, or +5 are not allowed. (However, a repetition factor of 1 is allowed.)

Likewise, it is possible to repeat groups of individual formats. For example, consider the following:

```
1000 FORMAT(I2,3X,F5.2,I2,3X,F5.2,I2,3X,F5.2,I2,3X,F5.2)
```

Since the pattern "I2,3X,F5.2" is repeated in this FORMAT statement, we may simplify the statement to

```
1000 FORMAT(4(I2,3X,F5.2))
```

The repetition factor 4 indicates that the pattern within parentheses is to be repeated four times.

The general form of this grouping of formats is:

```
r(list)
```

where

"r" is a nonzero, unsigned integer constant, the repetition factor

"list" is a list of individual formats (one or more), as usual separated by commas.

The effect of using this type of format description is as if the formats in the given list had been written out repeatedly.

NOTES.

1. An exception to this last statement occurs when the FORMAT statement is reused. This will be discussed shortly.
2. A repetition factor of 1 may be omitted. The format portions

   ```
   1(3X,2A1,I5)
   ```

   and

   ```
   (3X,2A1,I5)
   ```

   are identical in meaning. However, a repetition of 1 can be useful in affecting how the FORMAT statement is reused, as we will also discuss shortly.

The following illustrate straightforward uses of repetition factors and grouping:

```
1000 FORMAT(I5,3X,10(I2,2X))
2000 FORMAT(A10,2X,5(A2,2X,F4.2),4X,I5)
3000 FORMAT(' ',10X,'LIST OF DATA'/' ',10(I4,2X,I4))
```

In each case, the grouping provides a convenient shorthand for a much longer list of individual formats. Without the grouping, we might write:

```
1000 FORMAT(I5,3X,I2,2X,I2,2X,I2,2X,I2,2X,I2,2X,I2,2X,
    $       I2,2X,I2,2X,I2,2X,I2,2X)
2000 FORMAT(A10,2X,A2,2X,F4.2,A2,2X,F4.2,
    $       A2,2X,F4.2,A2,2X,F4.2,A2,2X,F4.2,4X,I5)
3000 FORMAT(' ',10X,'LIST OF DATA'/' ',I4,2X,I4,I4,2X,I4,
    $       I4,2X,I4,I4,2X,I4,I4,2X,I4,I4,2X,I4,I4,2X,I4,
    $       I4,2X,I4,I4,2X,I4,I4,2X,I4)
```

It is possible to use combinations of grouping and simple repetition factors such as:

```
1000 FORMAT(A20,3(I5,5A1))
2000 FORMAT(10(A4,2X),5I2,2(I2,3F5.1))
3000 FORMAT(5(A3,3(A1,I2,A2),F7.1))
```

Written longhand, these would be

```
1000 FORMAT(A20,I5,A1,A1,A1,A1,A1,I5,A1,A1,A1,A1,A1,
    $       I5,A1,A1,A1,A1,A1)
2000 FORMAT(A4,2X,A4,2X,A4,2X,A4,2X,A4,2X,A4,2X,A4,2X,A4,2X,
    $       A4,2X,A4,2X,I2,I2,I2,I2,I2,I2,F5.1,F5.1,F5.1,
    $       I2,F5.1,F5.1,F5.1)
3000 FORMAT(A3,A1,I2,A2,A1,I2,A2,A1,I2,A2,F7.1,
    $       A3,A1,I2,A2,A1,I2,A2,A1,I2,A2,F7.1,
    $       A3,A1,I2,A2,A1,I2,A2,A1,I2,A2,F7.1.
    $       A3,A1,I2,A2,A1,I2,A2,A1,I2,A2,F7.1
    $       A3,A1,I2,A2,A1,I2,A2,A1,I2,A2,F7.1)
```

CAUTION. For some systems, there is a limit of three levels of parentheses within the outer pair of parentheses.

FORMAT Statements and I/O Lists

Using the "control" type "/" and X formats, along with repetition factors and grouping, we may write very complex FORMAT statements. In this subsection, we examine exactly how the FORMAT statement and I/O statement work together to determine what gets read or printed. We do so in the context of the types of format we are presently familiar with (I, F, A, literal, X, /). The concepts will also apply to new types of format to be introduced later.

The computer will process the FORMAT statement and the list of variables in the I/O statement jointly. In getting the next individual format, it treats the FORMAT as if there were no repetition factors or grouping. However, as we will see shortly, the grouping does enter into the "reuse of format."

A rough algorithm may be expressed as follows ("I/O list" refers to the list of variables in the READ or WRITE statement).

```
loop
   get next individual format
   case
     1(end of FORMAT)
        case
          1(variables all processed) exit
          2(variables left) reuse FORMAT
        endcase
     2('control' format) process the format
     3('variable' format)
        case
          1(variables all processed) exit
          2(variables left) process next variable in I/O
             list, using given format
        endcase
   endcase
endloop
stop procesing of I/O statement
```

There are several noteworthy consequences of this algorithm:

1. After reading or writing the last variable in the variable list, the computer will process any remaining "control" formats. This may cause the printing of further messages or the skipping of records (due to literal or / formats). For example,

```
         WRITE(*,2000) COUNT
    2000 FORMAT(/'0THERE WERE ',I7,' BONUSES PAID.'//)
```

   (The message "BONUSES PAID." and the two slashes are not ignored.)

2. After all variables are processed, the I/O processing may terminate either by reaching the end of the FORMAT or by reaching a "variable-related" format. Thus, we are allowed to have "more FORMAT than we need." For example,

```
         INTEGER A(10,12),N
              .
              .
              .
         WRITE(*,1000) (A(3,J),J=1,N)
    1000 FORMAT(' ',12(I7,3X))
```

   (This example prints up to 12 numbers from the third row of A.)

3. There may be "less FORMAT than we need." If the computer reaches the end of the FORMAT statement with variables left to be processed, it will "reuse the FORMAT" as discussed below.

   CAUTION. It should be obvious that, if an I/O statement contains a variable, there must be at least one "variable-related" individual format in the corresponding FORMAT statement.

Reuse of FORMAT

When the end of the FORMAT statement is reached and there are still variables in the I/O list to be processed, the computer will "reuse the FORMAT." Exactly what this means depends on whether or not the FORMAT statement contains any grouping.

These FORMAT statements contain no grouping:

```
    1000 FORMAT(' ',I5,3X,F7.2,4X,A9)
    2000 FORMAT(10I7)
```

However, these similar FORMATs do contain grouping:

```
    1000 FORMAT(' ',I5,2(3X,F7.2,4X,A9))
    2000 FORMAT(10(I7,2X)
```

A FORMAT statement with no grouping contains only one set of parentheses, surrounding the entire list of formats.

In the simplest instance, the FORMAT contains no grouping. In this case, we may easily describe how the computer will reuse the FORMAT.

1. The computer will proceed to a new record. For reading, this means ignoring any further information on the present line of input, going on to the next input line. For printing, this means starting a new line of output.
2. The computer will go back to the first individual format in the FORMAT statement and resume processing from there (using the procedure outlined earlier).

Earlier, this process was utilized in reading and printing arrays, as in this example:

```
          INTEGER A(1000),N,I
             .
             .
          READ(*,1000) A
     1000 FORMAT(12I6)
             .
             .
          WRITE(*,2000) (I,A(I),I=1,N)
     2000 FORMAT(' ',I5,4X,I6,10X,I5,4X,I6,10X,I5,4X,I6)
```

When the FORMAT contains grouping, the process is similar. However, the computer does *not* automatically return to the beginning of the FORMAT statement.

1. The computer will proceed to a new record.
2. The computer will go back to the beginning of the group terminated by the next-to-last right parenthesis.

NOTE. After returning to the indicated location in the FORMAT the entire FORMAT from that point on is reused. In the examples that follow, the arrows highlight the "group terminated by the next-to-last right parenthesis," and the brackets indicate which portion of the FORMAT is then reused.

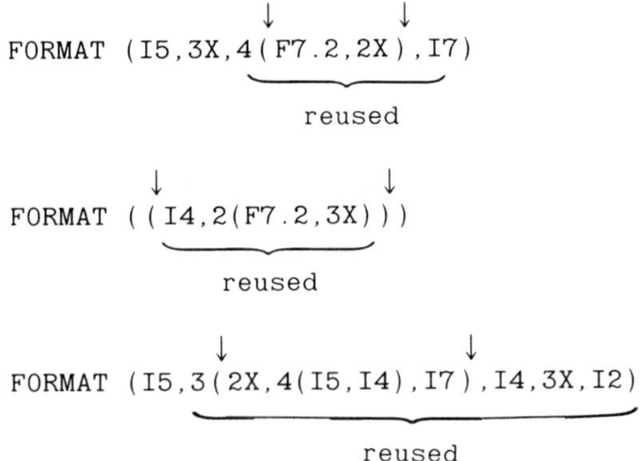

It is relatively easy, given a FORMAT, to determine which portion is reused. It is somewhat more difficult to write a FORMAT to achieve the desired results. The following examples illustrate some useful techniques.

Consider the FORMAT used in an earlier example:

```
     WRITE(*,2000) (I,A(I),I=1,N)
2000 FORMAT(' ',I5,4X,I6,10X,I5,4X,I6,10X,I5,4X,I6)
```

This is used to print elements of the array A, along with their subscripts, three per line. We may simplify the FORMAT to

```
2000 FORMAT(' ',I5,4X,I6,2(10X,I5,4X,I6))
```

However, this destroys the reuse of the FORMAT. To cause the entire FORMAT to be reused, as desired, we need to include an additional set of parentheses:

```
2000 FORMAT((' ',I5,4X,I6,2(10X,I5,4X,I6)))
```

Now the next-to-last right parenthesis terminates a group consisting of the entire FORMAT. (Notice that a "repetition factor" of 1 is very useful in this example.)

Another approach to this problem is to write

```
2000 FORMAT((' ',3(I5,4X,I6,10X)))
```

Strictly speaking, this is not the same as the original FORMAT; there is an extra "10X" at the end. However, this will not cause any problems.

This concept of including an "extra" set of parentheses in the FORMAT is very useful. This extra set serves no purpose other than to make the reuse of FORMAT occur in the desired manner. For example, a common error is writing code such as

```
     INTEGER A(500)
           .
           .
     WRITE(*,1000) A
1000 FORMAT(' ',10(3X,I8))
                ‾‾‾‾‾‾‾‾‾‾
                  reused
```

On the second and all subsequent lines, there will be no carriage-control character. The output will not line up properly. To fix this, we write

```
1000 FORMAT((' ',10(3X,I8)))
           ‾‾‾‾‾‾‾‾‾‾‾‾‾‾‾‾‾
                reused
```

As another example, consider this WRITE and FORMAT used to print headings along with two arrays.

```
      INTEGER ID(150),N,I
      REAL PAY(150)
        .
        .
      WRITE(*,1000) (ID(I),PAY(I),I=1,N)
 1000 FORMAT('1LIST OF EMPLOYEES AND PAY'/
     $       ' ---- -- --------- --- ---'//
     $       (' ',4X,I5,7X,F9.2))
```

The "extra" pair of parentheses in the third line of the FORMAT causes that line alone to be repeated. The portion of the FORMAT which prints headings is not reused.

Similar applications of FORMAT reuse are explored in the exercises.

Pitfalls

The major pitfall to avoid when using grouping occurs when the FORMAT is reused. As was pointed out in the previous examples, it may be necessary to include an extra set of parentheses whose sole purpose is to control which portion of the FORMAT is reused. Two common errors are exemplified by these FORMATs:

```
 1000 FORMAT(I7,3(2X,F7.2))
 2000 FORMAT(' ',10(5X,F5.2))
```

In both instances, if we do in fact desire that the whole FORMAT be reused, we must insert additional parentheses:

```
 1000 FORMAT((I7,3(2X,F7.2)))
 2000 FORMAT((' ',10(5X,F5.2)))
```

COMMENT. In the original (incorrect) version of the second example, the carriage-control character would be missing on the second and subsequent lines. The computer would take one of the spaces generated by the 5X format as carriage control, resulting in output in this form:

```
 xx.xx  xx.xx  .....
xx.xx  xx.xx  .....
xx.xx  xx.xx  .....
     and so on
```

REVIEW

"Variable-related" (repeatable) formats: I, F, A

"Control" (nonrepeatable) formats: literal, X, /

FORMAT statement: list of individual formats, which may be either:

an I, F, A, literal, X, or /
a repeated I, F, or A, such as 10I6
a group with a repetition factor, such as 10(I6,3X,I4)

Repetition factor: nonzero unsigned integer (may be omitted if 1).

COMMENT. List items are separated by commas. However, the commas may be omitted before and after slash formats (/).

Summary of I/O Processing

1. Terminate when either end of FORMAT or "variable-related" format is reached and all variables have been processed.
2. Reuse FORMAT (or portion of FORMAT) when end of FORMAT (with variables remaining in I/O list) is reached.
3. Otherwise simply process "control" format or "variable-related" format with next variable in I/O list.

Reuse of FORMAT

1. Proceed to next record.
2. Go back:
   (a) to beginning of FORMAT if no grouping;
   (b) otherwise, to start of group terminated by next-to-last right parenthesis.

NOTE. Programmer may have to insert "extra" parentheses to obtain reuse of desired portion of FORMAT.

EXERCISES

1. Assuming that X, Y, Z, and W are REAL variables with values 1.0, 2.0, 3.0, and 4.0, respectively, tell exactly what gets printed by each of the following.

(a)
```
      WRITE(*,2000) X
 2000 FORMAT(' ',F7.2,' IS X ',F7.2,' IS Y '/
     $       ' ','THE VALUE OF Z AND W ARE ',F7.2)
```
(b) `WRITE(*,2000)X,Y [same FORMAT as (a)]`

(c) `WRITE(*,2000)X,Y,Z`

(d) `WRITE(*,2000)X,Y,Z,W`

2. Repeat Exercise 1 with this FORMAT:

```
 2000 FORMAT((' ',2('NUMBER IS',F7.2),F7.2))
```

3. For each of the following FORMATs, create a FORMAT of similar meaning, with no grouping or repetition factors.

(a) `1000 FORMAT(3(I4,2X),2I5)`

(b) `2000 FORMAT(' ',3F7.2,2(4X,I5,3I2))`
(c) `3000 FORMAT(4F2.1,3(2F7.2,2X,2(I5,2X,I4)),4(I2,2X))`

4. For each of the following, tell which portion of the FORMAT would be reused if the end of the FORMAT were reached with variables left in the I/O list.
   (a) `1000 FORMAT(F7.2,3(F6.2,2X,I5),I7)`
   (b) `2000 FORMAT(' ',4('ARRAY ELEMENT IS',F10.4))`
   (c) `3000 FORMAT((' ',4('ARRAY ELEMENT IS',F10.4))`
   (d) `4000 FORMAT('1LIST'/'----'/' ',10I10)`
   (e) `5000 FORMAT('1LIST'/'----'/(' ',10I10))`
   (f) `6000 FORMAT(' ',10(I5,4X)/(' ',6X,10(I5,4X)))`
   (g) `7000 FORMAT(A20,(9I6,A3))`
5. Suppose we have a 7×9 INTEGER array ARR to be printed. Give a single WRITE and FORMAT for each of the following.
   (a) Print the array, one row per line, single spaced below the previous output (no labelling required).
   (b) Repeat (a), but print on a new page of output.
   (c) Repeat (b), but add appropriate row and column labels (ROW 1, COLUMN 3, and so on.)
6. Suppose that the array ARR of exercise 5 is 7×30. Repeat (a)–(c) of Exercise 5, printing each row of the array as three lines each containing ten numbers, with a blank line between rows.
7. (a) Give code to print an INTEGER array A of size 1000 in this form:

```
x x x x x x x x x x
  x x x x x x x x x
      and so on
```

   Ten numbers are printed on the first line, nine on each subsequent line.
   (b) Modify (a) to include a variable N which tells how many items from the array should be printed.
8. We have a 23×32 REAL array B, and variables M and N telling how many rows and columns, respectively, are in use.
   (a) Give a single WRITE and FORMAT to print row 7, twelve numbers per line.
   (b) Revise (a) to begin row 7 two lines below the previous line of output.
   (c) Give code to print the entire array on a new page. Each row should be printed as in (b). [*Caution*: As was discussed in Chapter 8, a nested implied DO is probably not appropriate because of the variable N telling how many columns to print.]
9. Repeat Exercise 8, but causing the second and subsequent lines printed for each row to contain only 11 numbers, indented similarly to the illustration in Exercise 7(a).

10.3 INDIVIDUAL FORMAT SPECIFICATIONS

In this section we examine some new format specifications. In addition, we present a more complete description of the familiar format types we have been using. (However, some advanced features are not covered.)

Numeric Editing

The term **editing** describes the action of an individual format during the processing of a READ or WRITE statement.

Output editing occurs when the format is used with a WRITE statement. It determines the form of the record being created by the WRITE statement. **Input editing**, used with a READ statement, determines how the data on the input record is interpreted by the READ statement. In describing how a particular format works, it is necessary to describe its action for both input editing and output editing.

For editing numeric data we may use the I, F, E, or G **edit descriptors** (formats). We discuss each of these in turn.

I Format

For editing INTEGER data, the I format is used. Its form is

Iw

The "w" indicates that the field to be edited occupies "w" positions. The corresponding item in the I/O list must be of the type INTEGER.

On input, any leading blanks are ignored; however, if the field is completely blank it is treated as zero. Any blanks other than leading blanks are treated as zeroes. (As a result, in creating data cards we should right justify the number within the allotted number of positions.) The data in the field must be in the form of an integer constant, with an optional sign.

For an I5 format, consider these possible input fields.

```
bb2b4
b-15b
+1327
b1327
```

In the first two, the blanks other than the leading blanks are treated as zeroes. Hence, these two data items will be interpreted as 204 and −150, respectively. Because the sign is optional, the final two examples have the same interpretation.

> **COMMENT.** Some more advanced features may be used to change this interpretation of blanks. However, it is generally more convenient to follow the practice of right justifying the input data.

On output, the Iw causes a field of width w to be created on the output record. The output field created consists of:

1. leading blanks (0 or more);
2. a minus sign, if the value is negative (some computers may also print plus signs); and
3. an unsigned integer constant with no leading zeroes.

Thus, the number will appear right justified, with the sign (if any) immediately prior to the first digit.

These rules imply that for an I6 format, these resulting fields are possible:

```
bbbbb0
bbbb-3
-19053
269471
```

COMMENT. If the number of characters needed to output the number is more than w, the entire field is filled with asterisks.

The output line created by this short program:

```
     INTEGER I,J
     I = 493706
     J = -35
     WRITE(*,3000) I,J
3000 FORMAT(' I = ',I5,' J = ',I2)
     STOP
     END
```

is

```
I = ***** J = **
```

The number 493706 requires six characters, and the number −35 requires three. However, the number +35 would require only two characters; the plus sign would not be printed.

F Format

One possible edit descriptor for REAL values is the F descriptor, whose form is

Fw.d

This indicates that the input or output field occupies "w" positions, and that the fractional part contains "d" digits.

There are several possible forms of input which may be used with this Fw.d format.

First, the input may consist of "w" characters with no explicit decimal point. In this case the rightmost "d" digits will be considered as constituting the fractional portion of the input. For example, the following strings, when read using an F8.3 format, yield the indicated values.

```
bb125652   125.652
bbbbb125      .125
bbb-3bbb    -3.
bbbb1bb3     1.003
bbbbbb32      .032
```

The data should be right justified within the field when using this form of input.

Second, the input may consist of "w" characters, including an explicit decimal point. In this case the explicit decimal point overrides the "d" of the format. With an F6.1 format, each of the following data items (except the last) yields a value of 1.5.

```
bbbb15
bbb1.5
1.5bbb
b1.5bb
+1.5bb
b1.52b
```

The last yields 1.52 as its input value.

Third, the data may appear in exponential form. For example, the following input data would be valid and would yield the indicated values. (Recall that the "exponent portion" indicates the power of ten by which the given number is to be multiplied.)

bb1.6E3	$1.6 \times 10^3 = 1600.0$
3.59E-2	.0359
.61Eb+1	6.1

The "w" in the Fw.d must be large enough to take in all the characters of the input data, including those in the exponent portion of the data.

The exponent portion contains:

the letter E

0 or more blanks

an integer constant, with optional sign

Of course, if the exponent is negative the minus sign must appear.

Alternatively, the exponent may appear simply as an integer constant which *must* contain a sign. These three examples have the same meaning as those given earlier:

```
bb1.6+3
b3.59-2
bb.61+1
```

Finally, the decimal point may be omitted; if so, the "d" in the Fw.d determines how many digits are in the fractional portion. For an F9.3 format, the data given below will generate the indicated values.

bbb1473E2	$1.473 \times 10^2 = 147.3$
bb1524E-1	0.1524
bb21325+2	2132.5

(Care is required when the decimal point is omitted in conjunction with an exponent. It is easy to create faulty data.)

On output, the Fw.d format creates a real number in the usual decimal fraction notation. The string of characters created consists of

1. 0 or more leading blanks;
2. possibly a minus sign (some computers may also print plus signs); and
3. the value of the number being output, containing a decimal point, and rounded to "d" digits to the right of the decimal point.

The number produced is right justified within the field. As with the I format, the entire field is filled with asterisks if the field width "w" is too small for the number to be output.

For example, for an internal value of 17.127, these formats yield the indicated output:

```
F9.3    bbb17.127
F6.3       17.127
F5.3        *****
F5.2        17.13
F5.1        b17.1
F5.0        bb17.
```

E Format

Another format which may be used for reading and writing REAL values is the E format, written as

Ew.d

On input, the Ew.d edit descriptor has *exactly* the same interpretation as the Fw.d.

On output, the Ew.d format will create a number printed in exponential form. This is especially convenient when printing very large or very small numbers. For example,

```
4600000000000000000000000000.0 and
0.000000000000000000000000012
```

would not be conveniently printed using the F format.

In the Ew.d, as in the Fw.d, the "w" indicates the total number of positions occupied on the output record. The fraction printed will be rounded to "d" decimal places. For example, for an E13.5 format these values yield the indicated output.

```
      1.63    bb0.16300E+01
  -.0173567   b-0.17357E-01
 16000000.2   bb0.16000E+08
      -0.15   b-0.15000E+00
```

Observe that:

1. The exponent will occupy four columns. This must be taken into account in determining the necessary value of "w". (Likewise, the decimal point and minus sign, if present, will occupy columns.)

2. The numbers are printed in *normalized* form, with no nonzero digits before the decimal point, and with the first digit following the decimal point not a zero.

COMMENTS.

1. On some computers, the 0 before the decimal point may not be printed.
2. On some computers, a plus sign may be printed for positive numbers.
3. The exponent is limited in this form to −99 to +99. For larger exponents, the printed number would be in a slightly different form. However, this is not likely to occur in student programs.
4. Finally, some computers would print the exponents without the letter E. In the examples just given, the numbers would appear as

```
bb0.16300+001 (exponent part is +001 rather than E+01)
b-0.17357-001
bb0.16000+008
b-0.15000+000
```

(The exponent still occupies four columns.)

As with the F and I formats, the field will be completely filled with asterisks if the width "w" allocated is too small. However, for the Ew.d format we may avoid this possibility, since we can determine precisely how wide a field is needed. In addition to the "d" digits of the fraction, we will want to allow:

4 columns for the exponent
1 column for the decimal point
1 column for the 0 before the decimal point
1 column for the sign

This, in writing Ew.d, we will always make sure that "w" is at least 7 larger than "d".

G Format

As we have mentioned, the E format is most useful when dealing with either very large or very small numbers. When the numbers are relatively small, the F format may be desirable. For example,

```
  17.13
-103.05
   0.01
```

are perhaps more readable than the equivalent exponential notation

```
 0.17130E+02
-0.10305E+03
 0.10000E-01
```

The purpose of the G format is to allow the computer to decide which form to use, based on the magnitude of the particular value being printed.

The form of the G edit descriptor is Gw.d. On input, it behaves exactly the same as Fw.d or Ew.d. On output, the interpretation is fairly complex. We can summarize what happens by an example. For the format G9.2, and the given values to be printed, we obtain the indicated results:

```
  0.01  b0.10E-01  same as E9.2
  0.15  b0.15bbbb  same as F5.2,4(' ')
  1.53  bb1.5bbbb  same as F5.1,4(' ')
 11.27  bb11.bbbb  same as F5.0,4(' ')
100.00  b0.10E+03  same as E9.2
```

To be more precise, if N is the absolute value of the number, then:

1. For $N < 0.1$ or $N \geq 10^d$, the result is the same as using Ew.d.
2. Otherwise, the result is the same as using

```
Fw'.d',4(' ')
```

Here w' is w-4, and d' depends on the size of N, as shown here:

```
case
   1(N<1) d' ← d
   2(N<10)d' ← d-1
   3(N<100) d' ← d-2
        .
        .
        .
   'd'(N<10^(d-1)) d' ← 1
   'd+1'(N<10^d) d' ← 0
endcase
```

The net effect is to print the given number in the space allotted for the fractional part, with blanks in the space allotted for the exponent part. The change in d' for different sized numbers ensures that there will be sufficient space to print the number.

The rules just given may be used, if necessary, to determine in advance what the output will look like. However, in a way, doing so violates the purpose of the G format, which is to let the computer decide on the appropriate form for the output. In brief:

> The output will be in an "appropriate" F format, if reasonable; otherwise in an E format.

Character Editing

The A format is used for reading and writing character data. Its general form is

Aw

As usual, the "w" indicates the width of the field which is read from an input record or created on an output record. As long as the value to be read or printed has length w (that is, stores w characters), the result is quite simple. On input, w characters will be read from the input record and placed into the indicated variable. On output, the w characters to be written will be placed on the output record. The following example illustrates this principle:

```
      CHARACTER*5 DEPT
      CHARACTER*9 EVAL
          .
          .
      READ(*,1000) DEPT
 1000 FORMAT(A5)
          .
          .
      EVAL='EXCELLENT'
      WRITE(*,2000) EVAL
 2000 FORMAT(' THIS PERSON DOES ',A9,' WORK.')
```

In each case the size of the variable is precisely the same as the "w" in the format. In the READ, the five characters on the input record will be placed into DEPT. The WRITE will print the nine characters of EVAL in the proper spot.

COMMENT. If we omit the "w" in the A format, the computer will assume a value of w just big enough for the values involved. The formats of the two examples just given could be written as

```
1000 FORMAT(A)
```

and

```
2000 FORMAT(' THIS PERSON DOES ',A,' WORK.')
```

Suppose we indicate the length of the item to be read or printed as "len." As we have indicated, when len = w there is no problem. The following algorithm summarizes what happens on input when len is not the same as w.

```
case
   1(len<w) reads the rightmost 'len' characters
        from the field of width w
   2(len>w) the w characters from the field
        will be placed in the variable,
        left justified with trailing blanks
endcase
```

Consider a data record as pictured below:

```
ABCDEFGHIJKLMNOPQRSTUVWXYZ
```

and this program segment:

```
      CHARACTER*6 X,Y,Z
      READ(*,1000) X,Y,Z
 1000 FORMAT(A6,A3,A8)
```

The format splits the input card into fields as indicated below by the vertical lines.

```
ABCDEF|GHI|JKLMNOPQ|RSTUVWXYZ
```

The action of the READ is:

1. For X, len = w (both are 6). Hence X receives the value 'ABCDEF'.
2. For Y, len = 6 but w = 3. The three characters from the field are placed into Y, left justified with trailing blanks. Y gets the value 'GHIbbb'.
3. For Z, len = 6 but w = 8. The rightmost six characters from the field are placed into Z; Z gets the value 'LMNOPQ'. The two leftmost characters are **truncated** (cut off).

Similarly, we may indicate what happens on output when len is not the same as w:

```
case
   1(len<w) the 'len' characters will appear
      right justified in a field of
      length w, with leading blanks.
   2(len>w) the leftmost w characters will
      be placed into the output field
endcase
```

Consider the program segment

```
      CHARACTER*5,X,Y,Z
      X = 'ABCDE'
      Y = 'FGHIJ'
      Z = 'KLMNO'
      WRITE(*,2000) X,Y,Z
 2000 FORMAT(' ',A5,A7,A3)
```

This will create an output line with fields of widths 5, 7, and 3 respectively.

1. For X, len = w = 5. The five characters of X are printed.
2. For Y, len = 5 but w = 7. The five characters of Y will be printed right justified.
3. For Z, len = 5 but w = 3. The leftmost three characters of Z will be printed. (The rightmost two characters (N and O) are truncated on the print line.)

The resulting output line, with field divisions indicated, is

```
ABCDE|bbFGHIJ|KLM
```

Positional and Literal Editing

The remaining edit descriptors we present are not used in conjunction with variables in the I/O list. Instead, they are what we have called **control** (or "nonrepeatable") descriptors. We consider the following: "apostrophe editing," H, X, T, and/.

Literals

There are two types of formats used to place messages on output records.

CAUTION. These edit descriptors may not be used in conjunction with input.

The first type is the familiar "apostrophe editing." The individual format consists of one or more characters enclosed in apostrophes (single quotes):

```
'string of characters'
```

In processing this type of format, the string of characters within the quotes (apostrophes) will be placed verbatim on the output record.

NOTES.

1. Within the quotes, blanks are significant. For example, the format

   ```
   'ABbbbCD'
   ```

   will cause seven characters to appear on the output line: A, B, three blanks, C, and D.
2. An actual apostrophe is indicated by placing two apostrophes in the message. For example,

   ```
   'DON''T'
   ```

   will cause the word DON'T to be printed.

The same effect given by using "apostrophe editing" may also be achieved with H editing. The form is

nHstring-of-length-n

For example, the apostrophe forms and H forms given here are equivalent:

```
'1'                 1H1
'SUM'               3HSUM
'bERRORS'           7HbERRORS
'EMPLOYEE LIST'     13HEMPLOYEE LIST
'ABbbbCD'           7HABbbbCD
'DON''T'            5HDON'T
```

Observe that in 5HDON'T the apostrophe appears only once; also that blank spaces are included in determining the value of "n."

COMMENT. The H format is not as convenient as apostrophe (literal) editing. The programmer must count the characters in the message in order to use the H format. The H descriptor is present in the language primarily for compatibility with earlier versions of FORTRAN. It is not suggested that you use it in your programs.

X Format

X format is an example of what is known as "positional editing." Its purpose is to determine the position from or to which the next character will be read or written. An X format determines the position for the next format processed.

The X format is written as

nX

It causes the next field to begin "n" places to the right of the end of the previous field. Consider the following illustration:

```
                 |← (15 spaces) →|
previous field         15X         next field
```

On input, the result is that 15 columns are skipped on the input record. On output, the results is that 15 blanks are placed into the output record.

COMMENT. There is a slight subtlety here. To illustrate it, consider the format

```
1000 FORMAT(9(I6,3X))
```

which might be used to read nine 6-digit numbers with three spaces between each. Now this is equivalent to

```
1000 FORMAT(I6,3X,I6,3X,I6,3X,I6,3X,I6,3X,
   $        I6,3X,I6,3X,I6,3X,I6,3X)
```

If we assume that a data record contains 80 columns, this looks like trouble. The format specifies a total of 81 columns. The final "3X" runs off the end of the record.

However, that 3X becomes operative only when it is followed by a transmittal of further data by the READ statement. It specifies that, *if* further data is read, it will be read from column 82. Since no further data is read, no error occurs.

Similarly, an X format is allowed to extend past the width of an output line, provided no further values are written to that line.

T Format

The T format, like the X format, is a "positional edit descriptor." It determines the position from which the next item is to be read or written. The form is

Tc

and the meaning is, essentially, "tab to character position c."

The following formats have the same effect:

```
1000 FORMAT(9X,I5)
2000 FORMAT(T10,I5)
```

In the first, the input record is read by "skipping nine spaces," then using the I5 format. The I5 format commences after the nine spaces.

In the second, the record is read by "tabbing to column 10," then using the I5 format. The I5 format commences at column 10, the character position reached by the use of the T10 descriptor.

Similarly, these formats have the same effect:

```
3000 FORMAT(F6.2,2X,I5,5X,I4)
3001 FORMAT(F6.2,T9,I5,T19,I4)
```

The T format can be especially useful on output. In determining its effect, we take into account that the carriage control character occupies character position 1. Hence, these formats have the same effect:

```
2000 FORMAT(' ',5X,A20,10X,I3,12X,F8.2)
2001 FORMAT(' ',T7,A20,T37,I3,T52,F8.2)
```

Either of these might be used to print NAME, AGE, and SALARY in appropriate columns. Consider, however, what we would have to do to each to move the NAME column two places to the left, the AGE column one place to the right, and leave the SALARY column alone. Using the T format, we simply change T7 to T5, change T37 to T38, and leave T52 alone. The corresponding adjustments using the X format are more difficult. (Why?)

COMMENTS.

1. Like the X, the T format really takes effect only when followed by a transmittal of values from or to the indicated position. In reading a record with 80 characters, "T81" would be allowed provided we do not follow it by the attempted reading of a variable.
2. The "c" indicated in the Tc format may be prior to the present position. For example, each of these has the same effect:

```
     READ(*,1000) I,J                READ(*,2000) J,I
1000 FORMAT(T2,I5,T10,I4)       2000 FORMAT(T10,I4,T2,I5)
```

3. When we "tab left" using Tc, with c less than the current position, we may cause fields to overlap. This can lead to quite complex results.

The following examples illustrate what can happen when Tc is used to "tab left."

```
     INTEGER I,J,K,L
     READ(*,1000) I,J,K,L
1000 FORMAT(T3,I2,T1,I5,T1,I4,T3,I4)
```

For an input record containing

```
123456789
```

I gets the value 34, J gets 12345, K gets 1234, and L gets 3456. Similarly, consider the following program segment.

```
      INTEGER I,J,K,L
      I = 111
      J = 2222
      K = 33
      L = 4444
      WRITE(*,2000) I,J,K,L
 2000 FORMAT(' ',T7,I3,T4,I4,T12,I2,T9,I4)
```

The output record has these fields:

```
Carriage
control─┐  |J  |  | L |
        bxxxxxxxxxxxx
              | I | |K |
```

Now the values are placed in the order I,J (which overwrites part of I), K, and finally L (which overwrites part of I and K). The resulting line of output is

```
bbb2222144443
```

In general, it is best to avoid "tabbing left."

/(Slash) Format

The slash format descriptor was covered in some detail in Section 10.1. Its action is:

1. On input, the remainder of the current record is skipped.
2. On output, the current record is complete; a new record is started.

REVIEW

Integer Editing

Iw—w columns

Input: blanks treated as zeroes

Output: right justified with leading blanks

**** if w too small

Real Editing

Fw.d—w columns, d digits after decimal point

Input may be:

1. right justified with assumed decimal point;

2. explicit decimal point (overrides "d"); or
3. either of above followed by exponent:
   (a) E±n, with + optional;
   (b) ±n, + not optional.

Output: right justified, with leading blanks, in usual decimal form.

Ew.d—w columns, d digits after decimal

Input: same as Fw.d

Output: normalized fraction with d digits, followed by exponent of form E±nn (4 columns for exponent)

Gw.d—w columns, d (or fewer) digits after decimal point

Input: same as Fw.d

Output: in "appropriate" F format if reasonable, otherwise same as Ew.d

Character Editing

Aw—w columns

Input: read w characters, place into variable
if len < w, left truncate
if len > w, right pad with blanks

Output: print w characters
if len < w, right justify in output field
if len > w, right truncate

A Input: read len characters

Output: print len characters

Literals (output only)

'string of characters' (apostrophe twice, for example, `'DON''T'`)
nHstring-of-length-n

Positional Editing

nX—position n places further to right in record

Tc—position at character position c
(on output, carriage control is position 1)

/—terminate present record, move to new record

EXERCISES

1. When would it be a good idea to use E format? What about G format?

2. In each of the following, you are given a program segment and an associated data record. Tell what values each variable is given. (I and J are INTEGER; X and Y are REAL; A, B, and C are CHARACTER*3.)

(a) Record: 123456789012345678901234567890

```
     READ(*,1000) I,X,Y,A,B,C
1000 FORMAT(I4,F6.2,E5.1,A2,A3,A4)
```

(b) Record: same as (a)

```
     READ(*,1000) B,I,J,X,Y
1000 FORMAT(A,I6,2X,I2,2G3.1)
```

(c) Record: same as (a)

```
     READ(*,1000) I,J,X,Y,A,B,C
1000 FORMAT(I4,T3,I4,T6,F6.3,T4,F6.3,
    $        T5,A3,T10,A,T7,A4)
```

(d) Record: 135675E-01bb3156+1253147

```
     READ(*,1000) X,Y
1000 FORMAT(F10.2,G8.3)
```

(e) Same as (d) with this record:

```
bbbbb123-33156E+1234
```

3. For each of the following, you are given values for various variables. Indicate exactly what gets printed by the given WRITE and FORMAT statements. (I and J are INTEGER; X and Y are REAL; A, B, and C are CHARACTER*3,*4, and *5, respectively.)

(a) X = 106154000.0, Y = −.00000000020417

```
     WRITE(*,2000) X,Y
2000 FORMAT(' ',F7.2,3X,F7.2)
```

(b) Same as (a) for the FORMAT

```
2000 FORMAT(' ',E13.6,3X,E11.4)
```

(c) Same as (a) for the FORMAT

```
2000 FORMAT(' ',E11.4,3X,E13.6)
```

(d) I = 141012, J = −3572, A = 'ABC', B = 'KLMN', C = 'PQRST'

```
     WRITE(*,3000) I,J,A,A,A
3000 FORMAT(' ',I10,I10,A3,A4,A2)
```

(e) Same values as (d).

```
     WRITE(*,3000) I,J,A,B,C
3000 FORMAT(' ',I5,2X,I5,2X,A,2X,A,2X,A)
```

(f) Same values as (d).

```
     WRITE(*,3000) J,C
3000 FORMAT(' ',T3,I4,T10,A4)
```

(g) Same values as (d).

```
     WRITE(*,3000) I,J,B
3000 FORMAT(' ',T7,I6,T9,I2,T6,A5)
```

(h) X = 147.3.

```
     WRITE(*,4000) X,X,X,X,X
4000 FORMAT(' ',F5.1,2X,F5.2,2X,F7.2,2X,E13.6,2X,E12.3)
```

4. Fill in the missing values in the following table. The left column contains "apostrophe editing" descriptors, the right column the equivalent H formats.

'DO NOT INCLUDE SIGN'	
'DON''T INCLUDE SIGN'	
	1H1
	6HERRORb
'bANDb'	
	3Hb=b
'PAYROLL FOR XYZ COMPANY, INC.'	
'NAME'	
	4H----
	5H----b

5. Consider this program segment.

```
     REAL X,Y,Z
     READ(*,1000) X,Y,Z
1000 FORMAT(F7.2,E10.3,2X,F5.1)
```

For each of the following, make up an appropriate input record so that the READ statement will give the indicated values to X, Y, Z. Be explicit on where blank spaces occur. For example, for X = Y = Z = 1.0, one possible answer is

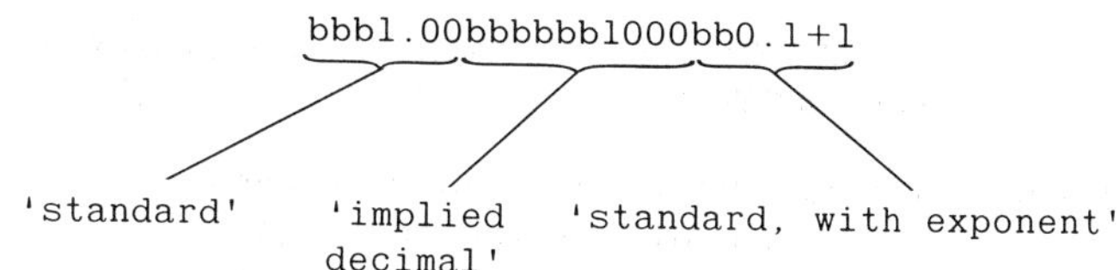

(a) X = Y = Z = 10.5. Use the "standard" form with explicit decimal point for each variable.
(b) X = Y = Z = 10.5. Use the "implied decimal" form for each.
(c) X = Y = Z = 1.5. Use exponential notation for each.
(d) X = .0000000012, Y = 152.3, Z = 16.4.

6. Follow the directions of Exercise 5 for this program segment:

```
     INTEGER I
     REAL X
     CHARACTER*3 A,B
     CHARACTER*7 C
     READ(*,5000) I,X,A,B,C
5000 FORMAT(I5,2X,F10.2,2X,A3,2X,A,2X,A5)
```

and these desired values:
(a) I = 100, X = .03, A = 'MAN', B = 'CAR', C = 'TABLE'.
(b) I = −1400, X = −.0003, A = B = C = completely blank.
(c) I = 0, X = 0.0, A = 'PEM', B = 'CAL', C = 'PRODUCT'.
(d) I = −11, X = 135000, A = 'bbA,' B = 'Bbb', C = 'AbBbCbD'.

7. For each data record described below, make up suitable declarations, READ, and FORMAT. Do the FORMAT twice, once using X formats and once using T formats. Which is easier?

(a)

```
xxxxxx...xxxxbbbbxxbbxxxxx.xx
name(20)cols      age salary
```

(b)

Columns	Field
4–17	Name (characters)
23–26	Age (integer)
29–39	Salary (two places after decimal)
	All others blank

8. The following program segments are being used to create tables containing several columns of information. After running the program some changes are needed, as described. Make the necessary changes to the segments.

(a)

```
      INTEGER SSNO,AGE,NODEP
      REAL SALARY,FEDTAX
      CHARACTER*20 NAME
            .
            .
      WRITE(*,3000) NAME,SSNO,AGE,SALARY,NODEP,FEDTAX
 3000 FORMAT(' ',3X,A20,7X,I9,8X,I2,10X,F9.2,10X,I2,7X,F8.2)
```

Changes: name to appear starting in first column
age to be moved one column to right
salary to be moved one column to left
all other figures to stay in present location

(b) Same as (a), but with this format:

```
 3000 FORMAT(' ',T7,A20,T35,I9,T50,I2,T65,F9.2,T88,I2,T97.F8.2)
```

(c) For the original program segment and format of (a), insert an additional field, containing the CHARACTER*4 variable DEPT. This field is to be in columns 1–4, with three spaces prior to the NAME field.

(d) Repeat (c) but using the format as given in (b).

11

DECLARATIONS

11.1 DOUBLE PRECISION VARIABLES

The FORTRAN language provides other variable types in addition to those we have considered so far. These types are DOUBLE PRECISION (discussed in this section) and COMPLEX (Section 11.2). In addition, the LOGICAL and CHARACTER types will be discussed in more detail in Section 11.3 and Chapter 12, respectively. Many FORTRAN compilers provide variations on these types. Frequently, for example, two or more sizes of integers will be provided. However, we suggest that programmers should normally restrict themselves to using only the standard types of variables.

Thus, to give a summary, the permissible variable types in FORTRAN are REAL, INTEGER, DOUBLE PRECISION, COMPLEX, LOGICAL, and CHARACTER. In all cases a variable may be specified to be of a given type by a statement of the form

type v

where type is any of the six permissible variable types (CHARACTER requires a length specification), and v is the variable name. In addition, in the standard language a variable whose name does not appear in a type statement is assumed to be INTEGER if its name begins with the letters I, J, K, L, M, or N. In all other cases, the type is assumed to be REAL, if not specified.

DOUBLE PRECISION in FORTRAN

DOUBLE PRECISION variables in FORTRAN are the same as REAL except that approximately twice as many significant figures are available in double precision. Double precision variables are declared using a type statement such as:

```
DOUBLE PRECISION X,Y,Z
```

where X, Y, and Z are the names of variables which are to be double precision. Double precision constants are written in exponential form using the letter D to indicate the exponent, as in

```
1.0D1
3.1415926D0
```

(On some systems writing a value using a large number of significant figures will cause the value to be stored as a double precision constant.)

FORTRAN supplies several functions which accept double precision arguments and return double precision results or which convert between double precision and other types. A list of some useful DOUBLE PRECISION library functions is found in Table 11.1. In addition, you may write double precision functions in a form very similar to real functions. The function header statement would be

```
DOUBLE PRECISION FUNCTION fname (arguments)
```

Within the body of the function there would be a statement assigning a value to the name of the function. The arguments of the function may be of any FORTRAN type and should be declared within the function.

Double precision variables may be read or written using either the usual F format or a special D format. The D format code requires two numeric values, w and d, and is written as

Dw.d

The meaning of the Dw.d is almost identicial to that of the Ew.d. On input, it works exactly like the Fw.d and Ew.d (see Section 10.3). However, in preparing our input data, we may want to write our exponents using D rather than E, as in this example

```
1.5D-3     rather than   1.5E-3
```

Similarly, on output using Dw.d the computer will write the character D where the E code would write the letter E. For example, the code D25.16 will cause the value 1.5 to be printed as

```
bbb0.1500000000000000Db01
```

where the b indicates spaces.

> **NOTE.** The D, of course, indicates "double precision." However, the computer does not enforce this. We may

1. use Ew.d to process a double precision variable, or Dw.d for a real variable; or

TABLE 11.1 SAMPLE OF DOUBLE PRECISION LIBRARY FUNCTIONS

Name	Type of Argument	Type of Result	Action
DSQRT	DP	DP	Square root of x
DSIN	DP	DP	Sine of x
DCOS	DP	DP	Cosine of x
DABS	DP	DP	Absolute value of x
SNGL	DP	REAL	Conversion to real
DBLE	REAL	DP	Conversion to double precision

DP stands for DOUBLE PRECISION in the table.

2. create data such as 1.5D-3 to be read into a real variable, or such as 1.5E-3 to be read into a double precision variable.

   However, this would probably cause confusion and it would be better to use D with double precision.

Examples

For an equation of the form $ax^2 + bx + c = 0$, the quadratic formula gives the solutions as

$$x1 = \frac{-b + \sqrt{b^2 - 4ac}}{2a} \qquad x2 = \frac{-b - \sqrt{b^2 - 4ac}}{2a}$$

We will assume that real solutions exist, that is, that $b^2 - 4ac$ is not negative. This program segment reads values for a, b, and c and calculates and prints the solutions. The double precision function DSQRT is used to calculate square roots and is included in the declarations. Also, we use the double precision constants 4.0D0 and 2.0D0 for the numbers 4 and 2 as shown here.

```
      DOUBLE PRECISION A,B,C,X1,X2,ROOT,DSQRT
            .
            .
      READ(*,1000) A,B,C
      ROOT = DSQRT(B*B-4.0D0*A*C)
      X1 = (-B+ROOT) / (2.0D0*A)
      X2 = (-B-ROOT) / (2.0D0*A)
      WRITE(*,2000) A,B,C,X1,X2
            .
            .
 1000 FORMAT(3D20.11)
 2000 FORMAT(' ',5(D20.11,5X))
```

Suppose we want a function to calculate the square root

$$\sqrt{X*Y}$$

Although X and Y are real, we want to perform double precision calculations. We may use the DBLE function as indicated below:

```
DOUBLE PRECISION FUNCTION ROOTPR(X,Y)
REAL X,Y
DOUBLE PRECISION DSQRT,DBLE
    .
    .

ROOTPR = DSQRT(DBLE(X)*DBLE(Y))
RETURN
END
```

Now let us write a function to calculate INNER, given by

$$\text{INNER} \leftarrow X(1)*Y(1) + X(2)*Y(2) + \cdots + X(N)*Y(N)$$

Although INNER, X, and Y are REAL, we wish the summation and the multiplication to be performed using DOUBLE PRECISION. We will use a temporary DOUBLE PRECISION variable called TSUM to contain the sum; this will be converted back to a REAL value using the function SNGL. The function follows.

```
      REAL FUNCTION INNER(X,Y,ASIZE,N)
      INTEGER ASIZE,N
      REAL X(ASIZE),Y(ASIZE)
      INTEGER I

      DOUBLE PRECISION TSUM,DBLE

C    WRITTEN BY ********, **/**/**

C    THIS FUNCTION CALCULATES THE INNER PRODUCT OF
C  THE ARRAYS X AND Y USING DOUBLE PRECISION VARIABLES.

C    THESE ARE THE PARAMETERS:

C        X-INPUT, REAL ARRAY-FIRST NUMBER
C        Y-INPUT, REAL ARRAY-SECOND NUMBER
C        ASIZE-INPUT, INTEGER-SIZE OF ARRAYS
C        N-INPUT, INTEGER-PORTION OF ARRAYS IN USE

      TSUM = 0.0D0
      DO 10 I = 1,N
         TSUM = TSUM + DBLE(X(I)) * DBLE(Y(I))
   10    CONTINUE
      INNER = SNGL(TSUM)
      RETURN
      END
```

The Need For Double Precision

Double precision is especially needed in those cases where the accuracy of the calculation would suffer using the limited number of significant figures available in

REAL values. Frequently in an involved sequence of calculations the accuracy of the result depends upon a few critical steps. If those steps are performed using double precision and the rest are performed using REAL, one can obtain an accurate result with computation time only slightly longer than it would be using only REAL calculations. These critical portions depend upon the specific calculation being performed, and even in some cases upon the particular values being used.

These questions are beyond the scope of this text. They belong to the branch of mathematics known as Numerical Analysis. However, we will consider two brief examples to illustrate the kinds of problems which can arise due to the limited precision of computer arithmetic.

COMMENT. For simplicity we phrase our examples in terms of REAL values having two digits of precision and DOUBLE precision having four digits. On actual computer systems the number of digits is higher (perhaps 7 and 14, for example). The examples given are, however, illustrative of the problem that exists.

As our first example, we will describe the solution of $.1x^2 - 2x + .1 = 0$ using two-digit decimal arithmetic.The standard algebraic approach to solving this equation would have us compute

$$X1 = \frac{2 + \sqrt{2^2 - 4(.1)(.1)}}{2(.1)} \quad \text{and} \quad x2 = \frac{2 - \sqrt{2^2 - 4(.1)(.1)}}{2(.1)}$$

The correct answers are $x1 = 19.9498\ldots$ and $x2 = 0.050125\ldots$. Using two-digit arithmetic the quantity under the square root sign becomes $4.0 - 0.04$. Now if we subtract 4.0 and 0.04 using only two digits, the result will be 4.0 (Why?) Thus $x1$ becomes 20.0, and $x2$ becomes 0.0. The error in $x1$ is only 0.25 percent, but the error in $x2$ is 100 percent.

By calculating the numerator of $x2$ using four significant digits, we obtain

$$2.000 - \sqrt{4.000 - 0.04} = 2.000 - \sqrt{3.960} = 2.000 - 1.990 = .0100$$

Now the rest of the $x2$ calculation may be done using two digits, yielding $.01/.2 = .05$, for an error of 0.25 percent. Doing a portion of the calculation in DOUBLE PRECISION (four digits) improves the accuracy of the result from 100 percent error to 0.25 percent error.

In this particular example the improved accuracy could also be obtained by using a modified algorithm. We could compute $x1$ as before and obtain 20.0. To compute $x2$ we note that $ax^2 + bx + c = a(x - x1)(x - x2)$ and thus $c = a^*x1^*x2$. Therefore, we can compute $x2$ as $c/(a^*x1)$ and obtain $x2 = .1/(.1^*20) = .1/2 = .05$. In other problems, however, alternative methods will not exist, and the careful use of double precision calculations will be needed to ensure accuracy.

For our second example, let us solve the linear system

$$85x + 27y = 86$$
$$96x + 34y = 97$$

using Cramer's rule and two significant decimal digits. First, the correct answers are

$$x = \frac{(86)(34) - (97)(27)}{(85)(34) - (96)(27)} = \frac{2924 - 2619}{2890 - 2592} = \frac{305}{298} = 1.0235 \cdots$$

$$y = \frac{(85)(97) - (96)(86)}{(85)(34) - (96)(27)} = \frac{8245 - 8256}{2890 - 2592} = -\frac{11}{298} = -.0369 \cdots$$

Using two significant figures, we get

$$x = \frac{(86)(34) - (97)(27)}{(85)(34) - (96)(27)} = \frac{2900 - 2600}{2900 - 2600} = \frac{300}{300} = 1.0$$

$$y = \frac{(85)(97) - (96)(86)}{(85)(34) - (96)(27)} = \frac{8200 - 8300}{2900 - 2600} = -\frac{100}{300} = -.333 \cdots$$

The solution for x has an error of about 0.24 percent, and y is in error by about 800 percent. The problem is that the computation of (85)(97) − (96)(86) should yield −11 but with two significant figures we get a value of −100. Notice that this error occurred even though all of our numbers in the original problem were represented exactly in our two-digit number system.

REVIEW

DOUBLE PRECISION

Constants: Use "D" exponential notation

```
1.563729431D5
```

Variables and functions: Declare using

```
DOUBLE PRECISION list of variables
and DOUBLE PRECISION FUNCTION fname (parameters).
```

I/O: May use F or D (or even E) format. D format on output uses "D" rather than "E" for exponential notation

Library functions: See Table 11.1 for partial list

Use of DOUBLE PRECISION. Used to obtain increased accuracy. For some numerical problems, only portions of the calculation need be done in double precision to greatly improve the overall accuracy.

EXERCISE

In this exercise you will write a program to measure the accuracy of some of the real library functions supplied by the vendor of the computer system you are using. To do this you need the real and double precision versions of the library functions. As an example, we will describe a test of the SIN function, using the DSIN function as a standard for comparison. The basic idea is to calculate the function SIN at a large number of values of the argument X, and compare the values of SIN(X) to the values of DSIN(X). Now X will be real, and since we need a double precision argument for DSIN we will write DSIN(DBLE(X)). The expression

```
A = DABS((DSIN(DBLE(X))-SIN(X))/DSIN(DBLE(X)))
```

gives the relative error in the SIN(X) if DSIN(DBLE(X)) is assumed correct. Write a program to determine the value of A for a large number, say 1000, of values of X in a range of interest. Compute and print the average of the A values and the largest of the A values. Use this method to estimate the accuracy of the SIN function for X between $-.1$ and $+.1$, X between 1.56 and 1.58, and X between 300.0 and 300.2. Repeat for the ATAN with X between $-.1$ and $+.1$, and X between 1.55 and 1.57. Compare your results with the claimed accuracy for real computations on the computer you are using.

Try some other functions such as the ALOG, EXP, and so forth. [*Warning:* watch out for divisions by zero.]

11.2 COMPLEX VARIABLES

In this section we discuss the FORTRAN implementation of the mathematical concept of **complex numbers**. If the reader is not familiar with the concept of complex numbers this section should be skipped.

Complex numbers in algebra are represented in many forms including

$$3+4i$$

$$5e^{\frac{i\pi}{4}}$$

and others. In the first form 3 is known as the *real part* of the number and 4 is known as the *imaginary part*. The symbol i represents the *imaginary unit* $\sqrt{-1}$. FORTRAN represents complex values as two real values, one representing the real part and one the imaginary part. COMPLEX variables are declared by statements like

```
COMPLEX A,B,C
```

A **complex constant** is written as two real values within parentheses, as for example (3.,4), (5.2E-3,2.7E2), or (3.12,4.56E-2). Complex variables and constants may be mixed with real values (but not with double precision values).

In mathematics there is no accepted method for saying one complex number is larger than another. For this reason, the only comparisons allowed between complex expressions in IF statements are .EQ. for equality and .NE. for inequality. Also, in mathematics there are many commonly used notations for representing complex numbers and no notation that is universally accepted. Therefore the FORTRAN language does not provide any special format codes for reading or writing complex values. Instead, the complex number is regarded as two real values and the format must provide two real format codes. For example, the complex variable C might be written using

```
WRITE(*,1000) C
```

where the FORMAT could be any of the following:

```
1000 FORMAT(' ',2F10.5)
1000 FORMAT(' ',F10.5,'+I*',F10.5)
1000 FORMAT(' ','(',F10.5,',',F10.5,')')
```

Table 11.2 gives a description of a few of the library functions that are provided in FORTRAN for manipulating complex values. The programmer may define his or her own complex functions by using declarations such as

```
COMPLEX FUNCTION fname(arg1,arg2, . . . )
```

As an example of the use of complex values consider the solution of the equation $Ax^2 + Bx + C = 0$ where A, B, and C are REAL values. A program segment to perform this computation is shown below:

```
      REAL A,B,C
      COMPLEX ROOT1,ROOT2,SD,CSQRT,CMPLX
           .
           .
      READ(*,1000) A,B,C
      SD = CSQRT(CMPLX(B*B-4.0*A*C,0.0))
      ROOT1 = (-B+SD) / (2.0*A)
      ROOT2 = (-B-SD) / (2.0*A)
      WRITE(*,2000) ROOT1,ROOT2
           .
           .
1000  FORMAT(3E10.0)
2000  FORMAT(' ','ROOT1 = ',F10.5,'+I*',F10.5/
     $       ' ','ROOT2 = ',F10.5,'+I*',F10.5)
```

Note that in this segment it is not necessary to consider the sign of $B^2 - 4AC$ since the square root of a negative is defined and will be computed as a complex value by the function CSQRT. The function CMPLX is needed since CSQRT expects a complex argument.

TABLE 11.2 LIBRARY FUNCTIONS USED WITH COMPLEX VALUES.

Function	Argument type	Result type	Computation
CSQRT	C	C	Square root of argument
CSIN	C	C	Sine of argument
CCOS	C	C	Cosine of argument
CABS	C	REAL	$\sqrt{a^2 + b^2}$, where arg=$a + bi$
CONJG	C	C	$a-bi$, where arg=$a+bi$
REAL	C	REAL	a, where arg=$a+bi$
AIMAG	C	REAL	b, where arg=$a+bi$
CMPLX	REAL, REAL	C	$a+bi$, where a is first argument and b is the second

C stands for COMPLEX in the table.

As we mentioned earlier, FORTRAN allows mixed COMPLEX and REAL operations. In a mixed real and complex addition or subtraction such as the computation of the numerators in ROOT1 and ROOT2, the reals are regarded as being added to the real part of the complex. With a multiplication or division, both the real and imaginary part of the complex number are multiplied or divided by the real. For example,

```
6.0 + (2.0,3.0)   gives  (8.0,3.0)
6.0 * (2.0,3.0)   gives  (12.0,18.0)
(6.0,8.0)/2.0     gives  (3.0,4.0)
```

Note that 50.0/(3.0,4.0) is

$$\frac{50}{3 + 4i} = \frac{50\,(3 - 4i)}{(3 + 4i)(3 - 4i)} = \frac{150 - 200i}{9 + 16} = \frac{150 - 200i}{25} = 6 - 8i$$

and thus 50.0/(3.0,4.0) yields (6.0,−8.0).

We can write a slightly more efficient (although less clear) solution to the quadratic equation. If the imaginary part of ROOT1 is not zero, then ROOT2 will be the complex conjugate of ROOT1. Thus we may modify our algorithm to:

```
SD ← CSQRT(CMPLX(B*B-4.*A*C,0.0))
ROOT1 ← (-B+SD)/(2.*A)
if imaginary part of ROOT1 = 0 then
   ROOT2 ← (-B-SD)/(2.*A)
else
   ROOT2 ← complex conjugate of ROOT1
endif
```

Note that FORTRAN provides the functions AIMAG and CONJG to compute the imaginary part and the complex conjugate, respectively. The IF-THEN-ELSE in FORTRAN would be

```
IF(AIMAG(ROOT1).EQ.0.0) THEN
   ROOT2 = (-B-SD)/(2.*A)
ELSE
   ROOT2 = CONJG(ROOT1)
ENDIF
```

Of course, we would include CONJG in our COMPLEX declaration.

REVIEW

Complex

Constants: Two REAL constants in parentheses

```
(3.0,4.0) for 3 + 4i
```

Variables and functions: Declare using

```
COMPLEX list of variables
```

and

```
COMPLEX FUNCTION fname(parameters)
```

I/O: as two REAL values
Library functions: see Table 11.2

Interaction of REAL with COMPLEX

Real number x is treated as complex number $x + 0i$

3.0 + (1.0,2.0)	is	(4.0,2.0)
3.0 * (1.0,2.0)	is	(3.0,6.0)
(6.0,4.0)/2.0	is	(3.0,2.0)

(Division by complex uses usual complex division.)

EXERCISES

1. Write a program which will read complex variables and print them in the form $a + ib$ and (p,θ), where $p = \sqrt{a^2 + b^2}$ and $\theta = \arctan(b/a)$.
2. The exponential and trigonometric functions are related by a formula $e^{i\theta} = \cos\theta + i \sin\theta$. Write a program to compute the quantity
$$A = \frac{|e^{i\theta} - (\cos\theta + i\sin\theta)|}{|e^{i\theta}|}$$
for 1000 values of θ between 0.0 and 10.0. Determine and print the largest value of A and the average of the A values. Compare these values to the claimed accuracy of the real arithmetic on the computer you are using. [*Hint:* See exercise in Section 11.1.]
3. Write a program which will read two integers NZ and NP, then read NZ complex values Z(1), Z(2), . . ., Z(NZ) and NP complex values P(1), P(2), . . ., P(NP). Compute the complex values
$$T(W) = \prod_{i=1}^{NZ} (W - Z(i)) / \prod_{i=1}^{NP} (W - P(i))$$
and the real values
$$A(W) = |T(W)| \text{ and } \phi(W) = \arctan\left[\frac{\text{imaginary part of } T(W)}{\text{Real part of } T(W)}\right]$$
Print the values of $A(W)$ and $\phi(W)$ for $W = 0.0$ to 10.0 by 0.1. Note that only one value of $T(W)$ need be present at any one time. You may assume that $|Z(i)|<1$ and $|P(i)|<1$.

   Such a computation can arise in electric circuit theory where the $T(W)$ is a "transfer function" and the Z's and P's are special values known as the zeros and poles of the transfer function. The quantities $A(W)$ and $\phi(W)$ are the so-called gain and phase shift of a circuit.

11.3 LOGICAL VARIABLES

Logical variables and functions were introduced in Section 4.3. This section collects together information on logical variables in the format used in Sections 11.1 and 11.2, and discusses two operators which were not discussed earlier.

Logical variables are declared using the statement

```
LOGICAL list of variables
```

A logical variable can have one of the two possible values .TRUE. and .FALSE.. These are also the only possible constants.

Logical variables can be read or written using the L format. (See Section 4.3 for details.)

Logcal expressions can be formed by using relational operators (.EQ., .NE., .LT., .LE., .GT., and .GE.) and logical operators (.NOT., .AND., and .OR.). (See Section 4.3 for details.)

.EQV and .NEQV.

We are not allowed to compare logical quantities using .EQ. or .NE.. However, special operators are provided to use in such comparisons. These are .EQV. (logically equivalent) and .NEQV. (not logically equivalent). The meanings are the same as we would expect for "equal" and "not equal."

> **COMMENT.** The .NEQV. relation applied to two logical values L1 and L2 yields what is sometimes called the *exclusive or* of the two values. The result is .TRUE. if either L1 or L2 is true, but not both.

These operators are of lowest precedence, lower than .OR.. As a result,

```
L1. EQV. L2 .OR. L3
```

has the same meaning as

```
L1 .EQV. (L2 .OR. L3)
```

> **CAUTION.** This is contrary to what we might expect, since .EQ. and the other relational operators have higher precedence than the logical operators. For integers I and J,
>
> ```
> I .EQ. J .OR. L3
> ```
>
> has the effect of
>
> ```
> (I .EQ. J) .OR. L3
> ```

REVIEW

Logical Values

Constants: .TRUE., .FALSE.

Declaration: LOGICAL list of variables

Function: LOGICAL FUNCTION fname(parameters)

I/O: use Lw

```
input: T or F somewhere in field
output: T or F, right justified
```

Logical Expressions

Form

constant, variable, array reference, function reference

single comparison (.EQ., .NE., .LT., .LE., .GT., .GE.)

combinations using (.NOT., .AND., .OR., .EQV., .NEQV.)

precedence:

```
.NOT.
.AND.
.OR.
.EQV., .NEQV.
```

EXERCISES

1. Fill in the following table:

L1	L2	L1 .NEQV. L2	(L1 .OR. L2) .AND. .NOT. (L1 .AND. L2)
.TRUE.	.TRUE.		
.TRUE.	.FALSE.		
.FALSE.	.TRUE.		
.FALSE.	.FALSE.		

Relate this to the comment on "exclusive or" in this section.

2. Fill in the following table:

L1	L2	L1 .EQV. L2 .OR. L3	L1 .AND. L2 .NEQV. L2
.TRUE.	.TRUE.		
.TRUE.	.FALSE.		
.FALSE.	.TRUE.		
.FALSE.	.FALSE.		

11.4 COMMON

One of the most convenient features of FORTRAN subprograms is that variables defined within a subprogram and not passed as arguments are **local** to the subprogram. This means that those variables cannot be referred to outside of the subprogram. Two local variables in different subprograms are completely different variables, even if the names are the same. Therefore one can write programs using subprograms without knowing anything about the local variable names used by the other subprograms.

As convenient and as powerful as this feature is, there are times when one wishes to have a name stand for a single unique variable which can be referenced throughout a program by several different subprograms. One approach is to pass these variables as arguments to the various subprograms. However, this can become cumbersome if there are many such variables.

The COMMON Statement

The COMMON statement

COMMON list of variables

provides a convenient mechanism for sharing variables among a number of program units. For example, suppose we wish to share the variables X and PAGENO, where X is REAL and PAGENO is INTEGER, among a main program and two subroutines S1 and S2. We will place the statements

```
REAL X
INTEGER PAGENO
COMMON X,PAGENO
```

in the declarations of the main program and in the declarations of each of the subroutines S1 and S2. The variable X in the main program will be the same as X in each of the subroutines, and likewise PAGENO will be shared among the three program units.

The statement

```
COMMON X,PAGENO
```

causes the variable X and PAGENO of the program unit containing the statement to be placed in a special area of the computer memory called the **blank** or **unnamed common** area. X is placed in the first available position and PAGENO in the second. Since the COMMON statement appears in the main program and each of the two subroutines, S1 and S2, the variable X in each of those units refers to the same memory location. As a result, the variable X in each of the three program units will be the same variable.

In addition to blank common, variables may be placed into **named common** areas using statements of the form

```
COMMON/name/ list of variables
```

For example, we may write

```
COMMON/ABC/ X,Y,Z
```

The name ABC is the name assigned to the common area. X, Y, and Z are variables placed into the named common area ABC. The name of a common area must obey the rules for FORTRAN names: six or fewer letters or digits with the first being a letter. The user can regard the overall common area as being divided into sections in which the blank common area is one section and each named common is a separate section.

Both simple variables and arrays may be placed into a common area. For example, the statements

```
REAL X,Y(3),Z
COMMON/A/ X,Y,Z
```

define the named common A with X being the first element, Y(1) the second, Y(2) the third, Y(3) the fourth, and Z the fifth. The variables may be of any type. However, if any variable in a given common area is of type CHARACTER then all variables in that common area must be CHARACTER type.

All program units referring to a given named common must define it with the same length, that is, the same number of storage units. (Some compilers relax this restriction.) The standard does permit definitions of blank common to have different lengths in different program units.

BLOCK DATA

In general, variables which appear in COMMON statements may not appear in DATA statements. However, if the COMMON block is a named common, it is possible to initialize the variables using a special construction called a **BLOCK DATA** subprogram. A **BLOCK DATA** subprogram consists of type, DIMENSION, COMMON, and other declarations. No other statements (such as assignment statements) may be present. The form is

```
BLOCK DATA name
      .
      .
      .
END
```

Suppose we wish to make the variables PAGENO and LINECT available to three subroutines HEADER, DETAIL, and INPUT. We could place the declarations

```
INTEGER PAGENO,LINECT
COMMON/PAGE/ PAGENO,LINECT
SAVE/PAGE/
```

in each of the HEADER, DETAIL, and INPUT routines.

The SAVE statement can reference a named common block as illustrated above. To do so, we write the common area's name inside slashes within the SAVE statement. In the statement

```
SAVE /A/,/B/,C,D
```

the A and B are names of COMMON blocks, while the C and D are normal variables. When the SAVE lists a common block, then it applies to all of the variables in the common block.

To initialize the variables we could write a separate BLOCK DATA routine.

```
BLOCK DATA PAGEVL
INTEGER PAGENO, LINECT
COMMON/PAGE/ PAGENO,LINECT
SAVE/PAGE/
DATA PAGENO, LINECT/1,45/
END
```

Note that the names of the BLOCK DATA subprogram and the common block are different, and must be different from any variable in the common block. (It is possible to omit the name of a BLOCK DATA subprogram, but only one such unnamed BLOCK DATA subprogram can be used in a single executable program.)

COMMENT. The BLOCK DATA subprogram may be placed at any location in our list of program units. One possible ordering would be

main
block data (1 or more)
other subprograms (1 or more)

The BLOCK DATA subprogram is never explicitly "CALLED." Its presence in the list of subprograms being processed is sufficient to accomplish the intialization (by the use of the DATA statement) of the variables in the named COMMON area.

Case Study 6 in Section 6.4 dealt with a program to maintain and use an inventory data base using two sets of parallel arrays ITEMS, PRICES, INVENT and CUSTID, CUSPCT, plus the simple variables NITEMS and NCUST. Many of the subroutines in that case study were designed with these arrays and variables passed as arguments. The design could be simplified considerably if these arrays and variables were placed in two common blocks, named say INVTRY and CUSTR, using declarations like

```
INTEGER ITEMS(250),INVENT(250),NITEMS
REAL PRICES(250)
COMMON/INVTRY/ NITEMS,ITEMS,INVENT,PRICES
```

and

```
INTEGER CUSTID(150),NCUST
REAL CUSPCT(150)
COMMON/CUSTR/ NCUST,CUSTID,CUSPCT
```

Some of the subprograms need only refer to one of the common areas while others will need to refer to both areas. For example, UPDATE need only refer to the INVTRY area, and DISC to the CUSTR area. On the other hand, INIT would refer to both.

The common blocks can be used as a structuring tool to group related data items. In fact, we have done this in the example above. The information about the inventory items is placed in the named common INVTRY, while the information about the customers is placed in the named common CUSTR.

Pitfalls

The COMMON statement is easy to use if all the program units that use COMMON blocks have exactly the same variables and arrays placed in each of the various COMMON blocks. Unfortunately, the FORTRAN language does not require this, and most FORTRAN compilers cannot check for consistent uses of COMMON statements. Suppose we have the following two subroutines:

```
     SUBROUTINE S1
     REAL X
     COMMON/JUNK/ X
     CALL S2(10000.0)
     WRITE(6,1000) X
1000 FORMAT(' ',E13.6)
     RETURN
     END
```

and

```
SUBROUTINE S2(Y)
REAL Y
INTEGER K
COMMON/JUNK/ K
K = Y
RETURN
END
```

Note that the first element of the common JUNK is defined as REAL in S1 but as INTEGER in S2. S2 assigns the value 10000 as an INTEGER to the first element in JUNK. S1 prints the value of that first element, but prints it as a REAL. According to the standard, the assignment of a value to K causes X to become undefined. On many systems what will happen is that a value for X will be printed but that value will be quite different from the value assigned to K. Frequently the value will be a REAL value with an extremely small magnitude.

Another problem could arise if an array is used in one subprogram but not in another. For example, suppose S1 declares the variables A, B, C as:

```
REAL A,B(2),C
COMMON/C1/ A,B,C
```

but S2 uses the declarations

```
REAL A,B,C
COMMON/C1/ A,B,C
```

C1 is declared by S1 to be four elements long, the elements being A, B(1), B(2), and C, while S2 declares C1 as being three elements long. Since the lengths of the two declarations of C1 are different, this is actually an illegal construction. However, some compilers will accept it, and if they do, then C in S2 is actually the same variable as B(2) in S1. This is probably not what was intended.

This second pitfall generally arises when programmers say to themselves, "The S2 subprogram does not use the B array, so I don't need to worry about its dimension." As we have indicated, this argument is erroneous and must be resisted. The safest thing to do when using COMMON is to use precisely the same series of declaration statements for the common variables in each subprogram. To facilitate this, it is a good idea to keep these declarations separate from those for other variables used in the subprogram.

REVIEW

COMMON Statement

Form

```
COMMON list of variables              (blank common)
COMMON/name/ list of variables        (named common)
```

Use:

1. Place identical COMMON statements (and declarations for the variables in the common block) in two or more program units. The program units then will share the variables in the common block.
2. May organize data by using more than one named common block.

SAVE

May include entire named common block by placing the name in slashes in the SAVE statement:

```
SAVE/PAGEVL/
```

BLOCK DATA

Form

```
BLOCK DATA name
  various declaration statements
END
```

Use:

1. May not include nondeclarations (such as assignment statements).
2. Used to initialize variables in common blocks using DATA statement.
3. Is not called; merely place it in with the other program units of the program.

EXERCISES

1. Using the common blocks INVTRY and CUSTR discussed in this section, redesign the program in Case Study 6 of Section 6.4.

2. Discuss how you might use the COMMON statement to redesign the following exercises:
- **(a)** Section 5.2, Exercise 12
- **(b)** Section 8.2, Exercise 14
- **(c)** Section 8.2, Exercise 15
- **(d)** Section 8.2, Exercise 16
- **(e)** Section 9.1, Exercise 4a

11.5 OTHER DECLARATIONS

In this section we will look at several declarations. A few of these have been introduced and used before but are included here for completeness.

PARAMETER

The parameter declaration is one which is quite useful in programs which depend upon the values of certain constants. The statement has the form

```
PARAMETER (name1=value1,name2=value2, . . .)
```

Name1, name2, and so forth are FORTRAN names and value1, value2, and so on are expressions. The statement defines name1, name2, . . . to be constants whose values are value1, value2, and so forth. The expressions in the parameter statement may contain constants and any previously defined parameters. The definition of the parameter remains in effect for the program unit containing the statement. For example, the statements

```
INTEGER NUM
REAL PI,TWOPI
PARAMETER (PI=3.1416,TWOPI=2.0*PI,NUM=50)
```

declare that the symbolic names PI, TWOPI, and NUM stand for the constants 3.1416, 6.2832, and 50, respectively. Once declared, the names may be used almost any place that a constant could be used, including DIMENSION statements.

For example, we might have statements such as

```
          REAL RADIUS(NUM),CIRCUM(NUM),AREA(NUM)
          INTEGER I
              .
              .
          DO 10 I = 1,NUM
             CIRCUM(I) = TWOPI * RADIUS(I)
             AREA(I) = PI * RADIUS(I)**2
   10        CONTINUE
```

COMMENT. These examples illustrate two common reasons for using the PARAMETER statement:

1. to give meaningful names to constants such as PI and TWOPI;
2. to simplify program modification. If we decide to increase the array size, we do not have to search through the whole program looking for every occurrence of the constant 50. (Some of these occurrences may not even refer to the array size, and so should not be changed.) We simply change the PARAMETER statement.

As another example of the second use of PARAMETER, consider the following. Suppose we are writing a program which depends upon the number of characters which can be printed on a line, and suppose our printer allows 132 characters per line. We might have such lines as

```
      DIMENSION LINE (133)
          .
          .
      DO 10 I = 1,133
          .
         DO 20 L = 1,132
             .
            WRITE(*,1000) LINE
                .
                .
 1000 FORMAT(133A1)
```

in our program. If we moved the program to another machine which has a printer with 120 characters per line, then we would want to change some of the 133 values to 121, and the 132 values to 120, in the program. There might, however, be other values 132 or 133 which are not determined by the line size and so would not be changed. If the program were fairly large, it could be difficult to identify just which constants should be changed.

Suppose we had defined parameters

```
      PARAMETER (LINSIZ=132,LINSZ1=LINSIZ+1)
```

and written our program in terms of them. The selected lines of code shown earlier would become

```
          DIMENSION LINE(LINSZ1)
            .
            .
          DO 10 I = 1,LINSZ1
            .
             DO 20 L = 1,LINSIZ
               .
                WRITE(*,1000) LINE
                  .
                  .
     1000 FORMAT(133A1)
```

(Unfortunately the named parameter cannot be used in a FORMAT statement.) Now if we changed the program we would only have to change the PARAMETER statement to

```
PARAMETER (LINSIZ=120,LINSZ1=LINSZ+1)
```

and examine the FORMATs for required changes. In the case of this FORMAT there would be no need to make a change unless LINSZ1 were greater then 133.

An example where we could have used a PARAMETER statement occurred in the function LOOKUP in Section 6.3. We had defined a variable TABSIZ and initialized it with the value 100 in a DATA statement. It would have been possible to make an error in our function and modify the variable TABSIZ. If the declarations within LOOKUP had been

```
INTEGER KEY,TABLE,NUMENT
INTEGER I,TABSIZ
PARAMETER (TABSIZ=100)
DIMENSION TABLE(1:TABSIZ)
```

then TABSIZ would be a named constant and any attempt to change its value could be detected by the FORTRAN compiler and flagged as an error. In addition, if we wished to modify the program to work with a different size of table, we would only have to change the PARAMETER statement.

COMMENT. The distinction between

```
DATA TABSIZ/100/
```

and

```
PARAMETER (TABSIZ=100)
```

is that in the former TABSIZ is a variable. It may be changed by the program. With the PARAMETER statement, we are simply giving a symbolic name to a constant. Although TABSIZ may still look like a variable, it is not.

For this reason, it would not be appropriate, in a DETAIL routine, to write code such as

```
PARAMETER (PAGENO=1,LINECT=45)
```

The DATA statement is needed here, because the page number and line count will need to change as the program is running.

SAVE

The SAVE statement was introduced in Section 4.2 and used again in Section 11.4. The statement has the form

SAVE name1,name2, . . .

where name1, name2, and so forth are each local variable names, local array names, or COMMON names enclosed in slashes. If a COMMON name is used, then the interpretation is that all variables in the common area are to be saved. If no names are listed then the statement is interpreted as if all the local variables and COMMONs referenced in the program unit are to be saved.

CAUTION. Only local variables or local array names (or COMMON names) may be used. Note that argument names or names of variables or arrays within COMMONs may not be used.

If a local variable or array is listed in a SAVE statement then the value of that variable is retained following a return from the subprogram. Thus, when the subprogram is reentered at a later time, the value of the variable is the same as it was when the return was performed. If a COMMON name is listed, then the values of all variables in the common are retained when a return is executed. In the case of a COMMON, however, another subprogram might reference the COMMON and change selected variable values or even cause selected variables to become undefined. If a COMMON name is listed in a SAVE statement, then that COMMON should be listed in a SAVE statement in every subprogram which references that COMMON area.

Some sample SAVE statements for the variables

```
REAL X,Y(100),A,B
COMMON/XYZ/ A,B
```

are:

```
SAVE X,Y or SAVE /XYZ/ or SAVE
```

The values of some variables are retained without SAVE statements being required. These include:

1. variables in blank common;
2. initially defined variables (using a DATA statement) that have not been redefined or become undefined; and

3. variables in a named common block where the common block is referenced in another program unit that either directly or indirectly called the subprogram from which the return is being executed.

DATA

The DATA statement has been introduced earlier (Section 4.2) and used in a number of examples. This statement provides initial values for variables. It is of the form

DATA name1,name2, . . . /value1,value2, . . ./

There are certain special forms that may be used in the list of names or list of values. If A is an array then a list of names such as

```
A(1), A(3), A(5), A(7)
```

can be written using an implied DO as

```
(A(I),I=1,7,2)
```

Also, if all elements of an array are to be initialized then we may simply place the name of the array in the list of names. If A is an array declared and dimensioned as

```
REAL A(3,2)
```

then the data statements

```
DATA A/ . . . /
```

and

```
DATA((A(I,J),I=1,3),J=1,2)/ . . . /
```

are equivalent. Notice that this implies that the values in the value list are placed into the array by columns.

The values in the value list are constants of the same type as the corresponding variables or array elements in the variable list. A number of identical adjacent values in the value list can be represented by the notation

```
n*v
```

where n is the number of values and v is the value. For example, the six elements of the array A used above can be initialized to zero using

```
DATA A/6*0.0/
```

IMPLICIT

As indicated earlier a variable or function which is not typed by appearing in an explicit type statement is REAL unless the first letter of the name is I, J, K, L, M, or N, in which case the variable is INTEGER. The IMPLICIT statement allows us to override this default typing of variable and function names. For example, the statement

```
      IMPLICIT REAL(A,B,C),INTEGER(I-N),DOUBLE PRECISION(D-H),
     $  CHARACTER*5(O-R)
```

would cause variables beginning with A, B, or C to be REAL; I, J, K, L, M, or N to be INTEGER; D, E, F, G, or H to be DOUBLE PRECISION; and O, P, Q, or R to be CHARACTER of length 5. The remaining letters S to Z would follow the default rule and would indicate REALs. The IMPLICIT statement must appear before any specification statement except for PARAMETER statements.

Our policy is to explicitly type all names, and thus we would not generally use the IMPLICIT statement.

EQUIVALENCE

The EQUIVALENCE statement is used to make two or more variables or array elements share the same memory locations. The statement provides the programmer with the power to manipulate values in nonstandard ways. However, if used in nonstandard ways, this statement can be a source of difficulty in transferrring programs from one computer system to another.

There are a few situations in which the statement is useful and which do not cause problems with program portability. One of these situations is when two large arrays are used in different portions of a program and there is no overlap of use. Then these arrays could be made to share the same memory area and thus reduce the total memory requirement. (This might be especially important when working with a relatively small computer.)

A sample of the statement is

```
      REAL A,B,C,X(2000),Y(2000)
      EQUIVALENCE (A,B,C), (X,Y)
```

As a result of this statement the variables A, B, and C share the same location, while the arrays X and Y share the same 2000 locations. The variables sharing a location do not have to be the same type; however, CHARACTER variables can only be equivalanced to other CHARACTER variables. The standard specifies that REAL, INTEGER, and LOGICAL variables require one storage unit and DOUBLE PRECISION and COMPLEX require two units.

Some care is required in using EQUIVALENCE. For example, consider

```
      REAL X(5),Y(3),Z(4)
      EQUIVALENCE (X,Z), (X(3),Y)
```

The first list (X,Z) causes this overlapping:

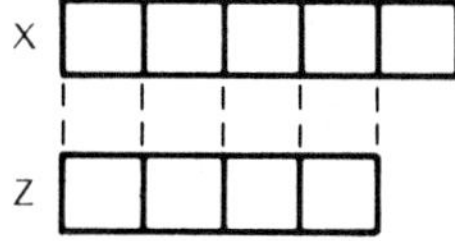

and the second list (X(3),Y) causes:

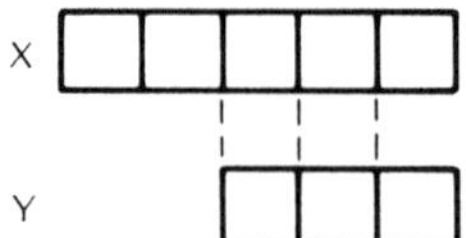

The net result is

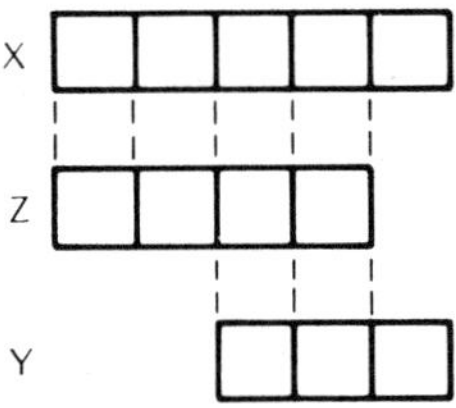

Observe that Z and Y will partially overlap, even though there is no explicit EQUIVALENCE involving them.

One standard conforming application would be a situation where the programmer wanted to refer to the columns of a two-dimensional array as one-dimensional arrays. For example, suppose a store sells three products and is open five days per week. The sales of each product for a given day could be entered in an element of an array SALES(5,3) where the row position indicates the day of the week and the column position the product.

The statements

```
      REAL SALES(5,3),PROD1(5),PROD2(5),PROD3(5)
      EQUIVALENCE (SALES(1,1),PROD1(1)),(SALES(1,2),PROD2(1)),
     $    (SALES(1,3),PROD3(1))
```

would cause the array PROD1 to be the same as the first column of the array SALES, and similarly for PROD2 and PROD3. This can be done since FORTRAN stores the elements of a two-dimensional array with the elements of a given column appearing in contiguous locations. We *cannot* equivalence a single-dimensional array to the rows of a two-dimensional array.

A final standard conforming use would be to equivalence a number of simple variables to the elements of an array. This would, for example, permit the initialization of the variables to be performed by a loop referencing the array elements.

EQUIVALENCE and COMMON

It is possible to use EQUIVALENCE in connection with variables which are also in COMMON. However, this should be done with great care. Likewise, care should be given when using EQUIVALENCE with variables of different types, as it may cause problems.

For example, consider

```
DOUBLE PRECISION D,E
REAL X(2)
EQUIVALENCE (D,X(1)),(E,X(2))
```

which forces this alignment

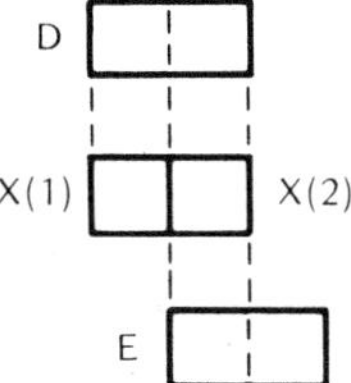

D and E wind up sharing space, which, while allowed, is probably not wise in most applications.

Similarly, consider

```
REAL X(3),Y(2),Z(2)
EQUIVALENCE (X(2),Y(1)),(Z(1),Y(2))
COMMON X,Z
```

The EQUIVALENCE causes

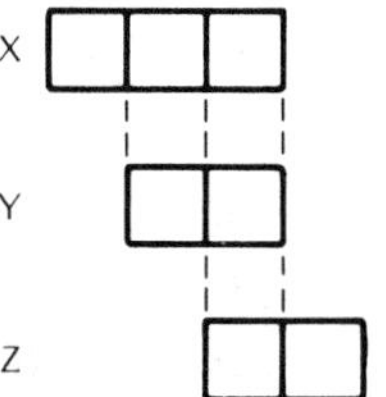

which is incompatible with the COMMON statement's requirement that Z follow X in the COMMON block memory.

Subprogram Arguments

Dummy arguments of a subprogram may not be used in COMMON, EQUIVALENCE, or SAVE statements. The fundamental idea is that these three statements specify details about the positioning or usage of variables in the computer memory. The dummy argument will be replaced by another variable or value when the subprogram is called, and the position or usage defined for the actual argument supplied at the time of the call may conflict with the position or usage defined by these statements.

REVIEW

PARAMETER (name1=value1,name2=value2, . . .)

Names: usual FORTRAN names

Values: constants (of appropriate type) or expressions which may use previously defined PARAMETER names

Uses: (a) meaningful names for constants; (b) easier modification when desired values for constants change

SAVE list

List may include:

1. local variables;
2. local array names; and
3. COMMON names in slashes

Causes values of indicated variables to be preserved upon return from the subprogram.

DATA name1, name2, . . ./value1,value2, . . ./

Names: variable names, array names, or implied DO's

Values: individual constants of appropriate type
n*v for repeated values

IMPLICIT type1(list1), . . .

Types: usual types (REAL, and so forth)

Lists: may be in forms such as A,B,C or A−C

Overrides default type convention

EQUIVALENCE (list1),(list2), . . .

Lists: may include variable names, array names, array elements
Items in each list are stored in same location in memory. (This may have other overlapping effects, especially if used in conjunction with COMMON.)

CAUTION. May not include dummy arguments in COMMON, EQUIVALENCE, or SAVE statements.

EXERCISES

1. In an earlier example (Section 4.3) we indicated that one use of LOGICAL variables could be to include debugging statements which would be printed if a logical variable, say DEBUG, was true. We could use DATA to initialize that variable to .TRUE. when the program was being tested. After testing was complete, we could change the initializations to .FALSE.. Could this variable be replaced by a named constant; if so, what declarations would be needed?

2. Discuss the difference between these approaches for a program where many subprograms refer to the same array. What are the strengths and weaknesses of each approach?

(a) Using PARAMETER in each subprogram to make references to the array size easy to modify.

(b) Using PARAMETER only in the main program, and using "adjustable dimension" concepts in the subprograms. This necessitates passing the array size as an argument to the subprograms.

(c) Placing a variable with the array size in a common block, using DATA in a BLOCK DATA subprogram to give the variable a value.

3. For the variables declared by

```
REAL X(3),Y(2),Z,A,B,C
COMMON /T/ X,A
```

what variables have their values saved as a result of each of the following?

(a) SAVE /T/

(b) SAVE Y,B

(c) SAVE Z,/T/,C

(d) SAVE

4. Give declarations and DATA for the following:

(a) For a REAL array A of size 200, set all odd-subscripted locations to 0.0, all others to 1.0

(b) For a 7 × 10 INTEGER array A, set the first five columns to 0, the others to 1.

(c) For the array of (b), initialize the first three columns to 13.

(d) For the array of (b), initialize the first two rows to 17, the final three rows to −3.

5. Give a diagram illustrating the overlap for each of the following:

(a)
```
REAL X,Y(3),Z(4)
EQUIVALENCE (X,Z(2)),(Y,Z)
```

(b)
```
INTEGER I(10),J(4),K(3)
EQUIVALENCE (I,J), (I(3),K(2))
```

(c)
```
INTEGER I(10),J(5,2)
EQUIVALENCE (I,J)
```

Hint: J is stored as column 1, then column 2.

6. Consider the following declarations

```
INTEGER NUMIN,NUMOUT,NUMTOT
INTEGER NUM(3)
COMMON NUMIN,NUMOUT,NUMTOT
EQUIVALENCE (NUM(1),NUMIN)
```

What are NUM(2) and NUM(3) equivalent to?

7. Explain why the following set of declarations is inconsistent.

```
INTEGER N(5),M(6),I,J,K
EQUIVALENCE (N(2),M(3))
EQUIVALENCE (N(4),I)
EQUIVALENCE (M(6),J)
EQUIVALENCE (I,J)
```

Can we say that any particular one of the EQUIVALENCE statements is wrong?

8. **(a)** Give code to declare a 100×4 INTEGER array VALUES. Using EQUIVALENCE, name the columns as ID, AGE, SALARY, and SEX (0=male, 1=female).

   (b) Give code to swap two people in this array (those at positions ROW1 and ROW2). Is swapping two rows of the VALUES array easier than working with the four column arrays individually?

   (c) Give code to sort the array in ascending order by salary.

12

ELEMENTARY CHARACTER MANIPULATION

12.1 ELEMENTARY CHARACTER OPERATIONS

We have been using CHARACTER variables and constants in limited ways beginning in Chapter 1. This chapter explores this data type in more detail.

NOTE. Not all the features we describe are available on every computer.

Constants and Variables

We begin with a description of the ways a program can refer to a character entity. First of all, we may have a **CHARACTER constant** such as the following:

```
'A'
'IOWA'
'POSITIVE'
' = '
```

A CHARACTER constant consists of one or more characters, enclosed in apostrophes (single quotes). The *length* of the constant is the number of characters, not including the enclosing quotes. The length must be greater than 0. For example,

```
'A'            has length 1
'IOWA'         has length 4
'POSITIVE'     has length 8
' = '          has length 3
```

Observe that blanks do count as characters in determining the length.

Apostrophes in a character constant are represented by two consecutive apostrophes. To represent the word DON'T we write

```
'DON''T' (length is 5, not 6)
```

A **CHARACTER variable** is a variable used to store character data. Variables are declared to be CHARACTER variables by a declaration of the form

```
CHARACTER*n variable list
```

The variable list consists of one or more variables, separated by commas. The "n" represents the length (in characters) of each of the variables in the lists. The length n is an unsigned, nonzero integer constant. For example, we might have

```
CHARACTER*20 NAME,NAMARR(35)
CHARACTER*2 STATE
CHARACTER*1 SEX,GRADE
```

This declares two variables, SEX and GRADE, of length 1, and one variable, STATE, of length 2. In addition, the variable NAME is of length 20, and the array NAMARR consists of 35 items, each of length 20. Note that when we write CHARACTER*20, the length 20 refers to each variable in the list that follows.

There is an alternate way to write the CHARACTER declaration. Rather than specifying the length for an entire list of variables, we may specify it separately for each variable. The declaration

```
CHARACTER NAME*20,NAMARR(35)*20,STATE*2,SEX*1,GRADE*1
```

has the same effect as the three separate statements given earlier.

Finally, the length may be omitted, as in

```
CHARACTER STATE*2,SEX,GRADE
```

If the length is omitted, a length of 1 is assumed.

Substrings

A **string** is a sequence of one or more characters. Thus, the value stored in a CHARACTER variable is a string. Each character in the string has a *position* within that string, numbered starting with 1.

Suppose that the variable RESULT presently contains the string

```
'FAIL'
```

Then the F is in position 1, the A in position 2, the I in position 3, and the L in position 4.

In determining position, any blanks are significant. For example, for the string

```
' = '
```

the length is 3, and the = is in position 2.

It is possible in FORTRAN to refer to a **substring** of a string that is stored in a variable (or an array element). A substring is a string of one or more consecutive characters from the original string. We identify the substring in FORTRAN by indicating three things:

1. var: the variable (or array element);
2. first: the position of the first character in the substring; and
3. last: the position of the last character in the substring.

The form is

```
var(first:last)
```

Suppose that the CHARACTER*12 variable STATE contains the value

```
'FLORIDAbbbbb'
```

Then the following substrings have the indicated values.

```
STATE(1:5)      'FLORI'
STATE(2:4)      'LOR'
STATE(7:7)      'A'
STATE(11:12)    'bb'
```

This example illustrates that

```
1≤first≤last≤len
```

where "len" is the length of the variable referred to. The actual form of "first" and "last" may be any integer expressions, provided the resulting values satisfy this limitation.

Suppose I,J, and K are INTEGER variables, A is a CHARACTER*14 variable, and B is a CHARACTER*7 array of size 17. We might have substring expressions of the following forms:

```
B(6)(1:3)        (characters 1-3 of B(6))
A(3:3)
A(1:I)
A(I:J)
B(I)(1:J)        (characters 1-J of B(I))
A(I+J:I+K+1)
```

The expressions may be as complicated as we like and may even include function calls:

```
A(1+MOD(I,J):12)
B(I+J)(1:INT(SQRT(REAL(K))))
```

COMMENT. We may omit either the "first" or the "last" (or both). For example, if A is a CHARACTER*11 variable,

```
A(:7)    is the same as A(1:7)
A(3:)    is the same as A(3:11)
A(:)     is the same as A(1:11), or just A
```

Using CHARACTER Values

In this subsection, we indicate how CHARACTER variables, constants, and substrings may be used in:

1. DATA statements;
2. READ and WRITE statements;
3. assignment statements; and
4. comparisons (in IF statements).

DATA

The DATA statement, of course, is used to give an initial value to a variable prior to running the program. The initialization takes place at compile time.

We have seen the DATA statement in forms similar to this:

```
CHARACTER*3 A,B
DATA A/'AMA'/,B/'ART'/
```

Two additional points are worth noting.

First, it is possible to use the DATA statement to initialize a substring of a variable, as in

```
CHARACTER*8 IDENT
DATA INDENT(3:5)/'PRO'/
```

(The first, second, sixth, seventh, and eight positions are *not* given any value.)

Secondly, the character constant being placed into the variable (or substring) may be longer or shorter than the required length. If so, truncation and padding (with blanks) will occur on the right. For example:

```
CHARACTER*3 A,B
DATA A/'APPLE'/,B/'GO'/
```

will cause A to have the value 'APP', with the last two characters truncated (cut off). B will have the value 'GOb,' right padded with blanks. Similarly,

```
CHARACTER*8 IDENT,TAG
DATA IDENT(3:5)/'PROD'/,TAG(2:4)/'A'/
```

will yield

```
IDENT — 'uuPROuuu'
TAG — 'uAbbuuuu'
```

(Here "b" stands for blank, "u" for undefined. Being blank is different from being undefined. An undefined variable, or portion of a variable, has not yet been given any value at all.)

I/O

We have discussed the use of the A format for reading and writing CHARACTER variables. At this point we merely observe that it is possible to use the substring notation in either a READ or WRITE statement, as in this example

```
      CHARACTER*7 IDENT
      DATA IDENT(2:4)/'-L-'/
          .
          .
      READ(*,1000) IDENT(1:1),IDENT(5:)
 1000 FORMAT(A1,A3)
          .
          .
      WRITE(*,2000) IDENT(:4),IDENT(3:3),IDENT
 2000 FORMAT(' ',A4,2X,A1,2X,A7)
```

If the data record contained J14A, the READ together with the DATA would cause IDENT to have the value 'J-L-14A', and the WRITE would print the three substrings 'J-L-', 'L', and 'J-L-14A'.

Assignment

The form of a character assignment statement is

var = exp

where "var" is a CHARACTER variable (or array element) and "exp" is a CHARACTER expression. We have previously seen assignment statements such as

```
GRADE = 'A'             ('exp' is a constant)
LNAME = NAME            ('exp' is a variable)
NAMES(I) = INNAME
OUTNAM = NAMES(I)       ('exp' is an array reference)
GRADE = GRADEF(AVE)     ('exp' is a CHARACTER function reference)
```

In addition to these four possibilities, the expression or the variable (or both) may be a substring reference.

Suppose data records contain section name, department name, and production data (mm/dd/yy). It is desired to determine identification codes of the form ddd-ss-yy, where ddd is the first three characters of the department, ss is the first two characters of the section, and yy is the year from the date. Code similar to this might be used:

```
CHARACTER IDENT*9,DEPT*15,SECTION*12,DATE*8
DATA IDENT(4:4)/'-'/,IDENT(7:7)/'-'/
   .
   .
   .
IDENT(1:3) = DEPT(1:3)      (or DEPT(:3))
IDENT(5:6) = SECTION(1:2)
IDENT(8:9) = DATE(7:8)      (or IDENT(8:) = DATE(7:))
```

Since the fourth and seventh positions of IDENT do not change, the DATA statement is used to assign values to them.

As with the DATA statement, it is possible that the length of the expression is different from that of the variable (or substring) into which the expression is to be placed. The action taken in this case is analogous to that for the DATA statement:

1. If the expression value is too long for the variable, the rightmost characters of the expression are removed (truncated).
2. If the expression value is too short, the value is right padded with blanks.

If A is CHARACTER*5, then

```
A = 'RESULT'        gives A the value 'RESUL'
A = 'PASS'          gives A the value 'PASSb'
A(2:4) = 'PASS'     gives A the value 'nPASn'
A(2:4) = 'F'        gives A the value 'nFbbn'
```

(Here 'b' stands for a blank, 'n' for "no change." The character positions which are not changed may remain undefined, if they were previously undefined.)

Concatenation

Just as we may combine numerical values by using operations such as addition, it is possible to use **concatenation** to combine character values. "Concatenation", which means "placing side by side" was discussed briefly in Section 2.1.

The expression on the right side of a character assignment statement may include the concatenation operator, which is written

```
//
```

Now let's suppose A is CHARACTER*3 and has value 'NEW', and B is CHARACTER*4, with value 'YORK'. Then the value of the expression

```
A // ' '// B
```

is the eight character string 'NEW YORK' formed by placing the values of A, the character constant ' ', and B side by side. We could include this in an assignment statement such as

```
STATE = A // ' ' // B
```

where STATE is a CHARACTER*8 variable.

It is possible to concatenate any number of variables, constants, substrings, array elements, and function references in an expression. Assuming that A is CHARACTER*7, B is a CHARACTER*5 function with four parameters, and C is a CHARACTER*3 array of size 17, we might write

```
D = A(2:4) // B(I,J,K,L) // C(7)(2:)
```

(The result is of length 3 + 5 + 2 = 10.)

Given three variables FIRST, MIDDLE, and LAST, containing a person's three given names, we might write

```
      NAME = LAST // ',' // FIRST(1:1) // '. '
     $            // MIDDLE(1:1) // '.'
```

to create a name of the form

```
'SMITH   , J. T.'
```

(Later we will learn techniques which may be used to "get rid of" the unwanted blanks which are part of the value of LAST.)

COMMENT. Parentheses are allowed in character expressions but have no effect. Writing

```
E = A // (B // (C // D))
```

is the same as writing

```
E = A // B // C // D
```

CAUTION. For the assignment statement

var = exp

none of the characters being given a value within "var" may be included in "exp." For example,

```
A(1:3) = A(2:2) // 'TH'
```

is not allowed. Since character positions 1, 2, and 3 are being given values by the assignment statement, A(2:2) may not appear on the right side.

This rules out some of the types of things we are used to doing with numerical variables, such as

```
TOTAL = TOTAL + WAGE
```

The analogous

```
STRING(1:20) = STRING(1:10) // WORD
```

is not allowed. However, we can easily achieve the same result by writing

```
STRING(11:20) = WORD
```

Comparisons

The final topic for this section is the comparison of CHARACTER values (in a logical expression, perhaps for an IF statement).

The simplest comparisons are

```
expl .EQ. exp2
expl .NE. exp2
```

We have used these types in simple forms such as these:

```
IF(OP.EQ.'+') THEN
IF(NAME.NE.LIST(I)) THEN
```

and so on. At this point we should observe that the "expressions" may be more complicated than this. In fact, they may include any of the ideas used in writing expressions for assignment statements:

```
CHARACTER constant
CHARACTER variable
CHARACTER array element
CHARACTER function reference
substring
concatenation
```

> **COMMENT.** If one expression is shorter than the other, the shorter expression is right padded with blanks in making the comparison. When compared, 'JOHNSON' and 'JOHNSON   ' are considered equal.

Suppose we have a loop which contains these steps:

```
loop
   read NAME,...
   if NAME is blank then exit endif
      .
      .
      .
endloop
```

The **exit** step may be coded as

```
IF(NAME.EQ.' ') THEN
   GO TO 400
ENDIF
```

even though the variable NAME is certainly more than one character long.

In addition to .EQ. and .NE., we may use the other four operators .GT., .GE., .LT., and .LE. in comparisons. Once again, the shorter expression will be right padded with blanks in doing the comparison.

COMMENT. The comparison is an "alphabetical" comparison:

1. 'A' comes before 'Z';
2. 'O' comes before '9'; and
3. 'b' comes before 'A' and before '0'.

However, there is no set rule on whether letters precede digits, or on how such characters as '.', '$', and so forth will relate either to each other or to the letters and digits.

The following are sample examples showing how the previous rules apply.

```
'JOHN'.LT.'JOHNSON' is .TRUE.
'JOHNS, C.'.LT.'JOHNSTON, R.' may vary from computer to computer
'J2C'.GT.'J1C' is .TRUE.
'J2C'.GT.'JAC' may vary
```

Let us consider a few applications of this concept.

Write a segment of code to count the blank words in a CHARACTER*8 array of size 48.

```
          INTEGER COUNT,I
          CHARACTER*8 ARR(48)       (or CHARACTER ARR(48)*8)
              .
              .
          COUNT = 0
          DO 100 I = 1,48
             IF(ARR(I).EQ.' ') COUNT = COUNT + 1
    100   CONTINUE
```

Write a segment of code to change the first letter of every word in the same array to the letter 'D'.

```
          DO 200 I = 1,48
             ARR(I)(1:1) = 'D'
    200   CONTINUE
```

Modify the previous example to change the first letter to 'D' only if the last letter is an I,J,K,M,or N.

The body of the loop becomes

```
       IF(ARR(I) (8:8).GE.'I' .AND.
     $    ARR(I) (8:8).LE.'N') ARR(I)(1:1)='D'
```

REVIEW

CHARACTER constants

'string of characters'

length is # of characters, cannot be 0

Declaration of CHARACTER variable

```
CHARACTER*n list of variables
```

or

```
CHARACTER var1*n1, var2*n2,...
    (default length is 1)
```

Example: CHARACTER NAME*20,WORD(25)*6,SEX,GRADE*2

Substrings

Form: var(first:last) (1≤first≤last≤size)
or array(subscript,...)(first:last)
default on first is 1, on last is size of variable or array element
Example: A(3:7), B(1:), C(6)(3:30), D(:12)

DATA

Form: DATA var/char.constant/
"var" may be variable, array element, or substring reference
Notes:

1. Right truncate if constant too long.
2. Right pad with blanks if constant too short.

I/O

May read or print variable, array element, or substring

Assignment

Form:var = exp
"var" is variable, array element, or substring reference
"exp" may include constant, variable, array element, function reference, or substring reference.
may combine using // (concatenation)
Notes:

1. Right truncate if expression has too many characters.
2. Right pad with blanks if expression has too few characters.

Comparisons

May use .EQ.,.NE.,.GT.,.GE.,.LT., or .LE. as relational operator ("relop")
Form: exp relop exp
"exp" may be any expression allowed in an assignment statement

Notes:

1. If unequal lengths, shorter expression is right padded with blanks for comparison.
2. .LT., etc., are based on "collating sequence" (basically alphabetical order, but computers may differ when comparisons involve digits or special symbols).

EXERCISES

1. Tell what values are given to each variable by the following declarations and DATA statements.

(a)
```
CHARACTER*2 A,B,C
DATA A/'X'/,B/'XY'/,C/'XYZ'/
```
(b)
```
CHARACTER NAME*12,ZIP*5,SEX*6
DATA NAME/' '/,ZIP/'01013'/,SEX/'MALE'/
```
(c)
```
CHARACTER SEX,CITY*12,DEPT*3
DATA SEX/'FEMALE'/,CITY/'NEW YORK'/,DEPT/'PER'/
```

2. Follow the instructions of Exercise 1.

(a)
```
   CHARACTER*7 A,B,C,D
   DATA A(:3)/'X'/,B(3:6)/'CANTOR'/,C(5:)/'HOG'/,
$  D(:)/'BASEBALL'/
```
(b)
```
CHARACTER*12 PRODCT
CHARACTER*7 STATE
DATA STATE(1:2)/'CA'/,PRODCT(7:)/'NYLON'/
```

3. Suppose that the variable A is CHARACTER*10, and that it is undefined when the assignment statements given below are executed. Show its contents after each assignment statement, using b for blank and u for undefined. (For example, for A(9:10) = 'R' the answer is 'uuuuuuuuRb').

(a) `A = ' '`
(b) `A = 'CAT'//' '//'DOG'`
(c) `A = ' '//'ARE'//'NOT'`
(d) `A(1:3) = 'SUM'`
(e) `A(1:3) = 'SO'`
(f) `A(1:3) = 'SOME'`
(g) `A(7:) = 'SUM'`
(h) `A(:) = ' '//'AX'`
(i) `A(4:8) = 'MIX'`

4. Follow the directions of Exercise 3, assuming also that CHARR is declared as

```
CHARACTER CHARR(10)*5
```

and that the words 'ONE','TWO',...,'TEN' are in the ten elements of CHARR.

(a) `A = CHARR(1)`
(b) `A = CHARR(1) (1:1)`
(c) `A = CHARR(3)//CHARR(10)`
(d) `A = CHARR(3)(1:5)//CHARR(10)(1:3)`
(e) `A = CHARR(3)(:5)//CHARR(10)`
(f) `A = CHARR(1)(1:4)//'-'//CHARR(10)(1:3)`
(g)
```
   A = CHARR(1)(:1)//CHARR(2)(:2)//CHARR(3)(:3)
$    //CHARR(4)(:4)//CHARR(5)(:5)
```

5. Write segments of FORTRAN code for the following. Include any necessary declarations.

(a) Look up a given name in a given array of names of size 10. Print either the subscript where found, or a message saying it was not found.

(b) Modify (a) to print the subscript as a word, such as:

```
IT WAS FOUND AT LOCATION ONE
```

(c) For a given name and a given array (size N) of names, print a list of those array entries which agree with this name in the first five characters.

(d) Print a message telling whether a given array of states adheres to this rule; there may be no nonblank entries following the first blank entry (if any).

(e) Given an array of words, delete any duplicates by changing them to blanks.

(f) Given an array of words, move all blank words (if any) to the end of the list.

6. For each part of Exercise 5, make appropriate decisions on parameters and indicate the necessary additions to write the FORTRAN segments as subprograms.

7. **(a)** Write a function to count the number of blanks in a string of length 20. [*Hint*: Use comparisons such as WORD(I:I).EQ.' '.]

(b) Write a function to locate the position of the first blank character in a given string of length 20 (for example, for 'JONES, ROBERT E.   'the answer is 7).

(c) Write a function to determine the length of a string of nonblanks starting at a given position POS in a given string of length 20.

8. Given a variable NAME which contains a name such as

```
JOHNSON, JOSEPH LAWRENCE
```

write code to obtain the proper value for a variable LAST which should contain only the last name.

Note: NAME is CHARACTER*25. It contains a last name terminated by a comma, then first and middle names. LAST is CHARACTER*12. [*Hint*: Use the ideas of Exercise 7(b).]

9. Give a function to create a magazine account number, given last name (ten characters), initials (two characters), city (ten characters), and date of expiration in the form mm/yy (five characters).

The account number is in a form such as

```
CRAJW-DEC89-SP
```

This consists of:

(1) first three letters of last name

(2) initials

(3) dash

(4) month of expiration (JAN,FEB, and so on.)

(5) year of expiration

(6) dash

(7) first and fourth characters of city

10. Give a function which has three parameters: a word of length 7, a character, and a position (1–7). Its answer consists of a word formed by replacing the character in the given position of the given word by the given character.

11. Give a function which, for a given word of length 8, places N blanks in the word starting at position POS.

For example, if the word is 'ABCDEFGH', N is 3, POS is 2, the answer is 'AbbbBCDE'.

12.2 MORE CHARACTER OPERATIONS

The previous section discussed CHARACTER constants, variables, and substrings, as well as some methods used to manipulate character data. In this section we examine COMMON and EQUIVALENCE as they relate to CHARACTER variables, and we look at CHARACTER values as parameters of subprograms.

EQUIVALENCE

In the EQUIVALENCE statement

```
EQUIVALENCE (listl),(list2),...
```

the lists may include CHARACTER variables and substring references. We are not allowed to equivalence a CHARACTER entity with any type of variable other than another CHARACTER entity. That is, if one of the lists contains a CHARACTER variable reference, then all other items in that particular list must also be of type CHARACTER.

Let us, then, consider a list of the form

(item1,item2,...)

where each item in the list is of type CHARACTER. The items may have different lengths. Since consecutive characters are stored consecutively in the computer memory, we may obtain overlapping other than that specifically stated. For example, consider

```
CHARACTER A*5,B*4,C*3
EQUIVALENCE (A,B(2:3)),(B(3:4),C)
```

These lists yield

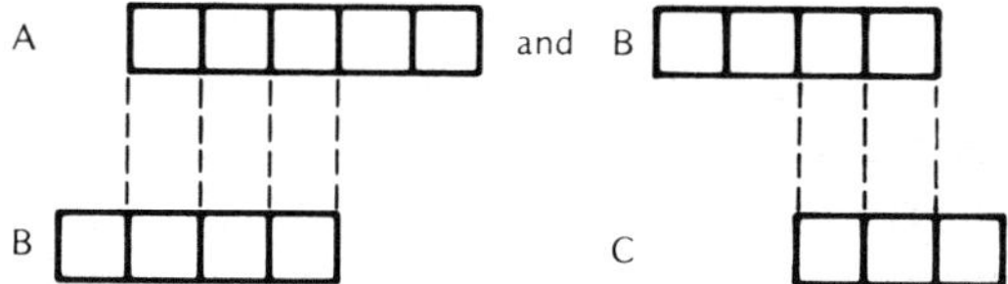

The net result is the following, with the resulting correspondences listed.

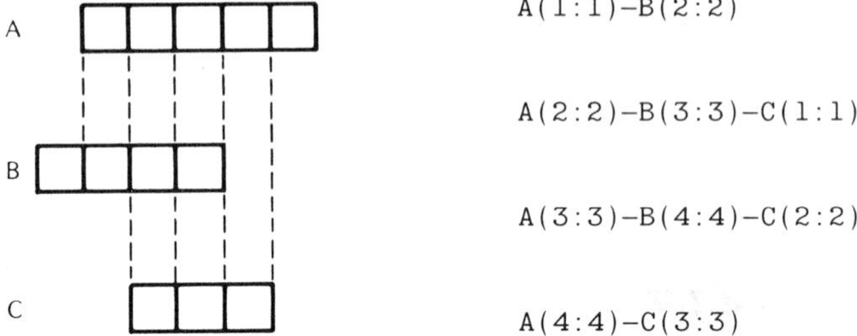

COMMENT. In many ways a CHARACTER variable looks much like an array. The correspondences shown above are reminiscent of those discussed for arrays in Chapter 11.

CAUTIONS.

1. Note that no dummy argument of a subprogram may be included in an EQUIVALENCE list.
2. We may not include contradictory EQUIVALENCE lists. For example, adding the list (A,C) to the previous example would be inconsistent with the other two lists, and would not be allowed.

In addition to variable names and substring references, an EQUIVALENCE statement may include array names, as in the following example.

```
CHARACTER A*10,B(5)*2,C*5,D(7)
EQUIVALENCE (A,B),(C(3:3),D(1))
```

COMMON

As discussed in Chapter 11, there are two types of COMMON blocks: **named** COMMON, and unnamed (or **blank**) COMMON. We may place CHARACTER variables and arrays in either type of COMMON block, subject to the following:

RULE. If any item in a given COMMON block is of type CHARACTER, then all elements in that given block must be of type CHARACTER.

We are not allowed to mix CHARACTER entities with any other type of entity in a COMMON block.

COMMON differs from EQUIVALENCE in that:

1. EQUIVALENCE is used to associate different items within the same subprogram or main program. We use COMMON to associate items from different program units.
2. We may not use substring references in the COMMON statement.

As was discussed in Chapter 11, we may refer to the same variable in a COMMON statement and in an EQUIVALENCE statement; however, the two references must be consistent. For example, this program segment is not allowed:

```
CHARACTER*3 A,B,C
COMMON A,C
EQUIVALENCE (A,B(1:1)),(B(2:2),C)
```

The EQUIVALENCE causes

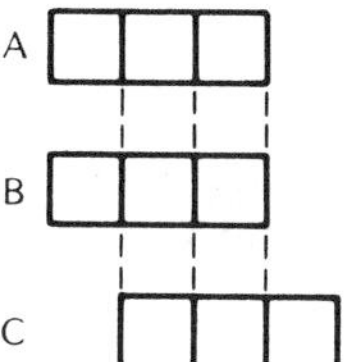

which is inconsistent with the COMMON statement's placement of C right after A.

CHARACTER Parameters

CHARACTER variables may be used as parameters for subprograms, and in fact we have done so in many earlier examples and exercises. In those previous problems, we have always taken care that the dummy argument and the actual argument are of the same length. For example, if the parameter in a subroutine is CHARACTER*3, we have passed an actual argument which is also CHARACTER*3.

FORTRAN actually relaxes this rule somewhat; if the actual argument's length is greater than that of the dummy argument in the subprogram, there is no problem. The parameter in the subprogram will refer to the leftmost character positions of the actual argument.

> **CAUTION.** On the other hand, the actual argument is not allowed to be shorter than the dummy argument.

Another useful feature in working with CHARACTER parameters is similar to a feature we have seen for arrays as parameters. In order to make our subprograms as general as possible, we learned how to use **adjustable dimensions** (Section 8.3).

In a similar fashion, any CHARACTER variable or array which is a parameter in a subprogram may be declared with a length of (*). For example,

```
INTEGER FUNCTION EX(A,B,C)
CHARACTER*(*) A,B,C
```

The parameters A, B, and C are not given explicit lengths within the subprogram. When the subprogram is invoked, their lengths will be based on the lengths of the corresponding parameters in the calling program. For the call

```
INTEGER EX,ANS
CHARACTER M*5,N,P*2
     .
     .
     .
ANS = EX(M,N,P)
```

the parameters A,B, and C would have lengths 5, 1, and 2, respectively.

Examples

In Section 12.4 we will consider some case studies using CHARACTER manipulation. Here we give some relatively simple examples.

It is sometimes convenient to use EQUIVALENCE to treat a string as an array of characters. (This is especially true if our particular computer does not support substring manipulations.)

For example, suppose someone has written a function BLCNT(ARR,N). Given a CHARACTER*1 array of size N, this function counts the blanks in that array. We may use this function to count the blanks in any CHARACTER variable, as illustrated in this simple program segment.

```
INTEGER BLCNT,BLANK1,BLANK2
CHARACTER NAME*20,CITY*14,NAMARR(20)*1,CITARR(14)*1
EQUIVALENCE (NAME,NAMARR), (CITY,CITARR)
    .
    .
READ(*,1000) NAME,CITY
    .
    .
BLANK1 = BLCNT(NAMARR,20)
BLANK2 = BLCNT(CITARR,14)
```

(It is assumed that there are other places in the program where it is more convenient to have the string NAME than the array NAMARR. If not, we could have simply used the arrays themselves in the main program.)

Suppose several routines share access to several items:

CARD, a CHARACTER*80 string
VOWEL, an array of vowels ('A','E','I','O','U')
LETTS, an array of letters ('A' to 'Z')
DIGITS, an array of digits ('0' to '9')
LENCT, an array of counters
VOWCT, an array of counters
HEAP, an array of characters
SUBSC, an array of subscripts relating to HEAP

We might have declarations which include

```
INTEGER LENCT(15),VOWCT(6),SUBSC(100)
CHARACTER CARD*80,VOWEL(6),LETTS(26),DIGITS(10),HEAP(1000)
COMMON/COUNT/ LENCT,VOWCT
COMMON/CHARS/ CARD,VOWEL,LETTS,DIGITS
COMMON/HEAPCH/ HEAP
COMMON/HEAPSS/ SUBSC
```

The several different named COMMONs are used to:

1. organize the various items, perhaps based on which subprograms share which items;
2. avoiding mixing CHARACTER items with other types.

We next write a general-purpose character lookup routine, which looks up a given string in an array of strings. We have written similar routines before. By using adjustable dimensions for the array and a length of (*) for both the string and the array, we may achieve good generality.

```
      INTEGER FUNCTION CHLOOK(KEY,ARRAY,ASIZE,N)
      INTEGER ASIZE,N,I
      CHARACTER*(*) KEY,ARRAY(ASIZE)

C   WRITTEN BY *******, **/**/**.

C   THIS INTEGER FUNCTION LOOKS UP A STRING OF ANY LENGTH
C IN AN ARRAY OF STRINGS. IT RETURNS THE POSITION
C OF THE FIRST OCCURRENCE (OR 0 IF NO OCCURRENCE).

C   THESE PARAMETERS ARE USED:

C      KEY-INPUT, CHARACTER- STRING WE ARE LOOKING FOR.
C      ARRAY-INPUT, CHARACTER ARRAY OF LENGTH ASIZE-
C            ARRAY IN WHICH TO SEARCH FOR STRING.
C      ASIZE-INPUT, INTEGER-LENGTH OF ARRAY.
C      N-INPUT, INTEGER-PORTION OF ARRAY IN USE.

      CHLOOK = 0
      DO 10 I = 1,N
         IF(KEY.EQ.ARRAY(I)) THEN
            CHLOOK = I
            GO TO 100
         ENDIF
   10    CONTINUE
  100 CONTINUE
      RETURN
      END
```

REVIEW

EQUIVALENCE(list1),(list2),...
- Each list may contain:
  - CHARACTER variables
  - substring references
  - CHARACTER array names or references
- May not mix CHARACTER with other types

COMMON
- May not mix CHARACTER with other types in a COMMON block
- No substring references allowed

Subprogram parameters
- Dummy argument length must be ≤ actual argument length; if less, then uses leftmost portion of actual argument
- Dummy argument length may be (*); will assume the length of the actual parameter

EXERCISES

1. For each of the following, give a diagram illustrating the correspondences resulting from the EQUIVALENCE and COMMON statements.

(a)
```
CHARACTER*3 A,B,C
COMMON A,B
EQUIVALENCE (A(2:2),C)
```
(b)
```
CHARACTER A*3,B*4,C*6
COMMON A,B
EQUIVALENCE (A,C)
```
(c)
```
CHARACTER A*5,B*7,C*9,D*11
EQUIVALENCE (A,C,D),(A(4:4),B)
```
(d)
```
CHARACTER N*1,M*2,P*10
COMMON N,M
EQUIVALENCE (N,P),(M,P(5:5))
```

2. Follow the instructions of Exercise 1.

(a)
```
CHARACTER A*10,B(10)*1
EQUIVALENCE (A,B)
```
(b)
```
CHARACTER A(3)*4,B*6,C*5
COMMON B,C
EQUIVALENCE (A,B)
```
(c)
```
CHARACTER ADDRES*25,STATE*2,ZIP*5
EQUIVALENCE (ADDRES(19:19),STATE),(ADDRES(21:21),ZIP)
```
(d)
```
CHARACTER A(20)*1,B*5,C*3,D
COMMON C,D
EQUIVALENCE (A,B,C)
```
(e)
```
CHARACTER A(20)*1,B*5,C*3,D
COMMON C,D
EQUIVALENCE (B,C),(B(3:3),D)
```

3. Write program segments for the following, using the general-purpose character lookup function, CHLOOK. Include declarations.

(a) Given a letter, tell its position in the alphabet ('A' is 1, 'B' is 2, and so on).

(b) Given a digit, tell its value ('0' is 0, '1' is 1, and so on).

(c) Given parallel arrays NAME and AGE, tell how old John Smith is (or print an error message if not there). Assume the arrays are size 200, and there are N slots filled.

(d) For the arrays of (c), add 1 to Mary Spain's age.

(e) Given an array WORDS containing words of length 10 and a new word NEW, add NEW to the end of the WORDS array if it is not already in the array. The WORDS array is of size 1000, and there are NWORDS words already in the array.

4. Write a program which, given a series of data records containing text, tells how many times each letter occurs.

[*Hint*: Use parallel arrays LETTS and COUNTS, where LETTS contains the letters 'A' to 'Z', and COUNTS counts the corresponding letter. Use the CHLOOK function.]

5. Write a program which, given a series of data lines each containing one word of length 10, counts how many times each word appears.

[*Hint*: See the hint for Exercise 4, together with Exercise 3(e).]

6. Someone has written two functions which each have these three input parameters:

a CHARACTER*1 array
the size of the array
a starting position within the array

The first, called BLANK, returns the subscript of the first blank in the array at or after the given starting position. The second, called NONBLK, does the same for the first nonblank at or after the starting position.

(a) Using these functions, give code to generate a name of the form

last, first initial. middle initial.

given variables

```
CHARACTER LAST*12,FIRST*12,MIDDLE*12
```

For example, if LAST is 'JONESbbbbbbb', FIRST is 'SUSANbbbbbbb', and MIDDLE is BARBARAbbbbb', the answer should be 'JONES, S.B.'.

You may assume that the names each begin with a nonblank. [*Hint*: Use EQUIVALENCE to equate the CHARACTER*12 variables with CHARACTER*1 arrays of size 12.]

(b) Repeat (a), but do not assume that the names begin with a nonblank. For example, LAST might be bbbJONESbbbb'.

7. (a) Using the functions described in Exercise 6, give code to determine whether or not the first word in a given string of size 400 begins with an 'A'.

(b) Give code to determine whether or not this word ends with a 'W'.

8. Some systems do not support substring operations. On these systems, we may obtain some of the same results using EQUIVALENCE.

(a) Give code to EQUIVALENCE a CHARACTER*80 variable A to a CHARACTER*1 array AARRAY of size 80. Do the same for B and BARRAY.

(b) Without using substring operations, give code to accomplish

```
A(1:10) = B(13:22)
```

(c) Without using substrings, give code to accomplish

```
      WRITE(*,2000) A(15:70)
2000  FORMAT(' ',A56)
```

(d) Without using substrings, give code to accomplish

```
      DO 20 I = 1,80
         DO 10 J = 1,80
            IF(A(I,I).EQ.B(J:J))THEN
               GO TO 30
            ENDIF
10       CONTINUE
20    CONTINUE
```

(e) Without using substrings or concatenation, give code to accomplish

```
      A = B(41:80) // B(1:40)
```

12.3 FUNCTIONS FOR CHARACTER MANIPULATION

In this section we examine some character manipulation functions which are supplied by many versions of FORTRAN. However, not all computers will include these features.

Length

This first function is an INTEGER function named LEN. It has one input parameter, of type CHARACTER. The function returns the length of the string supplied as a parameter. For example,

LEN('ABC') is 3
LEN(X//Y) is the length of X plus that of Y
LEN(A(3:7)) is 5

COMMENT. This function can be used to determine the length of parameters which have been declared in a subprogram using the (*) length designation.

Conversions

Two functions are supplied which provide conversions from CHARACTER to INTEGER and back. To understand how these functions work, we must discuss the **collating sequence** for characters.

Each FORTRAN compiler assigns an ordering, or **collating sequence**, for the characters which may be used in character strings. The only rules are:

1. The letters 'A' to 'Z' appear in order.
2. The digits '0' to '9' appear in order.

3. The character ' ' must precede 'A' and also must precede '0'.
4. No intermixing of letters and digits is allowed.

As we discussed in Section 12.1, outside of these rules computers may vary in their order. The functions **ICHAR** and **CHAR** are based on the order assigned by the particular computer on which the program is being run.

ICHAR is an INTEGER function with one parameter. This parameter must be a character string of length 1. The answer returned is that character's relative position within the ordering sequence. This answer will be

0 for the first in the sequence
1 for the second in the sequence
2 for the third in the sequence

.
.
.

$n-1$ for the last in the sequence (assuming n characters in the sequence)

The CHAR function is the *inverse* of the ICHAR function. That is, given the position in the sequence, it will give us the character that occupies that position.

CHAR is thus a CHARACTER*1 function with a single INTEGER parameter. The value of that parameter must lie in the range 0 to $n-1$, where "n" is the number of characters in the collating sequence.

On a particular computer, it might be that ICHAR('A') is 63. If so, then CHAR(63) would be 'A'. In fact, it is true that, for any character CH in the allowable set of characters,

```
CHAR(ICHAR(CH)) is CH
```

and for any integer I in the range 0 to $n-1$,

```
ICHAR(CHAR(I)) is I
```

On a computer with 123 allowable characters, we could use this program to determine the order of those characters in the collating sequence:

```
      INTEGER I
      CHARACTER*1 CHAR
      DO 10 I = 0,122
         WRITE(*,2000) I,CHAR(I)
   10    CONTINUE
      STOP
 2000 FORMAT(' CHARACTER # ',I3,' IS ',A1)
      END
```

COMMENT. If you run this program, you may find that some of the allowable characters do not print on the particular printing device you are using. For example, many printers do not print lower case letters.

ASCII Comparisons

Because different computers have different collating sequences, comparisons using .GT.,.LE., and so on may give different results on different computers. To circumvent this problem, a set of functions is provided which does comparisons based on a standardized collating sequence. This standardized collating sequence is known as the ASCII sequence.

Each of these functions is a LOGICAL function with two parameters. These parameters are of type CHARACTER (of any length). The two strings are compared as indicated by the function name, and either .TRUE. or .FALSE. is returned as the answer, based on this comparison.

The descriptions given here assume that S1 and S2 are the two strings to be compared:

```
LGE(S1,S2) is .TRUE. if S1≥S2, else .FALSE.
LGT(S1,S2) is .TRUE. if S1>S2, else .FALSE.
LLE(S1,S2) is .TRUE. if S1≤S2, else .FALSE.
LLT(S1,S2) is .TRUE. if S1<S2, else .FALSE.
```

NOTES.

1. The "L" in these function names stands for "lexically," which is roughly synonymous with "alphabetically." Thus LGE means "lexically greater than or equal to."
2. If one of S1 or S2 is shorter than the other, it is considered as being right padded with blanks for the comparison.

Locating Substrings

We have seen, especially in Chapter 6, the importance of "lookup" type operations in an array. The same type of operation is important in working with strings of characters. For example, we might want to know whether or not a particular character appears in a string and if so, in what position.

FORTRAN supplies a function which can be used to answer this type of question. In fact, it can answer more general questions concerning whether a particular string occurs as a substring.

The function described is the INTEGER function INDEX. It has two character arguments, which we will refer to as STRING and SUBST (short for "substring"). Using these names,

```
INDEX(STRING,SUBST)
```

returns the starting position within STRING of the occurrence of SUBST as a substring. For example,

```
INDEX ('ABC','A') is 1
INDEX ('ABC','B') is 2
INDEX ('ABC','C') is 3
```

If the substring occurs more than once, the first occurrence is indicated.

```
INDEX ('ABCABCA','A') is 1 (not 4 or 7)
INDEX ('ABCABCABC','CA') is 3
```

If the substring does not exist within the first argument, the answer is 0. (This is similar to what we have done with LOOKUP functions.)

```
INDEX('CRAFTY','FT') is 4
INDEX('CRAFTY','FI') is 0
INDEX('CRAFTY','SC') is 0
INDEX('A','ABC') is 0
```

Examples

As illustrations of some possible uses of these functions, we have the following examples.

Given a name of the form

last, first name middle initial.

obtain the last name alone in the variable LAST. To do so, we locate the comma, and use its position in a substring operation:

```
CHARACTER NAME*35,LAST*16
INTEGER ICOMMA
    .
    .
ICOMMA = INDEX(NAME,',')
LAST = NAME(1:ICOMMA-1)
```

Write a function BLPOS(STRING,STPOS) which returns the position of the first blank at or after position STPOS in the string STRING (or zero if no such blank). Again, we combine the INDEX function with substring operations. The idea is to look in the substring of STRING starting at position STPOS. The program follows:

```
      INTEGER FUNCTION BLPOS(STRING,STPOS)
      CHARACTER STRING*(*)
      INTEGER STPOS,POSN,INDEX

C   POSN <- INDEX IN THE SUBSTRING

      POSN = INDEX(STRING(STPOS:),' ')

C   ADJUST ANSWER, BY ADDING ON THE POSITIONS PRIOR TO
C THE SUBSTRING

      IF(POSN.EQ.0) THEN
         BLPOS = 0
      ELSE
         BLPOS = (STPOS-1) + POSN
      ENDIF
      RETURN
      END
```

Given a series of data records, count how many times each character of the allowable character set occurs. The ICHAR function returns a value which we will use as a subscript for an array of counters. Assuming 256 allowable characters, we will have a subscript range from 0 to 255, as shown in the following program.

```
      INTEGER COUNT(0:255),SUBSC,I
      CHARACTER*1 LINE(80)
      DATA COUNT/256*0/

C   READ AND COUNT

   10 CONTINUE
         READ(*,1000,END=500) LINE
         DO 20 I = 1,80
            SUBSC = ICHAR(LINE(I))
            COUNT(SUBSC) = COUNT(SUBSC) + 1
   20       CONTINUE
         GO TO 10

C   PRINT NON-ZERO ANSWERS

  500 CONTINUE
      DO 510 I = 0,255
         IF(COUNT(I).NE.0) THEN
            CALL DETAIL(CHAR(I),COUNT(I))
         ENDIF
  510    CONTINUE
      STOP
 1000 FORMAT(80A1)
      END
```

COMMENT. In the call to DETAIL, the parameter CHAR(I) is the Ith character (a call to the CHAR function). On the other hand, COUNT(I) is the Ith count (an array element).

REVIEW

Table of CHARACTER related functions.

Function Name	Type	Parameters	Comment
LEN	INTEGER	1-string	Length of string
ICHAR	INTEGER	1-single character	Relative position of character in collating sequence (0 to $n-1$)
CHAR	CHARACTER*1	1-integer (0 to $n-1$)	Character in the given position in the collating sequence

(continued)

Function Name	Type	Parameters	Comment
LGE LGT LLE LLT	LOGICAL	2-strings	Compares the two strings using the ASCII sequence
INDEX	INTEGER	2-strings	Gives the starting position of the 2nd parameter as a substring of the 1st parameter (0 if not there)

EXERCISES

1. Give the value of the following expressions:
   (a) `INDEX('MARTHA','ART')`
   (b) `INDEX('BALLOON','BALL')`
   (c) `INDEX('JONES, JR., JOHN',',')`
   (d) `INDEX('THIS STRING',' ')`
   (e) `INDEX('WORDS','ORDER')`
   (f) `INDEX('INDEX','X')`
   (g) `INDEX('RAPIDLY','DLE')`

2. Explain the difference between these two statements

```
IF(STRA.GE.STRB)THEN      IF(LGE(STRA,STRB))THEN
```

3. Write a function LAST10 which determines the last ten characters of a given string. For example

```
LAST10('THIS IS AN EXAMPLE') is 'AN EXAMPLE'
LAST10('0123456789') is '012345678'
LAST10('SHORT') is 'SHORTbbbbb'
```

Observe that the parameter will need to be given as (*) length.
   [*Hint*: Review the list of available functions.]

4. CHARACTER assignment statements give right truncation and padding. For example, if A is CHARACTER*3, then

```
A = 'G'    gives 'Gbb'
A = 'GOLD' gives 'GOL'
```

This exercise will explore obtaining left truncation and padding.
   (a) Suppose A is length 3, and B is length 7; give code to copy the final three characters of B into A.
   (b) Suppose A is length 12 and B is length 5. Give code to copy B into A, left padded with blanks.
   (c) Write a general-purpose LCOPY(A,B), which copies string B into string A, using left truncation and padding. Use the (*) length designation for A and B.

5. Give a general-purpose string-sorting routine SORT(ARRAY,ASIZE,N). ARRAY is an array of strings, ASIZE the actual array size, N the portion of the array in use. Use (*) length designation for ARRAY. Sort in ascending order based on the ASCII sequence.

6. Write a substring-counting routine COUNT(STRING,SUBST). It will count how many times SUBST occurs as a substring of STRING. For example,

```
COUNT('BANANA','A') is 3
COUNT('ABRACADABRA','BRA') is 2
COUNT('XYLOPHONE','PHONY') is 0
```

7. Write a substring-replacement routine REPL(STRING,SUB1,SUB2). This routine replaces the first occurrence of SUB1 in STRING by SUB2.

For example, if STRING is 20 characters long and contains 'THIS IS A STRINGbbbb', then for these values of SUB1 and SUB2 we get the indicated new value for STRING:

SUB1	SUB2	STRING
'IS'	'NOT IS'	'THIS NOT IS A STRING' (still length 20)
'IS'	'IS NOT'	'THIS IS NOT A STRING'
'STRING'	'S'	'THIS IS A Sbbbbbbbbb'
'HIS'	'HERE'	'THERE IS A STRINGbbb'
'HER'	'HIS'	No change

8. Modify Exercise 7 to replace all occurrences of SUB1 by SUB2.

9. Write a LOGICAL function CLOSE(CH1,CH2) which tells whether CH1 and CH2 are within three of each other in the collating sequence for the particular computer.

10. Modify Exercise 9 to consider characters close if one is near the end of the collating sequence and the other near the beginning. Make the length of the sequence (N) an additional parameter.

For example, if CH1 is the last character in the sequence, it would be "close" to the three before it, and also to the first three characters in the sequence.

11. Write a coding routine CODE(CHAR,OFFSET,N) which, given a character CHAR, returns a code for that character. The code should be the character OFFSET places further along in the collating sequence. Characters near the end will "wrap around" back to the beginning of the sequence. For this reason we have N, the length of the collating sequence, as an additional parameter.

12. **(a)** Write a REVERS(STRING,REVSTR) subroutine which reverses a given STRING to obtain REVSTR. For example, after a call

```
CALL REVERS('ABCD',X)
```

X would have the value 'DCBA'.

(b) Write a logical function PALIN(STRING) which tests STRING to see if it is a "palindrome." A palindrome is a string which reads the same forward or backward, such as 'MADAM'.

13. If the PALIN function of Exercise 12 is called by:

```
CHARACTER STRING*10
LOGICAL ANSWER,PALIN
STRING = 'MADAM'
ANSWER = PALIN(STRING)
```

the answer will be .FALSE., since STRING obtains the value 'MADAMbbbbb', which is not a palindrome. Revise the function PALIN to ignore trailing blanks in the input. (You might actually modify the REVERS routine instead.)

14. Write a function LASTNB(STRING) which obtains the position of the last nonblank in the given STRING. For example,

```
LASTNB('A CAT IS   ') is 8.
```

12.4 CASE STUDIES

Case Study #9

In this case study we write a function VALUE(STRING) which obtains the numerical value of a string of digits contained in the CHARACTER variable STRING. For simplicity, we make the following assumptions:

1. STRING contains nothing but valid digits and blanks.
2. The digits are left justified in STRING.
3. The digits are terminated by a blank.

The exercises explore ways to relax these restrictions.

For example,

```
Value('123b') is 123
Value('7bb') is 7
```

NOTE. This routine is similar to what is automatically done for us when we read using an I format. The character digits are given an interpretation as a numerical value.

There are a number of ways to approach this problem. The way we will choose is to look at the digits, one at a time, from the left. Each time we see a new digit, we will adjust our answer.

For example, suppose we "see" the following series of characters:

'3' at this point our value is 3

'7' we adjust the value to 37 based on this new digit

'6' we adjust to 376

'1' we adjust to 3,761

' ' the process terminates, since we have reached a blank, with a final value of 3,761

Thus the string '3761b' yields a value of 3,761.

It should be fairly clear to you that a loop is involved, and that this loop uses "general condition" loop control. In rough form:

```
loop
   CHAR ← next character of string
   if CHAR = ' ' then exit endif
   adjust value based on CHAR
endloop
return
```

Now when we "adjust the value" observe that we always take the previous value, multiply by 10, and add in the value of the particular digit which is in CHAR. (This is true also for the first digit, provided the initial value is 0.) Moreover, we may obtain the next character by using the substring notation STRING(I:I), where I takes on the values 1, 2, and so on. We obtain this refinement.

```
I ← 1
VALUE ← 0
loop
   CHAR ← STRING(I:I)
   if CHAR = ' ' then exit endif
   VALUE ← 10 * VALUE + value of the digit in CHAR
   I ← I + 1
endloop
return
```

The only portion still to be refined is the "value of the digit in CHAR" phrase. There are a number of ways to obtain this value. One is to use the general-purpose character lookup function CHLOOK(KEY,ARRAY,ASIZE,N) which we wrote in Section 12.2. To do so, we observe that, in the array

```
'0'  '1'  '2'  '3'  '4'  '5'  '6'  '7'  '8'  '9'
```

each digit's subscript is 1 more than its value. For example, '0' has subscript 1, '1' has subscript 2, and so on. Hence, we may write

"value of the digit in CHAR"

as

```
CHLOOK(CHAR,DIGITS,10,10) - 1
```

DIGITS will be set up as an array of size 10 containing the digits '0' through '9'.

Summarizing our variables, we have

Name	Type	Use	Comment
STRING	CHARACTER*(*)	String of digits	Input parameter
I	INTEGER	Substring index	
CHAR	CHARACTER*1	Single digit	STRING(I:I)
CHLOOK	INTEGER		Character lookup function
DIGITS	CHARACTER*1 array size 10		DATA:'0'–'9'

With this and our refined algorithm, we may easily write the following function.

```
      INTEGER FUNCTION VALUE(STRING)
      CHARACTER*(*) STRING
      CHARACTER*1 CHAR,DIGITS(10)
      INTEGER I,CHLOOK
      DATA DIGITS/'0','1','2','3','4','5','6','7','8','9'/

C   WRITTEN BY *******, **/**/**.

C   THIS FUNCTION FINDS THE VALUE OF A STRING
C OF DIGITS. THE PARAMETER:

C        STRING-INPUT, CHARACTER*(*)-A VALID STRING OF
C               DIGITS, LEFT JUSTIFIED, TERMINATED
C               BY A BLANK.

C   INITIALIZE

      I = 1
      VALUE = 0

C   FOR EACH NEW DIGIT, ADJUST THE ANSWER BASED ON THAT
C DIGIT'S VALUE.

   10 CONTINUE
         CHAR = STRING(I:I)
         IF(CHAR.EQ.' ') THEN
            GO TO 100
         ENDIF
         VALUE = 10*VALUE+(CHLOOK(CHAR,DIGITS,10,10)-1)
         I = I + 1
         GO TO 10
  100 CONTINUE
      RETURN
      END
```

Case Study #10

This case study explores some simple character manipulation ideas. It will format lines of text. For example, given the line

```
THIS  LINE  WAS  TYPED  IN  USING  ERRATIC SPACING.
```

The output will be

```
THIS LINE WAS TYPED IN USING ERRATIC SPACING.
```

This case study is a first step in the area known as text-formatting. The exercises will explore some other ideas along these lines.

The basic algorithm will be the following:

```
loop
   read an input line; if eof then exit endif
   set output line to all blanks
   one 'word' at a time, locate a word
     in the input line and move it to
     the proper spot in the output line
   print the input line and the output line
endloop
```

We will use these routines:

LOCATE—a routine to locate the next word of the input line and tell us how long it is

MOVE—a routine to move that word to the output line

DETAIL—a routine to print the answers

Since no editing of input is done, we will read the input line within the main program.

We will clearly need variables for the input and output lines. In addition, we will need several other variables in the main program. We obtain this tentative variable list:

	Name	Type	Use	Comment
Input:	INLINE	CHARACTER*80	Input line	Also printed
Output:	OUTLIN	CHARACTER*80	Output line	
Other:	INPOS	INTEGER	Position in input line	
	OUTPOS	INTEGER	Position in output line	
	LENGTH	INTEGER	Length of word	

The "pointer" variable INPOS will be used to keep track of how far we have searched through the INLINE string in our search for words. Likewise, the

OUTPOS pointer will keep track of where the next word found should be moved in the OUTLIN string.

We can now write a partially refined algorithm.

```
loop
   read INLINE; if eof then exit endif
   OUTLIN ← ' '
   loop
      use LOCATE to locate next word in INLINE
      if no more words then exit endif
      use MOVE to move the word to OUTLIN
   endloop
   call DETAIL(INLINE,OUTLIN)
endloop
```

To further refine the algorithm, we will need to discuss the parameters for the subprograms LOCATE and MOVE.

For LOCATE, we are writing a routine which will search for a "word" in a given string of characters. By a "word" we mean a sequence of one or more nonblank characters. We clearly need the following input information:

1. The string to be searched.
2. A position to start looking. (If we always started at position 1, we would always find the first word.)

Our answers include

3. The position where the next word starts.
4. The length of that word.

If there is no next word, the subroutine will set the starting position to 0 and not give a value to the length.

Thus we have a subroutine LOCATE(STRING,POS,START,LENGTH). To use this routine we must supply variables to match the parameters:

INLINE—will be the string
INPOS—will tell where to start looking
START—will be used to obtain the starting position (this must be added to our variable list)
LENGTH—will be used to obtain the length

We will therefore write

```
call LOCATE(INLINE,INPOS,START,LENGTH)
```

However, for this to work properly, we must make sure that INPOS has the proper value every time we call LOCATE. The first time its value should be 1. Each successive time its value should be the position right after the word we just found. With a little thought, we realize that the formula START+LENGTH gives the desired value for the second and all later passes through the loop.

Our algorithm now looks like this:

```
loop
   read INLINE; if eof then exit endif
   OUTLIN ← ' '
   INPOS ← 1
   loop
      call LOCATE(INLINE,INPOS,START,LENGTH)
      if START = 0 then exit endif
      use MOVE to move the word to OUTLIN
      INPOS ← START+LENGTH
   endloop
   call DETAIL(INLINE,OUTLIN)
endloop
```

For MOVE, we write a routine which moves (copies) a series of characters from one string to another. In the process the second string is modified. We have as parameters:

```
A – the 'source' string
APOS – the starting position in the A string
B – the 'destination' string
BPOS – the starting position in the B string
LENGTH – the length of the substring moved
```

Of these, all but B are input, while B is an update parameter.

Reasoning similar to that used for the LOCATE routine leads to a call of the form

```
call MOVE(INLINE,START,OUTLIN,OUTPOS,LENGTH)
```

In order for OUTPOS to have the proper value at each call, we initialize it to 1 before the inner loop, and update it to the value OUTPOS+LENGTH+1 within the loop. (The "+1" in this formula leaves a blank space between words.)

Our final smooth algorithm is

```
loop
   read INLINE; if eof then exit endif
   OUTLIN ← ' '
   INPOS ← 1
   OUTPOS ← 1
   loop
      call LOCATE (INLINE,INPOS,START,LENGTH)
      if START = then exit endif
      call MOVE (INLINE,START,OUTLIN,OUTPOS,LENGTH)
      INPOS ← START+LENGTH
      OUTPOS ← OUTPOS+LENGTH+1
   endloop
   call DETAIL(INLINE,OUTLIN)
endloop
```

This is easily coded in FORTRAN (see the Exercises).

COMMENTS.

1. The LOCATE and MOVE routines can be useful for other applications. For this reason, we have chosen to design them in more general form than this particular problem requires.
2. The main program requires no special knowledge of CHARACTER manipulations. Given a description of the LOCATE and MOVE subroutines, we could have written the main program as early as Chapter 4.

We now turn to the writing of the LOCATE and MOVE routines. The DETAIL routine is left as an exercise.

For the LOCATE routine we will use this rough algorithm:

1. Search for a nonblank, starting at position POS; if none is found set START to 0 and return.
2. Search for a blank, starting at the nonblank found in step 1.

Each of these steps will require a loop, whose primary form of control will be the count-control mechanism, since we do not wish to go past the end of STRING. We thus have

```
LAST ← LEN(STRING)
loop for I = POS to LAST
   if STRING(I:I) ≠ ' ' then exit endif
endloop
if I > LAST then
   START ← 0
   return
else
   START ← I
endif
```

followed by

```
loop for I = START to LAST
   if STRING(I:I) = ' ' then exit endif
endloop
LENGTH ← I-START
```

(If we "fall through" without finding a blank, I has the value LAST + 1 and the formula I − START is still correct.) The FORTRAN code is easily written, and is left as an exercise.

Finally, we write the MOVE routine. With substring operations it is very simple to write. In doing so, we take advantage of the fact that the word to be moved is known to exist in the source array. Moreover, we know it will fit into the destination array. (Why?) See Figure 12.1.

```
      SUBROUTINE MOVE(A,APOS,B,BPOS,LENGTH)
      CHARACTER*(*) A,B
      INTEGER APOS,BPOS,LENGTH
      INTEGER ALAST,BLAST

C   WRITTEN BY *******, **/**/**

C   THIS SUBROUTINE MOVES (COPIES) A SERIES OF CHARACTERS
C OF A GIVEN LENGTH FROM ONE STRING TO ANOTHER

C   THESE ARE THE PARAMETERS.

C       A-INPUT, CHARACTER*(*)-SOURCE STRING.
C       APOS-INPUT, INTEGER-STARTING POSITION IN
C            THE A STRING.
C       B-UPDATE, CHARACTER*(*)-DESTINATION STRING.
C       BPOS-INPUT, INTEGER-STARTING POSITION IN
C            THE B STRING.
C       LENGTH-INPUT, INTEGER-LENGTH OF STRING TO MOVE.

C   CALCULATE FINAL POSITIONS IN SOURCE AND DESTINATION STRINGS

      ALAST = APOS + LENGTH - 1
      BLAST = BPOS + LENGTH - 1

C  COPY

      B(BPOS:BLAST) = A(APOS:ALAST)
      RETURN
      END
```

Figure 12.1

EXERCISES

Exercises 1–6 refer to Case Study #9. However, some of the concepts used in Case Study #10 may be helpful.

1. Can you suggest a way to obtain the "value of the digit in CHAR" using one of the character functions of the previous section rather than the CHLOOK function?

2. The VALUE function as written requires the number to be terminated by a blank. Modify the function to remove this restriction. For example, VALUE('1235') should be 1,235.

3. Modify the VALUE function to handle an optional sign. For example,

```
VALUE('-100b') is -100
VALUE('+100b') is 100
VALUE('100b') is 100
```

4. Modify the VALUE function to accept leading blanks; as in the example,

```
VALUE('bbb123bb') is 123.
```

5. Combine Exercises 2–4. VALUE should work properly for strings of this form:

   0 or more blanks
   optional sign
   0 or more blanks
   string of digits
   optional blank

6. **(a)** Modify Case Study #9 to return, in addition to the value of the string of digits, an indication of whether or not any invalid character occurred (use a logical variable GOOD). For example,

```
STRING = '123Ab'     VALUE =  123    GOOD = .FALSE.
         '1011b'             1011           .TRUE.
         'A123b'                0           .FALSE.
```

   Observe that "VALUE" is the value determined up to the point where the invalid character occurred.

   (b) Modify (a) to also place a limit of nine digits on the string; for STRING = '1234567891', VALUE is 123456789 and GOOD is .FALSE..

   (c) Modify (b) to make the limit of the number of digits allowed a parameter.

Exercises 7–14 refer to Case Study #10.

7. Give FORTRAN code for the main program, the DETAIL routine, and the LOCATE routine of Case Study #10.

8. When we used the MOVE routine of Case Study #10, we could assume that LENGTH was short enough that neither ALAST nor BLAST would extend beyond the end of the A or B strings. (Why?) In other applications, this might not be so.
   Modify the MOVE routine to check for this possibility. If LENGTH is too long, it should set an output parameter GOOD to .FALSE. and not perform the move.

9. Modify the LOCATE routine of Case Study #10 to use the INDEX function (rather than a DO loop) to determine the length of the word once it is located.

10. Modify Case Study #10 to center the line of output within an allotted 80-column line.

11. Modify Case Study #10 to "justify" the output line. This means placing blanks between the words so that the last word ends in column 80 and the words are as evenly spaced as possible on the line.

12. Modify Case Study #10 to treat the character '#' as a "fill" character. For purposes of determining where a word begins and ends, it is to be treated as a regular character. However, on output it is to be replaced by a blank, as illustrated by this example:

```
 Input  - FILL###CHAR.       CREATES#    SPACES.
Output  - FILL    CHAR.  CREATES SPACES.
```

13. Modify Case Study #10 to treat periods properly. Two blank spaces should be left after each period which ends a word. The following computer statements illustrate this.

```
  Input - THE   3.2 IS NOT.   THE OTHER PERIOD IS.
 Output - THE 3.2 IS NOT.  THE OTHER PERIOD IS.
```

14. Combine Exercises 11–13 with the following considerations.

In general text-formatting, it is not enough to reformat each line individually. Rather, we must take a series of input lines and create a neat series of output lines. The output lines will be printed only when they are full, rather than at the end of each input line. Moreover, the text may contain more than one paragraph.

Write a program which incorporates all these features, using these guidelines:

(a) If a new input line begins with a word, it is a continuation of the previous paragraph.
(b) When a new input line begins with a blank, it is the start of a new paragraph.
(c) Paragraphs should be indented five spaces.
(d) All but the last line of the paragraph should be justified, as defined in Exercise 11.
(e) Totally blank lines should be output as they are.
(f) Only the output lines should be printed.

Exercises 15–23 do not specifically refer to case studies. However, they may utilize concepts or routines developed in the case studies.

15. Develop a program to count the total number of words in a series of input lines.

16. Develop a program which will tell how many times each word occurred in a series of input lines.

17. Develop a program to find the total value of a string containing zero or more numbers, separated by blanks or commas.

For example, for

```
'    13              23,17' the answer is 53
' -7, -3                45' the answer is 35
' ' the answer is 0
```

18. Develop a routine which will create a "printable" version of a dollar and cents figure given as a string of up to ten digits right justified. For example,

```
'1234567891'   yields   '$12,345,678.91'
'      7891'            '        $78.91'
'0000007891'            '        $78.91'
'         2'            '         $0.02'
'    135692'            '     $1,356.92'
```

19. Give a routine which essentially undoes what VALUE does. Given an INTEGER value, it creates a string of length 10, right justified. For example,

```
  231 yields '       231'
1,349        '      1349'
```

[*Hint*: Successive division of the value by 10, together with the MOD function, can be used to get the digits from right to left.]

20. (a) Modify Exercise 19 to convert the value to a string in a given base (up to base 16, perhaps). For example,

```
231 with base = 10 yields '        231'
 31 with base = 16 yields '         1F'
 52 with base =  8 yields '         64'
```

(b) In a similar fashion, modify Case Study #9 to treat the given string as a string of digits in a given base.

21. Write a base 2 to base 8 conversion routine. Its input will be a string representing a number in base 2; its output will be a string containing that same number in base 8. For example,

```
'101'       yields '5'
'10101'     yields '25'
'111010110' yields '726'
```

There is no limit on the length of the input string.

[*Hint*: When grouped by threes from the right, the triplets of binary digits yield the corresponding base 8 digit. For example,

```
' 10' '101'   (you may have to left pad the leftmost
 '2'   '5'     triplet with 0's).
```

22. Write a base 8 to base 2 routine similar to that in Exercise 21.

23. Exercise 20 of Section 6.4 dealt with rational numbers. You are to write a routine which will allow a free form of input. In particular, the rational number will appear as a pair of numbers separated by a slash and enclosed in parentheses. You may assume that the number is in valid form, but there are no other assumptions (concerning spacing, for example). Your routine has these parameters:

STRING: Input, CHARACTER*(*)—string containing the rational number

R: Output, INTEGER(2)—the rational, represented as numerator in R(1), denominator in R(2).

Valid strings might be any of the following:

```
'(  3/5)'
'(          3    /       5  )'
'(-7/       35)'
```

and so on.

13

FILE I/O

13.1 INTRODUCTION

In this chapter we explore FORTRAN commands for working with files. The presentation is not intended to be a complete discussion of file processing techniques. Indeed, whole textbooks have been written on that subject. Nor do we give an exhaustive description of the FORTRAN file processing commands. Our purpose is to indicate some methods for working with files using the FORTRAN language, expanding on what we learned in Chapter 5.

File Terminology

A **file** consists of a number of records. A record contains one or more values, frequently relating to one given entity. For example, we might have a record which contains the following **fields**:

name
social security number
date of birth
marital status
and so on

In this case, the record refers to a particular individual.

Files may appear in many forms. For example, a deck of data cards may constitute a file, with each data card being a single record of the file. Another example of a file is a printed report. In this case, each line printed is considered to be one record of the file.

It is frequently desirable to store and maintain data in a more convenient form. For example, we might want to have one program put some information on a file and later use that information as input to some other program. A printed report is not appropriate in this application. We could have the first program create a deck of punched cards to be read by the second program. However, this would require maintaining the deck of cards (which could be sizable) over an extended period of time.

Fortunately, there are more convenient storage media for files. Two of the most commonly used are **magnetic tape** and **magnetic disk**.

The magnetic tape used by the computer to store a data file is analogous to the tape used for sound recording. Indeed, many microcomputers use ordinary audio cassettes as a storage medium. The records of the file are placed on the tape, one after another, from first to last (see Figure 13.1). In reading a file which has been written on a tape, the computer will have to read the records in order (sequentially). As a result, a magnetic tape is referred to as a **sequential access** storage medium. A file stored on tape will be accessed sequentially.

Likewise, a magnetic disk is somewhat analogous to the phonograph records used to store sound. However, as illustrated in Figure 13.2, the data is stored on a series of concentric rings, rather than on one continuous spiral. The disk is rotated at a high rate of speed by a device called a disk drive. The **disk drive** mechanism includes a **read/write head** on an arm which may be moved to any of the concentric rings, or **tracks**, of the disk. This is again somewhat analogous to the audio record player arm, which may be moved to any groove on the record.

A magnetic disk is called a **direct access** storage medium. In order to access a particular record (perhaps record 735), it is not necessary to read all the records up to the record. The read/write head may be moved directly to the track (concentric ring) on which the desired record is located. Since the disk is being rotated by the disk drive, the desired record will pass under the read/write head soon after the head is in place. This direct access capability of the magnetic disk and disk drive does not, however, mean that the records of the file cannot be processed in order. If a file is stored on a disk, then it may be accessed either sequentially or directly.

FORTRAN Files

The FORTRAN language provides for two types of files: sequential access and direct access. However, the language makes no requirement that a sequential file reside on tape or a direct file on disk. In fact, FORTRAN makes no suppositions whatever about the particular storage mechanism the computer uses for the files. In the future, either type of file might in fact reside on some yet-to-be-invented storage medium.

In the area of file processing. FORTRAN is more system-dependent than in most other areas. The reason for this is that each computer system will designate the allowable **logical unit numbers** (or just **unit numbers**) and their meanings. In a

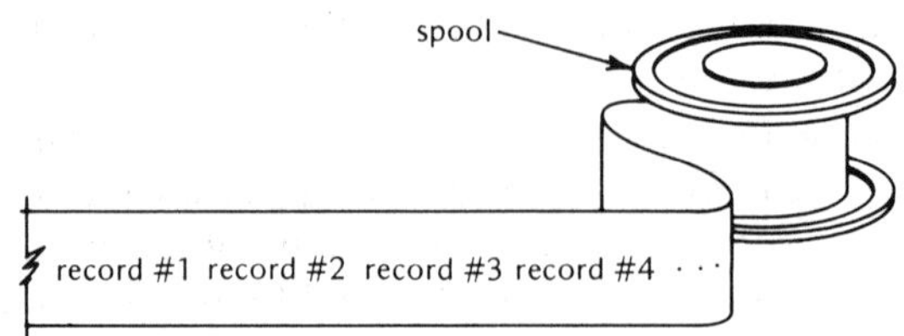

Figure 13.1

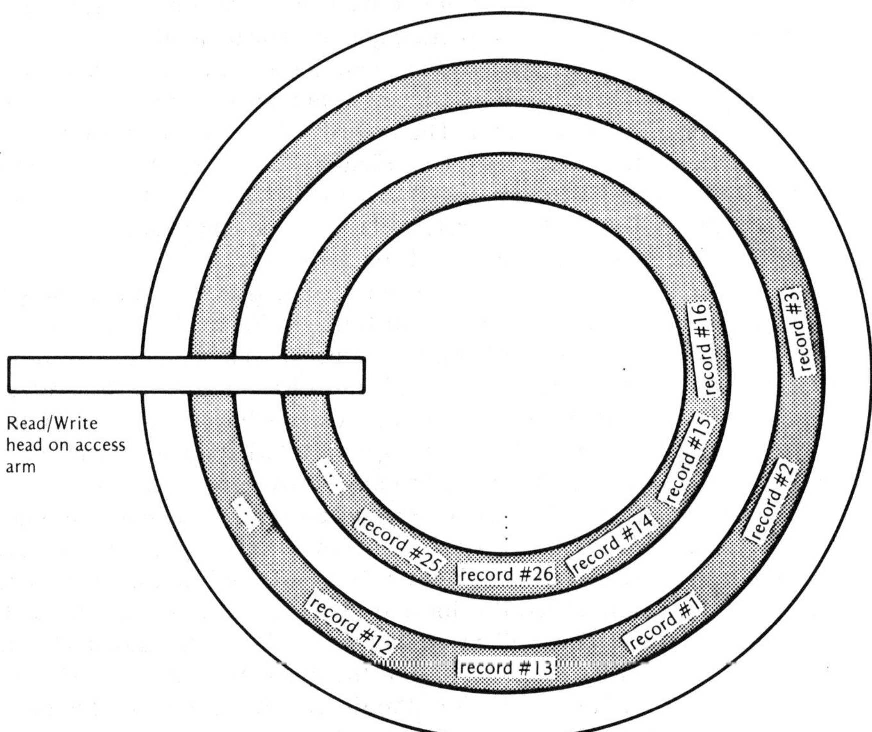

Figure 13.2

READ or WRITE the first number inside the parentheses is the unit number. For example, in

```
READ(5,1000) X
```

the unit number is 5.

On each system there are two special unit numbers, one for reading and one for writing, which are required to be available to the FORTRAN programmer. These are the units referred to by the READ(*,—) and WRITE(*,—). These are often units 5 and 6, respectively.

In addition to these numbers, each computer system will allow a selection of other unit numbers for use in FORTRAN programs. There may be certain restrictions on the use of these numbers. For example, numbers 12–18 on a particular system might be restricted to use for sequential access files.

Rather than trying to follow any particular computer system in our examples, we will simply assume that unit numbers 10–50 are available for unrestricted use. Hence we will use these numbers in our examples.

There is one further area of difficulty. The special unit numbers denoted by an asterisk (5 and 6 perhaps) have a preassigned meaning. Unit 6, for example, may refer to the system line printer. However, for the other unit numbers there must be a mechanism for specifying to which file they refer. For example, in one program written by programmer X, unit 14 may refer to a company payroll file. Programmer Y, on the other hand, may have written a program using unit 14 to refer to a parts inventory file. There must be some mechanism for establishing the proper correspondence when each of the programs is run.

> **COMMENT.** This is why the numbers are sometimes called logical unit numbers. The word "logical" in this context means "not physical." The numbers refer, not to some particular physical file or device, but to some "unit" whose actual meaning will be determined when the program runs.

There are generally two methods for establishing the connection between a unit number and the file to which it refers. The first method, called "preconnection," is accomplished using JCL (job control language). The second is to use the OPEN statement in the FORTRAN program. We will use this second approach, although there are instances in which the first method is preferable.

The basics of utilizing sequential and direct access files in FORTRAN programs are discussed in the next two sections. Section 13.4 will discuss some "frills" which are available to the programmer.

REVIEW

Terms

file
record
field
magnetic tape
magnetic disk
disk drive
read/write head
track
sequential access
direct access

unit number (logical unit number)
connection, preconnection

13.2 SEQUENTIAL FILE TECHNIQUES

FORTRAN Statements

We consider these five statements as they relate to FORTRAN sequential access files:

```
READ   OPEN    ENDFILE
WRITE  REWIND
```

In considering the details of the statements, it is helpful to visualize a **file pointer** which the system uses to keep track of where the program is within a given file.

The READ statement has the form

```
READ(unit,format, . . .) list of items to be read
```

The first two items inside the parentheses are the unit number and format label. These may, if desired, be followed by one or more of the following options:

```
END=label
ERR=label
IOSTAT=integer variable name
```

The options, if used, may be listed in any order.

> **COMMENT.** The words END, ERR, and IOSTAT are sometimes called **keywords**. It is possible to specify the unit and format using keywords UNIT and FMT, respectively. In this case there is no rule about the order of the five keywords. In any case, the unit number and format label must be specified.
>
> These are possible READ statements:

```
READ(23,1500,END=700,ERR=900) X,Y,Z
READ(40,3000) NAME,AGE
READ(*,2000,IOSTAT=STATUS,END=300) I,J,K
READ(25,4000,IOSTAT=IN1) ID1,DATA1
READ(FMT=4000,IOSTAT=IN1,UNIT=25) ID1,DATA1
```

As we know, the label in the END= option specifies a label to which the computer is to branch in case the end of file is reached. Likewise, the ERR=label option specifies a label to branch to in case of an error in the READ. (Each computer will have its own list of possible error conditions.)

The IOSTAT= specifies the name of an INTEGER variable (or array element) which will be automatically given a value based on the result of the READ:

0	if successful
positive	if an error occurred
negative	if end-of-file occurred

Similarly, the form of the WRITE statement is

```
WRITE(unit,format, . . .) list of items to be written
```

The options include ERR=label and IOSTAT=variable only. These options have the same meanings as for the READ statement.

COMMENT. We may use the IOSTAT= option to discover the nature of any error that occurs. By using it in conjunction with the ERR= option, we may branch to a portion of the program which prints the value of the IOSTAT variable prior to stopping. By consulting the manual for the particular computer involved, it will be possible to get an indication of what error occurred.

This comment applies to any use of the IOSTAT option. (See, for example, the OPEN statement below.)

Sample WRITE statements include

```
WRITE(25,1000) I,J
WRITE(FMT=1000,UNIT=25) I,J
WRITE(35,4000,IOSTAT=OUT1) NAME
WRITE(*,5000)
```

When the unit we are writing to refers to a printing device (as determined by the computer manufacturer), then the first character of the record written must be a **carriage-control** character. This first character will not be printed but will be used to determine vertical spacing as follows:

blank	one line
0	two lines
1	top of next page
+	not advanced (overprint previous line)

In general, unless we are writing to a unit connected to a printer device, or to a "printer-destined" file as defined in Section 5.1, we will *not* include a carriage-control character.

We will use the OPEN statement to connect a particular file to a given unit. Its form is

```
OPEN(unit, . . .)
```

with a list of options which includes the following:

```
IOSTAT=variable name
ERR=label
FILE=a character expression telling the filename
ACCESS='SEQUENTIAL'
```

Observe that, as usual, we may include UNIT= with the unit, in which case the unit number need not come first.

```
OPEN(25,FILE='PAYROLL-FILE',ACCESS='SEQUENTIAL')
OPEN(FILE='PAYROLL-FILE',UNIT=25,ACCESS='SEQUENTIAL')
OPEN(40,FILE='MASTER',IOSTAT=OPERR,ERR=900,ACCESS='SEQUENTIAL')
```

The ACCESS='SEQUENTIAL' is optional; FORTRAN assumes a default of sequential for the type of access.

The REWIND and ENDFILE statements have the form:

REWIND unit	ENDFILE unit
REWIND(unit,. . .)	ENDFILE(unit, . . .)

The forms with parentheses may include the options ERR= and IOSTAT=. The REWIND statement positions the file pointer to the beginning of the file. The ENDFILE places a special "endfile" record at the end of a file that has been created. In subsequent reading of the file, the END= option will use this to determine when end of file is reached.

Suppose each record of an existing student file named STUDENT.MASTER is 250 characters long and contains the following fields.

Position	Description
1–30	Name
31–39	Social security number (nine digits)
100–103	Quality point average (three digits, two after decimal)
125–127	Major (three character code)

Positions 40–99, 104–124, and 128–250 contain various other information.

We wish to create a file STUDENT.PARTIAL containing only the records of history majors (code 'HIS') with a quality point average in excess of 3.50. At the same time, we wish to print a list of the name, social security number, and quality point average of those students placed into this partial file.

The logic is very simple. We will use these variables:

Name	Type	Use	Comment
NAME	CHARACTER*30	Name	
SSNO	CHARACTER*9	Social security number	
QPA	REAL	Quality point average	
MAJOR	CHARACTER*3	Major	
MISC1	CHARACTER*60		Used to read positions 40–99
MISC2	CHARACTER*21		Used to read positions 104–124
MISC3	CHARACTER*123		Used to read positions 128–250

```
open (connect) and rewind files
loop
   read data from input file; if eof then exit endif
   if MAJOR='HIS' and QPA>3.50 then
      write data to output file
      call DETAIL(NAME,SSNO,QPA)
   endif
endloop
stop
```

The program is in Figure 13.3. We make several observations. First, we rewind each file after connecting it to ensure that the file pointer is at the beginning of the file. We use a DETAIL routine for the printing, since we want headings on the printed report. Both the READ and WRITE may use the same FORMAT, since the partial file record will have the same format as the original file. In particular, no carriage control is used with the WRITE statement. Finally, all file commands use the IOSTAT= and ERR= options to allow us to determine what error occurred, if any.

COMMENTS.

1. We do not include the error recovery as part of the algorithm itself.
2. By having more different labels in the various ERR= options, we could determine where the error occurred as well as what the error was.
3. We place the *error recovery* portion at the bottom of the program, outside the main program logic.

SEQUENTIAL ALGORITHMS

Sequential files are most useful for applications which require all, or most of, the records on the file. For applications which require only a small portion of the file, a direct file might be more useful. However, sequential files are generally more efficient both in terms of the actual space occupied on the storage medium and in the time required to process the entire file.

Because of these savings, sequential files are widely used. As a result, a number of techniques have been developed for efficient modification and utilization of this type of file. The **merge** algorithm discussed here is one example. Others are indicated in the exercises.

Suppose we have two nonempty files, each of which contains records in this format:

1–5	ID number
6–100	Other information

Each of these files is known to be in ascending order based on the ID number. Moreover, neither file contains any duplicates.

```
      CHARACTER NAME*30,SSNO*9,MAJOR*3,MISC1*60,MISC2*21,
     $  MISC3*123
      REAL QPA
      INTEGER ERRCOD

C    WRITTEN BY *******, **/**/**.

C    THIS PROGRAM CREATES A FILE, STUDENT.PARTIAL,
C CONTAINING THE RECORDS OF HISTORY MAJORS WITH A QUALITY
C POINT AVERAGE IN EXCESS OF 3.50. AT THE SAME
C TIME, A LIST OF THE STUDENTS PLACED INTO
C THIS PARTIAL FILE IS PRINTED. THE PARTIAL FILE
C IS MADE FROM THE STUDENT.MASTER FILE.

C    OPEN FILES ON UNITS 20 AND 30.

      OPEN(20,FILE='STUDENT.MASTER',ACCESS='SEQUENTIAL',
     $    IOSTAT=ERRCOD,ERR=900)
      REWIND(20,IOSTAT=ERRCOD,ERR=900)
      OPEN(30,FILE='STUDENT.PARTIAL',ACCESS='SEQUENTIAL',
     $    IOSTAT=ERRCOD,ERR=950)
      REWIND(30,IOSTAT=ERRCOD,ERR=950)

C    MAIN LOOP. READ MASTER, PLACE ON PARTIAL IF APPROPRIATE

   10 CONTINUE
         READ(20,1000,END=500,IOSTAT=ERRCOD,ERR=900)
     $      NAME,SSNO,MISC1,QPA,MISC2,MAJOR,MISC3
         IF(MAJOR.EQ.'HIS'.AND.QPA.GT.3.50) THEN
            WRITE(30,1000,IOSTAT=ERRCOD,ERR=950)
     $         NAME,SSNO,MISC1,QPA,MISC2,MAJOR,MISC3
            CALL DETAIL(NAME,SSNO,QPA)
         ENDIF
         GO TO 10

C    AFTER LOOP PLACE END-FILE MARKER ON CREATED FILE

  500 CONTINUE
      ENDFILE(30,IOSTAT=ERRCOD,ERR=950)
      STOP

C     'ERROR RECOVERY'

  900 CONTINUE
      WRITE(*,2000) ERRCOD
      STOP
  950 CONTINUE
      WRITE(*,3000) ERRCOD
      STOP

C    FORMATS

 1000 FORMAT(A30,A9,A60,F4.2,A21,A3,A123)
 2000 FORMAT(///' *** ERROR #',I5,' ON MASTER FILE ***')
 3000 FORMAT(///' *** ERROR #',I5,' ON PARTIAL FILE ***')
      END
```

Figure 13.3

Our goal is to create a combined file with these same properties: in order by ID number, with no duplicates. The technique we use is called "merging" the files and is similar to the action when two lanes of traffic merge into one.

The basic idea is to repeatedly compare ID's from the two files, always placing the lower one into the output file. Here is a very rough algorithm. (Record 1, ID1 refer to the data from the first file. Record 2, ID2 refer to the second file.)

```
read a record from each file to get started
loop
   case
      1(ID1<ID2) put record 1 on output file
         read another record from file 1
      2(ID1>ID2) put record 2 on output file
         read another record from file 2
      3(ID1=ID2) process a duplicate error
   endcase
endloop
???
```

Since we have not talked about how we will get out of the loop, it is not yet clear what steps may follow the loop.

There are a number of options for processing a duplicate record. For this example we choose to place the record from the first file on the output file and print an error message. Since both records have then been processed, we will read a new record from each of the two files.

The most straightforward method for handling loop exits is to simply leave the loop when either file runs out of records. When one file runs out, we simply copy the rest of the other file to the output file. This yields the following loop with four exits. The variable TYPE is used to distinguish among the four exits.

```
read record1, record2
loop
   case
      1(ID1<ID2) write record1 (on output file)
                 TYPE ← 1
                 read record1;
                    if eof then exit endif
      2(ID1>ID2) write record2
                 TYPE ← 2
                 read record2;
                    if eof  then exit endif
      3(ID1=ID2) write record 1
                 write error message
                 TYPE ← 3
                 read record 1;
                    if eof then exit endif
                 TYPE ← 4
                 read record 2;
                    if eof then exit endif
   endcase
endloop
```

Careful thought reveals the code for the second and fourth exits will be the same:

```
loop
   write record1
   read record1; if eof then exit endif
endloop
```

For the first exit the code is similar; however, the third is different. When the third exit is taken there is no record 2 available to be written to the output file, so we write

```
loop
   read record2; if eof then exit endif
   write record2
endloop
```

The complete program is in Figure 13.4. Several modifications and improvements are suggested in the exercises.

COMMENTS.

1. We have given TYPE a value just prior to each READ. When we reach step 500 it will have the proper value based on which exit was taken.
2. Exit means "leave the loop," proceeding to the step following the loop. For the loops beginning at labels 510, 520, and 530, the loop itself is the only thing within the branch of the decision structure. Thus the "step after" each of these loops is the step following the decision structure, namely the ENDFILE. Hence each of these exits is written using END=900.

```
      INTEGER ID1, ID2, TYPE
      CHARACTER*95 DATA1,DATA2

C   WRITTEN BY *******, **/**/**.

C   THIS PROGRAM MERGES TWO NONEMPTY FILES, INPUT.1
C AND INPUT.2, INTO A FILE, MERGED.FILE, IN ORDER
C BY I.D. NUMBER WITH NO DUPLICATES.
C   CONNECT FILES ON UNITS 30, 40, 50

      OPEN(30,FILE='INPUT.1',ACCESS='SEQUENTIAL')
      REWIND 30
      OPEN(40,FILE='INPUT.2',ACCESS='SEQUENTIAL')
      REWIND 40
      OPEN(50,FILE='MERGED.FILE',ACCESS='SEQUENTIAL')
      REWIND 50
```

Figure 13.4 ***(continued on p. 569)***

```
C    READ TWO RECORDS TO GET STARTED

      READ(30,1000) ID1,DATA1
      READ(40,1000) ID2,DATA2

C    IN LOOP, COMPARE; PUT SMALLER ID ON OUTPUT

   10 CONTINUE
         IF(ID1.LT.ID2) THEN
            WRITE(50,1000) ID1,DATA1
            TYPE = 1
            READ(30,1000,END=500) ID1,DATA1
         ELSE IF (ID1.GT.ID2) THEN
            WRITE(50,1000) ID2,DATA2
            TYPE = 2
            READ(40,1000,END=500) ID2,DATA2
         ELSE
            WRITE(50,1000) ID1,DATA1
            CALL ERROR(ID2)
            TYPE = 3
            READ(30,1000,END=500) ID1,DATA1
            TYPE = 4
            READ(40,1000,END=500) ID2,DATA2
         ENDIF
         GO TO 10

C    AFTER LOOP. EXITS 1 AND 3 COPY REST OF FILE 2

  500 CONTINUE
      IF(TYPE.EQ.1) THEN
  510    CONTINUE
            WRITE(50,1000) ID2,DATA2
            READ(40,1000,END=900)'ID2,DATA2
            GO TO 510
      ELSE IF (TYPE.EQ.3) THEN
  520    CONTINUE
            READ(40,1000,END=900) ID2,DATA2
            WRITE(50,1000) ID2,DATA2
            GO TO 520
      ELSE

C    EXITS 2 AND 4 COPY REST OF FILE 1

  530    CONTINUE
            WRITE(50,1000) ID1,DATA1
            READ(30,1000,END=900) ID1,DATA1
            GO TO 530
      ENDIF
  900 CONTINUE
      ENDFILE 50
      STOP
 1000 FORMAT(I5,A95)
      END
```

Figure 13.4 ***(continued)***

REVIEW

Options	Used in
END=label	READ
ERR=label	READ, WRITE, OPEN, REWIND, ENDFILE
IOSTAT=integer variable	READ, WRITE, OPEN, REWIND, ENDFILE
FILE=file name	OPEN
ACCESS='SEQUENTIAL'	OPEN
UNIT=unit[1]	READ, WRITE, OPEN, REWIND, ENDFILE
FORMAT=format label[1]	READ, WRITE

[1]keyword part is optional

Commands (. . . indicates zero or more options)
READ(unit,format, . . .) list
WRITE(unit,format, . . .) list
OPEN(unit, . . .)
REWIND unit or REWIND(unit, . . .)
ENDFILE unit or ENDFILE(unit, . . .)

EXERCISES

Exercises 1–9 refer to the examples in this section.

1. **(a)** Write the DETAIL routine for the program in Figure 13.3. The social security number should be printed in the form xxx-xx-xxxx.
(b) Write the ERROR routine for the program in Figure 13.4. Notice that it will be similar to a DETAIL routine.
(c) Modify the program of Figure 13.4 and (b) of this exercise, as follows. Instead of generating a printed error listing, create an ERROR.LIST file containing a copy of each of the faulty records from the second file.

2. Modify the program in Figure 13.3 to print different error messages identifying where the error occurred (at open, read, and so on).

3. **(a)** In the program in Figure 13.3, could QPA be treated as CHARACTER*3 and read using an A3 format? Explain any assumptions you would have to make.
(b) If QPA were a CHARACTER variable, show how to use EQUIVALENCE to simplify the READ and WRITE statements to something like what is indicated here

```
CHARACTER DATA*250, . . .
      .
      .
      .

READ(20,1000,END=500,IOSTAT=ERRCOD,ERR=900) DATA
```

It will still be necessary to refer to the name, social security number, major, and QPA at other points in the program.

4. Add "error recovery" to the program in Figure 13.3.

5. Rather than using the TYPE variable in Figure 13.3, we could use four different IOSTAT variables for the four READ statements in the loop. Prior to the loop, we would initialize each to zero. When we left the loop, we could tell which exit occurred by seeing which IOSTAT variable was positive.

   Make these suggested modifications. Do you think the resulting program would be more efficient?

6. Someone has suggested modifying case 3 (ID1 = ID2) of the merge algorithm as follows. Remove both the "write record 1" and the "read record 1" steps. This leaves only the call to ERROR and the "read record 2" steps. Moreover, it removes the **exit** which was different from the other three.

   Will the resulting algorithm work? Justify your answer.

7. The fact that three of the four exits in Figure 13.3 use similar code suggest writing that code as a subprogram.

   (a) Write such a subroutine. You may wish to use an INTEGER parameter UNITNO and a READ such as

   ```
   READ(UNITNO,1000,END=500) . . .
   ```

   This is allowed; the unit number may be given as either a constant or a variable.

   (b) Modify the main program of Figure 13.3 to use this subroutine. Can you revise the code for exit 3 so that it can also make use of the subroutine?

8. **(a)** The merge algorithm we wrote is made complex by the many different exits from the main loop. One way to avoid this is to stay in the loop until both files are exhausted.

   Modify the algorithm by changing each read statement as suggested below:

   read record 1; **if** eof **then** ID1 ← + ∞ **endif**

   After the main loop you will simply stop. What condition will be used to leave the loop when both files have reached end of file? Where will this exit step be placed?

   Explain why the resulting algorithm works. Note. By "+ ∞" we mean a number which is larger than any ID existing on either input file.

   (b) Is the resulting algorithm easier to understand? Is it more or less efficient than the original algorithm? Explain your answer.

   (c) Code the resulting algorithm in FORTRAN. Of course, your must choose a particular number to represent "+ ∞". [*Hint:* The PARAMETER statement might be appropriate in this context.]

9. (See Exercise 8.) Another approach to this problem is to arrange that each of the files to be merged will contain a trailer (dummy) record with an ID of "+ ∞." Modify the algorithm based on this assumption.

   Note: Place a trailer record on the output file; then it may be used in a later merge.

Exercises 10–11 expand on the merge algorithm.

10. In merging two files, we may consider the second file as containing a list of records to be added to the first file. The first file would be called a "master" file, and the second a "transaction" file. The purpose of the merge would be to add the transaction records to the master file. (After running the program, we would use operating system commands to replace the old master by the output from the merge.)

This suggests that it might be possible to perform other modifications of a master file. Each of the algorithms suggested in this exercise may be patterned after the merge algorithm.

(a) A master file has records consisting of item number, department, and quantity. A transaction file has records containing only an item number. Each record in the transaction file represents a record to be removed from the master file. Both files are in order by item number, with no duplicates.

Write an algorithm to create an output file consisting of the records in the master file, with the indicated records removed. Print an error message for any faulty transaction item numbers.

(b) The master file is the same as for (a). The transaction file contains a list of changes to be made. Each transaction record contains an item number and a new quantity for that item. Both files are in order by item number, with no duplicates.

Write an algorithm to create an output file consisting of the records in the master file, with the new quantity for each of the indicated items. Print an error message for any faulty transaction item numbers.

11. Combine the merge (add) with the delete and change algorithms of Exercise 10. The master file is the same as for Exercise 10. Each transaction record contains

transaction code (A=add, D=delete, C=change)
item number
department (blank for code D or C)
quantity (blank for code D)

Both files are in order by item number, with no duplicates.

Write an algorithm to create an output file containing the records of the master file with the indicated additions, deletions, and changes.

Exercises 12–15 refer to a sequential file DRUG.INVEN which contains these fields:

Description	Type	Number of Columns
Item number	Numeric	5
Item name	Character	16
Department code	Character	3
Inventory at each of 9 locations	Numeric array	4 columns each (36 in all)

The file is in ascending order by item number.

12. Write a program to create this file.

In order to create the file, you will read a set of input. Each record will have exactly the information which will be put on the file, plus an additional field which contains the total inventory for the entire chain (numeric, five columns). You will perform the following "correctness" checks:

(a) The item name field must begin with a nonblank character.

(b) The department code must be one of the following eight codes: COS, DRU, TOY, CRD, PRE, HHG, CLO, or BKS.

(c) The sum of the individual inventory amounts must equal the total inventory (this helps catch data entry errors).
(d) The item numbers must be in order.

In addition, perform the following "reasonableness" check:

(e) Each inventory amount must be between 0 and 5000, inclusive.
Records with no errors will be placed in the file; records with errors will *not*. All errors will be listed on an exception report, as illustrated below:

```
                         EXCEPTION REPORT        PAGE 1
                         --------- ------
ITEM NUMBER                  TYPE OF ERROR
---- ------                  ---- -- -----
   12345          BLANK ITEM NAME
                  BAD DEPT CODE
                  BAD INVENTORY AMT (STORE 2)
                  BAD INVENTORY AMT (STORE 9)
                  INCORRECT TOTAL
   12479          BAD INVENTORY AMT (STORE 6)
   13780          OUT OF ORDER (PREVIOUS ITEM=13792)
```

Notice that you should continue checking for further errors even after finding one error. Also, notice that the output is group indicated by item number. If the list for a single item spans two pages, print the item number in a form such as 79345(CONT.) on the new page.

13. Write programs to create partial files containing:
(a) All TOY items.
(b) All items whose item number is between 10000 and 40000, inclusive.
(c) All items where any single inventory amount is less than 10. The output record should contain only the item number, name, and department.

14. Write a program to create a file where each record contains item number and the total inventory for the entire chain.

15. Write a program to update the DRUG.INVEN file (see Exercise 11).
You have a DRUG.TRANS file containing this information: item number, item name, department code, inventory of each of nine locations, and transaction code. Except for the transaction code, the information format is precisely the same as that on the master file. The transaction code has the same meaning as in Exercise 11. The transaction record may leave blank any of the fields not actually being used in that type of transaction. You may assume that the information on the transaction record has already been edited.
The following are to be done for a "change" transaction:
(a) If the item name on the transaction record is not blank, then change the item name.
(b) If the department code on the transaction record is not blank, then change the department code.
(c) Add each element in the inventory array to the corresponding element in the master record.

Instead of creating an exception report, create an exception file. This file will have records containing all the fields of the transaction record, plus a code for the type of error:

- Trying to add a record already there.
- Trying to delete a record not there.
- Trying to change a record not there.

- A resulting inventory amount which is less than 0 or more than 5000. (For this error, leave the master record with the faulty inventories—assume the error will be corrected later.)

13.3 DIRECT FILE TECHNIQUES

Sequential files are convenient for the long-term storage of data. As long as a file is updated fairly infrequently, sequential access may be adequate. For example, a mailing list for an organization might be stored on a sequential file. Generally, this information will be used in its entirety to generate a set of mailing labels. Updating might occur only once a month or even less frequently.

Even when a file is updated frequently, sequential access may be appropriate. For example, the "hours worked" and other fields on a file used to generate payroll checks might change every week. However, in this case most of the records in the file will be modified. An algorithm which goes through the file sequentially making the changes would be fairly efficient.

Sequential files become inadequate in situations where frequent changes occur to records scattered throughout the file. As we discussed in the exercises of Section 13.2, each batch of changes requires us to go completely through the file. In addition, if we are using the file to "look up" records which are scattered at random throughout the file, we will want a direct access file. Even in applications where a sequential file is adequate, a direct file may be more convenient. For example, consider a conversational payroll system. Using a sequential file, a payroll clerk could enter the hours for each person on the file. However, he would have to do so in the same order as the records were listed on the file. With a direct file, the values could be entered in any desired order, perhaps by several payroll clerks, one per department.

As a result of these and similar considerations, direct files have become more and more important in computing. (This growth in importance is evidenced by the fact that the previous FORTRAN standard did not provide for direct file facilities.)

Direct File Commands

We now cover the OPEN, READ, and WRITE as used for direct files. The other commands covered in Section 13.2 (REWIND and ENDFILE) may not be used with a direct file.

The form of the OPEN is

```
OPEN(unit, . . .)
```

where, as usual, we may write UNIT=unit. The options are

ACCESS='DIRECT'	This *must* be included.
RECL=n	This *must* be included.
FORM='FORMATTED'	This *must* be included.
IOSTAT=variable	
ERR=label	
FILE=filename	

The last three listed have the same meaning they did for sequential files. The first three must be given, except that for an unformatted file the FORM = may be omitted (see Section 13.4). The RECL = n gives the record length in characters. All the records in the file will be of this same length. (However, if we write a record which would be shorter, the system will automatically right pad the record with blanks.) Any attempt to read or write a longer record is an error.

When a file is first created, the RECL = sets the record length. Any other programs which later access that file must specify the correct record length as set at creation time.

Each record on a direct file has a **record number**. This number is established when the record is first written on the file. The record number may never be changed, although any of the data on the record may be changed by writing the record again. The records may be placed on the file in any order; when we write record 4, records 1, 2, and 3 need not exist.

Both the READ and WRITE use the record number to determine which record on the file is being referred to. They have the forms

```
READ(unit,format, . . .)
WRITE(unit,format, . . .)
```

with options for each:

IOSTAT = variable

ERR = label

REC = record number (This *must* be present.)

(We may use UNIT = and FMT =, but *not* END =.)

The record number may be given as any INTEGER expression; in most cases it will be an INTEGER variable. It specifies the record to which the file is to be positioned for the READ or WRITE.

The following segment of code writes records numbered 1 to 100 onto a previously opened direct file on unit 25.

```
      INTEGER I,AGE
      CHARACTER NAME*20
         .
         .
      DO 50 I = 1,100
         READ (*,1000) NAME,AGE
         WRITE(25,1000,REC=I) NAME,AGE
   50    CONTINUE
```

This code segment writes records 105 and 106. The "slash" format (/) causes the system to move on to the next record number. Record 105 will contain I and J, record 106 K and L.

```
      INTEGER I,J,K,L
         .
         .
      WRITE(33,1000,REC=105) I,J,K,L
 1000 FORMAT(I5,I8/I7,I7)
```

This next code segment reads a sequential file on unit 23. This file contains a series of record numbers to be read from a direct file on unit 30.

```
      INTEGER RECNO
      CHARACTER NAME*30,ADDRESS*60
          .
          .
   10 CONTINUE
         READ(23,1000,END=500) RECNO
         READ(30,2000,REC=RECNO) NAME,ADDRESS
         WRITE(*,3000) RECNO,NAME,ADDRESS
         GO TO 10
  500 CONTINUE
          .
          .
 1000 FORMAT(I5)
 2000 FORMAT(A30,A60)
 3000 FORMAT(///' RECORD #:',I5,' HAS NAME AND ADDRESS '//
     $       ' ',A30/' ',A60)
```

Direct File Algorithms

The examples that follow illustrate the basic techniques for working with direct files. The major difficulty with direct files is that the program must know the proper record number. If this number is read from some other file, as in the previous example, then the person making up the data for the other file must know the record numbers of the records to be processed. There are a number of techniques which have been devised for this purpose. One of the simplest is illustrated by the following example.

A college maintains a student data file. Among other things, the file contains a five-digit student number, the total number of credits attempted to date, and the number of quality points earned to date.

When the file was originally created, it was decided to use the student number itself as the record number. The student number may be viewed as a **key** to the record, given the student number, we know which student's record we wish to see. In this case, we have the record number equal to the key.

The program in Figure 13.5 updates this file. To do so, it reads a sequential file containing a series of student numbers, credit hours attempted during one semester, and quality points earned during that semester. Using the given student number, it retrieves the student's record, updates the record, and writes it back onto the file.

We assume that the records on the master file are 280 characters long, with the semester hours in columns 101–103 and the quality points in columns 104–106.

> **COMMENT.** It would not be necessary to include the student number on the record, since this number is the same as the record number.

When the record number is the key, then we must know the key to obtain the record. Moreover, this key must be numerical, and the number of digits allowed in the key will be limited. There are many applications where it is more convenient to use an alphabetic key. For example, when students come in to check on their records,

```
      INTEGER STNO,SEMHRS,TOTHRS,SEMQP,TOTQP
      CHARACTER DATA1*100,DATA2*174

C   WRITTEN BY *******, **/**/**.

C   THIS PROGRAM, USING THE GIVEN STUDENT NUMBER
C OBTAINED FROM READING THE SEQUENTIAL FILE,
C RETRIEVES THE STUDENT'S RECORD ON THE
C DIRECT FILE, UPDATES THE RECORD, AND WRITES
C IT BACK ONTO THE DIRECT FILE.

C   OPEN FILES

      OPEN(20,FILE='SEMESTER',ACCESS='SEQUENTIAL')
      REWIND 20
      OPEN(30,FILE='STUDENT.MASTER',ACCESS='DIRECT',
     $   FORM='FORMATTED',RECL=280)

C   LOOP. READ SEMESTER RECORD, UPDATE STUDENT MASTER RECORD

   10 CONTINUE
         READ(20,1000,END=500) STNO,SEMHRS,SEMQP
         READ(30,2000,REC=STNO) DATA1,TOTHRS,TOTQP,DATA2
         TOTHRS = TOTHRS + SEMHRS
         TOTQP = TOTQP + SEMQP
         WRITE(30,2000,REC=STNO) DATA1,TOTHRS,TOTQP,DATA2
         GO TO 10
  500 CONTINUE
      STOP

C   FORMATS

 1000 FORMAT(I5,2I3)
 2000 FORMAT(A100,2I3,A174)
      END
```

Figure 13.5

they may not remember their student numbers. Either their name or their social security number might be a more convenient key.

As a similar example, consider a file which lists the local tax rate for each of the various cities, towns, and so forth in a given state. For such a file, the most convenient key would be the locality name, or perhaps an abbreviation of that name. If the file is set up with this alphabetical key, then some means must be provided in the program to determine the desired record number, given the locality name.

A number of techniques have been devised to handle these and other considerations when working with direct files. These techniques are beyond the scope of this text. However, keep in mind that, once the record number is calculated, the READ or WRITE will be just like those presented in our examples.

Missing Records

In our previous example, we have completely ignored the possibility that a given student number may not exist on the file. How this problem is handled will depend on the particular computer system being used.

One approach is for the programmer to ensure that this never occurs. For example, suppose a small company has approximately 500 employees and uses a three-digit "clock number" to identify these employees. We can set up a file containing 999 records:

```
      INTEGER I
      OPEN(20,FILE='EMPLOYEE',ACCESS='DIRECT',
     $    FORM='FORMATTED',RECL=300)
      DO 10 I = 1,999
          WRITE(20,*,REC=I)'*'
10        CONTINUE
      STOP
      END
```

The asterisk in column 1 of a record will be used to indicate that that record is empty. As employees are added, we rewrite the records with the particular employee's data. At this time we change the first character to some character other than an '*'. This allows us to determine whether or not a READ has obtained an active record:

```
READ(35,1000,REC=EMPNO) FLAG, . . .
IF (FLAG.EQ.'*') THEN
   (error message, next iteration)
ENDIF
```

COMMENT. This approach allows us to **delete** a record by putting an asterisk back in column 1.

The problem with this approach may be seen if the employee number being used as a record number were six digits long. We would have to set up a file with 999,999 records, most of which would be unused.

On some computer systems, it may be possible to avoid this problem by using the IOSTAT variable. For example, one particular system might set this variable to the value 8 when an attempted read of a nonexistent record occurs. If so, we may write code similar to the following

```
READ(35,1000,REC=EMPNO,IOSTAT=ERRFL)
IF(ERRFL.EQ.8) THEN
   (error message, next iteration)
ENDIF
```

NOTE. We will still need to use some method similar to that given above to delete a record.

To determine whether or not your particular computer does set the IOSTAT variable for this condition, you will need to consult the manufacturer's manual.

REVIEW

These options have the same meaning and use as for sequential files:

```
 FILE=filename
 IOSTAT=variable
 ERR=label
*UNIT=unit
*FMT=format label

*: keyword optional
```

Other options which must be used in OPEN command

```
ACCESS='DIRECT'
FORM='FORMATTED'
RECL=n (record length)
```

Other option which must be used in READ and WRITE

```
REC=record number (constant or variable telling record number)
```

EXERCISES

1. Give an OPEN command to connect a direct file named ATH.DEC to unit 17. This file contains records 100 characters long.

2. For the file of Exercise 1, give appropriate READ or WRITE statements to:

(a) Read record 103 into an INTEGER array A of size 10. Assume the record contains ten numbers each ten digits long.

(b) Write the array A mentioned in (a) onto record 75.

(c) Write an INTEGER array C of size 30 onto the successive records 17, 18, and 19, ten numbers per record.

3. A direct file named ACCOUNT.LIST contains a list of persons and companies to whom a church typically writes checks. Write the following set of routines for the church treasurer.

[*Note:* Record 1 contains a three-digit number, N, indicating the largest record number currently stored in the file. Each other record contains the account name (25 characters) as it is to appear on the checks. If the first character of the name is '*', the account has been deleted.

(a) Initialize the file. Create the file with N = 1.

(b) Addition. Given a new account name, add it to the end of the file.

(c) Printout. Print a list of the current contents of the file: record number and account name. Ignore deleted records.

(d) Deletion. Given a record number, mark it as deleted.

(e) Compression. Remove all deleted records, by copying valid data into them and adjusting N.

For example,

Before	After
5	3
SHIELDS, INC	SHIELDS, INC
*	SCRIPPS PUBL.
*	(records 4 and 5 will be
SCRIPPS PUB.	overwritten by the next
	two additions)

(f) Lookup. Given an account number (record number), determine the account name.

4. A direct file CHECK.LIST is being used to keep a list of checks written by a church. Record 1 contains three fields (3I4); first check number in the file; last check number in the file; last check number already printed and sent. For the other records, the check number is the record number, and the records contain these fields:

Columns	Description
1–6	Date (yymmdd)—870407 is April 7, 1987
7–9	Paid to whom (three-digit code)
10–11	Budget category (two-digit code)
12–17	Amount (ddddcc)—101345 is $1013.45

The "paid to whom" code refers to the file ACCOUNT.LIST of Exercise 3. The "budget category" code refers to a similar file BUDGET.CAT which lists budget category names (again with N on the first record).

Give subprograms for the following. Assume the main program has opened the files.

(a) New check. Given date, "paid to" code, "category" code, and amount, add a check to the end of the file. First, however, make sure that the given date is after the date of the last check written, and that both codes are valid. Set a LOGICAL output parameter GOOD to indicate success or failure.

(b) Check list. Create a printed list of the checks on the file, with these columns: date, number, paid to (name, not code), budget category (name), amount. As an optional extra, group indicate by date. Print the dates in the form mm/dd/yy.

(c) Partial list. Modify (b) to print only those checks whose date lies between two given dates, inclusive.

(d) Check print. Print any checks which have not yet been printed.

(e) Budget summary. Create a printed report showing how much was spent in each budget category between two given dates. You may assume that BUDGET.CAT file contains a field for use as an accumulator.

5. An employee file named EMP.MASTER contains records 1–999, with unused records beginning with an asterisk. For several applications we wish to access the records in alphabetical order by last name. Write the following collection of program segments to accomplish this (see also Exercise 6).

(a) Each record is 520 characters long and contains the last name in the first 18 columns. Give code to set up parallel arrays RECNO and NAME, where RECNO(I) is the record number and NAME(I) is the name of the Ith actual record. (Skip over unused records.)

(b) Sort the RECNO/NAME pairs into alphabetical order by name.
(c) Create a sequential file EMP.ALPHABETICAL which contains the sorted RECNO array, one number per record.

6. See Exercise 5. If we are given a list of record numbers to be processed, we may easily process a direct file in that order.

Use the EMP.ALPHABETICAL file to create a printed list of the name, hourly rate, department, clock number, marital status, and number of dependents in alphabetical order by last name. Make reasonable assumptions about the layout of the EMP.MASTER file.

7. See Exercise 5. Rather than creating a separate file to get an alphabetical listing, we could have each record in the EMP.MASTER file tell which record is next in alphabetical order. Each record might be in this form:

Columns	Description
1–18	Name
19–21	"NEXT"—a three-digit number telling which record number comes next in alphabetical order
22–520	Other data

Suppose that record 1000 contains only a single number ("First") which tells which record is first in alphabetical order. Also, suppose that the "NEXT" field for the person who is last contains the number −1.

(a) Write a program to print the file as in Exercise 6, using record 1000 to get started and using the "NEXT" field to move through the file.
(b) Can you devise algorithms for inserting a new employee or deleting an employee? Each of these will involve changing some of the "NEXT" fields in the file (and perhaps the "FIRST" field on record 1000).

13.4 OTHER FEATURES

Formats

We have consistently identified the format, for a formatted input or output by giving the label on a FORMAT statement. There are a number of other ways the format may be specified. For example, we may give the format as a character constant, as in this example:

```
READ(10,'(5I6)') I,J,K,L,M
```

This is equivalent to

```
     READ(10,1000) I,J,K,L,M
1000 FORMAT(5I6)
```

As another example, consider

```
     WRITE(*,1000) SUM
1000 FORMAT(' THE SUM IS ',I5)
```

When we write this format as a character constant, we must use two apostrophes for each apostrophe in the format, obtaining

```
WRITE(*,' ('' THE SUM IS '',I5) ') SUM
```

Rather than using a character constant as the format, we may use a character variable or even a character expression. For example, the following segment is equivalent to our first example above:

```
CHARACTER*25 RFORM
RFORM = '(5I6)'
READ(10,RFORM) I,J,K,L,M
```

The computer will use as its format the portion of the string from the left parenthesis to the matching right parenthesis. Anything after that right parenthesis is ignored.

A more useful application of this technique involves having the program read in the format to be used for some later I/O operation. Instead of the assignment statement of the last example, we might have

```
READ(*,5000) RFORM
```

This allows us to write programs with some flexibility in the formats used. Another application might be to pass a character variable containing a heading format to a general-purpose HEADER subroutine. Finally, we might use character assignment statements and substring operations to change the format as the program is running.

A special situation occurs when the format is given as a CHARACTER array name. In this case the entire array is considered as giving the format. For example, consider

```
CHARACTER*3 A(2)
A(1) = '(5I'
A(2) = '6)'
READ(10,A) I,J,K,L,M
```

The format is the entire array A as illustrated below:

```
 (5I 6)b
A(1) A(2)
```

Finally, the format may be given as an asterisk, as in

```
WRITE(*,*) A,X,I    or    PRINT *,NUM
```

We have used this approach extensively.

Other Options and Commands

The OPEN command has two additional keyword options. First, we have STATUS=character expression. The expression may have the value 'NEW', 'OLD', 'SCRATCH', or 'UNKNOWN'. The first two can be used to detect problems such as:

1. a program trying to use an "old" file which does not exist;
2. a program creating a "new" file when a file of that same name already exists.

Execution of an OPEN where the STATUS as given does not match the actual status will cause an error condition, which can be checked using the IOSTAT variable. A value of 'SCRATCH' indicates the file is a temporary file which is to be deleted when the program terminates. Using 'UNKNOWN' is the same as omitting the option.

The other option, BLANK=character expression, indicates whether blanks in the input record should be treated as zeroes (BLANK='ZERO') or as not being there (BLANK='NULL'). For example, using an I3 format, '2b3' is read as 203 or as 23 depending on this option's value.

In addition, the FORM=character expression may be either 'FORMATTED' or 'UNFORMATTED'. The default for sequential files is 'FORMATTED', so we omitted the keyword. We specified the keyword for direct files because in this case the default is 'UNFORMATTED'. Unformatted files are discussed later in this section.

There are three commands not covered earlier: BACKSPACE, CLOSE, and INQUIRE. The BACKSPACE has the same form as REWIND and ENDFILE:

```
BACKSPACE unit      or      BACKSPACE(unit, . . .)
```

with options IOSTAT and ERR. If may be used only with sequential files, and it moves the file pointer back to the previous record. (Nothing happens if the pointer is already at the first record of the file.)

The CLOSE statement disconnects a file from the unit to which it is connected. This frees the unit for connection to another file (and the file for connection to another unit). The form is

```
CLOSE(unit, . . .)
```

with options IOSTAT, ERR, and STATUS. The first two have the usual meaning. The STATUS=character expression specifies whether or not the file which was disconnected should be erased (STATUS='DELETE') or not (STATUS='KEEP'). The default is 'KEEP' (except, of course, for a 'SCRATCH' file).

The INQUIRE statement may be used to inquire about a particular file:

```
INQUIRE(FILE=filename, . . .)
```

or unit:

```
INQUIRE(unit, . . .)
```

There are many options, most of the form

keyword=variable (or array element)

The variable (or array element) will receive a value indicating the answer to the question indicated by the keyword. Among the keyword options are those listed in Table 13.1. In addition, there are the usual IOSTAT and ERR keywords. The INQUIRE statement would, for example, allow the program to obtain a file name

TABLE 13.1

Keyword	Variable or array element type	Question
EXIST=	logical	Does it (file or unit) exist? (.TRUE. means yes)
OPENED=	logical	Is it connected?
NUMBER=	integer	What unit is it connected to?
NAME=	character	What is the file name?
SEQUENTIAL= DIRECT=	character	May the file be connected as a sequential (direct) file? ('YES' or 'NO')
FORM=	character variable	'FORMATTED' or 'UNFORMATTED'?
FORMATTED= UNFORMATTED=	character	Is it formatted (unformatted)? ('YES' or 'NO')
RECL	integer	What is the record length?

from the user, then inquire about the file prior to issuing an open and beginning processing. The answers to the various questions might be used in the OPEN, in decision structures within the program, or perhaps to generate error messages.

Unformatted Files

Data is typically stored in the computer using **binary** (base 2) numbers. For example, the INTEGER variable I might contain the **bit** (binary digit) pattern

```
0000000000101101
```

to represent the number 45. If we use an I4 format to write this on a file, this bit pattern must be converted to the character string ' 45'. This takes time. Moreover, when a program later reads the number from the file, the '45' must be converted back into the bit pattern which represents the integer 45. Once again, the conversion takes time.

FORTRAN allows "unformatted" files, in which the bit patterns themselves may be stored on the file and later read directly. This will generally be a good deal faster than using a format. In addition, it may save space on the file. A major disadvantage is that a normal print of the file, using an operating system command, will not be readable. It will print binary patterns rather than the familiar character form.

To use an unformatted file, we specify FORM='UNFORMATTED' in the OPEN statement. (In addition, the meaning of the RECL= option will vary from system to system.) In our READ and WRITE statements we merely omit the format, as in these examples.

```
READ(10) I,J
READ(20,END=700) NAME,AGE
WRITE(27,IOSTAT=ERRCOD,REC=I) COMP,ADDR,STAT,AMT
```

The variables, no matter what their type, will be read or written using the particular computer's form of bit pattern representations.

CAUTIONS.

1. A file is either formatted or unformatted. No mixing is allowed. The READ and WRITE statements must be consistent with the file type.
2. In reading an unformatted record, the READ should include the same type of variables as were originally put in the record. If a WRITE statement has placed three integers on the record, the READ which reads the record should not try to read two real numbers and a character string.

REVIEW

Formats may be:
  1. label;
  2. character constant or expression;
  3. character array name; or
  4. * (list directed I/O—see Chapter 14)

Other OPEN options:
  STATUS='NEW', 'OLD', 'SCRATCH', or 'UNKNOWN'
  BLANK= 'ZERO' or 'NULL'
  FORM='FORMATTED' or 'UNFORMATTED'

Other commands:
  BACKSPACE unit or BACKSPACE(unit, . . .)
  CLOSE(unit, . . .)
    options: IOSTAT, ERR, STATUS='KEEP' or 'DELETE'
  *INQUIRE(FILE=filename, . . .)
  *INQUIRE(unit, . . .)
    *:see Table 13.1

Unformatted files
  OPEN—use FORM='UNFORMATTED'; see manual for meaning of RECL keyword
  READ and WRITE—leave out "format" option

14

ADDITIONAL FEATURES

This chapter provides a brief introduction to several additional statements and facilities present in FORTRAN. The chapter is not intended to be complete in the sense of discussing all of the remaining statements in FORTRAN, but merely to describe some of those which we have found to be useful in our own work. Additional statements covered are the COMPUTED and ASSIGNED GO TO, the arithmetic and logical IF statements, and PAUSE. Run time formats, the scale factor for REALs and DOUBLE PRECISION, and internal files are covered in the second part. The final portion deals with some selected topics concerning subprograms.

14.1 ADDITIONAL EXECUTABLE STATEMENTS

COMPUTED GO TO

The COMPUTED GO TO statement uses an INTEGER value to select a label from a list of labels, and then performs a transfer to that label. A sample of the form of the statement is

```
GO TO (10,20,30,20,50) ,K
```

If K is outside the range 1−5 (since there are five labels in the statement) the statement following the GO TO is executed. For K within the range 1−5, the Kth label in the list is selected. The labels may be the labels of any executable statements within the same program unit as the GO TO. Those statement labels must be the same as those that could appear in a regular GO TO at that point of the program.

Notice that the same label may appear more than once in the list. The sample given is equivalent to this series of statements:

```
IF (K.EQ.1) GO TO 10
IF (K.EQ.2 .OR.K.EQ.4) GO TO 20
IF (K.EQ.3) GO TO 30
IF (K.EQ.5) GO TO 50
```

ASSIGNED GO TO

It is possible to place a statement label in an INTEGER variable using a special statement called an ASSIGN statement. This statement is of the form

```
ASSIGN label TO integer variable
```

For example, we might have

```
ASSIGN 10 to K
```

This label can then be referenced by an ASSIGNED GO TO of the form

```
GO TO K
```

or of the form

```
GO TO K, (10,20,30,40)
```

To GO TO causes a transfer to the last label that was assigned to the variable K prior to the execution of the GO TO. If the second form of the ASSIGNED GO TO is used, the label which is assigned to the variable must be one of those in the list.

Logical IF

An older form of the IF statement in FORTRAN is the so-called logical IF. This statement is of the form

```
IF(l) s
```

where l is a logical expression and s is a statement. The logical expression is any which could be used in a normal IF( ) THEN statement. The statement, s, can be any executable statement except for another logical IF, a DO statement, an IF( ) THEN, ELSE, ELSE IF or ENDIF. The major use of the logical IF is to implement a simple IF,THEN,ELSE construction where the ELSE part is empty and the IF THEN action consists of a single assignment or READ or WRITE.

A few simple examples are

```
IF(A.LT.5.0) LOW = LOW + 1
IF(DEBUG) WRITE(*,1000) I,J,K
IF(X.GT.0.0.AND. X.LT.1.0) GO TO 50
```

Arithmetic IF

The original decision statement in FORTRAN was the arithmetic IF, which is of the form

```
IF(expression) label1, label2, label3
```

Label1, label2, and label3 are labels on executable statements, and may be, but do not have to be, all different. The expression may of be REAL, INTEGER, or DOUBLE PRECISION type. The action is to evaluate the expression and transfer control to the statement labeled label1, label2, or label3 if the expression is negative, zero, or positive, respectively. The use of this statement tends to make code difficult to understand. However, there are a few situations where one would in fact like to make a three-way decision, and where the statement can be useful. The case of solving a quadratic equation $ax^2 + bx + c = 0$ is an example. Here the character of the solution and the possible computer algorithms depend upon whether the quantity $b^2 - 4ac$ is negative, zero, or positive.

The statement will frequently be found in older programs, and so the reader should be familiar with it.

PAUSE

The PAUSE statement causes a FORTRAN program to temporarily halt execution. Upon such a halt, the user or operator can resume the program at the statement following the PAUSE by using some mechanism which is dependent upon the computer system being used. The major use of this statement would be to allow the user to modify the environment of a program, perhaps to manually start a device the program is controlling or to fix some condition such as a paper outage in a printer or terminal.

An optional string of up to five digits (or a character constant) may follow the PAUSE. If the string is used it will be displayed or made available to the user or operator in some system dependent manner. This string can be used to identify which of the PAUSEs in a program was executed.

The same types of strings may also be used following a STOP, and will be made available in the same manner as the PAUSE, although after a STOP the program cannot be resumed. This can be used, for example, to distinguish between error stops and normal completion of a program.

14.2 ADDITIONAL I/O FEATURES

Run Time Formats

The simplest type of format identifier in a READ or WRITE statement is the label of a FORMAT statement. However, this format identifier may also be an INTEGER variable, a CHARACTER array or variable name, a CHARACTER constant, or a CHARACTER expression. If the format identifier is an INTEGER variable then an ASSIGN statement must assign the label of a FORMAT statement to the variable, prior to executing the READ or WRITE. If a CHARACTER form is used its value must contain a left parenthesis, a group of valid format codes, and a right parenthesis, in that order. Only blanks may precede the opening left parenthesis.

The form with an INTEGER variable allows a program to select an appropriate predefined format during execution. This option can lead to shorter and perhaps clearer programs than simply selecting among a number of READ or WRITE statements referencing different FORMATs.

The option of using character expressions or variables allows a program to generate the format at execution time, or allows the format codes to be read as data. An application might be a program to print a series of values in which the program inserts E or F codes depending on the magnitude of the numbers involved. Another application would be to provide the appropriate format codes as part of a data file. Thus the program user could use the program with a wide range of different data formats simply by supplying the appropriate format codes. An example of such a program code is shown here:

```
      CHARACTER*80 DATFRM
      INTEGER I,J,M,N
      REAL X(10)
        .
        .
      READ(*,1000) M,N
      READ(*,1010) DATFRM
        .
      DO 10 I = 1,M
        READ(*,DATFRM) (X(J),J=1,N)
           computation using X values
   10   CONTINUE
        .
        .
 1000 FORMAT(2I2)
 1010 FORMAT(A80)
```

If there are three values per input card in F10.5 format, and we wish to read 15 cards, the first two cards could be:

```
15b3
(3F10.5)
```

Scaling (P Format)

Frequently one would like numbers with exponents to be printed with a significant digit to the left of the decimal point. This can be done using the code 1PE15.6. The 1P causes the number to be shifted left *one* decimal place before printing. On input, the action would be the opposite, with 1P causing a shift to the right by one place. When an exponent is present, the exponent will be adjusted so that the numerical value will not be changed. If there is no exponent, as in writing with an F format code, the shifting occurs and results in a change of value of the number printed.

The scale factor is set to zero when a READ or WRITE statement is executed, changed when a P code appears in a FORMAT, and applied to all the E, F, and D codes in the given FORMAT. Thus if a scale factor is used on a code in a FORMAT, and you do not want the remaining codes to be affected, the scale factor must be reset to zero, as for example in (1PE15.6,0PF10.5).

The scale factor can be used to scale values by factors of 10 upon input (if no exponent is used) but the programs would probably be clearer if the scaling were done by explicit multiplications and divisions instead.

List-directed I/O

As we know, the format specifier in a READ or WRITE statement can be the character '*', as in

```
WRITE(*,*) 'A = ',A,' B = ',B,' C = ',C
```

or

```
READ(5,*) A,B,C
```

The items to be written may be variables of any type—arrays, character constants, or expressions. The computer will write the values out using reasonable formats and as many records as needed. Character constants will be written without apostrophes surrounding them. Commas may be used to separate values, depending upon the particular computer system. If two or more adjacent values are identical, the computer may use the notation r*v to represent them. For example, 5*10 appearing in the output would mean the same as

10 10 10 10 10 or 10, 10 ,10 ,10 ,10

For input the items in the READ statement may be variable names, array names, or array elements. The values supplied may take as many records as needed to supply values for all elements in the list of the READ statement. The values are separated by spaces, commas, slashes, or ends of records. Character values must be enclosed in apostrophes. Spaces may not be used within values other than character values. Logical values are represented as T or F while complex values use parentheses and a comma to separate the real and imaginary parts. Adjacent identical values may use the notation r*v mentioned above. A null value is indicated by using commas as separators, as in 5,,6, which represents three values—5, null, and 6. If a variable or array element is matched by a null value, the original value of the variable or element is left unchanged. Note that the actions for output and input of character data are inconsistent, and information written using list-directed output might not be able to be read using list-directed input.

One of the more common uses of list-directed output is to write out intermediate values of variables during the testing and debugging of a program. It is a simple matter (since one does not have to worry about detailed format design) to insert

WRITE statements at critical points within a program and use character constants to label the values.

Internal Files

READ and WRITE statements can be used to transfer information between variables of any type and what are called internal files. This allows the powerful formatting capabilities of FORTRAN to be used for character manipulation.

An internal file is a character variable, character array, character array element, or a character substring. If the internal file is a character array, then each element of the array is regarded as one record. In the other cases the entire file is regarded as a single record. The READ and WRITE statements are the same as regular sequential READ and WRITE statements. The unit reference must be present and is the name of the internal file. The statements must include a format reference. The file pointer is positioned before the first (and in most cases the only record) before executing each READ or WRITE. The READ and WRITE transfer information in the usual direction. The READ obtains information from the internal file while the WRITE transfers information to the internal file.

As a first example, suppose we want to write a dollar amount contained in a real variable BALANC. Assume that BALANC is between 0.1 and 99,999.99 and we are to write it right justified in a ten-column field, with dollar signs in the left-most positions in the field. The following segment of code will do this:

```
      CHARACTER*10 FIELD

      WRITE(FIELD,'(F10.2)')BALANC
      IF(FIELD(4:4).NE.' ')THEN
        FIELD(2:2) = FIELD(3:3)
        FIELD(3:3) = FIELD(4:4)
        FIELD(4:4) = ','
      ENDIF
      DO 10 I = 1, 7
        IF(FIELD(I:I).EQ.' ')THEN
          FIELD(I:I) = '$'
          ENDIF
10        CONTINUE
      WRITE(*,'(A10)')FIELD
```

For a second example, suppose we want to read data records of two different types. The first contain two real numbers in columns 1–10 and 11–20 while the second contains two integers in the same columns. We will assume that the real numbers will always contain a decimal point. The following segment will set the variable RV to .TRUE. If the values are real and place them in the variables X and Y. If the values are integers, then RV is set to .FALSE. and the values are placed in I and J.

```
LOGICAL RV
REAL X,Y
INTEGER I, J
CHARACTER*20 DD

READ(*,'(A)')DD
RV = INDEX(DD(1:10), '.').NE.0
IF(RV) THEN
  READ(DD,'(2E10.0)')X,Y
ELSE
  READ(DD,'(2I10)')I,J
ENDIF
```

For our last example, suppose we have a positive integer number of up to ten digits and we wish to copy each digit of the number to an element of an integer array. This operation might be a preliminary step in computing a check digit for the number. (A check digit is a digit appended to a number. The value of the check digit is computed by applying some fixed algorithm to the digits of the number. Hopefully, if the number is changed, a recalculation of the check digit will give a value different from the check digit with the number. This would indicate that the value had been changed.)

```
INTEGER NUM, DIGITS(10)
CHARACTER*10 CNUM

WRITE(CNUM,'(I10)') NUM
READ(CNUM,'(10I1)') DIGITS
```

14.3 ADDITIONAL SUBPROGRAM FEATURES

EXTERNAL

It is possible to pass the name of a function or subroutine to a FORTRAN subprogram as an argument. As an example, one function might compute the sum of a number of values of another function F. In the following example, the argument F of SUM is the name of a REAL function with one REAL parameter.

```
      REAL FUNCTION SUM(START,FINAL,STEP,F)
      REAL START,FINAL,STEP,F,X

C  THIS FUNCTION SUMS THE VALUES OF A FUNCTION, F,
C FOR ARGUMENTS RUNNING FROM 'START' TO 'FINAL' IN
C INCREMENTS OF 'STEP'

      SUM = 0.0
      DO 10 X = START,FINAL,STEP
         SUM = SUM + F(X)
   10    CONTINUE
      RETURN
      END
```

When the compiler is translating SUM, it can tell that F is a function by the reference that occurs in the statement SUM = SUM + F(X). In a calling program the function SUM might be declared as

```
REAL SUM
```

and referenced in a line like

```
D = SUM(0.0,1.0,0.1,AA)
```

AA would also be declared as REAL, but the compiler would also need to distinguish AA from the name of a variable. Therefore the declaration

```
EXTERNAL AA
```

would appear in the calling program. In addition, the function AA with one real argument would have to be defined either in a library or in the program being compiled.

As another example, we might have this segment which uses the FORTRAN library sine function.

```
REAL SUM,SIN,ANS
EXTERNAL SIN
      .
      .
      .
ANS = SUM(-0.5,0.5,0.01,SIN)
```

Passing function names as arguments makes it possible to write general-purpose subprograms which can perform operations on functions. As examples, one might have subroutines to integrate a function between two limits, find the largest and smallest values of a function within an interval, or possibly differentiate a function at a point.

Multiple Entry

Occasionally one wants to write a number of subprograms in which a large amount of the code is the same within the routines. A multiple entry subprogram can be useful in these situations. As an example, suppose we wish to write two functions SUM2 and SUM3 with arguments A, ASIZE, and N. The parameter A is a real one-dimensional array (of size ASIZE), and N is an integer. SUM2 is to compute the sum of the squares of the first N elements of A and SUM3 the sum of the cubes. We could write SUM2 as

```
      REAL FUNCTION SUM2(A,ASIZE,N)
      INTEGER ASIZE,N
      REAL A(ASIZE)
      INTEGER I
      SUM2 = 0.0
      DO 10 I = 1,N
         SUM2 = SUM2 + A(I)**2
10       CONTINUE
      RETURN
      END
```

SUM3 would be similar.

It would be possible to combine the two functions into one multiple entry function in the form

```
      REAL FUNCTION SUM2(A,ASIZE,N)
      INTEGER ASIZE,N
      REAL A(ASIZE)
      INTEGER I,PWR
      PWR = 2
      GO TO 5
      ENTRY SUM3(A,ASIZE,N)
      PWR = 3
    5 SUM2 = 0.0
      DO 10 I = 1.N
         SUM2 = SUM2 + A(I)**PWR
   10    CONTINUE
      RETURN
      END
```

If the using program calls SUM2, the function is entered at the beginning and PWR is set to 2. If SUM3 is called, the function is entered at the ENTRY statement and PWR is set to 3.

If an ENTRY statement is encountered in the normal flow of execution it has no effect. For a multiple entry function one of the entry names must be assigned a value, while with a subroutine none of the entries is assigned a value. The calling program is written exactly the same whether or not multiple entries are used.

Note that the same effect for SUM2 and SUM3 can be obtained (at the expense of an additional function call) by defining SUM2 and SUM3 as

```
      REAL FUNCTION SUM2(A,ASIZE,N)
      INTEGER ASIZE,N
      REAL A(ASIZE)
      SUM2 = SUMN(A,ASIZE,N,2)
      RETURN
      END

      REAL FUNCTION SUM3(A,ASIZE,N)
      INTEGER ASIZE,N
      REAL A(ASIZE)
      SUM3 = SUMN(A,ASIZE,N,3)
      RETURN
      END

      REAL FUNCTION SUMN(A,ASIZE,N,PWR)
      INTEGER ASIZE,N,PWR
      REAL A(ASIZE)
      INTEGER I
      SUM = 0.0
      DO 10 I = 1,N
         SUMN = SUMN + A(I)**PWR
   10    CONTINUE
      RETURN
      END
```

Alternate Returns

In addition to multiple entries, a subroutine can contain multiple (or alternate) returns. Multiple returns can be used with subroutines but not with functions.

To use a subroutine which contains alternate returns, labels of executable statements are passed to the subroutine by a CALL statement of the form

```
CALL S1 (A,B,C,&100,&200)
```

The 100 and 200 are labels of executable statements in the calling program. The subroutine header would be of the form.

```
SUBROUTINE S1 (X,Y,Z,*,*)
```

where the *'s indicate that labels are to be passed. Within the subroutine the statement RETURN would function in the normal way, returning control to the statement following the CALL statement. On the other hand, RETURN 1 and RETURN 2 statements would cause control to transfer to the first or second statement label passed, respectively (in this case 100 or 200).

The multiple return can be used to provide error returns from a subroutine with the normal return indicating successful completion of the subroutine.

A similar action can be performed by using an INTEGER variable, say CODE, with CODE being set to 1 for a normal return and 2 or 3 for an error. The call statement would be replaced with

```
CALL S1(A,B,C,CODE)
GO TO (90,100,200),CODE
```

and within the subroutine the header would be

```
SUBROUTINE S1 (X,Y,Z,CODE)
          .
          .
          .
INTEGER CODE
CODE = 1
```

The normal returns would be unchanged, while RETURN 1 and RETURN 2 would be replaced by

```
CODE = 2
RETURN
```

and

```
CODE = 3
RETURN
```

respectively.

A

ANSWERS TO SELECTED EXERCISES

CHAPTER 1

Section 1.2

1. (a), (b), (e), (f), and (h). legal **(c)** illegal period **(d) and (i)** too many characters **(j)** illegal $

2. (a) integer **(b)** real **(c)** real **(d)** character **(k) and (m)** illegal comma **(l)** character

3. (b) (others are possible)

```
CHARACTER*12 NAME
INTEGER TEST1,TEST2,TEST3
REAL AVERAG
```

Section 1.3

1. (a) possible algorithm:

```
print instructions
loop
   prompt for side
   read SIDE
   if SIDE = 0 then
      exit
   endif
   AREA ← SIDE * SIDE
   print AREA
endloop
stop
```

Section 1.4

5. (a) Might include, for example:
near 0 boundary: 0.1, 0.5
easy to check: 2, 5
more realistic: 3.72, 5.03
bad data: −1, −0.1

7. Between line number 16 and 17 insert lines such as:

```
PRINT *, ' '
PRINT *,'Have a nice day.'
```

CHAPTER 2

Section 2.1

1. (a) 13 **(b)** 1 **(c)** 3.25 **(d)** 2.5 **(e)** 21 **(f)** −2 **(g)** −6 **(h)** 'AB' **(i)** 6 **(j)** 4 **(k)** 6.0 **(l)** 'X4*65 *3'

2. (a) 1.6 **(b)** 5 **(c)** 65 **(d)** 15 **(g)** 16 **(h)** 25.0 **(i)** 8.0

3. (a) `Y = A * X + B` **(b)** `T = 0.5 * A + R` **(c)** `W = (X + Y) / 2.0` **(g)** `W = (X + 3 * Y) /(R + A - 3)` **(i)** `B = P * (1 + R / REAL(K)) ** (K*Y)` **(j)** `X = Y ** (3 + 5 * K)`

4. (lower case b stands for blank space) **(a)** BBB **(b)** BBBbb **(c)** CCC **(d)** BBBBCCC **(e)** BBB**(g)** 'B'//C

5. (b)

```
REAL INCHES,CMS
CMS = 2.54 * INCHES
```

(d)

```
INTEGER YEARS,MONTHS,AGE
AGE = 12 * YEARS + MONTHS
```

(f)

```
INTEGER ATBAT,HITS
REAL BATAVG
BATAVG = REAL(HITS) / REAL(ATBAT)
```

Section 2.2

2. Replace lines 2–5 by a line: CALL INSTR, and place the PRINT statements from lines 2–5 in a subroutine something like this. You could also ask if instructions are wanted.

```
SUBROUTINE INSTR
  (print statements go here)
RETURN
END
```

5. No instructions will be printed. One possible solution is to change the IF condition to convey the concept: If the answer is either 'Y' or 'y' then print the instructions. (See Section 2.5 for details on how to do this.)

Section 2.3

1. (a)

```
if INCOME < 8000 then
    RATE ← .02
else
    RATE ← .045
endif
```

```
REAL INCOME,RATE
IF (INCOME.LT.8000) THEN
   RATE = .02
ELSE
   RATE = .045
ENDIF
```

(c)

```
if INCOME > 15000 then
    CTR ← CTR + 1
    TOTAL ← TOTAL + SALARY
endif
```

```
REAL INCOME,TOTAL
INTEGER CTR
IF (INCOME.GT.15000) THEN
   CTR = CTR + 1
   TOTAL = TOTAL + SALARY
ENDIF
```

(l)

```
if I/J > 4.7 then
    K ← I + J
else
    K ← I - J
endif
```

```
INTEGER I,J,K
IF (REAL(I)/REAL(J).GT.4.7) THEN
   K = I + J
ELSE
   K = I - J
ENDIF
```

2. (a) Boundary 8000.00 (also 0.00 for good data). Test cases: −0.01, 0, .01, 7999.99, 8000.00, 8000.01

7. Possible variable list and algorithm:

	Name	Type	Use	Comment
Input:	BALANC	REAL	Balance	Beginning balance, then running balance
	TYPE	CHARACTER*1	'W' or 'D'	Assumed valid
	AMOUNT	REAL	Amount of transaction	

```
print instructions
prompt for beginning balance
read BALANC
loop
   prompt for type, amount
   read TYPE,AMOUNT
   if TYPE = ' ' then
      exit
   endif
   if TYPE = 'W' then
      BALANC ← BALANC − AMOUNT
   else
      BALANC ← BALANC + AMOUNT
   endif
endloop
print BALANC
stop
```

Some test cases: type = W, D, bad (will treat as D)
resulting balance 0, .01, −.01 (error ignored)

Section 2.4

1. **(a)** `1 + SQRT(X)` **(b)** `SQRT(1 + X)` **(d)** `ABS(3 - 2 * X) + Y` **(h)** `(SQRT(R+S) - 5) / (5 - Y)`
2. **(b)** `ABS(3*K) - 5` **(c)** `ABS(3 * X - 5)` **(d)** `REAL (I+J) / REAL(K)` **(e)** `SQRT (REAL(J))`
3. *Hint:* Convert to cents, then round, then convert back to dollars.
4. **(a)** 1 **(b)** 2 **(d)** 0 **(e)** 5 **(g)** 0.3 **(h)** 1.4
7. **(a)**

```
INTEGER L,K
IF (MOD(L,K).EQ.0) THEN
   M = 1
ELSE
   M = MOD(L,K)
ENDIF
```

(c) *Hint:* $|x-y|$ is the distance between x and y

8. **(a)**

```
      INTEGER STATE,POP
      CHARACTER*15 CAPTAL
      READ(*,1000) STATE,POP,CAPTAL
 1000 FORMAT(I2,2X,I8,2X,A)
```

9. **(a)**

```
      WRITE(*,2000) 'The capital ofstate #',STATE,' is ', CAPTAL
      WRITE(*,3000) 'Its population is ',POP
 2000 FORMAT(' ',A,I2,A,A)
 3000 FORMAT(' ',A,I8)
```

10. **(a)**

```
      REAL AREA
      WRITE(*,1000) 'The area of the triangle is ',AREA
 1000 FORMAT(' ',A,F9.2)
```

11. **(a)**

```
      REAL AREA
      WRITE(*,1000) AREA
 1000 FORMAT(' ','The area of the triangle is ',F9.2)
```

Section 2.5

1. **(a)**
```
CHARACTER*1 STATUS,SEX
STATUS.EQ.'S' .AND. SEX.EQ.'F'
```
(b)
```
CHARACTER*1 STATUS,SEX
STATUS.NE.'S' .OR. SEX.NE.'F'
```
(c)
```
CHARACTER*1 STATUS,SEX
STATUS.NE.'S' .AND. SEX.NE.'F'
```
(i)
```
INTEGER I,J,K
MOD(I,10).EQ.0 .AND. MOD(J,10).EQ.0 .AND. MOD(K,10).EQ.0
```
(o)
```
REAL X,Y
(X.GT.0 .AND. Y.LE.0) .OR. (Y.GT.0 .AND. X.LE.0)
```
(other solutions are equally good)

(q)
```
INTEGER I
REAL X,Y
I.LT.0 .OR. (X.GT.5 .AND. Y.GT.5)
```
(parentheses optional)

2. **(a)** false **(b)** true **(c)** true
3. **(d)** `.NOT. (Y.LT.Z .OR. Y.GE.Z+4.0)` or `Y.GE.Z .AND. Y.LT.Z+4.0`
5. **(b)** algorithm segment:

```
AVERAG ← (TEST1 + TEST2) / 2
case
   1(TEST3 > AVERAG) print 'improving'
   2(TEST3 ≤ AVERAG − 5) print 'declining'
endif
```

(d) algorithm segment:

```
case
   1(TYPE = 'REGULAR')
```

(continued)

```
      if LOWEST ≥ 500 then
         CHARGE ← 0
      else
         CHARGE ← 5
      endif
   2(TYPE = 'SPECIAL')
      CHARGE ← 0.20 * NCHECK
   3(any other)
      CHARGE ← 0
endcase
```

6. (b)

```
INTEGER TEST1,TEST2,TEST3
REAL AVERAG
AVERAG = REAL(TEST1+TEST2)/2.0
IF (TEST3.GT.AVERAG) THEN
   PRINT *,'Improving'
ELSE IF (TEST3.LE.AVERAG-5) THEN
   PRINT *,'Declining'
ENDIF
```

9. (e) Test cases should contain all three types, plus error types (will be treated as VIP by the algorithm). For type 'REGULAR', test the boundary (lowest = 499.99, 500.00, 500.01). For type 'SPECIAL', test the boundary on how many checks there are (0 checks, 1 check, more than 1 check).

Section 2.6

1.

```
REAL FUNCTION SMALLR(X,Y)
REAL X,Y
IF (X.LE.Y) THEN
   SMALLR = X
ELSE
   SMALLR = Y
ENDIF
RETURN
END
```

3.

```
INTEGER FUNCTION SMALLS(I,J,K)
INTEGER I,J,K
SMALLS = I
IF (J.LT.SMALLS) THEN
   SMALLS = J
ENDIF
IF (K.LT.SMALLS) THEN
   SMALLS = K
ENDIF
RETURN
END
```

8. (a)

```
INTEGER FUNCTION LARGEF(I,J)
INTEGER I,J
IF (I.GE.J) THEN
 LARGEF = I
ELSE
   LARGEF = J
ENDIF
RETURN
END
```

(b)

```
INTEGER TRY, LARGEF, M, N
TRY = LARGEF(M,N)
```

10. (b)

```
REAL FUNCTION CHARGE(TYPE,LOWEST, NCHECK)
CHARACTER*7 TYPE
REAL LOWEST
INTEGER NCHECK
IF (TYPE.EQ.'REGULAR') THEN
   IF (LOWEST.GE.500) THEN
      CHARGE = 0
   ELSE
      CHARGE = 5
   ENDIF
ELSE IF (TYPE.EQ.'SPECIAL') THEN
   CHARGE = 0.20 * NCHECK
ELSE
   CHARGE = 0
ENDIF
RETURN
END
```

Unit tests: See answer to Exercise 9(e), Section 2.5.

11. (c) The test cases should include the following types of tests:
Which one is smallest (no ties): I, J, and K.
How many ties? None, two tied (I−J, I−K, or J−K), all three tied.

CHAPTER 3

Section 3.1

1.

```
   INTEGER IDNO,DEPTNO
   REAL RATE,SALES,TOTAL
   CALL INSTR
   TOTAL = 0
10 CONTINUE
      PRINT *,'Enter i.d. (0 to quit), department, rate, sales'
```

(continued)

```
        READ *,IDNO,DEPTNO,RATE, SALES
        IF (IDNO.EQ.0)THEN
           GO TO 500
        ENDIF
        TOTAL = TOTAL + SALES
        GO TO 10
  500 CONTINUE
      WRITE (*,1000) 'Total sales = ',TOTAL
      STOP
 1000 FORMAT(' ',A,F10.2)
      END
```

2. (a) `LARGE ← 0` / `SMALL ← 120` **(f)** `LARGE ← −53001` / `SMALL ← 1701`

3.

```
      CHARACTER*12 NAME
      CHARACTER*1 LETTER
      INTEGER PCTR,FCTR
      CALL INSTR
      PCTR = 0
      FCTR = 0
   10 CONTINUE
         PRINT *,'Enter name (blank to quit), letter grade'
         READ *,NAME,LETTER
         IF (NAME.EQ.' ') THEN
              GO TO 500
         ENDIF
         IF(LETTER.EQ.'F') THEN
            FCTR = FCTR+1
         ELSE
            PCTR = PCTR+1
         ENDIF
         GO TO 10
  500 CONTINUE
      WRITE(*,1000) PCTR,' passed and ',FCTR,' failed'
 1000 FORMAT('1',I5,A,I5,A)
      END
```

4.

```
call INSTR
loop
   prompt
   read NAME,AVE
   if NAME = ' ' then exit endif
   if AVE ≥ 60.0 then
      RESULT ← 'PASS'
   else
      RESULT ← 'FAIL'
   endif
   print NAME,AVE,RESULT
endloop
stop
```

6. (c)

```
call INSTR
OLDEST ← 0
loop
   prompt
   read IDNO,SEX,AGE,KIDS
   if IDNO = 0 then exit endif
   if AGE > OLDEST and KIDS=0 then
      OLDEST ← AGE
      OLDID ← IDNO
   endif
endloop
print OLDID,OLDEST
stop
```

7. (a)

```
call INSTR
prompt
read IDNO,INCOME,YEARS,DEPT
LARGE ← INCOME
LIDNO ←IDNO
loop
   prompt
   read IDNO,INCOME,YEARS,DEPT
   if IDNO=0 then exit endif
   if INCOME > LARGE then
      LARGE ← INCOME
      LIDNO ← IDNO
   endif
endloop
print LIDNO,LARGE
stop
```

Section 3.2

1. (a) −5, −4, −3, −2, −1, 0, 1, 2, 3, on termination is 4
(c) 1, 4, 7, on termination is 10
(d) no passes, on termination is 7
(e) 7, 5, 3, on termination is 1

2. (a)

```
SUM ← 0
loop for I = 1 to 87
   SUM ← SUM + I
endloop
print (or use) SUM
```

(d)
```
SUM ← 0
loop for I = 2 to 400 by 2
   SUM ← SUM + I
endloop
print (or use) SUM
```

3. (b) A possible algorithm is given here:
```
call INSTR
loop
   prompt
   read FIRST,LAST
   if FIRST = LAST = 0 then exit endif
   SUM ← SUMF(FIRST,LAST)
   print SUM
endloop
stop
```

5. (a)
```
      REAL Y,F,X
      INTEGER I,N
      Y = 0
      F = 1
      DO 10 I = 1,N
        Y = Y + F
        F = F*X/REAL(I)
10    CONTINUE
```

8. (b)
```
call HEADER
loop for FEET = 30 to 1 by -1
   INCHES ← FEET * 12
   print INCHES,FEET
endloop
stop
```

9. (a)
```
call INSTR
prompt
read M,N
PAGENO ← 1
loop for I = M to N
   DIVCTR ← NODIV(I)
   if time for new page then      (How can we refine
      call HEADER(PAGENO)          the condition?)
      PAGENO ← PAGENO + 1
   endif
   print I,DIVCTR
endloop
stop
```

15. (c)
```
      SUBROUTINE HEADER(PAGENO)
      INTEGER PAGENO
      WRITE(*,1000) 'ALPHABETICAL LIST OF EMPLOYEES',
     $              'page ',PAGENO
      WRITE(*,1001) '------------ ---- -- ----------',
     $              '----------'
      PRINT *,' '
      PRINT *,' '
      RETURN
1000  FORMAT('1',15X,A,10X,A,I4)
1001  FORMAT(' ',15X,A,10X,A)
      END
```

16. (b)
```
MATCH ← 0
loop for I = 1 to 1000
   NUMBER ← RND(1000)
   if NUMBER = I then
      MATCH ← MATCH + 1
   endif
endloop
print MATCH
stop
```

17. (a) Use RND(2), and treat a 1 as a head; a 2 as a tail.

(c)
```
COUNT ← 0
PREV ← RND(2)
loop for I = 2 to 1000   (Why start at 2?)
   TOSS ← RND(2)
   if TOSS ≠ PREV then
      COUNT ← COUNT + 1
   endif
   PREV ← TOSS
endloop
print COUNT
stop
```

18. (a) Since there are 11 outcomes 5, 6, 7, 8, 9, 10, 11, 12, 13, 14, and 15, we could use RND(11)+4. The +4 changes the values 1 through 11 to the desired values 5 through 15.

19. (b)
```
COUNT ← 0
loop for I = 1 to 15000
   ROLL1 ← RND(6) + RND(6)
   ROLL2 ← RND(6) + RND(6)
   if ROLL1 = ROLL2 then COUNT ← COUNT + 1 endif
endloop
PROB ← COUNT / 15000
print PROB
```

Section 3.3

2. (b)
```
10 CONTINUE
      PRINT *,'Enter 3 numbers'
      READ(*,1000) A,B,C
      Y = A*B*C
      IF(Y.LT.0.0) THEN
           GO TO 20
      ENDIF
      WRITE(*,2000) Y
      GO TO 10
20 CONTINUE
   W = 0
```

3.
```
loop
   read IDNO,NUMDEP,STATUS
   if IDNO=645 then exit endif
endloop
if STATUS='M' then
   ANSWER ← 'YES'
else
   ANSWER ← 'NO'
endif
print ANSWER
stop
```

5. (a)
```
BALANC ← 200.0
CTR ← 0
loop
   BALANC ← (.05*BALANC)+BALANC
   CTR ← CTR+1
   if BALANCE > 600.00 then exit endif
endloop
print CTR,BALANC
stop
```

9. (c)
```
      SUBROUTINE INPUT(N)
      INTEGER N
   10 CONTINUE
         PRINT *, 'Enter an integer from 3 to 10000'
         READ *, N
         IF (N.GT.2 .AND. N.LE.10000) THEN
            GO TO 100
         ENDIF
         PRINT *,'Invalid data, try again - ',N
         GO TO 10
  100 CONTINUE
      RETURN
      END
```

11. (a) 8 **(d)** infinite loop

13. *Hint.* See the key for exercise 17(c) in section 3.2.

15. (a)
```
      INTEGER FUNCTION RNDCTR(N,TOTAL)
      INTEGER N,TOTAL
      RNDCTR = 0
      SUM = 0
   10 CONTINUE
         IF (SUM.GT.TOTAL) THEN
            GO TO 500
         ENDIF
         SUM = SUM + RND(N)
         RNDCTR = RNDCTR + 1
         GO TO 10
  500 CONTINUE
      RETURN
      END
```

19.
```
      INTEGER FUNCTION GCD(M,N)
      INTEGER M,N,TRY
      IF (M.LE.N) THEN
         TRY = M
      ELSE
         TRY = N
      ENDIF
   10 CONTINUE
         IF (MOD(M,TRY).EQ.0 .AND. MOD(N,TRY).EQ.0) THEN
            GO TO 500
         ENDIF
         TRY = TRY - 1
         GO TO 10
  500 CONTINUE
      GCD = TRY
      RETURN
      END
```

22. (a) Assuming that each group is not empty, we can have a test plan which includes tests such as these:

- only 1 person in first group
- only 1 person in second group
- largest in first group is:
  - first in group
  - last in group
  - in middle of group
- IQ in second group is:
  - equal to largest in first
  - 1 less than largest in first
  - 1 more than largest in first

how many in second group are higher:
none
all
some, but not all

(We could also deal with the situation where the second group is empty, so we might test that situation. Dealing with the first group being empty is a little more subtle.)

CHAPTER 4

Section 4.1

1. legal
2. legal
3. illegal—parameters are integer in calling program; real in subprogram
4. legal
5. illegal—function is declared integer in calling program; real in function itself

Section 4.2

3.
```
SUBROUTINE VOLSUR(RADIUS,VOLUME,SURFAC)
REAL RADIUS,VOLUME,SURFAC
VOLUME = 4.0/3.0 * 3.14 * RADIUS ** 3
SURFAC = 4.0 * 3.14 * RADIUS ** 2
RETURN
END
```

6.
```
REAL FUNCTION TAXF(INCOME,NDEP)
REAL INCOME
INTEGER NDEP
REAL TAXINC
TAXINC = INCOME - 500 * NDEP
TAXINC = TAXINC - 0.1 * INCOME
IF (TAXINC .LT. 0) THEN
   TAXF = 0
ELSE IF (TAXINC .LE. 10000) THEN
   TAXF = 0.02 * TAXINC
ELSE
   TAXF = 200 + 0.025 * (TAXINC - 10000)
ENDIF
RETURN
END
```

9.
```
REAL FUNCTION RANGEF(NO1,NO2,NO3)
REAL NO1,NO2,NO3
REAL LARGE,SMALL
CALL MAXMIN(NO1,NO2,NO3,LARGE,SMALL)
RANGEF = LARGE - SMALL
RETURN
END
```

11. *Hint:* Integer division by a power of 10 "strips off" the right hand digits. For example, 29867÷100 is 298. Then the MOD function can be used to "capture" the right hand digit. For example, MOD(298,10) is 8.

17. *Hint:* The key to this problem is recognizing that the main program should supply parameters to the two functions, which will calculate the tuition and room and board. A step such as

```
TOTAL ← TUITF(???) + ROOMBD(???,???)
```

can be used, provided we supply the proper parameters. For the TUITF function, we need the main program's variable for the number of hours (NHOURS). Similar reasoning applies for the ROOMBD parameters.

20. *Note:* For test plans, we cannot hope to be completely exhaustive. Given below are some important tests.

(c) We need to exercise the boundaries on the taxable income (0 and 10000). It would be desirable to do so with different values for the number of dependents. Here are some tests:

income	# deps.	resulting taxable income
0	0	0
11111.00	0	9999.90
11112.00	0	10000.80
12222.00	2	9999.80
12223.00	2	10000.70

(d) Boundary on the comparison of first number to second:
first = second
first one less than second
first one greater than second

(e) Combinations on which is largest, which is smallest:
first, second first, third
second, first second, third
third, first third, second
All the same value (range is 0)
Two the same value, the other less:
first, second first third second, third
Two the same value, the other more:
first, second first, third second, third

21. (a)
```
      SUBROUTINE READID(IDNO)
      INTEGER IDNO
   10 CONTINUE
         PRINT *, 'Enter ID number (0 to stop)'
         READ *, IDNO
```

(continued)

```
      IF (IDNO .EQ. 0 .OR.
   $      (IDNO .GE. 10000 .AND. IDNO .LE. 99999)) THEN
         GO TO 100
      ENDIF
      PRINT *, 'Valid ID number must be from 10000 to 99999'
      PRINT *, 'Please reenter'
      GO TO 10
  100 CONTINUE
      RETURN
      END
```

Section 4.3

1. **(a)** .TRUE. **(b)** .TRUE. **(c)** .TRUE. **(d)** .FALSE. **(e)** .FALSE.

3. **(a)**

```
LOGICAL FUNCTION NOTEQ(L1,L2)
LOGICAL L1, L2
NOTEQ = (L1.OR.L2) .AND. .NOT.(L1.AND.L2)
RETURN
END
```

(b) We may use the function of part (a), as in

```
  EQUAL = .NOT. NOTEG(L1,L2)
```

(c) The first is

```
    NOTEG(L1,L2) .OR. EQUAL(L3,L4)
```

4. **(a)**

```
LOGICAL FUNCTION PASSF(T1,T2,T3,T4)
INTEGER T1,T2,T3,T4
PASSF = REAL(T1+T2+T3+T4)/4.0 .GE. 60
RETURN
END
```

Note: The assignment statement may be replaced with the following:

```
IF (REAL(T1+T2+T3+T4)/4.0 .GE. 60) THEN
   PASSF = .TRUE.
ELSE
   PASSF = .FALSE.
ENDIF
```

7. **(b)**

```
      INTEGER A,B
      CHARACTER*3 ANSWER
      LOGICAL RELPR
   10 CONTINUE
         CALL INPUT(A,B)
         IF (A .EQ. 0) THEN
            GO TO 100
         ENDIF
         IF (RELPR(A,B))THEN
            ANSWER = 'YES'
         ELSE
            ANSWER = 'NO'
         ENDIF
         PRINT *, ANSWER
         GO TO 10
  100 CONTINUE
      STOP
      END
```

(d) The test plan should include some cases where the numbers are prime and some cases where they are not prime, but do not have any factors in common (for example, 8 and 75). It should also include some which are equal, and some which have many factors in common (for example, 210 and 525).

9. **(a)**

```
LOGICAL FUNCTION BETWEN(VALUE,LOW,HIGH)
INTEGER VALUE,LOW,HIGH
IF (LOW .LE. VALUE .AND. VALUE .LE. HIGH) THEN
   BETWEN = .TRUE.
ELSE
   BETWEN = .FALSE.
ENDIF
RETURN
END
```

(b) *Hint:* the crucial steps might look something like this.

```
ONEOK = BETWEN(SCORE1,0,100)
TWOOK = BETWEN(SCORE2,0,100)
THROK = BETWEN(SCORE3,0,100)
IF (ONEOK .AND. TWOOK .AND. THROK) THEN
   GO TO 100
ENDIF
```

where going to the label 100 represents exiting the loop.

15. The algorithm might be the following:

```
read N
if N >= 2 then print 2 endif
loop for I = 3 to N by 2
   if PRIME(I) then print I endif
endloop
stop
```

20. **(a)**

```
SUBROUTINE ADD(DOL1,CENT1,DOL2,CENT2,DOLANS,CNTANS)
INTEGER DOL1,CENT1,DOL2,CENT2,DOLANS,CNTANS
DOLANS = DOL1 + DOL2
CNTANS = CNT1 + CNT2
IF (CNTANS .GE. 100) THEN
   DOLANS = DOLANS + 1
   CNTANS = CNTANS - 100
ENDIF
```

(continued)

```
      RETURN
      END
```

(f)
```
      LOGICAL FUNCTION LARGER(DOL1,CENT1,DOL2,CENT2)
      INTEGER DOL1,CENT1,DOL2,CENT2
      IF (DOL1 .GT. DOL2) THEN
         LARGER = .TRUE.
      ELSE IF (DOL1 .LT. DOL2) THEN
         LARGER = .FALSE.
      ELSE
         IF (CENT1 .GT. CENT2) THEN
            LARGER = .TRUE.
         ELSE
            LARGER = .FALSE.
         ENDIF
      ENDIF
      RETURN
      END
```

CHAPTER 5

Section 5.1

1. (a)
```
TOTAL ← 0
CTR ← 0
loop
   read NAME, SEX, WAGE; if eof then exit endif
   TOTAL ← TOTAL + WAGE
   CTR ← CTR + 1
endloop
AVERAG ← TOTAL / CTR
print AVERAG
stop
```

3. (b)
```
LARGE ← 0
loop
   read ID, INCOME, YEARS, DEPT; if eof then exit endif
   if INCOME > LARGE then
      LARGE ← INCOME
      LID ← ID
      LYEARS ← YEARS
      LDEPT ← DEPT
   endif
endloop
print LARGE,LID,LYEARS,LDEPT
stop
```

5. (a)
```
      INTEGER CTR
      REAL TOTAL,WAGE,AVERAG
      CHARACTER*1 SEX
      TOTAL = 0
      CTR = 0
   10 CONTINUE
         READ (*,*,END=500) NAME,SEX,WAGE
         TOTAL = TOTAL + WAGE
         CTR = CTR + 1
         GO TO 10
  500 CONTINUE
      AVERAG = TOTAL / REAL(CTR)
      PRINT *, 'Average wage is ', AVERAG
      STOP
      END
```

6. (c)
```
      INTEGER ID,YEARS,LID,LYEARS,STATUS
      REAL INCOME,LARGE
      CHARACTER*4 DEPT,LDEPT
      OPEN (10,FILE='PAYROLL.FILE')
      REWIND (10)
      LARGE = 0
   10 CONTINUE
         READ (10,*,IOSTAT=STATUS) ID,INCOME,YEARS,DEPT
         IF (STATUS .LT. 0) THEN
            GO TO 500
         ENDIF
         IF (INCOME .GT. LARGE) THEN
            LARGE = INCOME
            LID = ID
            LYEARS = YEARS
            LDEPT = DEPT
         ENDIF
         GO TO 10
  500 CONTINUE
      PRINT *, LARGE, LID, LYEARS, LDEPT
      STOP
      END
```

Section 5.2

3. (a)
```
      INTEGER I,J,K,C
      READ *,I,J,K
      PRINT *,I,J,K
      C = 0
   10 CONTINUE
```

(continued)

```
20     CONTINUE
          IF (I.GT.J) THEN
             GO TO 100
          ENDIF
          I = 2 * I
          C = C + 1
          GO TO 20
100    CONTINUE
       IF (I.GT.K) THEN
          GO TO 200
       ENDIF
       PRINT *,I,J,K
       J = J + 1000
       GO TO 10
200 CONTINUE
    PRINT *,C
    STOP
    END
```

4. (a) First version:

```
loop
   read BEGBAL, RATE; if eof then exit endif
   BALANC ← BEGBAL
   find how many years for BALANC tc exceed 2 * BEGBAL
   print input and answer
endloop
```

Second version obtained by refining the step "find how many years for BALANC to exceed 2* BEGBAL":

```
loop
   read BEGBAL, RATE; if eof then exit endif
   BALANC ← BEGBAL
   YEARS ← 0
   loop
      YEARS ← YEARS + 1
      BALANCE ← BALANC + RATE * BALANC
      if BALANC > 2 * BEGBAL then exit endif
   endloop
   print BEGBAL, RATE, YEARS
endloop
```

8. Non-refined version:

```
loop for I = 3 to 201 by 2
   find smallest divisor of I
   print I, answer
endloop
```

Refinement #1 using a function (algorithm for function given also):

```
loop for I = 3 to 201 by 2
   SMDIV ← SMDIVF(I)
   print I, SMDIV
endloop
```

for function: parameter is N, a number

```
DIVISR ← 3
loop
  if MOD(N,DIVISR) = 0 then exit endif
  DIVISR ← DIVISR + 2
endloop
SMDIVF ← DIVISR
```

Refinement #2 placing the code in line as a nested loop:

```
loop for I = 3 to 201 by 2
   DIVISR ← 3
   loop
     if MOD(I,DIVISR) = 0 then exit endif
     DIVISR ← DIVISR + 2
   endloop
   print I, DIVISR
endloop
```

13.

```
read NDEPT
loop for I = 1 to NDEPT
   read DEPT,NPROF
   loop for J = 1 to NPROF
      read ID, SALARY
      call DETAIL(DEPT,ID,SALARY,??)
   endloop
endloop
stop
```

Question: what other parameter could be passed to allow the DETAIL routine to know when to print the DEPT?

14.

```
loop for ROW = 1 to 6
   print ROW, 1
   loop for SEAT = 2 to 16
      print SEAT
   endloop
endloop
stop
```

16.

```
loop for N = 1 to 75
   SUM ← 0
   loop for I = 1 to N
      SUM ← SUM + I
   endloop
   print SUM, N*(N+1)/2
```

(continued)

```
      if SUM = N*(N+1)/2 then
         print 'formula works'
      else
         print 'formula is incorrect'
      endif
   endloop
```

18.
```
MONEY ← 0
loop for I = 1 to 1000
   loop
      DICE ← RND(6) + RND(6)
      if DICE = 2 or DICE = 7 or DICE = 11 then exit endif
   endloop
   if DICE = 2 or DICE = 11 then
      MONEY ← MONEY + 5
   else
      MONEY ← MONEY - 2
   endif
endloop
if MONEY > 0 then
   print MONEY 'was won in 1000 games'
else
   print MONEY 'was lost in 1000 games'
endif
```

Section 5.3

1. (a) The two conditions for exit are: TRY divides N evenly, and TRY is equal to N. If we ask whether TRY divides N evenly, this will always be true. (If TRY is equal to N, then the quotient is 1 with a remainder of 0.) Thus, we must distinguish between the exits by asking whether TRY is equal to N.

(b) This is subtle! In FORTRAN it is technically illegal to examine the variables that caused an end of file condition in the READ statement. Thus, if we reach end of file without finding IDNO 11457, the condition IDNO.EQ.11457 is illegal. (However, many FORTRAN compilers relax this restriction.) The recommended alternative is to use IOSTAT, and examine the status variable to see if end of file occurred.

2. (a)
```
loop
   read IDNO, NAME, ..., NCHILD, ...; if eof then exit endif
   if NAME = 'JOE JONES' then exit endif
endloop
if end of file occurred (use IOSTAT) then
   print 'Joe Jones is not in file'
else
   print NCHILD
endif
```

3. (a)
```
      INTEGER IDNO,AGE,YRMARR,NCHILD,STATUS
      REAL SALARY
      CHARACTER*20 NAME
      CHARACTER*5 ZIPCOD
      CHARACTER*1 BLOOD
      OPEN (10,FILE='EMPLOYEE.FILE')
      REWIND (10)
   10 CONTINUE
         READ(10,*,IOSTAT=STATUS) IDNO,NAME,AGE,ZIPCOD,YRMARR,
     $                  NCHILD,SALARY,BLOOD
         IF (STATUS .LT. 0) THEN
            GO TO 500
         ENDIF
         IF (NAME .EQ. 'JOE JONES') THEN
            GO TO 500
         ENDIF
         GO TO 10
  500 CONTINUE
      IF (STATUS .LT. 0) THEN
         PRINT *, 'Joe Jones is not in file'
      ELSE
         PRINT *, 'Joe Jones has ',NCHILD,' children'
      ENDIF
      STOP
      END
```

4. (a) There are tests having to do with where in the file JOE JONES is located:
first record
last record
in middle somewhere
not there

There are also tests related to "almost match" records, such as:
JOE JOHNSON
MOE JONES

7. (b)
```
POINT ← RND(6) + RND(6)
loop for I = 1 to 5
   ROLL ← RND(6) + RND(6)
   if ROLL = POINT then exit endif
endloop
if I > 5 then
   print 'no match'
else
   print 'there was a match in ', I, ' rolls'
endif
stop
```

8.
```
COUNT ← 0
loop for I = 1 to 1000
   loop for I = 1 to 5
      ROLL ← RND(6) + RND(6)
      if ROLL = 7 then exit endif
   endloop
   if I ≤ 5 then
      COUNT ← COUNT + 1
   endif
endloop
PCT ← COUNT / 1000
print PCT
```

CHAPTER 6

Section 6.1

2. (a)
```
COUNT ← 0
loop for I = 1 to 100
   if SALARY(I) > 15000 then
      COUNT ← COUNT + 1
   endif
endloop
print COUNT
```
(b)
```
loop for J = 1 to 1400
   if G(J) > 0 then
      print G(J)
   endif
endloop
```
(c)
```
SUM ← 0
loop for I = 1 to 750
   SUM  ← SUM + LO(I)
endloop
print SUM
```
(d)
```
LARGE ← GRADES(1)      (note: subscript is 1, not I!)
loop for I = 1 to 50
   if GRADES(I) > LARGE then
      LARGE ← GRADES(I)
   endif
endloop
print LARGE
```
3.
```
SUM ← 0
loop for I = 1 to 30
   read ID(I), AGE(I)
   SUM ← SUM + AGE(I)
endloop
AVERAG ← SUM / 30
loop for I = 1 to 30
   if AGE(I) > AVERAGE then
      print ID(I)
   endif
endloop
```

Section 6.2

1. (a)
```
SMALL ← A(1)
loop for I = 1 to N
   if A(I) < SMALL then
      SMALL ← A(I)
   endif
endloop
print SMALL
```
(b) One solution is just to add an extra variable to part (a) to keep track of where the SMALL variable gets its value.
```
SMALL ← A(1)
SMSUB ← 1
loop for I = 1 to N
   if A(I) < SMALL then
      SMALL ← A(I)
      SMSUB ← I
   endif
endloop
print SMSUB
```
Another solution is to observe that we can do without SMALL in this algorithm by observing the A(SMSUB) is the same as SMALL:
```
SMSUB ← 1
loop for I = 1 to N
   if A(I) < A(SMSUB) then
      SMSUB ← I
   endif
endloop
print SMSUB
```
2. (c) Here are two solutions. The second assumes that what we are looking for will not be found, then changes the answer if it is found.
```
loop for I = 1 to N
   if ARR(I) < 0 then
      exit
   endif
endloop
```
```
LOCAT ← 0
loop for I = 1 to N
   if ARR(I) < 0 then
      LOCAT ← I
      exit
```
(continued)

```
endloop
```

```
if I > N then
   LOCAT ← 0
else
   LOCAT ← I
endif
```

(d) *Hint.* See exercise 2(c). This time you are looking for a 0 rather than a negative number.

(e)
```
if N = 50 then
   print 'the array is already full'
else
   N ← N + 1
   ARR(N) ← NEWVAL
endif
```

4. (a)
```
loop for I = 1 to N
   AVE(I) ← (G1(I) + G2(I) + G3(I) + G4(I)) / 4
endloop
```

5. (a)
```
loop for I = 1 to N
   if ID(I) ≥ 0 then
      AVE(I) ← (G1(I) + G2(I) + G3(I) + G4(I)) / 4
   endif
endloop
```

6. (c) To find the total sales for each group, using an array TOTSAL of size 10:
```
loop for I = 1 to 10
   TOTSAL(I) ← 0
endloop
loop for I = 1 to NEMPL
   EMPGRP ← GROUP(I)
   TOTSAL(EMPGRP) ← TOTSAL(EMGGRP) + SALES(I)
endloop
```

7. (b) Here are two solutions:
```
loop for I = 1 to 50
   A(I + 50) ← B(I)
endloop
```

```
ASUB ← 51
loop for I = 1 to 50
   A(ASUB) ← B(I)
   ASUB ← ASUB + 1
endloop
```

8. (b)
```
loop for I = 200 to 800
   COUNT(I) ← 0
endloop
LARGE ← 0
loop
   read SCORE; if eof then exit endif
   COUNT(SCORE) ← COUNT(SCORE) + 1
   if COUNT(SCORE) > LARGE then
      LARGE ← COUNT(SCORE)
      FREQSC ← SCORE
   endif
endloop
```

9.
```
TEMP ← A(I)
A(I) ← A(J)
A(J) ← TEMP
```

10.
```
loop for I = 1 to 2
   swap A(I) with A(6-I)
endloop
```
(Use the technique in problem 9, either in-line or as a subroutine.)

13.
```
loop for I = 1 to N
   if A(I) is not equal to B(I) then exit endif
endloop
if I > N then
   print 'yes'
else
   print 'no'
endif
```

17.
```
P ← 0
loop for I = 1 to N
   P ← P + A(I) * B(I)
endloop
```

18.
```
LARGE ← A(7)
LGSUB ← 7
loop for I = 7 to N
   if A(I) > LARGE then
      LARGE ← A(I)
      LGSUB ← I
   endif
endloop
TEMP ← A(7)
A(7) ← A(LGSUB)
A(LGSUB) ← TEMP
```

20. (a)
```
loop
   call INPUT(ID,PAY,EOF)
   if EOF then exit endif
   TOTAL ← 0
   loop for I = 1 to 12
      TOTAL ← TOTAL + PAY(I)
   endloop
   call DETAIL(ID,PAY,TOTAL)
endloop
```

21. (a) In finding the smallest, we should test the cases where the smallest is the first, the last, and one of the middle elements of the array. Also, we should test where the smallest value is negative and where it is positive.

(d) Some questions leading to borderline tests:

How many are negative? none, exactly one, all, some but not all

Where is the first negative value of several that are in the array? In first position, in last position, in between.

Where is the only negative value in the array? In first position, in last position, in between.

(i) Borderlines on START and END: START = 1, START = 100, END = 1, END = 100, START = END, START 1 less than END.

For added thoroughness, we might try several instances of each of these general tests, as shown in this table:

START	END
1	10
1	1
1	2
1	100
25	100
99	100
100	100
24	24
93	94
68	68

(m) *Hint:* Exercise 13 is similar to exercise 2(c). Both involve searching for some condition. Thus, refer to the test plan for exercise 2(c) given above in the answer for exercise 21(d).

Section 6.3

1. (a) Parameters: *A*, an array of size 100; *N*, the portion in use. Notice that rather than printing the answer, we assign it to the function name.

```
      INTEGER FUNCTION SMALLF(A,N)
      INTEGER A(1:100),N
      INTEGER I,SMALL
      SMALL = A(1)
      DO 10 I = 1, N
         IF (A(I) .LT. SMALL) THEN
            SMALL = A(I)
         ENDIF
   10 CONTINUE
      SMALLF = SMALL
      RETURN
      END
```

(b)

```
      INTEGER FUNCTION SMSUBF(A,N)
      INTEGER A(1:100),N
      INTEGER I, SMALL,SMSUB
      SMALL = A(1)
      SMSUB = 1
      DO 10 I = 1, N
         IF (A(I) .LT. SMALL) THEN
            SMALL = A(I)
            SMSUB = I
         ENDIF
   10    CONTINUE
      SMSUBF = SMSUB
      RETURN
      END
```

or

(b)

```
      INTEGER FUNCTION SMSUBF(A,N)
      INTEGER A(1:100),N
      INTEGER I,SMALL,SMSUB
      SMSUB = 1
      DO 10 I = 1, N
         IF (A(I) .LT. A(SMSUB)) THEN
            SMSUB = I
         ENDIF
   10    CONTINUE
      SMSUBF = SMSUB
      RETURN
      END
```

2. (c)

```
      INTEGER FUNCTION LOCATF(ARR,N)
      INTEGER ARR(1:100),N
      INTEGER I
      DO 10 I = 1, N
         IF (ARR(I) .LT. 0) THEN
            GO TO 20
         ENDIF
   10    CONTINUE
   20 CONTINUE
      IF (I .GT. N) THEN
         LOCATF = 0
      ELSE
         LOCATF = I
      ENDIF
      RETURN
      END
```

or

```
      INTEGER FUNCTION LOCATF(ARR,N)
      INTEGER ARR(1:100),N
      INTEGER I
      LOCATF = 0
      DO 10 I = 1, N
         IF (ARR(I) .LT. 0) THEN
            LOCATF = I
            GO TO 20
         ENDIF
10       CONTINUE
20    CONTINUE
      RETURN
      END
```

4. (a) Parameters are the four grade arrays (input), the number of students (input), and the average array (output). Since there is a whole array of answers, we need a subroutine.

```
      SUBROUTINE GETAVE(G1,G2,G3,G4,N,AVE)
      INTEGER G1(1:100),G2(1:100),G3(1:100),G4(1:100),N
      REAL AVE(1:100)
      INTEGER I
      DO 10 I = 1,N
         AVE(I) = REAL(G1(I) + G2(I) + G3(I) + G4(I)) / 4.0
10       CONTINUE
      RETURN
      END
```

6. (c)

```
      SUBROUTINE FNDTOT(SALES,GROUP,NEMPL,TOTSAL)
      REAL SALES(1:100), TOTSAL(1:10)
      INTEGER GROUP(1:100), NEMPL
      INTEGER I, EMPGRP
      DO 10 I = 1, 10
         TOTSAL(I) = 0
10       CONTINUE
      DO 20 I = 1, NEMPL
         EMPGRP = GROUP(I)
         TOTSAL(EMPGRP) = TOTSAL(EMGGRP) + SALES(I)
20       CONTINUE
      RETURN
      END
```

7. (b)

```
      SUBROUTINE COPY(A,B)
      INTEGER A(1:100),B(1:100)
      INTEGER I
      DO 70 I = 1, 50
         A(I+50) = B(I)
70       CONTINUE
      RETURN
      END
```

13. Rather than printing the answer, we write a logical function whose value is true if the arrays are equal, false if not.

```
      LOGICAL FUNCTION EQUALF(A,B,N)
      INTEGER A(1:100),B(1:100),N
      INTEGER I
      DO 100 I = 1,N
         IF (A(I) .NE. B(I)) THEN
            GO TO 200
         ENDIF
100      CONTINUE
200   CONTINUE
      IF (I .GT. N) THEN
         EQUALF = .TRUE.
      ELSE
         EQUALF = .FALSE.
      ENDIF
      RETURN
      END
```

20. (a)

```
      INTEGER ID,I
      REAL PAY(1:12),TOTAL
      LOGICAL EOF
   10 CONTINUE
         CALL INPUT(ID,PAY,EOF)
         IF (EOF) THEN
            GO TO 100
         ENDIF
         TOTAL = 0
         DO 20 I = 1, 12
            TOTAL = TOTAL + PAY(I)
20          CONTINUE
         CALL DETAIL(ID,PAY,TOTAL)
         GO TO 10
100   CONTINUE
      STOP
      END
```

21. First way:

```
CHARACTER*1 BLANKS(1:50)
DATA BLANKS /50*' '/
```

Second way:

```
   CHARACTER*1 BLANKS(1:50)
   INTEGER I
```

(continued)

```
        DO 10 I = 1, 50
           BLANKS(I) = ' '
     10    CONTINUE
```

The first approach happens at compile time, prior to the program starting to run. The second happens at run time. If the value must be set *back* to blanks, we must use the second approach.

22. (c)
```
REAL X(1:100)
DATA X /25*1.0,59*6.5,16*17.2/
```

23. (c)
```
loop for I = 1 to 250 by 2
   A(I) ← 0
   A(I+1) ← 1
endloop
```
CAUTION: What would happen if the array were size 249 and we used this algori-thm? Can you think of a solution for odd-sized arrays?

(f) The idea of the algorithm is to use a count-controlled loop to move through the array, moving non-zeros to the front. We need a variable to count the number of non-zeros encountered. At the end, we fill the rest of the array with zeros.
```
NONZER ← 0
loop for I = 1 to 150
   if A(I) is not 0 then
      NONZER ← NONZER + 1
      A(NONZER) ← A(I)
   endif
endloop
loop for I = NONZER + 1 to 150
   A(I) ← 0
endloop
```

(h) *Hint:* Consider the problem of interchanging two values, where we used a temporary variable. You should be able to solve this with three temporary variables, working from right to left. Move $A(1)$, $A(2)$, and $A(3)$ to the temporaries. Then move $A(100)$ to $A(3)$, $A(99)$ to $A(2)$, $A(98)$ to $A(1)$, $A(97)$ to $A(100)$, $A(96)$ to $A(99)$, etc.

24. (a)
```
loop for N = 1 to 15
   FACT ← 1
   loop for I = 1 to N
      FACT ← FACT * I
   endloop
   print FACT
endloop
```

(b)
```
loop for N = 1 to 15
   FACT(N) ← 1
   loop for I = 1 to N
      FACT(N) ← FACT(N) * I
   endloop
endloop
```

(c)
```
FACT(1) ← 1
loop for N = 2 to 15
   FACT(N) ← N * FACT(N-1)
endloop
```

Section 6.4

3.
```
loop for I = 1 to NCUST
   if CUSTNO = CUSTID(I) then exit endif
endloop
if I > N then
   DISCNT ← 0
else
   PCT ← CUSPCT(I)
   case
      1(100<QUANT≤500) PCT ← PCT + .01
      2(QUANT>500) PCT ← 2.0 * (PCT + .01)
   endcase
   DISCNT ← PCT * GROSS
endif
```
In main program—no more "next iteration" for bad customer #.

4. UPDATE routine now has LOCAT, the subscript of the item, as an output parameter.
```
loop for I = 1 to NITEMS
   if ITEMNO = ITEMS(I) then exit endif
endloop
case
   1(I>NITEMS)
      error message (not found)
      BAD ← .TRUE.
   2(QUANT>INVENT(I))
      error message (insufficient inventory)
      BAD ← .TRUE.
   3(any other)
      LOCAT ← I
      INVENT(I) ← INVENT(I) - QUANT
      BAD ← .FALSE.
endcase
return
```
Main program changes:
add a variable LOCAT
```
call UPDATE(CUSTNO,ITEMNO,QUANT,BAD,NITEMS,ITEMS,INVENT,LOCAT)
if BAD then
   next iteration
endif
UNITPR ← PRICES(LOCAT)
```
(continued)

remove the UNITPR function from the program

9. For POLMLC, which multiplies a polynomial by a constant: input parameters are P, a polynomial, and C, a constant; output parameter is R, the resulting polynomial. The algorithm:

```
loop for I = 0 to N
   R(I) ← P(I) * C
endloop
return
```

For POLMLX, which multiplies a polynomial by X: input parameter is P, a polynomial; output parameter is R, the resulting polynomial. The algorithm:

```
DEGP ← POLDEG(P)
if DEGP = 50 then
   print 'result too large in POLMLX'
   stop
endif
loop for I = 1 to 50
   R(I) ← P(I-1)
endloop
R(0) ← 0
return
```

11. For POLEQU, which sees if two polynomials are equal: we will write a logical function with input parameters P and Q, two polynomials.

```
POLEQU ← .TRUE.
loop for I = 0 to 50
   if P(I) is not equal to Q(I) then
      POLEQU ← .FALSE.
      exit
   endif
endloop
return
```

14. (a)

```
loop for I = 1 to N-1
   LSUB ← I
   loop for J = I to N
      if ID(J) > ID(LSUB) then
         LSUB ← J
      endif
   endloop
   TEMP ← ID(I)
   ID(I) ← ID(LSUB)
   ID(LSUB) ← TEMP
   TEMP ← AGE(I)
   AGE(I) ← AGE(LSUB)
   AGE(LSUB) ← TEMP
endloop
```


CHAPTER 7

Section 7.1

1. (a) −5,−4,−3,−2,−1,0,1,2,3 final value is 4, IC is 9
   (c) 1,4,7 final value is 10, IC is 3
   (e) 7,5,3 final value is 1, IC is 3
   (g) 17.25,17.75,18.25,18.75,19.25 final value is 19.75, IC is 5

2. (a)

```
DO 10 I=1725,1950,50
      X=REAL(I)/100.0
```

   (c)

```
DO 10 I=3619,7234
   X=REAL(I)/1000.0
```

   (e)

```
DO 10, I=1900,100,-25
   X=REAL(100 I)/
```

3. (a)

```
SUM ← 0
loop for I = 1 to 87
   SUM ← SUM + I
endloop
```

   or

```
SUM ← (87*(87+1))/2
```

   (c)

```
SUM ← 0
loop for I = 1 to 200
   SUM ← SUM + 2*I
endloop
```

   or

```
SUM ← 0
loop for I = 2 to 400 by 2
   SUM ←SUM + I
endloop
```

   or

```
SUM ← 2*200(200+1)/2
```

   (e)

```
SUM ← 0
loop for I = 900 to 1 by -1
   SUM ← SUM + A(I)
endloop
```

4. (a)

```
print table headings
loop for F = 1 to 30
   IN ← 12 * F
   print F, IN
endloop
```

   (c)

```
read N
print table headings
loop for F = 1 to N
   IN ← 12 * F
   print F, IN
endloop
```

(e)
```
print table headings
loop for F = 1 to 20 by .5
   IN ← 12 * F
   print F, IN
endloop
```

6. (a)
```
SIGN = -1
SUM ← 0
loop for I = 1 to 401 by 2
   SIGN = -1 * SIGN
   SUM ← SUM + REAL(SIGN)/I
endloop
```

7. (b)
```
T ← X
X2 ← X * X
SINX ← T
loop for I = 3 to N by 2
   T ← (-1.0)*T*X2/(I*(I-1))
   SINX ← SINX + T
endloop
```

8. (a)
```
print headings
loop for N = 1 to 15
   FAC ← 1
   loop for I = 1 to n
      FAC ← FAC * I
   endloop
   print N, FAC
endloop
```

(c)
```
print headings
FAC ← 1
loop for N = 1 to 15
   FAC ← FAC * N
   FACT (N) ← FAC
endloop
```

11.
```
assume A,B,N defined
H ← (B-A)/N
AREA ← H/3 * (F(A) + F(B))
S ← 0.0
loop for I = 1 to N-1 by 2
   S ← S + F(A+I*H)
endloop
AREA ← AREA + 4*S
S ← 0.0
loop for I=2 to N-2 by 2
   S ← S + F(A+I*H)
endloop
AREA ← AREA + 2*S
```

CHAPTER 8

Section 8.1

1.
```
      INTEGER GR(10),I
      REAL AVG,SUM
       .
       .
      READ(*,100)GR
  100 FORMAT(10I4)
      SUM=0
      DO 10 I=1,10
         SUM = SUM + GR(I)
   10    CONTINUE
      AVG = SUM/10
      WRITE(*,110)AVG
  110 FORMAT(' ',F6.1)
       .
       .
```

2. (a)
```
      INTEGER DATA(500)
       .
       .
      READ(*,100)DATA
  100 FORMAT(7I5)
       .
       .
```

3. (a)
```
      REAL A(800)
      WRITE(*,100)A
  100 FORMAT(' ',F10.3)
```

(c)
```
      same as part (a) except
  100 FORMAT(' ',13F10.3)
```

5.
```
      INTEGER EMPNO(100),I,N
      REAL SALARY(100)
       .
       .
      DO 10 I=1,N
        WRITE(*,100)EMPNO(I),SALARY(I)
   10   CONTINUE
  100 FORMAT(' ',I10,2X,F12.2)
      or same declarations and format with
      WRITE(*,100)(EMPNO(I),SALARY(I),I=1,N)
```

6. (d)
```
      INTEGER ID(100),AGE(100),NOEMP,I
      CHARACTER*1 SEX(100)
      REAL SALARY(100)
       .
       .
```

(continued)

```
      READ(*,*)NOEMP
      IF (NOEMP.GT.100) THEN
         WRITE(*,*) 'NOEMP TOO LARGE'
         STOP
      ELSE
         READ(*,100)(ID(I),AGE(I),SEX(I),SALARY(I),I=1, NOEMP)
100      FORMAT(3(I10,I5,1X,A1,1X,F10.0))
      ENDIF
         .
         .
```

Section 8.2

1. (a)
```
loop for I=1 to 30
   loop for J=1 to 47
      A(I,J) ← 0
   endloop
endloop
```
(c)
```
S ← 0
loop for J=1 to 47
   C ← 0
   loop for I=1 to 30
      if A(I,J) > 0.0 then C ← C+1 endif
      S ← S + A(I,J)
   endloop
   print J,C
   endloop
   print S
```

2. (a)
```
      SUBROUTINE INIT(A,VAL)
      INTEGER A(30,47),VAL
      INTEGER I,J
      DO 10 I=1,30
         DO 20 J=1,47
            A(I,J) = VAL
20          CONTINUE
10       CONTINUE
      RETURN
      END
```

3. (a) A: output
VAL: input

4. (a) Add 2 additional parameters, say M and N
```
SUBROUTINE INIT(A,M,N,VAL)
INTEGER A(30,47),M,N,VAL
 .
 .
DO 10 I=1,M
   DO 20 J=1,N
   .
   .
```

5. (a)
```
MAX ← A(1,1)
loop for I=1 to 21
   loop for J=1 to 28
      if MAX < A(I,J) then MAX ← A(I,J) endif
   endloop
endloop
```

6. (a)
```
C ← 0
loop for I=1 to 15
   if A(I,I) > 0 then C ← C + 1 endif
endloop
```
(d)
```
S ← 0
loop for I=1 to 15
   S ← S + A(I,16-I)
endloop
```
(e)
```
MAX ← A(1,1)
loop for I=1 to 15
   loop for J=1 to I
      if A(I,J) > MAX then MAX ← A(I,J) endif
   endloop
endloop
```
(g)
```
SYM ← TRUE
loop for I=1 to 15
   loop for J=I+1 to 15
      if A(I,J) ≠ A(J,I) then SYM ← FALSE endif
   endloop
endloop
```

7. (a)
```
      INTEGER A(24,14),I,J
       .
       .
      READ(*,100)(A(I,J),J=1,14),I=1,24)
100   FORMAT(14I5)
```
or
```
      DO 10 I=1,24
         READ(*,100)(A(I,J),J=1,14)
10       CONTINUE
```

10. (a)
```
      SUBROUTINE MULT(A,M,N,C)
      REAL A(10,10),C
      INTEGER M,N
      INTEGER I,J
      DO 10 I=1,M
         DO 20 J=1,N
```
(continued)

```
            A(I,J) = C * A(I,J)
   20       CONTINUE
   10    CONTINUE
      RETURN
      END
```

Section 8.3

2. (a)

```
      SUBROUTINE INIT(A,NR,NC,M,N,VAL)
      INTEGER NR,NC,A(NR,NC),M,N,VAL
      INTEGER I,J
      DO 10 I=1,M
         DO 20 J=1,N
            A(I,J) = VAL
   20       CONTINUE
   10    CONTINUE
      RETURN
      END
```

4.

```
      INTEGER FUNCTION LOOKUP(A,N,KEY)
      INTEGER A(*),N,KEY
      INTEGER I
      LOOKUP=0
      DO 10 I=1,N
         IF(A(I).EQ.KEY)THEN
            LOOKUP=I
            RETURN
         ENDIF
   10    CONTINUE
      RETURN
      END
```

6.

```
      REAL FUNCTION ROWSUM(A,NR,NC,ROW)
      INTEGER NR,NC,ROW
      REAL A(NR,NC)
      REAL S
      INTEGER I
      S=0
      DO 10 I=1,NC
         S=S+A(ROW,I)
   10    CONTINUE
      ROWSUM=S
      RETURN
      END
```

CHAPTER 9

Section 9.1

4. (a) Variable List

Name	type	use
NAME	C*20	Student Name
ONAME	C*20	Old Student Name
COURSE	I	Course Number
GRADE	C*1	Letter Grade
NC	I	Number of Courses
NF	I	Number of F's
EOF	L	True for End of File

C=CHARACTER, I=INTEGER, L=LOGICAL

```
LINECT ← 45
call INPUT(NAME,COURSE,GRADE,EOF)
call SETUP(NAME,NC,NF,ONAME)
NEWGRP ← true
call DETAIL(NAME,COURSE,GRADE,NEWGRP)
NC ← NC + 1
if GRADE = 'F' then NF ← NF + 1 endif
loop
   call INPUT(NAME,COURSE,GRADE,EOF)
   if EOF then exit endif
   if NAME = ONAME then
      NEWGRP ← false
   else
      NEWGRP ← true
      print NC,NF
      call SETUP(NAME,NC,NF,ONAME)
   endif
   call DETAIL(NAME,COURSE,GRADE,NEWGRP)
   NC ← NC + 1
   if GRADE = 'F' then NF ← NF + 1 endif
endloop
print NC,NF
stop

subroutine DETAIL(NAME,COURSE,GRADE,NEWGRP)
(Note: DATA LINECT/45/)
if NEWGRP then LINECT ← LINECT + 3 endif
if LINECT ≥ 45 then
   print headings
   LINECT ← 6
endif
```

(continued)

```
if NEWGRP then
   print NAME,COURSE,GRADE
else
   print COURSE,GRADE
endif
LINECT ← LINECT + 1
return

subroutine SETUP(NAME,NC,NF,ONAME)
ONAME ← NAME
NC ← 0
NF ← 0
return
```

CHAPTER 10

Section 10.1

1.
```
    WRITE(6,100)I,J,K
100 FORMAT('0',I10 //// ' ',2I5 //////)
```

3.
```
    READ(5,100)I,J,K
100 FORMAT(I10/I10/I10)
```

Section 10.2

3. (a) `(I4,2X,I4,2X,I4,2X,I5,I5)`

4. (a) `3(F6.2,2X,I5),I7`

(b) `4(' ARRAY ELEMENT IS ',F10.4)`

5. (a)
```
    WRITE(6,100)((ARR(I,J),J=1,9),I=1,7)
100 FORMAT(' ',9I5)
```

(b) `100 FORMAT('1',9I5/(' ',9I5))`

6. (a)
```
    WRITE(6,100) ((ARR(I,J),J=1,30),I=1,7)
100 FORMAT(' ',10I5/' ',10I5/' ',10I5/)
```

7. (a)
```
    WRITE(6,100)A
100 FORMAT(' ',10I5/(' ',5X,9I5))
```

Section 10.3

2. (a)
```
I  1234
X  5678.90
Y  1234.5
A  '67'
B  '890'
C  '234'
```

CHAPTER 11

Section 11.3

1.
```
L1.NEQV.L2
  .FALSE.
  .TRUE.
  .TRUE.
  .FALSE.
```

Section 11.5

3. (a) `X(1),X(2),X(3),A`

(b) `Y(1),Y(2),B`

4. (a)
```
  REAL A(200)
  DATA (A(I),I=1,200,2) /100*0.0/,
 $     (A(I),I=2,200,2) /100*1.0/
```

6. NUM(2) EQUIVALENT TO NUMOUT
NUM(3) EQUIVALENT TO NUMTOT

CHAPTER 12

Section 12.1

1. (a) A has the value 'Xb'
B has the value 'XY'
C has the value 'XY'

2. (a) A has the value 'Xbbuuuu'
B has the value 'uuCANTu'

3. (a) A has the value 'bbbbbbbbbb'

(i) A has the value 'uuuMIXbbuu'

7. (b)
```
      INTEGER FUCNTION BPOS(STRING)
      CHARACTER*20 STRING
      INTEGER I
      BPOS = 0
      DO 100 I = 1,20
         IF(STRING(I:I).EQ.' ') THEN
            BPOS = I
            RETURN
         ENDIF
100      CONTINUE
      RETURN
      END
```

10.
```
CHARACTER*7 FUNCTION REPLC(WORD,CHAR,POS)
CHARACTER*7 WORD
CHARACTER CHAR
INTEGER POS
REPLC = WORD
REPLC(POS:POS) = CHAR
RETURN
END
```

Section 12.2

3. (b)
```
CHARACTER*1 NUMBER(10),DIGIT
INTEGER CHLOOK,VALUE
DATA NUMBER/'0','1','2','3','4','5','6','7','8','9'/
VALUE = CHLOOK(DIGIT,NUMBER,10,10)-1
```

8. (b)
```
      INTEGER I
      CHARACTER*80 A,B
      CHARACTER*1 AARRAY(80),BARRAY(80)
      EQUIVALENCE (A,AARRAY),(B,BARRAY)
      DO 10 I = 1,10
         A(I) = B(I+12)
10    CONTINUE
```

Section 12.3

1. (a) 2
1. (g) 0

Section 12.3

3.
```
CHARACTER*10 FUNCTION LAST10(STRING)
CHARACTER*(*) STRING
INTEGER LEN,N
N = LEN(STRING)
IF(N.GE.10) THEN
   LAST10 = STRING(N-9:N)
ELSE
   LAST10 = STRING
ENDIF
RETURN
END
```

9.
```
LOGICAL FUNCTION CLOSE(CH1,CH2)
CHARACTER*1 CH1,CH2
INTEGER IABS,ICHAR
CLOSE = IABS((ICHAR(CH1) - ICHAR(CH2))).LE.3
RETURN
END
```

CHAPTER 13

Section 13.2

8. (a) Here is a possible algorithm.

```
read record1,record2
loop
   case
      1(ID1 < ID2)
         write record1 (on output file)
         read record1; if eof then ID1 ← BIG endif
      2(ID1 > ID2)
         write record2
         read record2; if eof then ID2 ← BIG endif
      3(ID1 = ID2)
         if ID1 = BIG then exit endif
         write record1
         call ERROR(ID2)
         read record1; if eof then ID1 ← BIG endif
         read record2; if eof then ID2 ← BIG endif
   endcase
endloop
stop
```

The variable BIG must be set to a value larger than any permitted ID.

Section 13.3

1.
```
      OPEN(17,FILE = 'ATH.DEC',ACCESS = 'DIRECT',
     $     FORM = 'FORMATTED',RECL = 100)
```

2. (a)
```
         INTEGER A(10),I
         READ(17,1000,REC=103) (A(I),I=1,10)
    1000 FORMAT(10I10)
```

3. (d)

```
      SUBROUTINE DELETE(RECNUM)
      INTEGER RECNUM
      WRITE(40,1000 ,REC=RECNUM)
      RETURN
 1000 FORMAT('*')
      END
```

3. (e) A rough algorithm is given below:

```
read N from record 1
OUT ← 1
loop for IN = 2 to N
   read DATA from record IN
   if (1st char of DATA is not '*') then
      OUT ← OUT + 1
      write DATA to record OUT
   endif
endloop
write OUT to record 1
```

Index

A

B

C

G

U

V

W

X